SPURGEON'S
SERMONS

SPURGEON'S SERMONS

Charles Haddon Spurgeon

Volumes 3–4

Volume 3

Baker Books

A Division of Baker Book House Co
Grand Rapids, Michigan 49516

Reprinted by Baker Books
a division of Baker Book House Company
P.O. Box 6287, Grand Rapids, MI 49516-6287

Five-volume edition published 1996

Second printing, March 1999

Previously published in ten volumes

Originally published in 1883 under the title *Sermons of Rev. C. H. Spurgeon of London* by Robert Carter & Brothers, New York

Printed in the United States of America

ISBN 0-8010-1113-2

For information about academic books, resources for Christian leaders, and all new releases available from Baker Book House, visit our web site:

http://www.bakerbooks.com

PREFACE

I PRAYERFULLY commit this volume to the blessing of Almighty God, with the earnest hope that its reception by the American public may be as hearty as that obtained by its predecessors, and that the good resulting from its circulation may be far more abundant. The sermons herein contained are not essays laboriously written and laboriously heard, they are the verbatim reports of the extemporaneous utterances of a very busy man. A few minutes of revision is all that I can afford them, and hence the reader must be lenient toward the errors of the book. Week by week the sermons are issued in haste, almost as soon as they are delivered, while I am continually running hither and thither preaching the Word, and am therefore frequently unable so much as to glance at the proof-sheets. The eighteen Sermons at the close of the volume were delivered to immense audiences in the Royal Surrey Music Hall, and are purposely made as simple and elementary as possible. Without eloquence or learning, these discourses have riveted the attention of ten thousand at once, and have attracted princes of every nation and nobles of every rank, some of whom have not been unprofitable hearers, but have brought forth fruits meet for repentance. It is the Lord's doing, and it is marvelous in our eyes.

Brethren in the land of the West, I am linked to your great republic by ties which daily multiply; fellowships with the great and holy are the silken bands which bind me to your nation. May the old faith of the men from whose loins ye sprang be ever nourished among you. Ye are unfettered; no State Church spreads its upas shade over your churches, and no reverence for antiquated errors checks your progress. Let a brother beseech you to maintain the faith, once delivered to the saints, whole and inviolable. In our land we have been favored with some blessed gleams of sunshine; but those who know the signs of the times are led very frequently to tremble for the ark of the Lord. Arminianism secretly lurks among us. Our ministers prune the truth, and conceal the great distinguishing doctrines of grace, in a manner much to be lamented. Antinomianism, through its perversions of the truth, has done much to check the advance of sound opinions, and has made many good men so cautious of being too high, that they have run into the opposite extremes of error. May the Lord restore unto us all a pure language, and may the time come when the Gospel of the Lord Jesus shall universally prevail.

May the perusal of these Sermons confirm the wavering, and, by the influence of the Holy Spirit, guide the anxious to joy and peace.

To the sacred name of the Father, the Son, and the Holy Spirit, be glory for ever, so prays

THE AUTHOR.

CONTENTS

SERMON I

A FAITHFUL FRIEND

"There is a friend that sticketh closer than a brother."—PROVERBS, xviii. 24

CICERO has well said, "Friendship is the only thing in the world concerning the usefulness of which all mankind are agreed." Friendship seems as necessary an element of a comfortable existence in this world as fire or water, or even air itself. A man may drag along a miserable existence in proud solitary dignity, but his life is scarce life, it is nothing but an existence, the tree of life being stripped of the leaves of hope and the fruits of joy. He who would be happy here must have friends; and he who would be happy hereafter, must, above all things, find a friend in the world to come, in the person of God, the Father of his people.

Friendship, however, though very pleasing and exceedingly blessed, has been the cause of the greatest misery to men when it has been unworthy and unfaithful; for just in proportion as a good friend is sweet, a false friend is full of bitterness. "A faithless friend is sharper than an adder's tooth." It is sweet to repose in some one; but O! how bitter to have that support snapped, and to receive a grievous fall as the effect of your confidence. Fidelity is an absolute necessary in a true friend; we can not rejoice in men unless they will stand faithful to us. Solomon declares that "there is a friend that sticketh closer than a brother." That friend, I suppose, he never found in the pomps and vanities of the world. He had tried them all, but he found them empty; he passed through all their joys, but he found them "vanity of vanities." Poor Savage spoke from sad experience when he said,

> " You'll find the friendship of the world a show!
>   Mere outward show ! 'Tis like the harlot's tears,
>   The statesman's promise, or false patriot's zeal,
>   Full of fair seeming, but delusion all."

And so for the most part they are. The world's friendship is
ever brittle. Trust to it, and you have trusted a robber; rely
upon it, and you have leaned upon a thorn; ay, worse than
that, upon a spear which shall pierce you to the soul with
agony. Yet Solomon says he had found " a friend that sticketh closer than a brother." Not in the haunts of his unbridled
pleasures, nor in the wanderings of his unlimited resources,
but in the pavilion of the Most High, the secret dwelling-place
of God, in the person of Jesus, the Son of God, the Friend of
sinners.

It is saying a great thing to affirm that " there is a friend
that sticketh closer than a brother ;" for the love of brother
hood has produced most valiant deeds. We have read stories
of what brotherhood could do, which, we think, could hardly
be excelled in the annals of friendship. Timoleon, with his
shield, stood over the body of his slain brother, to defend him
from the insults of the foe. It was reckoned a brave deed of
brotherhood that he should dare the spears of an army in
defense of his brother's corpse. And many such instances
have there been, in ancient and modern warfare, of the attach-
ment of brethren. There is a story told of a Highland regi-
ment, who, while marching through the Highlands, lost their
way ; they were overtaken by one of the terrible storms which
will sometimes come upon travelers unawares, and blinded by
the snow, they lost their way upon the mountains. Well nigh
frozen to death, it was with difficulty they could continue their
march. One man after another dropped into the snow and
disappeared. There were two brothers, however, of the name
of Forsythe ; one of them fell prostrate on the earth, and
would have lain there to die, but his brother, though barely
able to drag his own limbs across the white desert, took him
on his back, and carried him along, and as others fell one by
one, this brave, true-hearted brother carried his loved one on
his back, until at last he himself fell down overcome with
fatigue, and died. His brother, however, had received such

warmth from his body that he was enabled to reach the end of his journey in safety, and so lived. Here we have an instance of one brother sacrificing his life for another. I hope there are some brothers 1 ere who would be prepared to do the same if they should ever be brought into the same difficulty. It is saying a great thing, to declare that "there is a friend that sticketh closer than a brother." It is putting that friend first of all in the list of loving ones; for, surely, next to a mother's love, there is, and there ought to be, no higher affection in the world than the love of a brother to one begotten of the same father, and dandled on the same knee. Those who have "grown in beauty side by side, and filled one house with glee," ought to love one another. And we think there have been many glorious instances and mighty proofs of the love of brethren. Yet, says Solomon, "there is a friend that sticketh closer than a brother."

To repeat our assertion, we believe that this friend is the blessed Redeemer, Jesus Christ. It shall be ours, first, *to prove*, this morning, *the fact* that he sticks closer than a brother; then, as briefly as we can, to show you *why he sticks closer than a brother;* and then to finish up by giving you *some lessons which may be drawn from the doctrine*, that Jesus Christ is a faithful Friend.

I. First, then, beloved, we assert that CHRIST IS "A FRIEND THAT STICKETH CLOSER THAN A BROTHER." And in order to prove this from facts, we appeal to such of you as have had him for a friend. Will you not, each of you, at once give your verdict, that this is neither more nor less than an unexaggerated truth? He loved you before all worlds; long ere the day star flung his ray across the darkness, before the wing of angel had flapped the unnavigated ether, before aught of creation had struggled from the womb of nothingness, God, even our God, had set his heart upon all his children. Since that time, has he once swerved, has he once turned aside, once changed? No; ye who have tasted of his love and know his grace, will bear me witness, that he has been a certain friend in uncertain circumstances.

> "He, near your side hath always stood,
> His loving-kindness. O! how good!"

You fell in Adam; did he cease to love you? No; he became the second Adam to redeem you. You sinned in practice, and brought upon your head the condemnation of God; you deserved his wrath and his utter anger; did he then forsake you? No!

> "He saw you ruined in the fall,
> Yet loved you notwithstanding all."

He sent his minister after you: you despised him; he preached the gospel in your ears: you laughed at him; you broke God's Sabbath, you despised his Word. Did he then forsake you? No!

> "Determined to save, he watched o'er your path,
> Whilst, Satan's blind slave, you sported with death."

And at last he arrested you by his grace, he humbled you, he made you penitent, he brought you to his feet, and he forgave all your sins. Since then, has he left you? You have often left him; has he ever left you? You have had many trials and troubles; has he ever deserted you? Has he ever turned away his heart, and shut up his bowels of compassion? No, children of God, it is your solemn duty to say " No," and bear witness to his faithfulness. You have been in severe afflictions and in dangerous circumstances; did your friend desert you then? Others have been faithless to you; he that eat bread with you has lifted up his heel against you; but has Christ ever forsaken you? Has there ever been a moment when you could go to him, and say, " Master, thou hast betrayed me?" Could you once, in the blackest hour of your grief, dare to impugn his fidelity? Could you dare to say of him, " Lord, thou hast promised what thou didst not perform?" Will you not bear witness now, " Not one good thing hath failed of all that the Lord God hath promised; all hath come to pass?" And do you fear he will yet forsake you? Ask, then, the bright ones before the throne—" Ye glorified spirits! did Christ forsake you? Ye have passed through Jordan's stream; did he leave you there? Ye have been baptized in the black flood of death; did he there forsake you? Ye have stood before the throne of God; did he then deny you?" And they answered, " No; through all the troubles of our life, in all the bitterness of death, in all the agonies of our expiring moments, and in all the terrors of God's judgment, he hath been with us, 'a friend that sticketh closer than a brother.'" Out of all the millions of God's redeemed, there is not one he hath forsaken. Poor they have been, mean and distressed, but he hath never abhorred their prayer, never turned aside from doing them good. He hath been ever with them.

> " For his mercy shall endure,
> Ever faithful, ever sure."

But I shall not longer stay, since I can not prove this to the ungodly, and to the godly it is already proven, for they know it by experience; therefore it is but little necessary that I should do more than just certify the fact that Christ is a faithful friend—a friend in every hour of need and every time of distress.

II. And now I have to tell you THE REASONS WHY WE MAY DEPEND UPON CHRIST AS BEING A FAITHFUL FRIEND.

There are some things in himself which render it certain that he will stick close to his people.

1. True friendship can only be made between true men. Hearts are the soul of honor. There can be no lasting friendship between bad men. Bad men may pretend to love each other, but their friendship is a rope of sand, which shall be broken at any convenient season ; but if a man have a sincere heart within him, and be true and noble, then we may confide in him. Spenser sings in fine old English verse—

> " Ne, certes can that friendship long endure,
> However gay and goodly be the style,
> That doth ill cause or evil end enure,
> For Vertue is the band that bindeth Harts most sure."

But who can find a stain in the character of Jesus, or who can tarnish his honor ? Has there ever been a spot on his escutcheon ? Has his flag ever been trampled in the dust ? Does he not stand the true witness in heaven, the faithful and just ? Is it not declared of him that he is God who can not lie ? Have we not found him so up to this moment ; and may we not, knowing that he is " Holy, holy, holy Lord," confide in him, that he will stick closer to us than a brother? His good-ness is the guaranty of his fidelity; he can not fail us.

2. *Faithfulness to us in our faults* is a certain sign of fidelity in a friend. You may depend upon that man who will tell you of your faults in a kind and considerate manner. Fawn-ing hypocrites, insidious flatterers, are the sweepings and offal of friendship. They are but the parasites upon that noble tree. But true friends put enough trust in you to tell you openly of your faults. Give me for a friend the man who will speak honestly of me before my face; who will not tell first one neighbor, and then another, but who will come straight to my house, and say, "Sir, I feel there is such-and-such a thing in you, which, as my brother, I must tell you of." That man is a true friend; he has proved himself to be so; for we never ge any praise for telling people of their faults; we rather hazard their dislike; a man will sometimes thank you for it, but he does not often like you any the better. Praise is a thing we all love. I met with a man the other day who said he was impervious to flattery; I was walking with him at the time, and turning round rather sharply, I said, "At any rate, sir, you seem to have a high gift in flattering yourself, for you are really doing so, in saying you are impervious to flattery." 'You can not flatter me," he said. I replied, "I can, if I like to try; and perhaps may do so before the day is out." I found I could not flatter him directly, so I began by saying what a fine child that was of his; and he drank it in as a precious draught; and when I praised this thing and that thing belonging to him, I could see that he was very easily flattered; not directly, but indirectly. We are all pervious to flattery; we like the soothing cordial, only it must not be labeled flattery; for we have a religious abhorrence of flattery if it be so called; call it by any other name, and we drink it in, even as the ox drinketh in water. Now, child of God, has Christ ever flattered you? Has he not told you of your faults right truly? Has he not pricked your conscience even upon what you thought to gloss over—your little secret sins? Has he not provoked conscience to thunder in your ears notes of terror, because of your misdeeds? Well, then, you may trust him, for he shows that faithfulness which renders a man right

trustworthy. Thus I have pointed out to you that there are reasons in himself for which we may trust him.

3. In the next place, *there are some things in his friend-ship which render us sure of not being deceived, when we put our confidence in him.* True friendship must not be of hasty growth. As quaint old Master Fuller says. " Let friend-ship creep gently to a height ; if it rush to it, it may soon run itself out of breath." It is even so. I think it was Joanna Baillie said,

> " Friendship is no plant of hasty growth.
> Though planted in esteem's deep fixed soil,
> The gradual culture of kind intercourse
> Must bring it to perfection."

In vain thou trustest the gourd over thy head, O Jonah ; it will not be of much use to thee ; it came up in a night, it may wither in a night. It is the strong stiff oak, of ages' growth, which shall abide the tempest ; which shall alike put out its wings to shield thee from the sun, and shall afterward find thee a hovel in its heart, if necessary, in its grey old age, when its branches tremble in the blast. Friendship is true when it begins ; but we must have a man's friendship long before we can say of him, that he will stick closer than a brother. And how long has Christ loved you ? That you can not tell. When the ages were not born he loved you ; when this world was an infant, wrapped in the swaddling clothes of mist, he loved you ; when the old pyramids had not begun to be builded, his heart was set upon you ; and ever since you have been born he has had a strong affection for you. He looked on you in your cradle, and he loved you then; he was affianced to you when you were an infant of a span long, and he has loved you ever since. Some of you I see with gray hairs, some with heads all bald with age ; he has loved you up till now, and will he now forsake you ? O ! no, his friendship is so old that it must last ; it has been matured by so many tem-pests, it has been rooted by so many winds of trouble, that it can not but endure ; it must stand. Even as the granite peak of the mountain shall not be melted, because, unlike the snow. it has braved the blast, and borne the heat of the burning sun ;

it has stood out always, catching in its face every blow from the face of nature, and yet been unmoved and uninjured. It shall last, for it has lasted. But when the elements shall melt, and in a stream of dissolving fire shall run away, then shall Christ's friendship still exist, for it is of older growth than they. He must be "a friend that sticketh closer than a brother;" for his friendship is a hoary friendship—hoary as his own head, of which it is said, "His head and his hair are white like snow, as white as wool."

4. But note, further, the *friendship which lasts does not take its rise in the chambers of mirth, nor is it fed and fattened there.* Young lady, you speak of a dear friend whom you acquired last night in a ball-room. Do not, I beseech you, misuse the word; he is not a friend if he was acquired merely there; friends are better things than those which grow in the hot-house of pleasure. Friendship is a more lasting plant than those. You have a friend, have you? Yes; and he keeps a pair of horses, and has a good establishment. Ah! but your best way to prove your friend is to know that he will be your friend when you have not so much as a mean cottage; and when, houseless and without clothing, you are driven to beg your bread. Thus you would make true proof of a friend. Give me a friend who was born in the winter time, whose cradle was rocked in the storm; he will last. Our fair weather friends shall flee away from us. I had rather have a robin for a friend than a swallow; for a swallow abides with us only in the summer time, but a robin cometh to us in the winter. Those are tight friends that will come the nearest to us when we are in the most distress; but those are not friends who speed themselves away when ill times come. Believer, hast thou reason to fear that Christ will leave you now? Has he not been with you in the house of mourning? You found your friend where men find pearls, "in caverns deep, where darkness dwells;" you found Jesus in your hour of trouble. It was on the bed of sickness that you first learned the value of his name; it was in the hour of mental anguish that you first did lay hold of the hem of his garment; and since then, your nearest and sweetest intercourse has been held with him in the hours of darkness. Well, then, such a friend, proved in

the house of sorrow—a friend who gave his heart's blood for you, and let his soul run out in one great river of gore—such a friend never can and never will forsake you; he sticketh closer than a brother.

5. Again, *a friend who is acquired by folly is never a lasting friend.* Do a foolish thing, and make a man your friend; 'tis but a confederacy in vice, and you will soon discover that his friendship is worthless; the friendships you acquire by doing wrong, you had better be without. O! how many silly friendships there are springing up, the mere fruit of a sentimentalism, having no root whatever, but like the plant of which our Saviour tells us, " It sprang up because it had no depth of earth." Jesus Christ's friendship is not like that; there is no ingredient of folly in it; he loves us discreetly, not winking or conniving at our follies, but instilling into us his wisdom. His love is wise; he hath chosen us according to the counsel of his wisdom; not blindly and rashly, but with all judgment and prudence.

Under this head I may likewise observe, that *the friendship of ignorance is not a very desirable one.* I desire no man to call himself my friend, if he doth not know me. Let him love me in proportion to his knowledge of me. If he loves me for the little he knows, when he knoweth more he may cast me aside. " That man," says one, " seems to be a very amiable man." " I am sure I can love him," says another, as he scans his features. Ay, but do not write " friend" yet; wait a wee bit, until you know more of him; just see him, examine him, try him, test him, and not till then enter him on the sacred list of friends. Be friendly to all, but make none your friends until they know you, and you know them. Many a friendship born in the darkness of ignorance, hath died suddenly in the light of a better acquaintance with each other. You supposed men to be different from what they were, and when you discovered their real character you disregarded them. I remember one saying to me, " I have great affection for you, sir," and he mentioned a certain reason. I replied, " My dear fellow, your reason is absolutely false; the very thing you love me for, I am not, and hope I never shall be." And so I said, " I really can not accept your friendship, if it be founded upon a misunderstanding of what I may have said." But our Lord Jesus never can forsake those whom once he loves, because he can discover nothing in us worse than he knew, for he knew all about us beforehand. He saw our leprosy, and yet he loved us; he knew our deceitfulness and unbelief, and yet he did press us to his bosom; he knew what poor fools we were, and yet he said he would never eave us nor forsake us. He knew that we should rebel against him and despise his counsel often times; he knew that even when we loved him our love would be cold and languid but he loved for his own sake. Surely, then, he will stick closer than a brother.

6. Yet again, *friendship and love, to be real, must not lie in words, but in deeds.* The friendship of bare compliment is the fashion of this age, because this age is the age of deceit. The world is the great house of sham. Go where you may in London, sham is staring you in the face; there are very few real things to be discovered. I allude not merely to tricks in business, adulterations in food, and such like. Deception is not confined to the tradesman's shop. It prevails throughout society; the sanctuary is not exempt. The preacher adopts a sham voice. You hardly ever hear a man speak in the pulpit in the same way he would speak in the parlor. Why, I hear my brethren, sometimes, when they are at tea or dinner, speak in a very comfortable decent sort of English voice, but when they get into their pulpits they adopt a sanctimonious tone, and fill their mouths with inflated utterance, or else whine most pitifully. They degrade the pulpit by pretending to honor it; speaking in a voice which God never intended any mortal to have. This is the great house of sham; and such little things show which way the wind blows. You leave your card at a friend's house; that is an act of friendship—the card! I wonder whether, if he were hard up for cash, you would leave your banker's book! You write " My dear sir," " Yours very truly;" it is a sham; you do not mean it. " Dear!" that is a sacred word; it ought to be used to none but those you regard with affection; but we tolerate false-hoods now, as if they were truths; and we call them courte-sies. Courtesies they may be; but untruths they are in many

cases. Now, Christ's love lieth not in words, but in deeds. He saith not, "My dear people;" but he let his heart out, and we could see what that was. He doth not come to us, and say, "Dearly beloved" simply; but he hangs upon the cross, and there we read "Dearly beloved" in red letters. He does not come to us with the kisses of his lips first—he giveth us blessings with both his hands; he giveth himself *for* us, and then he giveth himself *to* us. Trust no complimentary friend; rely upon the man who giveth you real tokens worth your having, who does for you deeds to show the truthfulness of his heart. Such a friend—and such is Jesus—"sticketh closer than a brother."

7. Once more, and I shall not weary you, I trust. *A purchased friend will never last long.* Give to a man nineteen times, and deny him the twentieth, and he shall hate you; for his love sprang only from your gifts. The love which I could buy for gold I would sell for dross; the friendship that I could buy for pearls I would dispense with for pebbles; it were of no value, and therefore the sooner lost the better. But O! believer, Christ's love was unpurchased love. Thou broughtest him no present. Jacob said, when his sons went to Egypt, "Take the man a present, a little oil, a little balm, a few nuts and almonds;" but you took Christ no presents. When you came to him you said,

> "Nothing in my hands I bring,
> Simply to thy cross I cling."

You did not even promise that you would love him; for you had such a faithless heart, you durst not say so. You asked him to make you love him; that was the most you could do. He loved you for nothing at all—simply because he would love you. Well, that love which so lived on nothing but its own resources, will not starve through the scantiness of your returns; the love which grew in such a rocky heart as this, will not die for want of soil. That love which sprang up in the barren desert, in your unirrigated soul, will never, never die for want of moisture: it must live, it can not expire. Jesus must be "a friend that sticketh closer than a brother."

8. Shall I stay to urge more reasons? I may but mention one other, namely, this—that *there can not, by any possibility,*

arise any cause which could make Christ love us less. You say, how is this? One man loves his friend, but he on a sudden grows rich, and now he says, I am a greater man than I used to be, I forget my old acquaintances. But. Christ can grow no richer; he is as rich as he can be, infinitely so. He loves you now; then it can not be possible that he will by reason of an increase in his own personal glory forsake you, for everlasting glories now crown his head : he can never be more glorious and great, and therefore he will love you still Sometimes, on the other hand, one friend grows poorer, and then the other forsakes him; but you never can grow poorer than you are, for you are " a poor sinner and nothing at all" now; you have nothing of your own; all you have is borrowed, all given you by him. He can not love you, then, less, because you grow poorer; for poverty that hath nothing is at least as poor as it can be, and can. never sink lower in the scale. Christ, therefore, must love thee for all thy nakedness and all thy poverty.

" But I may prove sinful," sayest thou. Yes, but thou canst not be more so than he foreknew thou wouldst be ; and yet he loved thee with the foreknowledge of all thy sins. Surely, then, when it happens it will occasion no surprise to him ; he knew it all beforehand, and he can not swerve from his love ; no circumstance can possibly arise that ever will divide the Saviour from his love to his people, and the saint from his love to his Saviour. He is " a friend that sticketh closer than a brother."

III. Now, then, AN INFERENCE TO BE DERIVED FROM THIS. Lavater says, " The qualities of your friends will be those of your enemies : cold friends, cold enemies, half friends, half enemies ; fervid enemies, warm friends." Knowing this to be a truth, I have often congratulated myself, when my enemies have spoken fiercely against me. Well, I have thought, " My friends love me hard and fast; let my enemies be as hot as they please; it only indicates that the friends are proportionately firm in affection. Then we draw this inference, that if Christ sticks close, and he is our friend, then our enemies will stick close, and never leave us till we die. O, Christian, because Christ sticks close, the devil will stick close too : he will be at you and with you; the dog of hell will never cease his howlings, till you reach the other side of Jordan; no place in this world' is out of bow-shot of that great enemy; till you have crossed the stream his arrows *can* reach you, and they will. If Christ gave himself for you, the devil will do all he can to destroy you; if Christ has been long-suffering to you, Satan will be persevering, in hopes that Christ may forget you; he will strive after you, and strive until he shall see you safely landed in heaven. But be not disappointed: the louder Satan roars, the more proof you shall have of Christ's love. "Give me," said old Rutherford, "give me a roaring devil rather than a sleeping one; for sleeping devils make me slumber, but roaring ones provoke me to run to my Master." O! be glad, then, if the world rant at thee, if thy foes attack thee fiercely. Christ is just as full of love to thee as they are of hatred. Therefore,

> "Be firm and strong;
> Be grace thy shield and Christ thy song."

And now I have a question to ask: that question I ask of every man and every woman in this place, and of every child too—Is Jesus Christ your friend? Have you a friend at court —at heaven's court? Is the judge of quick and dead your friend? Can you say that you love him, and has he ever revealed himself in the way of love to you? Dear hearer, do not answer that question for thy neighbor; answer it for thyself. Peer or peasant, rich or poor, learned or illiterate, this question is for each of you; therefore, ask it: Is Christ my friend? Did you ever consider that question? Have you ever asked it? O! to be able to say "Christ is my friend," is one of the sweetest things in the world. A man who had lived much in sin, one day casually entered a place of worship Before the sermon, this hymn was sung—

> "Jesus, lover of my soul."

The next day the man was met by an acquaintance who asked him how he liked the sermon. Said he, "I do not know, but there were two or three words that took such a hold of me that I did not know what to do with myself. The minister read that hymn, 'Jesus, lover of my soul.' Ah!" said he, though he was by no means a religious man, "to be able to say that, I would give up all I have got! But do you think," he asked "that Jesus ever will be the lover of such a man as I am? 'Jesus, lover of *my* soul!' O! could I say it." And then he buried his head in his hands and wept. I have every reason to fear that he went back to his sin, and was the same afterwards as before. But, you see, he had conscience enough to let him know how valuable it was to have Christ for his lover and his friend. Ah! rich man, thou hast many friends. There be some here who have learned the faithlessness of friends; there be some here who have toiled for their country's good, and deserve a meed of honor at their country's hands, who, for one mistake—or what, perhaps, was a mistake—have been neglected by too many who once appeared to be their most trusty adherents. O! put no confidence, ye great men and ye rich, in the adherence of your friends. David said in his haste, " All men are liars;" you may one day have to say it at your leisure. And O! ye kind and affectionate hearts, who are not rich in wealth, but who are rich in love—and that is the world's best wealth—put this golden coin among your silver ones, and it will sanctify them all. Get Christ's love shed abroad in your hearts, and your mother's love, your daughter's love, your husband's love, your wife's love, will become more sweet than ever. The love of Christ casts not out the love of relatives, but it sanctifies our loves, and makes them sweeter far. Remember, dear hearer, the love of men and women is very sweet; but all must pass away; and what will you do, if you have no wealth but the wealth that fadeth, and no love but the love which dies, when death shall come? O! to have the love of Christ! You can take that across the river of death with you; you can wear it as your bracelet in heaven, and set it up as a seal upon your hand; for his love is "strong as death and mightier than the grave." Good old Bishop Beveridge, I think it was, when dying, did not know his best friends. Said one, " Bishop Beveridge, do you know me?" Said he, " Who are you?" and when the name was mentioned, he said, " No." " But don't you know your wife, Bishop?" " What is her name?"

said he. Said she, "I am your wife." "I did not know I had got one," said he. Poor old man! his faculties all failed him. At last one stooped down and whispered, "Do you know the Lord Jesus Christ?" "Yes," said he, making ar effort to speak, "I have known him these forty years, and I never can forget him." It is marvelous how memory will hold the place with Jesus, when it will with no one else; and it is equally marvelous, that,

> "When all created things are dry,
>   Christ's fullness is the same."

My dear hearers, do think of this matter. O that you might get Christ for your friend; he will never be your friend while you are self-righteous; he will never be your friend while you live in sin. But do you believe yourselves guilty? Do you desire to leave off sin? Do you want to be saved? Do you desire to be renewed? Then let me tell you, my Master loves you! Poor, weak, and helpless worms, my Master's heart is full of love to you; his eyes at this moment are looking down with pity on you. "O! Jerusalem, Jerusa lem, Jerusalem!" He now bids me tell you that he died for all of you who confess yourselves to be sinners, and feel it. He bids me say to you, "Believe on the Lord Jesus Christ, and you shall be saved." He tells me to proclaim salvation full and free; full, needing nothing of yours to help it; free, needing nothing of yours to buy it.

> "Come, ye thirsty, come and welcome;
>   God's free bounty glorify:
> True belief and true repentance,
>   Every grace that brings us nigh—
> Without money,
> Come to Jesus Christ, and buy.'

There is nothing I feel that I fail so much in as addressing sin ners. O! I wish I could cry my heart out, and preach my heart out, to you and at you.

> "Dear Saviour, draw reluctant hearts,
>   To thee let sinners fly,
> And take the bliss thy love imparts;
>   And drink, and never die."

Farewell, with this one thought—we shall never ail of us meet together here again. It is a very solemn thought, but according to the course of nature and the number of deaths, if all of you were willing to come here next Sabbath morning, it is not at all likely that all of you would be alive; one out of this congregation will be sure to have gone the way of all flesh. Farewell, thou that are appointed to death; I know not where thou art—yon strong man, or yon tender maiden with the hectic flush of consumption on her cheek. I know not who is appointed to death; but I do now most solemnly take my farewell of such an one. Farewell, poor soul; and is it farewell for ever? Shall we meet in the land of the hereafter, in the home of the blessed; or do I bid you farewell now for ever? I do solemnly bid farewell to you for ever, if you live and die without Christ. But I can not bear that dreary thought; and I therefore say, poor sinner! stop and consider—consider thy ways, and now "turn ye, turn ye, why will ye die?" "Why will ye *die?*" "Why will *ye* die?" 'Why *will* ye die?" Ah! ye can not answer that question. May God help you to answer it in a better fashion, by saying, 'Here, Lord!

> Just as I am, without one plea,
> But that thy blood was shed for me,
> O Son of God I come to thee."

trust my soul in thy kind hands." The Lord bless you all for Christ's sake! Amen.

SERMON II

THE LEAFLESS TREE

" But yet in it shall be a tenth, and it shall return, and it shall be eaten
as a teil tree, and as an oak, whose substance is in them, when they cast their
leaves; so the holy seed shall be the substance thereof."—ISAIAH, vi. 13

OUR first business to-night will be briefly to explain the
metaphor employed in the text. The prophet was told that
despite all the remonstrances he was instructed to deliver, and
notwithstanding the eloquent earnestness of his lips, which
had been just touched by a live coal from off the altar, still the
people of Israel would persevere in their sins, and would therefore be certainly destroyed. He asked the question, " Lord,
how long ?" that is, How long will the people be thus impenitent ? How long will thy sore judgment thus continue ? and
he was informed that God would waste and destroy the cities
and their inhabitants, till the land should be utterly desolate.
Then it was added, for his comfort, " Yet in it shall be a
tenth." And so it happened; for when " Nebuchadnezzar carried away all Jerusalem," the historian gives this reservation—
" none remained save the poorer sort of the people of the land."
They were left by the captain of the guard, " to be vine-dress-
ers and husbandmen." Thus in it there was a tenth; this
small remnant of the people, however, was to be nearly destroyed too. " It shall return and shall be eaten ;" the sense
is, eaten up or consumed. The poor creatures left in the land,
many of them fled into Egypt at the time of the conspiracy of
Ishmael (not Ishmael, the son of Hagar, but an unworthy
member of the royal family of Judah), and there in Egypt
most of them were cut off and perished. " But," says God,
" although this tenth only shall be preserved, and then even
this small part shall he subjected to many perils, yet Israel

shall not be destroyed, for it shall be as a terebinth tree and as an oak;" their "substance is in them, when they cast their leaves," and so lose their verdure and their beauty; thus, in like manner, a holy seed, a chosen remnant, shall still be the substance of the children of Israel, when the fruitful land is stripped of its foliage, and that fair garden of earth is barren as the desert.

The figure is taken, first of all, from the terebinth or turpentine tree—here translated the teil tree. That tree is an evergreen, with this exception, that in very severe and inclement weather it loses its leaves; but even then the terebinth tree is not dead. And so of the oak; it loses its leaves every year, of course, but even then it is not dead. "So," says God, "you have seen the tree in winter, standing naked and bare, without any sign of life, its roots buried in the hard and frozen soil, and its naked branches exposed to every blast, without a bloom or a bud; yet the substance is in the tree when the leaves are gone. It is still alive, and it shall, by and by, in due season, bud and bloom; so," says he, "Nebuchadnezzar shall cut off all the leaves of the tree of Israel—take away the inhabitants, only a tenth shall be left, and they shall well nigh be eaten up; still the church of God and the Israel of God never shall be destroyed; they shall be like the terebinth tree and the oak, whose substance is in them, when they cast their leaves; so the holy seed shall be the substance thereof."

I hope I have made the meaning of the passage as plain as words can make it. Now, then, for the application—first, *to the Jews;* secondly, *to the Church;* thirdly, *to each believer.*

I. First, TO THE JEWS.

What a history is the history of the Jew! He has antiquity stamped upon his forehead. His is a lineage more noble than that of any knights or even kings of this our island, for he can trace his pedigree back to the very loins of Abraham, and through him to that patriarch who entered into the ark, and thence up to Adam himself. Our history is hidden in gloom and darkness; but theirs, with certainty, may be read from the first moment even down till now. And what a checkered history has been the history of the Jewish nation

Nebuchadnezzar seemed to have swept them all away with the huge broom of destruction; the tenth left was again given over to the slaughter; and one would have thought we should have heard no more of Israel; but in a little time they rose phœnix-like, from their ashes. A second temple was builded, and the nation became strong once more, and though often swept with desolations in the mean time, yet it did not abide, and the scepter did not depart from Judah, nor a lawgiver from between his feet, until Shiloh came. And, since then, how huge have been the waves that have rushed over the Jewish race! The Roman emperor razed the city to the ground, and left not a vestige standing; another emperor changed the name of Jerusalem into that of Eliah, and forbade a Jew to go within some miles of it, so that he might not even look upon his beloved city. It was plowed and left desolate. But is the Jew conquered? Is he a subjugated man? Is his country seized? No; he is still one of earth's nobles—distressed, insulted, spit upon; still it is written, "To the Jew first, and afterward to the Gentile." He claims a high dignity above us, and he has a history to come which will be greater and more splendid than the history of any nation that has yet existed. If we read the Scriptures aright, the Jews have a great deal to do with this world's history. They shall be gathered in; Messiah shall come, the Messiah they are looking for—the same Messiah who came once shall come again—shall come as they expected him to come the first time. They then thought he would come a prince to reign over them, and so he will when he comes again. He will come to be king of the Jews, and to reign over his people most gloriously; for when he comes, Jew and Gentile will have equal privileges, though there shall yet be some distinction afforded to that royal family from whose loins Jesus came; for he shall sit upon the throne of his father David, and unto him shall be gathered all nations. O!

> "Ye chosen seed of Israel's race,
> A remnant weak and small,"

ye may, indeed,

> "Hail him who saves you by his grace,
> And crown him Lord of all;"

your church shall never die, and your race shall never become extinct. The Lord hath said it. "The race of Abraham shall endure for ever, and his seed as many generations."

But why is it that the Jewish race is preserved? We have our answer in the text: "The holy seed is the substance thereof." There is something within a tree mysterious, hidden, and unknown, which preserves life in it when every thing outward tends to kill it. So in the Jewish race there is a secret element which keeps it alive. We know what it is: it is the "remnant according to the election of grace:" in the worst of ages there has never been a day so black but there was a Hebrew found to hold the lamp of God. There has always been found a Jew who loved Jesus; and though the race now despise the great Redeemer, yet there are not a few of the Hebrew race who still love Jesus, the Saviour of the uncircumcised, and bow before him. It is these few, this holy seed, that are the substance of the nation; and for their sake, through their prayers, because of God's love to them, he still says of Israel to all nations, "Touch not these mine anointed, do my prophets no harm. These are the descendants of Abraham, my friend. I have sworn, and will not repent; I will show kindness unto them for their father's sake, and for the sake of the remnant I have chosen."

Let us think a little more of the Jews than we have been wont; let us pray oftener for them. "Pray for the peace of Jerusalem; they shall prosper that love her." As truly as any great thing is done in this world for Christ's kingdom, the Jews will have more to do with it than any of us have dreamed. So much for the first point. The Jewish nation is like "a terebinth tree, and as an oak, whose substance is in them, when they cast their leaves; so the holy seed shall be the substance thereof."

II. And now, secondly, THE CHURCH OF CHRIST, whereof the Jewish people are but a dim shadow, and an emblem.

The church has had its trials; trials from without and trials within. It has had days of blood-red persecution, and of fiery trial; it has had times of sad apostacy, when an evil heart of unbelief and departing from the living God has broken out, and a root of bitterness springing up has troubled many, and thereby they have been defiled. Yet, blessed be God, through all the winters of the church she still lived, and she gives signs now of a sweeter spring-tide, a fresher greenness and a healthier condition than she has shown before for many a day. Why is it that the church is still preserved, when she looks so dead? For this reason: that there is in the midst of her—though many are hypocrites and impostors—a "chosen seed," who are "the substance thereof." You might have looked back a hundred years ago upon the professing church of Christ in this land, and what a sad spectacle it would have exhibited! In the Church of England there was mere formality; in the Independent and Baptist denominations there was truth, but it was dead, cold, lifeless truth. Ministers dreamed on in their pulpits, and hearers snored in their pews; infidelity was triumphant; the house of God was neglected and desecrated. The church was like a tree that had lost its leaves: it was in a wintry state. But did it die? No; there was a holy seed within it. Six young men were expelled from Oxford for praying, reading the Bible, and talking to poor people about Christ; and these six young men, with many others whom the Lord had hidden by fifties in the caves of the earth, secret and unknown—these young men, leaders of a glorious revival, came out, and though ridiculed and laughed at as Methodists, they brought forth a great and glorious revival, almost equaling the commencement of the gospel triumphs under Paul and the apostles, and very little inferior to the great Reformation of Luther, of Calvin, and Zwingle. And just now the church is to a great degree in a barren and lifeless state. But will she therefore die? You say that true doctrine is scarce, that zeal is rare, that there is little life and energy in the pulpit and true devotion in the pew, while formality and hypocrisy stalk over us, and we sleep in our cradles. But will the church die? No; she is like a teil tree and an oak; her substance is in her when she has lost her leaves; there is a holy seed in her still that is the substance thereof. Where these are we know not; some, I doubt not, are here in this church—some, I hope, are to be found in every church of professing Christians: and woe worth the day to the church that loses her holy seed; for she must die, like the oak blasted by the lightning, whose heart is

scorched out of it—broken down, because it has no substance
in it.

Let me now draw your attention, as a church connected
with this place, to this point—that the holy seed is the substance of the church. A great many of you might be compared to the bark of the tree; some of you are like the big
limbs; others are like pieces of the trunk. Well, we should
be very sorry to lose any of you; but we could afford to do
so without any serious damage to the life of the tree. Yet
there are some here—God knoweth who they are—who are
the substance of the tree. By the word "substance" is meant
the life, the inward principle. The inward principle is in the
tree, when it has lost its leaves. Now, God discerns some
men in this church, I doubt not, who are toward us like the
inward principle of the oak; they are the substance of the
church. I would feign hope that all the members of the
church in some degree contribute to the substance; but I can
not think so. I am obliged to say I doubt it; because when
one hath fallen and another, it makes us remember that a
church hath much in it that is not life. There be some
branches on the vine that be cut off, because they do not draw
sap from the heart of it, they are only branches bound on by
profession, pretended graftings that have never struck root
into the parent stock, and that must be cut off, and hewn
down, and cast into the fire. But there is a holy seed in the
church that is the substance of it.

Please to note here, that the life of a tree is not determined
by the shape of the branches, nor by the way it grows, but it
is the substance. The shape of a church is not its life. In one
place I see a church formed in an Episcopalian shape; in another place I see one formed in a Presbyterian shape; then,
again, I see one, like ours, formed on an Independent principle. Here I see one with sixteen ounces to the pound of doctrine; there I see one with eight, and some with very little clear
doctrine at all. And yet I find life in all the churches, in some
degree—some good men in all of them. How do I account
for this? Why, just in this way—that the oak may be alive,
whatever its shape, if it has got the substance. If there be
but a holy seed in the church, the church will live; and it is

astonishing how the church will live under a thousand errors, if there be but the vital principle in it. You will find good men among the denominations that you can not receive as being sound in faith. You say, "What! can any good thing come out of Nazareth?" and you go through, and find that there are even in them some true Nazarites of the right order. The very best of men found in the worst of churches! A church lives not because of its rubrics, and its canons, and its articles; it lives because of the holy seed that is in it as the substance. No church can die while it has a holy seed in it, and no church can live that has not the holy seed, for "the holy seed is the substance thereof."

Observe, again, that the substance of the oak is a hidden thing; you can not see it. When the oak or the terebinth is standing destitute of leaves, you know that life is there somewhere. But you can not see it. And very likely you can not and do not know the men that are the holy seed, the substance of the church. Perhaps you imagine the substance of the church lies in the pulpit. Nay, friend! Let us pray to God that such of us as are in the pulpit may be a part of that substance; but much of the substance of the church lies where you don't know any thing of it. There is a mine near Plymouth, where the men who work in it, two hundred and fifty feet below the surface, have a little shelf for their Bibles and hymn-books, and a little place where every morning, when they go down in the black darkness, they bow before God, and praise him whose tender mercies are over all his works. You never heard of these miners, perhaps, and do not know of them; but perhaps some of them are the very substance of the church. There sits Mr. Somebody in that pew; O! what a support he is to the church. Yes, in money matters, perhaps; but do you know, there is poor old Mrs. Nobody in the aisle that is most likely a greater pillar to the church than he, for she is a holier Christian, one who lives nearer to her God and serves him better, and she is "the substance thereof." Ah! that old woman in the garret who is often in prayer; that old man on his bed who spends days and nights in supplication; such people as these are the substance of the church. O! you may take away your prelates, your orators, and the best and greatest of those who stand among earth's mighty men, and their place could be supplied; but take away our intercessors; take away the men and women that breathe out prayer by night and day, and like the priests of old offer the morning and evening lamb as a perpetual sacrifice, and you kill the church at once. What are the ministers? They are but the arms of the church, and the lips of it. A man may be both dumb and armless, and yet live. But these, the heavenly seed, the chosen men and women who live near their God, and serve him with sacred fervent piety—these are the heart of the church; we can not do without them. If we lose them we must die. "The holy seed is the substance thereof."

Then, my hearer, thou art a church member. Let me ask thee—art thou one of the holy seed? Hast thou been begotten again to a lively hope? Has God made thee holy by the sanctifying influence of his Spirit, and by the justifying righteousness of Christ, and by the application to thy conscience of the blood of Jesus? If so, then thou art the substance of the church. They may pass by thee and not notice thee, for thou art little; but the substance is little; the life-germ within the grain of barley is too small for us, perhaps, to detect; the life within the egg is almost an animalcula—you can scarcely see it; and so the life of the church is among the little ones, where we can scarcely find it out. Rejoice, if you are much in prayer; you are the life of the church. But you, O you proud man, pull down your grand thoughts of yourself; you may give to the church, you may speak for the church, and act for the church, but unless you are a holy seed you are not the substance thereof, and it is the substance which is in reality of the greatest value.

But here let me say one thing before I leave this point. Some of you will say, "How is it that good men are the means of preserving the visible church?" I answer, the holy seed doth this, because it derives its life from Christ. If the holy seed had to preserve the church by its own purity and its own strength, the church would go to ruin to-morrow; but it is because these holy ones draw fresh life from Christ continually that they are able to be, as it were, the salvation of the body, and by their influence, direct and indirect, shed life over the whole visible church. The prayers of those living ones in Zion bring down many a blessing upon us; the groans and cries of these earnest intercessors prevail with heaven, and bring down very argosies of mercy from the gates of paradise. And besides, their holy example tends to check us and preserve us in purity; they walk among us like God's own favored ones, wrapped in white, reflecting his image wherever they go, and tending, under God, to the sanctifying of believers, not through their vaunting any self-righteousness, but by stirring up believers to do more for Christ, and to be more like him. "The holy seed shall be the substance thereof."

III. And now I come to the third point. This is true of EVERY INDIVIDUAL BELIEVER: his substance is in him when he has lost his leaves.

The Arminian says that when a Christian loses his leaves he is dead. "No," says God's Word, "he is not; he may look as if he were dead, and not have so much as here and there a leaf upon the topmost bough; but he is not dead. Their substance is in them even when they lose their leaves."

By losing their leaves allow me to understand two things Christian men lose their leaves when they lose their comforts, when they lose the sensible enjoyment of their Master's presence, and when their full assurance is turned into doubting. You have had many such a time as that, have you not? Ah! you were one day in such a state of joy, that you said you could

"Sit and sing yourself away
To everlasting bliss."

But a wintry state came, and your joy all departed, and you stood like a bare tree, after the wind had swept it in the time of winter, with just perhaps one sere leaf hanging by a thread on the topmost bough. But you were not dead then; no, your substance was in you, when you had lost your leaves. You could not see that substance, and good reason why, because your life was hid with Christ in God; you saw not your signs, but you had your substance still, though you could not discover it. There were no heavings of faith, but faith was there; there were no lookings out of hope, but though hope's

eyelids were shut, the eyes were there, to be opened afterwards; there was no lifting, perhaps, of the hand of ardent
prayer, but the hands and arms were there, though they hung
powerless by the side. God said, afterwards, "Strengthen
the feeble knees, and lift up the hands that hang down."
Your substance was in you when you had lost your leaves.
Good Baxter says—"We do not see graces, except when
they are in exercise; and yet they are as much there when
they are not in exercise as when they are." Saith he, "Let
a man take a walk into a wood; there lieth a hare or a rabbit
asleep under the leaves; but he can not see the creature until
it is frightened, and it runneth out, and then he seeth it to be
there." So if faith be in exercise you will perceive your evidence, but if faith be slumbering and still, you will be led to
doubt its existence; and yet it is there all the while.

> "Mountains when in darkness hidden,
> Are as real as in day,"

said one; and truly the faith of the Christian, when shrouded
by doubts and fears, is just as much there as when he rejoiceth devoutly in the display of it.

It is a common error of young converts that they attempt
to live by their experience, instead of tracing their life up
to its precious source. I have known persons rejoicing in
the fullest assurance one day, and sinking into the deepest
despondency the next. The Lord will sometimes strip you
of the leaves of evidence to teach you to live by faith, as
John Kent says—

> "If to-day he deigns to bless us
>   With a sense of pardoned sin;
> He to-morrow may distress us,
>   Make us feel the plague within;
>   All to make us
>   Sick of self and fond of him."

But, ah! there is a worse phase to the subject than this.
Some Christians lose their leaves not by doubts, but by sin.
This is a tender topic—one which needs a tender hand to
touch. O! there are some in our churches that have lost
their leaves by lust and sin. Fair professors once they were;

they stood green among the church, like the very leaves of
paradise; but in an evil hour they fell, the slaves of temptation. They were God's own people by many infallible marks
and signs; and if they were so, though it is grievous that
they should have lost their leaves, yet there is the sweet consolation, their substance is in them still: they are still the
Lord's, still his living children, though they have fallen into
the coma of sin, and are now in a fainting fit, having gone
astray from him, and having their animation suspended, while
life is still there. Some, as soon as they see a Christian do
any thing inconsistent with his profession, say, "That man is
no child of God; he can not be; it is impossible." Ay, but,
sir, remember what he thought who once said—"If a brother
err, ye that are spiritual restore such an one in the spirit of
meekness, considering thyself, lest thou also be tempted." It
is a fact, deny it who will, and abuse it, if you please, to your
own wicked purposes; I can not help it—it is a fact that
some living children of God have been allowed—and an awful allowance it is—to go into the very blackest sins. Do you
think David was not a child of God, even when he sinned?
It is a hard subject to touch; but it is not to be denied. He
had the life of God within him before; and though he sinned
—O! horrid and awful was the crime!—yet his substance
was in him when he lost his leaves. And many a child of
God has gone far away from his Master; but his substance is
in him. And how know we this? Because a dead tree never
lives again; if the substance be really gone, it never lives;
and God's holy Word assures us, that if the real life of grace
could die out in any one, it could never come again; for saith
the apostle, "it is impossible, if they have been once enlightened, and have tasted the heavenly gift, and have been made
partakers of the Holy Ghost"—if these fall away—"it is impossible to renew them again unto repentance." Their tree is
"dead, plucked up by the roots." And the apostle Peter
says—"For if, after they have escaped the corruption that is
in the world through lust, they are again turned back, their
last end shall be worse than the first." But now take David,
or take Peter, which you please. Peter we will have. O!
how foully did he curse his Master! With many an oath he

denied him. But had not Peter the life of God in him then ? Yes; and how do we know? Because when his Master looked upon him, he "went out and wept bitterly." Ah ! if he had been a dead man, hardened and without the substance in him, his Master might have looked to all eternity, and he would not have wept bitterly. How know I that David was yet alive ? Why, by this—that although there was a long long winter, and there were many prickings of conscience, like the workings of the sap within a tree, abortive attempts to thrust forward here and there a shoot before its time, yet when the hour was come, and Nathan came to him and said, "Thou art the man," had David been dead, without the life of God, he would have spurned Nathan from him, and might have done what Manasseh did with Isaiah, cut him in pieces in his anger; but instead of that he bowed his head and wept before God ; and still it is written, "The Lord hath put away thy sin, thou shalt not die." His substance was in him, when he lost his leaves. O ! have pity upon poor fallen brethren. O ! burn them not ; they are not dead logs; though their leaves are gone their substance is in them. God can see grace in their hearts when you can not see it ; he has put a life there that can never expire, for he has said, "I give unto my sheep *eternal* life," and that means a life that lives for ever ; "the water that I shall give him shall be in him a well of water springing up into *everlasting* life." You may choke the well up with big stones, but the water will find its way out yet, and well up notwithstanding. And so the heir of heaven may, to the grief of the church and to the injury of himself, most grievously transgress—and weep, my eyes, O weep for any that have done so, and O bleed, my heart, and thou hast bled, for any that have so sinned—but yet their "substance is in them, when they cast their leaves : so the holy seed"—that is, Christ within them, the Holy Ghost within them, the new creature within them—"the holy seed shall be the substance thereof." Poor backslider ! here is a word of comfort for you. I would not comfort you in your sins ; God forbid ! But if you know your sins and hate them, let me comfort you. Thou art not dead ! As Jesus said of the damsel, "She is not dead, but sleepeth," so let me say of

thee, "Thou art not dead; thou shalt yet l.ve." Dost thou
repent? Dost thou grieve over thy sin? That is the bud
that shows that there is life within. When a common sinner
sins he repents not, or if he doth repent it is with a legal repentance. His conscience pricks him, but he hushes it. He
does not leave his sin and turn from it.

But did you ever see a child of God after he had been
washed from a foul sin? He was a changed man. I know
such an one, who used to carry a merry countenance, and
many were the jokes he made in company; but when I met
him after an awful sin, there was a solemnity about his countenance that was unusual to him. He looked, I should say,
something like Dante, the poet, of whom the boys said, "There
is the man that has been in hell;" because he had written of
hell, and looked like it—he looked so terrible. And when we
spoke of sin there was such a solemnity about him; and when
we spoke of going astray the tears ran down his cheeks, as
much as to say, "I have been astray too." He seemed like
good Christian, after he had been in Giant Despair's castle.
Do you not remember, beloved, the guide who took the pilgrims up to the top of a hill called Clear, and he showed them
from the top of the hill a lot of men with their eyes put out,
groping among the tombs, and Christian asked what it meant.
Said the guide, "These are pilgrims that were caught in
Giant Despair's castle; the giant had their eyes put out, and
they are left to wander among the tombs to die, and their
bones are to be left in the court-yard." Whereupon John
Bunyan very naïvely says, "I looked, and saw their eyes full
of water, for they remembered they might have been there
too." Just as the man talked and spoke that I once knew.
He seemed to wonder why God had not left him to be an
apostate for ever, as the lot of Judas or Demas. He seemed
to think it such a startling thing that while many had gone
aside altogether from God's way, he should still have had his
substance in him, when he had lost his leaves, and that God
should still have loved him. Perhaps, beloved, God allows
some such men to live, and sin, and afterward repent, for this
reason. You know there are some voices needed in music
that are very rare, and when, now and then, such a voice is to

be heard, every one will go to hear it. I have thought that perhaps some of these men in heaven will sing soprano notes before the throne—choice, wondrous notes of grace, because they have gone into the depths of sin after profession; and yet he hath loved them when their feet made haste to perdition, and fetched them up, because he "loved them well." There are but few such; for most men will go foully into sin; they will go out from us because they are not of us, for if they had been of us they would doubtless have continued with us But there have been a few such—great saints, then great backsliding sinners, and then great saints again. Their substance was in them when they had lost their leaves. O! you that have gone far astray, sit and weep. You can not weep too much, though you should cry with Herbert—

> "O, who will give me tears? Come, all ye springs,
> Dwell in my head and eyes; come, clouds and rain!
> My grief hath need of all the watery things
> That nature hath produced."

You might well say,

> "Let every vein
> Suck up a river to supply mine eyes,
> My weary, weeping eyes; too dry for me,
> Unless they get new conduits, new supplies,
> To bear them out, and with my state agree."

But yet remember, "He hath not forsaken his people, neither hath he cut them off; for still he says,

> "Return, O wanderer, return,
> And seek an injured father's heart."

Return! return! return! Thy Father's bowels still move for thee. He speaks through the written oracles at this moment, saying, "How shall I give thee up, Ephraim? How shall I deliver thee, O Israel? How can I make thee as Admah? How can I set thee as Zeboim?" My bowels are moved; my repentings are kindled together; for I will heal their backslidings, I will receive them graciously, I will love them freely, for they are mine still. As the terebinth and as the oak, whose substance is in them when they cast their leaves, even so the holy seed within the elect and called vessels of mercy, is still the substance thereof.

And now, what have I to say to some of you that live in black sin, and yet excuse yourselves on account of the recorded falls of God's people? Sir, know this! Inasmuch as you do this, you wrest the Scriptures to your own destruction. If one man has taken poison, and there has been a physician by his side so skillful that he has saved his life by a heavenly antidote, is that any reason why thou, who hast no physician and no antidote, should yet think that the poison will not kill thee? Why, man, the sin that does not damn a Christian, because Christ washes him in his blood, will damn you. Said Brookes—and I will repeat his words and have done—" He that believeth and is baptized shall be saved, said the apostle, be his sins never so many; but he that believeth not shall be damned, be his sins never so few." Truly your sins may be little; but you are lost for them without Christ. Your sins may be great; but if Christ shall pardon them, then you shall be saved. The one question, then, I have to ask of thee, is—Hast thou Christ? For if thou hast not, then thou hast not the holy seed; thou art a dead tree, and in due time thou shalt be tinder for hell. Thou art a rotten-hearted tree, all touch-wood, ready to be broken in pieces; eaten by the worms of lust; and ah! when the fire shall take hold of thee, what a blazing and a burning! O! that thou hadst life! O! that God would give it to thee! O! that thou wouldst now repent! O! that thou wouldst cast thyself on Jesus! O! that thou wouldst turn to him with full purpose of heart! For then, remember, thou wouldst be saved—saved now, and saved for ever; for " the holy seed" would be " the substanc thereof."

SERMON III

THE SNARE OF THE FOWLER

"Surely he shall deliver thee from the snare of the fowler."—PSALM xci. 3

IF Moses wrote this Psalm he might represent the fowler as being in his case the king of Egypt, who sought to slay him, or the Amalekites, who pounced upon Israel in the plain, when they little expected it. If David penned it, he might have compared Saul to the fowler, for he himself says, he was hunted like a partridge upon the mountains. But we believe, if the verse be applicable to either of those cases, it was intended by the Psalmist not to have a private interpretation, but to be applicable to all time; and we believe it is spoken concerning that arch-enemy of souls, the great deceiver, Satan, of whom we just now sang,

> "Satan, the fowler, who betrays
> Unguarded souls a thousand ways."

"The prince of the power of this world, the spirit which still worketh in the children of disobedience," is like a fowler, always attempting to destroy us. It was once said by a talented writer, that the old devil was dead, and that there was a new devil now; by which he meant to say, that the devil of old times was a rather different devil from the deceiver of these times. We believe that it is the same evil spirit; but there is a difference in his mode of attack. The devil of five hundred years ago was a black and grimy thing well portrayed in our old pictures of that evil spirit. He was a persecutor, who cast men into the furnace, and put them to death for serving Christ. The devil of this day is a well-spoken gentleman: he does not persecute—he rather attempts to persuade and to beguile. He is not now so much the turious Romanist, so much as the insinuating unbeliever, attempting to overturn our religion, while at the same time he pretends he would make it more rational, and so more triumphant. He would only link worldliness with religion; and so he would really make religion void, under the cover of developing the great power of the gospel, and bringing out secrets which our forefathers had never discovered. Satan is always a fowler. Whatever his tactics may be, his object is still the same—to catch men in his net. Men are here compared to silly, weak birds, that have not skill enough to avoid the snare, and have not strength enough to escape from it. Satan is the fowler; he has been so and is so still; and if he does not now attack us as the roaring lion, roaring against us in persecution, he attacks us as the adder, creeping silently along the path, endeavoring to bite our heel with his poisoned fangs, and weaken the power of grace and ruin the life of godliness within us. Our text is a very comforting one to all believers, when they are beset by temptation. "Surely he shall deliver them from the snare of the fowler."

First, *a few words concerning the snare of the fowler;* secondly, *the deliverance;* and, thirdly, *the certainty of it;* dwelling upon that word *surely,* for it seems to be the diamond wherewith this precious golden promise is embellished. "*Surely* he shall deliver thee from the snare of the fowler."

I. First, then, THE SNARE OF THE FOWLER. It is an illustration too suggestive for me thoroughly to unravel. I must leave it for your meditations at home to enumerate the divers ways in which a fowler attempts to take his birds, and then you will have suggested to you the divers means which the evil spirit employs for the destruction of souls. Allow me, however, just to begin, and pass over two or three points connected with the fowler and with the evil one.

1. First, *the fowler's snare is intimately connected with secrecy.* "Surely in vain is the net spread in the sight of any bird." Therefore the fowler carefully covers up his trap; or, if the trap itself be uncovered he doth well beguile the bird, so that it is utterly ignorant of his intention to take it in the trap, little thinking that the food laid there for its banqueting is really placed there for its enticement and destruction. The

fowler, when he goes after his birds, is very careful lest they should discover him. We hear, for instance, that in the taking of wild ducks, in Lincolnshire, a man will hold before his mouth a piece of turf, in order that the smell of his breath may not be perceived by the birds, who are exceedingly wary. The temptations of the world are of this secret sort to a Christian, though not to the wicked man, for the wicked man sins with his eyes wide open; dashing into the net knowing it is a net, laying hold of iniquity with both his hands, even when destruction stareth him in the face. He will commit a sin that he knows is condemned even by the law of the land: he will rush into a crime, concerning the guilt of which no doubt can be entertained. Not so the Christian: he is taken by secrecy. "Ah!" says one, "if I thought such-and-such a thing were really wrong; if I were perfectly convinced of its wrongfulness, I would give it up." It is just there the difficulty lies. So would the bird say: "If I thought that really were a trap, I would not enter it; if I were perfectly persuaded that net would entangle me, I would not fly to such-and-such a spot; I would not approach there at all, if I were sure it would be my destruction." How many a professor there is who asks the question, "May I go to this place? May I go to that place?" and some of us answer "No," and we are called Puritans for it; but let those who have attempted to keep their godliness intact, while they pursued the pleasures of this world, stand up and make the mournful confession, that the healthiness of the two things can never exist together. We must either serve God wholly, or serve the evil one wholly. "If God be God, serve him; if Baal be God serve him." One, or else the other. Many a man has been entrapped into sin by Satan; not knowing that it was evil! Some one has hinted to him in business, for instance—"You may very safely do such-and-such a thing; all the shopkeepers in the street have done it; it is not actually dishonest; it improves the article, it really does; and although you can thus sell an article at a dearer rate than you ought to sell it, yet you need not tell the public; and if the article is all the better for it, it is quite fair and safe that you should adulterate it." And so the good easy man, not opening both his eyes, I think, but shutting one of them a little, lest he should see too well to be able to fill his pockets in the dark, is a little taken aside; and by-and-by he is led to discover that the act which he has done is the taking of him in the snare of the fowler, for he has been sinning against his God, and his God therefore punishes him for it with many stripes, and lays his rod upon him. I do not think that a Christian is so often betrayed into a sin that is palpable and known, as he is into a sin that is secret. If the devil comes to my door with his horns visible, I will never let him in; but if he comes with his hat on as a respectable gentleman, he is at once admitted. The metaphor may be very quaint, but it is quite true. Many a man has taken in an evil thing, because it has been varnished and glossed over, and not apparently an evil; and he has thought in his heart, there is not much harm in it; so he has let in the little thing, and it has been like the breaking forth of water— the first drop has brought after it a torrent. The beginning has been but the beginning of a fearful end. Take care, Christian, of things that are secret; take care of the common doings of the world, which are well enough for them, perhaps. We would not deny them their pleasures, for they have no others; but they are not good for you, for you have a finer life—a life of a finer texture and order than can exist in the haunts of ungodly persons. Remember, you are not to be a judge for others. Some men, especially those who are unconverted, can, without being led into sin, indulge in many gayeties and merriments; but the Christian is like the Englishman, who can not hope to survive long where the jungle fever reigns. The native can live there, but he can not. And so you who are twice-born men will find your piety ruined, by that which, to a worldly man, does not lead him into greater evil than that which he would naturally commit. You are to have a stricter rule on yourselves than others, and are to be more stern in your piety than the world would have you be; for sin is usually hidden, and the snare is not often made apparent. "Surely he shall deliver thee from the snare of the fowler."

2. In the second place, *the snare of the fowler is generally noted for its adaptation.* You do not find a fowler setting

the same snare for one bird as for another; he knows his bird and he adapts his bait to it. He would be an unwise fowler who should go to work with the same machinery to catch the lark that flies on high as the duck that swims along the stream. The fowler is wiser than that: he adapts his snare to the condition of the bird which he desires to take. Satan the fowler does just the same. There is one man here; he tempts him to drunkenness. Perhaps that would naturally be his sin, if left without grace in his heart; and Satan, knowing it to be his weak point, attempts to overcome him by surfeiting, gluttony, and drunkenness. Another man is utterly impervious to any temptation to that bestial habit; but, it may be, he is easily taken in another snare—the snare of lust; therefore Satan adapts his temptation to the hot blood of the man who naturally would be inclined to live a life of sin. Another one perhaps eschews every lascivious and sensual habit; then Satan comes to him, and adapts his temptation to the shape of pride. The man is naturally a melancholy man, full of solitude: Satan gets him, if he can, to wrap himself up in a solitary dignity, to say, "I am holy." "Lord, I thank thee, I am not as other men are." Or if a man is not naturally inclined to a very high degree of pride, Satan takes him with sloth. The man likes an easy life; Satan therefore adapts his bait to him by letting him sit still, fold his arms, and so perish by slothfulness: and mark this, he who sitteth still in the frost, when the snow is on the ground, in the depths of the wild regions of the frozen zone, must as surely perish by his idleness as if he drove a dagger to his heart. Satan knows that, and so adapts his bait accordingly. O! how often it happens, beloved, that you and I condemn a thing in another person which we allow in ourselves, perhaps without knowing it. We say of such a one, How proud he is! Well, our pride is not exactly of that shape; we have got another shaped pride, but the same article; labeled differently, but the same thing. Satan adapts the pride to each particular case. We are rich: he does not perhaps tempt us to the pride of riches, but he tempts us to the pride of mastership, and makes us harsh masters to our servants. Or if he does not tempt us to that pride, he perhaps enchants us with the pride of generosity and we are apt to boast of our kindness and of what we have given away. He will always adapt his trap to his man, and his bait to his bird. He will not tempt you all with the same temptation he would tempt me with; nor me with the temptation with which he would naturally assail another. "The snare of the fowler." A cunning enemy we have to deal with he knows our weak points; he has been dealing with men for these last six thousand years; he knows all about them. He is possessed of a gigantic intellect; though he be a fallen spirit; and he is easily able to discover where our sore places are, and there it is he immediately attacks us. If we be like Achilles, and can not be wounded anywhere but in our heel, then at the heel he will send his dart, and nowhere else. He will find out our easily besetting sin, and there, if he can, he will attempt to work our ruin and our destruction. Let us bless God that it is written, "Surely he shall deliver thee from the snare of the fowler."

3. In the next place, *the fowler's snare is frequently connected with pleasure, profit, and advantage.* In the bird's case it is for the seed scattered on the ground that he flies to the snare. It is some tempting bait which allures him to his death. And usually Satan, the fowler, uses a temptation wherewith to beguile us. "O!" says one, "I can not give up such-and-such a thing, it is so pleasant. Sir, you never knew the charms of such-and-such a pursuit, otherwise you could never advise me to relinquish it." Yes, my friend, but it is just the sweetness of it to you that makes it the more dangerous. Satan never sells his poisons naked; he always gilds them before he vends them. He knows very well that men will buy them and swallow them, if he does but gild them beforehand. Take care of pleasures; mind what you are at when you are at them. Many of them are innocent and healthful, but many of them are destructive. It is said that where the most beautiful cacti grow, there the most venomous serpents are to be found at the root of every plant. And it is so with sin. Your fairest pleasures will harbor your grossest sins. Take care; take care of your pleasures. Cleopatra's asp was introduced in a basket of flowers; so are our sins often brought to us in the flowers of our pleasures.

Satan offers to the drunkard the sweetness of the intoxicating cup, which rejoices him, when his brain is rioting in frolic, and when his soul is lifted up within him. He offers to the lustful man the scenes and pleasures of carnal mirth, and merriment, and delight, and so he leadeth him astray with the bait, concealing the hook which afterwards shall pain him. He gives to you and to me, each of us, the offer of our peculiar joy; he tickleth us with pleasures, that he may lay hold upon us, and so have us in his power. I would have every Christian be especially on his guard against the very thing that is most pleasing to his human nature. I would not have him avoid every thing that pleases him, but I would have him be on his guard against it. Just like Job, when his sons had been feasting in their houses. He did not forbid them doing it, but he said, " I will offer a sacrifice, lest my sons should have sinned in their hearts, and should have cursed God foolishly." He was more careful over them at the time of their feasting than at any other season. Let us be the same. Let us remember that the snare of the fowler is generally connected with some pretended pleasure or profit, but that Satan's end is not our pleasing, but our destruction.

4. In the next place, *sometimes the fowler very wisely employs the force of example.* We all know the influence of the decoy-duck, in endeavoring to bring others into the snare. How very often Satan, the fowler, employs a decoy to lead God's people into sin! You get with a man; you think him to be a true Christian; you have some respect for his character; he is a high professor, can talk religion by the yard, and can give you any quantity of theology you like to ask for. You see him commit a sin; ten to one but you will do the same, if you have much respect for him; and so he will lead you on. And mark, Satan is very careful in the men whom he chooses to be decoys. He never employs a wicked man to be a decoy for a good man. It is very seldom, when Satan would decoy a Christian into a snare, that he makes use of an open reprobate. No; he makes use of a man who is pretendedly religious, and who looks to be of the same quality as yourself, and therefore entices you astray. Let a bad man meet me in the street, and ask me to commit sin! The devil

knows better than to set him at any such work as that, because he knows I should pass by directly. If he wants his
errand well done, he sends one to me whom I call brother;
and so through the brotherhood of profession I am apt to give
him credence and pay him respect; and then if he goeth
astray, the force of example is very powerful, and so I may
easily be led into the net too. Take care of your best friends;
be careful of your companions. Choose the best you can;
then follow them no further than they follow Christ. Let your
course be entirely independent of every one else. Say with
Joshua, let others do what they will, "As for me and my
house we will serve the Lord."

5. Note, once more, that *sometimes the fowler, when he
faileth to take his bird by deceit and craft, will go a hawking
after it*—will send his hawk into the air, to bring down his
prey. It often happens, when the devil can not ruin a man by
getting him to commit a sin, he attempts to slander him; he
sends a hawk after him, and tries to bring him down by slan-
dering his good name. I will give you a piece of advice. I
know a good minister, now in venerable old age, who was
once most villainously lied against and slandered by a man
who had hated him only for the truth's sake. The good man
was grieved; he threatened the slanderer with a lawsuit, unless he apologized. He did apologize. The slander was
printed in the papers in a public apology; and you know what
was the consequence. The slander was more believed than if
he had said nothing about it. And I have learned this lesson
—to do with the slanderous hawk what the little birds do,
just fly up. The hawk can not do them any hurt while they
can keep above him—it is only when they come down that he
can injure them. It is only when by mounting he gets above
the birds, that the hawk comes sweeping down upon them,
and destroys them. If any slander you, do not come down
to them; let them slander on. Say, as David said concerning
Shimei, "If the Lord hath given him commandment to curse,
let him curse;" and if the sons of Zeruiah say, "Let us go
and take this dead dog's head," you say, "Nay, let him curse;"
and in that way you will live down slander. If some of us
turned aside to notice every bit of a sparrow that began

chirping at us, we should have nothing to do but to answer them. If I were to fight people on every doctrine I preach, I should do nothing else but just amuse the devil, and indulge the combative principles of certain religionists who like nothing better than quarreling. By the grace of God, say what you please against me, I will never answer you, but go straight on. All shall end well, if the character be but kept clean ; the more dirt that is thrown on it by slander, the more it shall glisten, and the more brightly it shall shine. Have you never felt your fingers itch sometimes to be at a man who slanders you ? I have. I have sometimes thought, "I can not hold my tongue now ; I must answer that fellow ;" but I have asked of God grace to imitate Jesus, who, "when he was reviled reviled not again," and by his strength let them go straight on The surest way in the world to get rid of a slander is just to let it alone and say nothing about it, for if you prosecute the rascal who utters it, or if you threaten him with an action, and he has to apologize, you will be no better off—some fools will still believe it. Let it alone—let it keep as it is ; and so God will help you to fulfill by your wisdom his own promise, "Surely he shall deliver thee from the snare of the fowler."

And now, ere I close this point, let me observe once more, the fowler, when he is determined to take his birds, uses all these arts at once, perhaps, and *besets the bird on every side.* So, you will remember, beloved, it is with you. Satan will not leave a stone unturned to ruin your soul for ever.

> "Amidst a thousand snares I stand,
> Upheld and guarded by thy hand."

Old Master Quarles says,

> The close pursuer's busy hands do plant
> Snares in thy substance ; snares attend thy want ;
> Snares in thy credit ; snares in thy disgrace ;
> Snares in thy high estate ; snares in thy base ;
> Snares tuck thy bed ; and snares surround thy board ;
> Snares watch thy thoughts ; and snares attach thy word
> Snares in thy quiet ; snares in thy commotion ;
> Snares in thy diet ; snares in thy devotion ;
> Snares lurk in thy resolves, snares in thy doubt ;
> Snares lie within thy heart, and snares without ;
> Snares are above thy head, and snares beneath ;
> Snares in thy sickness, snares are in thy death."

There is not a place beneath which a believer walks that free from snares. Behind every tree there is the Indian with his barbed arrow; behind every bush there is the lion seeking to devour; under every piece of grass there lieth the adder Everywhere they are. Let us be careful; let us gird our-selves with the might of God's omnipotence, and then shall his Holy Spirit keep us, so that we shall tread on the lion and the adder, the young lion and the dragon shall we trample under our feet, and we shall be " delivered from the snare of the fowler."

II. Now we pass to the second point—THE DELIVERANCE God delivers his people from the snare of the fowler. Two thoughts here: *from—out of.* First, he delivers them *from* the snare—does not let them get in it; secondly, when they do get in it, he delivers them *out of* it. The first promise is the most precious to some of us; the second is the best to others.

He shall deliver thee from the snare. How does he do that?

Very often by *trouble*. Trouble is often the means whereby God delivers us from snares. You have all heard the old story of the celebrated painter who was painting in St. Paul's, and who, looking at his work, went gradually back, inch by inch, to get a view of it, so that he might see the excellence of its proportions, until his feet were just on the edge of the platform upon which he stood; and he would have fallen down and been dashed in pieces upon the pavement beneath, but just at that moment a workman who stood there, desirous to save his life, and not knowing how to do it, hit upon an expe-dient which proved to be a very wise one. Instead of shout-ing out to his master, " Sir, you are in danger," which would most certainly have sent him backward, he took up a brush, and dipping it in a pot of paint, dashed it at the picture. The good man rushed forward in anger to chastise him; but when it was explained, he clearly saw that he had acted wisely Just so with God. You and I have often painted a fine pic-ture, and we have been walking backward admiring it. God knows that our backsliding will soon end in our destruction and he, by a sad providence, blasts our prospect, takes away

our child from us, buries our wife, removes some darling **object**
of our pleasures; and we rush forward and say, "Lord, why
is this?"—utterly unconscious that if it had not been for
trouble we might have been dashed in pieces, and our lives
would have been ended in destruction. I doubt not, many of
you have been saved from ruin by your sorrows, your griefs,
your troubles, your woes, your losses, and your crosses. All
these have been the breaking of the net that set you free from
the snare of the fowler.

At other times God keeps his people from the sin of the
fowler *by giving them great spiritual strength, a spirit of
great courage;* so that when they are tempted to do evil they
say, with decision, "How can I do this great wickedness and
sin against God?" O! that was a noble escape of Joseph,
when his mistress laid hold of his garment; that was a noble
escape of his, when his soul escaped like a bird out of the snare
of the fowler; and I doubt not there are many here who have
done deeds almost as noble as that of Joseph, who have had
grace within their hearts, so that they have turned away their
eyes from beholding folly, and when they have been tempted
to evil they have put their foot upon it, and said, "I can not,
I can not; I am a child of God; I can not and I must not;"
and though the thing was pleasing to themselves yet they abjured it. You remember the case of Mr. Standfast in Bunyan's
Pilgrim's Progress. Madame Bubble had greatly enticed
poor Mr. Standfast with her offers. He says, "There was one
in very pleasant attire, but old, who presented herself to me,
and offered me three things, to wit, her body, her purse, and
her bed. Now the truth is, I was both weary and sleepy: I
am also as poor as an owlet, and that perhaps the witch knew.
Well, I repulsed her once and again, but she put by my re-
pulses and smiled. Then I began to be angry; but she mat-
tered that nothing at all. Then she made offers again, and
said if I would be ruled by her, she would make me great and
happy; for, said she, I am the mistress of the world, and men
are made happy by me. Then I asked her her name, and she
told me it was Madame Bubble. This set me further from her;
but she still followed me with enticements. Then I betook
me, as you saw, to my knees, and with hands lifted up, and

cries, I prayed to him that had said he would help. So just as you came up the gentlewoman went her way. Then I continued to give thanks for this my great deliverance ; for I verily believe she intended no good, but rather sought to make stop of me in my journey." Thus God delivers his people from the snares of the fowler, by giving them the spirit of prayer as well as the spirit of courage, so that they call upon God in the day of trouble, and he delivers them.

And I have noticed one more very singular thing. Sometimes I, myself, have been saved from the snare of the fowler (I can not tell you how exactly), in this way. I have felt that if the temptation had come a week before, my mind was in that peculiar condition, that I should almost inevitably have been led away by it; but when it came, the mind, by passing through some process, had become in such a condition that the temptation was no temptation at all. We were just brought to such a state, that what might have ruined us before, we would not then look at. "No," we have said, "if you had offered me this some time ago it might have been accepted; but now God has, by some mysterious influence of his Spirit, turned my heart in another direction, and it is not even a temptation to me at all—not worthy of a moment's thought." So God delivers his people from the snare of the fowler.

But the second thought was, that *God delivers his people, even when they get into the snare.* Alas! my hearer, you and I know something about the net; we have been inside it, we have; we have not only seen it spread, we have been in its folds. We know something about the cage, for we have, unfortunately, been in the cage ourselves, even since we have known the Lord. The fowler's hand has been upon our neck; it has only been the sovereign grace of God that has prevented him from utterly destroying us. What a blessed thing it is, that if the believer shall, in an evil hour, come into the net, yet God will bring him out of it! Poor Christian and Hopeful got into the fowler's net when they entered into the castle of Giant Despair ; but the key of promise picked the lock, and they escaped. They were in the fowler's net, too, when Flatterer cast a net over them, and left them in the lane ; but there came one who, after he had beaten them full sore, took the net off, and then they went on their way, better men than they were before they were in the net. I know one who is in the net now. Some bird, one of God's own ones too, has been taken in the snare, and is now groaning and crying out, because, alas! alas! he has sinned. I have a person here, a good man, a professor of religion, and a truly worthy one! but alas! he has sinned, and at this hour the tears are in his eyes, and he is saying,

> " The tumult of my thoughts
>   Doth but increase my woe;
> My spirit languishes, my heart
>   Is desolate and low.
>
> " Turn, turn thee to my soul;
>   Bring thy salvation near;
> When will thy hand release my feet
>   Out of the deadly snare ?"

O backslider, be cast down, but do not despair; God will restore thee yet. Wanderer though thou hast been, hear what he says! "Return, O backsliding children; I will have mercy upon you." But you say you can not return. Then here is still a promise—" Surely he shall deliver thee from the snare of the fowler." Thou shalt yet be brought out from all the evil into which thou hast fallen, and though thou shalt never cease to repent thy ways even to thy dying day, yet he that hath loved thee will not cast thee away; he will receive thee; he will admit thee into his dwelling-place, and will even now restore thee to the number of his people, and give thee joy and gladness, that the bones which he has broken may rejoice. "Surely he shall deliver thee from the snare of the fowler."

There have been very remarkable instances of God delivering his people out of the snare of the fowler, as the following illustration will show :

" A young lady, who belonged to a church in the city of New York, married a young man who was not a Christian. He was a merchant, engaged in a lucrative business, and the golden stream of wealth flowed in upon him till he had amassed a large fortue. He accordingly retired from business, and went into the country. He purchased a splendid residence; fine trees waved their luxuriant foliage around it; here was a lake filled with fish, and there a garden full of rare shrubbery and flowers. Their house was fashionably and expensively furnished; and they seemed to possess all of earth that mortal could desire. Thus prospered, and plied with an interchange of civilities among her gay and fashionable neighbors, the piety of the lady declined, and her heart became wedded to the world. And it is not to be wondered at, that her three children, as they grew up, imbibed her spirit and copied her example. 'A severe disease,' it is said, 'demands a severe remedy;' and that God soon applied. One morning intelligence came that her little son had fallen into the fish-lake, and was drowned. The mother's heart was pierced with the affliction, and she wept and murmured against the providence of God. Soon afterwards, her only daughter, a blooming girl of sixteen, was taken sick of a fever and died. It seemed then as if the mother's heart would have broken. But this new stroke of the rod of a chastening Father seemed but to increase her displeasure against his will. The only remaining child, her eldest son, who had come home from college to attend his sister's funeral, went out into the fields soon afterwards, for the purpose of hunting. In getting over a fence, he put his gun over first to assist himself in springing to the ground, when it accidentally discharged itself and killed him! What then were that mother's feelings? In the extravagance of her grief, she fell down, tore her hair, and raved like a maniac against the providence of God. The father, whose grief was already almost insupportable, when he looked upon the shocking spectacle, and heard her frenzied ravings, could endure his misery no longer. The iron entered into his soul and he fell a speedy victim to his accumulated afflictions. From the wife and mother, her husband and all her children were now taken away. Reason returned, and she was led to reflection. She saw her dreadful backslidings, her pride, her rebellion; and she wept with the tears of a deep repentance. Peace was restored to her soul. Then could she lift up her hands to heaven, exclaiming, 'I thank thee, O Father!—the Lord hath given, the Lord hath taken away, and blessed be the name of the Lord.' Thus did he afflictions yield the peaceable fruit of righteousness, and her heavenly Father chasten her, 'not for his pleasure, but for her profit, that she might become partaker of his holiness.' "

So God delivered her soul out of the snare of the fowler She started afresh in the ways of righteousness, serving God with diligence and zeal, and growing up in his fear. By trouble and trial, by some means or another, God will surely deliver his people out of the snare of the fowler, even when they are in it.

III. And now, to conclude, I am to dwell for a moment or two upon that word "SURELY." The assurance of every truth of Scripture is just the beauty of it. If it were not sure, it were not precious; and it is precious just because it is sure.

Now, it says, "surely he shall deliver thee." Why? First, because he has promised to do it; and God's promises are bonds that never yet were dishonored. If he hath said he will, he will. Secondly, because Christ Jesus hath taken an oath that he will do it. In ages long gone by Christ Jesus became the shepherd of the sheep, and the surety of them too. "If any of them perish," said he, " at my hand, thou shalt require it;" and, therefore, because Christ is responsible, because he is the heavenly sponsor for all God's people, they must be kept: for otherwise Christ's bond were forfeited, and his oath were null and void. They must be kept, again, because otherwise the union that there is between all of them and Christ would not be a real one. Christ and his church are one—one body; but if any of the members of my body were cut off, I should be maimed, and if Christ could lose one of his children he would be a maimed Christ. " We are his body, the fullness of him that filleth all in all." If, then, the whole church were not gathered in, Christ would be an incomplete Christ, seeing he would want his fullness. They must all be saved, for God the Father has determined that they shall be; nay, the Son has sworn they shall be; and God the Holy Spirit vouches for it they shall be. None of God's people shall be cast away, or else the Bible is not true. The whole stability of the covenant rests on their final perseverance. The whole covenant of grace rests on this—

"He shall present our souls,
Unblemished and complete,
Before the glory of his face,
With joys divinely great."

And therefo e they must be preserved out of the snare o. the fowler, because otherwise the covenant would be null and void. If one should perish the oath would be broken; if one should be cast away the covenant would be void; and therefore they must be kept secure.

"His honor is engaged to save
The meanest of his sheep;
All that his heavenly Father gave,
His hands securely keep."

I have no time to enlarge upon that subject, which is big with glory, and might afford a topic for many discourses. I now close up by saying, Men and brethren, is this promise yours? "Surely he shall deliver thee." Are you the men ? "How can I tell?" you say. Do you believe on the Lord Jesus Christ? Do you, as a guilty sinner, cast yourself wholly on the blood and righteousness of the immaculate Redeemer? I do not ask you whether you are a Wesleyan, a Churchman, a Baptist, an Independent, or a Presbyterian; my only question is, Are you born again? Have you passed from death unto life? Are you "a new creature in Christ Jesus?" Is all your trust put in the Lord Jesus Christ? Has his life become your model, and does his Spirit dwell in your mortal body? If so, peace be unto you: this promise is yours. You may have been the worst of men; but if you have faith in Christ those sins are all forgiven, and you may take this promise to be yours for ever. But if you are self-righteous, self-sufficient, ungodly, careless, worldly, there is no such promise for you; you are in the snare, you shall be there, and you shall perish, unless you repent; for it is written, "Except ye repent ye shall all likewise perish." May God save you from perishing, by giving you an interest in the blood of Christ; and to the Father, the Son, and the Holy Ghost, be glory for ever and ever.

SERMON IV

THE FRUITLESS VINE

"And the word of the Lord came unto me, saying, Son of man, What is the vine-tree more than any tree, or than a branch which is among the trees of the forest?"—EZEKIEL, xv. 1, 2.

THE Jewish nation had arrogant ideas of themselves; when they sinned against God, they supposed that on account of the superior sanctity of their forefathers, or by reason of some special sanctity in themselves, they would be delivered, sin as they pleased. In consequence of the infinite mercy of Jehovah, which he had displayed toward them, in delivering them out of so many distresses, they gradually came to imagine that they were the favorite children of Providence, and that God could by no means ever cast them away. God, therefore, in order to humble their pride, tells them that they in themselves were nothing more than any other nation; and he asks them what there was about them to recommend them? " I have often called you a vine; I have planted you, and nurtured you in a very fruitful hill, but now you bring forth no fruit; what is there in you why I should continue you in my favor? If you imagine there is any thing about you more than about any other nation, your are mightily mistaken." " What is the vine-tree more than any tree, or than a branch which is among the trees of the forest?"

Let us remember that these things might be said without implying that God in the least degree alters his eternal purpose toward any chosen vessel of mercy; for the Israelitish nation was not chosen to eternal salvation, as a nation, but chosen to special privileges; a type and shadow of that eternal personal election which Christ has given to his church. From his own elect church God will never withdraw his love;

but from the outward and visible church he sometimes may. From his own people he never will take away his affection, but from professors, from those who merely stand in his people's external condition, and are not his children, he may, yea, and he will, withdraw every token of his favor. God humbles Israel, by reminding them that they had nothing which other nations had not; that, in fact, they were a contemptible nation, not worthy to be set side by side with the cedar of Babylon, or with the oak of Samaria; they were of no use, they were worthless, unless they brought forth fruit to him. He checks their pride and humbles them, with the parable we have here before us.

Beloved, we shall, by God's help, use this parable for ourselves, and learn two lessons from it. The first shall be *a lesson of humility for saints;* and the second, *a lesson of searching for all who are professors.*

I. First, here is A LESSON OF HUMILITY for all you who have " tasted that the Lord is gracious." " What is the vine-tree more than any tree, or than a branch which is among the trees of the forest ?"

In looking upon all the various trees, we observe that the vine is distinguished among them; so that, in the old parable of Jotham, the trees waited upon the vine-tree, and said unto it, " Come thou and reign over us." But merely looking at the vine, without regard to its fruitfulness, we should not see any kingship in it over other trees. In size, form, beauty, or utility, it has not the slightest advantage. We can do nothing with the wood of the vine. " Shall wood be taken thereof to do any work ? or will men make a pin of it to hang any vessel thereon ?" It is a useless plant apart from its fruitfulness. We sometimes see it in beauty, trained up by the side of our walls, and in the East it might be seen in all its luxuriance, and great care is bestowed in its training; but leave the vine to itself, and consider it apart from its fruitfulness, it is the most insignificant and despicable of all things that bear the name of trees. Now, beloved, this is for the humbling of God's people. They are called God's vine; but what are they by nature more than others ? Others are as good as they · yea, some others are even greater and better than they. They, by God's goodness, have become fruitful, have been planted in a good soil; the Lord hath trained them upon the walls of the sanctuary, and they bring forth fruit to his glory. But what are they without their God? What are they without the continual influence of the Spirit, begetting fruitfulness in them? Are they not the least among the sons of men, and the most to be despised of those that have been brought forth of women? Look upon this, believer.

> " What was there in thee to merit esteem,
>   Or give the Creator delight ?"

Yea, look upon thyself as thou art now. Doth not thy conscience reproach thee? Do not thy thousand wanderings stand before thee, and tell thee that thou art unworthy to be called his son? Does not the weakness of thy mental power, the frailty of thy moral power, thy continual unbelief, and thy perpetual backsliding from God, tell thee that thou art less than the least of all saints? And if he hath made thee any thing, art thou not thereby taught that it is grace, free, sovereign grace, which hath made thee to differ? Should any here, supposing themselves to be the children of God, imagine that there is some reason in them why they should have been chosen, let them know, that as yet they are in the dark concerning the first principles of grace, and have not yet learned the gospel. If ever they had known the gospel, they would, on the other hand, confess that they were less than the least— the offscouring of all things—unworthy, ill-deserving, undeserving, and hell-deserving, and ascribe it all to distinguishing grace, which has made them to differ; and to discriminating love, which has chosen them out from the rest of the world. Great Christian, thou wouldst have been a great sinner if God had not made thee to differ. O! thou who art valiant for truth, thou wouldst have been as valiant for the devil if grace had not laid hold of thee. A seat in heaven shall one day be thine; but a chain in hell would have been thine if grace had not changed thee. Thou canst now sing his love; but a licentious song might have been on thy lips, if grace had not washed thee in the blood of Jesus. Thou art now sanctified, thou art quickened, thou art justified; but what wouldst thou have been to-day if it had not been for the interposition of the divine hand? There is not a crime thou mightest not have committed; there is no: a folly into which thou mightest not have run. Even murder itself thou mightest have committed if grace had not kept thee. Thou shalt be like the angels; but thou wouldst have been like the devil if thou hadst not been changed by grace. Therefore, never be proud; all thy garments thou hast from above; rags were thine only heritage. Be not proud, though thou hast a large estate, a wide domain of grace; thou hadst once not a single thing to call thine own, except thy sin and misery. Thou art now wrapped up in the golden righteousness of the Saviour, and accepted in the garments of the beloved; but thou wouldst have been buried under the black mountain of sin, and clothed with the filthy rags of unrighteousness, if he had not changed thee. And art thou proud? Dost thou exalt thyself? O! strange mystery, that thou, who hast borrowed every thing, should exalt thyself; that thou, who hast nothing of thine own, but hast still to draw upon grace, shouldst be proud; a poor dependent pensioner upon the bounty of thy Saviour, and yet proud; one who hath a life which can only live by fresh streams of life from Jesus, and yet proud! Go, hang thy pride upon the gallows, as high as Haman; hang it there to rot, and stand thou beneath, and execrate it to all eternity; for sure of all things most to be cursed and despised is the pride of a Christian. He, of all men, has ten thousand times more reason than any other to be humble, and walk lowly with his God, and kindly and humbly toward his fellow-creatures. Let this, then, humble thee, Christian, that the vine-tree is nothing more than any other tree, save only for the fruitfulness which God has given it.

II. But now here comes A LESSON OF SEARCH. As the vine without its fruit is useless and worthless; so, too, the professor, without fruit, is useless and worthless; yea, he is the most useless thing in the wide world.

Now, let us dwell upon this point. *A fruitless profession.* And while I am preaching on it, let the words go round to each one, and let the minister, and let his deacons, and let his hearers all try their hearts and search their reins, and see whether they have a fruitless profession.

1. First, a fruitless professor. *How do we know him ? what is his character ?* Secondly. *What is the reason he is fruitless ?* Thirdly, *What is the estimation God holds him in ?* He is good for nothing at all. And, then, fourthly, *What will be his end ?* He is to be burned with fire.

First, *Where are we to find fruitless professors ?* Everywhere, dear friends, everywhere—down here, up there, everywhere; in pulpits and in pews. False professors are to be found in every church. Let us leave other denominations alone, then. They are to be found in this church; they are to be found in this present assembly. To whatever denomination you may belong, there are some false and fruitless professors in it. How know you that you may not belong to those who bring forth no fruit? There are fruitless professors to be found in every position of the church, and in every part of society. You may find the false professor among the rich; he hath much wealth, and he is hailed with gladness by the church. God hath given him much of this world's good; and therefore, the church, forgetful that God hath chosen the poor, giveth him honor, and what doth she get from him? She getteth but little to help her. Her poor are still neglected, and her means not in the least recruited by his riches. Or if she gain a portion of his riches, yet she getteth none of his prayers; nor is she in the least supported by his holy living, for he that hath riches often liveth in sin, and rolleth in uncleanness; and, then, weareth his profession as a uniform, wherewith to cover his guilt. Rich men have sometimes been false professors; and they are to be found among poor men too. Full many a poor man has entered into the church, and been cordially received. He has been poor, and they have thought it a good thing that poverty and grace should go together—that grace should cheer his hovel, and make his poverty-stricken home a glad one. But then, this poor man hath turned aside to follies, and hath degraded himself with drunkenness, hath sworn, and by unworthy conduct dishonored his God; or, if not, he hath been idle, and sat still, and been of little service to the church; and so he hath been false and fruitless in his profession.

False professors are to be found in the men that lead the

vanguard of God's army; the men who preach eloquently, whose opinion is law, who speak like prophets, and whose language seems to be inspired. They have brought forth the fruit of popularity, ay, and the fruit of philanthropy too, but their heart has not been right with God, therefore, the fruit, good in itself, was not fruit unto holiness; the moral benefit of their labors does not extend to everlasting life. They have not brought forth the fruits of the Spirit, seeing that they were not living branches of the living vine. Then there have been false professors in obscurity; modest people, who have said nothing, and seldom been heard of; they have glided into their pews on the Sunday morning, taken their seats, gone out, and satisfied themselves that by their presence they had fufilled a religious duty. They have been so silent, quiet, and retired. Lazy fellows, doing nothing. You may think that all the fruitless trees grow in the hedge outside of the garden. No they don't. There are some fruitless trees in the inside of it in the very center of it. There are some false professors to be found in obscurity as well as in publicity; some among the poor as well as among the rich.

And there are false professors to be found among men that doubt a great deal. They are always afraid they do not love Jesus, and always saying, " Ah, if I did but know I were his!

> " 'Tis a point I long to know,
> Oft it causes anxious thought."

Yes, and it ought to cause them anxious thought, too, if they are bringing forth no fruit and giving no " diligence to make their calling and election sure." Fruitless professors are to be found, on the other hand, among the confident men, who say, without a blush, " I know whom I have believed; I know I am a Christian, let who will doubt. I am sure and certain my sins can not destroy me, and my righteousness can not save me. I may do what I like; I know I am one of the Lord's." Ah! fruitless professor again; just as fruitless as the other man, who had all doubts and no faith, and did nothing for his Master.

And then there is the fruitless professor, who, when he is asked to pray at the prayer meeting, never does so; and who neglects family prayer. We will not say any thing about private devotion; no doubt he neglects that too: he is a fruitless one. Ah! but there may be another, who stands up and prays such an eloquent prayer for a quarter of an hour, perhaps, just as fruitless a professor as the silent one; with plenty of words, but no realities; many leaves, but no fruits; great gifts of utterance, but no gifts of consistency; able to talk well, but not to walk well; to speak piously, but not to walk humbly with his God, and serve him with gladness. I do not know your individual characters; but I know enough of you to say that your position, however honorable in the church, and your character, however fair before men, is not enough to warrant any of you in concluding at once that you are not a fruitless professor. For fruitless professors are of every character and every rank, from the highest to the lowest, from the most talented to the most illiterate, from the richest to the poorest, from the most retiring to the most conspicuous. Fruitless professors there are in every part of the church.

Now, shall I tell you who is a fruitless professor? The man who neglects private prayer, and does not walk with his God in public; that man whose carriage and conversation before God are hypocritical; who cheats in trade and robs in business, yet wraps it up, and comes out with a fair face, like the hypocrite with a widow's house sticking in his throat, and says, "Lord, I thank thee I am not as other men are!" There is a man for you, who brings forth no fruit to perfection. Another one is he who lives right morally and excellently, and depends upon his works, and hopes to be saved by his righteousness; who comes before God, and asks for pardon, with a lie in his right hand, for he has brought his own self-righteousness with him. Such a man is a fruitless professor; he has brought forth no fruit. That man, again, is a fruitless professor who talks big words about high doctrine, and likes sound truth, but he does not like sound living; his pretensions are high, but not his practice. He can bear to hear it said,

"Once in Christ, in Christ for ever."

But as for himself, he never was in Christ at all, for he neither loves nor serves his Master, but lives in sin that grace may abound. There is another fruitless vine for you.

But why need I stop to pick you out? May the Lord find you out to-night! There are many of you here, concerning whom the curse of Meroz might be uttered. "Curse ye Meroz, said the angel of the Lord, curse ye bitterly the inhabitants thereof, because they came not to the help of the Lord; to the help of the Lord against the mighty." Many of you are content to eat the fat and drink the sweet, and bring forth no fruit to God; nor do you serve him—lazy Issachars, crouching down like a strong ass between two burdens; neither speaking for Christ, nor praying for Christ, nor giving to Christ, nor living to Christ; but having a name to live, while you are dead; wrapping yourselves up in a profession, while you are not living to Christ, nor consecrating your being to him. Judge ye what I say; if ye were put into the sieve this night, how many of you would come out clean in this matter? Are there not many high-flying professors here, who fly high, but who do nothing; who can talk fast, but live as slowly as you like; who, perhaps, delight in hearing the truth, but who never practice the truth in serving their God, nor living to his honor? Such as you, sirs, are the most useless and worthless of all creatures in the world! For, like the vine, you would be honorable if you were fruitful; but without fruit, as the vine is despicable, so are you good for nothing but to be cast out and burned.

2. And now I come to the second question— *Why is it that these men are fruitless, and must be cast away?* The reason is, because they have no roots. Many, many professors have no roots; fine professors they are, beautiful to look at, but they have no roots whatever. Don't you remember your childish freak, when you had a little garden of your own; when you plucked some flowers, and put them in the ground, and said that was your garden; and when you went the next day, and found that all the flowers were withered and dead? Such are many professors—pretty flowers, plucked off without roots; having no adherence to the soil, drawing no sap and no nourishment from it. And therefore it is they die, and bring forth no fruit. You come to us; and say, "I wish to join

the church." We question you as far as we are able; you solemnly tell us that your hearts are right with God. We baptize you, receive you into our number; but then there was no root in many of you, and after a while you die; when the sun has risen with a burning heat you perish; or if you maintain a tolerably fair profession, yet there is never any fruit upon you, because you did not get the root first; you got the notion first, and then thought you would get the root afterward. I do tremble for many young people in my church—I will not exclude my own church. They get an idea into their heads that they are converted: the work was not true, not genuine, not real; it was an excitement; it was a stir in the conscience for a while, and it will not last. But the worst of it is, that though it does not last, they last as professors. When they have been received into the church, they say, "I am sure enough!" Preach about them as long as you please, you can not get at them. They are church members, they are baptized persons, they have passed the Rubicon; what do they want more? You can do little for them. I do tremble for these. For my most hard-hearted hearers I weep before God; but for these people I need to have four eyes to weep with. For who can make an impression upon them, when they are firmly persuaded that they are right, and have had the seal of the church that they are right, though they are deceiving themselves and others, and are still " in the gall of bitterness and in the bond of iniquity." My young friends, I do not want to check any of you in joining a church; but I do say to you, make sure work before you make a profession. I would say to as many of you as love the Lord, come forward and unite with God's people; but, I beseech you, do be sure; do " search your hearts and try your reins." Many have thought themselves converted when they were not; hundreds of thousands have had an impression, a kind of conversion, not real, which for a while endured, but afterward it passed away as summer's dream. It was but a little while ago that I had in my house a gentleman, an excellent man, and I believe a true child of God, who told me he had been brought seriously under impression, on account of sin, through hearing a sermon of late. " But," said he, " I was baptized in my childhood.

When I was but young, there was a revival in our village, in New England. Mine was the hardest heart in the village; but I was found out at last. There was scarcely a girl or boy that did not join the church, and I was at last brought under deep impression. I used to weep before God, and pray to him. I went to the minister and told him I was converted, deceived him, and was baptized." And then he went on to tell me that he had dived into the blackest crimes, and gone far away, even from the profession of religion; that after going to college he had been struck off the church-roll on account of wickedness, and that up to this time he had been an infidel, and had not so much as thought of the things of the kingdom. Take heed, many of you, that you do not get a sham religion. Many jump into godliness as they would into a bath; but they are very glad to jump out of it again, when they find the world pays them better. And many there are who will just come and say they are the Lord's, and they think they are, but there is no root in them, and therefore by-and-by their impressions pass away. O we have many fruitless professors in our midst, because they do not look well to their beginnings; they did not take heed at their starting point, they did not watch well the first dawn; they thought the little farthing rushlight of their own hopes was the dawning of the Sun of righteousness · they thought the bleeding of their own conscience was a killing by the hand of God, whereas it was a deeper, and better, and surer, and more entire work that they needed, than that which they received. Let us take heed, my brethren, that we do not put too much trust in our experiences, and take too much for granted while it is not yet proved in our beginnings; let us often go back and begin again; let us often go to Christ with the old cry,

> " Nothing in my hands I bring,
> Simply to thy cross I cling;"

for remember that these bad beginnings have had a great effect in making a man fruitless.

3. And again, thirdly— *What is God's estimation of fruitless professors?* I shall not ask you their own; for there are many men who are professors of religion, with whom you

might make your fortune very speedily if you could buy them at your price and sell them at their own. There are many, too, that have a very good opinion of themselves, which they have gained from the church. The minister thinks well of them; the church thinks well of them; they are respectable people; it is so nice to have them come, it helps the cause so, to see such respectable people sitting in the pews! Really, I do think he would do for a deacon! Everybody thinks well of him; everybody praises him. Now we have nothing to do with this kind of opinion to-night; our business is with God's opinion of such a man. And God's opinion of a man who makes a profession without being sincere, is this—that he is the most useless thing in the world. And now let me try to prove it. Is there any one that will prove that this man is of any use at all? I will ask the church—Here is a man that brings forth no fruit, and has only a profession. Members of the church, what is the use of this man? Will he comfort any of you in your distress? Will he hold up the pastor's hands in prayer, when he is weary? Will he lead the troops to battle? Will he be of any service to you? I see you unanimously lift up your hands, and say, "The man is of no use to us whatever, if he brings forth no fruit; if his life be not consistent with his profession; strike his name off the church-roll; let him go; he is of no use." Where has he gone to? He has gone to the world. Bring the worldling up. What do you think of this man? He makes a profession of religion. Is he of any use to you? "No," they say, "we do not want such a fellow as that. The man is Jack-of-both-sides; he is sometimes a professor of religion, and sometimes a sinner in the world. We will have nothing to do with him; turn him out of our company." Where shall we sell him then? How shall we dispose of him? He seems to be of no use either to the church or the world. Is he of any use to his family? Ask his eldest son. "John, is your father any good to you?" "No, sir; none at all. He used to pray the Lord to save us with seeming earnestness, and rise from his knees to give vent to his temper. Many a violent blow has he given me without any reasonable provocation. He was always a passionate man. He used to go to chapel on Sunday and take us with him and then we know what he used to do on Monday   he would get drunk, or swear. A deal of use he was ever to me! He made me an infidel, sir!" And his wife, " Well, what do you think of this good husband of yours? He has long made a profession of religion." " Ah! sir, it is not for me to say a word about my husband; but he has made me a miserable woman. I think I should have joined your church long ago, if it had not been for his miserable inconsistencies. But really he has grieved my heart; he has always been a stumbling-block to me; and what to do with him I do not know." Well, Jane, we will have you out of the kitchen. " What think you of your master; he makes a profession of religion, yet does not live a right life. What do you think of him?" " Well, I did think that Christians were a good sort of people, and that I should like to live with them; but if this be Christianity, sir, I will take five pounds a year less to live with a worldly man; that's all I can say." Well, what is the use of him? I suppose he does something in business. He is a grand professor. He keeps a shop; everybody thinks him a most respectable man. Has he not given a hundred pounds just now to the building of a new church? Is he not always known to subscribe liberally to ragged schools? We will ask his men. " What do you think of your master?" " What do we think of him? Why, we would think a great deal more of him if he would give us a half-crown a week more wages; for he is the worst paymaster in the parish." " That is nothing, perhaps. But what do you think of him?" " Why, that he is an unutterable cant! Some of us did go to a place of worship, but we are honest, and we would rather stay away than go with such a miserable hypocrite." I am describing real cases and not fictions. I need not to go further than between this and London Bridge to knock at the door and wake them up, some of them. What is the good of such professors? If they would speak fairly out, and say, "I am no Christian," there would be some sense in it. For if Baal be God, let Baal be served; and if the world be worth serving, let a man serve it out and out; and let him get the credit of candor—not cheating the devil. But if God be God, and a man live in sin, and talk about grace, then of what use is he? God himself will disown him. Ask him if this man has been of any use, and he replies, " No, of no use whatever." The vine is of no use unless it bring forth fruit ; and this man, making a profession, is worse than worthless, because he does not live up to it. My dear friends, I would not say an extravagant thing, but I will say this very coolly—if any of you, who make a profession of religion, are deceiving others, by not living up to it, I do request you—and I say it advisedly—I do request you to give up your profession, unless God give you grace to live up to it. Do not, I beseech you, halt between two opinions ; if God be God, serve him, and do it thoroughly ; do not tell lies about it. If Baal be God ; if he be a nice master ; if you would like to serve him, and win his wages, serve him ; but do not mix the two together ; be one thing, or else the other. Renounce your profession, and serve the devil thoroughly, or else keep your profession, and serve God with your heart— one thing, or else the other. I solemnly exhort you to choose which you will have, but never think that you can keep both ; for "no man can serve two masters." " Ye can not serve God and mammon."

4. And now let me close up by mentioning *what is to become of this fruitless tree ?* We are told it is to be devoured in the fire. When an old vine is pulled off the wall, after having brought forth no fruit, what becomes of it ? You know there is a lot of weeds raked up in the corner of the garden, and the gardener, without taking any notice of it, just throws the vine on the heap of weeds, and it is burned up. If it were any other kind of a tree he would at least reserve it for chopping up to make a fire within the master's house ; but this is much an ignominious thing, he throws it away in the corner, and burns it up with the weeds. If it were a stout old oak, it might have the funeral of the yule log, with honor in its burning, and brightness in its flame ; but the fruitless vine is treated with contempt, and left to smoulder with the weeds, the refuse, and rubbish. It is a miserable thing. Just so with professors ; all men that love not God must perish. But those who profess to love him, and do not, shall perish with singular igncminy. " They shall not come into the sepulchres of the kings." Something like that ancient king, of whom it was

said, " He shall be buried with the burial of an ass, drawn and cast foith beyond the gates of Jerusalem." The damnation of a professor will be the most horrible and ignominious sight that ever hell itself has seen! When Satan fell from heaven, with his black Satanic malice against God, there was a kind of grandeur in his devilry; there was an awful, terrific sublimity in his damnation; and when a great blasphemer and a hard swearer shall be sent at last to perdition, there shall be something of sublimity in it, because he has been consistent with his profession. But when a professor of religion finds himself in hell, it shall be the most miserable, contemptible, and yet terrible mode of damnation wherewith men were ever damned. I think I see honest blasphemers lifting themselves from their chains of fire, and hissing between their teeth at the minister who comes there, after having been a deceiver— " Aha! aha! aha! art thou here with us? Thou didst warn us cf our drunkenness, and tell us of our curse; ah! art thou come into the drunkard's hell thyself?" " Pshaw!" says another, " that is your strict Pharisee. Ah! I remember how he told me one night that I should perish, unless I made a profession of religion. Take that, sir!" and he spits upon him. " Thou art a loathsome thing. I perished; but I served my master well. Thou—thou didst pretend to serve God, and yet thou art a sneaking hypocrite!" Says another, yelling from the corner of the pit, " Let us have a Methodist hymn, sir; quote a promise from the Bible; tell us about election. Let us have a little of your fine preaching now." And round hell there goes the hiss, and the " aha! aha! aha!" and the yell of spitefulness and scorn upon the man who professed to be a Christian, but became a castaway, because his heart was not right in the matter. I confess, I should dread above all things the unutterable hell of hells of hypocritical apostates, of men that stand in the ranks, profess to love God, prate godliness, that sit in the pews and uphold Christianity, that take the sacrament, and speak about communion, that stand up to pray, and talk about being heard for their faith, who are all the while committing abominations, and under cover of their professions are cheating the poor, robbing the fatherless, and doing all kinds of iniquity. I confess, I as much dread the excess of their damnation, above the damnation of others, as I dread to be damned at all. It is as if in hell another hell had been made, to damn those that sin above others, to damn them after being damned—for hypocrites, for men who have been with us, and not of us; who professed to be Christ's, and yet have been mean deceivers after all. O! sirs, if ye would not make your chains more heavy, if ye would not stir the fire to a more furious heat, if ye would not make your yells more hideous, quit your professions this night, if ye are not worthy of them. Go out of this place, and send in your resignation to the church; or else, sirs, be honest, and bend your knee before God, and ask him to search you, and try you, and make you sincere and upright before him. Be one thing, or else the other; do not cloak yourself in the robes of sanctity to hide the corruptions that all the while fester beneath. Stand out, bold, brave sinners; and do not be mean, sneaking sinners, that wear the masks of saints. "What is the vine more than any other tree?" Without fruit it is worse than any other. It must perish more dolefully, more horribly than any other, if there be on it no fruit brought to perfection. Does not this shake us? Ah! it will shake you, very likely, that do not want the shaking; but the men that want arousing will keep just as they were. It will go into the hearts of some of you, like the cry, "Howl, Moab, howl, Moab!" but alas! Moab will not howl. You will weep for Kirhareseth, but Kirhareseth will not weep for herself. You will weep for your hypocritical friends; but they will rub their eyes, and say, "A strong sermon; but it has nothing to do with me." And they will go out with cool presumption; sin with one hand, and take the sacramental cup with the other; sing the lascivious song one night, and then sing,

"Jesus, lover of my soul,"

the day after. Meet Christ here, and take the devil yonder, and bid him God speed in all his freaks of devilry. Ah! sirs, sirs, sirs, take heed, take heed, I beseech you, of this matter. Let us each search our hearts, lest we should have been deceived. And may God bring us to a right understanding in this matter, that we may be clear before him. "Search me,

O God, and know my ways; try me, and know my thoughts, and see if there be any wicked thing in me; and lead me in the way everlasting."

And, now, I must not send you away until I have had a word with my friend in the aisle there. He says, "I like that, I like that; I am no professor, I am not; I am all right. No one can call me a hypocrite." Well, my dear friend, I am very glad you are not, because you say you are no Christian. But let me tell you, you must not expect to be a wonderful deal the better off for that. Suppose two men are brought up before the Lord Mayor, and one says, "Your worship, I am an honest man and not guilty;" and he blushes that an imputation should be cast on his character. Well, he is proved to be guilty, and gets committed to prison for three months. Up comes the other one, and says, "Your worship, I am a guilty man; I always was a rogue, and I always shall be; I don't make a profession at all." "I think I must give you six months," says his worship, "for really I think you must be the more determined rascal of the two." So if any of you say, "I do not make a profession, I shall be all right," let me tell you, that to make a lying profession is a very fearful thing; but for you to think of getting off because you make no profession at all, is equally bad. Take heed you do not deceive yourselves; it must be the new heart and the right spirit with God, or else, profession or no profession, we must perish. O! that God would give us grace to go to our houses, and cry to him for mercy, and would help us to repent of our sins, and bring us to put our trust simply and wholly upon the Lord Jesus Christ! So should we be saved now, and saved for ever.

SERMON V

SPIRITUAL REVIVAL THE WANT OF THE CHURCH

"O Lord, revive thy work."—HAB., iii. 2

ALL true religion is the work of God: it is pre-eminently so. If he should select out of his works that which he esteems most of all, he would select true religion. He regards the work of grace as being even more glorious than the works of nature; and he is, therefore, especially careful that it shall always be known, so that if any one dare to deny it, they shall do so in the teeth of repeated testimonies to the contrary, that God is indeed the author of salvation in the world and in the hearts of men, and that religion is the effect of grace, and is the work of God. I believe the Eternal might sooner forgive the sin of ascribing the creation of the heavens and of the earth to an idol, than that of ascribing the works of grace to the efforts of the flesh, or to any thing else but God. It is a sin of the greatest magnitude to suppose that there is aught in the heart which can be acceptable unto God, save that which God himself has first created there. When I deny God's work in creating the sun, I deny one truth; but when I deny that he works grace in the heart, I deny a hundred truths in one; for in the denial of that one great truth, that God is the author of good in the souls of men, I have denied all the doctrines which make up the great articles of faith, and have run in the very teeth of the whole testimony of sacred Scripture. I trust, beloved, that many of us have been taught, that if there be any thing in our souls which can carry us to heaven, t is God's work, and, moreover, that if there be aught that is good and excellent found in his church, it is entirely God's work, from first to last. We firmly believe that it is God who quickens the soul which was dead, positively "dead in tres passes and sins;" that it is God who maintains the life of that soul, and God who consummates and perfects that life in the home of the blessed, in the land of the hereafter. We ascribe nothing to man, but all to God. We dare not for a moment think that the conversion of the soul is effected either by its own effort or by the efforts of others; we conceive that there are means and agencies employed, but that the work is, both alpha and omega, wholly the Lord's. We think, therefore, that we are right in applying the text to the work of divine grace, both in the heart and in the church at large; and we think we can have no subject more appropriate for our consideration than the text. " O Lord, revive thy work!"

First, beloved, trusting that the Spirit of God will help me I shall endeavor to apply the text *to our own souls personally*, and then *to the state of the church at large*, for it well needs that the Lord should revive his work in its midst.

I. First, then, to OURSELVES. We should begin at home. We too often flog the church, when the whip should be laid on our own shoulders. We drag the church, like a colossal culprit, to the altar; we bind her, and try to execute her at once; we bind her hands fast, and tear off thongfull after thongfull of her quivering flesh—finding fault with her where there is none, and magnifying her little errors; while we too often forget ourselves. Let us, therefore, commence with ourselves, remembering that we are part of the church, and that our own want of revival is in some measure the cause of that want in the church at large.

Now, I directly charge the great majority of professing Christians—and I take the charge to myself also—with a need of a revival of piety in these days. I shall lay the charge before you very peremptorily, because I think I have abundant grounds to prove it. I believe that the mass of Christian men in this age need a revival, and my reasons are these:

In the first place, look at *the conduct and conversation* of too many who profess to be the children of God. It ill becomes any man who occupies the sacred place of a pulpit to flatter his hearers, and I shall not attempt **to** do so. The evil lies with too many of you who unite yourselves with Christian churches, and in practically protesting against your profession

It has become very common now-a-days to join a church; go where you may you find professing Christians who sit down at some Lord's table or another; but are there fewer cheats than there used to be? Are there less frauds committed? Do we find morality more extensive? Do we find vice entirely at an end? No, we do not. The age is as immoral as any that preceded it; there is still as much sin, although it is more cloaked and hidden. The outside of the sepulcher may be whiter; but within, the bones are just as rotten as before. Society is not one whit improved. Those men who, in our popular magazines, give us a true picture of the state of London life, are to be believed and credited, for they do not stretch the truth—they have no motive for so doing; and the picture which they give of the morality of this great city is certainly appalling. It is a huge criminal, full of sin; and I say this, that if all the profession in London were true profession, it would not be nearly such a wicked place as it is; it could not be, by any manner of means. My brethren, it is well known —and who dares deny it that is not too partial, and who will not speak willful falsehood?—it is well known that it is not in these days a sufficient guaranty even of a man's honesty, that he is a member of a church. It is a hard thing for Christian ministers to say, but we must say it, and if friends say it not, enemies will; and better that the truth should be spoken in our own midst, that men may see that we are ashamed of it, than that they should hear us impudently deny what we must confess to be true! O sirs, the lives of too many members of Christian churches give us grave cause to suspect that there is none of the life of godliness in them all! Why that reaching after money, why that covetousness, why that following of the crafts and devices of a wicked world, why that clutching here and clutching there, that grinding of the faces of the poor, that stamping down of the workman, and such like things, if men are truly what they profess to be? God in heaven knows that what I speak is true, and too many here know it themselves. If they be Christians, at least they want revival; if there be life in them, it is but a spark that is covered up with heaps of ashes; it needs to be fanned, ay, and it needs to be stirred also, that, haply, some of the ashes may be removed

and the spark may have place to live. The church wants revival in the persons of its members. The members of Christian churches are not what once they were. It is fashionable
to be religious now; persecution is taken away; and ah! I
had almost said, the gates of the church were taken away with
it. The church has, with few exceptions, no gates now; persons come in, and go out of it, just as they would march
through St. Paul's cathedral, and make it a very place of traf-
fic, instead of regarding it as a select and sacred spot, to be
apportioned to the holy of the Lord, and to the excellent of
the earth, in whom is God's delight. If this be not true, you
know how to treat it; you need not confess to sin you have
not committed; but if it be true, and true in your case, O !
humble yourselves under the mighty hand of God; ask him
to search and try you, that if you be not his child you may be
helped to renounce your profession, lest it should be to you
but the gaudy pageantry of death, and mere tinsel and gew-
gaw in which to go to hell. If you be his, ask that he may
give you more grace, that you may renounce these faults and
follies, and turn unto him with full purpose of heart, as the effect of a revived godliness in your soul.

Again: where the *conduct* of professing Christians is consistent, let me ask the question, Does not the *conversation* of
many a professor lead us either to doubt the truthfulness of
his piety, or else to pray that his piety may be revived? Have
you noticed the conversation of too many who think themselves Christians? You might live with them from the first
of January to the end of December, and you would never be
tired of their religion for what you would hear of it. They
scarcely mention the name of Jesus Christ at all. On Sabbath
afternoon all the ministers are talked over, faults are found
with this one and the other, and all kinds of conversation take
place, which they call religious, because it is concerning religious places. But do they ever talk of what he said and did,
and what he suffered for us here below? Do you often hear
the salutation addressed to you by your brother Christian,
"Friend, how doth thy soul prosper?" When we step into
each other's houses, do we begin to talk concerning the cause
and truth of God? Do you think that God would now stoop

from heaven to listen to the conversation of his church, as once he did, when it was said, "The Lord hearkened and heard, and a book of remembrance was written for them that feared the Lord and that thought upon his name?" I solemnly declare, as the result of thorough, and, I trust, impartial observation, that the conversation of Christians, while it can not be condemned on the score of morality, must almost invariably be condemned on the score of Christianity. We talk too little about our Lord and Master. That word sectarianism has crept into our midst, and we must say nothing about Christ, because we are afraid of being called sectarians. I am a sectarian, and hope to be so until I die, and to glory in it; for I can not see, now-a-days, that a man can be a Christian, thoroughly in earnest, without winning for himself the title. Why, we must not talk of this doctrine, because perhaps such a one disbelieves it; we must not notice such and such a truth in Scripture, because such and such a friend doubts or denies it; and so we drop all the great and grand topics which used to be the staple commodities of godly talk, and begin to speak of any thing else, because we feel that we can agree better on worldly things than we can on spiritual. Is not that the truth? and is it not a sad sin with some of us, that we have need to pray unto God, "O Lord, revive thy work in my soul, that my conversation may be more Christlike, seasoned with salt, and kept by the Holy Spirit?"

And yet a third remark here. There are some whose conduct is all that we could wish, whose conversation is for the most part unctuous with the gospel, and savory of truth; but even they will confess to a third charge, which I must now sorrowfully bring against them and against myself, namely, that there is *too little real communion with Jesus Christ*. If, thanks to divine grace, we are enabled to keep our conduct tolerably consistent, and our lives unblemished, yet how much have we to cry out against ourselves, from a lack of that holy fellowship with Jesus which is the high mark of the true child of God! Brethren, let me ask some of you how long it is since you have had a love-visit from Jesus Christ—how long since you could say, "My beloved is mine, and I am his: he feedeth among the lilies?" How long is it since "he brought you into his banqueting house, and his banner over you was love?" Perhaps some of you will be able to say, "It was but this morning that I saw him; I beheld his face with joy, and was ravished with his countenance." But I fear the greatest part of you will have to say, "Ah, sir, for months I have been without the shinings of his countenance." What have you been doing, then, and what has been your way of life? Have you been groaning every day? Have you been weeping every minute? "No!" Then you ought to have been. I can not understand how your piety can be of any very brilliant order, if you can live without the sunlight of Christ, and yet be happy. Christians will lose sometimes the society of Jesus; the connection between themselves and Christ will be at times severed, as to their own feeling of it; but they will always groan and cry when they lose their Jesus. What! is Christ thy Brother, and does he live in thine house, and yet thou hast not spoken to him for a month? I fear there is little love between thee and thy Brother, for thou hast had no conversation with him for so long. What! is Christ the Husband of his church, and has she had no fellowship with him for all this time? Brethren, let me not condemn you, let me not even judge you, but let your conscience speak. Mine shall, and so shall yours. Have we not too much forgotten Christ? Have we not lived too much without him? Have we not been contented with the world, instead of desiring Christ? Have we been, all of us, like that little ewe lamb that did drink out of the master's cup, and feed from his table? Have we not rather been content to stray upon the mountains, feeding anywhere but at home? I fear many of the troubles of our heart spring from want of communion with Jesus. Not many of us are the kind of men who, living with Jesus, his secrets must know. O! no; we live too much without the light of his countenance; and are too happy when he is gone from us. Let us, each of us, then, for I am sure we have each of us need, in some measure, put up the prayer, "O Lord, revive thy work!" Ah! methinks I hear one professor saying, "Sir, I need no revival in my heart; I am every thing I wish to be." Down on your knees, my brethren! down on your knees for him! He is the man that most needs to be prayed for. He says that he needs no revival in his soul; but he needs a revival of his humility, at any rate. If he supposes that he is all that he ought to be, and if he knows that he is all he wishes to be, he has very mean notions of what a Christian is, or of what a Christian should be, and very unjust ideas of himself. Those are in the best condition who, while they know they want reviving, yet feel their condition and groan under it.

Now, I think I have in some degree substantiated my charge, I fear with too strong arguments; and now let me notice, that the text has something in it which I trust that each of us has. Here is not only an evil implied in these words—"O Lord, revive thy work;" but there is an evil evidently felt. You see Habakkuk knew how to groan about it. "O Lord," said he, "revive thy work!" Ah! we many of us want revival, but few of us feel that we want it. It is a blessed sign of life within, when we know how to groan over our departures from the living God. It is easy to find by hundreds those that have departed, but you must count those by ones who know how to groan over their departure. The true believer, however, when he discovers that he needs revival, will not be happy; he will begin at once that incessant and continuous strain of cries and groans which will at last prevail with God, and bring the blessing of revival down. He will, days and nights in succession, cry, "O Lord, revive thy work!"

Let me mention some groaning times, which will always occur to the Christian who needs revival. I am sure he will always groan, *when he looks upon what the Lord did for him of old*. When he recollects the Mizars and the Hermons, and those places where the Lord appeared of old to him, saying, "I have loved thee with an everlasting love," I know he will never look back to them without tears. If he is what he should be as a Christian, or if he thinks he is not in a right condition, he will always weep when he remembers God's loving-kindness of old. O! whenever the soul has lost fellowship with Jesus, it can not bear to think of the "chariots of Aminadab;" it can not endure to think of "the banqueting house," for it hath not been there so long; and when it does think of it, it says,

> " The peaceful hours I then enjoyed,
> How sweet their memory still,
> But they have left an aching void
> The world can never fill."

When he hears a sermon which relates the glorious experience of the believer who is in a healthy state, he will put his hand upon his heart, and say, "Ah! such was my experience once; but those happy days are gone. My sun is set; those stars which once lit up my darkness are all quenched; O! that I might again behold him; O! that I might once more see his face; O! for those sweet visits from on high; O! for the grapes of Eschol once more." And by the rivers of Babylon you will sit down and weep. You will weep, when you remember your goings up to Zion—when the Lord was precious to you, when he laid bare his heart, and was pleased also to fill your heart with the fullness of his love. Such times will be groaning times, when you remember "the years of the right hand of the Most High."

Again, to a Christian who wants revival, *ordinances* will be also groaning times. He will go up to the house of God; but he will say of himself when he comes away, "Ah! how changed! When I once went with the multitude that kept holy day every word was precious. When the song ascended my soul had wings, and up it flew to its nest among the stars; when the prayer was offered, I could devoutly say, 'Amen;' but now the preacher preaches as he did before; my brethren are as profited as once they were; but the sermon is dry to me, and dull. I find no fault with the preacher; I know the fault is in myself. The song is just the same—as sweet the melody, as pure the harmony; but ah! my heart is heavy; my harp strings are broken, and I can not sing;" and the Christian will return from those blessed means of grace, sighing and sobbing, because he knows he wants revival. More especially at the Lord's Supper he will think, when he sits at the table, "O! what seasons I once had here! In breaking the bread and drinking the wine my Master was present." He will bethink himself how his soul was even carried to the seventh heaven, and the house was made "the very house of God and the gate of heaven." "But now," he says, "it is bread, dry bread to me; it is wine, tasteless wine, with none of the sweetness of paradise in it; I drink, but all in vain. No thoughts of Christ. My heart will not rise; my soul can not heave a thought half way to him!" And then the Christian will begin to groan again—"O Lord revive thy work!"

But I shall not detain you upon that subject. Those of you who know that you are in Christ, but feel that you are not in a desirable condition, because you do not love him enough, and have not that faith in him which you desire to have, I would just ask you this: Do you groan over it? Can you groan now? When you feel your heart is empty, is it "an aching void?" When you feel that your garments are stained, can you wash those garments with tears? When you think your Lord is gone, can you hang out the black flag of sorrow, and cry, "O my Jesus! O my Jesus! art thou gone?" If thou canst, then I bid thee do it. Do it, do it; and may God be pleased to give thee grace to continue to do it, until a happier era shall dawn in the reviving of thy soul!

And remark, in the last place, upon this point, that the soul, when it is really brought to feel its own sad estate, because of its declension and departure from God, *is never content without turning its groanings into prayer*, and without addressing the prayer to the right quarter: "O Lord, revive thy work!" Some of you, perhaps, will say, "Sir, I feel my need of revival; I intend to set to work this very afternoon, as soon as I shall retire from this place, to revive my soul." Do not say it; and, above all things, do not try to do it, for you never will do it. Make no resolutions as to what you will do; your resolutions will as certainly be broken as they are made, and your broken resolutions will but increase the number of your sins. I exhort you, instead of trying to revive yourself, to offer prayers. Say not, "I will revive myself," but cry, "O Lord, revive *thy* work!" And let me solemnly tell thee, thou hast not yet felt what it is to decline, thou dost not yet know how sad is thine estate, otherwise thou wouldest not talk of reviving thyself. If thou didst know thy own position, thou wouldest as soon expect to see the wounded soldier on the battle-field heal himself without medicine, or convey himself to the hospital when his limbs are shot away, as thou wouldest expect to revive thyself without the help of God. I bid thee not do any thing, nor seek to do any thing, until first of all thou hast addressed Jehovah himself by mighty prayer—until thou hast cried out, "O Lord, revive thy work!" Remember, he that first made you must keep you alive; and he that has kept you alive must restore more life to you. He that has preserved you from going down to the pit, when your feet have been sliding, can alone set you again upon a rock, and establish your goings. Begin, then, by humbling yourself— giving up all hope of reviving yourself as a Christian, but beginning at once with firm prayer and earnest supplication to God : "O Lord, what I can not do, do thou ! O Lord, revive thy work !"

Christian brethren, I leave these matters with you. Give them the attention they deserve. If I have erred, and in aught judged you too harshly, God shall forgive me, for I have meant it honestly. But if I have spoken truly, lay it to your hearts, and turn your houses into a "Bochim." Weep men apart, and women apart, husbands apart, and wives apart. Weep, weep, my brethren : "It is a sad thing to depart from the living God." Weep, and may he bring you back to Zion, that you may one day return like Israel, not with weeping, but with songs of everlasting joy !

II. And now I come to the second part of the subject, upon which I must be more brief. In THE CHURCH ITSELF, taken as a body, this prayer ought to be one incessant and solemn litany : "O Lord, revive thy work !"

In the present era there is *a sad decline of the vitality of godliness.* This age has become too much the age of form, instead of the age of life. I date the hour of life from this day one hundred years ago when the first stone was laid of this building in which we now worship God. Then was the day of life divine, and of power, sent down from on high. God had clothed Whitefield with power : he was preaching with a majesty and a might of which one could scarcely think mortal could ever be capable ; not because he was any thing in him·

self, but because his Master girded him with might. After Whitefield there was a succession of great and holy men. But now, sirs, we have fallen upon the dregs of time. *Men* are the rarest things in all this world; we have not many left now. We have no men in government hardly, to conduct our politics, and scarcely any men in religion. We have the *things* that perform their duties, as they are called; we have the good, and, perhaps, the honest things, who in the regular routine go on like pack-horses with their bells, for ever in the old style; but men who dare to be singular, because to be singular is generally to be right in a wicked world, are not very many in this age. Compared with the puritanic times even, where are our divines? Could we marshal together our Howes and our Charnocks? Could we gather together such names as I could mention about fifty at a time? I trow not. Nor could we bring together such a galaxy of grace and talent as that which immediately followed Whitefield. Think of Rowland Hill, Newton, Toplady, Doddridge, and numbers of others whom time would fail me to mention. They are gone, they are gone; their venerated dust sleeps in the earth, and where are their successors? Ask where, and echo shall reply, "Where?" There are none. Successors of them, where are they? God hath not yet raised them up, or, if he have, you have not yet found out where they are. There is preaching, and what is it? "O Lord, help thy servant to preach, and teach him by thy Spirit what to say." Then out comes the manuscript, and they read it. A pure insult to Almighty God! We have preaching, but it is of this order. It is not preaching at all. It is speaking very beautifully and very finely, possibly eloquently, in some sense of the word; but where is the right down preaching, such as Whitefield's? Have you ever read one of his sermons? You will not think him eloquent; you can not think him so. His expressions were rough, frequently very coarse and unconnected; there was very much declamation about him; it was a great part, indeed, of his speech. But where lay his eloquence? Not in the words you read, but in the tone in which he delivered them, and in the earnestness with which he felt them, and in the tears which ran down his cheeks, and in the pouring out of his soul. The reason why he was eloquent was just what the word means. He was eloquent, because he spoke right out from his heart—from the innermost depths of the man. You could see when he spoke that he meant what he said. He did not speak as a trade, or as a mere machine, but he preached what he felt to be the truth, and what he could not help preaching. When you heard him preach, you could not help feeling that he was a man who would die if he could not preach, and with all his might call to men and say, " Come! come! come to Jesus Christ, and believe on him!" Now, that is just the lack of these times. Where, where is earnestness now ? It is neither in pulpit nor yet in pew, in such a measure as we desire it; and it is a sad, sad age, when earnestness is scoffed at, and when that very zeal which ought to be the prominent characteristic of the pulpit is regarded as enthusiasm and fanaticism. I ask God to make us all such fanatics as most men laugh at—to make us all just such enthusiasts as many despise. We reckon it the greatest fanaticism in the world to go to hell, the greatest enthusiasm upon earth to love sin better than righteousness; and we think those neither fanatics nor enthusiasts who seek to obey God rather than man, and follow Christ in all his ways. We repeat, that one sad proof that the church wants revival is the absence of that death-like, solemn earnestness which was once seen in Christian pulpits.

The absence of sound doctrine is another proof of our want of revival. Do you know who are called Antinomians now, who are called " hypers," who are laughed at, who are rejected as being unsound in the faith ? Why, the men that once were the orthodox are now the heretics. We can turn back to the records of our Puritan fathers, to the articles of the Church of England, to the preaching of Whitefield, and we can say of that preaching, it is the very thing we love; and the doctrines which were then uttered are—and we dare to say it everywhere—the very self-same doctrines that he proclaimed. But because we choose to proclaim them, we are thought singular and strange ; and the reason is, because sound doctrine hath to a great degree ceased. It began in this way. First of all the truths were fully believed, but the angles were a little taken off. The minister believed election, but he did not use the word, for fear it should in some degree disturb the equanimity of the deacon in the green pew in the corner. He believed that all men were depraved, but he did not say it positively, because if he did, there was a lady who had subscribed so much to the chapel—she would not come again; so that while he did believe it, and did say it in some sense, he rounded it a little. Afterward it came to this. Ministers said, "We believe these doctrines, but we do not think them profitable to preach to the people. They are quite true : free grace is true; the great doctrines of grace that were preached by Christ, by Paul, by Augustine, by Calvin, and down to this age by their successors, are true; but they had better be kept back—they must be very cautiously dealt with; they are very high and dreadful doctrines, and they must not be preached; we believe them, but we dare not speak them out." After that it came to something worse. They said within themselves, "Well, if these doctrines will not do for us to preach, perhaps they are not true at all;" and going one step further, they said they dare not preach them. They did not actually say it, perhaps, but they began just to hint that they were not true; then they went one step further, giving us something which they said was the truth; and then they would cast us out of the synagogue, as if they were the rightful owners of it, and we were the intruders. So they have passed on from bad to worse; and if you read the standard divinity of this age, and the standard divinity of Whitefield's day, you will find that the two can not by any possibility stand together. We have got a "new theology." New theology? Why, it is any thing but a *The*ology; it is an ology which hath cast out God utterly and entirely, and enthroned man, as it is the doctrine of man, and not the doctrine of the everlasting God. We want a revival of sound doctrine once more in the midst of the land.

And the church at large, may be, wants *a revival of downright earnestness in its members.* Ye are not the men to fight the Lord's battles yet. Ye have not the earnestness, the zeal, which once the children of God had. Your forefathers were oaken men; ye are willow men. Our people, what are they many of them ?   Strong in doctrine when they are with strong-doctrine men ; but they waver when they get with others, and they change as often as they change their company ; they are sometimes one thing, and sometimes another.   They are not the men to go to the stake and die; they are not the men that know how to die daily, and so are ready for death when it comes.   Look at our prayer-meetings, with here and there a bright exception.   Go in.   There are six women ; scarcely ever enough members come to pray four times.   Look at them.   Prayer-meetings they are called ; *spare* meetings they ought to be called, for sparely enough they are attended.   And very few there are that go to our fellowship-meetings, or to any other meetings that we have to help one another in the fear of the Lord.   Are they attended at all ?   I would like to see a newspaper printed somewhere, containing a list of all the persons that went to those meetings during the week in any of our chapels.   Ah! my friends, if they should comprise all the Christians in London, you might find that a chapel or two would hold them all.   There are few enough that go.   We have not earnestness, we have not life, as we once had; if we had, we should be called worse names than we are; we should have viler epithets thrown at us, if we were more true to our Master; we should not have all things quite so comfortable, if we served God better.   We are getting the church to be an institution of our land—an honorable institution.   Ah! some think it a grand thing when the church becomes an honorable institution !   Methinks it shows the church has swerved, when she begins to be very honorable in the eyes of the world.   She must still be cast out, she must still be called evil, and still be despised, until that day shall come, when her Lord shall honor her because she has honored him—shall honor her, even in this world, in the day of his appearing.

Beloved, do you think it is true that the church wants reviving?   Yes, or no ?   " No," you say, " not to the extent that you suppose.   *We* think the church is in a good condition.   We are not among those who cry, ' The former days were better than these.' "   Perhaps you are not: you may be far wiser than we are, and therefore you are able to see those various signs of goodness which are to us so small that we are not able to discover them. You may suppose that the church is in a good condition ; if so, of course you can not sympathize with me in preaching from such a text, and urging you to use such a prayer. But there are others of you who are frequently prone to cry, "The church wants reviving." Let me bid you, instead of grumbling at your minister, instead of finding fault with the different parts of the church, to cry, "O Lord revive thy work!"   "O!" says one, "if we had another minister. O ! if we had another kind of worship. O ! if we had a different sort of preaching." Just as if that were all! It is, "O ! if the Lord would come into the hearts of the men you have got. O ! if he would make the forms you do use full of power." You do not want fresh ways or fresh machinery ; you want the life in what you have. There is an engine on a railway ; a train has to be moved. "Bring another engine," says one, "and another, and another." The engines are brought, but the train does not move at all. Light the fire, and get the steam up, that is what you want ; not fresh engines. We do not want fresh ministers, or fresh plans, or fresh ways, though many might be invented, to make the church better; we only want life in what we have got. Given, the very man who has emptied your chapel; given, the self-same person that brought your prayer-meeting low ; God can make the chapel crowded to the doors yet, and give thousands of souls to that very man. It is not a new man that is wanted ; it is the life of God in him. Do not be crying out for something new ; it will no more succeed, of itself, than what you have. Cry, "O Lord, revive thy work!" I have noticed in different churches, that the minister has thought first of this contrivance, then of that. He tried one plan, and thought that would succeed; then he tried another; that was not it. Keep to the old plan, but get life in it. We do not want anything new ; "the old is better"—let us keep to it. But we want the life in the old. "O!" men cry, "we have nothing but the shell; they are going to give us a new shell." No, sirs, we will keep the old one, but we will have the life in the shell too; we will have the old thing; but we must, or else we will throw the old away, have the life in the old. O! that God would give us life. The church wants fresh revivals

O! for the days of Cambuslang again, when Whitefield preached with power. O! for the days when in this place hundreds were converted sometimes under Whitefield's sermons. It has been known that two thousand credible cases of conversion have happened under one solitary discourse. O! for the age when eyes should be strained, and ears should be ready to receive the word of God, and when men should drink in the word of life, as it is indeed, the very water of life, which God gives to dying souls! O! for the age of deep feeling—the age of deep, thorough-going earnestness! Let us ask God for it; let us plead with him for it. Perhaps he has the man, or the men, somewhere, who will shake the world yet; perhaps even now he is about to pour forth a mighty influence upon men, which shall make the church as wonderful in this age, as it ever was in any age that has passed.

SERMON VI

THE ANXIOUS INQUIRER

"O that I knew where I might find him."—JOB, xxiii. 3.

WE will say nothing at this time concerning Job—we will leave the patriarch out of the question, and take these words as the exclamation forced from the aching heart of a sinner, when he finds that he is lost on account of sin, and can only be saved by Christ. "O that I knew where I might find him"—" my Saviour—that I might be saved by his love and blood!" There are some who tell us that a man can, if he pleases, in one moment obtain peace with God and joy in the Holy Ghost. Such persons may know something of religion in their own hearts; but I think they are not competent to be judges of others. God may have given them some peace through believing, and brought them immediately into a state of joy; he may have given them some repentance for sin, and then given them quickly to rejoice in Jesus; but I believe that, in many more cases, God begins by breaking the iron heart in pieces, and often makes a delay of days, of weeks, and of months, before he heals the heart which he has wounded, and gives life to the spirit which he has killed. Many of God's people have been, even for years, seeking peace, and finding none; they have known their sins, they have been permitted to feel their guilt, and yet, notwithstanding that they have sought earnestly with tears, they have not attained to a knowledge of their justification by faith in Christ. Such was the case with John Bunyan; for many a dreary month he walked the earth desolate, and said he knew himself to be lost without Christ; on his bended knees, with tears pouring like showers from his eyes, he sought mercy but he found none. Terrible words haunted him continually; dreadful passages of Scripture were quoted in his ears; and he found no consolation, until afterward God was pleased to appear to him in all the plenitude of grace, and give him to cast himself on the Saviour.

I think there may be some here who have been for some time under the hand of God—some who have been brought so far toward heaven as to know this, that they are undone unless Christ shall save them. I may be addressing some who have begun to pray; many a time the walls of their chamber have listened to their supplication; not once, nor twice, nor fifty times, but very often have they bent their knee in agonizing prayer: and yet up to this moment, so far as their own feelings are concerned, their prayers are unanswered, Christ has not smiled upon them, they have not received the application of his precious blood, and mayhap they are saying at this hour, "I am ready to give up all in despair; he said he would receive all that came to him, and he has apparently rejected me." Take heart, O mourner! I have a sweet message to thee; and I pray the Lord that thou mayest find Christ on the spot where thou art now standing or sitting, and rejoice in a pardon bought with blood.

I shall now proceed to consider the case of a man who is awakened, who is seeking Christ, but who at present has not, in his own apprehension, found him. First, I shall notice *some hopeful signs in this man's case;* secondly, I shall try to give *some reasons why it is that a gracious God delays an answer to prayer in the case of penitent sinners;* and then, thirdly, I shall close up by giving *some brief and suitable advice to those who have been seeking Christ, but have up to the present time found it a hopeless search.*

I. First, then, I notice, THERE ARE SOME VERY HOPEFUL SIGNS IN THE CASE OF THE MAN WHO HAS BEEN SEEKING CHRIST, THOUGH HE MAY NOT HAVE FOUND HIM.

And taking the text for a ground-work, we notice as one hopeful sign, *that the man has only one object, and that is Christ.* "O that I knew where I might find him!" The worldling's cry is, "Who will show us any good; this good, that good, or any other good—fifty kinds of good: who will show us these?" But the quickened sinner knows of only one good. "O that I knew where I might find HIM!" When the sinner is truly awakened to feel his guilt, if you could pour the gold of India at his feet, he would say, "Take it away: I want to find HIM." If you could then give him all the joys and delights of the flesh, he would tell you he had tried all these, and they but cloyed upon his appetite. His only cry is, "O that I knew where I might find HIM!"

> "These will never satisfy;
> Give me Christ or else I die."

It is a blessed thing for a man when he has brought his desires into a focus. When a man has fifty different desires, his heart resembles a pool of water, which is spread over a marsh, breeding miasma and pestilence; but when all his desires are brought into one channel, his heart becomes like a river of pure water, running along and fertilizing the fields. Happy is the man who hath one desire, if that one desire is set on Christ, though it may not yet have been realized. If it be his desire, it is a blessed sign of the divine work within him. Such a man will never be content with mere ordinances. Other men will go up to God's house, and when they have heard the sermon, they will be satisfied; but not so this man; he will say, "O that I knew where I might find HIM!" His neighbor who hears the sermon will be satisfied; but this man will say, "I want more than that; I want to find Christ in it." Another man will go to the sacramental table; he will eat the bread and drink the wine, and that will be enough for him; he will be contented with it. But the quickened sinner will say, "No bread, no wine will satisfy me; I want Christ; I must have him; mere ordinances are of no use to me; I want not the Saviour's clothes; I want himself; do not offer me these; you offer me the empty pitcher while I am dying of thirst; give me water, water, or I die. It is this I want." As we have it here in the text, "O that I knew where I might find him!"

Is this thy condition, my friend, at this moment? Hast thou but one desire, and is that after Christ? Then, as the Lord liveth, thou art not far from the kingdom of heaven. Hast thou but one wish in thy heart, and that one wish that

thou mayest be washed from all thy sins in Jesus' blood?
Canst thou really say, "I would give all I have to be a Christian; I would give up every thing I have and hope for, if I
might but feel that I have an interest in the person and death
of Christ?" Then, poor soul, despite all thy fears, be of good
cheer; the Lord loveth thee, and thou shalt come out into
daylight soon, and rejoice in the liberty wherewith Christ
makes men free.

There is another hopeful sign; not only that the man has
only one desire, but that it is *an intense one.* Hear the text
again! "O that I knew where I might find him!" There is
an "O" here: there is an intensity of desire. There are
some men who are mighty religious, but their religion is never
more than skin deep only, it never goes into their heart; they
can talk it finely, but they never feel it; it does not well up
from the heart, and that is a bad spring that only comes from
the lip; it is the true spring from the inmost heart of man
that can send forth living water. But this character is no
hypocrite: he means what he says. Other men will say,
"Yes, I should like to be a Christian; I should like to be pardoned; I should like to be forgiven." And so they would;
but they would like to go on in sin too. They would like to
be saved; yes, but they would like to live in sin; they would
like to hold with the hare and run with the hounds. They
have no desire whatever to give up their sins. They would
like to be pardoned for all their past transgressions, and then
go on just the same as before. Their wish is of no use, because it is so superficial. But when the sinner is really quickened, there is nothing superficial in him then. It is, "O
that I knew where I might find him!" coming from his very
heart. Art thou in that position, my friend? Is thy sigh a
real one? Is thy groan no mere fancy, but a real groan from
the heart? Is that tear which steals down thy cheek a real
tear, which comes from the grief of thy spirit? I think I hear
you saying, "Sir, if you knew me you would not ask me that
question, for my friends say I am miserable day after day, and
so indeed I am. I go to my chamber there, in the lean to, at
the top of the house, and often do I cry to God; ay, sir, I
cry in such a style, I would not have any one hear me; I cry

with groans and tears, that I may be brought near to God, I do mean what I say." Then, beloved, thou shalt be saved; so sure as it is a real emotion of thy heart, God will not let thee perish. Never was there a sinner whose inmost heart cried to God, who was not loved of God; never was there one who desired with all his might to be saved, and whose soul groaned out that desire in hearty prayer, who was cast away. His mercy may tarry, but it *shall* come. Pray on still; he will hear thee at last, and thou shalt yet " rejoice in hope of the glory of God."

But notice again, that in the text there is *an admission of ignorance*, which is also a very hopeful sign. " O that I *knew!*" Many people think they know every thing, and consequently know nothing. I think it is Seneca who says, " Many a man would have been a wise man, if he had not thought himself so; if he had but known himself to have been a fool, he would have become wise." The doorstep to the temple of wisdom is a knowledge of our own ignorance. He can not learn aright who has not first been taught that he knows nothing. A sense of ignorance is a very excellent sign of grace. It is a singular thing, that every man thinks himself qualified to be a doctor of divinity; a man who knows nothing of any other science, thinks he must understand this perfectly; and, alas! alas! for those who think they know so much about God's things, and have never been taught of God! Man's school is not God's school. A man may go to all the colleges in creation, and know as little of theology when he comes out as when he went into them. It is a good thing for a man to feel that he is only beginning to learn, and to be willing to submit his heart to the teaching of God's Spirit, that he may be guided in every thing by him. He that knoweth every thing need not think himself a Christian; he that boasteth that he can understand all mysteries needeth to fear. But the quickened soul says, " Teach thou me." We become little children when God begins to deal with us. Before, we were big, tall men and women, and so wise; but when he begins to deal with us, he cuts us down to the stature of children, and we are put on the form of humility, to learn the true lessons of wisdom, and then we are taught the great things of God. Happy art thou,

O man, if thou knowest thyself to know nothing. If God hath emptied thee of thy carnal wisdom, he will fill thee with heavenly; if he hath taught thee thine ignorance, he will teach thee his wisdom, and bring thee to himself; and if thou art taught to reject all thy knowings and findings-out, God will certainly reveal himself to thee.

There is one more hopeful sign in my text that I must mention. It is this: that the person I have spoken of *is quite careless where it is he finds Christ, so that he does find him.* Do you know, beloved, that people when they feel their sins, are the worst people in the world to stick up for sects? Other men can fight with broad-swords against their fellow-creatures; but a poor awakened sinner says, " Lord, I will meet thee anywhere." When we are whole-hearted, and have never felt our sins, we are the most respectable religionists in the world; we venerate every nail in the church door, and every word in the Book, and think so much of it, that we would not have any one differ from us—we would cut him off at once; but when we feel our sins we say, "Lord, if I could find thee anywhere, I would be glad; if I could find thee at the Baptist meeting-house, if I could find thee in the Independent chapel, I should be glad enough to go there. I have always attended a large, handsome church; but if I could find thee in that little despised meeting-house, I should be glad to go there; though it would be degrading my rank and respectability, there would I go to find my Saviour." Others think they would rather not have Christ, if Christ goes anywhere except to their own church; they must keep to their own sect, and can by no means overstep the line. It is a marvelous thing, but I believe I only speak the experience of many, when I say that there are very few of you were brought to know the Lord where you were in the habit of attending. You have attended there perhaps since; but it was not your father's church, not the church of the place where you were born and bred, but some other church, into which you strayed for a time, and where the arrows stuck fast in the heart of the King's enemies. I know it was so with me; I never thought of going to the despised chapel where I was first brought to know the Lord, but it snowed so hard that I could not go to a more respectable place, so I was obliged to go to the little meeting, and when I got in, the preacher read his text—" Look unto me, and be ye saved, all the ends of the earth." It was a blessed text, and blessedly applied: but if there had been any stickling as to going into places, I should not have been there. The awakened sinner says, " O that I knew where I might find him! Only let me know where; let the minister of it be the most despised in the world, I will go and hear him; let the sect to which he belongs be the most calumniated and slandered, there I will be found seeking him. If I can but find Christ, I will be content to find him anywhere." If divers can go into the deeps to bring up pearls, we should not be ashamed sometimes to dive deep to bring up precious jewels. Men will do any thing to get gold; they will work in the most muddy streams, or under the most scorching sun; surely, then, we ought not to mind how much we stoop, if we find that which is more precious than gold and silver, even " Jesus Christ, and him crucified." Is this also thy feeling? Then, beloved, I have not only a hope of thee, but I have a certainty of thee. If thou art brought to cry out, in all the senses I have mentioned. " O that I knew where I might find him!" then assuredly the Lord hath begun a good work in thee, and he will carry it on even unto the end.

II. But now, for the second point, I SHALL ENDEAVOR TO GIVE SOME REASONS WHY A GRACIOUS GOD DELAYS AN AN-SWER TO THE PRAYERS OF PENITENT SINNERS. Methinks I hear some one saying, " How is it that God does not give a man comfort as soon as he repents ? Why is it that the Lord makes some of his people wait in bondage till he gives them liberty ?"

In the first place, it is *to display his own sovereignty.* Ah that is a word that is not often mentioned in pulpits. Divin sovereignty is a very unfashionable doctrine. Few people care to hear of a God who doeth as he pleaseth, and is absolute monarch over man; who knoweth of no law but his own absolute will, which is always the will to do that which is right, to do good to those whom he hath ordained unto eter nal life, and to scatter mercy lavishly upon all creatures. But we do assert, that there is such a thing as divine sovereignty and more especially in the work of salvation. God said thus : " If I gave to all men peace as soon as they asked for it, they would begin to think they had a right to it. Now, I will make some of them wait, so that they may see that the mercy is absolutely in my hand, and that if I choose to withhold it altogether I might do so most justly; and I will make men see that it is a gift of my free grace, and not of their deserving." In some of our squares, where they are anxious to keep the right of way, you know they sometimes shut the gates, not because they would inconvenience us, but because they would preserve the right of way, and let the public see that although they let them through, yet they have no right of way, and might be excluded if the proprietors pleased. So with God : he says, " Man, if I save thee, it is entirely of my will and pleasure ; my grace I give, not because thou deservest it, for then it were no grace at all; but I give it to the most undeserving of men, that I may keep my claim to it." And I take it that this is the best way of proving God's sovignty, namely, his making delay between penitence and faith, or between penitence and that faith which brings peace with God and joy in the Holy Ghost. I think this is one very important reason.

But there is another. God sometimes delayeth manifesting his forgiving mercy to them, *in order that they may find out some secret sin*. There is something hidden in their hearts which they do not know of They come to God confessing their sins, and they think they have made a clean breast of all their transgressions. " Nay," saith God, " I will not give you pardon yet, or I will not apply it to your conscience yet ; there is a sin you have not yet discovered ;" and he sets the heart searching itself again, till Jerusalem is searched as with candles, and lo, there is some sin dragged out from the corner in which it was hidden. Conscience says, " I never knew this sin before ; I never felt it as a sin ; Lord, I repent." " Ah," saith the mighty Maker, " now I have proved thee and tried thee, and found out this dross, I will speak to thee the word of consolation and comfort." Art thou, then, a mourner, seeking rest, and not finding it ? I beseech thee, look into thine heart once more. Perhaps there is some hidden lust there, some secret sin. Look within once more; turn the traitor out. Then will God come and dwell in thy soul, and give unto thee the " peace that passeth all understanding."

Another reason is, *that he may make us more useful in after life.* A man is never made thoroughly useful unless he has suffering. I do not think there is much done by a man who is not a suffering man. We must first suffer in our heads and hearts the things we preach, or we shall never preach them with effect ; and if we are private Christians we can never be of use to our fellow men, unless we have passed through somewhat the same trials they have had to endure. So God makes some of his people wait a long time before he gives them the manifestation of their pardon, in order that they may comfort others in after days. "I need thee to be a consolation to others ; therefore I will make thee full of grief, and drunken with wormwood, so that when thou shalt in after years meet with the mourner, thou mayest say to him, I have suffered the same and endured the same." And there are none so fit to comfort others, as those who have once needed comfort themselves. Then take heart. Perhaps the Lord designs thee for a great work. He is keeping thee low in bondage, and doubt, and fear, that he may bring thee out more clearly, and make thy light like the light of seven days, and bring forth thy righteousness " clear as the sun, fair as the moon, and terrible as an army with banners." Wait, then, for God designs good to thee, and good to others through thee, by this delay.

But it often arises not so much from God as from ourselves. It is *ignorance of the way of salvation* which keeps many a man longer in doubt than he would be, if he knew more of it. I do not hesitate to affirm, that one of the hardest things for a sinner to understand is the way of salvation. It seems the plainest thing in all the world; nothing appears more easy than, " Believe on the Lord Jesus Christ, and thou shalt be saved." But when the sinner is led to feel himself a sinner, he finds it not so easy to understand as he thought. We tell a man that, with all their blackness, sinners are to be pardoned ; that, with all their sins, they are to be forgiven freely for Christ's sake. " But," says the man when he feels himself to be black, " do you mean to tell me that I am to be made whiter than snow? Do you mean to tell me that I who am lost am to be saved, not through any thing I do, or hope to do, but purely through what another did?" He can hardly believe it possible; he will have it, he must do something; he must do this, or that, or the other, to help Christ; and the hardest thing in the world is to bring a man to see that salvation is of the Lord alone, and not at all of himself; that it is God's free and perfect gift, which leaves nothing of ours to be added to it, but is given to us to cover us completely, from head to foot without any thing of our own. Men will conceive what God would not have them conceive, and they will not receive that which God would have them embrace. You know, it may be very easy to talk of certain cures, and to read of them. We may say "Such and such a medicine is very effective, and will work such and such a cure;" but when we are sick ourselves, we are often very dubious of the medicine, and if, having taken draught after draught of it, we find it does not cure us, perhaps we are brought to think, that though it may cure others, it can not cure us, because there has been such delay in the operation of it. So the poor soul thinks of the gospel, "Certainly it can not heal me;" and then he misunderstands the nature of the sacred medicine altogether, and begins to take the law instead of the gospel. Now the law never saved any yet, though it has condemned full many in its time, and will condemn us all, unless we have the gospel. If any man here should be in doubt on account of ignorance, let me, as plainly as I can, state the gospel. I believe it to be wrapt up in one word—*Substitution*. I have always considered, with Luther and Calvin, that the sum and substance of the gospel lies in that word, Substitution, Christ standing in the stead of man. If I understand the gospel, it is this: I deserve to be lost and ruined; the only reason why I should not be damned is this, that Christ was punished in my stead, and there is no need to execute a sentence twice for sin. On the other hand, I know I can not enter heaven, unless I have a perfect righteousness; I am absolutely certain I shall never have one of my own, for I find I sin every day; but then Christ had a perfect righteousness, and he said, "There, take my garment, put it on; you shall stand before God as if you were Christ, and I will stand before God as if I had been the sinner; I will suffer in the sinner's stead, and you shall be rewarded for works which you did not do, but which Christ did for you." I think the whole substance of salvation lies in the thought, that Christ stood in the place of man. The prisoner is in the dock; he is about to be taken away for death; he deserves to die; he has been a mighty criminal. But before he is taken away, the judge asks whether there is any possible plan whereby that prisoner's life can be spared. Up rises one who is pure and perfect himself, and has known no sin, and by the allowance of the judge, for that is necessary, he steps into the dock, and says, " Consider me to be the prisoner; pass the sentence on me, and let me die. Gentlemen of the court," says he, " consider the prisoner to be myself. I have fought for my country; I have dared, and deserved well of it; reward him as if he had done good, and punish me as if I had committed the sin." You say, " Such a thing could not occur in an earthly court of law." Ay, but it has happened in God's court of law. In the great court of King's Bench, where God is Judge of all, it has happened. The Saviour said, " The sinner deserves to die; let me die in his stead, and let him be clothed in my righteousness." To illustrate this, I will give you two instances. One is that of an ancient king, who passed a law against a crime, and the punishment of the crime was, that any one who committed it should have both his eyes put out. His own son committed the crime. The king, as a strict judge, said, " I can not alter the law; I have said that the loss of eyes shall be the penalty; take out one of mine and one of his." So, you see, he strictly carried out the law; but at the same time he was able to have mercy in part upon his son. But in the case of Christ we must go a little further. He did not say " Exact half the penalty of me, and half of the sinner;" he said, " Put both my eyes out; nail me to the tree; let me die; let me take all the guilt away, and then the sinner may go free." We have heard of another case, that of two brothers, one of whom had been a great criminal, and was about to die, when his brother, coming into court, decorated with medals, and having many wounds upon him, rose up to plead with the judge, that he would have mercy on the crimi nal for his sake. Then he began to strip himself and show his scars—how here and there on his big broad breast he had received saber cuts in defense of his country. " By these wounds," he said—and he lifted up one arm, the other having been cut away—" by these my wounds, and the sufferings I have endured for my country, I beseech thee, have mercy on him." For his brother's sake the criminal was allowed to escape the punishment that was hanging over his head. It was even so with Christ. "The sinner," he said, " deserves to die; then I will die in his stead. He deserves not to enter heaven, for he has not kept the law; but I have kept the law for him, he shall have my righteousness, and I will take his sin; and so the just shall die for the unjust, to bring him to God." I have thus run away from the subject somewhat, in order to clear up any ignorance that might exist in the minds of some of my hearers, as to this essential point of the gospel plan.

III. And now I am to give SOME ADVICE TO THOSE WHO HAVE BEEN SEEKING CHRIST, AND WHO HAVE NEVER FOUND HIM, HOW THEY MAY FIND HIM.

In the first place, let me say, *Go wherever Christ goes*. The sick man knew that Christ went to Bethesda, and there he lay. If Christ were to walk this earth again, and heal the sick, all the sick people would inquire, " Where does Christ walk to-morrow ?" and as soon as they found out where he would take his walks abroad, there they would be lying thick on the pavement, in the hope that as he passed by he would heal them. Go up, then, to Christ's house : it is there he meets with his people. Read his Word : it is there he blesses them, by applying sweet promises to them. Keep to the ordinances : do not neglect them. Christ comes to Bethesda pool : lie by the water. If you can not put in your foot, be where Christ comes. You know, Thomas did not get the blessing, for he was not there when Jesus came. Be not away from the house of God ; so that when he passes by he may haply look on thee, and say, " Thy sins are forgiven thee."

And whatever you do, when Christ passes by, *cry after him with all your might ;* never be satisfied until you do make him hear ; and if he frown on you seemingly, for the moment do not be stoppe l or stayed. If you are a little stirred by a sermon, pray over it ; do not lose the auspicious moment. If you hear any thing read which gives you some hope, lift up your heart in prayer at once ; when the wind blows, then should the sails be set up ; and it may happen that God may give you grace to cross the harbor's mouth, and you may find the haven inside, the haven of perpetual rest. There was a man, you know, who was born blind, and who wanted to have his sight. As he sat by the road-side one day, he heard that Jesus passed by, and when he heard that, he cried after him, " Jesus, thou son of David, have mercy on me." The people wanted to hear Christ preach, so they hushed the poor man ; but he cried again, " Thou Son of David, have mercy on me." The Son of David turned not his head ; he did not look upon the man, but continued his discourse ; but still the man shout-ed, " Jesus, thou Son of David, have mercy on me !" And then Jesus stopped. The disciples ran to the poor man, and said, " Be still, trouble not the Master." But he cried so much the more, " Jesus, thou Son of David, have mercy on me." And Jesus at last said, " What wilt thou that I shall do unto thee ?" He said, " Lord, that I may receive my sight." He received it, and " went on his way rejoicing." Now, your doubts say, " Hush ! do not pray any more ;" Satan says, " Be still ; do not cry any more." Tell your doubts and fears, and the demon too, that you will give Christ no rest till he turns his eyes upon you in love, and heals your diseases. Cry aloud unto him, O thou awakened sinner, when he passes by.

The next piece of advice I would give you is this : *think very much of Christ.* No way that I know of will get you faith in Christ so well as thinking of him. I would advise you, conscience-stricken sinner, to spend an hour in meditation on Christ. You do not want to spend an hour in meditation on yourself ; you will get very little good from that ; you may know beforehand that there is no hope for you in yourself. But spend an hour in meditation on Christ. Go, beloved, to thy closet, and sit down in that chamber of yours ; picture him in the garden ; think you see him there, sweating " great drops of blood, falling down to the ground." Then picture him standing in Pilate's hall ; think you see him with his

hands bound, his back pouring down rivers of gore; then fol
low him till you see him coming to the hill, Calvary; think
you see him hurled backward, and nailed to the tree; then
let your imagination, or rather your faith, bring before you
the cross lifted up, and dashed into its socket, when every
bone of Christ was put out of joint.   Look at him; look at his
thorn-crown, and see the beaded drops of blood trickling down
his cheek.

> "See from his head, his hands, his feet,
>   Sorrow and love flow mingling down."

I know of no means, under God, so profitable for getting faith,
as thoughts of Christ; for while you are looking at him you
will say, "Blessed Jesus, didst thou die? Surely, my soul, his
death is sufficient for thee."   He is able to save unto the uttermost all those who trust in him.   You may think of a doctrine for ever, and get no good from it, if you are not already
saved; but think of the person of Christ, and that will give
you faith.   Take him everywhere, wherever you go, and try
to meditate on him in your leisure moments, and then he will
reveal himself to you, and give you peace.   Ah! that is the
point where we feel that none of us have enough of Christ, not
even the best of Christians.   I went into a friend's house one
day, and he said to me, as a sort of hint, I suppose, "I have
known so and so these thirty years, without hearing any thing
of his religion."   Said I, "You will not know me thirty minutes without hearing something of mine."   It is a fact, that
many Christian people spend their Sunday afternoons in talking about common-place subjects, and Jesus Christ is scarcely
ever mentioned.   As for the poor ungodly world, of course
they neither say nor think any thing of him.   But O, thou
that knowest thyself to be a sinner, despise not the Man of
sorrows!   Let his bleeding hands drop on thee; look thou on
his pierced side; and, looking, thou shalt live; for, remember, it is only by looking to Christ we shall live, not by doing
any thing ourselves.   We must venture on Christ, and venture
wholly or else we never can be saved.

And this brings me to close up by saying to every awakened
sinner, if you would have peace with God, and have it now,
venture on Christ.   It is hardly fair to say venture, for it is no

venture; there is not a grain of hap-hazard in it; it is quite safe. He that trusteth himself to Christ need never fear "But," you will say, "how am I to trust Christ? What do you mean by trusting in Christ?" Why, I mean just what I say. Fully rely upon what Christ did, as the way of salvation. Yow know the negro, when he was asked how he believed, said, "Massa, dis is how I believe; I fall flat down on de promise; I can't fall no lower." He had just a right idea about believing. Believing is falling down on Christ, and looking to him to hold you up. Or, to illustrate it by an anecdote which I have often told: a boy at sea, who was very fond of climbing to the mast-head, one day climbed to the main-truck, and could not get down again. The sea was very rough, and it was seen that in a little while the boy would fall on the deck, and be dashed to pieces. His father saw but one way of saving his life. Seizing a speaking-trumpet, he cried out, "Boy, the next time the ship lurches, you fall into the sea." The next time the ship lurched the boy looked down, and, not much liking the idea of throwing himself into the sea, still held to the mast. The father, who saw that the boy's strength would soon fail him, took a gun in his hand, and cried out, "Boy, if you do not drop into the sea the next time the ship lurches, I'll shoot you!" The boy knew his father meant it, and the next time the ship lurched he leaped into the sea. It seemed like certain destruction, but out went a dozen brawny arms, and he was saved. The sinner, in the midst of the storm, thinks he must cling to the mast of his good works, and so be saved. Says the gospel, "Let go your good works, and drop into the ocean of God's love." "No," says the sinner, "it is a long way between me and God's love; I must perish if I trust to that; I must have some other reliance." "If you have any other reliance than that, you are lost." Then comes the thundering law, and declares to the sinner, that unless he gives up every dependence, he will be lost. And then comes the happy moment, when the sinner says, "Dear Lord, I give up all my dependence, and cast myself on thee; I take thee, Jesus, to be my one object in life, my only trust, the refuge of my soul." Can any of you say that in your hearts? I know there are some of you who can

But are there any who could not say it when they came here, but who can say it now? O, I would rejoice if one such were brought to God. I am conscious that I have not preached to you as I could desire; but if one such has been brought to believe and trust in the Saviour, it is enough; God will be glorified.

But alas! for such of you as will go away and say, "The man has talked about salvation, but what matters it to us?" Yes, go your way; you can afford to laugh to-day at God and his gospel; but, remember, men can not afford to scoff at boats when they are in a storm, although they may be on land. Death is after you, and will soon seize you; your pulse must soon cease to beat; strong as you are now, your bones are not of brass, nor your ribs of steel; you must lie on your lowly pallet, and there breathe out your last; or, if you be ever so rich, you must die on your curtained beds, and must depart from all your enjoyment into everlasting punishment. You will find it hard work to laugh at Christ then; you will find it dreadful work to scoff at religion then, in that day when death gets hold of you. I think I could almost stand by you and say, "Laugh now, scoffer." "Ah!" you would say, "I find it different from what I supposed; I can not laugh now— death is near me." Take warning, then, before death comes! take warning! He must be a poor ignorant man who does not insure his house before it is on fire; and he must be a fool of all fools, who thinks it unnecessary to seek the salvation of his soul till he comes to the last moment, and is in peril of his life. May God give you thought and consideration, so that you may be led to flee from sin, and fly to heaven; and may God the everlasting Father give you what I can not—give you his grace, which saveth the soul, and maketh sinners into saints, and landeth them in heaven. I can only close by repeating the words of the gospel—" He that believeth and is baptized shall be saved; he that believeth not shall be damned." Having said this, if I had said no more, I should have preached Christ's gospel to you. The Lord give you understanding in all things, and help you to believe; for Jesus Christ's sake!

SERMON VII

THE SINNER'S REFUGE.

"Then ye shall appoint you cities to be cities of refuge for you; that the slayer may flee thither, which killeth any person at unawares."—NUMBERS, xxxv. 11.

YOU are aware that the principle of blood revenge is a deep-seated one in the eastern mind. From the oldest ages it was always the custom with the Orientals, when a man was murdered or slain by chance-medley, for the nearest relative, his heir or any person related to him, to take revenge for him upon the person who, either intentionally or unintentionally, was the means of his death. This revenge was a very choice and special thing to the Oriental mind. The revenger of blood would hunt his victim for forty years—ay, until he died, if he was not able to reach him before—and would be at his heels all his life, that he might slay him. It was not necessary that the man-slayer should have any trial before a judge; the man was dead, and if he who killed him was not put to death, it was reckoned among some tribes to be legitimate to kill his father, or indeed any relative of his tribe; and until some relative of that tribe was put to death, as a revenge for the man who was slain, by accident or otherwise, a deadly feud existed between the two clans, which never could be quenched except by blood. Now, when God gave this law unto the Jews, he found all this deep-rooted love toward the system of the vengeance of blood by the nearest relative; and God acted wisely in this, as he has done in all things. There are two things mentioned in Scripture which I do not believe God ever approved, but which, finding they were deep-seated, he did not forbid to the Jews. One was polygamy: the practice of marrying many wives had become so established that though God abhorred the thing himself, yet he allowed and permitted it to his people, the Jews; because he foresaw they would inevitably have broken the commandment, even if he had made a command that they should have but one wife. It was even so with this matter of blood vengeance. It was so deeply seated in the mind, that God, instead of refusing to the Jews what they regarded as the privilege of taking vengeance, passed a commandment which rendered it impossible almost that a man should be killed, unless he were really a murderer; for he appointed six cities, at convenient distances, so that when one man killed another by chance-medley and committed homicide, he might at once flee to one of these cities; and though he must live there all his life, yet the avenger of blood could never touch him, if he were innocent. He must have a fair trial; but even if he were found innocent he must stay within the city, into which the avenger of blood could not by any possibility come. If he went out of the city the avenger might kill him; he was therefore to suffer perpetual banishment, even for causing death accidentally, in order that it might be seen how much God regarded the rights of blood, and how fearful a thing it is to put a man to death in any way. And we see that this prevented the likelihood of any one being killed who was not guilty; for as soon as one man struck another to the ground by accident, by a stone, or any other means, he fled to the city of refuge. He had a start of the pursuer; and if he arrived there, he was secure and safe.

Now, I wish to use this custom of the Jews as a metaphor and type, to set forth the salvation of men through Jesus Christ our Lord. I shall give you first an explanation, and then an exhortation.

I. WE SHALL ATTEMPT AN EXPLANATION OF THIS TYPE.

1. Note, *The person for whom the city of refuge was provided.* It was not provided for the willful murderer; if he fled there, he must be dragged out of it, and given up to the avenger after a fair trial, and the avenger of death was to kill him, and so have blood for blood, and life for life. But in case of accident, when one man had slain another, without malice or forethought, and had only committed homicide,

then the man fleeing there was perfectly safe. Here, how-ever, the type of Christ is not in keeping; Christ is not a city of refuge provided for men that are innocent, but a city pro-vided for men that are guilty—not for men who have acci-dentally transgressed, but for men who have willfully gone astray. Our Saviour has come into the world to save, not those who have by mistake and error committed sin, but those who have fearfully transgressed against his known command-ments, and have gone astray of their own free-will, their own perversity leading them to rebel against God.

2. *The avenger of blood.* In explaining this, I must, of course, take every part of the figure. The avenger of blood, I have said, was usually next of kin, but I believe any one of the family was held to be competent. If, for instance, my brother had been killed, it would have been my duty, as the first of the family, to avenge his blood, if possible, there and then; to go after the murderer, or the man who had caused death accidentally, and put him to death at once; and if I could not do that, it would be my business, and that of my father, and, indeed, of every male of the family, to hunt and pursue that man, until God should deliver him into our hand, so that we might put him to death. I mean not that it is our duty now, but it would have been under the old Jewish dis-pensation. It was allowed by the Jewish law, that those who were of the kith and kin of the man killed, should be the avengers of his blood. We find the type of this, then, for the sinner, in the law of God. Sinner, the law of God is the blood avenger against you; you have willfully transgressed, you have killed God's commandments, you have trampled them under foot; the law is the avenger of blood; that is after you, and it will have you; condemnation is hanging over your head now, and ere long it shall overtake you; though it reach you not in this life, yet, in the world to come, the avenger of blood, the Moses, the law shall have its vengeance upon you, and you shall be utterly destroyed.

3. But there *was a city of refuge* provided under the law; and *let me tell you a few things concerning this city.* You will remember there were six cities of refuge, in order that one of them might be at a convenient distance from any part

of the country. Now, there are not six Christs; there is but one; but then there is a Christ everywhere. "The word is nigh thee, in thy mouth, in thy heart; if thou wilt confess with thy mouth the Lord Jesus, and believe in thine heart, thou shalt be saved." The city of refuge was a priestly city —a city of the Levites, and it afforded protection to the manslayer for life. He might never go out of it, till the death of the then reigning high priest; after which he might go free, without being touched by the avenger of blood at all. But during the time of his sojourn there, he was housed and fed gratuitously; every thing was provided for him, and he was kept entirely safe. And I would have you mark that he was safe in this city, not because of the bolts or bars of the city, but simply because it was of divine appointment. Do you see the man running from the avenger? The avenger is after him, fast and furious; the man has just reached the borders of the city; in a moment the avenger halts; he knows it is of no use going any further after him, not because the city walls are strong, nor because the gates are barred, nor because an army standeth without to resist, but because God hath said the man shall be safe as soon as he has crossed the border, and has come into the suburbs of the city. Divine appointment was the only thing which made the city of refuge secure. Now, beloved, Jesus Christ is the divinely appointed way of salvation; whosoever amongst us shall make haste from our sins, and fly to Christ, being convinced of our guilt, and helped by God's Spirit to pursue the road, we shall, without doubt, find security; the course of the law shall not touch us, Satan shall not harm us, vengeance shall not reach us, for the divine appointment, stronger than gates of iron or brass, shieldeth every one of us who has "fled for refuge to the hope set before us in the gospel."

This city of refuge, I must have you note, too, had round it suburbs of a very great extent. Two thousand cubits were allowed for grazing land for the cattle of the priests, and a thousand cubits within these for fields and vineyards. Now, no sooner did the man reach the outside of the city, the suburbs, than he was safe; it was not necessary for him to get within the walls but the suburbs themselves were sufficient protection, Learn, hence, that if ye do but touch the hem of Christ's garment, ye shall be made whole; if ye do but lay hold of him with "faith as a grain of mustard seed," with faith which is scarcely a believing, but is truly a believing, you are safe.

> "A little genuine grace ensures
> The death of all our sins."

Get within the borders; lay hold of the hem of Christ' garments, and thou art secure.

We have some interesting particulars, also, with regard to the distance of these cities from the habitations of men in Judea. It is said, that wherever a homicide might occur, any man might get to a city of refuge within half a day. And verily, beloved, it is no great distance to the breast of Christ; it is but a simple renunciation of our own powers, and a laying hold of Christ, to be our all in all, that is required, in order to our being found in the city of refuge. And with regard to the roads to the city, we are told that they were strictly preserved. Every river was bridged; as far as possible, the road was made level, and every obstruction removed, so that the man who fled might find an easy passage to the city. Once a year the elders of the city went along the roads to keep them in order, so that nothing might occur, through the breaking down of bridges, or the stopping up of the highway, to impede the flight of any one, and cause him to be overtaken and killed. And wherever there were by-roads and turnings, there were fixed up hand-posts, and with this word upon them "Miklat"—"refuge"—pointing out the way in which the man should fly, if he wished to reach the city. And there were two people always kept on the road: so that in case the avenger of blood should overtake a man, they might come in the way and entreat the avenger to stay his hand, until the man had reached the city, lest haply innocent blood should be shed without a fair trial, and so the avenger should be proved guilty of murder; for the risk, of course, was upon the head of the avenger, if he put one to death that did not deserve to die. Now, beloved, I think this is a picture of the road to Christ Jesus. It is no round-about road of the law; it is no obeying this, that, and the other; it is a straight road: "Be

lieve and live." It is a road so hard, that no self-righteous
man can ever tread it; but it is a road so easy, that every sinner, who knows himself to be a sinner, might by it find his
way to Christ, and his way to heaven. And lest they should
be mistaken, God has set me and my brethren in the ministry,
to be like hand-posts in the way, to point poor sinners to Jesus;
and we desire ever to have on our lips, the cry "Refuge,
refuge, refuge!" Sinner, that is the way; walk thou therein
and be thou saved.

I think I have thus given the explanation. Christ is the
city of refuge, who preserves all those that flee to him for
mercy; he does that because he is the divinely appointed
Saviour, able to save unto the uttermost them that come unto
God by him.

II. WE HAVE AN EXHORTATION TO GIVE.

You must allow me to picture a scene. You see that man
in the field. He has been at work; he has taken an ox-goad
in his hand, to use it in some part of his husbandry. Unfortunately, instead of doing what he desires to do, he strikes a
companion of his to the heart, and he falls down dead! You
see the poor man with horror in his face; he is a guiltless
man; but, O! what misery he feels when he sees the corpse
lying at his feet! A pang shoots through his heart, such as
you and I have never felt—horror, dread, desolation! Yes,
some of us have felt something akin to it; we will not allude
to the when and the wherefore; but who can describe the
horror of a man at seeing his companion fall at his feet?
Words are incapable of expressing the anguish of his spirit;
he looks upon him, he takes him up—he ascertains that he is
really dead. What next! Do you not see him? In a moment he flies out of the field where he was at labor, and runs
along the road with all his might; he has many miles before
him, six long hours of hard running, and just as he passes the
gate, he turns his head, and there is the man's brother! He
has just come into the field, and seen his brother lying dead.
O! can you conceive how the man's heart palpitates with
fear? He has a little start upon the road. He just sees the
other, with red face, hot and fiery, rushing out of the field,
with the ox-goad in his hand, and running after him. The

way lies through the village where the man's father lives
how he rushes through the streets! He does not even stop
to bid good-by to his wife, nor kiss his children! But on, on
he flies for his very life. The relative calls his father, and his
other friends, and they all rush after him. Now, there is a
troop on the road; the man is still flying a-head—no rest for
him. Though one of his pursuers rests, the others still track
him. There is a horse in the village; they take it, and pursue
him. If they can find any animal that can assist their swiftness, they will take it. Can you not conceive him crying,
"O, that I had wings that I might fly?" See how he spurns
the earth beneath his feet! What to him the green fields on
either hand; what the brooks; he stops not even so much as
to wet his mouth. The sun is scorching him; but it is still
on, on, on! He casts aside one garment after another; still
he rushes on, and the pursuers are behind him. He feels like
the poor stag pursued by the hounds; he knows they are
eager for his blood, and that if they do but once overtake him
it will be a word, a blow—dead! See how he speeds his way!
Now, do you see him? A city is rising into sight; he can
see the towers of the city of refuge; his weary feet almost
refuse to carry him further; the veins are standing out on his
brow, like whipcords; the blood spirts from his nostrils; he
is straining to the utmost, as he rushes on, and faster he would
go if he were master of more strength. The pursuers are
after him—they have almost reached him; but see, and rejoice! He has just got to the outskirts of the city; there is
the line of demarcation; he leaps it, and falls senseless to the
ground; and there is joy in his heart. The pursuers come
and look at him; but they dare not slay him. The knife is
in their hand, and the stones too, to stone him or draw his
blood; but they dare not touch him. He is safe, he is secure;
his running has been just fast enough; he has just managed
to leap into the kingdom of life, and avoid death.

Sinner, that picture I have given thee is a picture of thyself, in all but the man's guiltlessness, for thou art a guilty
man. O! if thou didst but know that the avenger of blood
is after thee! O! that God would give thee grace that thou
couldst have a sense of thy danger to-night! thou wouldst

not then stop a solitary instant without flying to Christ. Thou wouldst say, even while sitting in thy pew, "Let me away, away, away, where mercy is to be found," and thou wouldst give neither sleep to thine eyes, nor slumber to thine eyelids, till thou hadst in Christ found a refuge for thy spirit. I am come, then, to exhort thee to-night. Let me pick out one of you to be a case for all the rest; there is a young man here who is guilty; the proofs of his guilt lie at his feet to-night He knows himself to be a great transgressor; he has foully offended against God's law. Young man, young man, certainly, as you are guilty, the avenger of blood is after you! O! he is a horrid thing, that avenger—God's fiery law; did you ever see it? It speaketh words of flame; it hath eyes like lamps of fire. If you could once see the law of God, and mark the dread keenness of its horrible sword, you might, as you sat in your pew, quiver to death itself in horror at your doom Sinner, bethink thee, if this avenger get hold of thee, it will not be temporal death merely; it will be death eternally. Sinner, remember, if the law doth get its hand on thee, thou art damned; and dost thou know what damnation means? Say, canst thou tell what are the billows of eternal wrath, and what the worm that never dies; what the lake of fire, what the pit that is bottomless? No, thou canst not know how dreadful these things are. Surely, if thou couldst, man, thou wouldst be up on thy feet, and off for life, eternal life. Thou wouldst be like that man in Bunyan's "Progress," who put his fingers in his ears, and ran away; and when his neighbors ran after him, he cried, "Eternal life, eternal life!" O, stolid stupidity—O, sottish ignorance—O, worse than brutal ignorance, that makes men sit down in their sins, and rest content. The drunkard quaffeth still his bowl; he knoweth not that in its dregs there lieth wrath. The swearer still indulgeth in his blasphemy; he knoweth not that one day his oaths shall return upon his own head. You will go your way, and eat the fat, and drink the sweet, and live merrily and happily; but, ah! poor souls, if ye knew that the avenger of blood was after you, you would not act so foolishly! Would you suppose that the man, after he had killed his neighbor, and when he saw the avenger coming, would coolly take his seat, and wait, when there was a city of refuge provided? No; such folly was reserved for such as you are; God has left that folly to be the topstone of the folly of the human race, to be the most glittering jewel in the crown of free will, to be consummate folly—the dress wherein free will doth robe itself. O! you will not fly to Christ, you will stop where you are, you will rest contented, and one day the law will seize you, and then wrath, eternal wrath, will lay hold upon you! How foolish is the man who wastes his time, and carelessly loiters, when the city of refuge is before him, and when the avenger of blood is after him!

Suppose, now, I take another case. I have a young man here who says, "Why, sir, it is no use in trying to be saved; I shall not think of prayer, or faith, or any thing of that sort because there is no city of refuge for me." Why, suppose that poor man who had killed his neighbor had said that; suppose he had sat still, and folded his arms, and said, "There is no city of refuge for me." You do not mean what you say. If you thought there was no city of refuge for you, I know what you would do; you would shriek, and cry, and groan. There is a kind of despair that some people have, which is a sham despair. I have met with many who say, "I do not believe I ever could be saved," and they seem not to care whether they are saved or not. Why, man, how foolish would he be, who would sit still, because he fancied there was no entrance for him into the city, and let the avenger slay him! But your folly is just as great and worse, if you sit still, and say, "He will never have mercy on me." He is as much a suicide who refuses the medicine, because he thinks it will not cure him, as the man who takes the dirk, and stabs himself to the heart. You have no right, sir, to let your despair triumph over the promise of God. He hath said it, and he means it: "Whosoever calleth on the name of the Lord shall be saved." If he has shown you your guilt, depend upon it, there is a city of refuge for you; haste thee to it; haste thee to it; may God help you to betake yourselves to it now! Ay, if men knew how dreadful is the wrath to come, and how terrible is judgment, how swiftly would they fly! There is not a hearer of mine here that would delay an hour to fly to Christ, if he di but know how fearful is his condition out of Christ. When God the Spirit once convinces us of our sin, there is no halting then; the Spirit says, "To-day, if you will hear his voice," and we say, "To-day, Lord, to-day, hear our voice!" There is no halting then; there is no pausing then; it is on, on, on, for our very life; and I beseech you, men, brethren, you, who have sinned against God, and know it; you that want to be delivered from the wrath to come, I beseech you, by him that liveth and was dead, flee to Christ; but take this exhortation, take heed it is Christ you flee to; for if the man who had slain his neighbor, had fled to another city, it would have been of no avail; had he fled to a city that was not an ordained city of refuge, he might have sped on with all the impetuosity of desire, and yet have been slain within the city gates. So, ye self-righteous ones, ye may fly on to your good works, ye may practice your baptism, and your confirmation, and your church going, and your chapel going; ye may be all that is good and excellent, but ye are flying to the wrong city, and the avenger of blood will find you, after all. Poor soul! remember Christ Jesus is the only refuge for a guilty sinner: his blood, his wounds, his agonies, his sufferings, his death, these, then, are the gates and walls of the city of salvation. But if we trust not in these, without a doubt, trust where we may, our hope shall be as a broken reed, and we shall perish after all.

I may have one here who is just awakened, just led to see his sin, as if it were a murdered corpse beneath his feet; it seems to me that God has sent me to that one man in particular. Man, God has shown you your guilt; he sent me to-night to tell you that there is a refuge for you; though you are guilty, he is good; though you have revolted and rebelled, he will have mercy on those that repent, and trust in the merits of his Son. And now he has bidden me say to you, "Fly, fly, fly!" In God's name, I say to you, fly to Christ. He has bidden me warn you to-night against delays; he has bidden me remind you that death surprises men when least they expect it; he has bidden me to warn you that the avenger will not spare, neither will his eye pity. His sword was forged for vengeance, and vengeance it will have. And he has bidden me exhort you by the terrors of the law, by the day of judgment, by the wrath to come, by the uncertainty of life, and by the nearness of death, this night to fly to Christ.

> " Haste, traveler, haste, the night comes on:
>   And thou far off from rest and home :
>   Haste, traveler, haste !"

But, O how much more earnest is our cry, when we say, " Haste, sinner, haste." Not only doth the night come on ; but, lo ! the blood avenger is behind. Already he has slain his thousands. Let the shrieks of souls, already damned, come up in your ears. Already the avenger has done wonders of wrath ; let the howlings of Gehenna startle you ; let the torments of hell amaze you. What ! will you stop with such a sword behind you ? will you pause with such an avenger in swift pursuit ? What ! young man, will you stop this night ? God has convinced you of your sin ; will you go to your rest this night without a prayer ? Will you live another day without fleeing to Christ ? No ; I think I see the Spirit of God in you to-night, and I think I hear what he makes you say. He makes you say, " No, God helping me, I give myself to Christ now ; and if he will not now shed abroad his love in my heart, yet this is my one resolve ; no slumber to my eyes will I afford till Christ shall look on me, and seal my pardon with his Spirit —the pardon bought with blood." But if thou sittest still, young man, and thou wilt do so, left to thy own free will, I can do no more for thee than this, I must weep for thee in secret. Alas! for thee, my hearer ; alas! for thee ; the ox led to the slaughter is more wise than thou ; the sheep that goeth to its death is not so foolish as thou art. Alas! for thee, my hearer, that thy pulse should beat a march to hell. Alas! that yonder clock, like the muffled drum, should be the music of the funeral march of thy soul. Alas! alas! that thou shouldst fold thine arms in pleasure, when the knife is at thy heart. Alas! alas! for thee, that thou shouldst sing, and make merriment, when the rope is about thy neck, and the drop is tottering under thee. Alas! for thee, that thou shouldst go thy way, and live merrily and happily, and yet be lost. Thou remindest me of the silly moth that dances round about the flame, singeing itself for a while, and then at last plunging to

!ts death. Such art thou! Young woman, with thy butter-
fly clothing, thou art leaping round the flame that shall destroy
thee. Young man, light and frothy in thy conversation, gay
in thy life, thou art dancing to hell; thou art singing thy way
to damnation, and promenading the road to destruction.
Alas! alas! that ye should be spinning your own winding
sheets; that ye should every day by your sins be building
your own gallows; that by your transgressions ye should be
digging your own graves, and working hard to pile the faggots
for your own eternal burning. O! that ye were wise, that ye
understood this, that ye would consider your latter end. O!
that ye would flee from the wrath to come. O! my hearers,
the wrath to come, the wrath to come! O, God! how terrible! these lips dare not venture to describe, this heart filleth
in agony; and, my hearers, are there not some of you that
will soon be in the wrath to come? Yes, yes! there are
some of you, who, if you were now to drop dead in your pews,
must be damned. Ah! ye know it; ye know it; ye dare not
deny it; I see you know; as you hang down your heads, you
seem to say it is true; I have no Christ to trust to, no robe of
righteousness to wear, no heaven to hope for. My hearer,
give me thine hand; never did father plead with son with
more impassioned earnestness than I would with thee. Why
wouldst thou sit still, when hell is burning in thy face. "Why
will ye die, O house of Israel!" O, God! must I preach to
these people in their place in hell; and must I continue to
preach to them, and be "a savor of death unto death to them,"
and not "a savor of life unto life?" And must I, must I, help
to make their hell more intolerable? Must it be so? Must
the people who now listen to us, like the people of Chorazin
and Bethsaida, have a more terrible doom than the people of
Sodom? Ah! yes, the Lord hath said it, and we believe it.
O! ye that are left to your own free will, to choose the way
to hell, as all men do when left alone—let these eyes run down
with tears for ye, because ye will not weep for yourselves.
Strange! strange! that I should feel more for some of your
souls than you do for yourselves! My God knoweth, there is
not a stone that I would leave unturned to save each one of
you there is nought that human strength could do, or human

study would learn, which I would not seek after, if I might but be the instrument of saving you from hell; and yet you act as though it concerned you not, whom it should concern the most; it is my business, but it is far more yours. Sirs, if ye be lost, remember, it is yourselves that will be lost; if ye perish, ye perish; I am clean of your blood. If ye flee not from the wrath to come, I have warned you; I could not bear to have he blood upon my head which some, even of those who like sound doctrine, I fear, will have at the last day of account. I tremble for some I know, that preach God's gospel, in some sense fully, but who never warn sinners. A member of my church said to me lately, "I heard such a one preach; a sound doctrine man he is called. I heard him preach for nine years, attending the theater all the time. I could curse, I could swear, I could sin, and I never heard a warning from that man's lips the whole nine years." Ah! my God, my God, let this world hiss me; let me wear the coat that sparkleth, and the cap that garnisheth a fool. Let earth condemn me, and let the fools of the universe spurn me; but free me from the blood of my hearers. By God's grace, again I register the vow, God helping me; the only thing I seek in this world is to be faithful to my hearers' souls. If you are damned, it is not for want of preaching to, nor for want of earnest warning. Young men and maidens, old men with gray hairs, merchants and tradesmen, servants, fathers, mothers, children, I have warned you this night, you are in danger of hell, and as God liveth, before whom I stand, you will be there soon, unless you flee from the wrath to come. Remember, none but Jesus can save you. But if God shall enable you to see your danger, and fly to Christ, he will have mercy upon you for ever, and the avenger of blood will never find you out. No, not even when the red lightnings shall be flashing from the hand of God in the day of judgment. That city of refuge shall shelter you, and in the heart of Jesus, triumphant, blessed, secure, you shall sing the righteousness and the blood of Christ who shelters sinners from the wrath to come.

SERMON VIII

THE DUMB SINGING

"Then the eyes of the blind shall be opened, and the ears of the deaf shall be unstopped. Then shall the lame man leap as an hart, and the tongue of the dumb sing; for in the wilderness shall waters break out, and streams in the desert."—ISAIAH, XXXV. 5, 6

WHAT a difference grace makes, whenever it enters the heart! We find here the blind spoken of; but they are not blind when once grace has touched their eyes; then "the eyes of the blind are opened." We read also of the deaf; but they are not deaf after grace has operated upon them · "the ears of the deaf are unstopped." Here are men who have been lame before; but when once the omnipotent influence of divine grace has come upon them, they leap like a hart. And those who were dumb once, so far from being dumb any longer, have experienced a change that must be radical, for its effects are surprising. The tongue of the dumb not simply speaks, but it sings.

Grace makes a great difference in a man, when it enters into him. How vain, then, are the boasts and professions of some persons, who assert themselves to be the children of God, and yet live in sin. There is no perceivable difference in their conduct; they are just what they used to be before their pretended conversion; they are not changed in their acts, even in the least degree, and yet they do most positively affirm that they are the called and living children of God, although they are entirely unchanged. Let such know that their pretensions are lies, and that falsehood is the only groundwork that they have for their hopes; for, wherever the grace of God is, it makes men to differ. A graceless man is not like a gracious man : and a gracious man is not like a graceless one

We are " new creatures in Christ Jesus." When God looks upon us with the eye of love, in conversion and regeneration, he makes us as opposite from what we were before as light is from darkness, as even heaven itself is from hell. God changes man. He works in him a change so great, that no reformation can even so much as thoroughly imitate it; it is an entire change—a change of the will, of the being, of the desires, of the hates, of the dislikings, and of the likings. In every respect the man becomes new when divine grace enters into his heart. And yet thou sayest of thyself, " I am converted," and remain what thou wast ! I tell thee once again to thy face, that thou sayest an empty thing; thou hast no ground for saying it. If grace permits thee to sin as thou wast wont to do, then that grace is no grace at all. That grace were not worth the having which permits a man to be, after he receives it, what he was before. No, we must ever hold and teach the great doctrine of sanctification. Where God really justifies he really sanctifies too ; and where there is the remission of sin, there is also the forsaking of it. Where God hath blotted out transgression, he also removeth our love of it, and maketh us seek after holiness, and walk in the ways of the Lord. I think we may fairly infer this from the text, as a prelude to the observations we have to make concerning it.

And now I shall want you, first of all, to notice *the sort of people whom God has chosen to sing his praises, and to sing them eternally.* Then, in the second place, I shall enter into *a more full description of the dumb people here described.* Then, thirdly, I shall try to notice *certain special times and seasons when those dumb people sing more sweetly than at others.*

I. First, then, THE PERSONS WHOM GOD HATH CHOSEN TO SING HIS SONGS FOR EVER. "The tongue of the *dumb* shall sing." We may make this the first point. There is no difference, by nature, between the elect and others; those who are now glorified in heaven, and who walk the golden streets clad in robes of purity, were by nature as unholy and defiled, and as far from original righteousness, as those who, by their own rejection of Christ, and by their love of sin, have brought themselves into the pit of eternal torment, as a punishment for their iniquities. The only reason why there is a difference between those who are in heaven and those who are in hell, rests with divine grace, and with divine grace alone. Those in heaven must inevitably have been cast away, had not everlasting mercy stretched out its hand and redeemed them. They were by nature not one whit superior to others. They would as certainly have rejected Christ, and have trodden under foot the blood of Jesus, as did those who were cast away, if grace, free grace, had not prevented them from committing this sin. The reason why they are Christians is not because they did naturally will to be so, nor because they did by nature desire to know Christ, or to be found of him; but they are now saints simply because God made them so. He gave them the desire to be saved; he put into them the will to seek after him; he helped them in their seekings, and afterward brought them to feel that peace which is the fruit of justification. But by nature they were just the same as others; and if there is any difference, we are obliged to say that the difference does not lie in their favor. In very many cases, we who now "rejoice in hope of the glory of God" were the very worst of men. There are multitudes that now bless God for their redemption, who once cursed him; who implored, as frequently as they dared to do, with oaths and swearing, that the curse of God might rest upon their fellows and upon themselves. Many of the Lord's anointed were once the very castaways of Satan, the sweepings of society, the refuse of the earth, those whom no man cared for, who were called outcasts, but whom God hath now called desired ones, seeing he hath loved them.

I am led to these thoughts from the fact that we are told here that those who sing were dumb by nature. Their singing does not come naturally from themselves; they were not born songsters; no, they were dumb ones, those whom God would have to sing his praises. It does not say the tongue of the stammerer, or the tongue of him that blasphemed, or the tongue of him that misused his tongue, but "the tongue of the dumb," of those who have gone furthest from any thought of singing, of those who have no power of will to sing—the tongue of such as these shall yet be made to sing God's praises. Strange choice that God has made! Strange, for its graciousness! strangely manifesting the sovereignty of his will! God would build for himself a palace in heaven of living stones: where did he get them? Did he go to the quarries of Paros? Hath he brought forth the richest and the purest marble from the quarries of perfection? No, ye saints, look to "the hole of the pit whence ye were digged, and to the rock whence ye were hewn!" Ye were full of sin; so far from being stones that were white with purity, ye were black with defilement, seemingly utterly unfit to be stones in the spiritual temple, which should be the dwelling-place of the Most High. And yet he chose you to be trophies of his grace, and of his power to save. When Solomon built for himself a palace, he built it of cedar: but when God would build for himself a dwelling for ever, he cut not down the goodly cedars, but he dwelt in a bush, and hath preserved it as his memorial for ever: "The God that dwelt in the bush." Goldsmiths make exquisite forms from precious metals; they fashion the bracelet and the ring from gold:—God maketh his precious things out of base material; and from the black pebbles of the defiling brooks he hath taken up stones, which he hath set in the golden ring of his immutable love, to make them gems to sparkle on his finger for ever. He hath not selected the best, but apparently the worst of men, to be the monuments of his grace; and when he would have a choir in heaven that should with tongues harmonious sing his praises —a chorus that should for ever chant hallelujahs louder than the noise of many waters, and like great thunders, he did not send Mercy down to seek earth's songsters, and cull from those who have the sweetest voices: he said, "Go, Mercy, and find out the dumb, and touch their lips, and make them sing. The virgin tongues that never sang my praise before, that have been silent till now, shall break forth in rhapsodies sublime, and they shall lead the song; even angels shall but attend behind, and catch the notes from the lips of those who once were dumb." "The tongue of the dumb shall sing" God's praises in heaven.

O! what a fountain of consolation this opens for you and for me! Ay, beloved, if God did not choose the base things of this world, he would never have chosen us; if he had respect unto the countenances of men, if he were a respecter ιf persons, where had you and I been this day ; we had never ρeen instances of his love and mercy. No, as we look upor ουrselves now, and remember what we once were, we are οften obliged to say,

> " Depths of mercy, can there be
> Mercy still reserved for me ?"

How many times we have sung at the Lord's table—at th sacramental supper of our Master—

> " Why was I made to hear thy voice
> And enter while there 's room,
> While thousands make a wretched choice,
> And rather starve then come ?"

And we have joined too in singing—

> " 'Twas the same love that spread the feast,
> That sweetly forced us in ;
> Else we had still refused to taste,
> And perished in our sin."

Grace is always grace, but it never seems so gracious as when we see it brought to our unworthy selves. Ay, my friends, you may be Arminians in your doctrine, but you never can be Arminians in your feelings ; you are obliged to confess that it is all of grace, and cast away the thought that it was of your foreseen faith or of your foreseen good works that the Lord chose you. We are obliged to come to this, to feel and know that it must have been of mercy, free mercy, and of that alone ; that we were not capable of doing good works without his grace preventing us before good works, and without his grace also in good works, enabling us to do them ; and, therefore, they never could have been the motive to divine love, nor the reason why it flowed toward us. O ! ye unworthy ones, ye saints that feel your deep natural depravity, and mourn over your ruin by the fall of Adam, lift up your hearts to God ! He hath delivered you from all the impediments which Adam cast upon you ; your tongue is loosed, it is loose now ; Adam made it dumb, but God hath loosed it ; your eyes that were blinded by Adam's fall are opened now ; he hath lifted you from the miry clay. What Adam lost for us, Christ hath regained for us ; he hath plucked us out of the pit, and " set us upon a rock, and established our goings, and hath put a new song into our mouth, even praise for evermore." Yes, "the tongue of the dumb shall sing."

And then just another hint here, before I leave this point. How this ought to give you encouragement in seeking to do good to others! Why, my brethren, I can never think any man too far gone for divine mercy, since I know that God saved me. Whenever I have felt desponding about any of my hearers, who have for a long time persevered in guilt, I have only had to reach down my own biography from the shelves of my memory and just think what I too was, till grace redeemed me, and brought me to my Saviour's feet; and then I have said, "It will be no wonder if that man is saved; after what he hath done for me, I can believe any thing of my Master. If he hath blotted out my transgressions, if he hath clean melted away my sin, then I can never despair of any of my fellow-creatures; I may of myself, but I can not of them." Remember, they may be dumb now, but he can make them sing. Your son John is a sad reprobate; keep on praying for him, mother; God can change his heart. Your daughter's heart seems hard as adamant; he who makes the dumb sing can make rocks melt. Believe in God for your children, as well as for yourselves; trust him; take their cases before his throne; rely upon him that he can save them, and believe that in answer to earnest prayer, he also will do it. And if you have neighbors that are full of the pestilence of sin, whose vices come up before you as a stench in your nostrils, yet fear not to carry the gospel to them; though they be harlots, drunkards, swearers, be not afraid to tell them of the Saviour's dying love. He makes the dumb sing; he does not ask even of them a voice to begin with; they are dumb, and he does not ask of them even the power of speech, but he gives them the power. O! if you have neighbors who are haters of the Sabbath, haters of God, unwilling to come to the house of God, despising Christ; if you find them as far gone as you can find them, recollect, he maketh the dumb to sing, and therefore, he can make them live. He wants no goodness in them to begin with; all he wants is just the rough, raw material, unhewn uncut, unpolished. And he does not want even good mate rial; bad as the material may be, he can make it into something inestimably precious, something that is worthy of the Saviour's blood. Go on; fear not! If the dumb can sing, then surely you can never say that any man need be cast away.

II. I am now to enter into *some rather more lucid description of these dumb people.* Who are they?

Well, sometimes I get a good thought out of old Master Cruden's Concordance. I believe that is the best commentary to the Bible, and I like to study it. I opened it lately at this passage, and I found Master Cruden describing different kinds of dumb people. He says there are four or five different sorts; but I shall name only four of them. The first sort of dumb people he mentions are those that can not speak; the second sort are those that won't speak; the third sort are those that dare not speak; and the fourth sort are those that have got nothing to say, and therefore they are dumb.

1. The first sort of people who shall sing are *those who can not speak.* This is the usual acceptation of the word dumb: the others are, of course, only figurative applications of the term. We call a man dumb when he can not speak. Now, spiritually, the man who is still in his trespasses and sins is dumb; and I will prove that. He is dead; and there is none so dumb as a dead man. We used to hear in our childhood that they buried none but deaf and dumb persons in certain churchyards. It was intended to tickle our childish fancies, and misled us a little; but the meaning was, that none but dead people were buried there; none are so dumb as those who are dead. "Shall the dead arise and praise thee? Shall thy loving-kindness be declared in the grave, or thy faithfulness in destruction?" The word of God assures us that unregenerate men are spiritually dead; it follows, then, that they must be spiritually dumb. They can not sing God's praises; they know him not, and, therefore, they can not exalt his glorious name. They can not confess their sins; they can utter the mere words of confession, but they can not really confess, for they do not know the evil of sin, nor have they been taught to feel what a bitter thing it is, and to know themselves as sinners. But "no man can call Jesus Lord, except by the Holy Ghost;" and these people can not do so truly. Perhaps, it may be,

they can talk well on the doctrines; but they can not speak them out of the fulness of their hearts, as living and vital principles which they know in themselves. They can not join in the songs, nor can they take part in the conversation of a Christian. If they sit down with the saints, perhaps they have culled a few phrases from the garden of the Lord, which they use and apply to certain things which they do not know any thing about. They talk a language the meaning of which they do not comprehend—like Milton's daughters reading a language to their father which they did not understand. Still, so far as the essence of the matter is concerned, they are dumb. But, hail to sovereign grace! "the tongue of the dumb shall sing!" God will have his darlings made what they should be. They are dumb by nature, but he will not leave them so; they can not now sing his praises, but they shall do it; they do not now confess their sins, but he will bring them on their knees yet, and make them pour out their hearts before him. They can not now talk the brogue of Canaan, nor speak the language of Sion, but they shall do it soon. Grace, omnipotent grace, will have its way with them. They shall be taught to pray; their eyes shall be made to flow with tears of penitence; and then, after that, their lips shall sing to the praise of sovereign grace.

I need not dwell upon this point, because I have many here that were dumb once, who can bless God that they can now sing. And does it not sometimes seem to you, beloved, a very strange thing, that you are what you are? I should think it must be the strangest thing in the world for a dumb man to speak, because he has no idea how a man feels when he is speaking; he has no notion of the thing at all. Like a man blind from his birth, he has no idea what kind of a thing sight can be. We have heard of a blind man, who supposed that the color scarlet must be very much like the sound of a trumpet: he had no other way of comparing it. So the dumb man has no notion of the way to talk. Do you not think it is a strange thing that you are what you are? You said once, "I will never be one of the canting Methodists. Do you think I shall ever make a profession of religion? What! I attend a prayer meeting? No." And you went along the streets in all your gayety of mirth, and said, "What! I become a little child, and give up my mind to simple faith, and not reason at all? What! am I to give up all argument about things, and simply take them for granted, because God has said them? Nay, that never can be." I will be bound to say, it will be a wonder to you as long as you are here, that you are the children of God; and even in heaven itself your greatest wonder will be that you were ever brought to know the Saviour.

2. But there is a sort of dumb people that *will not speak.* They are mentioned by Isaiah. He said of preachers in his day they were dumb dogs that would not bark. I bless God we are not now quite so much inundated by this kind of dumb people as we used to be. God has raised up, especially in the Church of England, of late, a large number of evangelical men, who are not afraid to preach the whole counsel of God. There are many such faithful preachers of the gospel to be found; and although we used to say we were the only evangelicals that preached the gospel, the time has come when "she that was barren keeps house, and has become the joyful mother of children." There is no reason why the Church of England should not be thoroughly evangelical; if it keeps to its articles, it ought to be. It is the most inconsistent church in the world, if it is not a Calvinistic one. It must be inconsistent, unless it keeps to those grand fundamental truths which are indeed a code of faith to be received by all believers—the truths which are written in its articles.

But, O! there are a great many among us Dissenters, and in the Church of England, too, that are dumb dogs. There are still plenty who do not know any thing about the gospel; who preach a vast deal about a great many things, but nothing about Jesus Christ; who buy their sermons cheap, and preach them at their ease; who ask God to tell them what to say, and then pull their manuscripts out of their pockets. We have had to mourn, especially in years gone by, that we could look from parish to parish, and find nobody but a dumb dog in the church, and in the pulpits of Dissenters too. And some men who might have spoken with a little earnestness, if they liked, let the people slumber under them, instead of preaching the word with true fidelity, as if they would not have to give account to God at the last. My aged grandfather tells a story, that I believe he himself could verify, of a person who once resided near him, and called himself a preacher of the gospel. He was visited by a poor woman, who asked him what was the meaning of the new birth? He replied, " My good woman, what do you come to me about that for? Nicodemus, a ruler of the Jews, did not know; he was a wise man, and did not know; and how do you think I should?" So she had to go away with only that answer. Time was when such an answer might have been given by a great many who were reckoned to be the authorized teachers of religion, but knew nothing really about the matter. They understood a great deal more about fox-hunting than about preaching, and more about farming their land than about the spiritual husbandry of God's church. But we bless God that there are not so many of that sort now; and we pray that the race may be come thoroughly extinct; that every pulpit, and every place of worship may be filled with a man who has a tongue of fire and a heart of flame, and shuns not to declare the whole counsel of God, neither seeking the smile of men nor dreading their frown. We have a promise that it shall be so. " The tongue of the dumb shall sing." And, ah! they do sing well too, when God makes them sing.

You remember Rowland Hill's story in "The Village Dialogues," about Mr. Merriman. Mr. Merriman was a sad scapegrace of a preacher; he was to be seen at every fair and revel, and used seldom to be found in his pulpit when he should have been; but when he was converted, he began to preach with tears running down his face—and how the church began to be crowded! The squire would not go and hear any of that stuff, and locked up his pew; and Mr. Merriman had a little ladder made outside the door, as he did not wish to break the door open; and the people used to sit on the steps, up one side and down the other, so that it made twice as much room as there was before.

No people make such good preachers as those who were dumb once. If the Lord opens their mouths, they will think they can not preach often enough, and earnestly enough, to make up for the mischief they did before. Chalmers himself might never have been so eloquent a preacher, had he not been for a long time a dumb dog. He preached morality, he said, till he made all the people in his parish immoral; he kept on urging them to keep God's law, till he made them break it; but when he turned round, and began to preach God's gospel, then the dumb began to sing. O! may God bring this about in every one of us! If we are dumb as professed ministers, may he open our mouths, and force us to speak forth his word, lest at the last day the blood of our hearers' souls should be found upon our skirts, and we should be cast away as unfaithful stewards of the gospel of Christ!

3. I now introduce you to a third sort of dumb people. They are dumb because *they dare not* speak; and they are good people, blessed souls. Here is one of them: "I was dumb with silence; I opened not my mouth, because thou didst it!" Ah! it is blessed to be dumb in that fashion. The Lord's servant will often have to be dumb under trials and troubles. When Satan tempts him to repine, he will put his finger to his lip and say, "Hush, murmuring heart, be still!" "Wherefore doth a living man complain, a man for the punishment of his sins?" Even the child of God will do like Job who sat down for seven days and nights, and said not a word, for he felt that his trouble was heavy, and he could say nothing It would have been as well if Job had kept his mouth shut all the next few days; he would not have said so much amiss as he did in some things that he uttered. It would have been well if he could always have kept silence. O! there are times when you and I, beloved, are obliged to keep the bridle on our tongues, lest we should murmur against God. We are in evil company; perhaps our spirits are hot within us, and we want to take vengeance for the Lord; we are like the friends of David, who wanted to take away the head of Shimei. "Let us take off this dead dog's head," we say; and then our Jesus tells us to put our sword into its scabbard, for the "servant o the Lord must not strive." How often have we thus been dumb! And sometimes when there have been slanders against our character, and men have calumniated us, O! how our fingers have itched to be at them! We have wanted to be at them at once, and let them see who was the strongest of the

two. But we have said, "No; our Master did not answer, and he 'left us an example that we should follow his steps.'" The chief priests accused him of many things, but he "answered them not a word." But we have found it hard sometimes to be dumb, like the sheep when it is brought to the shearer, or the lamb when it is in the slaughter-house. We could scarcely keep quiet. When we have been upon our beds in sickness, we have tried to quench every murmuring word; we have not let a sentence escape our lips, when we could possibly avoid it; but notwithstanding all that, we have found it hard work to keep dumb, though it is blessed work when we are enabled to do it. Now, ye who have been dumb under great weights of sorrow; ye whose songs have been suspended, because ye durst not open your lips, lest sighs should usurp the place of praise, come, listen to this promise, "The tongue of the dumb shall sing." Yes, though you are in the deepest trouble now, and are obliged to be silent, you shall sing yet. Though, like Jonah, you are in the whale's belly, carried down, as he called it, into the lowest hell; though the earth with her bars is about you for ever, and the weeds are wrapped about your head, yet you "shall look again toward his holy temple." Though you have hung your harp upon the willows, bless God you have not broken it; you will have use for it by-and-by; you shall take it down from its resting-place, and

> "Loud to the praise of sovereign grace,
> Bid every string awake."

If you have no songs in the night, yet he shall compass you about with songs of deliverance; if you can not sing his praises now, you shall do so by-and-by, when greater grace shall have come into your heart, or when delivering mercy shall be the subject of your song, in better days that are yet to come. But, blessed be God, we are not always to be silent in affliction; we are bound to sing. And I think we ought to sing even when we ought to be dumb; though we are dumb as to murmuring, we ought to sing God's praises. An old Puritan said, "God's people are like birds; they sing best in cages." He said, "God's people often sing the best when they are in the deepest trouble." Said old Master Brooks, "The deeper the flood was, the higher the ark went up to heaven." So it is with the child of God : the deeper his troubles, the nearer to heaven he goes, if he lives close to his Master. Troubles are called weights, and weights, you know, generally clog us and keep us down to the earth ; but there are ways, by the use of the laws of mechanics, by which you can make a weight lift you ; and so it is possible to make your troubles lift you nearer heaven, instead of making them sink you. Ah! we thank our God he has sometimes opened our mouth when we were dumb ; when we were ungrateful and did not praise him, he has opened our mouth by a trial, and though when we had a thousand mercies we did not praise him, when he sent a sharp affliction, then we began to do so. He has thus made the tongue of the dumb to sing.

4. We will mention one more kind of dumb people, and then we shall have done. There are *those who have nothing to say*, and, therefore, they are dumb. I will give you an instance : Solomon says in the Proverbs—" Open thy mouth for the dumb ;" and he shows by the context that he means those who in the court of judgment have nothing to plead for them- selves, and have to stand dumb before the bar. Like that man of old, who, when the king came in to see the guests, had not on a wedding garment, and when the king said, "Friend, how camest thou in hither ?" stood speechless, not because he could not speak, but because he had nothing to say. Have not you and I been dumb, and are we not now, when we stand on law terms with God, when we forget that Jesus Christ and his blood and righteousness were our full acquit- tal ? Are we not obliged to be dumb when the command- ments are laid bare before us, and when the law of God is brought home to our conscience ? There was a time with each of us, and not long ago with some here present, when we stood before Moses's seat, and heard the commandments read ; and when we were asked, "Sinner, canst thou claim to have kept these commandments ?" we were dumb. Then we were asked, "Sinner, canst thou give any atonement for the breach of these commandments ?" and we were dumb. We were asked, "Sinner, canst thou, by a future obedience, wipe out

thy past sin?" We knew it was impossible, and we were dumb. Then we were asked, "Canst thou endure the penalty; canst thou bear to welter for ever in the flames of hell? Canst thou suffer everlasting torments from the red right hand of an angry God? Canst thou dwell with everlasting burnings, and abide with eternal fires?" and we were dumb. And then we were asked the question, "Prisoner at the bar, hast thou any reason to plead why thou shouldst not be condemned?" and we were dumb. And we were asked, "Prisoner, hast thou any helper? hast thou any one that can deliver thee?" and we stood dumb, for we had nothing to say. Ay, but blessed be God, the tongue of the dumb can now sing. And shall I tell you what we can sing? Why, we can sing this: "Who shall lay any thing to the charge of God's elect?" Not God, for he has justified. "Who is he that condemneth?" Not Christ, for "he hath died, yea, rather hath risen again, who is also at the right hand of God, and maketh intercession for us." We who had not a word to say for ourselves, can now say every thing. We can say,

> "Bold shall I stand at that great day,
>   For who aught to my charge can lay?
>   Fully absolved by Christ I am,
>   From sin's tremendous curse and shame."

Yes, the dumb ones can sing. So shall you, poor dumb one: if God has made you dumb by taking away all the names of Baal out of your mouth—if he has taken away all your self-righteousness and all your trust in yourself, as truly as ever he has shut your mouth he will open it. If God has killed your self-righteousness, he will give you a better; if he has knocked down all your refuges of lies, he will build you up a good refuge. He has not come to destroy you; he has shut your mouth to fill it with his praise. Be of good cheer; look to Jesus; cast thine eyes to the cross; put thy confidence in him; and even thou, who thinkest thyself a castaway, even thou, poor, weeping Mary, even thou shalt yet sing of redeeming love.

IV. And now I have to conclude by just noticing *the occasions when the tongues of these dumb people sing the best*

When does the tongue of the dumb sing? Why, I think it sings always, little or much. It is always singing. If it is once set at liberty, it will never leave off. There are some of you people who say this world is a howling wilderness; well, you are the howlers—you make all the howling. If you choose to howl, I can not help it : I prefer the promise of my text— "Then shall the tongue of the dumb," not howl, but " sing." Yes, they do sing always, little or much ; sometimes it is in a ow hush-note; sometimes they have to go rather deep in the bass ; but there are other times, when they can mount to the highest notes of all. They have *special times of singing*. When they lose their burden at the foot of the cross, that is the time when they begin to sing. Never did a harp of heaven sound so sweetly as when touched by the finger of some returning prodigal, not even the songs of the angels seem to me to be so sweet as that first song of rapture which gushes forth from the inmost soul of the forgiven child of God. You know how John Bunyan describes it. He says, when poor Pilgrim lost his burden at the cross, he gave three great leaps, and went on his way singing. We have not forgotten those three great leaps; they were great leaps—leaps of praise. We have leaped many times since then with joy and gratitude ; but we think we never leaped so high as we did at the time when we saw our many sins all gone, and our transgressions covered up in the tomb of the Saviour. By the way, let me tell you a little story about that matter of John Bunyan. I am a great lover of John Bunyan, but I do not believe him infallible; for I met with a story the other day which I think a very good one. There was a young man in Edinburg who wished to be a missionary. He was a wise young man ; he thought—" Well, if I am to be a missionary, there is no need for me to transport myself far away from home; I may as well be a missionary in Edinburg." There's a hint to some of you ladies, who give away tracts in your district, and never give your servant Mary one. Well, this young man started. and determined to speak to the first person he met. He met one of those old fishwives; those of us who have seen them can never forget them ; they are extraordinary women indeed. So stepping up to her he said. " Here you are, coming with your burden on your back; let me ask you if you have got another burden, a spiritual burden!" "What!" she said; "do you mean that burden in John Bunyan's Pilgrim's Progress? Because if you do, young man, I have got rid of that many years ago, before you were born. But I went a better way to work than the Pilgrim did. The evangelist that John Bunyan talks about was one of your parsons that do not preach the gospel; for he said, 'Keep that light in thine eye and run to the wicket-gate.' Why, man alive! that was not the place for him to run to. He should have said, 'Do you see that cross? Run there at once! But instead of that, he sent the poor Pilgrim to the wicket-gate first; and much good he got by going there! He got tumbling into the slough, and was like to have been killed by it." "But did not you," he asked, "go through any Slough of Despond?" "Yes, young man, I did; but I found it a great deal easier going through with my burden off than with it on my back." The old woman was quite right. John Bunyan put the getting rid of the burden too far off from the commencement of the Pilgrimage. If he meant to show what usually happens, he was right; but if he meant to show what ought to have happened, he is wrong. We must not say to the sinner, "Now, sinner, if thou wilt be saved go to the baptismal pool; go to the wicket-gate; go to the church; do this or that." No, the cross should be right in front of the wicket-gate; and we should say to the sinner, "Throw thyself there, and thou art safe; but thou art not safe till thou canst cast off thy burden, and lie at the foot of the cross, and find peace in Jesus. Well, that is a time when we can sing.

And after that do God's people sing? Yes, they have sweet singing times in their house of communion. Oh! the music of that word "communion," when it is heard in the soul—communion with Jesus, fellowship with Jesus, whether in his sufferings, or in his glories! Those are singing times when the heart is lifted up to feel its oneness with Christ, and its vital union with him, and is enabled to "rejoice in hope of the glory of God," through communion with the Saviour.

Have not you had some precious singing times at the Lord's table? Ah! when the bread has been broken, and the wine

poured out, how often has it been to me a time of song, when
the people have all joined in singing,

> " Gethsemane, can I forget,
>   Or there thy conflict see,
> Thine agony and bloody sweat,
>   And not remember thee?
>
> " When to the cross I turn my eyes,
>   And rest on Calvary,
> O! Lamb of God, my sacrifice,
>   I must remember thee."

I am in the house of God, I think, every day. I believe
that David could not have prayed for more than I have
got, when he prayed that he might dwell in the house of the
Lord for ever; for I spend more of my time in the house of
God than I do anywhere else. But my best moments are at
the Lord's table. I do rejoice then, when I have no thought
of what I have to say to others, but simply to sit down
amongst the Lord's family, and taste my morsel of bread, and
have my sip of the wine. O! it is then the soul finds its
Saviour precious. I look forward for every month to come,
when I may once more sit at the table of my Master, and
spiritually eat his flesh and drink his blood, and feel that I
have indeed life in him, because I have got union with him.
Ah! those are singing times to the family of God. And so,
sometimes are preaching times and sometimes hearing times.
Prayer meetings are often special singing times; in fact, the
means of grace will very frequently be blessed of God to be
to us the occasion of song.

But lastly, my dear friends, for I can not stop to mention all
these singing times, the best we shall have will be when you
and I come to die. Ah! there are some of you that are like
what is fabled of the swan. The ancients said the swan never
sang in his life-time, but always sang just when he died. Now,
there are many of God's desponding children who seem to
go all their life under a cloud; but they get a swan's song
before they die. The river of their life comes running down,
perhaps black and miry with troubles, and when it begins to
touch the white foam of the sea there comes a little glistening

in its waters. So, beloved, though we may have oeen very much dispirited by reason of the burden of the way, when we get to the end we shall have sweet songs. Are you afraid of dying? O! never be afraid of that; be afraid of living. Living is the only thing which can do any mischief; dying never can hurt a Christian. Afraid of the grave? It is like he bath of Esther, in which she lay for a time, to purify herelf with spices, that she might be fit for her lord. The grave fits the body for heaven. There it lieth : and corruption, earth and worms, do but refine and purify our flesh. Be not afraid of dying; it does not take any time at all. All that death is, is emancipation, deliverance, heaven's bliss to a child of God. Never fear it; it will be a singing time. You are afraid of dying, you say, because of the pains of death. Nay, they are the pains of life—of life struggling to continue. Death has no pain; death itself is but one gentle sigh—the fetter is broken, and the spirit fled. The best moment of a Christian's life is his last one, because it is the one that is nearest heaven; and then it is that he begins to strike the key note of the song which he shall sing to all eternity. O! what a song will that be! It is a poor noise we make now; when we join the song perhaps we are almost ashamed to sing; but up there our voices shall be clear and good; and there

"Loudest of the crowd we'll sing,
 While heaven's resounding mansions ring
 With shouts of sovereign grace."

The thought struck me the other day, that the Lord will have in heaven some of those very big sinners that have gone further astray than any body that ever lived—the most extrardinary extravaganzas of vice—just to make the melody complete by singing some of those alto notes we sometimes hear, which you and I, because we have not gone so far astray, will never be able to utter. I wonder whether one has stepped into this chapel this morning, whom God has selected to take some of those alto notes in the scale of praise. Perhaps there is one such here. O! how will such a one sing, if grace, free grace, shall have mercy upon him!

And now, farewell, with just this solitary word : **My breth**

ren, the members of this church, strive together in your pray
ers, that God may bless you. Be not content with what you
are, however prosperous you may be; but seek to increase
more and more. Pray that you and your children may be
added to the church of Christ here, and may live to see others added too. Keep prayer going; do not neglect your
prayer meetings. Christmas Evans gives us a good idea about
prayer. He says, "Prayer is the rope in the belfry; we pull
it and it rings the bell up in heaven." And so it is. Mind you
keep that bell going. Pull it well. Come up to prayer meetings. Keep on pulling it; and though the bell is up so high
that you can not hear it ring, depend upon it, it can be heard
in the tower of heaven, and is ringing before the throne of
God, who will give you answers of peace according to your
faith. May your faith be large and plentiful, and so will your
answers be!

SERMON IX

FORETASTES OF THE HEAVENLY LIFE

"And they took of the fruit of the land in their hands, and brought it down unto us, and brought us word again, and said, It is a good land which the Lord our God doth give us."—DEUT., i. 25

You remember the occasion concerning which these words were written. The children of Israel sent twelve men as spies into the land of Canaan, who brought back with them the fruit of the land, amongst the rest a bunch of grapes from Eshcol too heavy to be borne by one man, and which, therefore, two of them carried on a staff between them. But I shall not remark upon the figure, but only say that as they learned of Canaan by the fruit of the land brought to them by the spies, so you and I, even while we are on earth, if we be the Lord's beloved, may learn something of what heaven is—a state to which we are to attain hereafter—by certain blessings which are brought to us on earth.

They were sure that the land of Israel was a *fertile land* when they saw the fruits which it produced, brought by their brethren, and when they ate thereof. Perhaps there was but little for so many, and yet those who did eat were made at once to understand that it must have been a goodly soil that produced such fruit. Now, then, beloved, we who love the Lord Jesus Christ have had clusters of the grapes of Eshcol. We have had some fruits of heaven even since we have been on earth, and by them we are able to judge of the richness of the soil of Paradise which bringeth forth such rare and choice fruits.

I shall, therefore, present to you some views of heaven in order to give you some idea how it is that the Christian on earth enjoys a foretaste of them.

Possibly, there are scarce two Christians who have the same
views of heaven; though they all expect the same heaven,
yet the most prominent feature in it is different to each different mind according to its constitution. Now, I will confess
what is to me the most prominent feature of heaven, judging
at the present moment. At another time I may love heaven
better for another thing: but lately I have learned to love
heaven as a *place of security*. We have seen high professors
turning from their profession, ay, and we have seen some of
the Lord's own beloved committing grievous faults and slips,
which have brought disgrace upon their character, and injury
to their souls. Now I have learned to look to heaven lately
as a place where we shall never, never sin—where our feet
shall be fixed firmly upon a rock—where there is neither trip-
ping nor sliding—where faults shall be unknown—where we
shall have no need to keep watch against an indefatigable enemy, because there is no foe that shall annoy us—where we
shall not be on our guard day and night watching against the
incursion of foes, for there "the wicked cease from troubling
and the weary are at rest." I have looked upon it as the land
of complete security, where the garment shall be always white,
where the face shall be always anointed with fresh oil, where
there is no fear of slipping or turning away, but where we
shall stand fast for ever. And I ask you, if that be a true
view of heaven—and I am sure it is one feature of it—do not
the saints even on earth enjoy some fruits of Paradise, even in
this sense? Do we not even in these huts and villages below
sometimes taste the joys of blissful security? The doctrine
of God's word is, that all who are in union with the Lamb are
safe, that all believers must hold on their way, that those who
have committed their souls to the keeping of Christ shall find
him a faithful and immutable keeper. On such a doctrine we
can enjoy security even on earth; not that high and glorious
security which renders us free from every slip and trip, but nevertheless a security well nigh as great, because it secures us
against ultimate ruin, and renders us certain that we shall attain to eternal felicity. And, beloved, have you never sat
down and reflected on the doctrine of the perseverance of the
saints? I trow you have. God has brought home to you a

sense of your security in the person of Christ. He has told you that your name is graven on his hand; he has whispered in your ear the promise, "Fear not, I am with thee." You have been led to look upon him, the great surety of the covenant, as faithful and true, and, therefore, bound and engaged to present you, the weakest of the family, with all the chosen race, before the throne of God; and in such sweet contemplation I am sure you have been drinking some of the juice of his spiced pomegranates; you have had some of the dainty fruits of Paradise; you have had some of the enjoyments which the perfect saints have above in a sense of security.

O how I love that doctrine of the perseverance of the saints I renounce the pulpit when I can not preach it, for the gospe seems to be a blank desert and a howling wilderness—a gospe as unworthy of God as it would be beneath even my accept ance, frail worm as I am—a gospel which saves me to-day and rejects me to-morrow—a gospel which puts me in Christ's family one hour, and makes me a child of the devil the next—a gospel which justifies and then condemns me—a gospel which pardons me, and afterward casts me to hell. Such a gospel is abhorrent to reason itself, much more to the God of the whole earth. But on the other ground of faith, that

> " He to the end must endure
> As sure as the earnest is given,"

we do enjoy a sense of perfect security even as we dwell in this land of wars and fightings. As the spies brought their brethren bunches of the grapes, so in the security we enjoy, we have a foretaste and earnest of the joy of Paradise.

In the next place, most probably the greater part of you love to think of heaven under another aspect: as *a place of perfect rest*. You sons of toil, you love the sanctuary because it is there you sit to hear God's word, and rest your wearied limbs. When you have wiped the hot sweat from your burning brow, you have often thought of heaven where your la bors shall be over; you have sung with sweet emphasis,

> " There shall I bathe my weary soul
> In seas of heavenly rest."

Rest, rest, rest,—this is what you want. And to me this idea of heaven is exceedingly beautiful. Rest I know I never shall have beneath this sky, while Christ's church is as barbarous as it is; for the most barbarous of masters is the church of Christ. I have served it, and am well-nigh hounded to my grave by Christian ministers perpetually requiring me to do impossibilities that they know no mortal strength can accomplish. Willing I am to labor till I drop, but more I can not do; yet I am perpetually assailed on this side and the other, till, go where I may, there seems no rest for me till I slumber in my grave; and I do look forward to heaven with some degree of happiness. There I shall rest from labors constant and perpetual, though much loved. And you, too, who have been toiling long to gain an object you have sought after— you have said if you could get it you would lie down and rest; you have toiled after a certain amount of riches, you have said if you could once gain a competence you would then make yourself at ease. Or, you have been laboring long to gain a certain point of character, and then you have said you would lay down your arms and rest. Ay, but you have not reached it yet; and you love heaven because heaven is the goal to the racer, the target of the arrow of existence; you love heaven because it will be the couch of time, ay, an eternal rest for the poor weary struggler upon earth. You love it as a place of rest; and do we never enjoy a foretaste of heaven upon earth in that sense? O, yes, beloved! blessed be God, "we who have believed do enter into rest." Our peace is like a river, and our righteousness like the waves of the sea. God may give to his people rest: even the rest that remaineth for the people of God. We have stormy trials and bitter troubles in the world; but we have learned to say, "Return unto thy rest, O my soul! for the Lord hath dealt bountifully with thee." Did you never, in times of great distress, climb up to your closet, and there on your knees pour out your heart before God? Did you never feel after you had so done that you had bathed yourself in rest, so that

> "Let cares like a wild deluge come,
> And storms of sorrow fall,"

you cared not one whit for them? For you had found a

shield in Christ; you had looked upon the face of God's anointed. Ah, Christian, that rest without a billow of disturbance, that rest so placid and serene, which in your deepest troubles you have been enabled to enjoy in the bosom of Christ, is to you a bunch of the mighty vintage of heaven, one grape of the heavenly cluster which you shall soon partake of in the land of the hereafter. Here, again, you see we can have a foretaste of heaven, and realize what it is even while here upon earth.

But that idea of rest will suit some indolent professors, and, therefore, let me just give the very opposite of it. I do think that one of the worst sins a man can be guilty of in this world is to be idle. I can almost forgive a drunkard, but a lazy man I do think there is very little pardon for. I think a man who is idle has as good a reason to be a penitent before God as David had when he was an adulterer, for the most abominable thing in the world is for a man to let the grass grow up to his ankles and do nothing. God never sent a man into the world to be idle. And there are some who make a tolerably fair profession, but who do nothing from one year's end to the other.

The next idea of heaven is, that it is *a place of uninterrupted service*. It is a place where they serve God day and night in his temple, and never know weariness, and never require to slumber. Do you know what is the deliciousness of work? For although we must complain when people expect impossibilities of us, it is the highest enjoyment of life to be busily engaged for Christ. Tell me the day I do not preach, I will tell you the day in which I am not happy; but the day in which it is my privilege to preach the gospel, and labor for God, is generally the day of my peaceful and quiet enjoyment after all. Service is delight. Praising God is pleasure. Laboring for him is the highest delight a mortal can know, O, how sweet it must be to sing his praises, and never feel that the throat is dry! O, how blessed to flap the wing for ever and never feel it flag! O, what sweet enjoyment to run upon his errands, evermore to circle round the throne of God in heaven while eternity shall last, and never once lay the head on the pillow, never once feel the throbbings of fatigue, never once the pangs that admonish us that we need to cease, but to keep on for ever like eternity's own self—a broad river rolling on with perpetual floods of labor! O, that must be enjoyment! That must be, indeed, a heaven, to serve God day and night in his temple! But you have served God on earth, and have had foretastes of that. I wish some of you knew the sweets of labor a little more, for although labor breedeth sweat, it breedeth sweets too—more especially labor for Christ. There is a satisfaction before the work; there is a satisfaction in the work; there is a satisfaction after the work, and there is a satisfaction in looking for the fruits of the work; and a great satisfaction when we get the fruits. Labor for Christ is, indeed, the robing-room of heaven; if it be not heaven itself, it is one of the most blissful foretastes of it. Thank God, Christian, if you can do any thing for your Master. Thank him if it is your privilege to do the least thing for him, for remember in so doing he is giving you a taste of the grapes of Eshcol. But you indolent people, you do not get the grapes of Eshcol, because you are too lazy to carry that big bunch. You would like it to come into your mouths without the trouble of gathering it; but you do not care to go forth and serve God. You sit still and look after yourselves, but what do you do for other people? You go to your place of worship; you talk about your Sunday-school and sick society, and so on. You never teach in the Sunday-school, and you never visit a sick person, and yet you take a great deal of credit to yourself while you do nothing at all. You will never know much of the enjoyments of heavenly glory until you know a little of the work of the kingdom of heaven on earth.

Now, let us proceed to some other points. Another view of heaven is, that it is *a place of complete victory and glorious triumph.* This is the battle-field; there is the triumphal procession. This is the land of the sword and the spear; that is the land of the wreath and the crown. This is the land of the garment rolled in blood and of the dust of the fight; that is the land of the trumpet's joyful sound—that is the place of the white robe and of the shout of conquest. O, what a thrill of joy shall shoot through the hearts of all the blessed when their conquests shall be complete in heaven, when death it self, the last of foes, shall be slain—when Satan shall be dragged captive at the chariot wheels of Christ—when he shall have overthrown sin and trampled corruption as the mire of the streets—when the great shout of universal victory shall rise from the hearts of all the redeemed! What a moment of pleasure shall that be! O, dear brethren, you and I have foretastes of even that. We know what conquests, what souls' battles we have even here. Did you never struggle against an evil heart, and at last overcome it? O, with what joy did you lift your eyes to heaven, the tears flowing down your cheeks, and say, " Lord, I bless thee that I have been able to overcome that sin." Did you ever have a strong temptation, and did you wrestle hard with it, and know what it was to sing with great joy, " My feet slipped; but thy mercy held me up?" Have you, like Bunyan's Christian, fought with old Apollyon, and have you seen him flap his dragon-wings and fly away? There you had a foretaste of heaven; you had just a guess of what the ultimate victory will be. In the death of that one Philistine you had the destruction of the whole army. That Goliath who fell beneath your sling and stone was but one out of the multitude who must yield their bodies to the fowls of heaven. God gives you partial triumphs that they may be the earnest of ultimate and complete victory. Go on and conquer, and let each conquest, though a harder one and more strenuously contested, be to you as a grape of Eshcol, a foretaste of the joys of heaven.

Furthermore, without doubt one of the best views we can ever give of heaven is, that it is *a state of complete acceptance with God*, recognized and felt in the conscience. I suppose that a great part of the joy of the blessed saints consists in a knowledge that there is nothing in them to which God is hostile; that their peace with God has not any thing to mar it; that they are so completely in union with the principles and thoughts of the Most High; that his love is set on them; that their love is set on him; that they are one with God in every respect. Well, beloved, and have we not enjoyed a sense of acceptance here below? Blotted and blurred by many doubts and fears, yet there have been moments when we have known ourselves as well accepted as we shall know ourselves to be even when we stand before the throne. There have been bright days with some of us, when we could " set to our seal" that God was true ; and, when afterward, feeling that the Lord knoweth them that are his, we could say, "And I know that I am his too." There have been moments when, with an unfaltering lip, we could say,

> " Now, I can call my Jesus mine;
> Now, I can all my joys resign ;
> Can tread the world beneath my feet,
> And all that earth calls good and great ;"

when we had such a view of the perfection of Christ's righteousness that we felt that God had accepted us, and could not do otherwise ; we had such a sense of the efficacy of the blood of Christ, we felt sure that our sins were all pardoned, and that they never could be mentioned unto us in mercy for ever. And, beloved, though I have spoken of other joys, let me say, this is the cream of all of them, to know ourselves accepted in God's sight. O ! to feel that I, a guilty worm, am now received in my Father's bosom ; that I, a lost prodigal, am now feasting at his table with delight ; that I, who once heard the voice of his anger, now listen to the notes of his love. This is joy—this is joy worth worlds. What more can they know up there than that ? And were it not that our sense of it were so imperfect, we might bring heaven down to earth, and might at least dwell in the suburbs of the celestial city, if we could not be privileged to go within the gates. So you see, again, we can have bunches of the grapes of Eshcol in that sense. Seeing that heaven is a state of acceptance, we, too, can know and feel that acceptance, and rejoice in it.

And, again, heaven is *a state of great and glorious manifestations*. You look forward to heaven as the place where you shall

> " See, and hear, and know
> All you desire and wish below."

You are now looking at it darkly through a glass : there you shall see face to face. Christ looks down on the Bible, and the

Bible is his looking-glass. You look into it, and see the face of Christ as in a mirror darkly; but soon you shall look upon himself, and see him face to face. You expect heaven as a place of peculiar manifestations. You believe that there he will unvail his face to you; that

> " Millions of years your wondering eyes
> Shall o'er your Saviour's beauties rove."

You are expecting to see his face, and never, never sin. You are longing to know the secrets of his heart. You believe that in that day you shall see him as he is, and shall be like him in the world of spirits. Well, beloved, though Christ does not manifest himself to us as he does to the bright ones there, have not you and I had manifestations even while we have been in this vale of tears? Speak, beloved; let your heart speak; hast thou not had visions of Calvary; has not thy Master sometimes touched thy eyes with eye-salve, and let thee see him on his cross? Hast thou not said

> " Here I'd sit for ever viewing
> Mercy stream in streams of blood!
> Precious drops my soul bedewing,
> Plead and claim my peace with God."

Have you not wept for joy and grief when you saw him bleeding out his life from his heart for you, and beheld him nailed to the tree for your sakes! O yes! I know you have had such manifestations of him. And have you not seen him in his risen glories? Have you not beheld him there exalted on his throne? Have you not by faith beheld him as the Judge of the quick and the dead, and as the Prince of the kings of the earth? Have you not looked through the dim future, and seen him with the crown of all the kingdoms on his head, with the diadems of all monarchies beneath his feet, and the scepters of all thrones in his hand? Have you not anticipated the moment of his most glorious triumphs, when he

> " Shall reign from pole to pole with illimitable sway?"

Yes, you have, and therein you have had foretastes of heaven. When Christ has thus revealed himself to you, you have looked within the vail, and, therefore, you have seen what is there, you have had some glimpses of Jesus while here; those glimpses of Jesus are but the beginning of what shall never end. Those joyous melodies of praise and thanksgiving are but the preludes of the notes of Paradise.

And now, lastly, the highest idea of heaven, perhaps, is the *idea of most hallowed and blissful communion.* I have not given you near half that I might have given you of the various characteristics of heaven, as described in God's word, but communion is the best. Communion! that word so little spoken of, so seldom understood. That word, communion! Dearly beloved, you hear us say, "And the communion of the Holy Ghost be with you all;" but there are many of you that do not know the meaning of that sweet heaven in a word. Communion! It is the flower of language; it is the honeycomb of words. Communion! You like to talk of corruption best, do you not? Well, if you like that filthy word, you are very willing to meditate upon it. I do so when I am forced to do it; but communion seems to me to be a sweeter word than that. You like to talk a great deal about affliction, don't you? Well, if you love the black word—ah! you have reason to love it; but if you love to be happy upon it, you may do so; but give me for my constant text and for my constant joy, communion. And I will not choose which kind of communion it shall be. Sweet Master, if thou givest me communion with thee in thy sufferings, if I have to bear reproach and shame for thy name's sake, I will thank thee; if I may have fellowship with thee in it, and if thou wilt give me to suffer for thy sake, I will call it honor, that so I can be a partaker of thy sufferings: and if thou givest me sweet enjoyments, if thou dost raise me up and make me to sit in heavenly places in Christ, I will bless thee. I will bless thee for ascension communion—communion with Christ in his glories. Do you not say the same? And for communion with Christ in death. Have you died unto the world, as Christ did die unto himself? And then have you had communion with him in resurrection? Have you felt that you are raised to newness of life, even as was he? And have you had communion with him in ascension, so that you could know yourself to be at heir to a throne in Paradise? If so, you have had the best earnest you can receive of the joys of Paradise. To be in heaven is to lean one's head upon the breast of Jesus. You have done it on earth? Then you know what heaven is. To be in heaven is to talk with Jesus, to sit at his feet, to let our heart beat against his heart. If you have had that on earth, you have had some of the grapes of heaven.

Cherish, then, these foretastes, of whatever kind they may have been in your individual case. Differently constituted, you will all look at heaven in a different light. Keep your foretaste just as God has given it to you. He has given each of you some one; if you love it, it is most suitable to your own condition. Treasure it up; think much of it. Think more of your Master. For, remember, it is "Christ in you the hope of glory," after all, that is your only foretaste of heaven; and the more fully prepared shall you be for the bliss of the joyous ones in the land of the happy.

SERMON X

PREACHING FOR THE POOR

"The poor have the gospel preached to them."—MATT., xi. 5

JOHN, the forerunner of Christ, had some followers who continued with him after Christ had come in the flesh, and openly manifested himself among the people. These disciples were in doubt as to whether Jesus was the Messiah or no. I believe that John himself had no doubt whatever upon the matter, for he had received positive revelations, and had given substantial testimonies on the subject. But in order to relieve their doubts, John said to his disciples, in some such words, "Go and ask him yourselves;" and, therefore, he dispatched them with this message, "Tell us whether thou art he that should come, or do we look for another?" Jesus Christ continuing his preaching for a while, said, "Stay and receive your answer;" and instead of giving them an affirmative reply, "I am that Messiah," he said, "Go and show John again those things which ye do hear and see: the blind receive their sight, and the lame walk, the lepers are cleansed, and the deaf hear, the dead are raised up, and the poor have the gospel preached to them." As much as to say, "That is my answer; these things are my testimonies—on the one hand, that I come from God, and, on the other hand, that I am *the Messiah*." You will see the truth and force of this reply, if you will observe that it was prophesied of the Messiah, that he should do the very things which Jesus at that moment was doing. It is said of Messias, in the 35th chapter of Isaiah, at the 5th and 6th verses: "Then the eyes of the blind shall be opened, and the ears of the deaf shall be unstopped. Then shall the lame man leap as an hart, and the tongue of the dumb sing; for in the widerness shall waters break out, and streams in the desert"

The Jews had forgotten this too much ; they only looked for a
Messiah who should be clothed with temporal grandeur and
dignity, and they overlooked the teaching of Isaiah, that he
should be "a man of sorrows and acquainted with grief."
And, besides that, you observe, they overlooked the miracles
which it was prophesied should attend the coming of the glorious one, the King of kings and Lord of lords. Jesus gave
this as his answer —a practical demonstration of John's problem, proving it to an absolute certainty. But he not only referred to the miracles, he gave them a further proof—"The
poor have the gospel preached to them." This, also, was one
evidence that he was Messias. For Isaiah, the great Mes-
sianic prophet, had said, "He shall preach the gospel unto the
meek ;" that is, the poor. And in that Jesus did so, it was
proved that he was the man intended by Isaiah. Beside, Zechariah mentions the congregation of the poor who attend on
nim, and therein evidently foretold the coming of Jesus Christ,
the preacher to the poor.

I shall not, however, dwell upon these circumstances this
morning; it must be apparent to every hearer, that here is
sufficient proof that Jesus Christ is the person who had been
foretold under the name of Shiloh, or Messiah. We all believe
that, and, therefore, there is little need that I should try to
prove what you have already received. I rather select my
text this morning as one of the constant marks of the gospel
in all ages and in every land. "The poor have the gospel
preached to them." This is to be its *semper eadem*, its constant
stamp. And we believe, where the poor have not the gospel
preached unto them, there is a departure from the dispensation of the gospel, the forsaking of this which was to be a
fundamental trait and characteristic of the gospel dispensation :
"The poor have the gospel preached to them."

I find that these words will bear three translations; I shall,
therefore, have three heads, which shall be composed of three
translations of the text. The first is that of *the authorized
version:* "The poor have the gospel preached to them ;" it is
also Tyndal's version. The second is *the version of Cranmer,
and the version of Geneva*, which is the best, "The poor
are evangelized," that is to say, they not only hear the gospel,

but they are influenced by it—the poor receive it. The last is the translation of *some eminent writers*, and above all of *Wyckliffe*, which amused me when I read it, although I believe it to be as correct as any of the others. Wyckliffe translates it—"pore men ben taken to prechynge of the gospel." The verb may be equally well translated in the active as in the passive sense : " The poor have taken to the preaching of the gospel." That is to be one of the marks of the gospel dispensation in all times.

I. First, then, THE AUTHORIZED VERSION, " The poor have the gospel preached to them." It was so in Christ's day; it is to be so with Christ's gospel to the end of time. Almost every impostor who has come into the world has aimed principally at the rich, and the mighty, and the respectable ; very few impostors have found it to be worth their while to make it prominent in their preaching that they preach to the poor. They went before princes to promulgate their doctrines ; they sought the halls of nobles, where they might expatiate upon their pretended revelations. Few of them thought it worth their while to address themselves to those who have been most wickedly called " the swinish multitude," and to speak to them the glorious things of the gospel of Christ. But it is one delightful mark of Christ's dispensation, that he aims first at the poor. " The poor have the gospel preached to them." It was wise in him to do so. If we would fire a building, it is best to light it at the basement; so our Saviour, when he would save a world, and convert men of all classes and all ranks, begins at the lowest rank, that the fire may burn upward, knowing right well that what is received by the poor will ultimately by his grace be received by the rich also. Nevertheless, he chose this to be given to his disciples, and to be the mark of his gospel—" the poor have the gospel preached unto them." Now, I have some things to say this morning, which I think are absolutely necessary if the poor are to have the gospel preached unto them.

In the first place, let me say, then, *that the gospel must be preached where the poor can come and hear it.* How can the poor have the gospel preached to them, if they can not come and listen to it ? and yet how many of our places of worship are there into which they can not come, and into which, if they could come, they would only come as inferior creatures. They may sit in the back seats, but are not to be known and recognized as any thing like other people. Hence the absolute necessity of having places of worship large enough to accommodate the multitude ; and hence, moreover, the obligation to go out into the highways and hedges. If the poor are to have the gospel preached unto them, then we must take it where they can get it. If I wanted to preach to English people, it would be of no use for me to go and stand on one of the peaks of the Himalayas, and begin preaching; they could not hear me there. And it is of little avail to build a gorgeous structure for a fashionable congregation, and then to think of preaching to the poor ; they can not come any more than the Hottentots can make the journey from Africa and listen to me here. I should not expect them to come to such a place, nor will they willingly enter it. The gospel should be preached, then, where the poor will come ; and if they will not come after it, then let it be taken to them. We should have places where there is accommodation for them, and where they are regarded and respected as much as any other rank and condition of men. It is with this view alone that I have labored earnestly to be the means of building a large place of worship, because I feel that although the bulk of my congregation in New Park-street chapel are poor, yet there are many poor who can, by no possibility, enter the doors, because we can not find room for the multitudes to be received. You ask me why I do not preach in the street. I reply, I would do so, and am constantly doing so in every place except London, but here I can not do it, since it would amount to an absolute breach of the peace: it is impossible to conceive what a multitude of people must be necessarily assembled. I trembled when I saw twelve thousand on the last occasion I preached in the open air ; therefore I have thought it best, for the present at least, to desist, until happily there shall be fewer to follow me. Otherwise my heart is in the open air movement ; I practice it everywhere else, and I pray God to give to our ministers zeal and earnestness, that they may take the gospel into the streets, highways and by-ways, and compel the people to come in, that the house may be filled.   O that God would give this characteristic mark of his precious grace, that the poor might have the gospel preached unto them.

"But," you reply, "there are plenty of churches and chapels to which they might come." I answer, yes, but that is only one half of the matter. *The gospel must be preached attractively* before the poor will have the gospel preached unto them. Why, there is no attraction in the gospel to the great mass of our race, as it is currently preached. I confess that when I have a violent headache, and can not sleep, I could almost wish for some droning minister to preach to me ; I feel certain I could go to sleep then, for I have heard some under the soporific influence of whose eloquence I could most comfortably snore. But it is not at all likely that the poor will ever go to hear such preachers as these. If they are preached to in fine terms—in grandiloquent language which they can not lay hold of—the poor will not have the gospel preached to them, for they will not *go* to hear it. They must have something attractive to them ; we must preach as Christ did ; we must tell anecdotes, and stories, and parables, as he did ; we must come down and make the gospel attractive. The reason why the old Puritan preachers could get congregations was this—they did not give their hearers dry theology ; they illustrated it ; they had an anecdote from this and a quaint passage from that classic author ; here a verse of poetry ; here and there even a quip or pun—a thing which now-a-days is a sin above all sins, but which was constantly committed by these preach ers, whom I have ever esteemed as the patterns of pulpit elo quence. Christ Jesus was an attractive preacher ; he sought above all means to set the pearl in a frame of gold, that it might attract the attention of the people. He was not willing to place himself in a parish church, and preach to a large con gregation of thirteen and a-half, like our good brethren in the city, but would preach in such a style that people felt they must go to hear him. Some of them gnashed their teeth in rage and left his presence in wrath, but the multitudes still thronged to him to hear and to be healed. It was no dull work to hear this King of preachers, he was too much in ear nest to be dull, and too humane to be incomprehensible. I be lieve that until t is is imitated, the poor will not have the gospel preached to them. There must be an interesting style adopted, to bring the people to hear. But if we adopt such a style they will call us clownish, vulgar, and so on. Blessed be God, we have long learned that vulgarity is a very different thing from what some men suppose. We have been so taught, that we are willing to be even clowns for Christ's sake, and so long as we are seeing souls saved we are not likely to alter our course. During this last week I have seen, I believe, a score of persons who have been in the lowest ranks, the very meanest sinners, the greatest of transgressors, who have, through preaching in this place, been restored and reclaimed. Do you think, then, that I shall shear my locks to please the Philistine? O, no; by the grace of God, Samson knoweth where his strength lieth, and is not likely to do that to please any man, or any set of men. Preaching must reach the popular ear; and to get at the people it must be interesting to them, and by the grace of God we hope it shall be.

But, in the next place, if the poor are to have the gospel preached unto them, *it must be preached simply.* It is a waste of time to preach Latin to you, is it not? To the multitude of people it is of no use delivering a discourse in Greek. Possibly five or six of the assembly might be mightily edified, and go away delighted; but what of that? The mass would retire unedified and uninstructed. You talk about the education of the people, don't you, and about the vast extent of English refinement? For the most part it is a dream. Ignorance is not buried yet. The language of one class of Englishmen is a dead language to another class; and many a word which is very plain to many of us, is as hard and difficult a word to the multitude as if it had been culled out of Hindostani or Bengali. There are multitudes who can not understand words composed of Latin, but must have the truth told them in round homely Saxon, if it is to reach their hearts. There is my friend the Rev. So-and-so, Doctor of Divinity; he is a great student; and whenever he finds a hard word in his books he tells it next Sunday to his congregation. He has a little intellectual circle, who think his preaching must be good, because they can not understand it, and who think it proves that he must be an intelligent man because all the pews are empty. They believe he must be a very useful member of society; in fact, they compare him to Luther, and think he is a second Paul, because nobody will listen to him, seeing it is impossible to understand him. Well, we conceive of that good man that he may have a work to do, but we do not know what it is. There is another friend of ours, Mr Cloudyton, who always preaches in such a style that if you should try to dissect the sermon for a week afterwards you could by no possibility tell what he meant. If you could look at things from his point of view you might possibly discover something; but it does appear by his preaching as if himself had lost his way in a fog, and were scattering a whole mass of mist about him everywhere. I suppose he goes so deep down into the subject that he stirs the mud at the bottom, and he can not find his way up again. There are some such preachers, whom you can not possibly understand. Now, we say. and say very boldly too, that while such preaching may be esteemed by some people to be good, we have no faith in it at all. If ever the world is to be reclaimed, and if sinners are to be saved, we can see no likelihood in the world of its being done by such means. We think the word must be un derstood before it can really penetrate the conscience and the heart; and we would always be preaching such as men can understand, otherwise the poor will not "have the gospel preached to them." Why did John Bunyan become the apostle of Bedfordshire and Huntingdonshire, and round about? It was because John Bunyan, while he had a surpassing genius, would not condescend to cull his language from the garden of flowers, but he went into the hayfield, and the meadow, and plucked up his language by the roots, and spoke out in the words that the people used in their cottages. Why is it that God has blessed other men to the stirring of the people, to the bringing about of spiritual revivals, to the renewal of the power of godliness? We believe it has always been owing to this, under God's Spirit, that they have adopted the phraseology of the people, and have not been ashamed to be despised because they talked as common people did.

But now we have something to say more important than

this. We may preach, very simply too, and very attractively, and yet it may not be true that "the poor have the gospel preached to them," for the poor may have something else preached to them beside the gospel. It is, then, highly im portant that we should each of us ask what the gospel is, and that when we think we know it we should not be ashamed to say, "this is the gospel, and I will preach it boldly, though all men should deny it." O! I fear that there is such a thing as preaching another gospel, "which is not another, but there be some that trouble us." There is such a thing as preaching science and philosophy attractively, but not preaching the gospel. Mark, it is not preaching, but it is preaching the gospel that is the mark of Christ's dispensation and of his truth. Let us take care to preach fully the depravity of man, let us dwell thoroughly upon his lost and ruined estate under the law, and his restoration under the gospel ; let us preach of these three things, for, as a good brother said, "The gospel lies in three things, the word of God only, the blood of Christ only, and the Holy Spirit only." These three things make up the gospel. " The Bible, the Bible alone the religion of Prot. estants; the blood of Christ the only salvation from sin, the only means of the pardon of our guilt ; and the Holy Spirit the only regenerator, the only converting power that will alone work in us to will and to do of his good pleasure." Without these three things there is no gospel. Let us take heed, then, for it is a serious matter, that when the people listen to us, it is *the gospel* that we preach, or else we may be as guilty as was Nero, the tyrant, who, when Rome was starving, sent his ships to Alexandria, where there was corn in plenty, not for wheat, but for sand to scatter in the arena for his gladiators. Ah! there be some who seem to do so—scattering the floor of their sanctuary not with the good corn of the kingdom, upon which the soul's of God's people may feed and grow thereby, but with sand of controversy, sand of logic, which no child of God can ever receive to his soul's profit. "The poor have the gospel preached to them." Let us take heed that it is the gospel. Hear, then, ye chief of sinners, the voice of Jesus. "This is a faithful saying, and worthy of all acceptation, that Christ Jesus came into the world to save sinners; of whom I am chief." "Him that cometh to me I will in no wise cast out." "Whosoever believeth and is baptized shall be saved." "For the Son of man is come to seek and to save that which was lost."

And just one more hint on this point, namely, this—it must be said of us, if we would keep true to Christ's rule and apostolic practice, that "the poor have the gospel *preached* to them." In these days there is a growing hatred of the pulpit. The pulpit has maintained its ground full many a year, but partially by its becoming inefficient, it is losing its high position. Through a timid abuse of it, instead of a strong, stiff use of the pulpit, the world has come to despise it; and now most certainly we are not a priest-ridden people one half so much as we are a press-ridden people. By the press we are ridden indeed. Mercuries, Dispatches, Journals, Gazettes, and Magazines, are now the judges of pulpit eloquence and style. They thrust themselves into the censor's seat, and censure those whose office it should rather be to censure them. The pulpit has become dishonored; it is esteemed as being of very little worth and of no esteem. Ah! we must always maintain the dignity of the pulpit. I hold that it is the Thermopylæ of Christendom; it is here that the battle must be fought between right and wrong; not so much with the pen, valuable as that is as an assistant, as with the living voice of earnest men, "contending earnestly for the faith once delivered unto the saints." In some churches the pulpit is put away; there is a prominent altar, but the pulpit is omitted. Now, the most prominent thing under the gospel dispensation is not the altar, which belonged to the Jewish dispensation. but the pulpit. "We have an altar, whereof they have no right to eat which serve the tabernacles;" that altar is Christ; but Christ has been pleased to exalt "the foolishness of preaching" to the most prominent position in his house of prayer. We must take heed that we always maintain preaching. It is this that God will bless; it is this that he has promised to crown with success. "Faith cometh by hearing, and hearing by the Word of God." We must not expect to see great changes, nor any great progress of the gospel, until there is greater esteem for the pulpit—more said of it and thought of

it. " Well," some may reply, " you speak of the dignity of
the pulpit ; I take it, you lower it yourself, sir, by speaking in
such a style to your hearers." Ah ! no doubt you think so.
Some pulpits die of dignity. I take it, the greatest dignity in
the world is the dignity of converts—that the glory of the
pulpit is, if I may use such a metaphor, to have captives at its
chariot-wheels, to see converts following it, and where there
are such, and those from the very worst of men ; there is a
dignity in the pulpit beyond any dignity which a fine mouthing of words and a grand selection of fantastic language could
ever give to it. " The poor have the gospel preached to
them."

II. Now, the next translation is, THE TRANSLATION OF GE-
NEVA, principally used by Calvin in his commentary ; and it is
also the translation of Thomas Cranmer, whose translation, I
believe, was at least in some degree molded by the Genevan
translation. He translates it thus : " The poor receive the
gospel." The Genevan translation has it, " The poor receive
the glad tidings of the gospel," which is a tautology, since
glad tidings mean the same thing as gospel. The Greek has
it, " The poor are evangelized." Now, what is the meaning
of this word " evangelized ?" They talk with a sneer in these
days of evangelical drawing-rooms and evangelicals, and so on.
It is one of the most singular sneers in the world, for to call a
man an evangelical by way of joke, is the same as calling a
man a gentleman by way of scoffing at him. To say a man is
one of the gospelers, by way of scorn, is like calling a man a
king by way of contempt. It is an honorable, a great, a glorious title, and nothing is more honorable than to be ranked
among the evangelicals. What is meant, then, by the people
being evangelized ? Old Master Burkitt, thinking that we
should not easily understand the word, says, that as a man is
said to be Italianized by living among the Italians, getting
their manners and customs, and becoming a citizen of the
state, so a man is evangelized when he lives where the gospel
is preached, and gets the manners and customs of those who
profess it. Now, that is one meaning of the text. One of the
proofs of our Saviour's mission is not only that the poor hear
the World, but are influenced by it and are gospelized. O

how great a work it is to gospelize any man, and to gospelize a poor man. What does it mean? It means, to make him *like* the gospel. Now, the gospel is holy, just, and true, and loving, and honest, and benevolent, and kind, and gracious. So, then, to gospelize a man is to make a rogue honest, to make a harlot modest, to make a profane man serious, to make a grasping man liberal, to make a covetous man benevolent, to make the drunken man sober, to make the untruthful man truthful, to make the unkind man loving, to make the hater the lover of hiss pecies, and, in a word, to gospelize a man is, in his outward character, to bring him into such a condition that he labors to carry out the command of Christ, " Love thy God with all thy heart, and thy neighbor as thyself." Gospelizing, furthermore, has something to do with an inner principle ; gospelizing a man means saving him from hell and making him a heavenly character ; it means blotting out his sins, writing a new name upon his heart—the new name of God. It means bringing him to know his election, to put his trust in Christ, to renounce his sins, and his good works too, and to trust solely and wholly upon Jesus Christ, as his Redeemer. O ! what a blessed thing it is to be gospelized ! How many of you have been so gospelized ? The Lord grant that the whole of us may feel the influence of the gospel. I contend for this, that to gospelize a man is the greatest miracle in the world. All the other miracles are wrapped up in this one. To gospelize a man, or, in other words, to convert him, is a greater work than to open the eyes of the blind ; for is it not opening the eyes of the blind soul that he may see spiritual matters, and understand the things of heavenly wisdom, and is not a surgical operation easier than an operation on the soul ? Souls we can not touch, although science and skill have been able to remove films and cataracts from the eyes. " The lame walk." Gospelizing a man is more than this. It is not only making a lame man walk, but it is making a dead man who could not walk in the right way, walk in the right way ever afterward. " The lepers are cleansed." Ah ! but to cleanse a sinner is greater work than cleansing a leper. " The deaf hear." Yes, and to make a man, who never listened to the voice of God, hear the voice of his Maker, is a miracle greater

than to make the deaf hear, or even to raise the dead. **Great**
though that be, it is not a more stupendous effort of divine
power than to save a soul, since men are naturally dead in
sins, and must be quickened by divine grace if they are saved.
To gospelize a man is the highest instance of divine might,
and remains an unparalleled miracle, a miracle of miracles.
" The poor are evangelized."

Beloved, there have been some very precious specimens of
poor people who have come under the influence of the gospel.
I think I appeal to the hearts of all of you who are now present, when I say there is nothing we more reverence and respect than the piety of the poor and needy. I had an engraving sent to me the other day which pleased me beyond
measure. It was an engraving simply but exquisitely executed. It represented a poor girl in an upper room, with a
lean-to roof. There was a post driven in the ground, on
which was a piece of wood, standing on which were a candle
and a Bible. She was on her knees at a chair, praying,
wrestling with God. Every thing in the room had on it the
stamp of poverty. There was the mean coverlet to the old
stump bedstead ; there were the walls that had never been
papered, and perhaps scarcely whitewashed. It was an upper
story to which she had climbed with aching knees, and where,
perhaps, she had worked away till her fingers were worn to
the bone, to earn her bread at needle-work. There it was
that she was wrestling with God. Some would turn away
and laugh at it ; but it appeals to the best feelings of man, and
moves the heart far more than does the fine engraving of the
monarch on his knees in the grand assembly. We have had
lately a most excellent volume, the Life of Captain Hedley
Vicars ; it is calculated to do great good, and I pray God to
bless it ; but I question whether the history of Captain Hedley Vicars will last as long in the public mind as the history of
the Dairyman's Daughter or the Shepherd of Salisbury Plain.
The histories of those who have come from the ranks of the
poor always lay hold of the Christian mind. O ! we love
piety anywhere ; we bless God when coronets and grace go
together ; but if piety in any place does shine more brightly
than anywhere else, it is in rags and poverty. When the poor

woman in the almshouse takes her bread and her wat⸀ , and
blesses God for both—when the poor creature who has not
where to lay his head, yet lifts his eye and says, " My Father
will provide,"· it is then like the glow-worm in the damp
leaves, a spark the more conspicuous for the blackness around
it. Their religion gleams in its true brightness, and is seen
in all its luster. It is a mark of Christ's gospel that the poor
are gospelized—that they can receive the gospel. True, it is,
the gospel affects all ranks, and is equally adapted to them
all; but yet we say, " If one class be more prominent than
another, we believe that in Holy Scripture the poor are most
of all appealed to." " O !" say some very often, " the converts
whom God has given to such a man are all from the lower
ranks; they are all people with no sense; they are all uneducated people that hear such and such a person." Very well,
if you say so; we might deny it if we pleased, but we do not
know that we shall take the trouble, because we thinc it no
disgrace whatever; we think it rather to be an honor that the
poor are evangelized, and that they listen to the gospel from
our lips. I have never thought it a disgrace at any time.
When any have said, " Look, what a mass of uneducated peo
ple they are." Yes, I have thought, and blessed be God they
are, for those are the very people that want the gospel most.
If you saw a physician's door surrounded by a number of ladies of the sentimental school, who are sick about three times
a week, and never were ill at all—if it were said he cured
them, you would say, " No great wonder too, for there never
was any thing the matter with them." But if you heard of
another man, that people with the worst diseases have come
to him, and that God has made use of him, and his medicine
has been the means of healing their diseases; you would then
say, " There is something in it, for the people that want it
most have received it." If, then, it be true that the poor will
come to hear the gospel more than others, it is no disgrace to
the gospel, it is an honor to it that those who most want it do
freely receive it.

III. And now I must close up by briefly dwelling on the
last point. It was the third translation, WYCKLIFFE'S TRANS-
LATION. To give it you in old English—" Poor men are

taking to the preaching of the gospel." "Ah!" say some "they had better remain at home, minding their plows or their blacksmith's hammer; they had better have kept on with their tinkering and tailoring, and not have turned preachers. But it is one of the honors of the gospel that poor men have taken to the preaching of it. There was a tinker once, and let the worldly-wise blush when they hear of it—there was a tinker once, a tinker of whom a great divine said he would give all his learning if he could preach like him There was a tinker once, who ne'er so much as brushed his back against the walls of a college, who wrote a Pilgrim's Progress. Did ever a doctor in divinity write such a book? There was a pot-boy once—a boy who carried on his back the pewter-pots for his mother, who kept the Old Bell. That man drove men mad, as the world had it, but led them to Christ, as we ' ave it, all his life long, until, loaded with honors he sank into his grave, with the good will of a multitude round about him, with an imperishable name written in the world's records, as well as in the records of the church. Did you ever hear of any mighty man, whose name stood in more esteem among God's people than the name of George Whitefield. And yet these were poor men, who, as Wyckliffe said, were taking to the preaching of the gospel. If you will read the life of Wyckliffe, you will find him saying there, that he believed that the Reformation in England was more promoted by the labors of the poor men, whom he sent out from Lutterworth than by his own. He gathered round him a number of the poor people whom he instructed in the faith, and then he sent them two and two into every village, as Jesus did. They went into the market-place and they gathered the people around; they opened the book and read a chapter, and then they left them a manuscript of it, which for months and years after the people would assemble to read, and would remember the gospellers that had come to tell them the gospel of Christ These men went from market-place to market-place, from town to town, and from village to village, and though their names are unknown to fame, they were the real reformers. You may talk of Cranmer and Latimer and Ridley; they did much, but the real reformers of the English nation were people whose names have perished from the annals of time, but are written in the records of eternity. God has blessed the poor man in preaching the truth. Far be it from me to depreciate learning and wisdom. We should not have had the Bible translated without learning, and the more learning a man can have, if he be a sanctified man, the better; he has so many more talents to lay out in his Master's service; but it is not absolutely necessary for preaching of the Word. Rough, un tamed, untaught energy, has done much in the church. A Boanerges has stood up in a village; he could not put three words together in grammatical English; but where the drowsy parson had for many a year lulled all his people into an unhal lowed rest, this man started up, like the herdsman Amos, and brought about a great awakening. He began to preach in some cottage; people thronged around him, then a house was built, and his name is handed down to us as the Rev. So-and-so, but then he was known as Tom the plowman, or John the tinker. God has made use of men whose origin was the most obscure, who seemed to have little, except the gifts of nature, which could be made use of in God's service; and we hold that this is no disgrace, but on the contrary an honor, that poor men are taking to preaching the gospel.

And now, beloved, I have opened my mouth for the dumb, and pleaded the cause of the poor, let me end by entreating the poor of the flock to consider the poor man's Christ; let me urge them to give him their thoughts, and may the Lord enable them to yield him their hearts. "He that believeth and is baptized shall be saved; but he that believeth not shall be damned."

May God bless the high and low, the rich and poor; yea, all of you, for his name's sake.

SERMON XI

SECRET SINS

" Cleanse thou me from secret faults."—PSALM xix. 12

SELF-RIGHTEOUSNESS arises partly from pride, but mainly from ignorance of God's law. It is because men know little or nothing concerning the terrible character of the divine law, that they foolishly imagine themselves to be righteous. They are not aware of the deep spirituality, and the stern severity of the law, or they would have other and wiser notions. Once let them know how strictly the law deals with the thoughts, how it brings itself to bear upon every emotion of the inner man, and there is not one creature beneath God's heaven who would dare to think himself righteous in God's sight in virtue of his own deeds and thoughts. Only let the law be revealed to a man ; let him know how strict the law is, and how infinitely just, and his self-righteousness will shrivel into nothing —it will become a filthy rag in his sight, whereas before he thought it to be a goodly garment.

Now, David, having seen God's law, and having praised it in his Psalm, which I have read in your hearing, he is brought by reflecting on its excellency to utter this thought, " Who can understand his errors ?" and then to offer this prayer, " Cleanse thou me from secret faults."

In the Lateran Council of the Church of Rome, a decree was passed that every true believer must confess his sins, all of them, once in a year to the priest, and they affixed to it this declaration, that there is no hope of pardon but in complying with that decree. What can equal the absurdity of such a decree as that ? Do they suppose they can tell their sins as easily as they can count their fingers ? Why, if we could receive pardon for all our sins by telling every sin we have com mitted in one hour, there is not one of us who would be able to enter heaven, since, besides the sins that are known to us and that we are able to confess, there are a vast mass of sins which are as truly sins as those which we do not observe, but which are secret and come not beneath our eye. O! if we had eyes like those of God, we should think very differently of ourselves. The sins that we see and confess are but like the farmer's small samples which he brings to market, when he has left his granary full at home. We have but a very few sins which we can observe and detect, compared with those which are hidden to ourselves and unseen to our fellow creatures. I doubt not it is true of all of us who are here, that in every hour of our existence in which we are active, we commit tens of thousands of unholinesses for which conscience has never reproved us, because we have never seen them to be wrong, seeing we have not studied God's laws as we ought to have done. Now, be it known to us all that sin is sin, whether we see it or not—that a sin secret to us is a sin as truly as if we knew it to be a sin, though not so great a sin in the sight of God as if it had been committed presumptuously, seeing that it lacks the aggravation of wilfulness. Let all of us who know our sins, offer this prayer after all our confessions : " Lord, I have confessed as many as I know, but I must add an et cetera after them, and say, ' Cleanse thou me from secret faults.' "

That, however, will not be the pith of my sermon this morning. I am going after a certain class of men who have sins not unknown to themselves, but secret to their fellow creatures. Every now and then we turn up a fair stone which lies upon the greensward of the professing church, surrounded with the verdure of apparent goodness, and to our astonishment we find beneath all kinds of filthy insects and loathsome reptiles, and in our disgust at such hypocrisy, we are driven to exclaim, " All men are liars ; there are none in whom we can put any trust at all." It is not fair to say so of all ; but really, the discoveries which are made of the insincerity of our fellow creatures are enough to make us despise our kind, because they can go so far in appearances, and yet have so little soundness of heart. To you, sirs, who sin secretly, and yet make a profession ; who break God's covenants in the dark and wear a mask of goodness in the light—to you, sirs, who shut the doors and commit wickedness in secret—to you I shall speak this morning. O may God also be pleased to speak to you, and make you pray this prayer, " Cleanse thou me from secret faults."

I shall endeavor to urge upon all pretenders present to give up, to renounce, to detest, to hate, to abhor all their secret sins. And, first, I shall endeavor to show *the folly of secret sins ;* secondly, *the misery of secret sins ;* thirdly, *the guilt of secret sins ;* fourthly, *the danger of secret sins ;* and then I shall try to apply some words by way of remedy, that we may all of us be enabled to avoid secret sins.

I. First, then, THE FOLLY OF SECRET SINS.

Pretender, thou art fair to look upon ; thy conduct outwardly upright, amiable, liberal, generous, and Christian ; but thou dost indulge in some sin which the eye of man has not yet detected. Perhaps it is private drunkenness. Thou dost revile the drunkard when he staggers through the street ; but thou canst thyself indulge in the same habit in private. It may be some other lust or vice, it is not for me just now to mention what it is. But, pretender, we say unto thee, thou art a fool to think of harboring a secret sin ; and thou art a fool for this one reason, that thy sin is not a secret sin ; *it is known*, and shall one day be revealed ; perhaps very soon. Thy sin is not a secret ; the eye of God hath seen it ; thou hast sinned before his face. Thou hast shut to the door, and drawn the curtains, and kept out the eye of the sun, but God's eye pierceth through the darkness ; the brick walls which surrounded thee were as transparent as glass to the eye of the Almighty ; the darkness which did gird thee was as bright as the summer's noon to the eye of him who beholdeth all things. Knowest thou not, O man, that " all things are naked and open to the eyes of him with whom we have to do ?" As the priest ran his knife into the entrails of his victim, discovered the heart and liver, and what else did lie within, so art thou, O man, seen by God, cut open by the Almighty ; thou hast no secret chamber where thou canst hide thyself thou hast no dark cellar where thou canst conceal thy soul. Dig deep, ay, deep as hell, but thou canst not find earth enough upon this globe to cover thy sin; if thou shouldst heap the mountains on its grave, those mountains would tell the tale of what was buried in their bowels. If thou couldst cast thy sin into the sea, a thousand babbling waves would tell the secret out. There is no hiding it from God. Thy sin is photographed in high heaven; the deed when it was done was photographed upon the sky, and there it shall remain, and thou shalt see thyself one day revealed to the gazing eyes of all men, a hypocrite, a pretender, who didst sin in fancied secret, observed in all thine acts by the all-seeing Jehovah. O what fools men are, to think they can do any thing in secret. This world is like the glass hives wherein bees sometimes work; we look down upon them, and we see all the operations of the little creatures. So God looketh down and seeth all. Our eyes are weak; we can not look through the darkness; but his eye, like an orb of flame, penetrateth the blackness, and readeth the thoughts of man, and seeth his acts when he thinks himself most concealed. O it were a thought enough to curb us all from sin, if it were truly applied to us—"Thou, God, seest me!" Stop thief! Drop thou that which thou hast taken to thyself. God seeth thee! No eye of detection on earth hath discovered thee, but God's eyes are now looking through the clouds upon thee. Swearer! scarce any for whom thou carest heard thy oath; but God heard it; it entered into the ears of the Lord God of Sabaoth. Ah! thou who leadest a filthy life, and yet art a respectable merchant, bearing among men a fair and goodly character, thy vices are all known; written in God's book. He keepeth a diary of all thine acts; and what wilt thou think on that day when a crowd shall be assembled, compared with which this immense multitude is but a drop of a bucket, and God shall read out the story of thy secret life, and men and angels shall hear it. Certain I am there are none of us who would like to have all our secrets read, especially our secret thoughts. If I should select out of this congregation the most holy man, should bring him forward and say, "Now, sir, I know all your thoughts, and am about to tell them," I am sure he would offer me the largest bribe that he could gather if I would be pleased to conceal at least some of them. "Tell," he would say, "of my acts; of them I am not ashamed; but do not tell my thoughts and imaginations—of them I must ever stand ashamed before God." What, then, sinner, will be thy shame when thy privy lusts, thy closet transgressions, thy secret crimes shall be gazetted from God's throne, published by his own mouth, and with a voice louder than a thousand thunders preached in the ears of an assembled world? What will be thy terror and confusion then, when all the deeds thou hast done shall be published in the face of the sun, in the ears of all mankind. O renounce the foolish hope of secrecy, for thy sin is this day recorded, and shall one day be advertised upon the walls of heaven.

II. In the next place, let us notice THE MISERY OF SECRET SINS.

Of all the sinners, the man who makes a profession of religion, and yet lives in iniquity, is the most miserable. A downright wicked man, who takes a glass in his hand, and says, "I am a drunkard, I am not ashamed of it," he shall be unutterably miserable in worlds to come, but brief though it be, he has his hour of pleasure. A man who curses and swears, and says, "That is my habit I am a profane man," and makes a profession of it, he has at least, some peace in his soul; but the man who walks with God's minister, who is united with God's church, who comes out before God's people, and unites with them, and then lives in sin, what a miserable existence he must have of it! Why, he has a worse existence than the mouse that is in the parlor, running out now and then to pick up the crumbs, and then back again to his hole. Such men must run out now and then to sin; and O! how fearful they are to be discovered! One day, perhaps, their character turns up; with wonderful cunning they manage to conceal and gloss it over; but the next day something else comes, and they live in constant fear, telling lie after lie, to make the last lie appear truthful, adding deception to deception, in order that they may not be discovered.

> "O! 'tis a tangled web we weave,
> When once we venture to deceive."

If I must be a wicked man, give me the life of a roystering sinner, who sins before the face of day; if I must sin, let me not act as a hypocrite and a coward; let me not profess to be God's and spend my life for the devil. This way of cheating the devil is a thing which every honest sinner will be ashamed of. He will say, " Now, if I do serve my master I will serve him out and out, I will have no sham about it; if I make a profession I will carry it out; but if I do not, if I live in sin, I am not going to gloss it over by cant and hypocrisy." One thing which has ham-stringed the church, and cut her very sinews in twain, has been this most damnable hypocrisy. O! in how many places have we men whom you might praise to the very skies, if you could believe their words, but whom you might cast into the nethermost pit if you could see their secret actions. God forgive any of you who are so acting! I had almost said, I can scarce forgive you. I can forgive the man who riots openly, and makes no profession of being better, but the man who fawns, and cants, and pretends and prays, and then lives in sin, that man I hate, I can not bear him, I abhor him from my very soul. If he will turn from his ways, I will love him, but in his hypocrisy he is to me the most loathsome of all creatures. 'Tis said the toad doth wear a jewel in her head, but this man hath none, but beareth filthiness about him, while he pretends to be in love with righteousness. A mere profession, my hearers, is but painted pageantry to go to hell in: it is like the plumes upon the hearse and the trappings upon the black horses which drag men to their graves, the funeral array of dead souls. Take heed above every thing of a waxen profession that will not stand the sun; take care of a life that needs to have two faces to carry it out; be one thing, or else the other. If you make up your mind to serve Satan, do not pretend to serve God; and if you serve God, serve him with all your heart. " No man can serve two *masters*," do not try it, do not endeavor to do it, for no life will be more miserable than that. Above all, beware of committing acts which it will be necessary to conceal. There is a singular poem by Hood, called " The Dream of Eugene Aram"— a most remarkable piece it is indeed, illustrating the point on which I am now dwelling. Aram has murdered a man and

cast his body into the river—" a sluggish water, black as ink,
the depth was so extreme." The next morning he visited the
scene of his guilt,

> " And sought the black accursed pool,
>   With a wild misgiving eye;
> And he saw the dead in the river bed,
>   For the faithless stream was dry."

Next he covered the corpse with heaps of leaves, but a
mighty wind swept through the wood and left the secret bare
before the sun.

> " Then down I cast me on my face,
>   And first began to weep,
> For I knew my secret then was one
>   That earth refused to keep,
> On land or sea, though it should be
>   Ten thousand fathoms deep."

In plaintive notes he prophesies his own discovery. He buried
his victim in a cave, and trod him down with stones, but when
years had run their weary round the foul deed was discovered
and the murderer put to death.

Guilt is a " grim chamberlain," even when his fingers are
not bloody red. Secret sins bring fevered eyes and sleepless
nights, until men burn out their consciences, and become in
very deed ripe for the pit. Hypocrisy is a hard game to play
at, for it is one deceiver against many observers; and for certain it is a miserable trade, which will earn at last, as its certain climax, a tremendous bankruptcy. Ah! ye who have
sinned without discovery, " be sure your sins will find you
out;" and bethink you it may find you out ere long. Sin,
like murder, will come out; men will even tell tales about
themselves in their dreams. God has sometimes made men so
pricked in their consciences, that they have been obliged to
stand forth and confess the story. Secret sinner! if thou
wantest the foretaste of damnation upon earth, continue in
thy secret sins; for no man is more miserable than he who
sinneth secretly, and yet trieth to preserve a character. Yon
stag, followed by the hungry hounds, with open mouths, is far
more happy than the man who is followed by his sins. You
bird taken in the fowler's net, and laboring to escape, is far

more happy than he who hath weaved around himself a web of deception, and labors to escape from it day by day by making the toils more thick and the web more strong. O! the misery of secret sins! Truly, one may pray, "Cleanse thou me from secret faults."

III. But now, next, the guilt, THE SOLEMN GUILT OF SECRET SIN.

Now, John, you do not think there is any evil in a thing unless some body sees it, do you? You feel that it is a very great sin if your master finds you out in robbing the till; but there is no sin if he should not discover it—none at all. And you, sir, you fancy it to be a very great sin to play a trick in trade, in case you should be discovered and brought before the court; but to play a trick and never be discovered, that is all fair—do not say a word about it, Mr. Spurgeon, it is all business; you must not touch business; tricks that are not discovered, of course you are not to find fault with them. The common measure of sin is the notoriety of it. But I do not believe in that. A sin is a sin, whether done in private or before the wide world. It is singular how men will measure guilt. A railway servant puts up a wrong signal, there is an accident; the man is tried and severely reprimanded. The day before he put up the wrong signal, but there was no accident, and therefore no one accused him for his neglect. But it was just the same, accident or no accident: the accident did not make the guilt, it was the deed which made the guilt, not the notoriety nor yet the consequence of it. It was his business to have taken care; and he was as guilty the first time as he was the second, for he negligently exposed the lives of men. Do not measure sin by what other people say of it; but measure sin by what God says of it, and what your own conscience says of it.

Now, I hold that secret sin, if any thing, is the worst of sin; because secret sin implies that the man who commits it has Atheism in his heart. You will ask how that can be. I reply, he may be a professing Christian, but I shall tell him to his face that he is a practical Atheist, if he labors to keep up a respectable profession before man, and then secretly transgresses. Why, is not he an Atheist, who will say there is a

God, yet at the same time thinks more of man than he does of God? Is it not the very essence of Atheism—is it not a denial of the divinity of the Most High when men lightly esteem him and think more of the eye of a creature than of the observation of their Creator? There are some who would not, for the life of them, say a wicked word in the presence of their minister, but they can do it, knowing God is looking at them. They are Atheists. There are some who would not trick in trade for all the world if they thought they should be discovered, but they can do it while God is with them; that is, they think more of the eye of man than of the eye of God; and they think it worse to be condemned by man than to be condemned by God. Call it by what name you will, the proper name of that is practical Atheism. It is dishonoring God; it is dethroning him; putting him down below his own creatures; and what is that, but to take away his divinity? Brethren, do not, I beseech you, incur the fearful guilt of secret sins. No man can sin a little in secret, it will certainly engender more sin; no man can be a hypocrite and yet be moderate in guilt; he will go from bad to worse, and still proceed, until when his guilt shall be published, he shall be found to be the very worst and the most hardened of men. Take heed of the guilt of secret sin. Ah, now, if I could preach as Rowland Hill did, I would make some people look to themselves at home, and tremble too! It is said that when he preached there was not a man in the window, or standing in the crowd, or perched up any where, but said, "There, he is preaching at me; he is telling me about my secret sins." And when he proclaimed God's omniscience, it is said men would almost think they saw God bodily present in the midst of them, looking at them. And when he had done his sermon, they would hear a voice in their ears, "Can any hide himself in secret places that I can not see him? saith the Lord. Do not I fill heaven and earth? saith the Lord." I would I could do that; that I could make every man look to himself, and find out his secret sin. Come, my hearer, what is it? Bring it forth to the daylight; perhaps it will die in the light of the sun. These things love not to be discovered. Tell thine own conscience, now, what it is. Look it in the face; confess it before God, and may he give thee grace to remove that sin and every other, and turn to him with full purpose of heart! But this know—that thy guilt is guilt discovered or undis-covered, and that, if there be any difference, it is worse, be-cause it has been secret. God save us from the guilt of secret sin! "Cleanse thou me from secret faults."

IV. And note, next, THE DANGER OF SECRET SIN. One danger is that a man can not commit a little sin in secret, with-out being by-the-by betrayed into a public sin. You can not, sir, though you may think you can, preserve a moderation in sin. If you commit one sin, it is like the melting of the lower glacier upon the Alps; the others must follow in time. As certainly as you heap one stone upon the cairn to-day, the next day you will cast another, until the heap, reared stone by stone, shall become a very pyramid. Set the coral insect at work, you can not decree where it shall stay its work. It will not build its rock just as high as you please, it will not stay until it shall be covered with weeds, until the weeds shall de-cay, and there shall be soil upon it, and an island shall be created by tiny creatures. Sin can not be held in with bit and bridle. "But I am going to have a little drink now and then. I am only going to be intoxicated once a week or so. No body will see it; I shall be in bed directly." You will be drunk in the streets soon. "I am only just going to read one lascivious book; I will put it under the sofa-cover when any one comes in." You will keep it in your library yet, sir. "I am only going into that company now and then." You will go there every day, such is the bewitching character of it; you can not help it. You may as well ask the lion to let you put your head into his mouth. You can not regulate his jaws, neither can you regulate sin. Once go into it, you can not tell when you will be destroyed. You may be such a fortunate individual, that, like Van Amburgh, you may put you head in and out a great many times; rest assured that one of these days it will be a costly venture. Again, you may labor to conceal your vicious habit, but it will come out, you can not help it. You keep your little pet sin at home; but mark this, when the door is ajar the dog will be out in the street; wrap im up in your bosom, put over him fold after fold of hypoc risy to keep him secret : the wretch will be singing some day when you are in company ; you can not keep the evil bird still. Your sin will gad abroad ; and what is more, you will not mind it some of these days. A man who indulges in sin privately, by degrees gets his forehead as hard as brass. The first time he sinned, the drops of sweat stood on his brow at the recollection of what he had done; the second time no hot sweat on his brow—only an agitation of the muscles ; the third time there was the sly, sneaky look, but no agitation ; the next time, he sinned a little further ; and by degrees he became the bold blasphemer of his God, who exclaimed, ' Who am I that I should fear Jehovah, and who is he that I should serve him ?" Men go from bad to worse. Launch your boat in the current—it must go where the current takes it. Put yourself in the whirlwind—you are but a straw in the wind : you must go which way the wind carries you—you can not control yourself. The balloon can mount, but it can not direct its course ; it must go which ever way the wind blows. If you once mount into sin, there is no stopping. Take heed, if you would not become the worst of characters, take heed of the little sins, which, mounting one upon another, may at last heave you from the summit and destroy your soul for ever. There is a great danger in secret sins.

But I have here some true Christians who indulge in secret sins. They say it is but a little one, and therefore do they spare it. Dear brethren, I speak to you, and I speak to myself, when I say this—let us destroy all our little secret sins. They are called little, and if they be, let us remember that it is the foxes, even the little foxes, that spoil our vines ; for our vines have tender shoots. Let us take heed of our little sins. A little sin, like a little pebble in the shoe, will make a traveler to heaven walk very wearily. Little sins, like little thieves, may open the door to greater ones outside. Christians, recollect that little sins will spoil your communion with Christ. Little sins, like little stains in silk, may damage the fine texture of fellowship ; little sins, like little irregularities in the machinery, may spoil the whole fabric of your religion. The one dead fly spoileth the whole pot of ointment. That one thistle may seed a continent with noxious weeds. Let us, brethren, kill our sins as often as we can find them. One said —"The heart is full of unclean birds; it is a cage of them." " Ah, but," said another divine, " you must not make that an apology, for a Christian's business is to wring their necks." And so it is; if there be evil things it is our business to kill them. Christians must not tolerate secret sins. We must not harbor traitors; it is high treason against the King of heaven. Let us drag them out to light, and offer them upon the altar, giving up the dearest of our secret sins at the will and bidding of God. There is a great danger in a little secret sin; therefore avoid it, pass not by it, turn from it and shun it; and God give thee grace to overcome it!

V. And now I come, in finishing up, to plead with all my might with some of you whom God has pricked in your consciences. I have come to intreat you, if it be possible, even to tears, that you will give up your secret sins. I have one here for whom I bless God; I love him, though I know him not. He is almost persuaded to be a Christian; he halteth between two opinions; he intendeth to serve God, he striveth to give up sin, but he findeth it a hard struggle, and as yet he knoweth not what shall become of him. I speak to him with all love: my friend, will you have your sin and go to hell, or leave your sin and go to heaven? This is the solemn alternative; to all awakened sinners I put it; may God choose for you, otherwise I tremble as to which you may choose. The pleasures of this life are so intoxicating, the joys of it so ensnaring, that did I not believe that God worketh in us to will and to do, I should despair of you. But I have confidence that God will decide the matter. Let me lay the alternative before you:—on the one hand there is an hour's merriment, a short life of bliss, and that a poor, poor bliss; on the other hand, there is everlasting life and eternal glory. On the one hand, there is a transient happiness, and afterward overwhelming woe; in this case there is a solid peace and everlasting joy, and after it overflowing bliss. I shall not fear to be called an Arminian, when I say, as Elijah did, " Choose you this day whom you will serve. If God be God, serve him; if Baal be God, serve him." But, now, make your choice deliberately; and may God help you to do it! Do not say you will take up with religion, without first counting the cost of it; remember, there is your lust to be given up, your pleasure to be renounced; can you do it for Christ's sake? Can you? I know you can not, unless God's grace shall assist you in making such a choice. But can you say, "Yes, by the help of God, earth's gaudy toys, its pomps, pageantries, gewgaws all these I renounce?

> "'These can never satisfy;
> Give me Christ or else I die.'"

Sinner, thou wilt never regret that choice, if God help thee to make it; thou wilt find thyself a happy man here, and thrice happy throughout eternity.

"But," says one, "sir, I intend to be religious, but I do not hold with your strictness." I do not ask you to do so; I hope, however, you will hold with *God's* strictness, and God's strictness is ten thousand times greater than mine. You may say that I am puritanical in my preaching; God will be puritanical in judging in that great day. I may appear severe, but I can never be so severe as God will be. I may draw the harrow with sharp teeth across your conscience, but God shall drag harrows of eternal fire across you one day. I may speak thundering things; God will not speak them, but hurl them from his hands. Remember, men may laugh at hell, and say there is none; but they must reject their Bibles before they can believe the lie. Men's consciences tell them that

> "There is a dreadful hell
> And everlasting pains,
> Where sinners must with devils dwell
> In darkness, fire, and chains."

Sir, will you keep your secret sins, and have eternal fire for them? Remember, it is of no use, they must all be given up, or else you can not be God's child. You can not by any means have both; it can not be God and the world, it can not be Christ and the devil; it must be one or the other. O, that God would give you grace to resign all; for what are they worth? They are your deceivers now, and will be your tormentors for ever. O! that your eyes were open to see the rottenness, the emptiness and trickery of iniquity. O! that God would turn you to himself. O! may God give you grace to cross the Rubicon of repentance at this very hour; to say, "Henceforth it is war to the knife with my sins; not one of them will I willingly keep, but down with them, down with them; Canaanite, Hittite, Jebusite, they shall all be driven out

> " 'The dearest idol I have known,
> Whate'er that idol be;
> Help me to tear it from its throne,
> And worship only thee.' "

But O! sir, I can not do it; it would be like pulling my eyes out." Ay, but hear what Christ says: " It were better for thee to enter into life with one eye, than having two eyes to be cast into hell fire." "But it would be like cutting my arm off." Ay, and it would be better for thee to enter into life halt or maimed, than to be cast into hell fire for ever. O! when the sinner comes before God at last, do you think he will speak as he does now? God will reveal his secret sins: the sinner will not then say, "Lord, I thought my secret sins so sweet, I could not give them up." I think I see how changed it will be then. "*Sir*," you say now, "*you are too strict;*" will you say that when the eyes of the Almighty are glowering on you? You say now, "*Sir, you are too precise;*" will you say that to God Almighty's face? "*Sir, I mean to keep such-and-such a sin.*" Can you say it at God's bar at last? You will not dare to do it then. Ah! when Christ comes a second time, there will be a marvelous change in the way men talk. Methinks I see him; there he sits upon his throne. Now, Caiaphas, come and condemn him now! Judas! come and kiss him now! What do you stick at, man? Are you afraid of him? Now, Barabbas! go; see whether they will prefer you to Christ now. Swearer, now is your time; you have been a bold man; curse him to his face now. Now, drunkard; stagger up to him now. Now, infidel; tell him there is no Christ now—now that the world is lit with lightning and the earth is shaken with thunder till the solid pillars thereof do bow themselves—tell God there is no God now; now laugh at the Bible; now scoff at the minister. Why men, what is the matter with you? Why, can't you do it? Ah! there you are; you have fled to the hills and to the rocks—"Rocks, hide us! mountains, fall on us hide us from the face of him that sitteth on the throne." **Ah!** where are now your boasts, your vauntings, and your glories? Alas! alas! for you, in that dread day of wonders.

Secret sinner, what will then become of thee? Go out of this place unmasked; go out to examine thyself, go out to bend thy knee, go out to weep, go out to pray. God give thee grace to believe! And O, how sweet and pleasant the thought, that this day sinners have fled to Christ, and men have been born again to Jesus! Brethren, ere I finish, I repeat the words at which so many have caviled—it is now or never, it is turn or burn. Solemnly in God's sight I say it; if it be not God's truth I must answer for it in the great day of account. Your consciences tell you it is true. Take it home, and mock me if you will; this morning I am clear of your blood; if any seek not God, but live in sin, I shall be clear of your blood in that day when the watchman shall have your souls demanded of him; O, may God grant that you may be cleared in a blessed manner! When I went down these pulpit stairs a Sabbath or two ago, a friend said to me words which have been in my mind ever since—"Sir, there are nine thousand people this day without excuse in the day of judgment." It is true of you this morning. If you are damned, it will not be for want of preaching to you, and it shall not be for want of praying for you. God knoweth that if my heart could break of itself, it would, for your souls, for God is my witness, how earnestly I long for you in the bowels of Christ Jesus. O, that he might touch your hearts and bring you to him! For death is a solemn thing, damnation is a horrible thing, to be out of Christ is a dreadful thing, to be dead in sins is a terrific thing. May God lead you to view these things as they are, and save you, for his mercy's sake! 'He that believeth and is baptized shall be saved."

> "Lord, search my soul, try every thought
> Though my own heart accuse me not
> Of walking in a false disguise,
> I beg the trial of thine eyes.
> Doth secret mischief lurk within?
> Do I indulge some unknown sin?
> O turn my feet whene're I stray,
> And lead me in thy perfect way."

SERMON XII

ELIJAH'S APPEAL TO THE UNDECIDED

"How long halt ye between two opinions? If the Lord be God, follow him; if Baal, then follow him."—1 KINGS, xviii. 21

IT was a day to be remembered, when the multitudes of Israel were assembled at the foot of Carmel, and when the solitary prophet of the Lord came forth to defy the four hundred and fifty priests of the false god. We might look upon that scene with the eye of historical curiosity, and we should find it rich with interest. Instead of doing so, however, we shall look upon it with the eye of attentive consideration, and see whether we can not improve by its teachings. We have upon that hill of Carmel, and along the plain, three kinds of persons. We have first the devoted servant of Jehovah, a solitary prophet; we have, on the other hand, the decided servants of the evil one, the four hundred and fifty prophets of Baal; but the vast mass of that day belonged to a third class —they were those who had not fully determined whether fully to worship Jehovah, the God of their fathers, or Baal, the god of Jezebel. On the one hand, their ancient traditions led them to fear Jehovah, and on the other hand, their interest at court led them to bow before Baal. Many of them, therefore, were secret and half-hearted followers of Jehovah, while they were the public worshipers of Baal. The whole of them at this juncture were halting between two opinions. Elijah does not address his sermon to the priests of Baal; he will have something to say to them by-and-by, he will preach them horrible sermons in deeds of blood. Nor has he aught to say to those who are the thorough servants of Jehovah, for they are not there; but his discourse is alone directed to those who are halting between two opinions.

Now, we have these three classes here this morning. We have, I hope, a very large number who are on Jehovah's side, who fear God and serve him; we have a number who are on the side of the evil one, who make no profession of religion, and do not observe even the outward symptoms of it; because they are both inwardly and outwardly the servants of the evil one But the great mass of my hearers belong to the third class— the waverers. Like empty clouds they are driven hither and thither by the wind; like painted beauties, they lack the fresh ness of life; they have a name to live and are dead. Procras- tinators, double-minded men, undecided persons, to you I speak this morning—" How long halt ye between two opin ions?" May the question be answered by God's Spirit in your hearts, and may you be led to say, "No longer, Lord, do I halt; but this day I decide for thee, and am thy servant for ever!"

Let us proceed at once to the text. Instead of giving the divisions at the commencement, I will mention them one by one as I proceed.

I. First, you will note that *the prophet insisted upon the distinction which existed between the worship of Baal and the worship of Jehovah.* Most of the people who were before him thought that Jehovah was God, and that Baal was God too; and that for this reason the worship of both was quite consistent. The great mass of them did not reject the God of their fathers wholly, nor did they bow before Baal wholly; but as polytheists, believing in many gods, they thought both Gods might be worshiped, and each of them have a share in their hearts. "No," said the prophet when he began, "this will not do, these are *two* opinions; you can never make them one, they are two contradictory things which can not be com- bined. I tell you that instead of combining the two, which i impossible, you are halting between the two, which makes a vast difference." "I will build in my house," said one of them, "an altar for Jehovah here, and an altar for Baal there I am of one opinion; I believe them both to be God." "No no," said Elijah, "it can not be so; they are *two*, and must be two. These things are not one opinion, but two opinions. No, you can not unite them." Have I not many here who say,

"I am worldly, but I am religious too ; I can go to the Music Hall to worship God on Sunday ; I went to the Derby races the other day : I go, on the one hand, to the place where I can serve my lusts ; I am to be met with in every dancing room of every description, and yet at the same time I say my prayers most devoutly.   May I not be a good churchman, or a right good dissenter, and a man of the world too ?   May I not, after all, hold with the hounds as well as run with the hare ?   May I not love God and serve the devil too—take the pleasure of each of them, and give my heart to neither ?   We answer—Not so, they are two opinions ; you can not do it, they are distinct and separate.   Mark Anthony yoked two lions to his chariot ; but there are two lions no man ever yoked together yet—the Lion of the tribe of Judah and the lion of the pit.   These can never go together.   Two opinions you may hold in politics, perhaps, but then you will be despised by every body, unless you are of one opinion or the other, and act as an independent man.   But two opinions in the matter of soul-religion you can not hold.   If God be God, serve him, and do it thoroughly ; but if this world be God, serve it, and make no profession of religion.   If you are a worldling, and think the things of the world the best, serve them ; devote yourself to them, do not be kept back by conscience ; spite your conscience, and run into sin.   But remember, if the Lord be your God, you can not have Baal too ; you must have one thing or else the other.   "No man can serve two *masters.*"   If God be served, he will be a master ; and if the devil be served he will not be long before he will be a master ; and "ye can not serve two *masters.*"   O ! be wise, and think not that the two can be mingled together.   How many a respectable deacon thinks that he can be covetous, and grasping in business, and grind the faces of the poor, and yet be a saint !   O ! liar to God and to man !   He is no saint ; he is the very chief of sinners !   How many a very excellent woman, who is received into church fellowship among the people of God, and thinks herself one of the elect, is to be found full of wrath and bitterness, a slave of mischief and of sin, a tattler, a slanderer, a busybody ; entering into other people's houses, and turning every thing like comfort out of the minds of those with whom she comes in contact—and yet she is the servant of God and of the devil too! Nay, my lady this will never an-swer; the two never can be served thoroughly. Serve your master, whoever he be. If you do profess to be religious, be so thoroughly; if you make any profession to be a Christian, be one; but if you are no Christian, do not *pretend* to be. If you love the world, then love it; but cast off the mask, and do not be a hypocrite. The double-minded man is of all men the most despicable; the follower of Janus, who wears two faces, and who can look with one eye upon the (so-called) Christian world with great delight, and give his subscription to the Tract Society, the Bible Society, and the Missionary Society, but who has another eye over there, with which he looks at the Casino, the Coal-hole, and other pleasures, which I do not care to mention, but which some of you may know more of than I wish to know. Such a man, I say, is worse than the most reprobate of men, in the opinion of any one who knows how to judge. Not worse in his open character, but worse really, because he is not honest enough to go through with that he professes. And how many such are there in Lon-don, in England; everywhere else! They try to serve both masters; but it can not be; the two things can not be recon-ciled; God and Mammon, Christ and Belial, these never can meet; there never can be an agreement between them, they never can be brought into unity, and why should you seek to do it? "*Two opinions*," said the prophet. He would not allow any of his hearers to profess to worship both. ◦ "No," said he, "these are two opinions, and you are halting between the two."

II. In the second place, *the prophet calls these waverers to an account for the amount of time which they had consumed in making their choice.* Some of them might have replied, "We have not had yet an opportunity of judging between God and Baal; we have not yet had time enough to make up our minds;" but the prophet puts away that objection, and he says, "*How long* halt ye between two opinions? How long? For three years and a half not a drop of rain has fallen at the command of Jehovah; is not that proof enough? Ye have been all this time, three years and a half, expecting, till 1 should come, Jehovah's servant, and give you rain ; and yet, though you yourselves are starving, your cattle dead, your fields parched, and your meadows covered with dust, like the very deserts, yet all this time of judgment, and trial, and affliction, has not been enough for you to make up your minds. *How long*, then," said he, " halt ye between two opinions ?"

I speak not, this morning, to the thoroughly worldly; with them I have now nothing to do ; another time I may address them. But I am now speaking to you who are seeking to serve God and to serve Satan ; you who are trying to be Christian worldlings, trying to be members of that extraordinary corporation, called the "religious world," which is a thing that never had an existence except in title. You are endeavoring, if you can, to make up your mind which it shall be ; you know you can not serve both, and you are coming now to the period when you are saying, "Which shall it be ? Shall I go thoroughly into sin, and revel in the pleasures of the earth, or become a servant of God ?" Now, I say to you this morning, as the prophet did, "*How long* halt ye?" Some of you have been halting until your hair has grown gray ; the sixtieth year of some you is drawing nigh. Is not sixty years long enough to make up your choice ? "*How long* halt ye?" Perhaps one of you may have tottered into this place, leaning on his staff, and you have been undecided up till now. Your eightieth year has come ; you have been a religious character outwardly, but a worldling truly ; you are still up to this date halting, saying, " I know not on which side to be." How long, sirs, in the name of reason, in the name of mortality, in the name of death, in the name of eternity, "*How long* halt ye between two opinions ?" Ye middle-aged men, ye said when ye were youths, "When we are out of our apprenticeship we will become religious ; let us sow our wild oats in our youth, and let us then begin to be diligent servants of the Lord." Lo ! ye have come to middle age, and are waiting till that quiet villa shall be built, and ye shall retire from business, and then ye think ye will serve God. Sirs, ye said that same when ye came of age, and when your business began to increase. I therefore solemnly demand of you, "How long halt ye between two opinions ?" How much time do you want ? O !

young man, thou saidst in thine early childhood, when a mother's prayer followed thee, " I will seek God when I come to manhood ;" and thou hast passed that day; thou art a man, and more than that, and yet thou art halting still. " How long halt ye between two opinions?" How many of you have been church-goers and chapel-goers for years! Ye have been impressed, too, many a time, but ye have wiped the tears from your eyes, and have said, "I will seek God and turn to him with full purpose of heart ;" and you are now just where you were. How many sermons do you want ? How many more Sundays must roll away wasted ? How many warnings, how many sicknesses, how many tollings of the bell to warn you that you must die ? How many graves must be dug for your family before you will be impressed ? How many plagues and pestilences must ravage this city before you will turn to God in truth ? " How long halt ye between two opinions ?" Would God ye could answer this question, and not allow the sands of life to drop, drop, drop from the glass, saying, " When the next goes I will repent," and yet that next one findeth you impenitent. You say, " When the glass is just so low, I will turn to God." No, sir, no ; it will not answer for you to talk so; for thou mayest find thy glass empty before thou thoughtest it had begun to run low, and thou mayest find thyself in eternity when thou didst but think of repenting and turning to God. How long, ye gray heads, how long, ye men of ripe years, how long, ye youths and maidens, how long will ye be in this undecided, unhappy state ? " How long halt ye between two opinions ?"

Thus we have brought you so far. We have noted that there are two opinions, and we have asked the question, How long time you want to decide ? One would think the question would require very little time, if time were all; if the will were not biassed to evil and contrary to good, it would re-quire no more time than the decision of a man who has to choose a halter or life, wealth or poverty ; and if we were wise, it would take no time at all ; if we understood the things of God, we should not hesitate, but say at once, " Now God is my God, and that for ever."

III. But *the prophet charges these people with the absurdity*

of their position.   Some of them said, "What! prophet, may
we not continue to halt between two opinions?   We are not
desperately irreligious, so we are better than the profane,
certainly we are not thoroughly pious; but, at any rate, a little piety is better than none, and the mere profession of it
keeps us decent, let us try both!"   "Now," says the prophet,
"how long halt ye?" or, if you like to read it so, "how long
limp ye between two opinions?"   (How long *wriggle* ye be
tween two opinions? would be a good word, if I might employ it.)   He represents them as like a man whose legs are
entirely out of joint; he first goes on one side, and then on
the other, and can not go far either way.   I could not describe it without putting myself into a most ludicrous posture.
"How long *limp* ye between two opinions?"   The prophet
laughs at them, as it were.   And is it not true, that a man
who is neither one thing or another is in a most absurd position?   Let him go among the worldlings; they laugh under
their sleeve, and say, "This is one of the Exeter Hall saints,"
or, "That is one of the elect."   Let him go among the Christian people, those that are saints, and they say, "How a man
can be so inconsistent, how he can come into our midst one
day, and the next be found in such and such society, we can
not tell."   Methinks even the devil himself must laugh at
such a man in scorn.   "There," says he, "I am every thing
that is bad; I do sometimes pretend to be an angel of light,
and put on that garb; but you do really excell me in every
respect, for I do it to get something by it, but you do not
get any thing by it.   You do not have the pleasures of
this world, and you do not have the pleasures of religion
either; you have the fears of religion without its hopes; you
are afraid to do wrong, and yet you have no hope of heaven;
you have the duties of religion without the joys; you have to
do just as religious people do, and yet there is no heart in the
matter; you have to sit down, and see the table all spread before you, and then you have not power to eat a single morsel
of the precious dainties of the gospel."   It is just the same
with the world; you dare not go into this or that mischief
that brings joy to the wicked man's heart; you think of what
society would say   We do not know what to make of you

I might describe you, if I might speak as the Americans do, but I will not. Ye are half one thing, and half the other. You come into the society of the saints, and try to talk as they talk; but you are like a man who has been taught French in some day-school in England; he makes a queer sort of French ified English, and Englishized French, and every one laughs at him. The English laugh at him for trying to do it, and the French laugh at him for failing in it. If you spoke your own language, if you just spoke out as a sinner, if you professed to be what you are, you would at least get the respect of one side; but now you are rejected by one class, and equally rejected by the other. You come into our midst, we can not receive you; you go amongst worldlings, they reject you too; you are too good for them, and too bad for us. Where are you to be put? If there were a purgatory, that would be the place for you; where you might be tossed on the one side into ice, and on the other into the burning fire, and that for ever. But as there is no such place as purgatory, and as you really are a servant of Satan, and not a child of God, take heed, take heed, how long you stay in a position so absurdly ridiculous. At the day of judgment, wavering men will be the scoff and the laughter even of hell. The angels will look down in scorn upon the man who was ashamed to own his Master thoroughly, while hell itself will ring with laughter. When that grand hypocrite shall come there—that undecided man, they will say, "Aha! we have to drink the dregs, but above them there were sweets; you have only the dregs. You dare not go into the riotous and boisterous mirth of our youthful days, and now you have come here with us to drink the same dregs; you have the punishment without the pleasure." O! how foolish will even the damned call you, to think that you halted between two opinions! "How long limp ye, wriggle ye, walk ye in an absurd manner, between two opinions?" In adopting either opinion, you would at least be consistent; but in trying to hold both, to seek to be both one and the other, and not knowing which to decide upon, you are limping between two opinions. I think a good translation is a very different one from that of the authorized version—"How long hop ye upon two sprays?" So the

Hebrew has it. Like a bird, which perpetually flies from bough to bough, and is never still. If it keeps on doing this, it will never have a nest. And so with you: you keep leaping between two boughs, from one opinion to the other ; and so between the two, you get no rest for the sole of your foot, no peace, no joy, no comfort, but are just a poor miserable thing all your life long.

IV. We have brought you thus far, then ; we have shown you the absurdity of this halting. Now, very briefly, the next point in my text is this. The multitude who had worshiped Jehovah and Baal, and who were now undecided, might reply, " *But how do you know that we do not believe that Jehovah is God ? How do you know we are not decided in opinion ?*" The prophet meets this objection by saying, " I know you are not decided in opinion, because *you are not decided in prac- tice.* If God be God, *follow him ;* if Baal, *follow* him. You are not decided in practice." Men's opinions are not such things as we imagine. It is generally said now-a-days, that all opinions are right, and if a man shall honestly hold his con- victions, he is, without doubt, right. Not so ; truth is not changed by our opinions; a thing is either true or false of it- self, and it is neither made true nor false by our views of it. It is for us, therefore, to judge carefully, and not to think that any opinion will do. Besides, opinions have influence upon the conduct, and if a man have a wrong opinion, he will, most likely, in some way or other, have wrong conduct, for the two usually go together. " Now," said Elijah, " that you are not the servants of God, is quite evident, for you do not follow him ; that you are not thoroughly servants of Baal either, is quite evident, for you do not follow him." Now I address myself to you again. Many of you are not the servants of God ; you do not follow him ; you follow him a certain dis- tance in the form, but not in the spirit ; you follow him on Sundays ; but what do you do on Mondays ? You follow him in religious company, in evangelical drawing-rooms, and so on ; but what do you do in other society ? You do not follow him. And, on the other hand, you do not follow Baal ; you go a little way with the world, but there is a place to which you dare not go ; you are too respectable to sin as others sin, or to go the whole way of the world. Ye dare not go to the atmost lengths of evil. "Now," says the prophet, twit.ing them upon this—"if the Lord be God, follow him. Let your conduct be consistent with your opinions ; if you believe the Lord to be God, carry it out in your daily life ; be holy, be prayerful, trust in Christ, be faithful, be upright, be loving ; give your heart to God, and follow him. If Baal be God, then follow him; but do not pretend to follow the other." Let your conduct back up your opinion ; if you really think that the follies of this world are the best, and believe that a fine fashionable life, a life of frivolity and gayety, flying from flower to flower, getting honey from none, is the most desirable, carry it out. If you think the life of the debauchee is so very desirable, if you think his end is to be much wished for, if you think his pleasures are right, follow them. Go the whole way with them. If you believe that to cheat in business is right, put it up over your door—"I sell trickery goods here ;" or if you do not say it to the public, tell your conscience so ; but do not deceive the public ; do not call the people to prayers when you are opening a "British Bank." If you mean to be religious, follow out your determination thoroughly; but if you mean to be worldly, go the whole way with the world. Let your conduct follow out your opinions. Make your life tally with your profession. Carry out your opinions whatever they be. But you dare not; you are too cowardly to sin as others do, honestly before God's sun ; your conscience will not let you do it—and yet you are just so fond of Satan, that you dare no leave him wholly and become thoroughly the servants of God. O do not let your character be like your profession ; either keep up your profession, or give it up : do be one thing or the other.

V. And now the prophet cries, "If the Lord be God, follow him; if Baal, then follow him," and in so doing, *he states the ground of his practical claim.* Let your conduct be consistent with your opinions. There is another objection raised by the crowd. "Prophet," says one, "thou comest to demand a practical proof of our affection ; thou sayest, Follow God. Now, if I believe God to be God, and that is my opinion, yet I do not see what claim he has to my opinions."

Now, mark how the prophet puts it: he says, "*If God be
God*, follow him." The reason why I claim that you should
follow out your opinion concerning God is, that God is God;
God has a claim upon you, as creatures, for your devout obedience. One person replies, "What profit should I have, if I
served God thoroughly? Should I be more happy? Should
I get on better in this world? Should I have more peace of
mind?" Nay, nay, that is a secondary consideration. The
only question for you is, "If God be God follow him." Not
if it be more advantageous to you; but, " if *God be God*, follow
him." The secularist would plead for religion on the ground
that religion might be the best for this world, and best for the
world to come. Not so with the prophet; he says, "I do not
put it on that ground, I insist that it is your bounden duty, if you
believe in God, simply because he is God, to serve him and obey
him. I do not tell you it is for your advantage—it may be, I
believe it is—but that I put aside from the question; I demand
of you that you follow God, if you believe him to be *God*. If
you do not think he is God; if you really think that the devil is
God, then follow him; his pretended godhead shall be your plea,
and you shall be consistent; but if God be God, if he made
you, I demand that you serve him; if it is he who puts the
breath into your nostrils, I demand that you obey him. If
God be really worthy of your worship, and you really think
so, I demand that you either follow him, or else deny that he
is God at all." Now, professor, if thou sayest that Christ's
gospel is the gospel, if thou believest in the divinity of the
gospel, and puttest thy trust in Christ, I demand of thee to
follow out the gospel, not merely because it will be to thy advantage, but because the gospel is divine. If thou makest a
profession of being a child of God, if thou art a believer, and
thinkest and believest religion is the best, the service of God
the most desirable, I do not come to plead with thee because
of any advantage thou wouldst get by being holy; it is on this
ground that I put it, that the Lord is God; and if he be God,
it is thy business to serve him. If his gospel be true, and thou
believest it to be true, it is thy duty to carry it out. If thou
sayest Christ is not the Son of God, carry out thy Jewish or
thy infidel convictions, and see whether it will end well. If

thou dost not believe Christ to be the Son of God, if thou art a Mohammedan, be consistent, carry out thy Mohammedan convictions, and see whether it will end well. But, take heed, take heed! If, however, thou sayest God is God, and Christ the Saviour, and the gospel true; I demand of thee, only on this account, that thou carry it out. What a strong plea some would think the prophet might have had, if he had said, "God is your fathers' God, therefore follow him!" But no, he did not come down to that; he said, "If God be God—I do not care whether he be your fathers' God or not—follow him." "Why do you go to chapel?" says one, "and not to church?" "Because my father and grandfather were dissenters." Ask a churchman, very often, why he attends the establishment "Well, our family were always brought up to it; that is why I go." Now, I do think that the worst of all reasons for a particular religion, is that of our being brought up to it. I never could see that at all. I have attended the house of God with my father and my grandfather; but I thought, when I read the Scriptures, that it was my business to judge for myself. I knew that my father and my grandfather took little children in their arms, and put drops of water on their faces, and they were baptized. I took up my Bible, and I could not see any thing about babes being baptized. I picked up a little Greek; and I could not discover that the word "baptized" meant to sprinkle; so I said to myself, "Suppose they are good men, they may be wrong; and though I love and revere them, yet it is no reason why I should imitate them." And therefore I left them, and became what I am to-day, a Baptist minister, so called, but I hope a great deal more a Christian than a Baptist. It is seldom I mention it; I only do so by way of illustration here. Many a one will go to chapel, because his grandmother did. Well, she was a good old soul, but I do not see that she ought to influence your judgment. "That does not signify," says one, "I do not like to leave the church of my fathers." No more do I; I would rather belong to the same denomination with my father; I would not willfully differ from any of my friends, or leave their sect and denomination; but let God be above our parents; though our parents are at the very top of our hearts, and we love them and reverence them,

and in all other matters pay them strict obedience, yet, with
regard to religion, to our own Master we stand or fall, and we
claim to have the right of judging for ourselves as men, and
then we think it our duty, having judged, to carry out our
convictions.   Now I am not going to say, "If God be your
mother's God, serve him;" though that would be a very good
argument with some of you; but with you waverers, the only
plea I use is, "If God be God, serve him;" if the gospel be
right, believe it; if a religious life be right, carry it out; if not,
give it up.   I only put my argument on Elijah's plea—"If God
be God, follow him; but if Baal, then follow him."

VI. And now I make my appeal to the halters and waverers, with some questions, which I pray the Lord to apply.
Now I will put this question to them: "*How long halt ye?*"
I will tell them; ye will halt between two opinions, all of you
who are undecided, *until God shall answer by fire.*   Fire was
not what these poor people wanted that were assembled there.
When Elijah says, that "the God that answereth by fire let
him be God," I fancy I hear some of them saying, "No; the
God that answereth by water let him be God; we want rain
badly enough."   "No," said Elijah, "if rain should come,
you would say that it was the common course of providence;
and that would not decide you."   I tell you, all the providences that befall you undecided ones will not decide you.
God may surround you with providences; he may surround
you with frequent warnings from the death-bed of your fellows; but providences will never decide you.   It is not the
God of rain, but the God of fire that will do it.   There are
two ways in which you undecided ones will be decided by-
and-bye.   You that are decided for God will want no decision; you that are decided for Satan will want no decision;
you are on Satan's side, and must dwell for ever in eternal
burning.   But these undecided ones want something to decide them, and will have either one of the two things; they
will either have the fire of God's Spirit to decide them, or else
the fire of eternal judgment, and that will decide them.   I
may preach to you, my hearers; and all the ministers in the
world may preach to you that are wavering, but you will
never decide for God through the force of your own will

None of you, if left to your natural judgment, to the use of your own reason, will ever decide for God. You may decide for him merely as an outward form, but not as an inward spiritual thing, which should possess your heart as a Christian, as a believer in the doctrine of effectual grace. I know that none of you will ever decide for God's gospel, unless God decide you; and I tell you that you must either be decided by the descent of the fire of his Spirit into your hearts now, or else in the day of judgment. O! which shall it be? O! that the prayer might be put up by the thousand lips that are here: "Lord, decide me now by the fire of thy Spirit; O! let thy Spirit descend into my heart, to burn up the bullock, that I may be a whole burnt offering to God; to burn up the wood and the stones of my sin; to burn up the very dust of worldliness; ah, and to lick up the water of my impiety, which now lieth in the trenches, and my cold indifference, that seek to put out the sacrifice."

> "O make this heart rejoice or ache!
>   Decide this doubt for me;
> And if it be not broken, break,
>   And heal it. if it be.

> "O sovereign grace, my heart subdue;
>   I would be led in triumph too,
> A willing captive to my Lord,
>   To sing the triumphs of his word."

And it may be, that whilst I speak, the mighty fire, unseen by men, and unfelt by the vast majority of you, shall descend into some heart which has of old been dedicated to God by his divine election, which is now like an altar broken down, but which God, by his free grace, will this day build up. O! I pray that that influence may enter into some hearts, that there may be some go out of this place, saying,

> ' 'Tis done, the great transaction's done,
>   I am my Lord's, and he is mine;
> He drew me, and I followed on,
>   Glad to obey the voice divine."

> "Now rest, my undivided heart,
>   Fixed on this stable center, rest."

O! that many may say that! But remember, if it be not so, the day is coming—*dies iræ*, the day of wrath and anger—when ye shall be decided of God; when the firmament shall be lit up with lightnings, when the earth shall roll with drunken terror, when the pillars of the universe shall shake, and God shall sit, in the person of his Son, to judge the world in righteousness. You will not be undecided then, when, "Depart ye cursed," or "Come, ye blessed," shall be your doom. There will be no indecision then, when you shall meet him with joy or else with terror—when, "rocks hide me, mountains on me fall," shall be your doleful shriek; or else your joyful song shall be, "The Lord is come." In that day you will be decided; but till then, unless the living fire of the Holy Spirit decide you, you will go on halting between two opinions. May God grant you his Holy Spirit, that you may turn unto him and be saved!

SERMON XIII

SALVATION OF THE LORD

"Salvation is of the Lord." —JONAH, ii. 9

JONAH learned this sentence of good theology in a strange college. He learned it in the whale's belly, at the bottom of the mountains, with the weeds wrapped about his head, when he supposed that the earth with her bars was about him for ever. Most of the grand truths of God have to be learned by trouble; they must be burned into us with the hot iron of affliction, otherwise we shall not truly receive them. No man is competent to judge in matters of the kingdom, until first he has been tried; since there are many things to be learned in the depths which we can never know in the heights. We discover many secrets in the caverns of the ocean, which, though we had soared to heaven, we never could have known. He shall best meet the wants of God's people as a preacher who has had those wants himself; he shall best comfort God's Israel who has needed comfort; and he shall best preach salvation who has felt his own need of it. Jonah, when he was delivered from his great danger, when, by the command of God the fish had obediently left its great deeps and delivered its cargo upon dry land, was then capable of judging; and this was the result of his experience under his trouble—"Salvation is of the Lord."

By salvation here we do not merely understand the special salvation which Jonah received from death; for according to Dr. Gill, there is something so special in the original, in the word salvation having one more letter than it usually has, when it only refers to some temporary deliverance, that we can only understand it here as relating to the great work of the salvation of the soul which endureth for ever. That "sal-

vation is of the Lord," I shall this morning try to show as best
I can. First, I shall endeavor to *explain the doctrine ;* then I
shall try to show you *how God has guarded us from making
any mistakes, and has hedged us up to make us believe the gospel ;* then I shall dwell upon t*he influence of this truth upon
men;* and shall close up by showing you *the counterpart of
the doctrine.* Seeing every truth hath its obverse, so hath
this.

I. First, then, to begin by explanation, let us EXPOUND THIS
DOCTRINE—the doctrine that salvation is of the Lord, or of
Jehovah. We are to understand by this, that the whole of
the work whereby men are saved from their natural estate of
sin and ruin, and are translated into the kingdom of God and
made heirs of eternal happiness, is of God, and of him only.
"Salvation is of the Lord."

To begin, then, at the beginning, *the plan of salvation is
entirely of God.* No human intellect and no created intelligence assisted God in the planning of salvation; he contrived
the way, even as he himself carried it out. The plan of salvation was devised before the existence of angels. Before the
day-star flung its ray across the darkness, when as yet the unnavigated ether had not been fanned by the wing of seraph,
and when the solemnity of silence had never been disturbed
by the song of angel, God had devised a way whereby he
might save man, whom he foresaw would fall. He did not
create angels to consult with them; no, of himself he did it.
We might truly ask the question, " With whom took he counsel ? Who instructed him, when he planned the great architecture of the temple of mercy ? With whom took he counsel
when he digged the deeps of love, that out of them there
might well up springs of salvation ? Who aided him?"
None. He himself, alone, did it. In fact, if angels had then
been in existence, they could not have assisted God ; for I can
well suppose that if a solemn conclave of those spirits had
been held, if God had put to them this question, " Man will
rebel; I declare I will punish; my justice, inflexible and
severe, demands that I should do so ; but yet I intend to have
mercy ;" if he had put the question to the celestial squadrons
of mighty ones, " How can those things be ? How can justice

have its demands fulfilled, and how can mercy reign?" the
angels would have sat in silence until now; they could not
have dictated the plan; it would have surpassed angelic intellect to have conceived the way whereby righteousness and
peace should meet together, and judgment and mercy should
kiss each other. God devised it, because without God it could
not have been devised. It is a plan too splendid to have been
the product of any mind except of that mind which afterward
carried it out. "Salvation" is older than creation; it is "of
the Lord."

And as it was of the Lord in planning so *it was of the Lord
in execution.* No one has helped to provide salvation; God
has done it all himself. The banquet of mercy is served up
by one host; that host is he to whom the cattle on a thousand
hills belong. But none have contributed any dainties to that
royal banquet; he hath done it all himself. The royal bath
of mercy, wherein black souls are washed, was filled from the
veins of Jesus; not a drop was contributed by any other
being. He died upon the cross, and as an expiator he died
alone. No blood of martyrs mingled with that stream; no
blood of noble confessors and of heroes of the cross entered
into the river of atonement; that is filled from the veins of
Christ, and from nowhere else beside. He hath done it wholly.
Atonement is the unaided work of Jesus. On yonder cross I
see the man who "trod the winepress alone;" in yonder garden I see the solitary conqueror, who came to the fight single-
handed, whose own arm brought salvation, and whose omnipotence sustained him. "Salvation is of the Lord," as to its
provisions; Jehovah—Father, Son, and Spirit—hath provided
every thing.

So far we are all agreed: but now we shall have to separate
a bit. "Salvation is of the Lord," *in the application of it.*
"No," says the Arminian, "it is not; salvation is of the Lord,
inasmuch as he does all for man that he can do; but there is
something that man must do, which if he does not do, he must
perish." That is the Arminian way of salvation. Now last
week I thought of this very theory of salvation, when I stood
by the side of that window of Carisbrooke castle, out of which
King Charles of unhappy and unrighteous memory, attempted

to escape. I read in the guide book that every thing was provided for his escape; his followers had means at the bottom of the wall to enable him to fly across the country, and on the coast they had their boats lying ready to take him to another land; in fact every thing was ready for his escape. But here was the important circumstance: his friends had done all they could; he was to do the rest; but that doing the rest was just the point and brunt of the battle. It was to get out of the window, out of which he was not able to escape by any means, so that all his friends did for him went for nothing, so far as he was concerned. So with the sinner. If God had provided every means of escape, and only required him to get out of his dungeon, he would have remained there to all eternity. Why, is not the sinner by nature dead in sin? And if God requires him to make himself alive, and then afterward he will do the rest for him, then verily, my friends, we are not so much obliged to God as we had thought for; for if he require so much as that of us, and we can do it, we can do the rest without his assistance. The Romanists have an extraordinary miracle of their own about St. Dennis, of whom they tell the lying legend that after his head was off he took it up in his hands and walked with it two thousand miles; whereupon, said a wit, "So far as the two thousand miles go, it is nothing at all; it is only the first step in which there is any difficulty." So I believe, if that is taken, all the rest can be easily accomplished. And if God does require of the sinner—dead in sin —that he should take the first step, then he requireth just that which renders salvation as impossible under the gospel as ever it was under the law, seeing man is as unable to believe as he is to obey, and is just as much without power to come to Christ as he is without power to go to heaven without Christ. The power must be given to him of the Spirit. He lieth dead in sin; the Spirit must quicken him. He is bound hand and foot and fettered by transgression; the Spirit must cut his bonds, and then he will leap to liberty. God must come and dash the iron bars out of their sockets, and then he can escape from the window, and make good his escape afterward; but unless the first thing be done for him, he must perish as surely under the gospel as he would have done under the law. I would cease to preach, if I believed that God, in the matter of salvation, required any thing whatever of man which he himself had not also engaged to furnish. For how many have I frequently hanging upon my lips of the worst of characters—men whose lives have become so horribly bad, that the lip of morality would refuse to give a description of their character? When I enter my pulpit am I to believe that these men are to do something before God's Spirit will operate upon them? If so, I should go there with a faint heart, feeling that I never could induce them to do the first part. But now I come to my pulpit with a sure confidence— God the Holy Spirit will meet with these men this morning. They are as bad as they can be; he will put a new thought into their hearts; he will give them new wishes; he will give them new wills, and those who hated Christ will desire to love him; those who once loved sin will, by God's divine Spirit, be made to hate it; and here is my confidence, that what they can not do, in that they are weak through the flesh, God sending his Spirit into their hearts will do for them, and in them, and so they shall be saved.

Well then, says one, that will make people sit still and fold their arms. Sir, it will not. But if men did so I could not help it; my business, as I have often said in this place before, is not to prove to you the reasonableness of any truth, nor to defend any truth from its consequences; all I do here, and I mean to keep to it, is just to assert the truth, because it is in the Bible; then, if you do not like it, you must settle the quarrel with my Master, and if you think it unreasonable, you must quarrel with the Bible. Let others defend Scripture and prove it to be true; they can do their work better than I could; mine is just the mere work of proclaiming. I am the messenger; I tell the Master's message; if you do not like the message, quarrel with the Bible, not with me; so long as I have Scripture on my side I will dare and defy you to do any thing against me. " Salvation is of the Lord." The Lord has to apply it, to make the unwilling willing, to make the ungodly godly, and bring the vile rebel to the feet of Jesus, or else salvation will never be accomplished. Leave that one thing undone, and you have broken the link of the chain, the rery link which was just necessary to its integrity. Take away the fact that God begins the good work, and that he sends us what the old divines call preventing grace—take that away, and you have spoilt the whole of salvation; you have just taken the key-stone out of the arch, and down it tumbles. There is nothing left then.

And now on the next point we shall a little disagree again. " Salvation is of the Lord," *as the sustaining of the work in any man's heart.* When a man is made a child of God he does not have a stock of grace given to him with which to go on for ever, but he has grace for that day; and he must have grace for the next day, and grace for the next, and grace for the next, until days shall end, or else the beginning shall be of no avail. As a man does not make himself spiritually alive, so neither can he keep himself so. He can feed on spiritual food, and so preserve his spiritual strength; he can walk in the commandments of the Lord, and so enjoy rest and peace, but still the inner life is dependent upon the Spirit as much for its after existence as for its first begetting. I do verily believe that if it should ever be my lot to put my foot upon the golden threshold of Paradise, and put this thumb upon the pearly latch, I should never cross the threshold unless I had grace given me to take that last step whereby I might enter heaven. No man of himself, even when converted, hath any power, except as that power is daily, constantly, and perpetually infused into him by the Spirit. But Christians often set up for independent gentlemen; they get a little stock of grace in hand, and they say, " My mountain standeth firm, I shall never be moved." But ah ! it is not long before the manna begins to be putrid. It was only meant to be the manna for the day, and we have kept it for the morrow, and therefore it fails us. We must have fresh grace.

> " For day by day the manna fell;
> O to learn that lesson well."

So look day by day for fresh grace. Frequently too the Christian wants to have grace enough for a month vouchsafed to him in one moment. " O !" he says, " what a host of troubles I have coming—how shall I meet them all ? O ! that I had grace enough to bear me through them all !" My dear friends, you will have grace enough for your troubles, as they come one by one. "As thy days, so shall thy strength be;" but thy strength shall never be as thy months, or as thy weeks. Thou shalt have thy strength as thou hast thy bread. "Give us this day our daily bread." Give us this day our daily grace. But why is it you will be troubling yourself about the things of to-morrow? The common people say, "Cross a bridge when you come to it." That is good advice. Do the same. When a trouble comes, attack it, and down with it, and master it; but do not begin now to forestall your woes. "Ah! but I have so many," says one. Therefore I say, do not look further before thee than thou needest. "Sufficient unto the day is the *evil* thereof." Do as the brave Grecian did, who, when he defended his country from Persia, did not go into the plains to fight, but stood in the narrow pass of Thermopylæ; there, when the myriads came to him, they had to come one by one, and he felled them to the earth. Had he ventured into the plain he would have been soon devoured, and his handfull would have been melted like a drop of dew in the sea. Stand in the narrow pass of to-day, and fight thy troubles one by one; but do not rush into the plains of to-morrow, for there thou wilt be routed and killed. As the evil is sufficient so will the grace be. "Salvation is of the Lord."

But, lastly, upon this point. *The ultimate perfection of salvation is of the Lord.* Soon, soon, the saints of earth shall be saints in light; their hairs of snowy age shall be crowned with perpetual joy and everlasting youth; their eyes suffused with tears shall be made bright as stars, never to be clouded again by sorrow; their hearts that tremble now are to be made joyous and fast, and set for ever like pillars in the temple of God. Their follies, their burdens, their griefs, their woes, are soon to be over; sin is to be slain, corruption is to be removed, and a heaven of spotless purity and of unmingled peace is to be theirs for ever. But it must still be by grace. As was the foundation such must the top-stone be; that which laid on earth the first beginning must lay in heaven the top-most stone. As they were redeemed from their filthy conversation by grace, so they must be redeemed from death and the grave by grace too, and they must enter heaven singing

> " Salvation of the Lord alone ;
> Grace is a shoreless sea."

There may be Arminians here, but they will not be Arminians there; they may here say, "It is of the will of the flesh," but in heaven they shall not think so. Here they may ascribe some little to the creature ; but there they shall cast their crowns at the Redeemer's feet, and acknowledge that he did it all. Here they may sometimes look a little at themselves, and boast somewhat of their own strength ; but there, " Not unto us, not unto us," shall be sung with deeper sincerity and with more profound emphasis than they have even sung it here below. In heaven, when grace shall have done its work, this truth shall stand out in blazing letters of gold, "Salvation is of the Lord."

II. Thus I have tried to expound the gospel. Now shall I show you HOW GOD HAS HEDGED THIS DOCTRINE ABOUT.

Some have said salvation in some cases is the result of *natural temperament*. Well, sir, well; God has effectually answered your argument. You say that some people are saved because they are naturally religious and inclined to be good ; unfortunately I have never met with any of that class of persons yet ; but I will suppose for a moment that there are such people. God has unanswerably met your objection ; for, strange to say, the great number of those who are saved are just the most unlikely people in the world to have been saved, while a great number of those who perish were once just the very people whom, if natural disposition had any thing to do with it, we should have expected to see in heaven. Why, there is one here who in his youth was a child of many follies. Often did his mother weep over him, and cry and groan over her son's wanderings ; for what with a fierce high spirit that could brook neither bit nor bridle, what with perpetual rebellions and ebullitions of hot anger, she said, " My son, my son, what wilt thou be in thy riper years? Surely thou wilt dash in pieces law and order, and be a disgrace to thy father's name." He grew up ; in youth he was wild and wanton, but, wonder of wonders, on a sudden he became a new man changed, altogetl.er changed; no more like what he was before than angels are like lost spirits. He sat at her feet, he cheered her heart, and the lost, fiery one became gentle, mild, humble as a little child, and obedient to God's commandments. You say, wonder of wonders! But there is another here He was a fair youth: when but a child he talked of Jesus; often when his mother had him on her knee he asked her questions about heaven; he was a prodigy, a wonder of piety in his youth. As he grew up, the tear rolled down his cheek under any sermon; he could scarcely bear to hear of death without a sigh; sometimes his mother caught him, as she thought, in prayer alone. And what is he now? He has just this very morning come from sin; he has become the debauched desperate villain, has gone far into all manner of wickedness and lust, and sin, and has become more damnably corrupt than other men could have made him; only his own evil spirit, once confined, has now developed itself; he has learned to play the lion in his manhood, as once he played the fox in his youth. I do not know whether you have ever met with such a case; but it very frequently is so. I know I can say that in my congregation some abandoned wicked fellow has had his heart broken, and been led to weep, and has cried to God for mercy, and renounced his vile sin; whilst some fair maiden by his side hath heard the same sermon, and if there was a tear she brushed it away; she still continues just what she was, "without God and without hope in the world." God has taken the base things of the world, and has just picked his people out of the very roughest of men, in order that he may prove that it is not natural disposition, but that "salvation is of the Lord" alone.

Well, but some say, it is *the minister* they hear who converts men. Ah! that is a grand idea, full sure. No man but a fool would entertain it. I met with a man some time ago who assured me that he knew a minister who had a very large amount of converting power in him. Speaking of a great evangelist in America, he said, "That man, sir, has got the greatest quan tity of converting power I ever knew a man to have; and Mr. So-and-so in a neighboring town I think is second to him." At that time this converting power was being exhibited; two hundred persons were converted by the converting power of this second best, and joined to the church in a few months. I went to the place some time afterwards—it was in England—and I said, "How do your converts get on?" "Well," said he, "I can not say much about them." "How many out of those two hundred whom you received in a year ago stand fast?" "Well," he said, "I am afraid not many of them; we have turned seventy of them out for drunkenness already." "Yes," I said, "I thought so: that is the end of the grand experiment of converting power." If I could convert you all, any one else might unconvert you; what any man can do another man can undo; it is only what God does that is abiding.

No, my brethren; God has taken good care it shall never be said conversion is of man, for usually he blesses those who seem to be the most unlikely to be useful. I do not expect to see so many conversions in this place as I had a year ago, when I had far fewer hearers. Do you ask why? Why, a year ago I was abused by every body; to mention my name was to mention the name of the most abominable buffoon that lived. The mere utterance of it brought forth oaths and cursing; with many men it was a name of contempt, kicked about the street as a foot-ball; but then God gave me souls by hundreds, who were added to my church, and in one year it was my happiness to see not less than a thousand personally who had then been converted. I do not expect that now. My name is somewhat esteemed now, and the great ones of the earth think it no dishonor to sit at my feet; but this makes me fear lest my God should forsake me now that the world esteems me. I would rather be despised and slandered than aught else. This assembly that you think so grand and fine, I would readily part with, if by such a loss I could gain a greater blessing. "God has chosen the base things of the world;" and, therefore, I reckon that the more esteemed I may be, the worse is my position, so much the less expectation shall I have that God will bless me. He hath but his " treasure in earthen vessels, that the excellency of the power may be of God, and not of man." A poor minister began to preach once, and all the world spoke ill of him; but God blessed him. By-and-bye they turned round and petted him. He was the man—a wonder! God left him! It has often been the same. It is for us to recollect, in all times of popularity, that "Crucify him, crucify him" follows fast upon the heels of "Hosanna," and that the crowd to-day, if dealt faithfully with, may turn into the handful of to-morrow; for men ove not plain speaking. We should learn to be despised, earn to be contemned, learn to be slandered, and then we shall learn to be made useful by God. Down on my knees I have often fallen, with the hot sweat rising from my brow, under some fresh slander poured upon me; in an agony of grief my heart has been well-nigh broken; till at last I learned the art of bearing all and caring for none. And now my grief runneth in another line. It is just the opposite. I fear lest God should forsake me, to prove that he is the author of salvation, that it is not in the preacher, that it is not in the crowd, that it is not in the attention I can attract, but in God, and in God alone. And this thing I hope I can say from my heart: if to be made as the mire of the streets again, if to be the laughing-stock of fools and the song of the drunkard once more will make me more serviceable to my Master, and more useful to his cause, I will prefer it to all this multitude, or to all the applause that man could give. Pray for me, dear friends, pray for me, that God would still make me the means of the salvation of souls; for I fear he may say, "I will not help that man, lest the world should say *he* has done it," for "salvation is of the Lord," and so it must be, even to the world's end.

III. And now WHAT IS, WHAT SHOULD BE, THE INFLUENCE OF THIS DOCTRINE UPON MEN?

Why, first, with sinners, this doctrine is *a great battering ram against their pride.* I will give you a figure. The sinner in his natural estate reminds me of a man who has a strong and well-nigh impenetrable castle into which he has fled There is the outer moat; there is a second moat; there are the high walls; and then afterward there is the dungeon and keep, into which the sinner will retire. Now, the first moat that goes round the sinner's trusting place is his good works. "Ah!" he says, "I am as good as my neighbor; twenty shil-

ings in the pound down, ready money, I have always paid; I
am no sinner; 'I tithe mint and cummin;' a good respectable.
gentleman I am indeed." Well, when God comes to work
with him, to save him, he sends his army across the first moat;
and as they go througl it, the cry, "Salvation is of the Lord;"
and the moat is dried up, for if it be of the Lord, how can it
be of good works? But when that is done, he has a second
intrenchment—ceremonies. "Well," he says, "I will not trust
n my good works, but I have been baptized, I have been confirmed; do not I take the sacrament? That shall be my trust."
"Over the moat! Over the moat!" And the soldiers go
over again, shouting, "Salvation is of the Lord." The second
moat is dried up; it is all over with that. Now they come to
the next strong wall; the sinner, looking over it, says, "I can
repent, I can believe, whenever I like; I will save myself by
repenting and believing." Up come the soldiers of God, his
great army of conviction, and they batter this wall to the
ground, crying, "'Salvation is of the Lord.' Your faith and
your repentance must all be given you, or else you will neither
believe nor repent of sin." And now the castle is taken; the
man's hopes are all cut off; he feels that it is not of self; the
castle of self is overcome, and the great banner upon which
is written "Salvation is of the Lord" is displayed upon the
battlements. But is the battle over? O no; the sinner has
retired to the keep, in the center of the castle; and now he
changes his tactics. "I can not save myself," says he, "therefore I will despair; there is no salvation for me." Now this
second castle is as hard to take as the first, for the sinner sits
down and says, "I can't be saved, I must perish." But God
commands the soldiers to take this castle too, shouting, "Salvation *is* of the Lord;" though it is not of man, *it is of God ;*
"he is able to save, even to the uttermost," though you can
not save yourself. This sword, you see, cuts two ways; it cuts
pride down, and then it cleaves the skull of despair. If any
man say he can save himself, it halveth his pride at once; and
if another man say he can not be saved, it dasheth his despair
co the earth; for it affirms that he can be saved, seeing, "Salvation *is* of the Lord." That is the effect this doctrine has
upon the sinner may it have that effect on you!

But what influence has it upon the saint? Why, it is the keystone of all divinity. *I will defy you to be heterodox* if you believe this truth. You must be sound in the faith if you have learned to spell this sentence—"Salvation is of the Lord;" and if you feel it in your soul *you will not be proud;* you can not be; you will cast every thing at his feet, confessing that you have done nothing, save what he has helped you to do and therefore the glory must be where the salvation is. If you believe this *you will not be distrustful.* You will say, " My salvation does not depend on my faith, but on the Lord; my keeping does not depend on myself, but on God who keepeth me; my being brought to heaven rests not now in my own hands, but in the hands of God;" you will, when doubts and fears prevail, fold your arms, look upward and say,

> " And now my eye of faith is dim,
>   I trust in Jesus, sink or swim."

If you can keep this in your mind *you may always be joyful.* He can have no cause for trouble who knows and feels that his salvation is of God. Come on, legions of hell; come on, demons of the pit!

> " He that has helped me bears me through,
>   And makes me more than conqueror too."

Salvation resteth not on this poor arm, else should I despair, but on the arm of yon Omnipotent—that arm on which the pillars of the heavens do lean. " Whom should I fear? The Lord is my strength and my life; of whom shall I be afraid?"

And this, may by grace, *nerve you to work for God.* If you had to save your neighbors you might sit down and do nothing; but since "salvation is of the Lord," go on and prosper. Go and preach the gospel; go and tell the gospel everywhere. Tell it in your house, tell it in the street, tell it in every land and every nation; for it is not of yourself, it is " of the Lord." Why do not our friends go to Ireland to preach the gospel? Ireland is a disgrace to the Protestant church. Why do not they go and preach there? A year or so ago a number of our brave ministers went over there to preach; they did right bravely; they went there, and they came back again, and that is about the sum total of the glorious expedition against Popery. But why come back again? Because they were stoned, good easy men! Do they not think that the gospel ever will spread without a few stones? But they would have been killed! Brave martyrs they! Let them be enrolled in the red chronicle. Did the martyrs of old, did the apostles shrink from going to any country because they would have been killed? No, they were ready to die: and if half a dozen ministers had been killed in Ireland, it would have been the finest thing in the world for liberty in future; for after that the people dare not have touched us; the strong arm of the law would have put them down; we might have gone through every village of Ireland afterwards, and been at peace; the constabulary would soon have put an end to such infamous mur der; it would have awakened the Protestantism of England to claim the liberty which is our right there as we give it else- where. We shall never see any great change till we have some men in our ranks who are willing to be martyrs. That deep ditch can never be crossed till the bodies of a few of us shall fill it up; and after that it will be easy work to preach the gospel there. Our brethren should go there once more. They can leave their white cravats at home, and the white feather too, and go forth with a brave heart and a bold spirit; and if the people mock and scoff, let them mock and scoff on. George Whitefield said, when he preached on Kennington Common, where they threw dead cats and rotten eggs at him, " This is only the manure of Methodism, the best thing in the world to make it grow; throw away as fast as you please." And when a stone cut him on the forehead, he seemed to preach the better for a little blood-letting. O! for such a man to dare the mob, and then the mob would not need to be dared. Let us go there, recollecting that "salvation is of the Lord," and let us in every place and at every time preach God's Word, believing that God's Word is more than a match for nan's sin, and God will yet be master over all the earth.

My voice fails me again, and my thoughts too, I was weary this morning, when I came into this pulpit, and I am weary now. Sometimes I am joyous and glad, and feel in the pul- pit as if I could preach for ever; at other times I feel glad to close; but yet with such a text I would that I could have finished up with all the might that mortal lip could sun.mon. O! to let men know this, that their salvation is of God! Swearer, swear not against him in whose hand thy breath is! Despiser, despise not him who can save you or destroy you. And thou hypocrite, seek not to deceive him from whom salvation comes, and who therefore knows right well whether thy salvation come from him.

IV. And now in concluding, let me just tell you WHAT IS THE OBVERSE OF THIS TRUTH. Salvation is of God: then *damnation is of man.* If any of you are damned, you will have no one to blame but yourselves; if any of you perish, the blame will not lie at God's door; if you are lost and cast away, you will have to bear all the blame and all the tortures of conscience yourself; you will lie for ever in perdition, and reflect, " I have destroyed myself; I have made a suicide of my soul; I have been my own destroyer; I can lay no blame to God." Remember, if saved, you must be saved by God alone, though if lost you have lost yourselves. "Turn ye, turn ye why will ye die, O house of Israel." With my last faltering sentence I bid you stop and think. Ah! my hearers, my hearers! it is an awful thing to preach to such a mass as this. But the other Sunday, as I came down stairs, I was struck with a memorable sentence, uttered by one who stood there. He said, "There are 9000 people this morning without excuse in the day of judgment." I should like to preach so that this always might be said; and if I can not, O may God have mercy on me, for his name's sake! But now remember! Ye have souls; those souls will be damned, or saved. Which will it be? Damned they must be for ever, unless God shall save you; unless Christ shall have mercy upon you, there is no hope for you. Down on your knees! Cry to God for mercy. Now lift up your heart in prayer to God. May now be the very time when you shall be saved. Or ever the next drop of blood shall run through your veins, may you find peace! Remember, that peace is to be had now. If you feel now your need of it, it is to be had now. And how? For the mere asking for it. "Ask, and it shall be given you; seek, and ye shall find."

Bɪt if your ears refuse
  The language of his grace,
Your hearts grow hard, like stubborn Jews,
  That unbelieving race,

The Lord with vengeance drest,
  Shall lift his hand and swear,
You that despised my promised rest
  Shall have no portion there."

O! that ye may not be despisers, lest ye " wonder and perish!" May ye now fly to Christ, and be accepted in the beloved. It is my last best prayer. May the Lord hear it!
Amen.

SERMON XIV

REGENERATION

"Except a man be born again, he can not see the kingdom of God." — JOHN, iii. 3

In daily life our thoughts are most occupied with things that are most necessary for our existence. No one murmured that the subject of the price of bread was frequently on the lips of men at a time of scarcity, because they felt that the subject was one of vital importance to the mass of the population, and therefore they murmured not, though they listened to continual declamatory speeches, and read perpetual articles in the newspapers concerning it. I must offer the same excuse, then, for bringing before you this morning the subject of regeneration. It is one of absolute and vital importance; it is the hinge of the gospel; it is the point upon which most Christians are agreed, yea, all who are Christians in sincerity and truth. It is a subject which lies at the very basis of salvation. It is the very groundwork of our hopes for heaven; and as we ought to be very careful of the basement of our structure, so should we be very diligent to take heed that we are really born again, and that we have made sure work of it for eternity. There are many who fancy they are born again who are not. It well becomes us, then, frequently to examine ourselves; and it is the minister's duty to bring forward those subjects which lead to self-examination, and have a tendency to search the heart and try the reins of the children of men.

To proceed at once, I shall first make some remarks upon *the new birth ;* secondly, I shall note *what is meant by not being able to see the kingdom of God if we are not born again ;* then I shall go further on to note *why it is that " except a are born again we can not see the kingdom of God ;"* and then *expostulate with men* as God's ambassador before I close.

I. First, then, THE MATTER OF REGENERATION. In endeavoring to explain it, I must have you notice, first of all, *the figure that is employed.* It is said a man must be born again. I can not lllustrate this better than by supposing a case. Suppose that in England there should be a law passed, that admission to royal courts, preference in office, and any privileges that might belong to the nation, could only be given to persons who were born in England—suppose that birth in this land was made a *sine qua non,* and it was definitely declared that whatever men might do or be, unless they were native born subjects of England they could not enter into her maj esty's presence, and could enjoy none of the emoluments or offices of the state, nor any of the privileges of citizens. I think if you suppose such a case I shall be able to illustrate the difference between any changes and reforms that men make in themselves and the real work of being born again. We will suppose, then, that some man—a red Indian, for instance—should come to this country, and should endeavor to obtain the privileges of citizenship, well knowing that the rule is absolute and can not be altered, that a man must be a born subject, or else he can not enjoy them. Suppose he says, " *I will change my name,* I will take up the name of an Englishman ; I have been called by my high-sounding title among the Sioux ; I have been called the son of the Great Westwind, or some such name ; but I will take an English name, I will be called a Christian man, an English subject." Will that admit him ? You see him coming to the palace gates and asking for admission. He says, " I have taken an English name." " But are you an Englishman born and bred ?" " I am not," says he. " Then the gates must be shut against you, for the law is absolute ; and though you may have the name of even the royal family itself upon you, yet because you have not been born here you must be shut out." That illustration will apply to all of us who are here present. At least, nearly the whole of us bear the professing Christian name ; living in England, you would think it a disgrace to you if you were not called Christian. You are not heathen, you are not infidel ; you are neither Mohammedans nor Jews; you think that the name, Christian, is a creditable one to you, and you have taken it. Be ye quite assured that the name of a Christian is not the nature of a Christian, and that your being born in a Christian land, and being recognized as professing the Christian religion is of no avail whatever, unless there be something more added to it—the being born again as a subject of Jesus Christ.

"But," says this red Indian, "I am prepared to *renounce my dress*, and to become an Englishman in fashion; in fact, I will go to the very top of the fashion; you shall not see me in any thing differing from the accepted style of the present day. May I not, when I am arrayed in court dress, and have decorated myself as etiquette demands, come in before her majesty? See, I'll doff this plume, I will not shake this tomahawk, I renounce these garments. The moccasin I cast away for ever; I am an Englishman in dress, as well as name." He comes to the gate, dressed out like one of our own countrymen; but the gates are still shut in his face, because the law required that he must be born in the country; and without that, whatever his dress might be, he could not enter the palace. So how many there are of you, who do not barely take the Christian name upon you, but have adopted Christian manners; you go to your churches and your chapels, you attend the house of God, you take care that there is some form of religion observed in your family; your children are not left without hearing the name of Jesus! So far so good; God forbid that I should say a word against it! But remember, it is bad because you do not go further. All this is of no avail whatever for admitting you into the kingdom of heaven, unless this also is complied with—the being born again. O! dress yourselves never so grandly with the habiliments of godliness; put the chaplet of benevolence upon your brow, and gird your loins with integrity; put on your feet the shoes of perseverance, and walk through the earth an honest and upright man; yet, remember, unless you are born again, "that which is of the flesh is flesh," and you, not having the operations of the Spirit in you, still have heaven's gates shut against you, because you are not born again.

"Well," but says the Indian, "I will not only adopt the

dress, but I will *learn the language ;* I will put away my brogue and my language that I once spoke, in the wild prairie or in the woods, far away from my lips. I shall not talk of the Shu-Shuh-gah, and of the strange names wherewith I have called my wild fowl and my deer, but I will speak as you speak, and act as you act; I will not only have your dress, but precisely your manners, I will talk just in the same fashion, I will adopt your brogue, I will take care that it shall be grammatically correct; will you not then admit me? I have become thoroughly Englishized; may I not then be received?" "No," says the keeper of the door, "there is no admittance; for except a man be born in this country, he can not be admitted." So with some of you; you talk just like Christians. Perhaps you have a little too much cant about you; you have begun so strictly to imitate what you think to be a godly man, that you go a little beyond the mark, and you gloss it so much that we are able to detect the counterfeit. Still you pass current among most men as being a right down sort of Christian man. You have studied biographies, and sometimes you tell long yarns about divine experience; you have borrowed them from the biographies of good men; you have been with Christians, and know how to talk as they do; you have caught a puritanical twang, perhaps; you go through the world just like professors; and if you were to be observed, no one would detect you. You are a member of the church; you have been baptized; you take the Lord's Supper; perhaps you are a deacon, or an elder; you pass the sacramental cup round; you are just all that a Christian can be, except that you are without a Christian heart. You are whitewashed sepulchres, still full of rottenness within, though garnished fairly on the outside. Well, take heed, take heed! It is an astonishing thing, how near the painter can go to the expression of life, and yet the canvas is dead and motionless; and it is equally astonishing how near a man may go to a Christian, and yet, through not being born again, the absolute rule shuts him out of heaven; and with all his profession, with all the trappings of his professed godliness, and with all the gorgeous plumes of experience, yet must he be borne away from heaven's gates.

You are uncharitable Mr. Spurgeon. I do not care what

you say about that I never wish to be more charitable **than** Christ. I did not say this; Christ said it. If you have **any** quarrel with him, settle it there; I am not the maker of **this** truth, but simply the speaker of it. I find it written, "**Except** a man be born again, he can not see the kingdom of God." I₁ your footman should go to the door, and deliver your message correctly, the man at the door might abuse him never so much, but the footman would say, "Sir, d, not abuse me, I can not help it; I can only tell you what my master told me. I am not the originator of it." So if you think me uncharitable, remember you do not accuse me, you accuse Christ; you are not finding fault with the messenger, you are finding fault with the message; Christ has said it—" Except a man be born again." I can not dispute with you, and shall not try. That is simply God's Word. Reject it at your peril. Believe it and receive it, I entreat you, because it comes from the lips of the Most High.

But now note *the manner in which this regeneration is obtained*. I think I have none here so profoundly stupid as to be Puseyites I can scarcely believe that I have been the means of attracting one person here, so utterly devoid of every remnant of brain, as to believe the doctrine of baptismal regeneration. Yet I must just hint at it. There be some who teach that by a few drops of water sprinkled on an infant's brow the infant becomes regenerate. Well, granted. And now I will find out your regenerate ones twenty years afterward. The champion of the prize ring is a regenerated man. O ! yes, he was regenerated, because in infancy he was baptized; and, therefore, if all infants in baptism are regenerated, the prize-fighter is a regenerated man. Take hold of him and receive him as your brother in the Lord. Do you hear that man swearing and blaspheming God ? He is regenerate; believe me, he is regenerate; the priest put a few drops of water on his brow, and he is a regenerated man. Do you see the drunkard reeling down the street, the pest of the neighborhood, fighting every body, and beating his wife, worse than the brute. Well, he is regenerate, he is one of those Puseyite's regenerates—O ! goodly regenerate ! Mark you the crowd assembled in the streets ! The gallows is erected,

Palmer is about to be executed; the man whose name should be execrated through all eternity for his villainy! Here is one of the Puseyite's regenerates. Yes, he is regenerate because he was baptized in infancy; regenerate, while he mixes his strychnine; regenerate while he administers his poison slowly, that he may cause death, and infinite pain, all the while he is causing it. Regenerate, forsooth! If that be regeneration, such regeneration is not worth having; if that be the thing that makes us free of the kingdom of heaven, verily, the gospel is indeed a licentious gospel; we can say nothing about it. If that be the gospel, that all such men are regenerate and will be saved, we can only say, that it would be the duty of every man in the world to move that gospel right away, because it is so inconsistent with the commonest principles of morality, that it could not possibly be of God, but of the devil.

But some say all are regenerate when they are baptized. Well, if you think so, stick to your own thoughts; I can not help it. Simon Magus was certainly one exception; he was baptized on a profession of his faith; but so far from being regenerated by his baptism, we find Paul saying, " I perceive that thou art in the gall of bitterness, and in the bond of iniquity." And yet he was one of those regenerates, because he had been baptized. Ah! that doctrine only needs to be stated to sensible men, and they will at once reject it. Gentlemen that are fond of a filagree religion, and like ornament and show; gentlemen of the high Beau Brummel school will very likely prefer this religion, because they have cultivated their taste at the expense of their brain, and have forgotten that what is consistent with the sound judgment of a man can not be consistent with the Word of God. So much for the first point.

Neither is a man regenerated, we say, in the next place, *by his own exertions*. A man may reform himself very much, and that is well and good; let all do that. A man may cast away many vices, forsake many lusts in which he indulged, and conquer evil habits; but no man in the world can make himself to be born in God; though he should struggle never so much, he could never accomplish what is beyond his power

And, mark you, if he could make himself to be born again, still he would not enter heaven, because there is another point in the condition which he would have violated—"unless a man be born of the *Spirit*, he can not see the kingdom of God." So that the best exertions of the flesh do not reach this high point, the being born again of the Spirit of God.

And now we must say, that regeneration consists in this God the Holy Spirit, in a supernatural manner—mark, by the word supernatural I mean just what it strictly means; supernatural, more than natural—works upon the hearts of men, and they by the operations of the divine Spirit become regenerate men; but without the Spirit they never can be regenerated. And unless God the Holy Spirit, who "worketh in us to will and to do," should operate upon the will and the conscience, regeneration is an absolute impossibility, and therefore so is salvation. "What!" says one, "do you mean to say that God absolutely interposes in the salvation of every man to make him regenerate?" I do indeed; in the salvation of every person there is an actual putting forth of the divine power, whereby the dead sinner is quickened, the unwilling sinner is made willing, the desperately hard sinner has his conscience made tender; and he who rejected God and despised Christ, is brought to cast himself down at the feet of Jesus. This is called fanatical doctrine, mayhap; that we can not help; it is scriptural doctrine, that is enough for us. " Except a man be born of the Spirit he can not see the kingdom of God; that which is born of the flesh is flesh, and that which is born of the Spirit is spirit." If you like it not, quarrel with my Master, not with me; I do but simply declare his own revelation, that there must be in your heart something more than you can ever work there. There must be a divine operation; call it a miraculous operation, if you please; it is in some sense so. There must be a divine interposition, a divine working, a divine influence, or else, do what you may, without that you perish, and are undone; "for except a man be born again, he can not see the kingdom of God." The change is radical; it gives us new natures, makes us love what we hated and hate what we loved, sets us in a new road; makes our habits different, our thoughts different, makes us

different i1 private, and different in public. So that being in
Christ it is fulfilled : " If any man be in Christ he is a new
creature ; old things are passed away, behold all things are
become new."

II. And now I must come to the second point. I trust I have
explained regeneration, so that all may see what it is. Now
WHAT DOES THE EXPRESSION, " SEEING THE KINGDOM OF GOD,"
MEAN ? It means two things. To see the kingdom of God on
earth is to be a member of the mystical church—it is to enjoy
the liberty and privileges of the child of God. To see the
kingdom of heaven means to have power in prayer, to have
communion with Christ, to have fellowship with the Holy
Ghost ; and to bring forth and produce all those joyous and
blessed fruits which are the effect of regeneration. In a
higher sense, " to see the kingdom of God," means to be admitted into heaven. Except a man be born again, he can not
know about heavenly things on earth, and he can not enjoy
heavenly blessings for ever—" he can not see the kingdom of
God."

III. I think I may just pass over the second point without
remark, and proceed to notice, in the third place, WHY IT IS
THAT " UNLESS A MAN BE BORN AGAIN, HE CAN NOT SEE THE
KINGDOM OF GOD." And I will confine my remarks to the
kingdom of God in the world to come.

Why, he can not see the kingdom of God, because *he would
be out of place in heaven*. A man that is not born again could
not enjoy heaven. There is an actual impossibility in his nature, which prevents him from enjoying any of the bliss of
Paradise. You think, mayhap, that heaven consists in those
walls of jewels, in those pearly gates, and gates of gold ; not
so, that is the habitation of heaven. Heaven dwells there,
but that is not heaven. Heaven is a state that is made here,
that is made in the heart ; made by God's Spirit within us,
and unless God the Spirit has renewed us, and caused us to be
born again, we can not enjoy the things of heaven. Why, it
is a physical impossibility that ever a swine should deliver a
lecture on astronomy ; every man will clearly perceive that it
must be impossible that a snail should build a city ; and there
is just as much impossibility that a sinner unmended, should

enjoy heaven. Why, there would be nothing there for him to enjoy; if he could be put into the place where heaven is, he would be miserable; he would cry, "Let me away, let me away; let me away from this miserable place!" I appeal to yourselves; a sermon is too long for you very often; the singing of God's praises is dull, dry work; you think that going up to God's house is very tedious. What will you do where they praise God day without night? If just a short discourse here is very wearying, what will you think of the eternal talkings of the redeemed through all ages of the wonders of redeeming love? If the company of the righteous is very irksome to you, what will be their company throughout eternity? I think many of you are free to confess that psalm-singing is not a bit to your taste, that you care naught about any spiritual things; give you your bottle of wine, and set you down at your ease, that is heaven for you! Well, there is no such a heaven yet made; and therefore there is no heaven for you. The only heaven there is, is the heaven of spiritual men, the heaven of praise, the heaven of delight in God, the heaven of acceptance in the beloved the heaven of communion with Christ. Now, you do not understand any thing about this; you could not enjoy it if you were to have it; you have not the capabilities for doing so. You, yourselves, from the very fact of your not being born again, are your own barrier to heaven, and if God were to open the gate wide, and say, "Come in," you could not enjoy heaven, if you were admitted; for unless a man be born again, there is an impossibility, a moral impossibility, of his seeing the kingdom of God. Suppose there are some persons here who are entirely deaf, who have never heard sounds; well, I say they can not hear singing. Do I when I say it, say a cruel thing? It is their own disability that prevents them. So when God says you can not see the kingdom of heaven, he means that it is your own disability for the enjoyment of heaven, that will prevent you ever entering there.

But there are some other reasons; there are reasons why

> "Those holy gates for ever bar
> Pollution, sin, and shame."

There are reasons, besides those in yourselves, why you can not see the kingdom of God, unless you are born again. *Ask yon spirits* before the throne: "Angels, principalities, and powers, would ye be willing that men who love not God, who believe not in Christ, who have not been born again, should dwell here?" I see them, as they look down upon us, and hear them answering, "No! Once we fought the dragon, and expelled him because he tempted us to sin; we must not and we will not, have the wicked here. These alabaster walls must not be soiled with black and lustful fingers; the white pavement of heaven must not be stained and rendered filthy by the unholy feet of ungodly men. No!" I see a thousand spears bristling, and the fiery faces of a myriad seraphs thrust over the walls of Paradise. "No, while these arms have strength, and these wings have power, no sin shall ever enter here." I address myself moreover to the saints in heaven, re deemed by sovereign grace: "Children of God, are ye willing that the wicked should enter heaven as they are, without being born again? Ye love men, say, say, say, are ye willing that they should be admitted as they are?" I see Lot rise up, and he cries, "Admit them into heaven! No! What! must I be vexed with the conversation of Sodomites again, as once I was?" I see Abraham; and he comes forward, and he says, "No; I can not have them here. I had enough of them while I was with them on earth—their jests and jeers, their silly talkings, their vain conversation, vexed and grieved us. We want them not here." And, heavenly though they be, and loving as their spirits are, yet there is not a saint in heaven who would not resent with the utmost indignation the approach of any one of you to the gates of paradise, if you are still unholy, and have not been born again.

But all that were nothing. We might perhaps scale the ramparts of heaven, if they were only protected by angels, and burst the gates of paradise open, if only the saints de- fended them. But there is another reason than that—*God has said it himself*—"Except a man be born again, he can not see the kingdom of God." What sinner, wilt thou scale the battlements of paradise when God is ready to thrust thee down to hell? Wilt thou with impudent face brazen him out?

God has said it, God hath said it, with a voice of thunder, "Ye shall not see the kingdom of heaven." Can ye wrestle with the Almighty? Can ye overthrow Omnipotence? Can ye grapple with the Most High? Worm of the dust! canst thou overcome thy Maker? Trembling insect of an hour, shaken by the lightnings when far overhead they flash far athwart the sky, wilt thou dare the hand of God? Wilt thou venture to defy him to his face? Ah! he would laugh at thee. As the snow melteth before the sun, as wax runneth at the fierceness of the fire, so wouldst thou, if his fury should once lay hold of thee. Think not that thou canst overcome him. He has sealed the gate of Paradise against thee, and there is no entrance. The God of justice says, "I will not reward the wicked with the righteous; I will not suffer my goodly, godly Paradise to be stained by wicked ungodly men. If they turn I will have mercy upon them; but if they turn not, as I live, I will rend them in pieces, and there shall be none to deliver." Now, sinner, canst thou brazen it out against him! Wilt thou rush upon the thick bosses of Jehovah's bucklers? Wilt thou try to scale his heaven when his arrow is stringed upon the bow to reach thine heart? What! when the glittering sword is at thy neck and ready to slay thee? Wilt thou endeavor to strive against thy Maker? No potsherd, no; contend with thy fellow potsherd. Go, crawling grasshopper; go, fight with thy brothers; strive with them, but come not against the Almighty. He hath said it, and you never shall, you never shall enter heaven, unless you are born again. Again, I say, quarrel not with me; I have but delivered my Master's message. Take it, disbelieve it if you dare; but if you believe it, rail not at me, for it is God's message, and I speak in love to your soul, lest, lacking it, you should perish in the dark, and walk blindfold to your everlasting perdition.

IV. Now, my friends, A LITTLE EXPOSTULATION WITH YOU; and then farewell. I hear one man say, "Well, well, well, I see it. *I will hope that I shall be born again after I am dead.*" O, sir, believe me, you will be a miserable fool for your pains. When men die their state is fixed.

> " Fixed as their everlasting state,
>   Could they repent, 'tis now too late."

Our life is like that wax melting in the flame ; death puts its stamp on it, and then it cools, and the impress never can be changed. You to day are like the burning metal running forth from the cauldron in the mold ; death cools you in your mold, and you are cast in that shape throughout eternity. The voice of doom crieth over the dead, " He that is holy let him be holy still ; he that is unjust let him be unjust still ; he that is filthy, let him be filthy still." The damned are lost for ever ; they can not be born again ; they go on cursing, ever being cursed ; ever fighting against God, and ever being trampled beneath his feet ; they go on ever mocking, ever being laughed at for their mockery ; ever rebelling and ever being tortured with the whips of conscience, because they are ever sinning. They can not be regenerated because they are dead.

" Well," says another, " *I will take care that I am regenerated first before I die.*" Sir, I repeat again, thou art a fool in talking thus ; how knowest thou that thou shalt live ? Hast thou taken a lease of thy life, as thou hast of thy house ? Canst thou insure the breath within thy nostrils ? Canst thou say in certainty that another ray of light shall ever reach thine eye ? Canst thou be sure that, as thine heart is beating a funeral march to the grave, thou wilt not soon beat the last note ; and so thou shalt die where thou standest or sittest now ? O, man ! if thy bones were iron, and thy sinews brass, and thy lungs steel, then mightest thou say, " I shall live." But thou art made of dust ; thou art like the flower of the field ; thou mayest die now. Lo ! I see death standing yonder, moving to and fro the stone of time upon his scythe, to sharpen it ; to-day, to-day, for some of you he grasps the scythe—and away, away, he mows the fields, and you fall one by one. You must not, and you can not live. God carries us away as a flood, like a ship in a whirlpool ; like the log in a current, dashed onward to the cataract. There is no stopping any one of us ; we are all dying now ! and yet you say you will be regenerated ere you die ! Ay sirs, but are you regenerated now ? For if not, it may be too late to hope for to

morrow. To-morrow you may be in hell, sealed up for ever
by adamantine destiny, which never can be moved.

"Well," cries another, "*I do not care much about it ;* for
I see very little in being shut out of Paradise." Ah, sir, it is
because thou dost not understand it. Thou smilest at it now ;
but there will be a day when thy conscience will be tender,
when thy memory will be strong, when thy judgment will be
enlightened, and when thou wilt think very differently from
what thou dost now. Sinners in hell are not the fools they are
on earth ; in hell they do not laugh at everlasting burnings ;
in the pit they do not despise the words "eternal fire." The
worm that never dieth, when it is gnawing, gnaws out all joke
and laughter ; you may despise God now, and despise me now,
for what I say, but death will change your note. O, my
hearers, if that were all, I would be willing. You may despise
me, yes, you may ; but O! I beseech you, do not despise yourselves ; O! be not so fool-hardy as to go whistling to hell, and
laughing to the pit ; for when you are there, sirs, you will find
it a different thing from what you dream it to be now. When
you see the gates of Paradise shut against you, you will find it
to be a more important matter than you judge of now. You
came to hear me preach to-day, as you would have gone to the
opera or play-house ; you thought I should amuse you. Ah!
that is not my aim, God is my witness, I came here solemnly
in earnest, to wash my hands of your blood. If you are
damned, any one of you, it shall not be because I did not warn
you. Men and women, if ye perish, my hands are washed in
innocency ; I have told you of your doom. I again cry, repent, repent, repent, for "unless ye repent ye shall all likewise
perish." I came here determined this morning, if I must use
rough words, to use them ; to speak right on against men, and
for men too ; for the things we say against you now are really
for your good. We do but warn you, lest you perish. But ah!
I hear one of you saying, "I do not understand this mystery ;
pray explain it to me." Fool, fool, that thou art ; do you see
that fire ? We are startled up from our beds, the light is at
the window ; we rush down stairs ; people are hurrying to and
fro ; the street is trampled thick with crowds : they are rushing toward the house, which is in a burst of flame. The fire-

men are at their work ; a stream of water is pouring upon the house ; but hark ye ! hark ye ! there is a man up stairs; there is a man in the top room ; there is just time for him to escape, and barely. A shout is raised—" Aho ! fire ! fire ! fire ! aho !" —but the man does not make his appearance at the window. See, the ladder is placed against the walls ; it is up to the window sill—a strong hand dashes in the casement ! What is the man after, all the while ? What ! is he tied down in his bed ? Is he a cripple ? Has some fiend got hold of him, and nailed him to the floor ? No, no, no ; he feels the boards getting hot beneath his feet, the smoke is stifling him, the flame is burning all around, he knows there is but one way of escape, by that ladder ! What is he doing ? He is sitting down— no, you can not believe me—he is sitting down and saying, " The origin of this fire is very mysterious ; I wonder how it is to be discovered ; how shall we understand it ?" Why, you laugh at him ! You are laughing at yourselves. You are seeking to have this question and that question answered, when your soul is in peril of eternal life ! O ! when you are saved, it will be time then to ask questions; but while you are now in the burning house, and in danger of destruction, it is not your time to be puzzling yourselves about free will, fixed fate, predestination absolute. All these questions are good and well enough afterward for those that are saved. Let the man on shore try to find out the cause of the storm ; your only business now is to ask, " What must I do to be saved ? And how can I escape from the great damnation that awaiteth me ?"

But ah ! my friends, I can not speak as I wish. I think I feel, this morning, something like Dante, when he wrote his " *Il Inferno*." Men said of him that he had been in hell ; he looked like it. He had thought of it so long, that they said, " He has been in hell," he spoke with such an awful earnestness. Ah ! if I could, I would speak like that too. It is only a few days more, and I shall meet you face to face ; I can look over the lapse of a few years, when you and I shall stand face to face before God's bar. " Watchman, watchman," saith a voice, " didst thou warn them ? didst thou warn them ?" Will any of you then say I did not ? No, even the most abandoned of you will, at that day, say, "We laughed, we scoffed at it, we cared not for it; but. O Lord, we are obliged to speak the truth; the man was in earnest about it; he told us of our doom, and he is clear." Will you say so? I know you will.

But yet this one remark—to be cast out of heaven is an awful thing. Some of you have parents there; you have dear friends there; they grasped your hand in death, and said, "Farewell, until we meet you." But if you never see the kingdom of God, you can never see them again. "My mother," says one, "sleeps in the graveyard; I often go to the tomb and put some flowers upon it, in remembrance of her who nursed me; but must I never see her again?" No, never again; no, never, unless you are born again. Mothers, you have had infants that have gone to heaven; you would like to see your family all around the throne; but you will never see your children more, unless you are born again. Will you bid adieu this day to the immortal? Will you say farewell this hour to your glorified friends in Paradise? You must say so, or else be converted. You must fly to Christ, and trust in him, and his Spirit must renew you, or else you must look up to heaven, and say, "Choir of the blest! I shall never hear you sing; parents of my youth, guardians of my infancy, I love you, but between you and myself there is a great gulf fixed; I am cast away, and you are saved." O, I beseech you, think on these matters; and when you go away, let it not be to for-get what I have said. If you are at all impressed this morn-ing, put not away the impression; it may be your last warn-ing; it will be a sorrowful thing to be lost with the notes of the gospel in your ears, and to perish under the ministry of truth.

SERMON XV

SPIRITUAL RESURRECTION

"And you hath he quickened, who were dead in trespasses and sins."—
EPHESIANS, ii. 1

IT might naturally be expected that I should have selected
the topic of the resurrection on what is usually called the
Easter Sabbath. I shall not do so ; for although I have read
portions which refer to that glorious subject, I have had
pressed on my mind a subject which is not the resurrection of
Christ, but which is in some measure connected with it—the
resurrection of lost and ruined man by the Spirit of God in
this life.

The apostle is here speaking, you will observe, of the church
at Ephesus, and, indeed, of all those who were chosen in Christ
Jesus, accepted in him, and redeemed with his blood ; and he
says of them, "You hath he quickened, who were dead in
trespasses and sins."

What a solemn sight is presented to us by a dead body !
When last evening trying to realize the thought, it utterly
overcame me. The thought is overwhelming, that soon this
body of mine must be a carnival for worms ; that in and out
of these places, where my eyes are glistening, foul things, the
offspring of loathsomeness, shall crawl ; that this body must be
stretched in still, cold, abject, passive death, must then become a noxious, nauseous thing, cast out even by those that
loved me, who will say, "Bury my dead out of my sight."
Perhaps you can scarcely, in the moment I can afford you, appropriate the idea to yourselves. Does it not seem a strange
thing, that you, who have walked to this place this morning,
shall be carried to your graves ; that the eyes with which you
now behold me shall soon be glazed in everlasting darkness ,

that the tongues, which just now moved in song, shall soon
be silent lumps of clay; and that your strong and stalwart
frame, now standing in this place, will soon be unable to move
a muscle, and become a loathsome thing, the brother of the
worm and the sister of corruption? You can scarcely get
hold of the idea; death doth such awful work with us, it is
such a Vandal with this mortal fabric, it so rendeth to pieces
this fair thing that God hath builded up, that we can scarcely
bear to contemplate his works of ruin.

Now, endeavor, as well as you can, to get the idea of a
corpse, and when you have so done, please to understand,
that that is the metaphor employed in my text to set forth
the condition of your soul by nature. Just as the body is
dead, incapable, unable, unfeeling, and soon about to become
corrupt and putrid, so are we if we be unquickened by divine
grace; dead in trespasses and sins, having within us death,
which is capable of developing itself in worse and worse stages
of sin and wickedness, until all of us here, left by God's grace,
should become loathsome beings; loathsome through sin and
wickedness, even as the corpse through natural decay. Understand, that the doctrine of the holy Scripture is, that man
by nature, since the fall, is dead; he is a corrupt and ruined
thing; in a spiritual sense, utterly and entirely dead. And if
any of us shall come to spiritual life, it must be by the quickening of God's Spirit, vouchsafed to us sovereignly through
the good will of God the Father, not for any merits of our
own, but entirely of his own abounding and infinite grace.

Now, this morning, I trust I shall not be tedious; I shall
endeavor to make the subject as interesting as possible, and
also endeavor to be brief. The general doctrine of this
morning is, that every man that is born into the world is dead
spiritually, and that spiritual life must be given by the Holy
Spirit, and can be obtained from no other source. That general doctrine, I shall illustrate in rather a singular way. You
remember that our Saviour raised three dead persons; I do
not find that during his lifetime he caused more than three
resurrections. The first was the young maiden, *the daughter
of Jairus*, who, when she lay on her bed dead, rose up to life
at the single utterance of Christ, " *Talitha cumi!*" The

second was the case of *the widow's son*, who was on his bier,
about to be carried to his tomb; and Jesus raised him up to life
by saying, "Young man, I say unto thee, arise." The third,
and most memorable case, was that of *Lazarus*, who was not
on his bed, nor on his bier, but in his tomb, ay, and corrupt too;
but notwithstanding that, the Lord Jesus Christ, by the voice
of his omnipotence, crying, "Lazarus come forth," brought
him out of the tomb.

I shall use these three facts as illustrations of *the different
states of men*, though they be all thoroughly dead; secondly,
as illustrations of *the different means of grace used for raising
them*, though, after all, the same great agency is employed;
and, in the third place, as illustrations of *the after experience
of quickened men;* for though that to a great degree is the
same, yet there are some points of difference.

I. I shall begin by noticing, then, first of all, THE CONDITION
OF MEN BY NATURE. Men by nature are all dead. There is
Jairus's daughter; she lies on her bed; she seems as if she
were alive; her mother has scarce ceased to kiss her brow, her
hand is still in her father's loving grasp, and he can scarcely
think that she is dead; but dead she is, as·thoroughly dead
as she ever can be. Next comes the case of the young
man brought out of his grave; he is more than dead, he has
begun to be corrupt, the signs of decay are upon his face, and
they are carrying him to his tomb; yet though there are more
manifestations of death about him, he is no more dead than
the other. He is just as dead; they are both dead, and death
really knows of no degrees. The third case goes further still
in the manifestation of death; for it is the case of which Martha,
using strong words, said, "Lord, by this time he stinketh; for
he hath been dead four days." And yet, mark you, the daughter of Jairus was as dead as Lazarus; though the manifestation of death was not so complete in her case. All were dead
alike. I have in my congregation some blessed beings, fair to
look upon; fair, I mean, in their character, as well as their
outward appearance; they have about them every thing that
is good and lovely; but mark this, if they are unregenerate
they are dead still. That girl, dead in the room, upon her
bed, had little about her that could show her death. Not yet

had the loving finger closed the eyelid; there seemed to be
a light still lingering in her eye; like a lily just nipped off, she
was as fair as life itself. The worm had not yet begun to gnaw
her cheek, the flush had not yet faded from her face; she
seemed well-nigh alive. And so is it with some I have here.
Ye have all that heart could wish for, except the one thing
needful; ye have all things save love to the Saviour. Ye are
not yet united to him by a living faith. Ah! then, I grieve to
say it, ye are dead! ye are dead! As much dead as the worst
of men, although your death is not so apparent. Again, I have
in my presence young men who have grown to riper years
than that fair damsel who died in her childhood. You have
much about you that is lovely, but you have just begun to indulge in evil habits; you have not yet become the desperate
sinner; you have not yet become altogether noxious in the
eyes of other men; you are but beginning to sin, you are like
the young man carried out on his bier; you have not yet become the confirmed drunkard; you have not yet begun to
curse and blaspheme God; you are still accepted in good society; you are not yet cast out; but you are dead, thoroughly
dead, just as dead as the third and worst case. But I dare
say I have some characters that are illustrations of that case
too. There is Lazarus in his tomb, rotten and putrid; and so
there are some men not more dead than others, but their death
has become more apparent, their character has become abominable, their deeds cry out against them, they are put out of
decent society, the stone is rolled to the mouth of their tomb,
men feel that they can not hold acquaintance with them, for
they have so utterly abandoned every sense of right, that we
say, "Put them out of sight, we can not endure them!" And
yet these putrid ones may live; these last are not more dead
than the maiden upon her bed, though death has more fully revealed itself in their corruption. Jesus Christ must quicken
the one as well as the other, and bring them all to know and
love his name.

1. Now, then, I am about to enter into the minutiæ of the
difference of these three cases. I will take the case of the
young maiden. I have her here to-day; I have many illustrations of her present before me; at least, I trust so. Now, will

you allow me to point out all the differences? Here is the young maiden; look upon her; you can bear the sight; she is dead, but O! *beauty lingereth there;* she is fair and lovely, though the life hath departed from her. In the young man's case there is no beauty; the worm hath begun to eat him; his honor hath departed. In the third case, there is absolute rottenness. But here there is beauty still upon her cheek. Is she not amiable? Is she not lovely? Would not all love her? Is she not to be admired, even to be imitated? Is she not fairest of the fair? Ay, that she is; but God the Spirit has not yet looked upon her; she has not yet bent her knee to Jesus, and cried for mercy; she has every thing, except true religion. Alas! for her; alas! that so fair a character should be a dead one. Alas! my sister; alas! that thou, the benevolent, the kind one, should yet be, after all, dead in thy trespasses and sins. As Jesus wept over that young man who had kept all the commandments, and yet one thing he lacked, so weep I over thee this morning. Alas! thou fair one, lovely in thy character, and amiable in thy carriage, why shouldst thou lie dead? For dead thou art, unless thou hast faith in Christ. Thine excellence, thy virtue, and thy goodness, shall avail thee nought; thou art dead, and dead thou must be, unless he make thee live.

Note, too, that in the case of this maiden, whom we have introduced to you, the daughter of Jairus, *she is yet caressed;* she has only been dead a moment or two, and the mother still presses her cheek with kisses. O! can she be dead? Do not the tears rain on her, as if they would sow the seeds of life in that dead earth again?—earth that looks fertile enough to bring forth life with but one living tear? Ay, but those salt tears are tears of barrenness. She liveth not; but she is still caressed. Not so the young man; he is put on the bier; no man will touch him any more, or else he will be utterly defiled. And as for Lazarus, he is shut up with a stone. But this young maiden is still caressed; so it is with many of you; you are loved even by the living in Sion; God's own people love you; the minister has often prayed for you; you are admitted into the assemblies of the saints, you sit with them as God's people, you hear as they hear, and you sing as they sing. Alas! for you; alas! for you, that you should still be dead! O! it grieves me to the heart, to think that some of you are all that heart could wish, except that one thing; yet lacking that which is the only thing that can deliver you. You are caressed by us, received by the living in Sion into their company and acquaintance, approved of and accepted; alas! that you should yet be without life! O! in your case, if you are saved, you will have to join with even the worst in saying " I have been quickened by divine grace, or else I had never lived."

And now will you look at this maiden again? Note, *she has no grave clothes on her yet ;* she is dressed in her own raiment; just as she retired to her bed a little sick, so lieth she there; not yet have the napkin and the shroud been wrapped about her; she still weareth the habiliments of sleep; she is not yet given up to death. Not so the young man yonder— he is in his grave clothes; not so Lazarus—he is bound hand and foot. But this young maiden hath no grave clothes upon her. So with the young person we wish to speak of this morning; she has as yet no evil habits, she hath not yet reached that point; the young man yonder has begun to have evil habits; and yon gray-headed sinner is bound hand and foot by them; but as yet she appeareth just like the living, she acteth just like the Christian; her habits are fair, goodly, and comely; there seemeth to be little ill about her. Alas! alas! that thou shouldst be dead, even in thy fairest raiment. Alas! thou who hast set the chaplet of benevolence on thy brow, thou who dost gird thyself with the white robes of outward purity, if thou art not born again, thou art dead still. Thy beauty shall fade away like a moth; and in the day of judgment thou wilt be severed from the righteous, unless God shall make thee live. O! I could weep over those young ones who seem at present to have been delivered from forming any habits which could lead them astray, but who are yet unquickened and unsaved O! would to God, young man and young woman, you might in early years be quickened by the Spirit.

And will you notice, yet once more, that this young maiden's death was *a death confined to her chamber.* Not so with the young man; he was carried to the gate of the city and much people saw him. Not so Lazarus; the Jews came to weep at his tomb. But this young woman's death is in her chamber. Ay, so it is with the young woman or young man I mean to describe now. His sin is as yet a secret thing, kept to himself; as yet there has been no breaking forth of iniquity, but only the conception of it in the heart; just the embryc of lust, not as yet broken out into act. The young man has not yet drained the intoxicating cup, although he has had some whisperings of the sweetness of it; he has not yet run into the ways of wickedness, though he has had temptations thrust upon him; as yet he has kept his sin in his chamber, and most of it has been unseen. Alas! my brother, alas! my sister, that thou who in thine outward carriage art so good, should yet have sins in the chamber of thine heart, and death in the secrecy of thy being, which is as true a death as that of the grossest sinner, though not so thoroughly manifested Would to God that thou couldst say, " And he hath quickened me, for with all my loveliness, and all my excellence, I was by nature dead in trespasses and sins." Come, let me just press this matter home. I have some in my congregation that I look upon with fear. O! my dear friends, my much loved friends, how many there are among you, I repeat, that are all that the heart could wish, except that one thing—that you love not my Master. O! ye young men who come up to the house of God, and who are outwardly so good ; alas! for you, that you should lack the root of the matter. O! ye daughters of Sion, who are ever at the house of prayer, O! that ye should yet be without grace in your heart! Take heed, I beseech you, ye fairest, youngest, most upright, and most honest; when the dead are separated from the living, unless ye be regenerated, ye must go with the dead ; though ye be never so fair and goodly, ye must be cast away, unless ye live.

2. Thus, I have done with the first case ; now we will go to the young man, who stands second. He is not more dead than the other, but *he is further gone.* Come, now, and stop the bier; you can not look upon him! Why, the cheek is sunken —there is a hollowness there ; not as in the case of the maiden, whose cheek was still round and ruddy. And the eye—O ! what a blackness is there ! Look on him ; you can see that

the gnawings of the worm will soon burst forth; corruption hath begun its work. So it is with some young men I have here. They are not what they were in their childhood, when their habits were proper and correct; but mayhap they have just been enticed into the house of the strange woman; they have just been tempted to go astray from the path of rectitude; their corruption is just breaking forth; they disdain now to sit at their mother's apron-strings; they think it foul scorn to keep to the rules that bind the moral! They! they are free, they say, and they will be free; they will live a jolly and a happy life; and so they run on in boisterous yet wicked merri ment, and betray the marks of death about them. They have gone further than the maiden; she was still fair and comely; but here there is something that is the afterwork of death. The maiden was caressed, but the young man is untouched he lieth on the bier, and though men bear him on their shoulders, yet there is a shrinking from him; he is dead, and it is known that he is dead. Young man, you have got as far as that; you know that good men shrink from you. It was but yesterday that your mother's tears fell fast and thick as she warned your younger brother to avoid your sin; your very sister, when she kissed you but this morning, prayed to God that you might get good in this house of prayer; but you know that of late she has been ashamed of you; your conversation has become so profane and wicked, that even she could scarce endure it. There are houses in which you were once welcome; where you once bowed your knee with them at the family prayer, and your name was mentioned too; but now you do not choose to go there, for when you go, you are treated with reserve. The good man of the house feels that he could not let his son go with you, for you would contaminate him; he does not sit down now side by side with you, as he used to do, and talk about the best things; he lets you sit in the room as a matter of mere courtesy; he stands far away from you, as it were; he feels that you have not a spirit congenial with his own. You are a little shunned; you are not quite avoided; you are still received among the people of God, yet there is a coldness that manifests that they under stand that you are not a living one.

And note, too, that this young man, though carried out to his grave, was not like the maiden; she was in the garments of life, but *he was wrapped in the cerements of death.* So many of you have begun to form habits that are evil; you know that already the screw of the devil is tightening on your finger. Once it was a screw you could slip off or on; you said you were master of your pleasures—now your pleasures are master of you. Your habits are not now commendable, you know they are not; you stand convicted while I speak to you this morning; you know your ways are evil. Ah! young man, though thou hast not yet gone so far as the open profligate and desperately profane, take heed, thou art dead! thou art dead! and unless the Spirit quicken thee, thou shalt be cast into the valley of Gehenna, to be the food of that worm which never dieth, but eateth souls throughout eternity. And ah! young man, I weep, I weep over thee; thou art not yet so far gone, that they have rolled the stone against thee; thou art not yet become obnoxious; thou art not yet the staggering drunkard, nor yet the blasphemous infidel; thou hast much that is ill about thee, but thou hast not gone all the lengths yet. Take heed; thou wilt go further still; there is no stopping in sin. When the worm is there, you can not put your finger on it, and say, "Stop; eat no more." No, it will go on to your utter ruin. May God save you now, ere you shall come to that consummation for which hell so sighs, and which heaven can alone avert.

One more remark concerning this young man. The maiden's death was in her chamber; *the young man's death was in the city gates.* In the first case I described, the sin was secret. But, young man, yours is not. You have gone so far that your habits are openly wicked; you have dared to sin in the face of God's sun. You are not as some others—seemingly good; but you go out and openly say, "I am no hypocrite; I dare to do wrong. I do not profess to be righteous; I know I am a scapegrace rascal. I have gone astray, and I am not ashamed to sin in the street." Ah! young man, young man! Thy father, perhaps is saying now, "Would God that I had died for him—would God that I had seen him buried in his grave, ere he should have gone to such a length in wickedness

Would God that when I first saw him, and mine eye was glad-
dened with my son, I had seen him the next minute smitten
with disease and death! O, would to God that his infant
spirit had been called to heaven, that he might not have lived
to bring in this way my gray hairs in sorrow to the grave!"
Your sport in the city gates is misery in your father's house;
your open merriment before the world brings agony into a
mother's heart. O, I beseech you, stay. O, Lord Jesus!
touch the bier this morning! Stop some young man in his
evil habits, and say unto him, "Arise." Then will he join
with us in confessing that those who are alive have been quickened by Jesus, through the Spirit, though they were dead in
trespasses and sins.

3. Now we come to the third and last case—LAZARUS DEAD
AND BURIED. Ah! dear friends, I can not take you to see Lazarus in his grave. Stand, O stand away from him. Whither
shall we flee to avoid the noxious odor of that reeking corpse?
Ah, whither shall we flee? There is no beauty there; we
dare not look upon it. There is not even the gloss of life left.
O, hideous spectacle! I must not attempt to describe it;
words would fail me, and you would be too much shocked.
Nor dare I tell the character of some men present here. I
should be ashamed to tell the things which some of you have
done. This cheek might mantle with a blush to tell the deeds
of darkness which some of the ungodly of this world habitually practice. Ah, the last stage of death, the last stage of
corruption, O, how hideous; but the last stage of sin, hideous far more! Some writers seem to have an aptitude for
puddling in this mud, and digging up this miry clay; I confess
that I have none. I can not describe to you the lusts and
vices of a full-grown sinner. I can not tell you what are the
debaucheries, the degrading lusts, the devilish, the bestial sins
into which wicked men will run, when spiritual death has
had its perfect work in them, and sin has manifested itself in
all its fearful wickedness. I may have some here. They are
not Christians. They are not, like the young maiden, still
fondled, nor even like the young man, still kept in the funeral
procession: no, they have gone so far that decent people avoid
them. Their very wife, when they go into the house, rushes

up stairs to be out of the way. They are scorned. Such a one is the harlot, from whom one's head is turned in the very street. Such a one is the openly profligate, to whom we give wide quarters, lest we touch him. He is a man that is far gone. The stone is rolled before him. No one calls him respectable. He dwelleth, perhaps, in some back slum of a dirty lane; he knoweth not where to go. Even as he stands in this place, he feels that if his next-door neighbor knew his guilt he would give him a wide berth, and stand far away from him; for he has come to the last stage; he has no marks of life; he is utterly rotten. And mark; as in the case of the maiden, the sin was in the chamber, secret; in the next case it was in the open streets, public; but in this case it is secret again. It is in the tomb. For you will mark that men, when they are only half gone in wickedness, do it openly; but when they are fully gone their lust becomes so degrading that they are obliged to do it in secret. They are put into the grave, in order that all may be hidden. Their lust is one which can only be perpetrated at midnight; a deed which can only be done when shrouded by the astonished curtains of darkness. Have I any such here? I can not tell that I have many; but still I have some. Ah! in being constantly visited by penitents I have sometimes blushed for this city of London. There are merchants whose names stand high and fair. Shall I tell it here? I know it on the best authority, and the truest, too. There are some who have houses large and tall, who on the exchange are reputable and honorable, and every one admits them and receives them into their society; but ah! there are some of the merchants of London who practice lusts that are abominable. I have in my church and congregation—and I dare say what men dare to do—I have in my congregation women whose ruin and destruction have been wrought by some of the most respected men in respectable society. Few would venture on so bold a statement as that; but if you boldly do the thing, I must speak of it. It is not for God's ambassador to wash his mouth beforehand; let him boldly reprove, as men do boldly sin. Ah! there are some that are a stench in the nostrils of the Almighty; some whose character is hideous beyond all hideousness. They have to be cov

ered up in the tomb of secrecy; for men would scout them
from society, and hiss them from existence, if they knew all.
And yet—and now comes a blessed interposition—yet this
last case may be saved as well as the first, and as easily too.
The rotten Lazarus may come out of his tomb, as well as the
slumbering maiden from her bed. The last, the most corrupt, the most desperately abominable, may yet be quickened;
and he may join in exclaiming, "And I have been quickened,
though I was dead in trespasses and sins." I trust you will
understand what I wish to convey—that the death is the same
in all cases; but the manifestation of it is different; and that
the life must come from God, and from God alone.

II. And now I will go on to another point—THE QUICKEN-
ING. These three persons were all quickened, and they were
all quickened by the same being—that is by Jesus. But they
were all quickened in a different manner. Note, first, the
young maiden on her bed. When she was brought to life, it
is said, "Jesus took her by the hand and said, Maiden, arise."
It was a still small voice. Her heart received its pulse again,
and she lived. It was the gentle touching of the hand—no
open demonstration—and the soft voice was heard, "Arise."
Now usually when God converts young people in the first
stage of sin, before they have formed evil habits, he does it
in a gentle manner; not by the "terrors of the law, the tempest, fire and smoke," but he makes them like Lydia, "whose
heart the Lord opened" that she received the word. On such
"it droppeth like the gentle dew from heaven upon the place
beneath." With hardened sinners grace cometh down in
showers that rattle on them; but in young converts it often
cometh gently. There is just the sweet breathing of the
Spirit. They perhaps scarcely think it is a true conversion;
but true it is, if they are brought to life.

Now note the next case. Christ did not do the same thing
with the young man that he did with the daughter of Jairus.
No; the first thing he did was, he put his hand, not on him, mark
you, but *on the bier;* "and they that bare it stood still," and
after that, without touching the young man, he said in a louder
voice, "Young man, I say unto thee, arise!" Note the difference; the young maiden's new life was given to her secretly

The young man's was given more publicly. It was done in the very street of the city. The maiden's life was given gently by a touch; but in the young man's case it must be done, not by the touching of him, but by the touching of the bier. Christ takes away from the young man his means of pleasure. He commands his companions, who by bad example are bearing him on his bier to his grave, to stop, and then there is a partial reformation for a while; after that there comes the strong outspoken voice, "Young man, I say unto thee, arise!"

But now comes the worst case; and will you please at your leisure at home to notice what preparations Christ made for the last case of Lazarus? When he raised the maiden, he walked up into the chamber, smiling, and said, "She is not dead, but sleepeth." When he raised the young man, he said to the mother, "Weep not." Not so when he came to the last case; there was something more terrible about that: it was *a man in his grave corrupting*. It was on that occasion you read, "Jesus wept;" and after he had wept, it is said that "he groaned in his spirit;" and then he said, "Take away the stone;" and then there came the prayer, "I know that thou hearest me always." And then, will you notice, there came, what is not expressed so fully in either of the other cases. It is written, "Jesus cried with a loud voice, Lazarus, come forth!" It is not written that he cried with the loud voice to either of the others. He spake to them; it was his word that saved all of them; but in the case of Lazarus, he cried to him in a loud voice. Now I have, perhaps, some of the last characters here—the worst of the worst. Ah, sinner, may the Lord quicken thee! But it is a work that makes the Saviour weep. I think when he comes to call some of you from your death in sin who have gone to the utmost extremity of guilt, he comes weeping and sighing for you. There is a stone there to be rolled away—your bad and evil habits; and when that stone is taken away, a still small voice will not do for you; it must be the loud crashing voice, like the voice of the Lord, which breaketh the cedars of Lebanon, "Lazarus, come forth!" John Bunyan was one of those rotten ones. What strong means were used in his case. Terrible dreams, fearful convulsions, awful shakings to and fro—all had to be employed to

make him live. And yet some of you think, when God is ter
rifying you by the thunders of Sinai, that he really does not
love you. It is not so: you were so dead that it needed a
loud voice to arrest your ears.

III. This is an interesting subject: I wish I could dilate
upon it, but my voice fails me; and, therefore, permit me to
go to the third point very briefly. THE AFTER-EXPERIENCE
OF THESE THREE PEOPLE WAS DIFFERENT—at least, you gather
it from the commands of Christ. As soon as the maiden was
alive, Christ said, "Give her meat;" as soon as the young man
was alive, "he delivered him to his mother;" as soon as Lazarus was alive, he said, "Loose him, and let him go." I think
there is something in this. When young people are converted
who have not yet acquired evil habits; when they are saved
before they become obnoxious in the eyes of the world, the
command is, "*Give them meat.*" Young people want instruction; they want building up in the faith; they generally lack
knowledge; they have not the deep experience of the older
man; they do not know so much about sin, nor even so much
about salvation as the older man that has been a guilty sinner;
they need to be fed. So that our business as ministers, when
the young lambs are brought in, is to remember the injunc-
tion, "Feed my lambs;" take care of them; give them plenty
of meat. Young people, search after an instructive minister;
seek after instructive books; search the Scriptures, and seek
to be instructed: that is your principal business. "Give her
meat."

The next case was a different one. He gave the young man
up to his mother. Ah! that is just what he will do with you
young man, if he makes you live. As sure as ever you are
converted, he will give you up to your mother again. You
were with her when you first as a babe sat on her knee; and
that is where you will have to go again. O, yes; grace knits
together again the ties which sin has loosed. Let a young
man become abandoned; he casts off the tender influence of a
sister and the kind associations of a mother; but if he is converted, one of the first things he will do will be to find the
mother out, and the sister out, and he will find a charm in
their society that he never knew before. You that have gone

into sin, let this be your business, if God has saved you. Seek good company. Just as Christ delivered the young man to his mother, do you seek after your mother, the church. Endeavor as much as possible to be found in the company of the righteous; for, as you were carried before to your grave by bad companions, you need to be led to heaven by good ones.

And then comes the case of Lazarus. "*Loose him, and let him go*." I do not know how it is that the young man never was loosed, I have been looking through every book I have about the manners and customs of the East, and have not been able to get a clew to the difference between the young man and Lazarus. The young man, as soon as Christ spoke to him, "sat up and began to speak;" but Lazarus, in his grave-clothes, lying in the niche of the tomb, could do no more than just shuffle himself out from the hole that was cut in the wall, and then stand leaning against it. He could not speak; he was bound about in a napkin. Why was it not so with the young man? I am inclined to think that the difference lay in the difference of their wealth. The young man was the son of a widow. Very likely he was only wrapped up in a few common things, and not so tightly bound about as Lazarus. Lazarus was of a rich family; very likely they wrapped him up with more care. Whether it was or not, I do not know. What I want to hint at is this: when a man is far gone into sin, Christ does this for him—he breaks off his evil habits. Very likely the old sinner's experience will not be a feeding experience. It will not be the experience of walking with the saints. It will be as much as he can do to pull off his grave-clothes, to get rid of his old habits: perhaps to his death he will have to be rending off bit after bit of the cerements in which he has been wrapped. There is his drunkenness; O what a fight he will have with that! There is his lust, what a combat he will have with that, for many a month! There is his habit of swearing; how often will an oath come into his mouth, and he will have as hard work as he can to thrust it down again! There is his pleasure-seeking; he has given it up; but how often will his companions be after him, to get him to go with them. His life will be ever afterward a loosing and letting go ; for he will need it till he cometh up to be with God for ever and ever.

And now, dear friends, I must close by asking you this question, *Have you been quickened ?* And I must warn you that, good, or bad, or indifferent, if you have never been quickened you are dead in sins, and must be cast away at the last. I must bid you, however, who have gone the furthest into sin, not to despair; Christ can quicken you as well as the best. O that he would quicken you and lead you to believe! O that he now would cry to some, "Lazarus, come forth!" and make some harlot virtuous, some drunkard sober. O that he would bless the word, especially to the young and amiable and lovely, by making them now the heirs of God and the children of Christ!

And now but one thing I have to say to those who are quickened ; and then adieu this morning, and may God bless you! My dear friends, you who are quickened, let me advise you to take care of the devil ; he will be sure to be after you. Keep your mind always employed, and so you will escape him. O be aware of his devices ; seek to " keep the heart with all diligence, for out of it are the issues of life." The Lord bless you, for Jesus' sake.

SERMON XVI

CONFESSION OF SIN

A SERMON WITH SEVEN TEXTS

My sermon this morning will have seven texts, and yet I pledge myself that there shall be but three different words in the whole of them ; for it so happens that the seven texts are all alike, occurring in seven different portions of God's holy Word. I shall require, however, to use the whole of them to exemplify different cases ; and I must request those of you who have brought your Bibles with you to refer to the texts as I shall mention them.

The subject of this morning's discourse will be this—con-FESSION OF SIN. We know that this is absolutely necessary to salvation. Unless there be a true and hearty confession of our sins to God, we have no promise that we shall find mercy through the blood of the Redeemer. " Whosoever confesseth his sins and forsaketh them shall find mercy." But there is no promise in the Bible to the man who will not confess his sins. Yet, as upon every point of Scripture there is a liability of being deceived, so more especially in the matter of confession of sin. There be many who make a confession, and a confession before God, who, notwithstanding, receive no blessing, because their confession has not in it certain marks which are required by God to prove it genuine and sincere, and which demonstrate it to be the work of the Holy Spirit. My text this morning consists of three words, " I have sinned." And you will see how these words, in the lips of different men, indicate very different feelings. While one says, " I have sinned," and receives forgiveness ; another we shall meet with says, " I have sinned," and goes his way to blacken himself with worse crimes than before, and dive into greater depths of sin than heretofore he had discovered.

THE HARDENED SINNER

PHARAOH—"I have sinned"—EXODUS, ix. 27.

I. The first case I shall bring before you is that of the *hard-ened sinner*, who, when under terror, says, "I have sinned." And you will find the text in the book of Exodus, the 9th chapter, and 27th verse : " And Pharaoh sent, and called for Moses and Aaron, and said unto them, I have sinned this time : the Lord is righteous, and I and my people are wicked."

But why this confession from the lips of the haughty ty-rant ? He was not often wont to humble himself before Je-hovah. Why doth the proud one bow himself? You will judge of the value of his confession when you hear the cir-cumstances under which it was made. " And Moses stretched forth his rod toward heaven ; and the Lord sent thunder and hail, and the fire ran along upon the ground ; and the Lord rained hail upon the land of Egypt. So that there was hail, and fire mingled with the hail, very grievous, such as there was none like it in all the land of Egypt since it became a na-tion." " Now," says Pharaoh, whilst the thunder is rolling through the sky, while the lightning flashes are setting the very ground on fire, and while the hail is descending in big lumps of ice, now, says he, " I have sinned." He is but a type and specimen of multitudes of the same class. How many a hardened rebel on ship-board, when the timbers are strained and creaking, when the mast is broken, and the ship is drift-ing before the gale, when the hungry waves are opening their mouths to swallow the ship up alive, and quick as those that go into the pit—how many a hardened sailor has then bowed his knee, with tears in his eyes, and cried, " I have sinned !" But of what avail and of what value was his confession ? The repentance that was born in the storm died in the calm ; that repentance of his that was begotten amid the thunder and the lightning, ceased so soon as all was hushed in quiet, and the man who was a pious mariner when on board ship, became the most wicked and abominable of sailors when he placed his foot on *terra firma.* How often, too, have we seen this in a storm of thunder and lightning? Many a man's cheek is blanched when he hears the thunder rolling; the tears start to his eyes, and he cries, "O God, I have sinned!" while the rafters of his house are shaking, and the very ground beneath him reeling at the voice of God which is full of majesty. But alas, for such a repentance! When the sun again shines, and the black clouds are withdrawn, sin comes again upon the man, and he becomes worse than before. How many of the same sort of confessions, too, have we seen in times of cholera, and fever, and pestilence! Then our churches have been crammed with hearers, who, because so many funerals have passed their door, or so many have died in the street, could not refrain from going up to God's house to confess their sins. And under that visitation, when one, two, and three have been lying dead in the house, or next door, how many have thought they would really turn to God! But, alas! when the pestilence had done its work, conviction ceased; and when the bell had tolled the last time for a death caused by cholera, then their hearts ceased to beat with penitence, and their tears did flow no more.

Have I any such here this morning? I doubt not I have hardened persons who would scorn the very idea of religion, who would count me a cant and hypocrite if I should endeavor to press it home upon them, but who know right well that religion is true, and who feel it in their times of terror! If I have such here this morning, let me solemnly say to them, "Sirs, you have forgotten the feelings you had in your hours of alarm; but, remember, God has not forgotten the vows you then made." Sailor, you said, if God would spare you to see the land again, you would be his servant; you are not so, you have lied against God, you have made him a false promise, for you have never kept the vow which your lips did utter. You said, on a bed of sickness, that if he would spare your life you would never again sin as you did before; but here you are, and this week's sins shall speak for themselves. You are no better than you were before your sickness. Couldst thou lie to thy fellow-man, and yet go unreproved? And thinkest thou that thou wilt lie against God, and yet go unpunished? No; the vow, however rashly made is registered in heaven and though it be a vow which man can not perform, yet, as it is a vow which he has made himself, and made voluntarily too, he shall be punished for the non-keeping it; and God shall execute vengeance upon him at last, because he said he would turn from his ways, and then when the blow was removed he did it not. A great outcry has been raised of late against tickets-of-leave; I have no doubt there are some men here, who before high heaven stand in the same position as the ticket-of-leave men stand to our government. They were about to die, as they thought; they promised good behavior if they might be spared, and they are here to-day on ticket-of-leave in this world: and how have they fulfilled their promise? Justice might raise the same outcry against them as they do against the burglars so constantly let loose upon us. The avenging angel might say, "O God, these men said, if they were spared they would be so much better; if any thing they are worse. How have they violated their promise, and how have they brought down divine wrath upon their heads!" This is the first style of penitence; and it is a style I hope none of you will imitate, for it is utterly worthless. It is of no use for you to say, "I have sinned," merely under the influence of terror, and then to forget it afterwards.

THE DOUBLE-MINDED MAN.

BALAAM—"I have sinned."—NUMBERS, xxii. 34.

II. Now for a second text. I beg to introduce to you another character—the *double minded man*, who says, "I have sinned," and feels that he has, and feels it deeply too, but who is so worldly-minded that he "loves the wages of unrighteousness." The character I have chosen to illustrate this, is that of *Balaam*. Turn to the book of Numbers, the 22d chapter and the 34th verse: "And Balaam said unto the angel of the Lord, I have sinned."

"I have sinned," said Balaam; but yet he went on with his sin afterward. One of the strangest characters of the whole world is Balaam. I have often marveled at that man; he seems really in another sense to have come up to the lines of Ralph Erskine,

> "To good and evil equal bent,
> And both a devil and a saint."

For he did seem to be so.   At times no man could speak more eloquently and more truthfully, and at other times he exhibited the most mean and sordid coveteousness that could disgrace human nature.   Think you see Balaam; he stands upon the brow of the hill, and there lie the multitudes of Israel at his feet; he is bidden to curse them, and he cries, " How shall I curse whom God hath not cursed ?"   And God opening his eyes, he begins to tell even about the coming of Christ, and he says, " I shall see him but not now: I shall behold him but not nigh." And then he winds up his oration by saying—" Let me die the death of the righteous, and let my last end be like his !" And ye will say of that man, he is a hopeful character.   Wait till he has come off the brow of the hill, and ye will hear him give the most diabolical advice to the king of Moab, which it was even possible for Satan himself to suggest.   Said he to the king, " You can not overthrow these people in battle, for God is with them; try and entice them from their God." And ye know how with wanton lusts they of Moab tried to entice the children of Israel from allegiance to Jehovah; so that this man seemed to have the voice of an angel at one time, and yet the very soul of a devil in his bowels.   He was a terrible character; he was a man of two things, a man who went all the way with two things to a very great extent.   I know the Scripture says, " No man can serve two masters." Now this is often misunderstood.   Some read it, " No man can *serve two* masters."   Yes he can ; he can serve three or four. The way to read it is this : " No man can serve two *masters*." They can not both be masters.   He can serve two, but they can not both be his master.   A man can serve two who are not his masters or twenty either ; he may live for twenty different purposes, but he can not live for more than one master purpose—there can only be one master purpose in his soul. But Balaam labored to serve two; it was like the people of whom it was said, "They feared the Lord, and served other gods."   Or like Rufus, who was a loaf of the same leaven ;

for you know our old king Rufus painted God on one side of his shield, and the devil on the other, and had underneath the motto, "Ready for both; catch who can." There are many such, who are ready for both. They meet a minister, and how pious and holy they are; on the Sabbath they are most respectable and upright people in the world, as you would think; indeed, they affect a drawling in their speech which they think to be eminently religious. But on a week day, if you want to find the greatest rogues and cheats, they are some of those men who are so sanctimonious in their piety. Now, rest assured, my hearers, that no confession of sin can be genuine, unless it be a whole hearted one. It is of no use for you to say, "I have sinned," and then to keep on sinning. "I have sinned," say you, and it is a fair, fair face you show; but, alas! alas! for the sin you will go away and commit. Some men seem to be born with two characters. I remarked when in the library at Trinity College, Cambridge, a very fine statue of Lord Byron. The librarian said to me, "Stand here, sir." I looked, and I said, "what a fine intellectual countenance! What a grand genius he was!" "Come here," he said, "to the other side." "Ah! what a demon! There stands the man that could defy the deity." He seemed to have such a scowl and such a dreadful leer in his face; even as Milton would have painted Satan when he said—"Better to reign in hell than serve in heaven." I turned away and said to the librarian, "Do you think the artist designed this?" "Yes," he said, "he wished to picture the two characters—the great, the grand, the almost superhuman genius that he possessed, and yet the enormous mass of sin that was in his soul." There are some men here of the same sort. I dare say, like Balaam, they would overthrow every thing in argument with their enchantments; they could work miracles; and yet at the same time there is something about them which betrays a horrid character of sin, as great as that which would appear to be their character for righteousness. Balaam, you know, offered sacrifices to God upon the altar of Baal; that was just the type of his character. So many do; they offer sacrifices to God on the shrine of Mammon; and while they will give to the building of a church, and distribute to the poor, they will at the other door of their counting-house grind the poor for bread, and press the very blood out of the widow, that they may enrich themselves. Ah! it is idle and useless for you to say, "I have sinned," unless you mean it from your heart. That double minded man's confession is of no avail.

THE INSINCERE MAN

SAUL—"I have sinned."—1 SAMUEL, xv. 24

III. And now a third character, and a third text. In the first book of Samuel, the 15th chapter and 24th verse: "And *Saul* said unto Samuel, I have sinned."

Here is the *insincere man*—the man who is not like Balaam, to a certain extent sincere in two things; but the man who is just the opposite—who has no prominent point in his character at all, but is molded everlastingly by the circumstances that are passing over his head. Such a man was *Saul*. Samuel reproved him, and he said, "I have sinned." But he did not mean what he said; for, if you read the whole verse, you will find him saying, "I have sinned: for I have transgressed the commandment of the Lord, and thy words; *because I feared the people:*" which was a lying excuse. Saul never feared any body; he was always ready enough to do his own will—he was the despot. And just before, he had pleaded another excuse, that he had saved the bullocks and lambs to offer to Jehovah, and therefore both excuses could not have been true. You remember, my friends, that the most prominent feature in the character of Saul was his insincerity. One day he fetched David from his bed, as he thought, to put him to death in his house. Another time he declares, "God forbid that I should do aught against thee, my son David." One day, because David saved his life, he said, "Thou art more righteous than I; I will do so no more." The day before he had gone out to fight against his own son-in-law, in order to slay him. Sometimes Saul was among the prophets, easily turned into a prophet, and then afterward among the witches; sometimes in one place, and then another, and insincere in every thing. How many such we have in every Christian assembly; men who are very easily molded! Say what you please to them, they always agree with you. They have affectionate dispositions, very likely a tender conscience; but then the conscience is so remarkably tender, that when touched it seems to give, and you are afraid to probe deeper—it heals as soon as it is wounded. I think I used the very singular comparison once before, which I must use again: there are some men who seem to have India-rubber hearts. If you do but touch them, there is an impression made at once; but then it is of no use, it soon restores itself to its original character. You may press them whichever way you wish; they are so elastic you can always effect your purpose; but then they are not fixed in their character, and soon return to be what they were before. O sirs, too many of you have done the same; you have bowed your heads in church, and said, "We have erred and strayed from thy ways:" and you did not mean what you said. You have come to your minister; you have said, "I repent of my sins;" you did not then feel you were a sinner; you only said it to please him. And now you attend the house of God: no one more impressible than you; the tear will run down your cheek in a moment, but yet, notwithstanding all that, the tear is dried as quickly as it is brought forth, and you remain to all intents and purposes the same as you were before. To say, "I have sinned," in an unmeaning manner, is worse than worthless, for it is a mockery of God thus to confess with insincerity of heart.

I have been brief upon this character, for it seemed to touch upon that of Balaam; though any thinking man will at once see there was a real contrast between Saul and Balaam, even though there is an affinity between the two. Balaam was the great bad man, great in all he did; Saul was little in every thing, except in stature—little in his good and little in his vice; and he was too much of a fool to be desperately bad, though too wicked to be at any time good: while Balaam was great in both: the man who could at one time defy Jehovah, and yet at another time could say, "If Balak would give me his house full of silver and gold, I can not go beyond the word of the Lord my God, to do less or more."

THE DOUBTFUL PENITENT

ACHAN—" I have sinned."—JOSHUA, vii. 20

IV. And now I have to introduce to you a very interesting case ; it is the case of the doubtful penitent, in the case of *Achan*, in the book of Joshua, the 7th chapter and the 20th verse : " And Achan answered Joshua, Indeed I have sinned."

You know that Achan stole some of the prey from the city of Jericho—that he was discovered by lot, and put to death. I have singled his case out as the representative of some whose characters are doubtful on their death-beds ; who do repent apparently, but of whom the most we can say is, that we hope their souls are saved at last, but indeed we can not tell. Achan, you are aware, was stoned with stones, for defiling Israel. But I find in the Mishna, an old Jewish exposition of the Bible, these words, " Joshua said to Achan, The Lord shall trouble thee *this* day." And the note upon it is—" He said *this* day, implying that he was only to be troubled in this life, by being stoned to death, but that God would have mercy on his soul, seeing that he had made a full confession of his sin." And I, too, am inclined, from reading the chapter, to concur in the idea of my venerable and now glorified predecessor, Dr. Gill, in believing that Achan really was saved, although he was put to death for the crime, as an example. For you will observe how kindly Joshua spoke to him. He said, " My son, give, I pray thee, glory to the Lord God of Israel, and make confession unto him ; and tell me now what thou hast done ; hide it not from me." And you find Achan making a very full confession. He says, " Indeed I have sinned against the Lord God of Israel, and thus and thus have I done : when I saw among the spoils a goodly Babylonish garment, and two hundred shekels of silver, and a wedge of gold of fifty shekels weight, then I coveted them, and took them ; and, behold, they are hid in the earth in the midst of my tent, and the silver under it." It seems so full a confession, that if I might be allowed to judge, I should say, " I hope to meet Achan, the sinner, before the throne of God." But I find Matthew Henry has no such opinion ; and many other expositors consider that as his body was destroyed, so was his soul. I have, therefore, selected his case, as being one of doubtful repentance. Ah! dear friends, it has been my lot to stand by many a death-bed, and to see many such a repentance as this. I have seen the man, when worn to a skeleton, sustained by pillows in his bed, and he has said, when I have talked to him of judgment to come, "Sir, I feel I have been guilty, but Christ is good; I trust in him." And I have said within myself, "I believe the man's soul is safe." But I have always come away with the melancholy reflection that I had no proof of it beyond his own words; for it needs proof in acts and in future life, in order to sustain any firm conviction of a man's salvation. You know that great fact, that a physician once kept a record of a thousand persons who thought they were dying, and whom he thought were penitents; he wrote their names down in a book as those who, if they had died, would go to heaven they did not die, they lived; and he says that out of the whole thousand he had not three persons who turned out well afterward, but they returned to their sins again, and were as bad as ever. Ah! dear friends, I hope none of you will have such a death-bed repentance as that; I hope your minister or your parents will not have to stand by your bedside, and then go away and say, "Poor fellow! I hope he is saved." But alas! death-bed repentances are such flimsy things; such poor, such trivial grounds of hope, that I am afraid, after all, his soul may be lost." O! to die with a full assurance; O! to die with an abundant entrance, leaving a testimony behind that we have departed this life in peace! That is a far happier way than to die in a doubtful manner, lying sick, hovering between two worlds, and neither ourselves nor yet our friends knowing to which of the two worlds we are going. May God grant us grace to give in our lives evidences of true conversion, that our case may not be doubtful.

THE REPENTANCE OF DESPAIR.

JUDAS—"I have sinned."—MATTHEW, xxvii. 4

V. I shall not detain you too long, I trust, but I must now give you another bad case; the worst of all. It is the *repent-*

ance of despair. Will you turn to the 27th chapter of Matthew and the 4th verse? There you have the dreadful case of the repentance of despair. You will recognize the character the moment I read the verse: "And Judas said, I have sinned." Yes, Judas the traitor, who had betrayed his Master, when he saw that his Master was condemned, " repented, and brought again the thirty pieces of silver to the chief priests and elders, saying, I have sinned in that I have betrayed innocent blood, and cast down the pieces in the temple, and went" and what?—" and *hanged himself.*" Here is the worst kind of repentance of all; in fact, I know not that I am justified in calling it repentance; it must be called remorse of conscience. But Judas did confess his sin, and then went and hanged himself. O! that dreadful, that terrible, that hideous confession of despair. Have you never seen it? If you never have, then bless God that you never were called to see such a sight. I have seen it once in my life, I pray God I may never see it again—the repentance of the man who sees death staring him in the face, and who says, "I have sinned." You tell him that Christ has died for sinners; and he answers, "There is no hope for me; I have cursed God to his face; I have defied him; my day of grace I know is past; my con- science is seared with a hot iron; I am dying, and I know I shall be lost!" Such a case as that happened long ago, you know, and is on record—the case of Francis Spira—the most dreadful case, perhaps, except that of Judas, which is upon record in the memory of man. O! my hearers, will any of you have such a repentance? If you do, it will be a beacon to all persons who sin in future; if you have such a repentance as that, it will be a warning to generations yet to come. In the life of Benjamin Keach—and he also was one of my prede- cessors—I find the case of a man who had been a professor of religion, but had departed from the profession, and had gone into awful sin. When he came to die, Keach, with many other friends went to see him, but they could never stay with him above five minutes at a time; for he said, "Get ye gone; it is of no use your coming to me; I have sinned away the Holy Ghost; I am like Esau, I have sold my birthright, and though I seek it carefully with tears, I can never find it again."

And then he would repeat dreadful words, like these: "**My** mouth is filled with gravel-stones, and I drink wormwood day and night. Tell me not, tel. me not of Christ! I know he is a Saviour, but I hate him, and he hates me. I know I must die; I know I must perish!" And then followed doleful cries, and hideous noises, such as none could bear. They returned again in his placid moments, only to stir him once more, and make him cry out in his despair, "I am lost! I am lost! It is of no use your telling me any thing about it!" Ah! there may be a man here who may have such a death as that; let me warn him, ere he come to it; and may God the Holy Spirit grant that that man may be turned unto God, and made a true penitent, and then he need not have any more fear; for he who has had his sins washed away in a Saviour's blood, need not have any remorse for his sins, for they are pardoned through the Redeemer.

THE REPENTANCE OF THE SAINT.

JOB—"I have sinned."—JOB, vii. 20.

VI. And now I come into daylight. I have been taking you through dark and dreary confessions; I shall detain you there no longer, but bring you out to the two good confessions which I have read to you. The first.is that of Job in 7th chapter at the 20th verse: "I have sinned; what shall I do unto thee, O thou preserver of men?" This is the *repentance of the saint.* Job was a saint, but he sinned. This is the repentance of the man who is a child of God already, an acceptable repentance before God. But as I intend to dwell upon this in the evening, I shall now leave it, for fear of wearying you. David was a specimen of this kind of repentance, and I would have you carefully study his penitential Psalms, the language of which is ever full of weeping humility and earnest penitence

THE BLESSED CONFESSION

THE PRODIGAL—"I have sinned."—LUKE, xv. 18

VII. I come now to the last instance, which I shall mention; it is the case of the prodigal. In Luke xv. 18, we find the prodigal says: "Father, I have sinned." O, here is *a blessed confession!* Here is that which proves a man to be a regenerate character—"Father, I have sinned." Let me picture the scene. There is the prodigal; he has run away from a good home and a kind father, and he has spent all his money with harlots, and now he has none left. He goes to his old companions, and asks them for relief. They laugh him to scorn. "O," says he, "you have drunk my wine many a day; I have always stood paymaster to you in all our revelries; will you not help me?" "Get you gone," they say; and he is turned out of doors. He goes to all his friends with whom he had associated, but no man gives him any thing. At last a certain citizen of the country said,—"You want something to do, do you? Well, go and feed my swine." The poor prodigal, the son of a rich landowner, who had a great fortune of his own, has to go out to feed swine; and he a Jew, too! the worst employment (to his mind), to which he could be put. See him there, in squalid rags, feeding swine; and what are his wages? Why, so little that he " would fain have filled his belly with the husks that the swine did eat, but no man gave to him." Look, there he is, with the fellow-commoners of the sty, in all his mire and filthiness. Suddenly a thought, put there by the good Spirit, strikes his mind. "How is it," says he, "that in my father's house there is bread enough and to spare, and I perish with hunger? I will arise and go to my father, and say unto him, Father, I have sinned against heaven and before thee, and am no more worthy to be called thy son: make me as one of thy hired servants." Off he goes. He begs his way from town to town. Sometimes he gets a lift on a coach perhaps, but at other times he goes trudging his way up barren hills and down desolate vales all alone. And now at last he comes to the hill outside the village, and sees his father's house down below. There it is; the old poplar tree against it, and there are the stacks round which he and his brother used to run and play; and at the sight of the old homestead all the feelings and associations of his former life rush upon him, and tears run down his cheeks, and he is almost ready to run away again. He says, "I wonder whether father's dead. I dare say mother broke her heart

when I went away, I always was her favorite. And if they
are either of them alive, they will never see me again; they
will shut the door in my face. What am I to do? I can not
go back, I am afraid to go forward." And while he was thus
deliberating his father had been walking on the house-top looking out for his son; and though he could not see his father
his father could see him. Well, the father comes down stairs
with all his might, runs up to him, and whilst he is thinking
of running away, his father's arms are round his neck, and he
falls to kissing him, like a loving father indeed, and then the
son begins,—" Father, I have sinned against heaven and in
thy sight, and am no more worthy to be called thy son," and
he was going to say, " Make me as one of thy hired servants."
But his father put his hand on his mouth. " No more of that,"
says he; " I forgive you all; you shall not say any thing about
being my servant—I will have none of that. Come along,"
says he, " come in, poor prodigal. Ho," said he to the servants, " bring hither the best robe, and put it on him, and put
shoes on his poor bleeding feet; and bring hither the fatted
calf, and kill it; and let us eat and be merry: for this my
son was dead, and is alive again, he was lost, and is found.
And then they began to be merry." O, what a precious reception for one of the chief of sinners! Good Matthew Henry
says—" His father saw him, there were eyes of mercy; he ran
to meet him, there were legs of mercy; he put his arms round
his neck, there were arms of mercy; he kissed him, there
were kisses of mercy; he said to him—there were words of
mercy—'Bring hither the best robe,' there were deeds of
mercy, wonders of mercy—all mercy. O, what a God of
mercy he is!"

Now, prodigal, you do the same. Has God put it into your
heart? There are many who have been running away a long
time now. Does God say " return?" O, I bid you return, then,
for as surely as ever thou dost return he will take thee in.
There never was a poor sinner yet who came to Christ, whom
Christ turned away. If he turns you away you will be the
first. O, if you could but try him! " Ah, sir, I am so black,
so filthy, so vile." Well, come along with you—you can not
be blacker than the prodigal. Come to your father's house,

and as surely as he is God he will keep his word—" Him that cometh unto me I will no wise cast out."

O, if I might hear that some had come to Christ this morning, I would indeed bless God! I must tell here, for the honor of God and Christ, one remarkable circumstance, and then I have done. You will remember that one morning I mentioned the case of an infidel who had been a scorner and scoffer, but who, through reading one of my printed sermons, had been brought to God's house and then to God's feet. Well, last Christmas day, the same infidel gathered together all his books, and went into the market-place at Norwich, and there made a public recantation of all his errors, and a profession of Christ, and then taking up all his books which he had written, and had in his house, on evil subjects, burned them in the sight of the people. I have blessed God for such a wonder of grace as that, and pray that there may be many more such, who, though they be born prodigal, will yet return home, saying, " I have sinned."

SERMON XVII

FAITH

"Without faith it is impossible to please God."—HEBREWS, xi. 6

THE old Assembly's Catechism asks, "What is the chief
end of man?" and its answer is, "To glorify God, and to en
joy him for ever." The answer is exceedingly correct; but
it might have been equally truthful if it had been shorter.
The chief end of man is "to please God;" for in so doing—we
need not say it, because it is an undoubted fact—in so doing
he will please himself. The chief end of man, we believe, in
this life and in the next, is to please God his Maker. If any
man pleases God, he does that which conduces most to his own
temporal and eternal welfare. Man can not please God without bringing to himself a great amount of happiness; for if
any man pleases God, it is because God accepts him as his son,
gives him the blessings of adoption, pours upon him the bounties of his grace, makes him a blessed man in this life, and in-
sures him a crown of everlasting life, which he shall wear, and
which shall shine with unfading luster, when the wreaths of
earth's glory have all been melted away; while, on the other
hand, if a man does not please God, he inevitably brings upon
himself sorrow and suffering in this life; he puts a worm and
a rottenness in the core of all his joys; he fills his death-pillow
with thorns, and he supplies the eternal fire with faggots of
flame which shall for ever consume him. He that pleases God
is, through divine grace, journeying. onward to the ultimate
reward of all those that love and fear God; but he who is ill-
pleasing to God must, for Scripture has declared it, be banished from the presence of God, and consequently from the
enjoyment of happiness. If, then, we be right in saying that
to please God is to be happy, the one important question is,

how can I please God? and there is something very solemn in the utterance of our text: " Without faith it is impossible to please God." That is to say, do what you may, strive as earnestly as you can, live as excellently as you please, make what sacrifices you choose, be as eminent as you can for every thing that is lovely and of good repute, yet none of these things can be pleasing to God unless they be mixed with faith. As the Lord said to the Jews, " With all your sacrifices you must offer salt ;" so he says to us, " With all your doings you must bring faith, or else ' without faith it is impossible to please God.' "

This is an old law ; it is as old as the first man. No sooner were Cain and Abel born into this world, and no sooner had they attained to manhood, than God gave a practical proclamation of this law, that " without faith it is impossible to please him." Cain and Abel, one bright day, erected an altar side by side with each other. Cain fetched of the fruits of the trees and of the abundance of the soil, and placed them upon his altar ; Abel brought of the firstlings of the flock, and laid it upon his altar. It was to be decided which God would accept. Cain had brought his best, but he brought it without faith ; Abel brought his sacrifice, but he brought it with faith in Christ. Now, then, which shall best succeed ? The offerings are equal in value ; so far as they themselves are concerned they are alike good. Upon which will the heavenly fire descend ? Which will the Lord God consume with the fire of his pleasure ? O ! I see Abel's offering burning, and Cain's countenance has fallen, for unto Abel and unto his offering the Lord had respect, but unto Cain and his offering the Lord had no respect. It shall be the same till the last man shall be gathered into heaven. There shall never be an acceptable offering which has not been seasoned with faith. Good though it may be, as apparently good in itself as that which has faith, yet unless faith be with it God never can and never will accept it, for he here declares, " Without faith it is impossible to please God."

I shall endeavor to pack my thoughts closely this morning, and be as brief as I can, consistently with a full explanation of the theme. I shall first have an *exposition* of what is faith secondly, I shall have an *argument*, that without faith it is im possible to be saved ; and thirdly, I shall ask a *question*— Have you that faith which pleases God ? We shall have, then, an exposition, an argument, and a question.

I. First, for the EXPOSITION. What is faith ?

The old writers, who are by far the most sensible—for you will notice that the books that were written about two hun-dred years ago by the old Puritans have more sense in one line than there is in a page of our new books, and more in a page than there is in a whole volume of our modern divinity —the old writers tell you, that faith is made up of three things : first, knowledge, then assent, and then what they call affiance, or the laying hold of the knowledge to which we give assent and making it our own by trusting in it.

1. Let us begin, then, at the beginning. The first thing in faith is *knowledge.* A man can not believe what he does not know. That is a clear, self-evident axiom. If I have never heard of a thing in all my life, and do not know it, I can not believe it. And yet there are some persons who have a faith like that of the fuller, who when he was asked what he be-lieved, said, "I believe what the church believes." "What does the church believe ?" "The church believes what I believe." "And pray what do you and the church believe ?" "Why we both believe the same thing." Now this man be-lieved nothing, except that the church was right, but in what he could not tell. It is idle for a man to say, "I am a be-liever," and yet not to know what he believes ; but yet I have seen some persons in this position. A violent sermon has been preached, which has stirred up their blood ; the minister has cried, " Believe ! believe ! believe !" and the people on a sud-den have got it into their heads that they were believers, and have walked out of their place of worship and said, " I am a believer." And if they were asked, " Pray what do you be-lieve ?" they could not give a reason for the hope that was in them. They believe they intend to go to chapel next Sunday ; they intend to join that class of people ; they intend to be very violent in their singing and very wonderful in their rant ; therefore they believe they shall be saved ; but what they be-ieve they can not tell. Now, I hold no man's faith to be sure

faith, unless he knows what he believes. If he says, " I be lieve," and does not know what he believes, how can that be true faith ? The apostle has said, " How can they believe on him of whom they have not heard ? and how can they hear without a preacher ? and how can they preach except they be sent ?" It is necessary, then, to true faith, that a man should know something of the Bible. Believe me, this is an age when the Bible is not so much thought of as it used to be. Some hundred years ago the world was covered with bigotry, cruelty, and superstition. We always run to extremes, and we have just gone to the other extreme now. It was then said, " One faith is right, down with all others by the rack and by the sword !" Now it is said, " However contradictory our creeds may be, they are all right." If we did but use our common sense we should know that it is not so. But some reply, " Such-and-such a doctrine need not be preached, and need not be believed." Then, sir, if it need not be preached it need not be revealed. You impugn the wisdom of God, when you say a doctrine is unnecessary ; for you do as much as say that God has revealed something which was not neces- sary, and he would be as unwise to do more than was neces- sary as if he had done less than was necessary. We believe that every doctrine of God's Word ought to be studied by men, and that their faith should lay hold of the whole matter of the sacred Scriptures, and more especially upon all that part of Scripture which concerns the person of our all-blessed Redeemer. There must be some degree of knowledge before there can be faith. " Search the Scriptures," then, " for in them ye think ye have eternal life, and they are they which testify of Christ ;" and by searching and reading cometh knowledge, and by knowledge cometh faith, and through faith cometh salvation.

2. But a man may know a thing, and yet not have faith. I may know a thing, and yet not believe it. Therefore *assent* must go with faith : that is to say, what we know we must also agree unto, as being most certainly the verity of God. Now, in order to faith it is necessary that I should not only read the Scriptures and understand them, but that I should receive them in my soul as being the very truth of the living God

and should devoutly with my whole heart receive the whole of Scripture as being inspired of the Most High, and the whole of the doctrine which he requires me to believe to my salvation. You are not allowed to halve the Scriptures, and to believe what you please; you are not allowed to believe the Scriptures with a half-heartedness, for if you do this willfully, you have not the faith which looks alone to Christ. True faith gives its full assent to the Scriptures; it takes a page and says, "No matter what is in the page, I believe it;" it turns over the next chapter and says, "Herein are some things hard to be understood, which they that are unlearned and unstable do wrest, as they do also the other Scriptures, to their destruction; but, hard though it be, I believe it." It sees the Trinity; it can not understand the Trinity in Unity, but it believes it. It sees an atoning sacrifice; there is something difficult in the thought, but it believes it; and whatever it be which it sees in revelation, it devoutly puts its lips to the book, and says, "I love it all; I give my full, free, and hearty assent to every word of it, whether it be the threatening, or the promise, the proverb, the precept, or the blessing. I believe that since it is all the word of God it is all most assuredly true." Whosoever would be saved must know the Scriptures, and must give full assent unto them.

3. But a man may have all this, and yet not possess true faith; for the chief part of faith lies in the last head, namely, in an *affiance* to the truth; not the believing it merely, but the taking hold of it as being ours, and in the resting on it for salvation. Recumbency on the truth was the word which the old preachers used. You will understand that word. Leaning on it; saying, "This is truth, I trust my salvation on it." Now, true faith in its very essence rests in this—a leaning upon Christ. It will not save me to know that Christ is a Saviour; but it will save me *to trust* him to be *my* Saviour. I shall not be delivered from the wrath to come, by believing that his atonement is sufficient, but I shall be saved by making that atonement my trust, my refuge, and my all. The pith, the essence of faith lies in this—a casting one's-self on the promise. It is not the life-buoy on board the ship that saves the man when he is drowning, nor is it his belief that it is an ex-

cellent and successful invention. No! He must have it around
his loins, or his hand upon it, or else he will sink. To use an
old and hackneyed illustration . suppose a fire in the upper
room of a house, and the people gathered in the street. A
child is in the upper story : how is he to escape? He can
not leap down—that were to be dashed to pieces. A strong
man comes beneath, and cries, " Drop into my arms." It is a
part of faith to know that the man is there ; it is another
part of faith to believe that the man is strong ; but the essence
of faith lies in the dropping down into the man's arms. That
is the proof of faith, and the real pith and essence of it. So,
sinner, thou art to know that Christ died for sin ; thou art
also to understand that Christ is able to save, and thou art to
believe that ; but thou art not saved, unless in addition to that
thou puttest thy trust in him to be thy Saviour, and to be
thine for ever. As Hart says in the hymn, which really ex-
presses the gospel,

> " Venture on him, venture wholly ;
>   Let no other trust intrude ;
>   None but Jesus
>   Can do helpless sinners good."

This is the faith which saves; and however unholy may have
been your lives up to this hour, this faith, if given to you at this
moment, will blot out all your sins, will change your nature,
make you a new man in Christ Jesus, lead you to live a holy
life, and make your eternal salvation as secure as if an angel
should take you on his bright wings this morning, and carry
you immediately to heaven. Have you that faith ? That is
the one all-important question ; for while with faith men are
saved, without it men are damned. As Brookes hath said in one
of his admirable works, " He that believeth on the Lord Jesus
Christ, shall be saved, be his sins never so many ; but he that
believeth not in the Lord Jesus must be damned, be his sins
never so few." Hast thou faith ? For the text declares,
" Without faith it is impossible to please God."

II. And now we come to the ARGUMENT, why, without faith,
we can not be saved.

Now there are some gentlemen present who are saying

"Now we shall see whether Mr. Spurgeon has any logic in
him." No, you won't, sirs, because I never pretend to exer
cise it. I hope I have the logic which can appeal to men's
hearts; but I am not very prone to use the less powerful logic
of the head, when I can win the heart in another manner.
But if it were needful, I should not be afraid to prove that I
know more of logic and of many other things than the little
men who undertake to censure me. It were well if they
knew how to hold their tongues, which is at least a fine part
of rhetoric. My argument shall be such as I trust will appeal
to the heart and conscience, although it may not exactly
please those who are always so fond of syllogistic demonstration,

> "Who could a hair divide
> Between the west and north-west side."

1. "Without faith it is impossible to please God." And I
gather it from the fact, that there never has been the case of
a man recorded in Scripture who did please God without
faith. The 11th chapter of the Hebrews is the chapter of the
men who pleased God. Listen to their names: "by faith
Abel offered unto God a more excellent sacrifice;" "by faith
Enoch was translated;" "by faith Noah built an ark;" "by
faith Abraham went out into a place that he should afterward
receive;" "by faith he sojourned in the land of promise;"
'by faith Sarah bore Isaac;" "by faith Abraham offered up
Isaac;" "by faith Moses gave up the wealth of Egypt;" "by
faith Isaac blessed Jacob;" "by faith Jacob blessed the sons
of Joseph;" "by faith Joseph, when he died, made mention
of the departure of the children of Israel;" "by faith the Red
Sea was dried up;" "by faith the walls of Jericho fell down;"
"by faith the harlot Rahab was saved;" "and what shall I
more say? for the time would fail me to tell of Gideon, and
of Barak, and of Samson, and of Jephtha, of David also, and
Samuel, and of the prophets." But all these were men of
faith. Others mentioned in Scripture have done something
but God did not accept them. Men have humbled themselves,
and yet God has not saved them. Ahab did, and yet his sins
were never forgiven. Men have repented, and yet have not
been saved, because theirs was the wrong repentance. Judas

repented, and went and hanged himself, and was not saved.
Men have confessed their sins, and have not been saved.
Saul did it. He said to David, "I have sinned against thee,
my son David;" and yet he went on as he did before. Multitudes have confessed the name of Christ, and have done many
marvelous things, and yet they have never been pleasing to
God, from this simple reason, that they had not faith. And
if there be not one mentioned in Scripture, which is the his
tory of some thousand years, it is not likely that in the other
two thousand years of the world's history there would have
been one, when there was not one during the first four thou
sand.

2. But the next argument is, *faith is the stooping grace*,
and nothing can make a man stoop without faith. Now, unless man does stoop, his sacrifice can not be accepted. The
angels know this. When they praise God, they do it vailing
their faces with their wings. The redeemed know it. When
they praise God, they cast their crowns before his feet. Now,
a man that has not faith proves that he can not stoop; for he
has not faith for this reason, because he is too proud to believe. He declares he will not yield his intellect, he will not
become a child and believe meekly what God tells him to believe. He is too proud, and he can not enter heaven, because
the door of heaven is so low that no one can enter in by it
unless they will bow their heads. There never was a man
who could walk into salvation erect. We must go to Christ
on our bended knees; for though he is a door big enough for
the greatest sinner to come in, he is a door so low that men
must stoop if they would be saved. Therefore, it is that faith
is necessary, because a want of faith is certain evidence of
absence of humility.

3. But now for other reasons. Faith is necessary to salva
tion, because we are told in Scripture that *works can not save.*
To tell a very familiar story, that even the poorest may not
misunderstand what I say. A minister was one day going to
preach. He climbed a hill on his road. Beneath him lay the
villages, sleeping in their beauty, with the corn fields motionless in the sunshine; but he did not look at them, for his attention was arrested by a woman standing at her door, and

who, upon seeing him, came up to him with the greatest anxiety, and said, "O, sir, have you any keys about you? I have broken the key of my drawers, and there are some things that I must get directly." Said he, "I have no keys." She was disappointed, expecting that every one would have keys. "But suppose," he said, "I had some keys, they might not fit your lock, and therefore you could not get the articles you want. But do not distress yourself, wait till some one else comes up. But," said he, wishing to improve the occasion, "have you never heard of the key of heaven?" "Ah! yes," she said, "I have lived long enough and have gone to church long enough to know that if we work hard and get our bread by the sweat of our brow, and act well toward our neighbors, and behave, as the catechism says, lowly and reverenly to all our betters, and if we do our duty in that station of life in which it has pleased God to place us, and say our prayers regularly, we shall be saved." "Ah!" said he, "my good woman, that is a broken key, for you have broken the commandments, you have not fulfilled all your duties. It is a good key, but you have broken it." "Pray, sir," said she, believing that he understood the matter, and looking frightened, "what have I left out?" "Why," said he, "the all-important thing, the blood of Jesus Christ. Don't you know it is said, the key of heaven is at his girdle; he openeth, and no man shutteth; he shutteth, and no man openeth?" And explaining it more fully to her, he said, "It is Christ, and Christ alone, that can open heaven to you, and not your good works." "What, minister," said she, "are our good works useless then?" "No," said he, "not after faith. If you believe first, you may have as many good works as you please; but if you believe you will never trust in them, for if you trust in them you have spoiled them, and they are not good works any longer. Have as many good works as you please; still, put your trust wholly in the Lord Jesus Christ, for if you do not, your key will never unlock heaven's gate." So, then, my hearers, we must have true faith, because the old key of works is so broken by us all that we never shall enter Paradise by it. If any of you pretend that you have no sins, to be very plain with you, you deceive yourselves, and the truth is not in you. If you conceive that by your good works you shall enter heaven, never was there a mcre fell delusion, and you shall find at the last great day that your hopes are worthless, and that like sere leaves from the autumn trees your noblest doings shall be blown away, or kindled into a flame wherein you yourselves must suffer for ever. Take heed of your good works; get them after faith, but remember, the way to be saved is simply to believe in Jesus Christ.

4. Again: without faith it is impossible to be saved, and to please God, because without faith there is *no union to Christ*. Now, union to Christ is indispensable to our salvation. If I come before God's throne with my prayers, I shall never get them answered unless I bring Christ with me. The Molossians of old, when they could not get a favor from their king, adopted a singular expedient; they took the king's only son in their arms, and falling on their knees, cried, " O king, for thy son's sake grant our request." He smiled and said, " I deny nothing to those who plead my son's name." It is so with God. He will deny nothing to the man who comes, having Christ at his elbow; but if he comes alone he must be cast away. Union to Christ is, after all, the great point in salvation. Let me tell you a story to illustrate this. The stupendous falls of Niagara have been spoken of in every part of the world; but while they are marvelous to hear of, and wonderful as a spectacle, they have been very destructive to human life, when by accident any have been carried down the cataract. Some years ago two men, a bargeman and a collier, were in a boat, and found themselves unable to manage it, it being carried so swiftly down the current that they must both inevitably be borne down and dashed to pieces. Persons on the shore saw them, but were unable to do much for their rescue. At last, however, one man was saved by floating a rope to him, which he grasped. The same instant that the rope came into his hand a log floated by the other man. The thoughtless and confused bargeman instead of seizing the rope laid hold on the log. It was a fatal mistake; they were both in imminent peril, but the one was drawn to shore because he had a connection with the people on the land, whilst the other, clinging to the log, was borne irresistibly along and never heard of

afterward. Do you not see that here is a practical illustration? Faith is a connection with Christ. Christ is on the shore, so to speak, holding the rope of faith, and if we lay hold of it with the hand of our confidence he pulls us to shore; but our good works, having no connection with Christ, are drifted along down the gulf of fell despair. Grapple them as tightly as we may, even with hooks of steel, they can not avail us in the least degree. You will see, I am sure, what I wish to show you. Some object to anecdotes; I shall use them till they have done objecting to them. The truth is never more powerfully set forth to men than by telling them, as Christ did, a story of a certain man with two sons, or a certain householder who went a journey, divided his substance, and gave to some ten talents, to another one.

Faith, then, is a union with Christ. Take care you have it; for if not, cling to your works, and there you go floating down the stream! Cling to your works, and there you go dashing down the gulf! Lost because your works have no hold on Christ and no connection with the blessed Redeemer! But thou, poor sinner, with all thy sin about thee, if the rope is round thy loins, and Christ has a hold of it, fear not!

> " His honor is engaged to save
> The meanest of his sheep;
> All that his heavenly Father gave,
> His hands securely keep."

5. Just one more argument, and then I have done with it. " Without faith it is impossible to please God," because it is impossible to preserve holiness without faith. What a multitude of fair-weather Christians we have in this age! Many Christians resemble the nautilus, which in fine smooth weather swims on the surface of the sea, in a splendid little squadron, like the mighty ships; but the moment the first breath of wind ruffles the waves, they take in their sails and sink into the depths. Many Christians are the same. In good company, in evangelical drawing-rooms, in pious parlors, in chapels and vestries, they are tremendously religious; but if they are exposed to a little ridicule, if some should smile at them and call them Methodist or Presbyterian, or some name of re-

proach, it is all over with religion till the next fine day. Then when it is fine weather, and religion will answer their purpose, up go the sails again, and they are as pious as before. Believe me, that kind of religion is worse than irreligion. I do like a man to be thoroughly what he is—a downright man ; and if a man does not love God, do not let him say he does ; but if he be a true Christian, a follower of Jesus, let him say it and stand up for it ; there is nothing to be ashamed of it in it ; the only thing to be ashamed of is to be hypocritical. Let us be honest to our profession, and it will be our glory. Ah ! what would you do without faith in times of persecution ? You good and pious people that have no faith, what would you do if the stake were again erected in Smithfield, and if once more the fires consumed the saints to ashes—if the Lollard's tower were again opened, if the rack were again plied, or even if the stocks were used, as they have been used by a Protestant church, as witness the persecution of my predecessor, Benjamin Keach, who was once set in the stocks at Aylesbury for writing a book against infant baptism. If even the mildest form of persecution were revived, how would the people be scattered abroad ! And some of the shepherds would be leaving their flocks.

III. And now, in conclusion, THE QUESTION, the vital question. Dear hearer, have you faith ? Dost thou believe on the Lord Jesus Christ with all thy heart ? If so, thou mayest hope to be saved. Ay, thou mayest conclude with absolute certainty that thou shalt never see perdition. Have you faith ? Shall I help you to answer that question ? I will give you three tests, as briefly as ever I can, not to weary you, and then farewell this morning. He that has faith has renounced his own righteousness. If thou puttest one atom of trust in thyself thou hast no faith ; if thou dost place even a particle of reliance upon any thing else but what Christ did, thou hast no faith. If thou dost trust in thy works, then thy works are antichrist, and Christ and antichrist can never go together Christ will have all or nothing ; he must be a whole Saviour or no Saviour at all. If then, you have faith, you can say,

> " Nothing in my hands I bring,
> Simply to the cross I cling "

Then true faith may be known by this, that it begets a great esteem for the person of Christ. Dost thou love Christ? Couldst thou die for him? Dost thou seek to serve him? Dost thou love his people? Canst thou say

> "Jesus, I love thy charming name,
> 'Tis music to my ear."

O! if thou dost not love Christ thou dost not believe in him: for to believe in Christ, begets love. And yet more: he that has true faith will have true obedience. If a man says he has faith and has no works, he lies; if any man declares that he believes on Christ, and yet does not lead a holy life, he makes a mistake; for while we do not trust in good works, we know that faith always begets good works. Faith is the father of holiness, and he has not the parent who loves not the child. God's blessings are blessings with both his hands. In the one hand he gives pardon: but in the other hand he always gives holiness; and no man can have the one, unless he has the other.

And now, dear hearers, shall I down upon my knees, and entreat you for Christ's sake to answer this question in your own silent chamber: Have you faith? O! answer it, Yes— or No. Leave off saying, "I do not know," or "I do not care." Ah! ye *will* care one day, when the earth is reeling, and the world is tossing to and fro; ye will care when God shall summon you to judgment, and when he shall condemn the faithless and the unbelieving. O! that ye were wise—that ye would care now, and if any of you feel your need of Christ, let me beg of you, for Christ's sake, now to seek faith in him who is exalted on high to give repentance and remission, and who, if he has given you repentance, will give you remission too. O sinners, who know your sins! "believe on the Lord Jesus, and ye shall be saved." Cast yourselves upon his love and blood, his doing and his dying, his miseries and his merits: and if you do this you shall never fall, but you shall be saved now, and saved in that great day, when not to be saved will be horrible indeed. "Turn ye, turn ye; why will ye die, O house of Israel?" Lay hold on him, touch the hem of his garment, and ye shall be healed. May God help you so to do; for Christ's sake! Amen and Amen.

SERMON XVIII

RAHAB'S FAITH

'By faith the harlot Rahab perished not with them that believed not, when she had received the spies with peace. —HEBREWS, xi. 31

In almost every capital of Europe there are varieties of triumphal arches or columns, upon which are recorded the valiant deeds of the country's generals, its emperors, or its monarchs. You will find, in one case, the thousand battles of a Napoleon recorded, and in another, you find the victories of a Nelson pictured. It seems, therefore, but right, that faith, which is the mightiest of the mighty, should have a pillar raised to its honor, upon which its valiant deeds should be recorded. The apostle Paul undertook to raise the structure, and he erected a most magnificent pillar in the chapter before us. It recites the victories of faith. It begins with one triumph of faith, and then proceeds to others. We have, in one place, faith triumphing over *death ;* Enoch entered not the gates of hades, but reached heaven by another road from that which is usual to men. We have faith, in another place, wrestling with *time ;* Noah, warned of God concerning things not seen as yet, wrestled with time, which placed his deluge a hundred and twenty years away ; and yet, in the confidence of faith, he believed against all rational expectation, against all probability, and his faith was more than a match for probability and time too. We have faith triumphing over *infirmity*—when Abraham begetteth a son in his old age. And then we have faith triumphing over *natural affection*, as we see Abraham climbing to the top of the hill and raising the knife to slay his only and beloved son at the command of God. We see faith, again, entering the lists with the infirmities of *old age* and the pains of the last struggle, as we read, " By faith Jacob when he was dying, blessed both the sons of Joseph, and wor shiped, leaning on the top of his staff." Then we have faith combating the allurements of a wealthy court. "By faith Moses esteemed the reproach of Christ greater riches than the treasures in Egypt." We see faith dauntless in courage when Moses forsook Egypt, not fearing the wrath of the king, and equally patient in suffering when he endured as seeing him who is invisible. We have faith dividing seas, and casting down strong walls. And then, as though the greatest victory should be recorded last, we have faith entering the lists with sin, holding a tournament with iniquity, and coming off more than a conqueror. "Rahab perished not with them that believed not, when she had received the spies with peace." That this woman was no mere hostess, but a real harlot, I have abundantly proved to every candid hearer while reading the chapter. I am persuaded that nothing but a spirit of distaste for free grace would ever have led any commentator to deny her sin.

I do think this triumph of faith over sin is not the least here recorded, but that if there be any superiority ascribable to any one of faith's exploits, this is, in some sense, the greatest of all. What! faith, didst thou fight with hideous lust? What! wouldst thou struggle with the fiery passion which sendeth forth flame from human breasts? What! wouldst thou touch with thy hallowed fingers foul and bestial debauchery? "Yea," says faith, "I did encounter this abomination of iniquity; I delivered this woman from the loathsome chambers of vice, the wily snares of enchantment, and the fearful penalty of transgression; yea, I brought her off saved and rescued, gave her purity of heart, and renewed in her the beauty of holiness; and now her name shall be recorded in the roll of my triumphs as a woman full of sin, yet saved by faith."

I shall have some things to say this morning concerning this notable victory of faith over sin, such as I think will lead you to see that this was indeed a supereminent triumph of faith. I will make my divisions alliterative, that you may recollect them. This woman's faith was *saving faith, singular faith, stable faith, self-denying faith, sympathising faith,* and *sanctifying faith.* Let no one run away, when I shall have ex

‚ounded the first point, and miss the rest, for you can not apprehend the whole power of her faith unless you remember each of those particulars I am about to mention.

I. In the first place, this woman's faith was SAVING FAITH. All the other persons mentioned here were doubtless saved by faith; but I do not find it specially remarked concerning any of them that they perished not through their faith; while it is particularly said of this woman, that she was delivered amid the general destruction of Jericho purely and only through her faith. And, without doubt, her salvation was not merely of a temporal nature, not merely a deliverance of her body from the sword, but redemption of her soul from hell. O! what a mighty thing faith is, when it saves the soul from going down to the pit! So mighty is the ever-rushing torrent of sin, that no arm but that which is as strong as Deity can ever stop the sinner from being hurried down to the gulf of black despair, and, when nearing that gulf, so impetuous is the torrent of divine wrath, that nothing can snatch the soul from perdition but an atonement which is as divine as God himself. Yet faith is the instrument of accomplishing the whole work. It delivers the sinner from the stream of sin, and so, laying hold upon the omnipotence of the Spirit, it rescues him from that great whirlpool of destruction into which his soul was being hurried. What a great thing it is to save a soul! You can never know how great it is unless you have stood in the capacity of a saviour to other men. Yon heroic man who, yesterday, when the house was burning, climbed the creaking stair-case, and, almost suffocated by the smoke, entered an upper chamber, snatched a babe from its bed and a woman from the window, bore them both down in his arms, and saved them at the peril of his own life, *he* can tell you what a great thing it is to save a fellow-creature. Yon noble-hearted youth who, yesterday, sprang into the river, at the hazard of himself, and snatched a drowning man from death, he felt, when he stood upon the shore, what a great thing it was to save life. Ah! but you can not tell what a great thing it is to save a soul. It is only our Lord Jesus Christ who can tell you that, for he is the only one who has ever been the Saviour of sinners. And remember, you can only know how great a thing faith is by knowing the infinite value of the salvation of a soul. "Now by faith, the harlot Rahab was delivered." That she was really saved in a gospel sense as well as temporally, seems to me to be proved from her reception of the spies which was an emblem of the entrance of the word into her heart, and her hanging out of the scarlet thread was an evidence of faith, not unaptly picturing faith in the blood of Jesus the Redeemer. But who can measure the length and breadth of that word—*salvation*. Ah! it was a mighty deed which faith accomplished when h bore her off in safety. Poor sinner! take comfort. The same faith which saved Rahab can save thee. Art thou literally one of Rahab's sisters in guilt? She was saved, and so mayest thou be, if God shall grant thee repentance. Woman! art thou loathsome to thyself? Dost thou stand at this moment in this assembly, and say, "I am ashamed to be here; I know I have no right to stand among people who are chaste and honest?" I bid thee still remain; yea, come again and make this thy Sabbath house of prayer. Thou art no intruder! Thou art welcome! For thou hast a sacred right to the courts of mercy. Thou hast a sacred right; for here *sinners* are in vited, and thou art such. Believe in Christ, and thou, like Rahab, shalt not perish with the disobedient, but even thou shalt be saved.

And now there is some gentleman in the audience who says, "There's a gospel for you; it is a kind of sanctuary for wicked men, unto which the worst of people may run and be saved." Yes, that is the stale objection which Celsus used against Ori gen in his discussion. "But," said Origen, "it is true, Celsus that Christ's gospel is a sanctuary for thieves, robbers, mur derers, and harlots. But know this, it is not a sanctuary merely, it is an hospital too; for it heals their sins, delivers them from their diseases, and they are not afterwards what they were before they received the gospel." I ask no man to-day to come to Christ, and then continue his sins. If so, I should ask him to do an absurdity. As well might I talk of delivering a Prometheus, while his chains are allowed to re main upon him and bind him to his rock. It can not be. Christ taketh away the vulture from the conscience, but he taketh away the chains too, and maketh the man wholly free when he doeth it all. Yet, we repeat it again, the chief of sinners are as welcome to Christ as the best of saints. The fountain filled with blood was opened for black ones; the robe of Christ was woven for naked ones; the balm of Calvary was compounded for sick ones; life came into the world to raise the dead. And O! ye perishing and guilty souls, may God give you Rahab's faith, and you shall have this salvation, and shall with her stand yonder, where the white-robed spotless hosts sing unending hallelujah to God and the Lamb.

II. But mark, Rahab's faith was a SINGULAR FAITH. The city of Jericho was about to be attacked; within its walls there were hosts of people of all classes and characters, and they knew right well that if their city should be sacked and stormed they would all be put to death; but yet, strange to say, there was not one of them who repented of sin, or who even asked for mercy, except this woman who had been a harlot. She, and she alone was delivered, a solitary one among a multitude. Now, have you ever felt that it is a very hard thing to have a singular faith? It is the easiest thing in the world to believe as every body else believes, but the difficulty is to believe a thing alone, when no one else thinks as you think; to be the solitary champion of a righteous cause when the enemy mustereth his thousands to the battle. Now, this was the faith of Rahab. She had not one who felt as she did, who could enter into her feelings and realize the value of her faith. She stood alone. O! it is a noble thing to be the lonely follower of despised truth. There be some who could tell you a tale of standing up alone. There have been days when the world poured continually a river of infamy and calumny upon them, but they stemmed the torrent, and, by continued grace, made strong in weakness, they held their own until the current turned, and they, in their success, were praised and applauded by the very men who sneered before. Then did the world accord them the name of "great." But where lay their greatness? Why, in this, that they stood as firm in the storm as they stood in the calm—that they were as content to serve God alone as they were to run by fifties. To be good we must be singular. Christians must swim against the stream. Dead fish always float down the stream, but the living fish forces its way against the current. Now, worldly religious men will go just as every body else goes. That is nothing. The thing is, to stand alone. Like Elijah, when he said, "I only am left, and they seek my life;" to feel in one's self that we believe as firmly as if a thousand witnesses stood up by our side. O! there is no great right in a man, no strong-minded right, unless he dares to be singular. Why, the most of you are as afraid as you ever can be to go out of the fashions, and you spend more money than you ought because you think you must be respectable. You dare not move in opposition to your brethren and sisters in the circle in which you move; and therefore you involve yourselves in difficulties. You are blindfolded by the rich fabric of fashion, and therefore many a wrong thing is tolerated because it is customary. But a strong-minded man is one who does not try to be singular, but who *dares* to be singular, when he knows that to be singular is to be right. Now, Rahab's faith, sinner as she was, had this glory, this crown about its head, that she stood alone, "faithful among the faithless found."

And why should not God vouchsafe the same faith to thee my poor, sinning, but contrite hearer? You live in a back street, in a house which contains none but Sabbath breakers, and irreligious men and women. But if you have grace in your heart you will dare to do right. You belong to an infidel club; if you should make them a speech after your own conscience, they would hiss you; and if you forsook their company, they would persecute you. Go and try them. Dare them. See, whether you can do it; for if you are afraid of men, you are taken in a snare which *may prove* your *grief* and *is now* your *sin*. Mark you, the chief of sinners can make the most daring of saints; the worst men in the devil's army, when they are converted, make the truest soldiers for Jesus. The forlorn hope of Christendom has generally been led by men who have proved the high efficacy of grace to an eminent degree by having been saved from the deepest sins. Go on, and the Lord give you that high and singular faith!

III. Furthermore, this woman's faith was A STABLE FAITH, which stood firm in the midst of trouble. I have heard of a church clergyman who was once waited upon by his church warden, after a long time of drought, and was requested to put up the prayer for rain. "Well," said he, "my good man, I will offer it, but it's not a bit of use while the wind is in the east, I'm sure." There are many who have that kind of faith: they believe just so far as probabilities go with them, but when the promise and the probability part, then they follow the probability and part with the promise. They say, "The thing is likely, therefore I believe it." But that is no faith, it is sight. True faith exclaims, "The thing is unlikely, yet I believe it." This is real faith. Faith is to say, that "mountains, when in darkness hidden, are as real as in day." Faith is to look through that cloud, not with the eye of sight, which seeth naught, but with the eye of faith, which seeth every thing, and to say, "I trust him when I can not trace him; I tread the sea as firmly as I would the rock; I walk as securely in the tempest as in the sunshine, and lay myself to rest upon the surging billows of the ocean as contentedly as upon my bed." The faith of Rahab was the right sort of faith, for it was firm and enduring.

I will just have a little talk with Rahab this morning, as I suppose old Unbelief did commune with her. Now, my good woman, don't you see the absurdity of this thing? Why, the people of Israel are on the other side of Jordan, and there is no bridge: how are they to get over? Of course they must go up higher toward the fords; and then Jericho will be for a long time secure. They will take other cities before coming to Jericho; and, besides, the Canaanites are mighty, and the Israelites are only a parcel of slaves; they will soon be cut in pieces, and there will be an end of them; therefore, do not harbor these spies. Why put your life in jeapordy for such an improbability? "Ah," says she, "I do not care about the Jordan; my faith can believe across the Jordan, or else it were only a dry-land faith." By-and-by, they march through the Jordan dry shod, and then faith gets firmer confidence. "Ah!" says she, secretly within herself, what she would willingly have said to her neighbors, "will you not now believe? will you not now sue for mercy?" "No," they say; "the walls of Jericho are strong; can the feeble host resist us? And lo on the morrow the troops are out, and what do they

do ? They simply blow a number of rams' horns ; her neigh
bors say, " Why, Rahab, you do not mean to say you believe
now ? They are mad." The people just go round the city,
and all hold their tongues, except the few priests blowing
rams' horns. " Why, it is ridiculous. It were quite a new
thing in warfare to hear of men taking a city by blowing rams'
horns." That was the first day ; probably the next day Ra
hab thought they would come with scaling-ladders and mount
the walls ; but no, rams' horns again, up to the seventh day ·
and this woman kept the scarlet thread in the window all the
time, kept her father and mother, and brothers and sisters in
the house, and would not let them go out ; and on the seventh
day, when the people made a great shout, the wall of the city
fell flat to the ground ; but her faith overcame her womanly
timidity, and she remained within, although the wall was tumbling to the ground. Rahab's house stood alone upon the
wall, a solitary fragment amid a universal wreck, and she
and her household were all saved. Now would you have
thought that such a rich plant would grow in such poor soil—
that strong faith could grow in such a sinful heart as that of
Rahab ? Ah ! but here it is that God exercises his great hus
bandry. " My Father is the husbandman," said Christ. Any
husbandman can get a good crop out of good soil ; but God is
the husbandman who can grow cedars on rocks, who can not
only put the hyssop upon the wall, but put the oak there too
and make the greatest faith spring up in the most unlikely position. All glory to his grace ! the great sinner may become
great in faith. Be of good cheer, then, sinner ! If Christ
should make thee repent, thou hast no need to think that thou
shalt be the least in the family. O ! no ; thy name may yet
be written among the mightiest of the mighty, and thou mayest stand as a memorable and triumphant instance of the
power of faith.

IV. This woman's faith was A SELF-DENYING FAITH. She
dared to risk her life for the sake of the spies. She knew
that if they were found in her house she would be put to
death ; but though she was so weak as to do a sinful deed to
preserve them, yet she was so *strong* that she would run the
risk of being put to death to save these two men. It is some-

thing to be able to deny ourselves. An American once said
" I have got a good religion ; it's the right sort of religion ; I
do not know that it costs me a cent a year ; and yet I believe
I am as truly a religious man as any body." " Ah !" said one
who heard it, "the Lord have mercy on your miserable stingy
soul for if you had been saved you would not have been con
tent with a cent a year"—a halfpenny per annum ! I hazard
this assertion, that there is nothing in the faith of that man
who does not exercise self-denial. If we never give any thing
to Christ's cause, work for Christ, deny ourselves for Christ,
the root of the matter is not in us. I might call some of you
hypocrites : you sing,

> " And if I might make some reserve,
>   And duty did not call,
> I love my God with zeal so great,
>   That I could give him all."

Yes, *but you would not, though ;* you know better than that,
for you do not, as it is, give all, no, nor yet half, nor yet the
thousandth part. I suppose you think you are *poor* yourselves,
though you have got some thousand pounds odd a year, and
so you keep it yourself, under the notion that " he that giveth
to the poor lendeth to the Lord." I don't know how else it
's you make your religion square with itself, and be at all consistent. This woman said, "If I must die for these men, I
will ; I am prepared, bad name as I have, to have a worse
name still ; as a traitor to my country I am prepared to be
handed down to infamy, if it be necessary, for having betrayed
my country in taking in these spies, for I know it is God's will
it should be done, and do it I will at every hazard." O men
and brethren, trust not your faith, unless it has self-denial
with it. Faith and self-denial, like the Siamese twins, are
born together, and must live together, and the food that nour-
isheth one must nourish both. But this woman, poor sinner
as she was, would deny herself. She brought her life, even as
that other woman, who was a sinner, brought the alabaster box
of precious ointment, and broke it on the head of Christ.

V. Not to detain you too long, another point very briefly.
This woman's faith was A SYMPATHISING FAITH. She did not

believe for herself only ; she desired mercy for her relations
Said she, " I want to be saved, but that very desire makes me
want to have my father saved, and my mother saved, and my
brother saved, and my sister saved." I know a man who
walks seven miles every Sabbath to hear the gospel preached
at a certain place—a place where they preach *the* gospel. You
know that very particular, superfine sort—*the* gospel, a gospel,
he spirit of which consists in bad temper, carnal security, ar
rogance and a seared conscience. But this man was one day
met by a friend, who said to him, " Where is your wife ?"
" *Wife ?*" said he to him. " What ! does she not come with
you ?" " O ! no," said the man ; " she never goes anywhere."
" Well, but," said he, " don't you try to get her to go, and
the children ?" " No ; the fact of it is, I think, if I look to
myself, that is quite enough." " Well," said the other, " and
you believe that you are God's elect, do you ?" " Yes."
" Well, then," said the other, " I don't think you are, because
you are worse than a heathen man and a publican, for you
don't care for your own household ; therefore I don't think
you give much evidence of being God's elect, for they love
their fellow-creatures." So sure as our faith is real, it will
want to bring others in. You will say, " You want to make
proselytes." Yes ; and you will reply, that Christ said to the
Pharisees, " Ye compass sea and land to make one proselyte."
Yes, and Christ did not find fault with them for doing so :
what he found fault with them for was this—" When ye have
found him ye make him tenfold more the child of hell than
yourselves."

The spirit of proselyting is the spirit of Christianity, and we
ought to be desirous of possessing it. If any man will say, " I
believe such and such a thing is true, but I do not wish any
one else to believe it, I will tell you, it is a lie ; he does not
believe it, for it is impossible, heartily and really to believe a
thing, without desiring to make others believe the same. And
I am sure of this, moreover, it is impossible to know the value
of salvation without desiring to see others brought in. Said
that renowned preacher, Whitefield, " As soon as I was converted, I wanted to be the means of the conversion of all that
I had ever known. There were a number of young men that

I had played cards with, that I had sinned with, and transgressed with: the first thing I did was, to go to their houses to see what I could do for their salvation, nor could I rest until I had the pleasure of seeing many of them brought to the Saviour." This is a first-fruit of the Spirit. It is a kind of instinct in a young Christian. He must have other people feel what he feels. Says one young man, in writing to me this week, "I have been praying for my fellow-clerk in the office; I have desired that he might be brought to the Saviour, but at present there is no answer to my prayers."

Do not give a penny for that man's piety which will not spread itself. Unless we desire others to taste the benefits we have enjoyed, we are either inhuman monsters or outrageous hypocrites; I think the last is most likely. But this woman was so strong in faith that all her family were saved from destruction. Young woman! you have a father, and he hates the Saviour. O! pray for him. Mother! you have a son: he scoffs at Christ. Cry out to God for him. Ay, my friends—young people like myself—we little know what we owe to the prayers of our parents. I feel that I shall never be able sufficiently to bless God for a praying mother. I thought it was a great nuisance to be had in at such a time to pray, and more especially to be made to cry, as my mother used to make me cry. I would have laughed at the idea of any body else talking to me about these things; but when she prayed, and said, "Lord, save my son Charles," and then was overcome, and could not get any further for crying, you could not help crying too; you could not help feeling; it was of no use trying to stand against it. Ah! and there you are young man! Your mother is dying, and one thing which makes her death-bed bitter is, that you scoff God and hate Christ. O! it is the last stage of impiety, when a man can think lightly of a mother's feelings. I would hope there are none such here, but that those of you who have been so blessed, as to have been begotten and brought forth by pious men and women may take this into consideration—that to perish with a mother's prayers is to perish fearfully; for if a mother's prayers do not bring us to Christ, they are like drops of oil dropped into the flames of hell that will make them burn more

fiercely upon the soul for ever and ever. Take l eed of rushing to perdition over your mother's prayers!

There is an old woman weeping—do you know why? I
believe she has sons too, and she loves them. I met with a
little incident in company, the other day, after preaching
There was a little boy at the corner of the table, and his father
asked him, "Why does your father love you, John?" Said
the dear little lad, very prettily, "Because I'm a good boy."
"Yes," said the father, "he would not love you if you were
not a good boy." .I turned to the good father and remarked
that I was not quite sure about the truth of the last remark,
for I believed he would love him if he were ever so bad.
"Well," he said, "I think I should." And said a minister at
the table, "I had an instance of that yesterday. I stepped
into the house of a woman who had a son transported for life,
and she was as full of her son Richard as if he had been prime
minister, or had been her most faithful and dutiful son." Well,
young man, will you kick against love like that—love that will
bear your kicks, and will not turn round against you, but love
you straight on still? But perhaps that woman—I saw her
weep just now—had a mother, who has gone long ago, and
she was married to a brutal husband, and at last left a poor
widow; she calls to mind the days of her childhood, when the
big Bible was brought out and read around the hearth, and
"Our Father which art in heaven" was their nightly prayer.
Now, perhaps, God is beginning some good thing in her heart.
O! that he would bring her now, though seventy years of age,
to love the Saviour! Then would she have the beginning of
life over again in her last days, which will be made her best
days.

VI. One more head, and then we have done. Rahab's faith
was a SANCTIFYING FAITH. Did Rahab continue a harlot after
she had faith? No, no, she did not. I do not believe she was a
harlot at the time the men went to her house, though the name
still stuck to her, as such ill names will; but I am sure she was
not afterward, for Salmon the prince of Judah married her,
and her name is put down among the ancestors of our Lord
Jesus Christ. She became after that a woman eminent for
piety walking in the fear of God. Now, you may have a

dead faith which will ruin your soul. The faith that will save you is a faith which sanctifies. "Ah!" says the drunkard, "I like the gospel, sir; I believe in Christ;" then he will go over to the Blue Lion to-night, and get drunk. Sir, that is not the believing in Christ that is of any use. "Yes," says another, "I believe in Christ;" and when he gets outside he will begin to talk lightly, frothy words, perhaps lascivious ones, and sin as before. Sir, you speak falsely; you do not believe in Christ. That faith which saves the soul is a real faith, and a real faith sanctifies men. It makes them say, "Lord, thou hast forgiven me my sins; I will sin no more. Thou hast been so merciful to me, I will renounce my guilt; so kindly hast thou treated me, so lovingly hast thou embraced me, Lord, I will serve thee till I die; and if thou wilt give me grace, and help me so to be, I will be as holy as thou art." You can not have faith, and yet live in sin. To believe is to be holy. The two things must go together. That faith is a dead faith, a corrupt faith, which lives in sin that grace may abound. Rahab was a sanctified woman. O that God might sanctify some that are here! The world has been trying all manner of processes to reform men: there is but one thing that ever will reform them, and that is, faith in the preached gospel. But in this age preaching is much despised. You read the newspaper; you read the book; you hear the lecturer; you sit and listen to the pretty essayist; but where is the preacher? Preaching is not taking out a manuscript sermon, asking God to direct your heart, and then reading pages prepared beforehand. That is reading—not preaching. There is a good tale told of an old man whose minister used to read. The minister called to see him, and said, "What are you doing John?" "Why, I'm prophesying, sir." "Prophesying; how is that? You mean you are reading the prophecies?" "No, I don't; I'm prophesying; for you read preaching, and call it preaching, and I read prophecies, and, on the same rule, that is prophesying." And the man was not far from right. We want to have more outspoken, downright utterances of truth and appeals to the conscience, and until we get these, we shall never see any very great and lasting reforms. But by the preaching of God's word, foolishness though it seem to some, harlots are reformed, thieves are made honest, and the worst of men brought to the Saviour. Again let me affectionately give the invitation to the vilest of men, if so they feel themselves to be,

> " Come, ye needy, come and welcome,
>   God's free bounty glorify :
> True belief and true repentance—
>   Every grace that brings us nigh—
> Without money,
> Come to Jesus Christ and buy."

Your sins will be forgiven, your transgressions cast away, and you shall henceforth go and sin no more, God having renewed you, and he will keep you even to the end. May God give his blessing, for Jesus' sake! Amen.

SERMON XIX

THE BLOOD-SHEDDING

"Without shedding of blood is no remission."—HEBREWS, ix 22

I WILL show you three fools. One is yonder soldier, who has been wounded on the field of battle, grievously wounded, well nigh unto death; the surgeon is by his side, and the soldier asks him a question. Listen, and judge of his folly. What question does he ask? Does he raise his eyes with eager anxiety and inquire if the wound be mortal, if the practitioner's skill can suggest the means of healing, or if the remedies are within reach and the medicine at hand? No, nothing of the sort; strange to tell, he asks, "Can you inform me with what sword I was wounded, and by what Russian I have been thus grievously mauled? I want," he adds, "to learn every minute particular respecting the origin of my wound." The man is delirious or his head is affected. Surely such questions at such a time are proof enough that he is bereft of his senses.

There is another fool. The storm is raging, the ship is flying impetuous before the gale, the dark scud moves swiftly over head, the masts are creaking, the sails are rent to rags, and still the gathering tempest grows more fierce. Where is the captain? Is he busily engaged on the deck, is he manfully facing the danger, and skillfully suggesting means to avert it? No, sir, he has retired to his cabin, and there with studious thoughts and crazy fancies he is speculating on the place where this storm took its rise. "It is mysterious, this wind; no one ever yet," he says, "has been able to discover it." And, so reckless of the vessel, the lives of the passengers, and nis own life, he is careful only to solve his curious questions. The man is mad, sir; take the rudder from his hand; he is clean gone mad! If he should ever run on shore, shut him up as a hope less lunatic.

The third fool I shall doubtless find among yourselves. You are sick and wounded with sin, you are in the storm and hurricane of Almighty vengeance, and yet the question which you would ask of me, this morning, would be, "Sir, what is the origin of evil?" You are mad, sir, spiritually mad; that is not the question you would ask if you were in a sane and healthy state of mind; your question would be, "How can I get rid of the evil?" Not, "How did it come into the world?" but "How am I to escape from it?" Not, "How is it that hail descends from heaven upon Sodom?" but "How may I, like Lot, escape out of the city to a Zoar?" Not, "How is it that I am sick?" but "Are there medicines that will heal me? Is there a physician to be found that can restore my soul to health?" Ah! you trifle with subtleties while you neglect certainties. More questions have been asked concerning the origin of evil than upon any thing else. Men have puzzled their heads, and twisted their brains into knots, in order to understand what men can never know—how evil came into this world, and how its entrance is consistent with divine goodness? The broad fact is this, there is evil; and your question should be, "How can I escape from the wrath to come, which is engendered of this evil?" In answering that question this verse stands right in the middle of the way (like the angel with the sword, who once stopped Balaam on his road to Barak), "Without shedding of blood is no remission." Your real want is to know how you can be saved; if you are aware that your sin must be pardoned or punished, your question will be, "How can it be pardoned?" and then point blank, in the very teeth of your inquiry, there stands out this fact, "Without shedding of blood there is no remission." Mark you, this is not merely a Jewish maxim; it is a world-wide and eternal truth. It pertaineth not to the Hebrews only, but to the Gentiles likewise. Never in any time, never in any place, never in any person, can there be remission apart from shedding of blood. This great fact, I say, is stamped on nature; it is an essential law of God's moral government, it is one of the fundamental principles which can neither be shaken

nor denied.   Never can there be any exception to it; it stands
the same in every place throughout all ages—"Without shedding of blood there is no remission." It was so with the Jews;
they had no remission without the shedding of blood. Some
things under the Jewish law might be cleansed by water or
by fire, but in no case where absolute sin was concerned was
there ever purification without blood—teaching this doctrine,
that blood, and blood alone, must be applied for the remission
of sin.   Indeed, the very heathen seem to have an inkling of
this fact.   Do not I see their knives gory with the blood of
victims ?   Have I not heard horrid tales of human immola-
tions, of holocausts, of sacrifices ; and what mean these, but
that there lies deep in the human breast, deep as the very existence of man, this truth, " that without shedding of blood
there is no remission."   And I assert once more, that even in
the hearts and consciences of my hearers there is something
which will never let them believe in remission apart from a
shedding of blood.   This is the grand truth of Christianity,
and it is a truth which I will endeavor now to fix upon your
memory ; and may God by his grace bless it to your souls.
" Without shedding of blood is no remission."
    First, let me show you the blood-shedding, before I begin
to dwell upon the text.   Is there not a special blood-shedding
meant ?   Yes, there was a shedding of most precious blood,
to which I must forthwith refer you.   I shall not tell you now
of massacres and murders, nor of rivers of blood of goats and
rams.   There was a blood-shedding once, which did all other
shedding of blood by far outvie ; it was a man—a God—that
shed his blood at that memorable season.   Come and see it.
Here is a garden dark and gloomy ; the ground is crisp with
the cold frost of midnight ; between those gloomy olive trees
I see a man, I hear him groan out his life in prayer ; hearken,
angels ; hearken, men, and wonder ; it is the Saviour groaning
out his soul !   Come and see him.   Behold his brow !   O
heavens! drops of blood are streaming down his face and from
his body ; every pore is open, and it sweats ! but not the sweat
of men that toil for bread : it is the sweat of one that toils for
heaven—he " sweats great drops of blood !"   That is the
blood-shedding, without which there is no remission.   Follow

that man further; they have dragged him with sacrilegious
hands from the place of his prayer and his agony, and tney
have taken him to the hall of Pilate; they seat him in a chair
and mock him; a robe of purple is put on his shoulders in
mockery; and mark his brow—they have put about it a crown
of thorns, and the crimson drops of gore are rushing down his
cheeks! Ye angels! the drops of blood are running down his
cheeks! But turn aside that purple robe for a moment. His
back is bleeding. Tell me, demons, who did this? They lift
up the thongs still dripping clots of gore; they scourge and
tear his flesh, and make a river of blood to run down his
shoulders! That is the shedding of blood, without which there
is no remission. Not yet have I done; they hurry him
through the streets; they fling him on the ground; they nail
his hands and feet to the transverse wood, they hoist it in the
air, they dash it into its socket, it is fixed, and there he hangs
the Christ of God. Blood from his head, blood from his hands
blood from his feet! In agony unknown he bleeds away hi
life: in terrible throes he exhausts his soul. " Eloi, Eloi, lama
sabacthani." And then see! they pierce his side, and foi th-
with runneth out blood and water! This is the shedding of
blood, sinners and saints, this is the awful shedding of blcod,
the terrible pouring out of blood, without which, for you, and
for the whole human race, there is no remission.

I have then, I hope, brought my text fairly out: witLout
this shedding of blood there is no remission. Now I shall
come to dwell upon it more particularly.

Why is it that the story doth not make men weep? I told
it ill, you say. Ay, so I did; I will take all the blame. But,
sirs, if it were told as ill as men could speak, were our hearts
what they should be, we should bleed away our lives in sor
row. O, it was a horrid murder that! It was not an act of
regicide; it was not the deed of a fratricide, or of a parricide
it was—what shall I say?—I must make a word—a deicide
the killing of a God; the slaying of him who became incar
nate for our sins. O, if our hearts were but soft as iron, we
must weep; if they were but tender as the marble of the
mountains, we should shed great drops of grief; but they are
harder than the nether millstone; we forget the griefs of him

that died this ignominious death ; we pity not his sorrows, nor do we account the interest we have in him as though he suffered and accomplished all for us. Nevertheless, here stands the principle—" Without shedding of blood is no remission."

Now, I take it, there are two things here. First, there is *a negative expressed:* " No remission without shedding of blood." And then there is *a positive implied,* forsooth, with shedding of blood there is remission.

I. First, I say, here is A NEGATIVE EXPRESSED; there is no remission without blood—without the blood of Jesus Christ. This is of divine authority ; when I utter this sentence I have divinity to plead. It is not a thing which you may doubt, or which you may believe ; it must be believed and received, otherwise you have denied the Scriptures, and turned aside from God. Some truths I utter, perhaps, have little better basis than my own reasoning and inference, which are of little value enough ; but this I utter, not with quotations from God's Word to back up my assertion, but from the lips of God himself. Here it stands in great letters, " There is no remission." So divine its authority. Perhaps you will kick at it : but remember, your rebellion is not against me, but against God. If any of you reject this truth, I shall not controvert ; God forbid I should turn aside from proclaiming his gospel, to dispute with men. I have God's irrevocable statute to plead now, here it stands : " Without shedding of blood there is no remission." You may believe or disbelieve many things the preacher utters ; but this you disbelieve at the peril of your souls. It is God's utterance : will you tell God to his face you do not believe it ? That were impious. The negative is divine in its authority ; bow yourselves to it, and accept its solemn warning.

But some men will say that God's way of saving men, by shedding of blood, is a cruel way, an unjust way, an unkind way ; and all kinds of things they will say of it. Sirs, I have nothing to do with your opinion of the matter ; it is so. If you have any faults to find with your Maker, fight your battles out with him at last. But take heed before you throw the gauntlet down ; it will go ill with a worm when he fighteth his Maker, and it will go ill with you when you contend with him. The doctrine of atonement when rightly understood and faithfully received, is delightful, for it exhibits boundless love, immeasurable goodness, and infinite truth; but to unbelievers it will always be a hated doctrine. So it must be, sirs; you hate your own mercies; you despise your own salvation. I tarry not to dispute with you; I affirm it in God's name: " Without shedding of blood there is no remission."

And note *how decisive this is in its character:* " Without shedding of blood there is no remission." " But, sir, can't I get my sins forgiven by my repentance? if I weep, and plead, and pray, will not God forgive me for the sake of my tears?" " No remission," says the text, "without shedding of blood " " But, sir, if I never sin again, and if I serve God more zealously than other men, will he not forgive me for the sake of my obedience?" " No remission," says the text, " without shedding of blood." " But, sir, may I not trust that God is merciful, and will forgive me without the shedding of blood?" " No," says the text, " without shedding of blood there is no remission;" none whatever. It cuts off every other hope. Bring your hopes here, and if they are not based in blood, and stamped with blood, they are as useless as castles in the air and dreams of the night. "There is no remission," says the text, in positive and plain words; and yet men will be trying to get remission in fifty other ways, until their special pleading becomes as irksome to us as it is useless for them. Sirs, do what you like, say what you please, but you are as far off remission when you have done your best, as you were when you began, except you put confidence in the shedding of our Saviour's blood, and in the blood-shedding alone, for without it there is no remission.

And note again, *how universal it is in its character.* "What! may not I get remission without blood-shedding?" says the king; and he comes with the crown on his head; " may not I n all my robes, with this rich ransom, get pardon without the blood-shedding?" " None," is the reply; "none." Forthwith comes the wise man, with a number of letters after his name— " Can I not get remission by these grand titles of my learning?" "None; none." Then comes the benevolent man—" I have dispersed my money to the poor, and given my body to feed them; shall not I get remission?" "None," says the text. "Without shedding of blood there is no remission." How this puts every one on a level! My lord, you are no bigger than your coachman; Sir squire, you are no better off than John that plows the ground; minister, your office does not serve you with any exemption—your poorest hearer stands on the very same footing. "Without shedding of blood there is no remission." No hope for the best, any more than for the worst, without this shedding of blood! O! I love the gospel, for this reason among others, because it is such a leveling gospel. Some persons do not like a leveling gospel; nor would I, in some senses of the word. Let men have their rank, and their titles, and their riches, if they will; but I do like, and I am sure all good men like, to see rich and poor meet together, and feel that they are on a level; the gospel makes them so. It says "Put up your money-bags, they will not procure remission; roll up your diploma, that will not get you remission; forget your farm and your park, they will not get you remission; just cover up that escutcheon, that coat of arms will not get remission. Come, ye ragged beggars, filthy off-scourings of the world, penniless; come hither; here is remission as much for you, ill-bred and ill-mannered though ye be, as for the noble, the honorable, the titled and the wealthy. All stand on a level here; the text is universal: "Without shedding of blood there is no remission."

Mark, too, *how perpetual my text is.* Paul said, "there is no remission;" I must repeat this testimony too. When thousands of years have rolled away, some minister may stand on this spot and say the same. This will never alter at all; it will always be so, in the next world as well as this: no remission without shedding of blood. "O! yes, there is," says one, "the priest takes the shilling, and he gets the soul out of purgatory." That is a mere pretense; it never was in. But without shedding of blood there is no real remission. There may be tales and fancies, but there is no true remission without the blood of propitiation. Never, though you strained yourselves in prayer; never, though you wept yourselves away in tears; never, though you groaned and cried till your heart-strings break; never in this world, nor in that which is to come, can the forgiveness of sins be procured on any other ground than redemption by the blood of Christ, and never can the conscience be cleansed but by faith in that sacrifice. The fact is, beloved, there is no use for you to satisfy your hearts with any thing less than what satisfied God the Father. Without the shedding of blood nothing would appease his justice and without the application of that same blood nothing can purge your consciences.

II. But as there is no remission without blood-shedding, it IS IMPLIED THAT THERE IS REMISSION WITH IT. Mark it well, this remission is a present fact. The blood having been already shed, the remission is already obtained. I took you to the garden of Gethsemane and the mount of Calvary to see the blood-shedding. I might now conduct you to another garden and another mount to show you the grand proof of the remission. Another garden, did I say ? Yes, it is a garden fraught with many pleasing and even triumphant reminiscences. Aside from the haunts of this busy world, in it was a new sepulcher, hewn out of a rock where Joseph of Arimathea thought his own poor body should presently be laid. But there they laid Jesus after his crucifixion.

He had stood surety for his people, and the law had demanded his blood ; death had held him with strong grasp and that tomb was, as it were, the dungeon of his captivity when, as the good Shepherd, he laid down his life for the sheep. Why, then, do I see in that garden an open, untenanted grave ? I will tell you. The debts are paid, the sins are canceled, the remission is obtained. How, think you ? That great Shepherd of the sheep hath been brought again from the dead by the blood of the everlasting covenant, and in him also we have obtained redemption through his blood. There, beloved, is proof the first.

Do you ask further evidence ? I will take you to mount Olivet. You shall behold Jesus there with his hands raised like the high priest of old to bless his people, and while he is blessing them, he ascends, the clouds receiving him out of their sight. But why, you ask, O why hath he thus ascended, and whither is he gone ? Behold he entereth, not into the holy place made with hands, but he entereth into heaven it self with his own blood, there to appear in the presence of God for us. Now, therefore, we have boldness to draw near by the blood of Christ. The remission is obtained, here is proof the second. O believer, what springs of comfort are there here for thee.

And now let me commend this remission by the shedding of blood to those who have not yet believed. Mr. Innis, a great Scotch minister, once visited an infidel who was dying. When he came to him the first time, he said, " Mr. Innis, I am relying on the mercy of God; God is merciful, and he will never damn a man for ever." When he got worse and was nearer death, Mr. Innis went to him again, and he said, " O! Mr. Innis, my hope is gone; for I have been thinking, if God be merciful, God is just too; and what if, instead of being merciful to me, he should be just to me? What would then become of me? I must give up my hope in the mere mercy of God; tell me how to be saved!" Mr. Innis told him that Christ had died in the stead of all believers—that God could be just, and yet the justifier through the death of Christ. " Ah!" said he, " Mr. Innis, there is something solid in that; I can rest on that; I can not rest on any thing else;" and it is a remarkable fact that none of us ever met with a man who thought he had his sins forgiven unless it was through the blood of Christ. Meet a Mussulman; he never had his sins forgiven; he does not say so. Meet an infidel; he never knows that his sins are forgiven. Meet a legalist; he says, " I hope they will be forgiven;" but he does not pretend they are. No one ever gets even a fancied hope apart from this, that Christ, and Christ alone, must save by the shedding of his blood.

Let me tell a story to show how Christ saves souls. Mr. Whitefield had a brother, who had been like him an earnest Christian, but he had backslidden; he went far from the ways of godliness; and one afternoon, after he had been recovered from his backsliding, he was sitting in a room in a chapel-house. He had heard his brother preach the day before, and his poor conscience had been cut to the very quick. Said Whitefield's brother, when he was at tea, " I am a lost man," and he groaned and cried, and could neither eat nor drink

Said Lady Huntingdon, who sat opposite, "What did you say, Mr. Whitefield?" "Madam," said he, "I said I am a lost man." "I'm glad of it," said she; "I'm glad of it." "Your ladyship, how can you say so? It is cruel to say you are glad that I am a lost man." "I repeat it, sir," said she; "I am heartily glad of it." He looked at her, more and more astonished at her barbarity. "I am glad of it," said she, "because it is written, 'The Son of man came to seek and to save that which was lost.'" With the tears rolling down his cheeks, he said, "What a precious Scripture; and how is it that it comes with such force to me? O! madam," said he, "madam, I bless God for that; then he will save me; I trust my soul in his hands; he has forgiven me." He went outside the house, felt ill, fell upon the ground, and expired. I may have a lost man here this morning. As I can not say much, I will leave you, good people; you do not want any thing.

Have I a lost man here? Lost man! Lost woman! Where are you? Do you feel yourself to be lost? I am so glad of it; for there is remission by the blood-shedding. O sinner, are there tears in your eyes? Look through them. Do you see that man in the garden? That man sweat drops of blood for you. Do you see that man on the cross? That man was nailed there for you. O! if I could be nailed on a cross this morning for you all, I know what you would do: you would fall down and kiss my feet, and weep that I should have to die for you. But sinner, lost sinner, Jesus died for you—for *you;* and if he died for you, you can not be lost. Christ died in vain for no one. Are you, then, a sinner? Are you convinced of sin because you believe not in Christ? I have authority to preach to you. Believe in his name and you can not be lost. Do you say you are no sinner? Then I do not know that Christ died for you. Do you say that you have no sins to repent of? Then I have no Christ to preach to you. He did not come to save the righteous; he came to save the wicked. Are you wicked? Do you feel it? Are you lost? Do you know it? Are you sinful? Will you confess it? Sinner! if Jesus were here this morning he would put out his bleeding hands, and say, "Sinner, I died for you; will you be lieve me?" He is not here in person; he has sent his servant to tell you. Won't you believe him? "O!" but you say, "I am such a sinner!" "Ah!" says he, "that is just why I died for you, because you are a sinner." "But," you say, "I do not deserve it." "Ah!" says he, "that is just why I did it." Say you, "I have hated him." "But," says he, "I have always loved you." "But, Lord, I have spat on thy minister, and scorned thy word." "It is all forgiven," says he, "all washed away by the blood which did run from my side. Only believe me; that is all I ask. And that I will give you. I will help you to believe." "Ah!" says one, "but I do not want a Saviour." Sir, I have nothing to say to you except this, "The wrath to come! the wrath to come!" But there is one who says, "Sir, you do not mean what you say? Do you mean to preach to the most wicked men or women in the place?" I mean what I say. There she is! She is a harlot; she has led many into sin, and many into hell. There she is; her own friends have turned her out of doors; her father called her a good-for-nothing hussey, and said she should never come to the house again. Woman! dost thou repent? Dost thou feel thyself to be guilty? Christ died to save thee, and thou shalt be saved. There he is. I can see him. He was drunk; he has been drunk very often. Not many nights ago I heard his voice in the street, as he went home at a late hour on Saturday night, disturbing every body; and he beat his wife too. He has broken the Sabbath; and as to swearing, if oaths be like soot, his throat must want sweeping bad enough, for he has cursed God often. Do you feel yourself to be guilty, my hearer? Do you hate your sins, and are you willing to forsake them? Then I bless God for you. Christ died for you. Believe! I had a letter a few days ago from a young man who heard that during this week I was going to a certain town. Said he, "Sir, when you come do preach a sermon that will fit me; for do you know, sir, I have heard it said that we must all think ourselves to be the wickedest people in the world, or else we can not be saved. I try to think so, but I can not, because I have not been the wickedest. I want to think so, but I can not. I want to be saved, but I do not know how to repent enough." Now, if I have the pleasure of seeing him I shall tell him, God does not require a man to think himself the wickedest in the world, because that would sometimes be to think a falsehood ; there are some men who are not so wicked as others are. What God requires is this, that a man should say, " I know more of myself than I do of other people ; I know little about them, and from what I see of myself, not of my actions, but of my heart, I do think that there can be few worse than I am. They may be more guilty openly, but then I have had more light, more privileges, more opportunities, more warnings, and therefore I am still guiltier." I do not want you to bring your brother with you and say, "I am more wicked than he is ;" I want you to come yourself, and say, " Father, I have sinned ;" you have nothing to do with your brother William, whether he has sinned more or less; your cry should be, "Father, I have sinned." You have nothing to do with your cousin Jane, whether or not she has rebelled more than you. Your business is to cry, " Lord have mercy upon me a sinner !" That is all. Do you feel yourselves lost ? Again, I say,

" Come, and welcome, sinner, come !"

To conclude. There is not a sinner in this place who knows himself to be lost and ruined, who may not have all his sins forgiven, and "rejoice in the hope of the glory of God." You may, though black as hell, be white as heaven this very instant. I know that 'tis only by a desperate struggle that faith takes hold of the promise, but, the very moment a sinner believes, that conflict is past. It is his first victory and a blessed one. Let this verse be the language of your heart ; adopt it and make it your own :

" A guilty, weak, and helpless worm,
In Christ's kind arms I fall ;
He is my strength and righteousness,
My Jesus and my all."

SERMON XX

JUSTIFICATION BY GRACE

"Being justified freely by his grace, through the redemption that is in Christ Jesus."—ROMANS, iii. 24.

THE hill of comfort is the hill of Calvary; the house of consolation is builded with the wood of the cross; the temple of heavenly cordials is founded upon the riven rock, riven by the spear which pierced its side. No scene in sacred history ever gladdens the soul like the scene on Calvary.

> "Is it not strange, the darkest hour
> That ever dawned on sinful earth
> Should touch the heart with softer power
> For comfort, than an angel's mirth?
> That to the cross the mourner's eye should turn,
> Sooner than where the stars of Bethlehem burn?"

Nowhere does the soul ever find such consolation as on that very spot where misery reigned, where woe triumphed, where agony reached its climax. There grace hath dug a fountain, which ever gusheth with waters pure as crystal, each drop capable of alleviating the woes and the agonies of mankind. Ye have had your seasons of woe, my brethren and my sisters in Christ Jesus; and ye will confess it was not at Olivet that ye ever found comfort, not on the hill of Sinai, nor on Tabor; out Gethsemane, Gabbatha, and Golgotha have been a means of comfort to you. The bitter herbs of Gethsemane have often taken away the bitters of your life; the scourge of Gabbatha hath often scourged away your cares, and the groans of Calvary have put all other groans to flight.

We have, this morning then, a subject which I trust may be the means of comforting God's saints, seeing it takes its rise at the cross, and thence runs on in a rich stream of perennial blessings to all believers. You note, we have in our text, first of all, *the redemption of Christ Jesus ;* secondly, *the justification of sinners flowing from it ;* and then thirdly, *the manner of the giving of this justification,* "freely by his grace."

I First, then, we have THE REDEMPTION THAT IS IN OR BY CHRIST JESUS.

The figure of redemption is very simple, and has been very frequently used in Scripture. When a prisoner has been taken captive, and has been made a slave by some barbarous power, it has been usual, before he could be set free, that a ransom price should be paid down. Now, we being, by the fall of Adam, prone to guiltiness, and, indeed, virtually guilty, we were by the irreproachable judgment of God given up to the vengeance of the law ; we were given to the hands of justice ; justice claimed us to be his bond-slaves for ever, unless we could pay a ransom, whereby our souls could be redeemed. We were, indeed, poor as owlets, we had not wherewith to bless ourselves. We were as our hymn hath worded it, "bankrupt debtors ;" an execution was put into our house ; all we had was sold ; we were left naked, and poor, and miserable, and we could by no means find a ransom ; it was just then that Christ stepped in, stood sponsor for us, and, in the room and stead of all believers, did pay the ransom price, that we might in that hour be delivered from the curse of the law and the vengeance of God, and go our way, clean, free, justified by his blood.

Let me just endeavor to show you some qualities of the redemption that is in Christ Jesus. You will remember *the multitude* he has redeemed ; not me alone, nor you alone, but "a multitude that no man can number," which shall as far exceed the stars of heaven for number, as they exceed all mortal reckoning. Christ hath bought for himself some out of every kingdom, and nation, and tongue, under heaven ; he hath redeemed from among men some of every rank, from the highest to the lowest ; some of every color—black and white ; some of every standing in society, the best and the worst. For some of all sorts hath Jesus Christ given himself a ransom that they might be redeemed unto himself.

Now, concerning this ransom, we have to observe, that it was *all paid*, and all paid *at once*. When Christ redeemed nis people, he did it thoroughly; he did not leave a single debt unpaid, nor yet one farthing for them to settle afterwards. God demanded of Christ the payment for the sins of all his people; Christ stood forward, and to the utmost farthing paid whate'er his people owed. The sacrifice of Calvary was not a part payment; it was not a partial exoneration, it was a complete and perfect payment, and it obtained a complete and perfect remittal of all the debts of all believers that have lived, do live, or shall live, to the very end of time. On that day when Christ hung on the cross, he did not leave a single farthing for us to pay as a satisfaction to God; he did not leave, from a thread even to a shoe-latchet, that he had not satisfied. The whole of the demands of the law were paid down there and then by Jehovah Jesus, the great high priest of all his people. And blessed be his name, he paid it all at once too. So priceless was the ransom, so princely and munificent was the price demanded for our souls, one might have thought it would have been marvelous if Christ had paid it by instalments; some of it now, and some of it then. Kings' ransoms have sometimes been paid part at once, and part in dues afterwards, to run through years. But not so our Saviour: once for all he gave himself a sacrifice; at once he counted down the price, and said, "It is finished," leaving nothing for him to do, nor for us to accomplish. He did not drivel out a part-payment, and then declare that he would come again to die, or that he would again suffer, or that he would again obey; out down upon the nail, to the utmost farthing, the ransom of all his people was paid, and a full receipt given to them, and Christ nailed that receipt to his cross, and said, "It is done, it is done; I have taken away the handwriting of ordinances, I have nailed it to the cross; who is he that shall condemn my people, or lay any thing to their charge? for I have blotted out like a cloud their transgressions, and like a thick cloud their sins!"

And when Christ paid all this ransom, will you just notice, that *he did it all himself!* He was very particular about that. Simor the Cyrenian, might bear the cross; but Simon, the

Cyrenian, might not be nailed to it. That sacred circle of Calvary was kept for Christ alone. Two thieves were with him there; not righteous men, lest any should have said that the death of those two righteous men helped the Saviour. Two thieves hung there with him, that men might see that there was majesty in his misery, and that he could pardon men and show his sovereignty, even when he was dying. There were no righteous men to suffer; no disciples shared his death; Peter was not dragged there to be beheaded, John was not nailed to a cross side by side with him; he was left there alone. He says, "I have trodden the wine-press alone; and of the people there was none with me." The whole of the tremendous debt was put upon his shoulders; the whole weight of the sins of all his people was placed upon him. Once he seemed to stagger under it: "Father, if it be possible." But again he stood upright: "Nevertheless, not my will, but thine be done." The whole of the punishment of his people was distilled into one cup; no mortal lip might give it so much as a solitary sip. When he put it to his own lips, it was so bitter, he well nigh spurned it: "Let this cup pass from me." But his love for his people was so strong, that he took the cup in both his hands, and

> "At one tremendous draught of love
> He drank damnation dry,"

for all his people. He drank it all, he endured all, he suffered all; so that now for ever there are no flames of hell for them, no racks of torment; they have no eternal woes; Christ hath suffered all they ought to have suffered, and they must, they shall go free, The work was completely done by himself, without a helper.

And note, again, *it was accepted*. In truth, it was a goodly ransom. What could equal it? A soul "exceeding sorrowful even unto death;" a body torn with torture; a death of the most inhuman kind; and an agony of such a character that tongue can not speak of it, nor can even man's mind imagine its horror. It was a goodly price. But say, was it accepted? There have been prices paid sometimes, or rather offered, which never were accepted by the party to whom they were offered, and therefore the slave did not go free. But this was accepted. The evidence I will show you. When Christ declared that he would pay the debt for all his people, God sent the officer to arrest him for it; he arrested him in the garden of Gethsemane, and seizing upon him, he dragged him to the bar of Pilate, to the bar of Herod, and to the judgment seat of Caiaphas; the payment was all made, and Christ was put into the grave. He was there, locked up in durance vile, until the acceptance should have been ratified in heaven. He slept there a portion of three days in his tomb. It was declared that the ratification was to be this: the surety was to go his way as soon as his suretyship engagements had been fulfilled. Now let your minds picture the buried Jesus. He is in the sepulcher. 'Tis true he has paid all the debt, but the receipt is not yet given; he slumbers in that narrow tomb. Fastened in with a seal upon a giant stone, he sleeps still in his grave; not yet has the acceptance been given from God; the angels have not yet come from heaven to say, "The deed is done, God has accepted thy sacrifice." Now is the crisis of this world; it hangs trembling in the balance. Will God accept the ransom, or will he not? We shall see. An angel comes from heaven with exceeding brightness; he rolls away the stone; and forth comes the captive, with no manacles upon his hands, with the grave-clothes left behind him; free, never more to suffer, never more to die. Now,

> "If Jesus had not paid the debt,
> He ne'er had been at freedom set."

If God had not accepted his sacrifice, he would have been in his tomb at this moment; he never would have risen from his grave. But his resurrection was a pledge of God's accepting him. He said, "I have had a claim upon thee to this hour; that claim is paid now; go thy way." And death gave up his royal captive, the stone was rolled into the garden, and the Conqueror came forth, leading captivity captive.

And, moreover, God gave a second proof of acceptance; *for he took his only-begotten Son to heaven*, and set him at his right hand, far above all principalities and powers; and therein he meant to say to him, "Sit upon the throne, for thou hast

done the mighty deed ; all thy works and all thy miseries are
accepted as the ransom of men." O my beloved, think what
a grand sight it must have been when Christ ascended into
glory; what a noble certificate it must have been of his Father's acceptance of him ! Do you not think you see the scene
on earth ? It is very simple. A few disciples are standing
upon a hill, and Christ mounts into the air in slow and solemn
movement, as if an angel sped his way by gentle degrees, like
mist or exhalation from the lake into the skies. Can you imagine what is going on up yonder ? Can you for a moment
conceive how, when the mighty Conqueror entered the gates
of heaven, the angels met him ;

> " They brought his chariot from on high,
>   To bear him to his throne ;
>   Clapped their triumphant wings, and cried,
>   ' The glorious work is done !' "

Can you think how loud were the plaudits when he entered
the gates of heaven ? Can you conceive how they pressed on
one another, to behold how he came conquering and red from
the fight ? Do you see Abraham, Isaac, Jacob, and all the
saints redeemed, come to behold the Saviour and the Lord ?
They had desired to see him, and now their eyes behold him
in flesh and blood, the conqueror over death and hell ! Do
you think you see him, with hell at his chariot-wheels, with
death dragged as a captive through the royal streets of heaven ? O, what a spectacle was there that day ! No Roman
warrior ever had such a triumph ; none ever saw such a ma
jestic sight. The pomp of a whole universe, the royalty of
entire creation, cherubim and seraphim, and all powers create,
did swell the show ; and God himself, the Everlasting One,
crowned all, when he pressed his Son to his bosom, and said,
" Well done, well done ; thou hast finished the work which I
gave thee to do. Rest here for ever, mine accepted one."
Ah, but he never would have 1 ad that triumph, if he had not
paid all the debt. Unless his Father had accepted the ransom-
price, the ransomer had never been so honored ; but because
it was accepted, therefore did he so triumph. So far, then,
concerning the ransom.

II. And now, by the help of God's Spirit, let me address my-self to THE EFFECT OF THE RANSOM ; being justified—"justi fied freely by his grace through the redemption."

Now, *what is the meaning of justification?* Divines will puzzle you, if you ask them. I must try the best I can to make justification plain and simple, even to the comprehension of a child. There is not such a thing as justification to be had on earth for mortal men, except in one way. Justification, you know, is a forensic term ; it is employed always in a legal sense. A prisoner is brought to the bar of justice to be tried. There is only one way whereby that prisoner can be justified ; that is, he must be found not guilty ; and if he is found not guilty, then he is justified—that is, he is proved to be a just man. If you find that man guilty, you can not justify him. The Queen may pardon him, but she can not justify him. The deed is not a justifiable one, if he were guilty concerning it ; and he can not be justified on account of it. He may be par-doned ; but not royalty itself can ever wash that man's char-acter. He is as much a real criminal when he is pardoned as before. There is no means among men of justifying a man of an accusation which is laid against him, except by his being proved not guilty. Now, the wonder of wonders is, that we are proved guilty, and yet we are justified : the verdict has been brought in against us, guilty ; and yet, notwithstanding, we are justified. Can any earthly tribunal do that ? No ; it remained for the ransom of Christ to effect that which is an impossibility to any tribunal upon earth. We are all guilty. Read the 23d verse, immediately preceding the text—"For all have sinned, and come short of the glory of God." There the verdict of guilty is brought in, and yet we are immediately afterward said to be justified freely by his grace.

Now, allow me to explain *the way whereby God justifies a sinner.* I am about to suppose an impossible case. A pris-oner has been tried, and condemned to death. He is a guilty man ; he can not be justified, because he is guilty. But now, suppose for a moment that such a thing as this could happen —that some second party could be introduced, who could take all that man's guilt upon himself, who could change places with that man, and by some mysterious process, which, of course, is impossible with men, become that man; or take that man's character upon himself; he, the righteous man, putting the rebel in his place, and making the rebel a righteous man. We can not do that in our courts. If I were to go before a judge, and he should agree that I should be committed for a year's imprisonment, instead of some wretch who was condemned yesterday to a year's imprisonment, I could not take his guilt. I might take his punishment, but not his guilt. Now, what flesh and blood can not do, that Jesus Christ by his redemption did. Here I stand, the sinner. I mention myself as the representative of you all. I am condemned to die. God says, "I will condemn that man; I must, I will—I will punish him." Christ comes in, puts me aside, and stands himself in my stead. When the plea is demanded, Christ says, "Guilty;" takes my guilt to be his own guilt. When the punishment is to be executed, forth comes Christ. "Punish me," he says; "I have put my righteousness on that man, and I have taken that man's sins on me. Father, punish me, and consider that man to have been me. Let him reign in heaven; let me suffer misery. Let me endure his curse, and let him receive my blessing." This marvelous doctrine of the changing of places of Christ with poor sinners, is a doctrine of revelation, for it never could have been conceived by nature. Let me, lest I should have made a mistake, explain myself again. The way whereby God saves a sinner is not, as some say, by passing over the penalty. No; the penalty has been all paid. It is the putting of another person in the rebel's place. The rebel must die; God says he must. Christ says, "I will be substitute for the rebel. The rebel shall take my place; I will take his." God consents to it. No earthly monarch could have power to consent to such a change. But the God of heaven had a right to do as he pleased. In his infinite mercy he consented to the arrangement. "Son of my love," said he, "you must stand in the sinner's place; you must suffer what he ought to have suffered; you must be accounted guilty, just as he was accounted guilty; and then I will look upon the sinner in another light. I will look at him as if he were Christ; I will accept him as if he were my only-begotten Son, full of grace and truth. I will give him a crown in heaven, and I will take him to my heart for ever and ever." This is the way we are saved; "Being justified freely by his grace, through the redemption which is in Christ Jesus."

And now, let me further go on to *explain some of the characteristics* of this justification. As soon as a repenting sinner is justified, remember, he is justified for all his sins. Here stands a man all guilty. The moment he believes in Christ, his pardon at once he receives, and his sins are no longer his; they are cast into the depths of the sea. They were laid upon the shoulders of Christ, and they are gone. The man stands a guiltless man in the sight of God, accepted in the beloved. "What!" say you, "do you mean that literally?" Yes, I do, that is the doctrine of justification by faith. Man ceases to be regarded by divine justice as a guilty being; the moment he believes in Christ his guilt is all taken away. But I am going a step further. The moment the man believes in Christ, he ceases to be guilty in God's esteem; but what is more, he becomes righteous, he becomes meritorious; for, in the moment when Christ takes his sins he takes Christ's righteousness; so that, when God looks upon the sinner who but an hour ago was dead in sins, he looks upon him with as much love and affection as he ever looked upon his Son. He himself has said it—"As the Father loved me, so have I loved you." He loves us as much as his Father loved him. Can you believe such a doctrine as that? Does it not pass all thought? Well, it is a doctrine of the Holy Spirit; the doctrine whereby we must hope to be saved. Can I to any unenlightened person illustrate this thought better? I will give him the parable we have given to us in the prophets—the parable of Joshua the high priest. Joshua comes in, clothed in filthy garments, those filthy garments repsesenting his sins. Take away the filthy garments; that is pardon. Put a miter on his head; clothe him in royal raiment; make him rich and fair; that is justification. But where do *these* garments come from? and where do those rags go to? Why, the rags that Joshua had on go to Christ, and the garments put on Joshua are the garments that Christ wore. The sinner and Christ do just what Jonathan and David did. Jonathan put his robes

on David, David gave Jonathan his garments; so Christ takes
our sins, we take Christ's righteousness; and it is by a glorious substitution and interchange of places that sinners go free
and are justified by his grace.

"But," says one, "no one is justified like that till he dies."
Believe me, he is.

> "The moment a sinner believes
> And trusts in his crucified God,
> His pardon at once he receives;
> Salvation in full, through his blood."

If that young man over there has really believed in Christ
this morning, realizing by a spiritual experience what I have
attempted to describe, he is as much justified in God's sight
now as he will be when he stands before the throne. Not the
glorified spirits above are more acceptable to God than the
poor man below, who is once justified by grace. It is a perfect washing, it is perfect pardon; perfect imputation; we are
fully, freely, and wholly accepted, through Christ our Lord.
Just one more word here, and then I will leave this matter of
justification. Those who are once justified are justified irre-
versibly. As soon as a sinner takes Christ's place, and Christ
takes the sinner's place, there is no fear of a second change.
If Christ has once paid the debt, the debt is paid, and it will
never be asked for again; if you are pardoned, you are pardoned once for ever. God does not give man a free pardon
under his own sign-manual, and then afterward retract it and
punish man: that be far from God so to do. He says, "I have
punished Christ; you may go free." And after that we may
"rejoice in hope of the glory of God," that "being justified
by faith we have peace with God, through our Lord Jesus
Christ." And now I hear one cry, "That is an extraordinary
doctrine." Well, so some may think; but let me say to you,
it is a doctrine professed by all Protestant churches, though
they may not preach it. It is the doctrine of the Church
of England, it is the doctrine of Luther, it is the doctrine of
the Presbyterian church; it is professedly the doctrine of all
Christian churches; and if it seems strange in your ears, it is
because your ears are estranged, and not because the doctrine
is a strange one. It is the doctrine of holy writ, that none

can condemn whom God justifies, and that none can accuse those for whom Christ hath died; for they are totally free from sin. So that, as one of the prophets has it, God sees no sin in Jacob nor iniquity in Israel. In the moment they believe, their sins being imputed to Christ, they cease to be theirs, and Christ's righteousness is imputed to them and accounted theirs, so that they are accepted.

III. And now I close up with the third point, upon which I shall be brief, and I hope very earnest : THE MANNER OF GIVING THE JUSTIFICATION. John Bunyan would have it, that there are some whose mouths are set a watering for this great gift of justification. Are there not some here who are saying, "O ! if I could be justified ! But, sir, can I be justified ? I have been a drunkard, I have been a swearer, I have been every thing that is vile. Can I be justified ? Will Christ take my black sins, and am I to take his white robes ?" Yes, poor soul, if thou desirest it ; if God has made *thee* willing, if thou dost confess thy sins, Christ is willing to take thy rags, and give thee his righteousness, to be thine for ever. "Well, but how is it to be obtained?" says one; "must I be a holy man for many years, and then get it ?" Listen ! "Freely by his grace ;" "freely," because there is no price to be paid for it ; "by his grace," because it is not of our deservings. "But, O sir, I have been praying, and I do not think God will forgive me, unless I do something to deserve it." I tell you, sir, if you bring in any of your deservings, you shall never have t. God gives away his justification freely ; and if you bring any thing to pay for it, he will throw it in your face, and will not give his justification to you. He gives it away freely. Old Rowland Hill once went preaching at a fair ; he noticed the chapmen selling their wares by auction ; so Rowland said, "I am going to hold an auction too, to sell wine and milk, without money and without price. My friends over there," said he, "find a great difficulty to get you up to their price; my difficulty is to bring you down to mine." So it is with men. If I could preach justification to be bought by you at a sovereign a piece, who would go out of the place without being justified ? If I could preach justification to you by walking a hundred miles, would we not be pilgrims to-morrow morn ing, every one of us ? If I were to preach justification which would consist in whippings and torture, there are very few here who would not whip themselves, and that severely too But when it is freely, freely, freely, men turn away. " What ! am I to have it for nothing at all, without doing any thing?" Yes, sir, you are to have it for nothing, or else not at all ; it is " freely." " But may I not go to Christ, lay some claim to his mercy, and say, Lord, justify me because I am not so bad as others ?" It will not do, sir, because it is " by his grace." " But may I not indulge a hope, because I go to church twice a-day ?" No, sir, it is " by his grace." " But may I not offer this plea, I mean to be better ?" No, sir ; it is " by his grace." You insult God by bringing your counterfeit coin to pay for his treasures. O ! what poor ideas men have of the value of Christ's gospel, if they think they can buy it ! God will not have your rusty farthings to buy heaven with. A rich man once, when he was dying, had a notion that he could buy a place in heaven by building a row of alms-houses. A good man stood by his bedside, and said, " How much more are you going to leave ?" " Twenty thousand pounds." Said he, " That would not buy enough for your foot to stand on in heaven ; for the streets are all made of gold there, and there-fore of what value can your gold be ? it would be accounted nothing of, when the very streets are paved with it." Nay, friends, we can not buy heaven with gold nor good works, nor prayers, nor any thing in the world. But how is it to be got ? Why it is to be got for asking only. As many of us as know ourselves to be sinners may have Christ for asking for him. Do you know that you want Christ ? You may have Christ ! " Whosoever will, let him come and take of the water of life freely." But if you cleave to your own notions, and say, " No, sir, I mean to do a great many good things, and then I will believe in Christ." Sir, you will be damned if you hold by such delusions. I earnestly warn you. You can not be saved so. " Well, but are we not to do good works ?" Cer-tainly you are ; but you are not to trust in them. You must trust in Christ wholly, and then do good works afterward. " But," says one, " I think if I were to do a few good works, it would be a little recommendation when I came." It would not, sir; they would be no recommendation at all. Let a beggar come to your house in white kid gloves, and say he is very badly off, and wants some charity; would the white kid gloves recommend him to your charity? Would a good new hat that he has been buying this morning recommend him to your charity? "No," you would say, "you are a miserable impostor; you do not want any thing, and you shall not have any thing either! Out with you!"

The best livery for a beggar is rags, and the best livery for a sinner to go to Christ in, is for him to go just as he is, with nothing but sin about him. "But no," say you, "I must be a little better, and then I think Christ will save me." You can not get any better, try as long as you please. And be-sides—to use a paradox—if you were to get better, you would be all the worse; for the worse you are, the better to come to Christ. If you are all unholy, come to Christ; if you feel your sin, and renounce it, come to Christ; though you have been the most debased and abandoned soul, come to Christ; if you feel yourself to have nothing about you to recommend you come to Christ.

> "Venture on him, venture wholly;
> Let no other trust intrude."

I do not say this to urge any man to continue in sin. God forbid! If you continue in sin, you must not come to Christ; you can not; your sins will hamper you. You can not be chained to your galley-oar—the oar of your sins—yet come to Christ, and be a free man. No, sir, it is repentance; it is the immediate leaving off the sin. But mark thee, neither re-pentance, nor leaving off thy sin, can save thee. It is Christ, Christ, Christ—Christ only.

But I know you will go away, many of you, and try to build up your own Babel-tower, to go to heaven. Some of you will go one way to work, and some another. You will go the ceremony way: you will lay the foundation of the structure with infant baptism, build confirmation on it, and the Lord's Supper. "I shall go to heaven," you say; "do not I keep Good Friday and Christmas-day? I am a better man than those dissenters. I am a most extraordinary man. Do I not say more prayers than any one?" You will be a long while going up that treadmill before you get an inch higher. That is not the way to get to the stars. One says, "I will go and study the Bible, and believe right doctrine; and I have no doubt that by believing right doctrine I shall be saved." Indeed you will not! You can be no more saved by believing right doctrine than you can by doing right actions. "There," says another, "I like that; I shall go and believe in Christ, and live as I like." Indeed you will not! For if you believe in Christ he will not let you live as your flesh liketh; by his Spirit he will constrain you to mortify its affections and lusts. If he gives you the grace to make you believe, he will give you the grace to live a holy life afterward. If he gives you faith, he gives you good works afterward. You can not believe in Christ, unless you renounce every fault, and resolve to serve him with full purpose of heart. Methinks at last I hear a sinner say, "Is that the only door? And may I venture through it? Then I will. But I do not quite understand you; I am something like poor Tiff, in that remarkable book 'Dred.' They talk a great deal about a door, but I can not see the door; they talk a great deal about the way, but I can not see the way. For if poor Tiff could see the way, he would take these children away by it. They talk about fighting, but I do not see any one to fight, or else I would fight." Let me explain it then. I find in the Bible, "This is a faithful saying, and worthy of all acceptation, that Christ Jesus came into the world to save sinners." What have you to do, but to believe this and trust in him? You will never be disappointed with such a faith as that. Let me give you over again an illustration I have given hundreds of times, but I can not find another so good, so I must give it again. Faith is something like this. There is a story told of a captain of a man-of-war, whose son— a young lad—was very fond of running up the rigging of the ship; and one time, running after a monkey, he ran up the mast, till at last he got on the main-truck. Now, the main-truck, you are aware, is like a large round table put on the mast, so that when the boy was on the main-truck there was plenty of room for him; but the difficulty was—to use the best explanation I can—that he could not reach the mast that was under the table; he was not tall enough to get down from this main-truck, reach the mast, and so descend. There he was on the main-truck; he managed to get up there, somehow or other, but down he never could get. His father saw that, and he looked up in horror; what was he to do? In a few moments his son would fall down, and be dashed to pieces. He was clinging to the main-truck with all his might, but in a little time he would fall down on the deck, and there he would be a mangled corpse. The captain called for a speaking-trumpet; he put it to his mouth, and shouted, "Boy, the next time the ship lurches, throw yourself into the sea." It was, in truth, his only way of escape; he might be picked up out of the sea, but he could not be rescued if he fell on the deck. The poor boy looked down on the sea; it was a long way; he could not bear the idea of throwing himself into the roaring current beneath him; he thought it looked angry and dangerous. How could he cast himself down into it? So he clung to the main-truck with all his might, though there was no doubt that he must soon let go and perish. The father called for a gun, and pointing it up at him, said, "Boy, the next time the ship lurches, throw yourself into the sea, or I'll shoot you!" He knew his father would keep his word; the ship lurched on one side, over went the boy splash into the sea, and out went brawny arms after him; the sailors rescued him, and brought him on deck. Now, we, like the boy, are in a position of extraordinary danger, by nature, which neither you nor I can possibly escape of ourselves. Unfortunately, we have got some good works of our own, like that main-truck, and we cling to them so fondly that we never will give them up. Christ knows that unless we do give them up, we shall be dashed to pieces at last, for that rotten trust must ruin us. He, therefore, says, "Sinner let go thine own trust, and drop into the sea of my love." We look down, and say, "Can I be saved by trusting in God? He looks as if he were angry with me, and I could not trust him." Ah! will not mercy's tender cry persuade you?—"He that believeth shall be saved." Must the weapon of destruction be pointed directly at you? Must you hear the dreadful threat—"He that believeth not shall be damned?" It is with you *now* as with that boy;

your position is one of imminent peril in itself, and your slight-
ing the Father's counsel is a matter of more terrible alarm, it
makes peril more perilous. You must do it, or else you
perish! Let go your hold! That is faith when the poor
sinner lets go his hold, drops down, and so is saved; and the
very thing which looks as if it would destroy him, is the means
of his being saved. O! believe on Christ, poor sinners; be-
ieve on Christ. Ye who know your guilt and misery come,
cast yourselves upon him; come, and trust my Master, and as
he lives, before whom I stand, ye shall never trust him in
vain; but ye shall find yourselves forgiven, and go your way
rejoicing in Christ Jesus.

SERMON XXI

MANASSEH

' Then Manasseh knew that the Lord he was God."—2 CHRON. xxxiii. 13

MANASSEH is one of the most remarkable characters whose history is written in the sacred pages. We are accustomed to mention his name in the list of those who greatly sinned, and yet found great mercy. Side by side with Saul of Tarsus, with that great sinner who washed the feet of Jesus with her tears, and wiped them with the hairs of her head, and with the thief that died upon the cross—a forgiven sinner at the eleventh hour—we are wont to write the name of Manasseh, who " shed innocent blood very much," and notwithstanding that, was forgiven and pardoned, finding mercy through the blood of a Saviour who had not then died, but whom God foresaw should die, and the merits of whose sacrifice he therefore imputed to so great a transgressor as Manasseh.

Without preface we shall enter on the history of Manasseh this morning, and consider him in a threefold light : first, as *a sinner*, then as *an unbeliever*, and thirdly, as *a convert*. It may be there shall be some Manasseh within these walls now ; and if in describing the case of this ancient king of Israel I shall in some degree describe him, I trust he will take to himself the same consoling truths which were the means of the comfort of Manasseh when in the dungeon of repentance.

I. First, then, we shall consider MANASSEH IN HIS SIN.

1. And we note, first, that he belonged to that class of sinners who stand first in the phalanx of evil—namely, those *who sin against great light, against a pious education and early training*. Manasseh was the son of Hezekiah, a man

who had some faults, but of whom it is nevertheless said, "He did right in the sight of the Lord." To a great degree he walked before God with a perfect heart, even as did David his father. We can not suppose that he neglected the education of his son Manasseh. He was the son of his old age. You will remember that at a time of heavy sickness God promised him that he should have his life prolonged fifteen years. Three years after that event Manasseh was born, and he was, therefore, only twelve years old when his father died ; still he was old enough to remember the pious prayers of a father and a mother, and had arrived at sufficient maturity to understand right from wrong, and to have received those early impressions which we believe are, in most cases, eminently useful for after life. And yet Manasseh pulled down what his father had built up, and built up the idol temples which his father had pulled down. Now, it is a notorious fact, that men who do go wrong after a good training, are the worst men in the world. You may not know, but it is a fact, that the late lamented murder of Williams at Erromanga, was brought about by the evil doings of a trader who had gone to the island, and who was also the son of a missionary. He had become reckless in his habits, and treated the islanders with such barbarity and cruelty, that they revenged his conduct upon the next white man who put his foot on their shore ; and the beloved Williams, one of the last of the martyrs, died a victim of the guilt of those who had gone before him. The worst of men are those who, having much light, still run astray. You shall find among the greatest champions of the camp of hell, men who were brought up and educated in our very ranks. It is not necessary that I should mention names ; but any of you that are acquainted with those who are the leaders of infidelity at the present time will at once recognize the fact. And such men actually make the very worst of infidels ; while the best of Christians often come from the very worst of sinners. Our John Bunyans have come from the pot-house and the tap-room, from the bowling-alley, or places lower in the scale ; our best of men have come from the very worst of places, and have been the best adapted to reclaim sinners, because they themselves had stepped into the kennel, and had nevertheless been washed in a Saviour's cleansing blood. And so it is true that the worst of the enemies of Christ are those who are nourished in our midst, and like the viper of old, which the husbandman nursed in his bosom, turn round to sting the bosom which has nurtured them. Such a one was Manasseh.

2. In the next place, *Manasseh as a sinner was a very bold one.* He was one of those men who do not sin covertly, but who, when they transgress, do not seem to be at all ashamed, who are born with brazen foreheads, and lift their faces to heaven with insolence and impudence. He was a man who, if he would set up an idol, as you would see by reading this chapter, did not set it up in an obscure part of the land, but put it in the very temple of God; and when he would desecrate the name of the Most High, he did not privily go to his chapel, where he might worship some evil deity, but he put the deity into the very temple itself, as if to insult God to his very face. He was a desperado in sin, and went to the utmost limit of it, being very bold, and desperately set on mischief. Now, whether it be for right or wrong, boldness is always sure to win the day. Give me a coward—you give me nothing; give me a bold man, and you give me one that can do something, whether for Christ's cause or for the devil's. Manasseh was a man of this kind. If he cursed God, it was with a loud voice; it was not in hole or corner, but upon his throne, that he issued proclamations against the Most High, and in the most daring manner insulted the Lord God of Israel. And yet, dear friends, this man was saved, notwithstanding all this. This greatest sinner, this man who had trampled on his father's prayers, who had wiped from his brow the tears which had been shed there by an anxious parent, who had stifled the convictions of his conscience, and had gone to an extremity of guilt, in bold, open, and desperate sin, yet this man was at last, by divine grace, humbled and brought on his knees to acknowledge that God was God alone. Let no man, therefore, despair of his fellow. I never do, since I think and hope that God has saved me. I am persuaded that, live as long as I may, I shall never see the individual of whom I can say, "That man is a hopeless case." I

may peradventure meet with the person who has been so
exhorted and so warned, and has so put off all the sweet woo-
ings of his conscience, that he has become seared and hardened,
and consequently apparently hopeless; but I shall never meet
a man who has sinned so desperately that I can say of him he
never can be saved. Ah! no; that arm of mercy which was
long enough to save me is long enough to save you; and if he
could redeem you from your transgression, assuredly there are
none sunk lower than you were, and therefore you may believe that his arm of mercy can reach them. Above all, let no
man despair of himself. Whilst there is life there is hope.
Give not up yourselves into Satan's arms. He tells you that
your death-warrant is sealed, that your doom is cast, and that
you never can be saved. Tell him to his face that he is a liar,
for that Jesus Christ " is able to save unto the uttermost them
that come unto God by him, seeing that he ever liveth to
make intercession for them."

3. Again, Manasseh was a sinner of that peculiar caste which
we suspect is not to be found very frequently. He was one of
those who *had the power of leading others* to a very large extent astray from the truth and religion of God. He was a king,
and had, therefore, great influence; what he commanded was
done. Among the rank of idolaters Manasseh stood first, and it
was the song and glory of the false priests that the king of Judah was on the side of the gods of the heathen. He was the
leader—the first man in the battle. When the troops of the
ungodly went to war against the God of the whole earth,
Manasseh led the vanguard and cheered them on. He was
their great Goliath, challenging all the armies of the living
God. Many among the wicked stood back and feared the
conflict; but he never feared. " He spake and it was done;
he commanded, and it stood fast;" and therefore he was bold
and arrogant in leading others astray. There are some such
still alive—men not content with treading the broad road
themselves, but seeking to entice others into it. And O, how
active they are in their efforts! They will go from house to
house, and distribute those publications which are impure and
polluting; they will stand in our streets and endeavor to draw
around them the young, ay, men and women just fresh come

from the house of God, or going to God's sanctuary, to tell
them that dreary story that there is no God, or the dismal
falsehood that there is no future, but that we must all die like
dogs and suffer annihilation. There are some such who never
seem to be happy unless when they are leading others astray.
It is not enough for them to go alone against God, but they
must sin in company. Like the woman in the Proverbs, they
hunt for precious life, and like hounds thirsting for blood, they
are seeking after men to destroy them. Society now is like
Prometheus: it is, to a great extent, bound hand and foot by
the very customs that surround it, and like Prometheus, we
have upon us the winged hound of hell perpetually tapping
at our heart and swallowing the life-blood of our spirit. I
mean we have that accursed infidelity which seeks to lead
men from God and drive them from their Maker. But, nevertheless, leaders among them have yet been saved. Manasseh, the leader of those who hated God, was yet humbled,
and made to love the Most High.

Do you ask me whether such cases ever occur now ? I answer, yes they do; too rarely, but they do happen. Yesterday I received something which cheered my heart very much,
and made me bless my God, that notwithstanding all opposition, he had still made me of some little use in the world. I
received a long letter from a certain city, from one who has
been one of the leaders of the secular society in that place.
The writer says, " I purchased one of the pamphlets entitled
' Who is this Spurgeon ?' and also your portrait (or a portrait
sold as yours) for 3d. I brought these home, and exhibited
them in my shop window. I was induced to do so from a feeling of derisive pleasure. The title of the pamphlet is, naturally, suggestive of caricature, and it was especially to incite
that impression that I attached it to your portrait and placed
it in my window. But I also had another object in view. I
thought by its attraction to improve my trade. I am not at
all in the book or paper business, which rendered its exposure
and my motive the more conspicuous. I have taken it down
now : *I am taken down too.* * * * I had bought one of
your sermons of an old infidel a day or two previous. In that
sermon I read these words :—' They go on ; that step is safe

—they take it ; the next is safe—they take it ; their foot hangs
over a gulf of darkness.' I read on, but the word darkness stag·
gered me. It was all dark with me. 'True, the way has been
safe so far, but I am lost in bewilderment. No, no, no, I will not
risk it.' I left the apartment in which I had been musing, and
as I did so, the three words, 'Who can tell ?' seemed to be whispered at my heart. I determined not to let another Sunday pass
without visiting a place of worship. How soon my soul might
be required of me I knew not, but felt that it would be mean,
base, cowardly, not to give it a chance. Ay, my associates may
laugh, scoff, deride, call me coward, turncoat, I will do an act of
justice to my soul. I went to the chapel; I was just stupefied
with awe. What could I want there ? The doorkeeper opened
his eyes wider, and involuntarily demanded, 'It's Mr. ——
isn't it ?' 'Yes,' I said, 'it is.' He conducted me to a seat, and
afterward brought me a hymn-book. I was fit to burst with
anguish. 'Now,' I thought, 'I am here, if it be the house of
God, heaven grant me an audience, and I will make full sur·
vender. O God, show me some token by which I may know
that thou art, and that thou wilt in no wise cast out the vile
deserter who has ventured to seek thy face and thy pardoning
mercy.' I opened the hymn-book to divert my mind from
feelings that were rending me, and the first words that caught
my eyes were,

> " ' Dark, dark indeed the grave would be,
> Had we no light, O God, from thee.' "

After giving some things which he looks upon as evidences that
he is a true convert of religion, he closes up by saying, " O sir,
tell this to the poor wretch whose pride, like mine, has made him
league with hell ; tell it to the hesitating and to the timid ; tell
it to the cooling Christian, that God is a very present help to
all that are in need. * * * Think of the poor sinner who
may never look upon you in this world, but who will live to
bless and pray for you here, and long to meet you in the world
exempt from sinful doubts, from human pride, and backsliding
hearts." Ah, he need not ask my forgiveness ; I am happy, too
happy, in the hope of calling him " brother" in the Christian
church. This letter is from a place many miles from this city,

and fr.m a man who had no small standing among the ranks of those who hate Christ. Ah! there have been Manassehs saved, and there shall be yet. There have been men who hated God, who have leaped for joy, and said,

> "I'm forgiven, I'm forgiven,
> I'm a miracle of grace,"

and have kissed the very feet which once they scorned and scoffed, and could not bear to hear the mention of.

There is one fact concerning Manasseh which stamps him as being a very prince of sinners, namely this : "He caused his children to pass through the fire in the valley of the son ot Hinnom," and dedicated his sons unto Tophet. This was a dreadful sin ; for though Manasseh repented, we find that his son Amon followed in the steps of his father in his wickedness but not in his righteousness. Listen! "Amon was two-and-twenty years old when he began to reign, and reigned two years in Jerusalem. But he did that which was evil in the sight of the Lord, as did Manasseh his father: for Amon sacrificed unto all the carved images which Manasseh his father had made, and served them ; and humbled not himself before the Lord, as Manasseh his father had humbled himself; but Amon trespassed more and more." Children will imitate their fathers in their vices, seldom in their repentance ; if parents sin, their children will follow them, without much doubt; but when they repent and turn to God, it is not easy to lead a child back in the way which it has once forsaken. Are there any here, who, like that ancient Carthaginian, have dedicated their sons to the opposition of their enemy. You remember one who dedicated his son Hannibal from his very birth to be the everlasting enemy of the Romans. There may be such a man here, who has dedicated his offspring to Satan, to be the everlasting enemy of Christ's gospel, and is trying to train up and tutor him in a way which is contrary to the fear of the Lord. Is such a man hopeless ? His sin is dreadful, his state is dreary, his sin without repentance will assuredly damn him ; but so long as he is here, we still will preach repentance to him, knowing that Manasseh was brought to know God, and was forgiven all his manifold sins.

II. The second aspect in which we are to regard Manasseh is as an UNBELIEVER ; for it appears that Manasseh did not believe that Jehovah was God alone ; he was, therefore, a believer in false gods, but an unbeliever, so far as the *truth* is concerned. Now, does it not strike you at the outset, that while Manasseh was an unbeliever in the truth, he must have been a very credulous person to believe in the all imaginary deities of the heathen ? In fact, the most credulous persons in the world are unbelievers. It takes ten thousand times more faith to be an unbeliever than to be a believer in revelation. One man comes to me and tells me I am credulous, because I believe in a great First Cause who created the heavens and the earth, and that God became man and died for sin. I tell him I may be, and no doubt am very credulous, as he conceives credulity, but I conceive that which I believe is in perfect consistency with my reason, and I therefore receive it. " But," saith he, " *I* am not credulous—not at all." Sir, I say, I should like to ask you one thing. You do not believe the world was created by God ? " No." You must be amazingly credulous, then, I am sure. Do you think this Bible exists without being made ? If you should say I am credulous because I believe it had a printer and a binder, I should say you were infinitely more credulous, if you assured me that it was made at all. And should you begin to tell me one of your theories about creation—that atoms floated through space, and came to a certain shape, I should resign the palm of credulity to you. You believe, perhaps, moreover, that man came to be in this world through the improvement of certain creatures. I have read, you say, that there were certain monads—that these monads improved themselves until they came to be small animalculæ—that afterward they grew into fishes—that these fishes wanted to fly, and then wings grew—that by-and-bye they wanted to crawl, and then legs came, and they became lizards, and by divers steps they then became monkeys, and then the monkeys became men, and you believe yourself to be cousin-german to an ourang-outang. Now, I may be very credulous, but really not so credulous as you are. I may believe very strange things ; I may believe that, with the jaw-bone of an ass, Samson slew a thousand men ; I

may believe that the earth was drowned with water, and many
other strange things, as you call them; but as for your creed,
your non-creed, "'tis strange, 'tis passing strange, 'tis wonderful," and it as much outvies mine in credulity, if I be credulous,
as an ocean outvies a drop. It requires the hardest faith in the
world to deny the Scriptures, because the man, in his secret
heart, knows they are true, and, go where he will, something
whispers to him, "You may be wrong—perhaps you are,"
and it is as much as he can do, to say, "Lie down, conscience! down with you; I must not let you speak, or I could
not deliver my lecture to-morrow, I could not go among my
friends, I could not go to such-and-such a club; for I can
not afford to keep a conscience, if I can not afford to keep a
God."

   And now let me tell you what I conceive to be the reasons
why Manasseh was an unbeliever. In the first place, I conceive that the *unlimited power* which Manasseh possessed had
a very great tendency to make him a disbeliever in God. I
should not wonder if an autocrat—a man with absolute do-
minion, should deny God; I should think it only natural.
You remember that memorable speech of Napoleon's. He
was told that man proposed, but that God disposed. "Ah!"
said Napoleon, "I propose and dispose too;" and therein he
arrogated to himself the very supremacy of God. We do not
wonder at it, because his victories had so speedily succeeded
each other, his prowess had been so complete, his fame so
great, and his power over his subjects so absolute. Power always, as I believe, except in the heart which is rightly gov-
erned by grace, has a tendency to lead us to deny God. It is
that noble intellect of such-and-such a man which has led him
into discussion; he has twice, thrice, four, five, six, seven
times, come off more than conqueror in the field of controversy; he looks round and says, "I am, there is none beside
me; let me take up whatever I please, I can defend it; there
is no man can stand against the blade of my intellect; I can
give him such a home thrust as will assuredly overcome him;"
and then, like Dr. Johnson, who often took up the side of the
question he did not believe, just because he liked to get a victory that was hard to win, so do these men espouse what they

believe to be wrong, because they conceive it gives them the finest opportunity of displaying their abilities. "Let me," says some mighty intellect, "fight with a Christian; I shall have hard enough work to prove my thesis, I know I shall have a great difficulty to undermine the bastions of truth which he opposes to bear against me; so much the better; it were worth while to be conquered by so stout an opposition, and if I can overcome my antagonist, if I can prove myself to have more logic than he has, then I can say, 'tis glorious; 'tis glorious to have fought against an opponent with so much on his side, and yet to have come off more than conqueror." I do believe the best man in the world is very hard to be trusted with power; he will, unless grace keeps him, make a wrong use of it before long. Hence it is that the most influential of God's servants are almost invariably the most tried ones, because our heavenly Father knows that if it were not for great trials and afflictions we should begin to set ourselves up against him, and arrogate to ourselves a glory which we had no right to claim.

But another reason why Manasseh was an unbeliever, I take it, was *because he was proud*. Pride lieth at the root of infidelity; pride is the very germ of opposition to God. The man saith, "Why should I believe? The Sunday-school child reads his Bible, and says it is true. Am I, a man of intellect, to sit side by side with him, and receive a thing as true simply at the dictum of God's Word? No, I will not; I will find it out for myself, and I will not believe simply because it is revealed to me, for that were to make myself a child." And when he turns to the page of revelation, and reads thus, "Except ye be converted and become as little children, ye can in nowise enter into the kingdom of heaven," he says, "Pshaw! I shall not be converted then; I am not going to be a child; I am a man, and a man I will be, and I would rather be lost a man than saved a child. What! am I to surrender my judgment, and sit down tacitly to believe in God's Word?" "Yes," says God's Word, "thou art; thou art to become as a child, and meekly to receive my Word." "Then," says he, in his arrogance and pride, "I will not," and like Satan, he declares it were better to rule in hell than serve in heaven, and he goes away an unbeliever, because to believe is too humbling a thing.

But perhaps the most potent reason for Manasseh's unbelief lies here *that he loved sin too well.* When Manasseh built the altars for his false gods, he could sin easily, and keep his conscience; but he felt Jehovah's laws so stringent, that if he once believed in the one God he could not sin as he did. He read it thus: " Remember the Sabbath-day to keep it holy; thou shalt not kill; thou shalt not steal;" and so on. Manasseh wanted to do all these things, and therefore he would not believe because he could not believe and keep his sin. The very reason why we have much unbelief is because we have much love of sin. Men will have no God, because God interferes with their lusts. They could not go on in their sins, if they once believed there was an everlasting God above them, or professed to believe it, for all do believe it, whether they say so or not; and because the thought of God checks them in their impiety and their lust, therefore they cry out, "There is no God," and say it with their lips as well as in their hearts. I believe it was this that led Manasseh to persecute the saints of God; for among his sins it is written, " he shed innocent blood very much." It is a tradition among the Jews that the prophet Isaiah was sawn in sunder by Manasseh, on account of a rebuke which he gave him for his sin. Isaiah was not wont to be very timid, and he told the king of his lusts, and therefore placing him between two planks, he cut him in sunder from head to foot. It is just the reason why men hate God, and hate his servants, because the truth is too hot for them. Send you a preacher who would not tell you of your sins, and you would hear him peaceably; but when the gospel comes with power, then it is that men can not bear it; when it trenches upon that pleasure, that sin, or that lust, then they will not believe it. Ye would believe the gospel, if ye could believe it and live in your sins too. O! how many a drunken reprobate would be a Christian, if he might be a drunkard and a Christian too! How many a wicked wretch would turn believer, if he might believe and yet go on in his sins! But because faith in the everlasting God can never stand side by side with sin, and because the gospel cries, " Down with it!

down with it! down with your sin," therefore it is that men turn round and say, "Down with the gospel." It is too hot for you, O ye sinful generation; therefore ye turn aside from it, because it will not tolerate your lusts, nor indulge your iniquity.

III. We look, then, at Manasseh as an unbeliever, and now we have our last most pleasing task of looking at Manasseh as A CONVERT. Hear it, O heavens, and listen, O earth! The Lord God hath said it. Manasseh shall be saved. He on his throne of cruelty has just appended his name to another murderous edict against the saints of God; yet he shall be humbled; he shall ask for mercy and shall be saved. Manasseh hears the decree of God; he laughs. "What! I play the hypocrite, and bend my knee? Never! It is not possible: and when the godly hear of it, they all say, 'It is not possible.' What! Saul among the prophets? Manasseh regenerated? Manasseh made to bow before the Most High? The thing is impossible." Ah! it is impossible with man, but it is possible with God; God knows how to do it. The enemy is at the gates of the city; a hostile king has just besieged the walls of Jerusalem; Manasseh flees from his palace and hides himself among the thorns; he is there taken, carried captive to Babylon, and shut up in prison. And now we see what God can do. The proud king is proud no longer, for he has lost his power; the mighty man is mighty no more, for his might is taken from him; and now in a low dungeon listen to him. It is no more the blasphemer, no more the hater of God; but see him cold on the floor! Manasseh bows his knee, and with the tears rolling down his cheeks, he cries, "O God! my father's God! an outcast comes to thee; a hellhound stained with blood throws himself at thy feet; I, a very demon, full of filthiness, now prostrate myself before thee! O my God, canst thou, wilt thou have mercy on such a wretch as I?" Hear it, ye heavens! Listen yet again. See, from the skies the angel flies with mercy in his hand. Ah! whither speeds he? It is to the dungeon of Babylon. The proud king is on his knee, and mercy comes and whispers in his ear —"Hope!" He starts from his knees, and cries, "Is there hope?" And down he falls again. Once more he pleads, and

mercy whispers that sweet promise, uttered once by the murdered Isaiah—" I, even I, am he that blotteth out thy transgressions for my name's sake, and will not remember thy
sins." O! do you see him? His very heart is running over
in his eyes. O! how he weeps for joy, and yet for sorrow
that he ever could have sinned against a God so kind. A moment more, and the dungeon is opened; the king of Babylon,
moved by God, bids him go free, and he returns to his king
dom and throne, a happier and a better man than he had ever
been before. I think I see him coming into Jerusalem. There
are his statesmen and favorites, crying to him, " Come in, Manasseh; the bowl shall be filled, and we will have a merry
night to-night; we will bow before the shrine of Ashtaroth,
and thank her that she has set thee at liberty; lo, the horses
of the sun are ready; come and pay thy devotions to him
that shines on the earth, and leads the host of heaven!" Methinks I see their astonishment when he cries, " Stand back!
stand back! ye are my friends no longer, until ye become
God's friends; I have dandled you on my knees, and, vipers,
you have stung me with the poison of asps; I made you my
friends, and you have led me down to the gulf of hell. But I
know it now. Stand back till ye are better men; and I will
find others to be my courtiers." And there the poor saints,
hidden in the back streets of the city, so frightened because
the king has come back, are holding meetings of solemn
prayer, crying unto God that no more murderous, persecut-
ing edicts might go forth. And lo, a messenger comes and
says, " The king is returned;" and while they are looking at
him, wondering what the messenger is about to say, he adds,
" He has returned, not Manasseh as he went, but as a very
angel. I saw him with his own hands dash Ashtaroth in
pieces; I heard him cry, ' The horses of the sun shall be
hoofed; sweep out the house of God; we will hold a pass-
over there; the morning and evening lamb shall again burn
on Jehovah's altars, for he is God, and beside him there is
none else.' " O! can you conceive the joy of believers on that
auspicious day? Can you think how they went up to God's
house with joy and thanksgiving? And on the next Sabbath
they sung, as they had never sung before, " O come let us

sing unto the Lord, let us make a joyful noise unto the rock of our salvation," while they remembered that he who had persecuted the saints of God aforetime, now defended that very truth which once he abhorred. There was joy on earth, ay, and there was joy in heaven too; the bells of heaven rang merry peals the day Manasseh prayed; the angels of heaven flapped their wings with double alacrity the day Manasseh repented; earth and heaven were glad, and even the Almighty on his throne smiled gracious approbation, while he again said, "I, even I, am he that blotteth out thy transgressions for my name's sake, and will not remember thy sins."

And now are you curious to know what were the bases of the faith of Manasseh—what were the rocks on which he built his trust in God? I think they were two. He believed in God, first, *because he had answered his prayer;* and secondly, *because he had forgiven his sin.* I have sometimes said, when I have become the prey of doubting thoughts, "Well, now I dare not doubt whether there be a God, for I can look back in my diary and say, on such a day in the depths of trouble I bent my knee to God, and or ever I had risen from my knees the answer was given me." And so can many of you say; and therefore whatever others may say, you know there is a God, because he answered your prayer. You heard of that holy man, Mr. Müller, of Bristol. If you were to tell George Müller there was not a God, he would weep over you. "Not a God?" he would say; "why, I have seen his hand. Whence came those answers to my prayers?" Ah! sirs, ye may laugh at us for credulity; but there are hundreds here who could most solemnly assert that they have asked of God for divers matters, and that God has not failed them, but granted their request. This was one reason why Manasseh knew that the Lord he was God.

The other reason was, that *Manasseh had a sense of pardoned sin.* Ah! that is a delightful proof of the existence of a God. Here comes a poor miserable wretch: his knees are knocking together, his heart is sinking within him, he is giving himself up to despair. Bring the physicians to him! they cry, "We fear his mind is infirm. We believe he will at last have to be taken to some lunatic asylum;" and they apply their remedies, but he is none the better, but rather grows worse. On a sudden this poor creature, afflicted with a sense of sin, groaning on account of guilt, is brought within the sound of the sacred Word; he hears it—it increases his misery; he hears again—his pain becomes doubled; till at last every one says his case is utterly hopeless. Suddenly, on a happy morning which God had ordained, the minister is led to some sweet passage. Perhaps it is this: "Come now, and let us reason together; though your sins be as scarlet, they shall be white as snow; though they be red like crimson, they shall be as wool." The Spirit applies it, and the poor man goes home light as air, and says to his wife and children, "Come rejoice with me." "Why?" say they. "Because," says he, "my sins are forgiven." "How do you know that?" "O!" says he, " I have a sense of pardoning love within my heart, which all the doubters in the world could not gainsay; and if all the earth should rise up against me and say I should be condemned, I could say, 'I know there is now no condemnation for me.'" Have you ever felt pardoning blood applied? You will never doubt God, I know, if you have. Why, dear friends, if the poorest old woman in the world should be brought before an infidel of the wisest order, having a mind of the greatest caliber, and he should endeavor to pervert her, I think I see her smile at him, and say, "My good man, it is of no use at all, for the Lord has appeared unto me of old, saying, 'Yea I have loved thee with an everlasting love,' and so you may tell me what you please: I have had a sense of blood-bought pardon shed abroad in my heart, and I know that he is God, and you can never beat it out of me." As good Watts says, when we have once such an assurance as that,

> " Should all the forms that men devise
>   Assault my faith with treacherous art,
> I'd call them vanity and lies,
>   And bind the gospel to my heart."

O! if you have a sense that sin is forgiven, you can never doubt the existence of a God; for it will be said of you, "Then *he* knew that the Lord he was God."

And now I gather up my strength for just one moment, to

speak to those of you who desire to know what you must do to be saved. My hearer, no question can be more important than that; none is so requisite to ask. Alas! there are too many who never ask it, but who go sailing down to the gulf of black despair, listening to the syren song of procrastination and delay. But if you have been brought to ask the question solemnly and seriously, " What must I do to be saved? "I am happy, thrice happy to be able to tell you God's own word, " He that believeth on the Lord Jesus Christ and is baptized, shall he saved; he that believeth not," the Scripture saith, " shall be damned." " Not of works, lest any man should boast." " But sir," you say, " I have many good works, and would trust in them." If you do, you are a lost man. As old Matthew Wilks most quaintly said once, speaking in his usual tone—" You might as well try to sail to America in a paper boat, as to go to heaven by your own works; you will be swamped on the passage if you attempt it." We can not spin a robe that is long enough to cover us; we can not make a righteousness that is good enough to satisfy God. If you would be saved, it must be through what Christ did, and not what you did. You can not be your own Saviour; Christ must save you, if you are saved at all. How then can you be saved by Christ? Here is the plan of salvation. It is written— " This is a faithful saying, and worthy of all acceptation, that Christ Jesus came into the world to save sinners." Do you feel that you are a sinner? Then believe that Jesus Christ came to save you; for so sure as ever you feel you are a sinner, it is a fact that Christ died for you; and if he died for you, you shall not perish, for I can not conceive that Christ would die in vain. If he did die for you, you shall most assuredly be pardoned and saved, and shall one day sing in heaven. The only question is, Did he die for you? He most certainly did if you are a sinner; for it is written—I will repeat it again —" It is a faithful saying, that Christ Jesus came to save sinners." Poor sinner, believe! My dear friend, give me thine hand! I wish I could put it inside Christ's hand. O! embrace him! embrace him! lest haply the clouds of night should come upon thee, and the sun should set ere thou hast found him. O! lay hold on him, lest death and destruction should overtake thee; fly to this mountain, lest thou be consumed; and remember, once in Christ, thou art safe beyond hazard.

"Once in Christ, in Christ for ever,
Nothing from his love can sever."

O! believe him! believe him, my dear, dear hearers for Jesus sake! Amen.

SERMON XXII

WHY ARE MEN SAVED?

Nevertheless he saved them for his name's sake."—PSALM cvi. 8

In looking upon the works of God in creation, there are two questions which at once occur to the thoughtful mind, and which must be answered before we can procure a clew to the philosophy and science of creation itself. The first one is the question of authorship: "Who made all these things?" And the next question is that of design: "For what purpose were all these things created?" The first question, "Who made all these things?" is one which is easily answered by a man who has an honest conscience and a sane mind; for when he lifts his eyes up yonder to read the stars, he will see those stars spell out in golden letters this word—*God;* and when he looks below upon the waves, if his ears are honestly opened, he will hear each wave proclaiming—*God.* If he looks to the summits of the mountains, they will not speak, but with a dignified answer of silence they seem to say,

"The hand that made us is divine."

If we listen to the rippling of the freshet at the mountain side, to the tumbling of the avalanche, to the lowing of the cattle, to the singing of the birds, to every voice and sound of nature, we shall hear this answer to the question, "God is our maker; he hath made us, and not we ourselves."

The next question, as to design—"Why were these things made?"—is not so easy to answer apart from Scripture; but when we look at Scripture we discover this fact—that as the answer to the first question is God, so the answer to the second question is the same. Why were these things made? The answer is, for God's glory, for his honor, and for his pleasure.

No other answer can be consistent with reason. Whatever other replies man may propound, no other can be really sound. If they will for one moment consider that there was a time when God had no creatures—when he dwelt alone, the mighty maker of ages, glorious in an uncreated solitude, divine in his eternal loneliness—" I am and there is none beside me"—can any one answer this question—Why did God make creatures to exist?—in any other way than by answering it thus: " He made them for his own pleasure and for his own glory?" You may say he made them for his creatures; but we answer, there were then no creatures to make them for. We admit that the answer may be a sound one *now*. God makes the harvest for his creatures; he hangs the sun in the firmament to bless his creatures with light and sunshine; he bids the moon walk in her course by night, to cheer the darkness of his creatures upon earth. But the first answer, going back to the origin of all things, can be nothing else than this: " For his pleasure they are and were created." " He made all things for himself and by himself."

Now, this which holds good in the works of creation, holds equally good in the works of salvation. Lift up your eyes on high; higher than those stars which glimmer on the floor of heaven; look up, where spirits in white, clearer than light, shine like stars in their magnificence; look there, where the redeemed with their choral symphonies " circle the throne of God rejoicing," and put this question : " Who saved those glorified beings, and for what purpose were they saved?" We tell you that the same answer must be given as we have previously given to the former question—"*He* saved them;" " he saved them for his name's sake." The text is an answer to the two great questions concerning salvation : Who saved men, and why are they saved? " He saved them for his name's sake."

Into this subject I shall endeavor to look this morning. May God make it profitable to each of us, and may we be found among the number who shall be saved " for his name's sake." Treating the text verbally—and that is the way most will understand—here are four things. First, *a glorious Saviour*— '*He* saved them ;" secondly, *a favored people*—" He saved *them ;*" thirdly, *a divine reason why he saved them-* -" for his name's sake ;" and fourthly, *an obstruction conquered,* in the word " nevertheless," implying that there was some difficulty that was removed. " Nevertheless he saved them for his name's sake." A Saviour ; the saved ; the reason ; the obstruction removed.

I. First, then, here is A GLORIOUS SAVIOUR—" *He* saved them." Who is to be understood by that pronoun " he ?" Possibly many of my hearers may answer, " Why, the Lord Jesus Christ is the Saviour of men." Right, my friends ; but not all the truth. Jesus Christ is the Saviour ; but not more so than God the Father, or God the Holy Ghost. Some persons who are ignorant of the system of divine truth think of God the Father as being a great being full of wrath, and anger, and justice, but having no love ; they think of God the Spirit perhaps as a mere influence proceeding from the Father and the Son. Now, nothing can be more incorrect than such opinions. It is true the Son redeems me, but then the Father gave the Son to die for me, and the Father chose me in the everlasting election of his grace. The Father blots out my sin ; the Father accepts me and adopts me into his family through Christ. The Son could not save without the Father any more than the Father without the Son ; and as for the Holy Spirit, if the Son redeems, know ye not that the Holy Ghost regenerates. It is he that makes us new creatures in Christ, who begets us again unto a lively hope, who purifies our soul, who sanctifies our spirit, and who, at last, presents us spotless and faultless before the throne of the Most High, accepted in the beloved. When thou sayest " Saviour," remember there is a Trinity in that word—the Father, the Son, and the Holy Ghost—this Saviour being three persons under one name. Thou canst not be saved by the Son without the Father, nor by the Father without the Son, nor by the Father and Son without the Spirit. But as they are one in creation, so are they one in salvation, working together in one God for our salvation, and unto that God be glory everlasting, world without end, Amen.

But, note here, how this divine being claims salvation wholly to himself. " Nevertheless HE saved them." But,

Moses, where art thou? Didst not thou save them, Moses? Thou didst stretch thy rod over the sea, and it clave in halves; thou didst lift up thy prayer to heaven, and the frogs came, and the flies swarmed, and the water was turned into blood, and the hail smote the land of Egypt. Wast not thou their Saviour, Moses? And thou, Aaron, thou didst offer the bullocks which God accepted; thou didst lead them, with Moses, through the wilderness. Wast not thou their Saviour? They answer, "Nay, we were the instruments, but *he* saved them." God made use of us, but unto his name be all the glory, and none unto ourselves. But, Israel, thou wast a strong and mighty people; didst thou not save thyself? Perhaps it was by thine own holiness that the Red Sea was dried up; perhaps the parted floods were frightened at the piety of the saints that stood upon their margin; perhaps it was Israel that delivered itself. Nay, nay, saith God's Word; *he* saved them; they did not save themselves, nor did their fellow-men redeem them. And yet, mark you, there are some who dispute this point, who think that men save themselves, or, at least, that priests and preachers can help to do it. We say that the preacher, under God, may be the instrument of arresting man's attention, of warning him and arousing him; but the preacher is nothing; God is every thing. The most mighty eloquence that ever distilled from the lips of seraphic preacher is nothing apart from God's Holy Spirit. Neither Paul, nor Apollos, nor Cephas, are any thing: God gave the increase, and God must have all the glory. There are some we meet with here and there who say, "I am Mr. So-and-so's convert; I am a convert of the Rev. Dr. this or that." Well, if you are sir, I can not give you much hope of heaven. Only God's converts go there; not proselytes of man, but the redeemed of the Lord. O! it is very little to convert a man to our own opinions; it is something to be the means of converting him to the Lord our God. I had a letter some time ago from a good Baptist minister in Ireland, who very much wanted me to come over to Ireland, as he said, to represent the Baptist interest, because it was low there, and perhaps it might lead the people to think a little more of Baptists. I told him I would not go across the street merely to do that, much less would I cross the Irish Channel. I should not think of going to Ireland for that; but if I might go there to make Christians, under God, and be the means of bringing men to Christ, I would leave it to them what they should be afterward, and trust to God's Holy Spirit to direct and guide them as to what denomination they should consider nearest akin to God's truth. Bretnren, I might make all of you Baptists, perhaps, and yet you would be none the better for it; I might convert you all in that way, but such a conversion would be that you would be washed to greater stains, converted into hypocrites, and not into saints I have seen something of wholesale conversion. Great reviv alists have risen up; they have preached thundering sermons that have made men's knees knock together. "What a wonderful man!" people have said. "He has converted so many under one sermon." But look for his converts in a month, and where will they be? You will see some of them in the alehouse, you will hear others of them swear, you will find many of them rogues and cheats, because they were not God's converts, but only man's. Brethren, if the work be done at all, it must be done of God, for if God do not convert there is nothing done that shall last, and nothing that shall be of any avail for eternity.

But some reply, "Well, sir, but men convert themselves." Yes, they do, and a fine conversion it is. Very frequently they convert themselves. But, then, that which man did, man undoes. He who converts himself one day, unconverts himself the next; he tieth a knot which his own fingers can loosen. Remember this—you may convert yourselves a dozen times over, but "that which is born of the flesh is flesh," and "can not see the kingdom of God." It is only "that which is born of the Spirit" that "is spirit," and is therefore able to be gathered at last into the spirit realm, where only spiritual things can be found before the throne of the Most High. We must reserve this prerogative wholly to God. If any man state that God is not Creator, we call him infidel; if any man entrench upon this doctrine, that God is not the absolute maker of all things, we hiss him down in a moment; but he is an infidel of the worst kind, because more specious, who puts God out of the mercy throne, instead of putting him out of

the creation throne, and who tells men that they may convert
themselves, whereas God doth it all. "*He*" only, the great
Jehovah—Father, Son, and Holy Ghost—"he saved them for
his name's sake."

Thus have I endeavored to set out clearly the first truth of
the divine and glorious Saviour.

II. Now, secondly, THE FAVORED PERSONS—"He saved
them." Who are they? You will reply, "They were the
most respectable people that could be found in the world;
they were a very prayerful, loving, holy, and deserving
people; and, therefore, because they were good he saved
them." Very well, that is your opinion, I will tell you what
Moses says—"Our fathers understood not thy wonders in
Egypt; they remembered not the multitudes of thy mercies;
but provoked him at the sea, even at the Red Sea. Nevertheless he saved them." Look at the seventh verse, and you
will have their character. In the first place, they were a stupid
people—"Our fathers understood not thy wonders in Egypt."
In the next place, they were an ungrateful people—"they remembered not the multitude of thy mercies." In the third
place, they were a provoking people—"they provoked him at
the sea, even at the Red Sea." Ah, these are the people
whom free grace saves, these are the men and these the women
whom the God of all grace condescends to take to his bosom
and to make anew.

Note, first, *that they were a stupid people.* God sends his
gospel not always to the wise and prudent, but unto fools:

> "He takes the fool and makes him know
> The wonders of his dying love."

Do not suppose, my hearer, because you are very unlettered
and can scarcely read—do not imagine, because you have
always been brought up in extreme ignorance, and have
scarcely learned to spell your name, that therefore you can
not be saved. God's grace can save you, and then enlighten
you. A brother minister once told me a story of a man who
was known in a certain village as a simpleton, and was always
considered to be soft in the head; no one thought he could
ever understand any thing. But one day he came to hear the

gospel preached. He had been a drunken fellow, having wit enough to be wicked, which is a very common kind of wit. The Lord was pleased to bless the Word to his soul, so that he became a changed character; and what was the marvel of all was, his religion gave him a something which began to develop his latent faculties. He found he had something to live for, and he began to try what he could do. In the first place he wanted to read his Bible, that he might read his Saviour's name; and after much hammering and spelling away, at last he was able to read a chapter. Then he was asked to pray at a prayer-meeting; here was an exercise of his vocal powers. Five or six words made up his prayer, and down he sat abashed. But by continually praying in his own family at home, he came to pray like the rest of the brethren, and he went on till he became a preacher, and singular enough, he had a fluency—a depth of understanding, and a power of thought, such as are seldom found among ministers who only occasionally occupy pulpits. Strange it was, that grace should even tend to develop his natural powers, giving him an object, setting him devoutly and firmly upon it, and so bringing out all his resources that they were fully shown. Ah, ignorant ones, ye need not despair. He saved them; not for *their* sakes—there was nothing in them why they should be saved. He saved them, not for their wisdom's sake; but, ignorant though they were, understanding not the meaning of his miracles, " he saved them for his name's sake."

Note, again, *they were a very ungrateful people*, and yet he saved them. He delivered them times without number, and worked for them mighty miracles; but they still rebelled. Ah, that is like you, my hearer. You have had many deliverances from the borders of the grave; God has given you house and food day after day, and provided for you, and kept you to this hour; but how ungrateful you have been! As Isaiah said, " The ox knoweth his owner, and the ass his master's crib: but my people doth not know, Israel doth not consider." How many there are of this character, who have favors from God, the history of which they could not give in a year; but yet what have they ever done for him? They would not keep a horse that did not work for them, nor as much as a dog that would not notice them. But here is God; he has kept them day by day, and they have done a great deal against him, but they have done nothing for him. He has put the bread into their very mouths, nurtured them, and sustained their strength, and they have spent that strength in defying him, in cursing his name and breaking his Sabbath, "nevertheless he saved them." Some of this sort have been saved. I hope I have some here now who will be saved by conquering grace, made new men by the mighty power of God's Spirit. "Nevertheless he saved them." When there was nothing to recommend them, but every reason why they should be cast away for their ingratitude, "nevertheless he saved them."

And note, once more, *they were a provoking people*—"They provoked him at the sea, even at the Red Sea." Ah! how many people there are in this world that are a provoking people to God! If God were like man, who among us would be here to-day? If we are provoked once or twice, up goes the hand. With some men their passions stir at the very first offense; others, who are somewhat placid, will bear offense after offense, till at last they say, "there is an end of every thing, and I can bear that no longer; you must stay it, or else I must stay you!" Ah! if God had that temper, where would we be? Well might he say, "My thoughts are not as your thoughts; I am God, I change not, or else ye sons of Jacob had been consumed." They were a provoking people, "nevertheless he saved them." Have you provoked him? Take heart; if you repent, God has promised to save you; and what is more, he may this morning give you repentance, and even give you remission of sins, for he saves provoking people for his name's sake. I hear one of my hearers say, "Well, sir, that is encouraging sin with a vengeance!" Is it, indeed, sir? Why? "Because you are talking to the very worst of men, and you are saying that they may yet be saved." Pray, sirs, when I spoke to the worst of men, did I speak to *you* or not? You say "No; I am one of the most respectable and best of men." Well, then, sir, I have no need to preach to you, for you think you do not need any. "The whole have no need of a physician, but they that are sick." But these poor people, whom you say I am encouraging in sin, need

to be spoken to. I will leave you. Good-morning to you!
You keep to your own gospel, and I wonder whether you will
find your way to heaven by it. Nay, I do not wonder, I know
you will not, unless you are brought as a poor sinner to take
Christ at his word, and be saved for his name's sake. But I
say farewell to you, and I will keep on in my course. But
why did you say I encourage men in sin? I encourage them
to turn from it. I did not say he saved the provoking people
and then let them still provoke him as they had done before.
I did not say he saved the wicked people, and then let them
sin as they did before. But you know the meaning of the
word " saved ;" I explained it the other morning. The word
" saved" does not merely mean taking men to heaven ; it
means more—it means saving them from their sin; it means
giving them a new heart, new spirits, new lives; it means mak
ing them into new men. Is there any thing licentious in say
ing that Christ takes the worst of men to make them into
saints? If there be, I can not see it. I only wish he would
take the worst of this congregation and make them into the
saints of the living God, and then there would be far less
licentiousness. Sinner, I comfort thee ; not in thy sin, but in
thy repentance. Sinner, the saints of heaven were once as
bad as thou hast been. Art thou a drunkard, a swearer, an
unclean person? "Such were some of them ; but they have
been washed—but they have been sanctified." Is thy robe
black? Ask them whether their robes were ever black?
They will tell you, " Yes, we have washed our robes." If
they had been black, they would not have wanted washing.
" We have washed our robes and made them white in the
blood of the Lamb." Then, sinner, if they were black, and
were saved, why not thyself?

> " Are not his mercies rich and free ?
> Then say, my soul, why not for thee ?
> Our Jesus died upon the tree,
> Then why, my soul, why not for thee ?"

Take heart, penitents ; God will have mercy on you. " Nev
ertheless he saved them for his name's sake."

III. Now we come to the third point—THE REASON OF SAL-
VATION : " He saved them for his name's sake." There is no
other reason why God should save a man, but for his name's
sake; there is nothing in a sinner which can entitle him to salvation, or recommend him to mercy ; it must be God's own
heart which must dictate the motive why men are to be saved.
One person will say, " God will save me because I am so upright." Sir, he will do no such thing. Says another, " God
will save me because I am so talented." Sir, he will not.
Your talent ! Why, thou driveling, self-conceited idiot, thy
talent is nothing compared with that of the angel that once
stood before the throne, and sinned, and who is now cast into
the bottomless pit for ever ! If he would save men for their
talent, he would have saved Satan ; for he had talents enough.
As for thy morality and goodness, they are but filthy rags, and
he will never save thee for aught thou doest. None of us would
ever be saved, if God expected any thing of us : we must be
saved purely and solely for reasons connected with himself,
and lying in his own bosom. Blessed be his name, he saves
us for " his name's sake." What does that mean ? I think it
means this : the name of God is his person, his attributes, and
his nature. For his nature's sake, for his very attributes'
sake, he saved men ; and, perhaps, we may include this also :
" My name is in him"—that is, in Christ ; he saves us for the
sake of Christ, who is the name of God. And what does that
mean ? I think it means this :

He saved them, first, that he might manifest his nature.
God was all love, and he wanted to manifest it ; he did show
it when he made the sun, the moon, and the stars, and scattered flowers over the green and laughing earth. He did
show his love when he made the air balmy to the body, and
the sunshine cheering to the eye. He gives us warmth even
in winter, by the clothing and by the fuel which he has stored
in the bowels of the earth. But he wanted to reveal himself
still more. " How can I show them that I love them with all
my infinite heart ? I will give my Son to die to save the very
worst of them, and so I will manifest my nature." And God
has done it ; he has manifested his power, his justice, his love,
his faithfulness, and his truth ; he has manifested his whole

self on the great platform of salvation. It was, so to speak, the balcony on which God stepped to show himself to man—the balcony of salvation—here it is he manifests himself by saving men's souls.

He did it, again, to vindicate his name. Some say God is cruel; they wickedly call him tyrant. "Ah!" says God, "but I will save the worst of sinners, and vindicate my name; I will blot out the stigma; I will remove the slur; they shall not be able to say that, unless they be filthy liars, for I will be abundantly merciful. I will take away this stain, and they shall see that my great name is the name of Love." And said he again, "I will do this for my name's sake; that is, to make these people love my name. I know if I take the best of men, and save them, they will love my name; but if I take the worst of men, O, how they will love me! If I go and take some of the offscouring of the earth, and make them my children, O, how they will love me! Then they will cleave to my name; they will think it more sweet than music; it will be more precious to them than the spikenard of the eastern merchants; they will value it as gold, yea, as much fine gold. The man who loves me best is the man who hast most sins forgiven: he owes much, therefore he will love much." This is the reason why God often selects the worst of men to make them his. Saith an old writer, "All the carvings of heaven were made out of knots; the temple of God, the King of heaven, is a cedar one, but the cedars were all knotty trees before he cut them down." He chose the worst, that he might display his workmanship and his skill, to make unto himself a name; as it is written, "It shall be unto me for a name; for an everlasting sign that shall not be cut off." Now, dear hearers, of whatever class you are, here is something I have to offer well worthy of your consideration, namely— that if saved, we are saved for the sake of God, for his name's sake, and not for our own.

Now, this puts all men on a level with regard to salvation. Suppose that in coming into this garden, the rule had been that every one should have made mention of my name as the key of admittance; the law is, no man is to be admitted for his rank or title, but only by the use of a certain name. Up comes a lord; he makes use of the name and comes in; up comes a beggar, all in patches; he makes use of the name—the law says it is only the use of the name that will admit you—he makes use of it and he enters, for there is no distinction. So, my lady, if you come, with all your morality, you must make use of his name; if you come, poor, filthy inhabitant of a cellar or a garret, and make use of his name, the doors will fly wide open, for there is salvation for every one who makes mention of the name of Christ, and for none other. This pulls down the pride of the moralist, abases the self-exaltation of the self-righteous, and puts us all, as guilty sinners, on an equal footing before God, to receive mercy at his hands, " for his name's sake," and for that reason alone.

IV. I have detained you too long; let me close by noticing obstacles removed, in the word " nevertheless." I shall do that in somewhat of an interesting form by way of parable.

Once on a time, Mercy sat upon her snow-white throne, surrounded by the troops of love. A sinner was brought before her, whom Mercy designed to save. The herald blew the trumpet, and after three blasts thereof, with a loud voice, he said, " O heaven, and earth, and hell, I summon you this day to come before the throne of Mercy, to tell why this sinner should not be saved." There stood the sinner, trembling with fear; he knew that there were multitudes of opponents, who would press into the hall of Mercy, and with eyes full of wrath, would say, " He must not, and he shall not escape; he must be lost!" The trumpet was blown, and Mercy sat placidly on her throne, until there stepped in one with a fiery countenance; his head was covered with light; he spoke with a voice like thunder, and out of his eyes flashed lightning ! " Who art thou?" said Mercy. He replied, " I am Law; the law of God." " And what hast thou to say ?" " I have this to say," and he lifted up a stony tablet, written on both sides; " these ten commands this wretch has broken. My demand is blood; for it is written, ' The soul that sinneth it shall die.' Die he, or Justice must." The wretch trembles, his knees knock together, the marrow of his bones melts within him, as if it were ice dissolved by fire, and he shakes with very fright. Already he thought he saw the thunderbolt launched at him, he saw the lightning penetrate into his soul, hell yawned before him in imagination, and he thought himself cast away for ever. But Mercy smiled, and said, "Law, I will answer thee. This wretch deserves to die ; Justice demands that he should perish —I award thee thy claim." And, O ! how the sinner trembles. " But there is one yonder who has come with me to-day, my King, my Lord ; his name is Jesus ; he will tell you how the debt can be paid, and the sinner can go free." Then Jesus spake, and said, " O Mercy, I will do thy bidding. Take me, Law ; put me in a garden ; make me sweat drops of blood ; then nail me to a tree ; scourge my back before you put me to death ; hang me on the cross ; let blood run from my hands and feet ; let me descend into the grave ; let me pay all the sinner oweth ; I will die in his stead." And the Law went out and scourged the Saviour, nailed him to the cross, and coming back with his face all bright with satisfaction, stood again at the throne of Mercy, and Mercy said, " Law, what hast thou now to say ?" " Nothing," said he ; " fair angel, nothing." "What ! not one of these commands against him ?" " No, not one. Jesus, his substitute, has kept them all—has paid the penalty for his disobedience ; and now, instead of his condemnation, I demand, as a debt of Justice, that he be acquitted." " Stand thou here," said Mercy ; " sit on my throne ; I and thou together will now send forth another summons." The trumpet rang again. " Come hither, all ye who have aught to say against this sinner, why he should not be acquitted ;" and up comes another—one who often troubled the sinner—one who had a voice not so loud as that of the Law, but still piercing and thrilling—a voice whose whispers were like the cuttings of a dagger. " Who art thou ?" says Mercy. " I am Conscience ; this sinner must be punished ; he has done so much against the law of God that he must be punished ; I demand it ; and I will give him no rest till he is punished, nor even then, for I will follow him even to the grave, and persecute him after death with pangs unutterable." " Nay," said Mercy, " hear me ;" and while he paused for a moment, she took a bunch of hyssop and sprinkled Conscience with the blood, saying, " Hear me, Conscience, 'The blood of

Jesus Christ, God's Son, cleanseth us from all sin.' Now hast thou aught to say?" "No," said Conscience, "nothing—

> " 'Covered is his unrighteousness;
> From condemnation he is free.'

Henceforth I will not grieve him; I will be a good conscience unto him, through the blood of our Lord Jesus Christ." The trumpet rang a third time, and growling from the innermost vaults, up there came a grim black fiend, with hate in his eyes, and hellish majesty on his brows. He is asked, "Hast thou any thing against that sinner?" "Yes," said he, "I have; he has made a league with hell, and a covenant with the grave, and here it is, signed with his own hand. He asked God to destroy his soul in a drunken fit, and vowed he would never turn to God; see, here is his covenant with hell!" "Let us look at it," said Mercy; and it was handed up, while the grim fiend looked at the sinner, and pierced him through with his black looks. "Ah! but," said Mercy, "this man had no right to sign the deed; a man must not sign away another's property. This man was bought and paid for long beforehand; he is not his own; the covenant with Death is disannulled, and the league with hell is rent in pieces. Go thy way, Satan." "Nay," said he, howling again, "I have something else to say: that man was always my friend; he listened ever to my insinuations; he scoffed at the gospel; he scorned the majesty of heaven: is he to be pardoned, while I repair to my hellish den, for ever to bear the penalty of guilt?" Said Mercy, "Avaunt, thou fiend; these things he did in the days of his unregeneracy; but this word 'nevertheless' blots them out. Go thou to thy hell; take this for another lash upon thyself—the sinner shall be pardoned, but thou—never, treacherous fiend!" And then Mercy, smilingly turning to the sinner, said, "Sinner, the trumpet must be blown for the last time!" Again it was blown, and no one answered. Then stood the sinner up, and Mercy said, "Sinner, ask thyself the question—ask thou of heaven, of earth, of hell—whether any can condemn thee?" And the sinner stood up, and with a bold, loud voice, said, "Who shall lay any thing to the charge of God's elect?" And he looked into hell, and Satan lay there, biting his iron bonds; and he looked on earth, and earth was silent; and in the majesty of faith the sinner did even climb to heaven itself, and he said, "Who shall lay any thing to the charge of God's elect? God?" And the answer came, "No; he justifieth." "Christ?" Sweetly it was whispered, "No; he died." Then turning round, the sinner joyfully exclaimed, "Who shall separate me from the love of God, which is in Christ Jesus our Lord?" And the once condemned sinner came back to Mercy; prostrate at her feet he lay, and vowed henceforth to be hers for ever, if she would keep him to the end, and make him what she would desire him to be. Then no longer did the trumpet ring, but angels rejoiced, and heaven was glad, for the sinner was saved.

Thus, you see, I have, what is called, dramatized the thing; but I don't care what it is called; it is a way of arresting the ear, when nothing else will. "Nevertheless;" there is the obstruction taken away! Sinner, whatever be the "nevertheless," it shall never the less abate the Saviour's love; not the less shall it ever make it, but it shall remain the same.

> "Come, guilty soul, and flee away
>   To Christ and heal thy wounds;
> This is the glorious gospel-day
>   Wherein free grace abounds:
>   Come to Jesus, sinner, come."

On thy knee weep out a sorrowful confession; look to his cross, and see the substitute; believe, and live. Ye almost demons, ye that have gone furthest into sin, now, Jesus says, "If you know your need of me, turn unto me, and I will have mercy upon you: and to our God, for he will abundantly pardon."

SERMON XXIII

PARTICULAR ELECTION

" Wherefore the rather, brethren, give diligence to make your calling and election sure : for if ye do these things, ye shall never fall : for so an entrance shall be ministered unto you abundantly into the everlasting kingdom of our Lord and Saviour Jesus Christ."—2 PETER, i. 10, 11

It is exceedingly desirable that in the hours of worship and in the house of prayer our minds should be as much as possible divested of every worldly thought. Although the business of the week will very naturally struggle with us to encroach upon the Sabbath, it is our business to guard the Sabbath from the intrusion of our worldly cares, as we would guard an oasis from the overwhelming irruption of the sand. I have felt, however, that to-day we should be surrounded with circumstances of peculiar difficulty in endeavoring to bring our minds to spiritual matters ; for of all times, perhaps the most unlikely for getting any good in the sanctuary, if that depends upon mental abstraction, are election times. So important, in the minds of most men, are political matters, that very naturally, after the hurry of the week, combined with the engrossing pursuit of elections, we are apt to bring the same thoughts and the same feelings into the house of prayer, and speculate, perhaps, even in the place of worship, whether a conservative or a liberal shall be returned for our borough, or whether for the city of London there shall be returned Lord John Russell, Baron Rothschild, or Mr. Currie I thought, this morning, " Well, it is of no use my trying to stop this great train in its progress. People are just now going on at an express rate in these matters ; I think I will be wise, and instead of endeavoring to turn them off the line, I will turn the points. so that they may still continue their pursuits with the same swiftness as ever, but in a new direction It shall be the same line ; they shall still be traveling in earnest toward election, but perhaps I may have some skill to turn the points, so that they shall be enabled to consider election in a rather different manner."

When Mr. Whitefield was once applied to to use his influence at a general election, he returned answer to his lordship who requested him, that he knew very little about *general* elections, but that if his lordship took his advice he would make his own *particular* " calling and election sure ;" which was a very proper remark. I would not, however, say to any persons here present, despise the privilege which you have as citizens. Far be it from me to do it. When we become Christians, we do not leave off being Englishmen ; when we become professors of religion we do not cease to have the rights and privileges which citizenship has bestowed on us. Let us, whenever we shall have the opportunity of using the right of voting, use it as in the sight of Almighty God, knowing that for every thing we shall be brought into account, and for that among the rest, seeing that we are intrusted with it. And let us remember that we are our own governors, to a great degree, and that if at the next election we should choose wrong governors, we shall have nobody to blame but ourselves, however wrongly they may afterward act, unless we exercise all prudence and prayer to Almighty God to direct our hearts to a right choice in this matter. May God so help us, and may the result be for his glory, however unexpected that result may be to any of us !

Having said so much, let me, then, turn the points, and draw you to a consideration of your own particular calling and election, bidding you in the words of the apostle, " the rather, brethren, give diligence to make your calling and election sure : for if ye do these things, ye shall never fall : for so an entrance shall be ministered unto you abundantly into the everlasting kingdom of our Lord and Saviour Jesus Christ." We have here, first of all, *two fundamental points in religion* —" calling and election ; we have here, secondly, *some good advice*—" to make your calling and election *sure*," or, rather, to assure ourselves that we are *called and elected ;* and then, in the third place, we have *some reasons given us why we should use this diligence to be assured of our election*—because, on the one hand, we shall so be kept from falling, and on the other hand, we shall attain unto "an abundant entrance into the everlasting kingdom of our Lord and Saviour Jesus Christ."

I. First of all, then, there are the TWO IMPORTANT MATTERS IN RELIGION—secrets, both of them, to the world—only to be understood by those who have been quickened by divine grace : "CALLING AND ELECTION."

By the word "calling" in Scripture, we understand two things—one, the *general call*, which in the preaching of the gospel is given to every creature under heaven ; the second call (that which is here intended) is the *special call*—which we call the effectual call, whereby God secretly, in the use of means, by the irresistible power of his Holy Spirit, calls out of mankind a certain number, whom he himself hath before elected, calling them from their sins to become righteous, from their death in trespasses and sins to become living spiritual men, and from their worldly pursuits to become the lovers of Jesus Christ. The two callings differ very much. As Bunyan puts it, very prettily, "By his common call, he gives nothing ; by his special call, he always has something to give ; he has also a brooding voice, for them that are under his wing ; and he has an outcry, to give the alarm when he seeth the enemy come." What we have to obtain, as absolutely necessary to our salvation, is a special calling, made in us, not to our ears but to our hearts, not to our mere fleshly understanding, but to the inner man, by the power of the Spirit. And then the other important thing is election. As without calling there is no salvation, so without election there is no calling. Holy Scripture teaches us that God hath from the beginning chosen us who are saved unto holiness through Jesus Christ. We are told that as many as are ordained unto eternal life believe, and that their believing is the effect of their being ordained to eternal life from before all worlds. However much this may be disputed, as it frequently is, you must first deny the authenticity and full inspiration of the holy Scriptures before you can legitimately and truly deny it. And since, without doubt, I have many here who are members of the Episcopal church, allow me to say to them what I have often said before, " You, of all men, are the most inconsistent in the world, unless you believe the doctrine of election, for if it be not taught in Scripture there is this one thing for an absolute certainty, it is taught in your Articles." Nothing can be more forcibly expressed, nothing more definitely laid down, than the doctrine of predestination in the Book of Common Prayer ; although we are told what we already know, that the doctrine is a high-mystery, and is only to be handled carefully by men who are enlightened. However, without doubt, it is the doctrine of Scripture, that those who are saved are saved because God chose them to be saved, and are called as the effect of that first choice of God. If any of you dispute this, I stand upon the authority of holy Scripture ; ay, and if it were necessary to appeal to tradition, which I am sure it is not, and no Christian man would ever do it, yet I would take you upon that point ; for I can trace this doctrine through the lips of a succession of holy men, from this present moment to the days of Calvin, thence to Augustine, and thence on to Paul himself; and even to the lips of the Lord Jesus Christ. The doctrine is, without doubt, taught in Scripture, and were not men too proud to humble themselves to it, it would universally be believed and received as being no other than manifest truth. Why, sirs, do you not believe that God loves his children ? and do you not know that God is unchangeable ? therefore, if he loves them now he must always have loved them. Do you not believe that if men be saved God saves them ? And if so, can you see any difficulty in admitting that because he saves them there must have been a purpose to save them—a purpose which existed before all worlds ? Will you not grant me that ? If you will not, I must leave you to the Scriptures themselves ; and if they will not convince you on the point, then I must leave you unconvinced.

It will be asked, however, why is *calling* here put before *election*, seeing election is eternal, and calling takes place in time ? I reply, because calling is first to us. The first thing which you and I can know is our calling : we can not tell whether we are elect until we feel that we are called. We must, first of all, prove our calling, and then our election is sure most certainly. "Moreover, whom he did predestinate, them he also called: and whom he called, them he also justified: and whom he justified, them he also glorified." Calling comes first in our apprehension. We are by God's Spirit called from our evil estate, regenerated and made new creatures, and then, looking backward, we behold ourselves as being most assuredly elect because we were called.

Here, then, I think I have explained the text. There are the two things which you and I are to prove to be sure to ourselves—whether we are *called* and whether we are *elected*. And O, dear friends, this is a matter about which you and I should be very anxious. For consider what an *honorable* thing it is to be elected. In this world it is thought a mighty thing to be elected to the House of Commons; but how much more honorable to be elected to eternal life; to be elected to "the church of the first born, whose names are written in heaven;" to be elected to be a compeer of angels, to be a favorite of the living God, to dwell with the Most High, among the fairest of the sons of light, nearest to the eternal throne! Election in this world is but a short-lived thing, but God's election is *eternal*. Let a man be elected to a seat in the House: seven years must be the longest period that he can hold his election; but if you and I be elected according to the divine purpose, we shall hold our seats when the day-star shall have ceased to burn, when the sun shall have grown dim with age, and when the eternal hills shall have bowed themselves with weakness. If we be chosen of God and precious, then are we chosen for ever; for God changeth not in the objects of his election. Those whom he hath ordained he hath ordained to eternal life, "and they shall never perish, neither shall any man pluck them out of his hand." It is worth while to know ourselves elect, for nothing in this world can make a man more *happy* or more valiant than the knowledge of his election. "Nevertheless," said Christ to his apostles, " rejoice not in this, but rather rejoice that your names are written in heaven"—that being the sweetest comfort, the honeycomb that droppeth with the most precious drops of all, the knowledge of our being chosen by God. And this, too, beloved, makes a man *valiant*. When a man by diligence has attained to the assurance of his election, you can not make him a coward, you can never make him cry craven even in the thickest battle; he holds the standard fast and firm, and cleaves his foes with the cimeter of truth. " Was not I ordained by God to be the standard bearer of this truth? I must, I will stand by it, despite you all." He saith to every enemy, " Am I not a chosen king? Can floods of water wash out the sacred unction from a king's bright brow? No, never! And if God hath chosen me to be a king and a priest unto God for ever and ever, come what may or come what will—the lion's teeth, the fiery furnace, the spear, the rack, the stake, all these things are less than nothing, seeing I am chosen of God unto salvation." It has been said that the doctrine of necessity makes men weak. It is a lie. It may seem so in theory, but in practice it has always been found to be the reverse. The men who have believed in destiny, and have held fast and firm by it, have always done the most valiant deeds. There is one point in which this is akin even with Mohammed's faith. The deeds that were done by him were chiefly done from a firm confidence that God had ordained him to his work. Never had Cromwell driven his foes before him if it had not been in the stern strength of this almost omnipotent truth; and there shall scarcely be found a man strong to do great and valiant deeds unless, confident in the God of providence, he looks upon the accidents of life as being steered by God, and give himself up to God's firm predestination, to be borne along by the current of his will, contrary to all the wills and all the wishes of the world. " Wherefore the rather, brethren, give diligence to make your calling and election sure.'

II. Come, then, here is the second point—GOOD ADVICE. " Make your calling and election sure." Not toward God, for they are sure to him; make them sure to yourself. Be quite certain of them; be fully satisfied about them. In many of our dissenting places of worship very great encouragement is held out to doubting. A person comes before the pastor, and says, " O! sir, I am so afraid I am not converted: I tremble lest I should not be a child of God. O! I fear I am not one of the Lord's elect." The pastor will put out his hands to him and say, "Dear brother, you are all right so long as you can doubt." Now, I hold, that is altogether wrong. Scripture never says, "He that doubteth shall be saved," but "He that believeth." It may be true that the man is in a good state; it may be true that he wants a little comfort; but his doubts are not good things, nor ought we to encourage him in his doubts. Our business is to encourage him out of his doubts, and by the grace of God to urge him to " give *all* diligence to make his calling and election *sure*;" not to doubt it, but to be sure of it. Ah! I have heard some hypocritical doubters say, "O! I have had such doubts whether I am the Lord's," and I have thought to myself, "And so have I very great doubts about you." I have heard some say they do tremble so because they are afraid they are not the Lord's people; and the lazy fellows sit in their pews on the Sunday, and just listen to the sermon; but they never think of giving diligence, they never do good, perhaps are inconsistent in their lives, and then talk about doubting. It is quite right they should doubt, it is well they should; and if they did not doubt we might begin to doubt for them. Idle men have no right to assurance. The Scripture says, "Give diligence to make your calling and election sure."

Full assurance is an excellent attainment. It is profitable for a man to be certain in this life, and absolutely sure of his own calling and election. But how can he be sure? Now, many of our more ignorant hearers imagine that the only way they have of being sure of their election is by some revelation, some dream, or some mystery. I have enjoyed very hearty laughs at the expense of some people who have trusted in their visions. Really, if you had passed among so many shades of ignorant professing Christians as I have, and had to resolve so many doubts and fears, you would be so infinitely sick of dreams and visions that you would say, as soon as a person began to speak about them, "Now, do just hold your tongue." "Sir," said a woman, "I saw blue lights in the front parlor when I was in prayer, and I thought I saw the Saviour in the corner and I said to myself, I am safe." (Mr. Spurgeon here narrated a remarkable story of a poor woman who was possessed with a singular delusion.)   And yet there are tens of thousands of people in every part of the country, and members too of Christian bodies, who have no better ground for their belief that they are called and elected, than some vision equally ridiculous, or the equally absurd hearing of a voice.   A young woman came to me some time ago she wanted to join the church, and when I asked her how she knew herself to be converted, she said she was down at the bottom of the garden, and she thought she heard a voice, and she thought she saw something up in the clouds that said to her so-and-so.   "Well," I said to her, " that thing may have been the means of doing good to you, but if you put any trust in it, it is all over with you."   A dream, ay, and a vision, may often bring men to Christ; I have known many who have been brought to him by them, beyond a doubt, though it has been mysterious to me how it was; but when men bring these forward as a proof of their conversion, *there* is the mistake; because you may have fifty thousand dreams and see fifty thousand visions, and you may be a fool for all that, and all the bigger sinner for having seen them.   There is better evidence to be had than all this: "Give diligence to make your calling and election sure."

"How then," says one, " am I to make my calling and election sure ?"   Why, thus:—If thou wouldst get out of a doubting state, get out of an idle state ; if thou wouldst get out of a trembling state, get out of an indifferent lukewarm state ; for lukewarmness and doubting, and laziness and trembling, very naturally go hand in hand.   If thou wouldst enjoy the eminent grace of the full assurance of faith under the blessed Spirit's influence and assistance, do what the Scripture tells thee—" Give diligence to make your calling and election sure." Wherein shalt thou be diligent?

Note how the Scripture has given us a list.   Be diligent in your *faith*.   Take care that your faith is of the right kind— that it is not a creed, but a credence—that it is not a mere belief of doctrine, but a reception of doctrine into your heart, and the practical light of the doctrine in your soul.   Take care that your faith results from necessity—that you believe in Christ because you have nothing else to believe in.   Take care t is simple faith, hanging alone on Christ, without any other dependence but Jesus Christ and him crucified. And when thou hast given diligence about that, give diligence next to thy *courage.* Labor to get *virtue ;* plead with God that he would give thee the face of a lion, that thou mayest never be afraid of any enemy, however much he may jeer or threaten thee, but that thou mayest with a consciousness of right, go on, boldly trusting in God. And having, by the help of the Holy Spirit, obtained that, study well the Scriptures, and get *knowledge ;* for a knowledge of doctrine will tend very much to confirm your faith. Try to understand God's Word, get a sensible, spiritual idea of it. Get, if you can, a system of divinity out of God's Bible. Put the doctrines together. Get real, theological knowledge, founded upon the infallible Word. Get a knowledge of that science which is most despised, but which is the most necessary of all, the science of Christ and of him crucified, and of the great doctrines of grace. And when thou hast done this, " add to thy knowledge *temperance.*" Take heed to thy body : be temperate there. Take heed to thy soul : be temperate there. Be not drunken with pride ; be not lifted up with self-confidence. Be temperate. Be not harsh toward thy friends, nor bitter to thine enemies. Get temperance of lip, temperance of life, temperance of heart, temperance of thought. Be not passionate : be not carried away by every wind of doctrine. Get temperance, and then add to it by God's Holy Spirit, *patience ;* ask him to give thee that patience which endureth affliction, which, when it is tried, shall come forth as gold. Array yourself with patience, that you may not murmur in your sicknesses; that you may not curse God in your losses, nor be depressed in your afflictions. Pray without ceasing, until the Holy Ghost has nerved you with patience to endure unto the end. And when you have that, get *godliness.* Godliness is something more than religion. The most religious men may be the most godless men, and sometimes a godly man may seem to be irreligious. Let me just explain that seeming paradox. A real *religious* man is a man who sighs after sacraments, attends churches and chapels, and is outwardly good but goes no further. A godly man is a man who does not ook so much to the dress as to the person: he looks not to the outward form, but to the inward and spiritual grace; he is a godly man, as well as attentive to religion. Some men, however, are godly, and to a great extent despise form; they may be godly, without some degree of religion; but a man can not be fully righteous without being godly in the true neaning of each of these words, though not in the general vulgar sense of them. Add to thy patience an eye to God; live in his sight; dwell close to him; seek for fellowship with him; and thou hast got godliness. And to that add *brotherly love*. Be loving towards all the members of Christ's church; have a love to all the saints of every denomination. And then add to that *charity*, which openeth its arms to all men, and loves them; and when you have got all these, then you will know your calling and election, and just in proportion as you practice these heavenly rules of life, in this heavenly manner, will you come to know that you are called and that you are elect. But by no other means can you attain to a knowledge of that, except by the witness of the Spirit, bearing witness with your spirit that you are born of God, and then witnessing in your conscience that you are not what you were, but are a new man in Christ Jesus, and are therefore called, and therefore elected.

A man over there says he is elect. He gets drunk. Ay, you are elect by the devil, sir; that is about your only election. Another man says, "Blessed be God, I do not care about evidences a bit; I am not so legal as you are!" No, I dare say you are not: but you have no great reason to bless God about it, for, my dear friend, unless you have these evidences of a new birth take heed to yourself. "God is not mocked: whatsoever a man soweth, that shall he also reap." "Well," says another, "but I think that doctrine of election a very licentious doctrine." Think on as long as you please; but please to bear me witness that as I have preached it to-day there is nothing licentious about it. Very likely you are licentious, and you would make the doctrine licentious if you believed it; but "to the pure all things are pure." He who receiveth God's truth in his heart doth not often pervert it and turn aside from it unto wicked ways. No man, let me repeat, has any right to believe himself elect of God, unless he has been renewed by God; no man has any right to believe himself called, unless his life be in the main consistent with his vocation, and he walk worthy of that whereunto he is called. Out upon an election that lets you live in sin! Away with it! away with it! That was never the design of God's Word; and it never was the doctrine of Calvinists either Though we have been lied against and our teachings perverted, we have always stood by this—that good works, though they do not procure nor in any degree merit salvation, yet are the necessary evidences of salvation; and unless they be in men the soul is still dead, uncalled, and unrenewed. The nearer you live to Christ, the more you imitate him, the more your life is conformed to him, and the more simply you hang upon him by faith, the more certain you may be of your election in Christ and of your calling by his Holy Spirit. May the Holy One of Israel give you the sweet assurance of grace, by affording you " tokens for good" in the graces which he enables you to manifest.

III. And now I shall close up by giving you THE APOSTLE'S REASONS WHY YOU SHOULD MAKE YOUR CALLING AND ELECTION SURE.

I put in one of my own to begin with. It is because, as I have said, *it will make you so happy*. Men who doubt their calling and election can not be full of joy: but the happiest saints are those who know and believe it. You know our friends say this is a howling wilderness, and you know my reply to it is, that they make all the howling themselves: there would not be much howling if they were to look up a little more and down a little less, for by faith they would make it blossom like the rose, and give to it the excellence and glory of Carmel and Sharon. But why they howl so much is because they do not believe. Our happiness and our faith are to a great degree proportionate; they are Siamese twins to the Christian; they must flourish or decay together.

> " When I can say my God is mine,
>   Then I can all my griefs resign;
>   Can tread the world beneath my feet,
>   And all that earth calls good or great."

> • When gloomy doubts prevail,
>   1 fear to call him mine;
> The streams of comfort seem to fail,
>   And all my hopes decline.'

Only faith can make a Christian lead a happy life.

But now for Peter's reasons. First, because " *if ye do these things ye will never fall.*" "Perhaps," says one, " in attention to election we may forget our daily walk, and like the old philosopher who looked up to the stars, we may walk on and tumble into the ditch !" " Nay, nay," says Peter, " if you take care of your calling and election, you shall not trip; but with your eyes up there, looking for your calling and election, God will take care of your feet, and you shall never fall." Is it not very notable, that, in many churches and chapels, you do not often hear a sermon about *to-day;* it is always either about old eternity, or else about the millennium ; either about what God did before man was made, or else about what God will do when all are dead and buried ? Pity they do not tell us something about what we are to do to-day, now in our daily walk and conversation ! Peter removes this difficulty. He says, " This point is a practical point; for you can only answer your election for yourself by taking care of your practice ; and while you are so taking care of your practice and assuring yourself of your election, you are doing the best possible thing to keep you from falling." And is it not desirable that a true Christian should be kept from falling ? Mark the difference between *falling* and *falling away.* The true believer can never fall away and perish ; but he may fall and injure himself. He shall not fall and break his neck ; but a broken leg is bad enough without a broken neck. " Though he fall he shall not be utterly cast down ;" but that is no reason why he should dash himself against a stone. His desire is, that day by day he may grow more holy ; that hour by hour he may be more thoroughly renewed, until, conformed to the image of Christ, he may enter int bliss eternal. If, then, you take care of your calling and election, you are doing the best thing in the world to prevert you from falling ; for in so doing you shall never fall.

And now, the other reason, and then I shall have almost concluded. "*For so an entrance shall be ministered unto you abundantly into the everlasting kingdom of our Lord and Saviour Jesus Christ.*" An "abundant entrance" has sometimes been illustrated in this way. You see yonder ship. After a long voyage, it has neared the haven, but is much injured; the sails are rent to ribbons, and it is in such a forlorn condition that it can not come up to the harbor: a steam-tug is pulling it in with the greatest possible difficulty. That is like the righteous being "scarcely saved." But do you see that other ship? It has made a prosperous voyage; and now, laden to the water's edge, with the sails all up and with the white canvas filled with the wind, it rides into the harbor joyously and nobly. That is an "abundant entrance;" and if you and I are helped by God's Spirit to add to our faith virtue, and so on, we shall have at the last "an abundant entrance into the kingdom of our Lord Jesus Christ." There is a man who is a Christian; but, alas! there are many inconsistencies in his life for which he has to mourn. He lies there, dying on his bed. The thought of his past life rushes upon him. He cries, "O Lord, have mercy upon me, a sinner," and the prayer is answered; his faith is in Christ, and he shall be saved. But O! what griefs he has upon his bed. "O, if I had served my God better! And these children of mine—if I had but trained them up better, 'in the nurture and admonition of the Lord!' I am saved," says he; "but alas, alas! though it be a great salvation, I can not enjoy it yet. I am dying in gloom, and clouds, and darkness. I trust, I hope, I shall be gathered to my fathers, but I have no works to follow me—or very few indeed; for though I am saved, I am but just saved—saved 'so as by fire.' " Here is another one; he too is dying. Ask him what his dependence is: he tells you, "I rest in none else but Jesus." But mark him as he looks back to his past life. "In such a place," says he, "I preached the gospel, and God helped me." And though with no pride about him—he will not congratulate himself upon what he has done—yet doth he lift his hands to heaven, and he blesses God that throughout a long life he has been able to keep his garments white; that he has served his Master; and now, like a shock of corn fully ripe, he is about to be gathered in o his Master's garner. Hark to him! It is not the feeble lisp of the trembler; but with "victory! victory! victory!" for his dying shout, he shuts his eyes, and dies like a warrior in his glory. That is the "abundant entrance." Now, the man that "gives diligence to make his calling and election sure," shall insure for himself "an abundant entrance into the kingdon of our Lord Jesus Christ."

What a terrible picture is hinted at in these words of the apostle—"saved so as by fire!" Let me try and present it to you. The man has come to the edge of Jordan; the time has arrived for him to die. He is a believer—just a believer; but his life has not been what he could wish; not all that he now desires that it had been. And now stern death is at him, and he has to take his first step into the Jordan. Judge of his horror when the flames surround his foot. He treads upon the hot sand of the stream; and the next step he takes, with his hair well nigh on end, with his eye fixed on heaven on the other side of the shore, his face is yet marked with horror. He takes another step, and he is all bathed in fire Another step, and he is up to his very loins in flames—"saved, so as by fire." A strong hand has grasped him, that drags him onward through the stream. But how dreadful must be the death even of a Christian, when he is saved "so as by fire!" There on the river's brink, astonished, he looks back and sees the liquid flames through which he has been called to walk, as a consequence of his indifference in this life. Saved he is—thanks to God; and his heaven shall be great, and his crown shall be golden, and his harp shall be sweet, and his hymns shall be eternal, and his bliss unfading;—but his dying moment, the last article of death, was blackened by sin; and he was saved "so as by fire!" Mark the other man; he too has to die. He has often feared death. He dips his foot in Jordan; and his body trembles, his pulse waxes faint, and even his eyes are well nigh closed. His lips scarcely speak, but still he says "Jesus, thou art with me, thou art with me, passing through the stream!" He takes another step, and the waters now begin to refresh him. He dips his hand and tastes the stream, and tells those who are watching him in tears, that to die is blessed. "The stream is sweet," he says, "it is not bitter : it is blessed to die." Then he takes another step, and when he is well nigh submerged in the stream, and lost to vision, he says,

> "And when ye hear my heart-strings break,
> How sweet the minutes roll!
> A mortal paleness on my cheek,
> But glory in my soul!"

That is the "abundant entrance" of the man who has manfully served his God—who, by his divine grace, has had a path unclouded and serene—who, by diligence, has "made his calling and election sure;" and, therefore, as a reward, not of debt, but of grace, hath entered heaven with higher honors and with greater ease than others equally saved, but not saved in so splendid a manner.

Just one thought more. It is said that the entrance is to be "ministered to us." That gives me a sweet hint that, I find, is dwelt upon by Doddridge. Christ will open the gates of heaven ; but the heavenly train of virtues—the works which follow us—will go up with us and minister an entrance to us. I sometimes think, if God should enable me to live and die for the good of these congregations, so that many of them shall be saved, how sweet it will be to enter heaven, and when I shall come there, to have an entrance ministered unto me, not by Christ alone, but by some of you for whom I have ministered. One shall meet me at the gate, and say, "Minister, thou wast the cause of my salvation!" And another, and another, and another, shall all exclaim the same. When Whitefield entered heaven—that highly honored servant of the Lord—I think I can see the hosts rushing to the gates to meet him. There are thousands there that have been brought to God by him. O how they open wide the gates; and how they praise God that he has been the means of bringing them to heaven ; and how do they minister unto him an abundant entrance! There will be some of you, perhaps, in heaven, with starless crowns : for you never did good to your fellow-creatures ; you never were the means of saving souls ; you are to have crowns without stars. But "they that turn many to righteousness" shall "shine as the stars, for ever and ever;"

and an entrance shall be abundantly ministered to them I do want to get a heavy crown in heaven—not to wear, but to have all the more costly gift to give to Christ. And you ought to desire the same, that you may have all the more honors, and so have the more to cast at his feet, with, "Not unto us, but unto thy name, O Christ, be the glory!" "Rather, brethren, give all diligence to make your calling and election sure."

And now, to conclude. There are some of you with whom this text has nothing to do. You can not make "your calling and election sure," for you have not been called; and you have no right to believe that you are elected, if you have never been called. To such of you, let me say, do not ask whether you are elected first, but ask whether you are called. And go to God's house, and bend your knee in prayer; and may God, in his infinite mercy, call you! And mark this—if any of you can say,

> "Nothing in my hands I bring,
> Simply to the cross I cling;"

if any of you, abjuring your self-righteousness, can now come to Christ and take him to be your all in all; you are called, you are elect. "Make your calling and election sure," and go on your way rejoicing! May God bless you; and to Father, Son, and Holy Spirit, be glory for evermore! Amen.

SERMON XXIV

MERCY, OMNIPOTENCE, AND JUSTICE

"The Lord is slow to anger, and great in power, and will not at all acquit
the wicked."—NAHUM, i. 3

WORKS of art require some education in the beholder, before they can be thoroughly appreciated. We do not expect
that the uninstructed should at once perceive the varied ex-
cellencies of a painting from some master hand; we do not
imagine that the superlative glories of the harmonies of the
prince of song will enrapture the ears of clownish listeners.
There must be something in the man himself, before he can
understand the wonders either of nature or of art. Certainly
this is true of character. By reason of failures in our character
and faults in our life, we are not capable of understanding all
the separate beauties, and the united perfection of the character of Christ, or of God, his Father. Were we ourselves as
pure as the angels in heaven, were we what our race once was
in the garden of Eden, immaculate and perfect, it is quite certain that we should have a far better and nobler idea of the
character of God than we can by possibility attain unto in our
fallen state. But you can not fail to notice, that men, through
the alienation of their natures, are continually misrepresenting
God, because they can not appreciate his perfection. Does
God at one time withhold his hand from wrath? Lo, they
say that God hath ceased to judge the world, and looks upon
it with listless phlegmatic indifference. Does he at another
time punish the world for sin? They say he is severe and
cruel. Men *will* misunderstand him, because they are imperfect themselves, and are not capable of admiring the character
of God.

Now, this is especially true with regard to certain lights and shadows in the character of God, which he has so marvelously blended in the perfection of his nature : that although we can not see the exact point of meeting, yet (if we have been at all enlightened by the Spirit) we are struck with wonder at the sacred harmony.   In reading holy Scripture, you can say of Paul, that he was noted for his zeal—of Peter, that he will ever be memorable for his courage—of John, that he was noted for his lovingness.   But did you ever notice, when you read the history of our Master, Jesus Christ, that you never could say he was notable for any one virtue at all ?   Why was that ?   It was because the boldness of Peter did so outgrow itself as to throw other virtues into the shade, or else the other virtues were so deficient that they set forth his boldness.   The very fact of a man being noted for something is a sure sign that he is not so notable in other things ; and it is because of the complete perfection of Jesus Christ, that we are not accustomed to say of him that he was eminent for his zeal, or for his love, or for his courage.   We say of him that he was a perfect character ; but we are not able very easily to perceive where the shadows and the lights blended, where the meekness of Christ blended into his courage, and where his loveliness blended into his boldness in denouncing sin.   We are not able to detect the points where they meet ; and I believe the more thoroughly we are sanctified, the more it will be a subject of wonder to us how it could be that virtues which seemed so diverse were in so majestic a manner united in one character.

It is just the same of God ; and I have been led to make the remarks I have made on my text, because of the two clauses thereof which seem to describe contrary attributes.   You will notice that there are two things in my text : he is " slow to anger," and yet he " will not at all acquit the wicked."   Our character is so imperfect that we can not see the congruity of these two attributes.   We are wondering, perhaps, and saying, " How is it he is slow to anger, and yet will not acquit the wicked ?"   It is because his character is perfect that we do not see where these two things melt into each other—the infallible righteousness and severity of the ruler of the world, and his loving-kindness, his long-suffering, and his tender mercies. The absence of any one of these things from the character of God would have rendered it imperfect; the presence of them all, though we may not see how they can be congruous with each other, stamps the character of God with a perfection elsewhere unknown.

And now I shall endeavor this morning to set forth these two attributes of God, and the connecting link. "*The Lord is slow to anger;*" then comes the *connecting link*, "great in power." I shall have to show you how that "great in power" refers to the sentence foregoing and the sentence succeeding. And then we shall consider the next attribute—"He will not at all acquit the wicked:" *an attribute of justice.*

I. Let us begin with the first characteristic of God. He is said to be "SLOW TO ANGER." Let me declare the attribute and then trace it to its source.

God is "slow to anger." When Mercy cometh into the world, she driveth winged steeds; the axles of her chariot-wheels are glowing hot with speed; but when Wrath cometh, it walketh with tardy footsteps; it is not in haste to slay, it is not swift to condemn. God's rod of mercy is ever in his hands outstretched; God's sword of justice is in its scabbard: not rusted in it—it can be easily withdrawn—but held there by that hand that presses it back into its sheath, crying, "Sleep, O sword, sleep; for I will have mercy upon sinners, and will forgive their transgressions." God hath many orators in heaven; some of them speak with swift words. Gabriel, when he cometh down to tell glad tidings, speaketh swiftly; angelic hosts, when they descend from glory, fly with wings of lightning, when they proclaim, "Peace on earth, good will toward men;" but the dark angel of Wrath is a slow orator; with many a pause between, where melting Pity joins her languid notes, he speaks; and when but half his oration is completed he often stays, and withdraws himself from his rostrum, giving way to Pardon and to Mercy; he having but addressed the people that they might be driven to repentance, and so might receive peace from the scepter of God's love.

Brethren, I shall just try to show you now how God 's slow to anger.

First, I will prove that he is " slow to anger;" *because he*

never smites without first threatening. Men who are passionate and swift in anger give a word and a blow; sometimes the
blow first and the word afterward. Oftentimes kings, when
subjects have rebelled against them, have crushed them first,
and then reasoned with them afterward; they have given no
time of threatening, no period of repentance; they have allowed no space for turning to their allegiance; they have at
once crushed them in their hot displeasure, making a full
end of them. Not so God: he will not cut down the tree that
doth much cumber the ground, until he hath digged about it,
and dunged it; he will not at once slay the man whose character is the most vile; until he has first hewn him by the prophets he will not hew him by judgments; he will warn the
sinner ere he condemn him; he will send his prophets, " rising
up early and late," giving him " line upon line, and precept
upon precept, here a little and there a little." He will not
smite the city without warning; Sodom shall not perish, until
Lot hath been within her. The world shall not be drowned,
until eight prophets have been preaching in it, and Noah, the
eighth, cometh to prophesy of the coming of the Lord. He
will not smite Nineveh until he hath sent a Jonah. He will
not crush Babylon till his prophets have cried through its
streets. He will not slay a man until he hath given many
warnings, by sicknesses, by the pulpit, by providences, and by
consequences. He smites not with a heavy blow at once; he
threateneth first. He doth not in grace, as in nature, send
lightnings first and thunder afterward; but he sendeth the
thunder of his law first, and the lightning of execution follows
it. The lictor of divine justice carries his axe bound up in a
bundle of rods, for he will not cut off men, until he has reproved them, that they may repent. He is " slow to anger."

But again: God is also *very slow to threaten.* Although he
will threaten before he condemns, yet he is slow even in his
threatening. God's lips move swiftly when he promises, but
slowly when he threatens. Long rolls the pealing thunder,
slowly roll the drums of heaven, when they sound the death-
march of sinners; sweetly floweth the music of the rapid notes
which proclaim free grace, and love, and mercy. God is slow
to threaten. He will not send a Jonah to Nineveh, until

Nineveh has become foul with sin ; he will not even tell Sodom
it shall be burned with fire, until Sodom has become a reeking
dung-hill, obnoxious to earth as well as heaven ; he will not
drown the world with a deluge, or even threaten to do it, until
the sons of God themselves make unholy alliances and begin
to depart from him. He doth not even threaten the sinner by
his conscience, until the sinner hath oftentimes sinned. He
will often tell the sinner of his sins, often urge him to repent ;
but he will not make hell stare him hard in the face, with all
its dreadful terror, until much sin has stirred up the lion from
his lair, and made God hot with wrath against the iniquities
of man. He is slow even to threaten.

But, best of all, when God threatens, *how slow he is to sentence the criminal!* When he has told them that he will
punish unless they repent, how long a space he gives them, in
which to turn unto himself! "He doth not afflict willingly,
nor grieve the children of men for naught ;" he stayeth his
hand ; he will not be in hot haste, when he hath threatened
them, to execute the sentence upon them. Have you ever observed that scene in the garden of Eden at the time of the
fall? God had threatened Adam that if he sinned he should
surely die. Adam sinned : did God make haste to sentence
him? 'Tis sweetly said, "The Lord God walked in the garden in the cool of the day." Perhaps that fruit was plucked
at early morn, mayhap it was plucked at noontide ; but God
was in no haste to condemn ; he waited till the sun was well
nigh set, and in the cool of the day came, and as an old ex-
positor has put it very beautifully, when he did come he did
not come on wings of wrath, but he "*walked* in the garden in
the cool of the day." He was in no haste to slay. I think I
see him, as he was represented then to Adam, in those glorious
days when God walked with man. Methinks I see the wonderful similitude in which the Unseen did vail himself : I see it
walking among the trees so slowly—ay, if it were right to give
such a picture—beating its breast, and shedding tears that it
should have to condemn man. At last I hear its doleful voice :
"Adam, where art thou ? Where hast thou cast thyself, poor
Adam ? Thou hast cast thyself from my favor ; thou hast cast
thyself into nakedness and into fear ; for thou art hiding thy

self. Adam, where art thou?   I pity thee.   Thou thoughtest
to be God.   Before I condemn thee I will give thee one note
of pity.   Adam, where art thou?"   Yes, the Lord was slow
to anger, slow to write the sentence, even though the command had been broken, and the threatening was therefore of
necessity brought into force.   It was so with the flood: he
threatened the earth, but he would not fully seal the sentence,
and stamp it with the seal of heaven, until he had given space
for repentance.   Noah must come, and through his hundred
and twenty years must preach the word; he must come and
testify to an unthinking and an ungodly generation; the ark
must be builded, to be a perpetual sermon; there it must be
upon its mountain-top, waiting for the floods to float it, that it
might be an every-day warning to the ungodly.   O heavens,
why did ye not at once open your floods?   Ye fountains of
the great deep, why did ye not burst up in a moment?   God
said, "I will sweep away the world with a flood:" why, why
did ye not rise?   " Because," I hear them saying with gurgling
notes, "because, although God had threatened, he was slow to
sentence, and he said in himself, ' Haply they may repent;
peradventure they may turn from their sin;' and therefore did
he bid us rest and be quiet, for he is slow to anger."

And yet once more: even when the sentence against a sin
ner is signed and sealed by heaven's broad seal of condemnation, even then *God is slow to carry it out.*   The doom of
Sodom is sealed; God hath declared it shall be burned with
fire.   But God is tardy.   He stops.   He will himself go down
to Sodom, that he may see the iniquity of it.   And when he
gets there guilt is rife in the streets.   'Tis night, and the crew
of worse than beasts besiege the door.   Does he then lift his
hands?   Does he then say, " Rain hell out of heaven, ye skies?"
No, he lets them pursue their riot all night, spares them to the
last moment, and though when the sun was risen the burning
hail began to fall, yet was the reprieve as long as possible.
God was not in haste to condemn.   God had threatened to
root out the Canaanites; he declared that all the children of
Ammon should be cut off; he had promised Abraham that he
would give their land unto his seed for ever, and they were to
be utterly slain ; but he made the children of Israel wait four

hundred years in Egypt, and he let these Canaanites live all through the days of the patriarchs; and even then, when he led his avenging ones out of Egypt, he stayed them forty years in the wilderness, because he was loth to slay poor Canaan. "Yet," said he, "I will give them space. Though I have stamped their condemnation, though their death warrant has come forth from the court of King's Bench, and must be executed, yet will I reprieve them as long as I can:" and he stops, until at last mercy had had enough, and Jericho's melting ashes and the destruction of Ai betokened that the sword was out of its scabbard, and God had awaked like a mighty man, and like a strong man full of wrath. God is slow to execute the sentence, even when he has declared it.

And ah! my friends, there is a sorrowful thought that has just crossed my mind. There are some men yet alive who are sentenced now. I believe that Scripture bears me out in a dreadful thought which I just wish to hint at. There are some men that are condemned before they are finally damned; there are some men whose sins go before them unto judgment, who are given over to a seared conscience, concerning whom it may be said that repentance and salvation are impossible. There are some few men in the world who are like John Bunyan's man in the iron cage, can never get out. They are like Esau—they find no place of repentance, though, unlike him, they do not seek it, for if they sought it they would find it. Many there are who have sinned "the sin unto death," concerning whom we can not pray; for we are told, "I do not say that ye shall pray for it." But why, why, why are they not already in the flame? If they be condemned, if mercy has shut its eye forever upon them, if it never will stretch out its hand, to give them pardon, why, why, why are they not cut down and swept away? Because God saith, "I will not have mercy upon them, but I will let them live a little while longer; though I have condemned them I am loth to carry the sentence out, and will spare them as long as it is right that man should live; I will let them have a long life here, for they will have a fearful eternity of wrath for ever." Yes, let them have their little whirl of pleasure; their end shall be most fearful. Let them beware, for although God is slow to anger he is sure in it.

If God were not slow to anger, would he not have smitten this huge city of ours, this behemoth city?—would he not have smitten it into a thousand pieces, and blotted out the remembrance of it from the earth? The iniquities of this city are so great, that if God should dig up her very foundations, and cast her into the sea, she well deserveth it. Our streets at night present spectacles of vice that can not be equaled. Surely there can be no nation and no country that can show a city so utterly debauched as this great city of London, if our midnight streets are indications of our immorality. You allow in your public places of resort—I mean you—my lords and ladies—you allow things to be said in your hearing, of which your modesty ought to be ashamed. Ye can sit in theaters to hear plays at which modesty should blush; I say naught of piety. That the ruder sex should have listened to the obscenities of *La Traviata* is surely bad enough, but that ladies of the highest refinement, and the most approved taste, should dishonor themselves by such a patronage of vice is indeed intolerable. Let the sins of the lower theaters escape without your censure, ye gentlemen of England, the lowest bestiality of the nethermost hell of a play-house can look to your opera-houses for their excuse. I thought that with the pretensions this city makes to piety, for sure, they would not have so far gone, and that after such a warning as they have had from the press itself—a press which is certainly not too religious—they would not so indulge their evil passions. But because the pill is gilded, ye suck down the poison; because the thing is popular, ye patronize it: it is lustful, it is abominable, it is deceitful! Ye take your children to hear what yourselves never ought to listen to. Ye yourselves will sit in gay and grand company, to listen to things from which your modesty ought to revolt. And I would fain hope it does, although the tide may for a while deceive you. Ah! God only knoweth the secret wickedness of this great city; it demandeth a loud and a trumpet voice; it needs a prophet to cry aloud, "Sound an alarm, sound an alarm, sound an alarm," in this city; for verily the enemy groweth upon us, the power of the evil one is mighty, and we are fast going to perdition, unless God shall put forth his hand and roll back the black torrent of iniquity that

streameth down our streets.   But God is slow to anger, and
doth still stay his sword.   Wrath said yesterday, "Unsheath
thyself, O sword;" and the sword struggled to get free.   Mercy
put her hand upon the hilt, and said, "Be still!"   "Unsheath
thyself, O sword!"   Again it struggled from its scabbard
Mercy put her hand on it, and said, "Back!"—and it rattled back again.   Wrath stamped his foot, and said, "Awake,
O sword, awake!"   It struggled yet again, till half its blade
was outdrawn;   "Back, back!" said Mercy, and with manly
push she sent it back rattling into its sheath; and there it
sleeps still, for the Lord is "slow to anger, and plenteous
mercy."

Now I am *to trace this attribute of God to its source:* why
is he slow to anger?

He is slow to anger because *he is infinitely good.*   Good is
his name; "good"-God.   Good is his nature; because he is
slow to anger.

He is slow to anger, again, *because he is great.*   Little
things are always swift in anger; great things are not so.
The surly cur barks at every passer-by, and bears no insult;
the lion would bear a thousand times as much; and the bull
sleeps in his pasture, and will bear much, before he lifteth up
his might.   The leviathan in the sea, though he makes the
deep to be hoary when he is enraged, yet is slow to be stirred
up, while the little and puny are always swift in anger.   God's
greatness is one reason of the slowness of his wrath.

II. But to proceed at once to the link.   A great reason why
he is slow to anger, is because he is GREAT IN POWER.   This is
to be the connecting link between this part of the subject and
the last, and therefore I must beg your attention.   I say that
this word *great in power* connects the first sentence to the
last; and it does so in this way.   The Lord is slow to anger;
and he is slow to anger because he is great in power.   "How
say you so?" says one.   I answer, he that is great in power
has power over himself; and he that can keep his own temper
down, and subdue himself, is greater than he who rules a city,
or can conquer nations.   We heard but yesterday, or the day
before, mighty displays of God's power in the rolling thunder which alarmed us   and when we saw the splendor of his

might in the glistening lightning, when he lifted up the gates of heaven and we saw the brightness thereof, and then he closed them again upon the dusty earth in a moment—even then we did not see any thing but the hidings of his power, compared with the power which he has over himself. When God's power doth restrain himself, then it is power indeed, the power to curb power, the power that binds omnipotence is omnipotence surpassed. God is great in power, and therefore doth he keep in his anger. A man who has a strong mind can bear to be insulted, can bear offenses, because he is strong. The weak mind snaps and snarls at the little; the strong mind bears it like a rock; it moveth not, though a thousand breakers dash upon it, and cast their pitiful malice in the spray upon its summit. God marketh his enemies, and yet he moveth not; he standeth still, and letteth them curse him, yet is he not wrathful. If he were less of a God than he is, if he were less mighty than we know him to be, he would long ere this have sent forth the whole of his thunder, and emptied the magazines of heaven; he would long ere this have blasted the earth with the wondrous mines he hath prepared in its lower surface; the flame that burneth there would have consumed us, and we should have been utterly destroyed. We bless God that the greatness of his power is just our protection; he is slow to anger because he is great in power.

And, now, there is no difficulty in showing how this link unites itself with the next part of the text. "He is great in power, and will not at all acquit the wicked." This needs no demonstration in words; I have but to touch the feelings, and you will see it. The greatness of his power is an assurance, and an assurance that he will not acquit the wicked. Who among you could witness the storm on Friday night without having thoughts concerning your own sinfulness stirred in your bosoms? Men do not think of God the punisher, or Jehovah the avenger, when the sun is shining, and the weather calm; but in times of tempest, whose cheek is not blanched? The Christian oftentimes rejoiceth in it; he can say, "My soul is well at ease, amid this revelry of earth; I do rejoice in it; it is a day of feasting in my Father's hall, a day of high-feast and carnival in heaven, and I am glad.

" The God that reigns on high,
  And thunders when he please,
That rides upon the stormy sky,
  And manages the seas,

This awful God is ours,
  Our Father and our love,
He shall send down his heavenly powers
  To carry us above."

But the man who is not of an easy conscience will be ill at ease when the timbers of the house are creaking, and the foundations of the solid earth seem to groan. Ah! who is he then that doth not tremble? Yon lofty tree is riven in half; that lightning flash has smitten its trunk, and there it lies for ever blasted, a monument of what God can do. Who stood there and saw it? Was he a swearer? Did he swear then? Was he a Sabbath-breaker? Did he love his Sabbath-breaking then? Was he haughty? Did he then despise God? Ah! how he shook then! Saw you not his hair stand on end? Did not his cheek blanch in an instant? Did he not close his eyes and start back in horror when he saw that dreadful spectacle, and thought God would smite him too? Yes, the power of God, when seen in the tempest, on sea or on land, in the earthquake or in the hurricane, is instinctively a proof that he will not acquit the wicked. I know not how to explain the feeling, but it is nevertheless the truth; majestic displays of omnipotence have an effect upon the mind of convincing even the hardened, that God, who is so powerful, " will not at all acquit the wicked." Thus have I just tried to explain and make bare the link of the chain.

III. The last attribute, and the most terrible one, is, " HE WILL NOT AT ALL ACQUIT THE WICKED." Let me unfold this. first of all; and then let me, after that, endeavor to trace it also to its source, as I did the first attribute.

God " will not acquit the wicked." How prove I this? I prove it thus. Never once has he pardoned an unpunished sin; not in all the years of the Most High, not in all the days of his right hand, has he once blotted out sin without punishment. What! say you, were not those in heaven pardoned? Are there not many transgressors pardoned, and do they not escape without punishment? Has he not said, "I have blotted out thy transgressions like a cloud, and like a thick cloud thine iniquities?" Yes, true, most true, and yet my assertion is true also—not one of all those sins that have been pardoned were pardoned without punishment. Do you ask me why and how such a thing as that can be the truth? I point you to yon dreadful sight on Calvary; the punishment which fell not on the forgiven sinner fell there. The cloud of justice was charged with fiery hail; the sinner deserved it; it fell on him; but, for all that, it fell, and spent its fury; it fell there, in that great reservoir of misery; it fell into the Saviour's heart. The plagues, which need should light on our ingratitude, did not fall on us, but they fell somewhere; and who was it that was plagued? Tell me, Gethsemane; tell me, O Calvary's summit, who was plagued. The doleful answer comes, "*Eli, Eli, lama sabachthani?*" "My God, my God, why hast thou forsaken me?" It is Jesus suffering all the plagues of sin. Sin is still punished, though the sinner is delivered.

But, you say, this has scarcely proved that he will not acquit the wicked. I hold it has proved it, and proved it clearly. But do ye want any further proof that God will not acquit the wicked? Need I lead you through a long list of terrible wonders that God has wrought—the wonders of his vengeance? Shall I show you blighted Eden? Shall I let you see a world all drowned—sea monsters whelping and stabling in the palaces of kings? Shall I let you hear the last shriek of the last drowning man as he falls into the flood and dies, washed by that huge wave from the hill-top? Shall I let you see death riding upon the summit of a crested billow, upon a sea that knows no shore, and triumphing because his work is done; his quiver empty, for all men are slain, save where life floats in the midst of death in yonder ark? Need I let you see Sodom with its terrified inhabitants, when the volcano of almighty wrath spouted fiery hail upon it? Shall I show you the earth opening its mouth to swallow up Korah, Dathan, and Abiram? Need I take you to the plagues of Egypt? Shall I again repeat the death-shriek of Pharaoh, and the drowning of his host? Surely, ye need not to be told of cities that are in ruins, ⲟr of nations that have been cut off in a day; ye need not to be told how God has smitten the earth from one side to the other, when he has been wroth, and how he has melted mountains in his hot displeasure. Nay, we have proofs enough in history, proofs enough in Scripture, that "he will not at all acquit the wicked." If ye wanted the best proof, however, ye should borrow the black wings of a miserable imagination, and fly beyond the world, through the dark realm of chaos, on, far on, where those battlements of fire are gleaming with a horrid light—if through them, with a spirit's safety, ye would fly, and would behold the worm that never dies, the pit that knows no bottom, and could you there see the fire unquenchable, and listen to the shrieks and wails of men that are banished for ever from God—if, sirs, it were possible for you to hear the sullen groans and hollow moans, and shrieks of tortured ghosts, then would ye come back to this world, amazed and petrified with horror, and you would say, "Indeed he will not acquit the wicked." You know, hell is the argument of the text; may you never have to prove the text by feeling in yourselves the argument fully carried out, "He will not at all acquit the wicked."

And now we *trace this terrible attribute to its source*. Why is this?

We reply, God will not acquit the wicked, *because he is good*. What! doth goodness demand that sinners shall be punished? It doth. The Judge must condemn the murderer, because he loves his nation. "I can not let you go free; I can not, and I must not; you would slay others, who belong to this fair commonwealth, if I were to let you go free; no, I must condemn you from the very loveliness of my nature." The kindness of a king demands the punishment of those who are guilty. It is not wrathful in the legislature to make severe laws against great sinners; it is but love toward the rest that sin should be restrained. Yon great flood-gates, which keep back the torrent of sin, are painted black, and look right horrible; like horrid dungeon gates, they affright my spirit; but are they proofs that God is not good? No, sirs; if ye could open wide those gates, and let the deluge of sin flow on us, then would you cry "O God, O God! shut-to the gates of

punishment again, let law again be established, set up the pillars, and swing the gates upon their hinges; shut again the
gates of punishment, that this world may not again be utterly
destroyed by men who have become worse than brutes." It
needs for very goodness' sake that sin should be punished.
Mercy, with her weeping eyes (for she hath wept for sinners),
when she finds they will not repent, looks more terribly stern
in her loveliness than Justice in all his majesty; she drops the
white flag from her hand, and saith—" No; I called, and they
refused; I stretched out my hand, and no man regarded; let
them die, let them die;" and that terrible word from the lip
of Mercy's self is harsher thunder than the very damnation
of Justice. O, yes, the goodness of God demands that men
should perish, if they will sin.

And again, *the justice of God demands it.* God is infinitely just, and his justice demands that men should be punished, unless they turn to him with full purpose of heart.
Need I pass through all the attributes of God to prove it?
Methinks I need not. We must all of us believe that the God
who is slow to anger and great in power is also sure not to
acquit the wicked. And now just a home-thrust or two with
you. What is your state this morning? My friend, man or
woman, what is thy state? Canst thou look up to heaven and
say, "Though I have sinned greatly I believe Christ was
punished in my stead,

> " My faith looks back to see
>   The burden he did bear
> When hanging on the cursed tree,
>   And knows her guilt was there?"

Can you by humble faith look to Jesus, and say, " My substitute, my refuge, my shield; thou art my rock, my trust; in
thee do I confide?" Then, beloved, to you I have nothing to
say, except this, Never be afraid when you see God's power;
for now that you are forgiven and accepted, now that by faith
you have fled to Christ for refuge, the power of God need no
more terrify you, than the shield and sword of the warrior
need terrify his wife or his child. " Nay," saith the woman,
" is he strong? He is strong for me. Is his arm brawney,

and are all his sinews fast and strong? Then are they fast and strong for me. While he lives, and wears a shield, he will stretch it over my head; and while his good sword can cleave foes, it will cleave my foes too, and ransom me." Be of good cheer; fear not his power.

But hast thou never fled to Christ for refuge? Dost thou not believe in the Redeemer? Hast thou never confided thy soul to his hands? Then, my friends, hear me; in God's name, hear me just a moment. My friend, I would not stand in thy position for an hour, for all the stars twice spelt in gold! For what is thy position? Thou hast sinned, and God will not acquit thee; he will punish thee. He is letting thee live; thou art reprieved. Poor is the life of one that is reprieved without a pardon! Thy reprieve will soon run out; thine hour-glass is emptying every day. I see on some of you death has put his cold hand, and frozen your hair to whiteness. Ye need your staff: it is the only barrier between you and the grave now; and you are, all of you, old and young, standing on a narrow neck of land, between two boundless seas—that neck of land, that isthmus of life, narrowing every moment, and you, and you, and you, are yet unpardoned. There is a city to be sacked, and you are in it—soldiers are at the gates; the command is given that every man in the city is to be slaughtered save he who can give the password. "Sleep on, sleep on; the attack is not to-day; sleep on, sleep on." "But it is to-morrow, sir." "Ay, sleep on, sleep on; it is not till to-morrow; sleep on, procrastinate, procrastinate." "Hark! I hear a rumbling at the gates; the battering-ram is at them; the gates are tottering." "Sleep on, sleep on; the soldiers are not yet at your doors; sleep on, sleep on; ask for no mercy yet; sleep on, sleep on!" "Ay, but I hear the shrill clarion sound; they are in the streets. Hark, to the shrieks of men and women! They are slaughtering them; they fall, they fall, they fall!" "Sleep on; they are not yet at *your* door." "But hark, they are at the gate; with heavy tramp I hear the soldiers marching up the stairs!" "Nay, sleep on, sleep on; they are not yet in your room." "Why, they are there; they have burst open the door that parted you from them, and there they stand!" "No, sleep on, sleep on; the sword is not yet at your throat; sleep on, sleep on!" It *is* at your throat, you start with horror. Sleep on, sleep on! But you are gone! "Demon, why toldest thou me to slumber? It would have been wise in me to have escaped the city when first the gates were shaken. Why did I not ask for the pass-word before the troops came? Why, by all that is wise, why did I not rush into the streets, and cry the password when the soldiers were there? Why stood I till the knife was at my throat? Ay, demon that thou art, be cursed; but I am cursed with thee for ever!" You know the application; it is a para-ble ye can all expound; ye need not that I should tell you that death is after you, that justice must devour you, that Christ crucified is the only password that can save you; and yet you have not learned it—that with some of you death is nearing, nearing, nearing, and that with all of you he is close at hand! I need not expound how Satan is the demon, how in hell you shall curse him and curse yourselves because you procrastinated—how, that seeing God was slow to anger you were slow to repentance—how, because he was great in power, and kept back his anger, therefore you kept back your steps from seeking him; and here you are what you are!

Spirit of God, bless these words to some souls that they may be saved! May some sinners be brought to the Saviour's feet, and cry for mercy! We ask it for Jesus' sake. **Amen.**

SERMON XXV

CHRIST—THE POWER AND WISDOM OF GOD

"Christ the power of God, and the wisdom of God."—1 Cor., i. 24

UNBELIEF toward the gospel of Christ is the most unreasonable thing in all the world, because the reason which the unbeliever gives for his unbelief is fairly met by the character and constitution of the gospel of Christ. Notice that before this verse we read—"The Jews required a sign, the Greeks seek after wisdom." If you met the Jew who believed not on Christ in the apostle's day, he said, "I can not believe, because I want a sign;" and if you met the Greek, he said, "I can not believe, because I want a philosophic system, one that is full of wisdom." "Now," says the apostle, "both these objections are untenable and unreasonable. If you suppose that the Jew requires a sign, that sign is given him : Christ is the power of God. The miracles that Christ wrought upon earth were signs more than sufficiently abundant; and if the Jewish people had but the will to believe, they would have found abundant signs and reasons for believing in the personal acts of Christ and his apostles." And let the Greeks say, "I can not believe, because I require a wise system : O Greek, Christ is the wisdom of God. If thou wouldst but investigate the subject, thou wouldst find in it profoundness of wisdom—a depth where the most gigantic intellect might be drowned. It is no shallow gospel, but a deep, and a great deep too, a deep which passeth understanding. Thine objection is ill-founded ; for Christ is the wisdom of God, and his gospel is the highest of all sciences. If thou wishest to find wisdom, thou must find it in the word of revelation."

Now, this morning, we shall try to bring out these two

thoughts of the gospel; and it may be that God shall bless what we shall say to the removing of the objection of either Jew or Greek; that the one requiring a sign may see it in the *power* of God in Christ, and that he who requireth wisdom may behold it in the *wisdom* of God in Christ. We shall understand our text in a threefold manner: Christ, that is, *Christ personally*, is " the power of God and the wisdom of God;" Christ, that is, *Christ's gospel*, is " the power of God and the wisdom of God;" Christ, that is, *Christ in the heart, true religion*, is " the power of God and the wisdom of God."

I. First, to begin, then, with CHRIST PERSONALLY. Christ considered as God and man, the Son of God equal with his Father, and yet the man, born of the Virgin Mary. Christ, in his complex person, is " the power of God and the wisdom of God." *He is the power of God from all eternity.* " By his word were the heavens made, and all the host of them." "The Word was God, and the Word was with God." " All things were made by him, and without him was not any thing made that was made." The pillars of the earth were placed in their everlasting sockets by the omnipotent right hand of Christ; the curtains of the heavens were drawn upon their rings of starry light by him who was from everlasting the All-glorious Son of God. The orbs that float aloft in ether, those ponderous planets, and those mighty stars, were placed in their positions, or sent rolling through space by the eternal strength of nim who is " the first and the last." " the Prince of the kings of the earth." Christ is the power of God, for he is the Creator of all things, and by him all things exist.

But *when he came to earth*, took upon himself the fashion of a man, tabernacled in the inn, and slept in the manger, he still gave proof that he was the Son of God; not so much so when, as an infant of a span long, the immortal was the mortal, and the infinite became a babe; not so much so in his youth, but afterward when he began his public ministry, he gave abundant proofs of his power and Godhead. The winds hushed by his finger uplifted, the waves calmed by his voice, so that they became solid as marble beneath his tread; the tempest, cowering at his feet, as before a conqueror whom it knew and obeyed; these things, these stormy elements, the wind, the tempest, and the water, gave full proof of his abundant power. The lame man leaping, the deaf man hearing, the dumb man singing, the dead rising, these, again, were proofs that he was the " power of God." When the voice of Jesus startled the shades of Hades, and rent the bonds of death, with " Lazarus, come forth !" and when the carcass rotten in the tomb woke up to life, there was proof of his divine power and Godhead. A thousand other proofs he afforded ; but we need not stay to mention them to you who have Bibles in your houses, and who can read them every day. At last he yielded up his life, and was buried in the tomb. Not long, however, did he sleep; for he gave another proof of his divine power and Godhead, when starting from his slumber, he affrighted the guards with the majesty of his grandeur, not being holden by the bonds of death, they being like green withes before our conquering Samson, who had meanwhile pulled up the gates of hell, and carried them on his shoulders far away.

That he is the *power* of God *now*, Scripture very positively affirmeth ; for it is written, " he sitteth at the right hand of God." He hath the reins of Providence gathered in his hands; the fleet coursers of Time are driven by him who sits in the chariot of the world, and bids its wheels run round ; and he shall bid them stay when it shall please him. He is the great umpire of all disputes, the great Sovereign Head of the church, the Lord of heaven, and death, and hell ; and by-and-by we shall know that he shall come,

> " On fiery clouds and wings of wind,
>   Appointed Judge of all mankind ;"

and then the quickened dead, the startled myriads, the divided firmaments, the " Depart, ye cursed," and the " Come, ye blessed," shall proclaim him to be the power of God, who hath power over all flesh, to save or to condemn, as it pleaseth him.

But he is equally " the *wisdom* of God." The great things that he did *before all worlds* were proofs of his wisdom. He planned the way of salvation ; he devised the system of atonement and substitution ; he laid the foundations of the great plan of salvation. There was wisdom. But he built the heavens by wisdom, and he laid the pillars of light, whereon the firmament is balanced, by his skill and wisdom. Mark the world ; and learn, as ye see all its multitudinous proofs of the wisdom of God, and there you have the wisdom of Christ; for he was the creator o. it. And *when he became a man*, he gave proofs enough of wisdom. Even in childhood, when he made the doctors sit abashed by the questions that he asked, he showed that he was more than mortal. And when the Phari-see and Sadducee and Herodian were all at last defeated, and their nets were broken, he proved again the superlative wis-dom of the Son of God. And when those who came to take him, stood enchained by his eloquence, spell-bound by his mar-velous oratory, there was again a proof that he was the wis-dom of God, who could so enchain the minds of men. And now that he intercedeth before the throne of God, now that he is our Advocate before the throne, the pledge and surety for the blessed, now that the reins of government are in his hands, and are ever wisely directed, we have abundant proofs that the wisdom of God is in Christ, as well as the power of God. Bow before him, ye that love him ; bow before him, ye that desire him ! Crown him, crown him, crown him ! He is worthy of it, unto him is everlasting might; unto him is unswerving wisdom : bless his name; exalt him ; clap your wings, ye seraphs ; cry aloud, ye cherubim ; shout, shout, shout, to his praise, ye ransomed host above. And ye, O men that know his grace, extol him in your songs for ever ; for he is Christ, the power of God and the wisdom of God.

II. But now Christ, that is, CHRIST'S GOSPEL, is the power and the wisdom of God.

1. Christ's gospel is *a thing of divine power*. Do you want proofs of it ? Ye shall not go far. How could Christ's gos-pel have been established in this world as it was, if it had not in itself intrinsic might ? By whom was it spread ? By mi-tered prelates, by learned doctors, by fierce warriors, by ca-liphs, by prophets ? No ; by fishermen, untaught, unlettered ; save as the Spirit gave them utterance, not knowing how to preach or speak. How did they spread it ? By the bayonet, by their swords, by the keen metal of their blades ? Did they drive their gospel into men at the point of the lance, and with the cimeter ? Say, did myriads rush to battle, as they did

when they followed the crescent of Mohammed, and did they convert men by force, by law, by might? Ah! no. Nothing but their simple words, their unvarnished eloquence, their rough declamation, their unhewn oratory; these it was, which, by the blessing of God's Spirit, carried the gospel round the world within a century after the death of its founder.

But what was this gospel which achieved so much? Was it a thing palatable to human nature? Did it offer a paradise of present happiness? Did it offer delight to the flesh and to the senses? Did it give charming prospects of wealth? Did it give licentious ideas to men? No; it was a gospel of morality most strict, it was a gospel with delights entirely spiritual—a gospel which abjured the flesh, which, unlike the coarse delusion of Joe Smith, cut off every prospect from men of delighting themselves with the joys of lust. It was a gospel holy, spotless, clean as the breath of heaven; it was pure as the wing of angel; not like that which spread of old, in the days of Mohammed, a gospel of lust, of vice, and wickedness, but pure, and consequently not palatable to human nature. And yet it spread. Why? My friends, I think the only answer I can give you is, because it has in it the power of God.

But do you want another proof? How has it been maintained since then? No easy path has the gospel had. The good bark of the church has had to plow her way through seas of blood, and those who have manned her have been bespattered with the bloody spray; yea, they have had to man her and keep her in motion, by laying down their lives unto the death. Mark the bitter persecution of the church of Christ from the time of Nero to the days of Mary, and further on, through the days of Charles the Second, and of those kings of unhappy memory, who had not as yet learned how to spell "toleration." From the dragoons of Claverhouse, right straight away to the gladiatorial shows of Rome, what a long series of persecutions has the gospel had! But, as the old divines used to say, "The blood of the martyrs" has been "the seed of the church." It has been, as the old herbalists had it, like the herb camomile, the more it is trodden on, the more it grows; and the more the church has been ill-treated, the more it has prospered. Behold the mountains where the

Albigenses walk in their white garments; see the stakes of mithfield, not yet forgotten; behold ye the fields among the towering hills, where brave hands kept themselves free from despotic tyranny.   Mark ye the Pilgrim Fathers, driven by a government of persecution across the briny deep.   See what vitality the gospel has.   Plunge her under the wave, and she rises, the purer for her washing; thrust her in the fire, and she comes out, the more bright for her burning; cut her in sunder, and each piece shall make another church; behead her, and like the hydra of old, she shall have a hundred heads for every one you cut away.   She can not die, she must live; for she has the power of God within her.

Do you want another proof?   I give you a better one than the last.   I do not wonder that the church has outlived persecution so much as I wonder she has outlived the unfaithfulness of her professed teachers.   Never was church so abused as the church of Christ has been, all through her history; from the days of Diotrephes, who sought to have the pre-eminence, even to these later times, we can read of proud, arrogant prelates, and supercilious, haughty lords over God's inheritance.   Bonners, Dunstans, and men of all sorts, have come into her ranks, and done all they could to kill her; and with their lordly priestcraft they have tried to turn her aside And what shall we say to that huge apostacy of Rome?   A thousand miracles that ever the church outlived that!   When her pretended head became apostate, and all her bishops disciples of hell, and she had gone far away, wonder of wonders, that she should come out, in the days of the glorious Reformation, and should still live.   And, even now, when I mark the supineness of many of my brethren in the ministry—when I mark their utter and entire inefficiency of doing aught for God—when I see their waste of time, preaching now and then on the Sunday, instead of going to the highways and hedges and preaching the gospel everywhere to the poor—when I see the want of unction in the church itself, the want of prayerfulness—when I see wars and fightings, factions and disunions—when I see hot blood and pride, even in the meetings of the saints; I say it is a thousand thousand miracles that the church of God should be alive at all, after the unfaithfulness of her members, her ministers, and her bishops. She has the power of God within her, or else she would have been destroyed; for she has got enough within her own loins to work her destruction.

"But," says one, "you have not yet proved it is the power of God to my understanding." Sir, I will give you another proof. There are not a few of you, who are now present, who would be ready, I know, if it were necessary, to rise in your seats and bear me witness that I speak the truth. There are some who, not many months ago, were drunkards; some who were loose livers; men who were unfaithful to every vow which should keep man to truth, and right, and chastity, and honesty, and integrity. Yes, I repeat, I have some here who look back to a life of detestable sin. You tell me, some of you, that for thirty years even (there is one such present now) you never listened to a gospel ministry, nor ever entered the house of God at all; you despised the Sabbath, you spent it in all kinds of evil pleasures, you plunged headlong into sin and vice, and your only wonder is, that God has not cut you off long ago, as cumberers of the ground; and now you are here, as different as light from darkness. I know your characters, and have watched you with a father's love; for, child though I am, I am the spiritual father of some here whose years outcount mine by four times the number; and I have seen you honest who were thieves, and you sober who were drunkards. I have seen the wife's glad eye sparkling with happiness; and many a woman has grasped me by the hand, shed her tears upon me, and said, "I bless God; I am a happy woman now; my husband is reclaimed, my house is blessed; our children are brought up in the fear of the Lord." Not one or two, but scores of such are here. And, my friends, if these be not proofs that the gospel is the power of God, I say there is no proof of any thing to be had in the world, and every thing must be conjecture. Yes, and there worships with you this day (and if there be a secularist here, my friend will pardon me for alluding to him for a moment), there is in the house of God this day one who was a leader in your ranks, one who despised God, and ran very far away from right. And here he is! It is his honor this day to own himself a

Christian; and I hope, when this sermon is ended, to grasp him by the hand, for he has done a valiant deed; he has bravely burned his papers in the sight of all the people, and has turned to God with full purpose of heart. I could give you proofs enough, if proofs were wanted, that the gospel has been to men the power of God and the wisdom of God. More proofs I could give, yea, thousands, one upon the other.

But we must notice the other points. Christ's gospel is the *wisdom* of God. Look at the gospel itself and you will see it to be wisdom. The man who scoffs and sneers at the gospel, does so for no other reason but because he does not understand it. We have two of the richest books of theology extant that were written by professed infidels—by men that were so, I mean, before they wrote the books. You may have heard the story of Lord Lyttleton and West. I believe they determined to refute Christianity; one of them took up the subject of Paul's conversion, and the other, the subject of the resurrection; they sat down, both of them, to write books to ridicule those two events, and the effect was, that in studying the subject, they, both of them, became Christians, and wrote books which are now bulwarks to the church they hoped to have overthrown. Every man who looks the gospel fairly in the face, and gives it the study it ought to have, will discover that it is no false gospel, but a gospel that is replete with wisdom, and full of the knowledge of Christ. If any man will cavil at the Bible, he must cavil. There are some men who can find no wisdom anywhere, except in their own heads. Such men, however, are no judges of wisdom. We should not set a mouse to explain the phenomena of astronomy, nor should we set a man who is so foolish as to do nothing but cavil to understand the wisdom of the gospel. It needs that a man should at least be honest, and have some share of sense, or we can not dispute with him at all. Christ's gospel, to any man who believes it, is the wisdom of God.

Allow me just to hint that to be a believer in the gospel is no dishonor to a man's intellect. While the gospel can be understood by the poorest and the most illiterate, while there are shallows in it where a lamb may wade, there are depths where leviathan may swim. The intellect of Locke found am-

ple space in the gospel ; the mind of Newton submitted to re
ceive the truth of inspiration as a little child, and found a
something in its majestic being higher than itself, unto which
it could not attain.   The rudest and most untaught have been
enabled, by the study of the holy Scripture of God's truth to
enter the kingdom; and the most erudite have said of the
gospel, it surpasses thought.   I was thinking the other day
what a vast amount of literature must be lost if the gospel
be not true.   No book was ever so suggestive as the Bible.
Large tomes we have in our libraries which it takes all our
strength to lift, all upon holy Scripture; myriads upon myriads of smaller volumes, tens of thousands of every shape and
size, all written upon the Bible; and I have thought that the
very suggestiveness of Scripture, the supernatural suggestiveness of holy Writ, may be in itself a proof of its divine wisdom, since no man has ever been able to write a book which
could have so many commentators and so many writers upon
its text as the Bible has received, by so much as one millionth
part.

III.   Christ in a man, the gospel in the soul, is the power of God and the wisdom of God.   We will picture the Christian from his beginning to his end.   We will give a short map
of his history.   He begins there, in that prison-house, with
huge iron bars, which he can not file ; in that dark, damp cell,
where pestilence and death are bred.   There, in poverty and
nakedness, without a pitcher to put to his thirsty lips, without
a mouthful even of dry crust to satisfy his hunger, that is
where he begins—in the prison chamber of conviction, powerless, lost and ruined.   Between the bars I thrust my hand to
him, and give to him in God's name the name of Christ to
plead.   Look at him ; he has been filing away at these bars
many and many a day, without their yielding an inch; but
now he has got the name of Christ upon his lips ; he puts his
hands upon the bars, and one of them is gone, and another, and
another; and he makes a happy escape, crying, "I am free, I
am free, I am free! Christ has been the power of God to me,
in bringing me out of my trouble."   No sooner is he free, however, than a thousand doubts meet him.   This one cries, "You
are not elect;" another cries, "You are not redeemed;"

another says, "You are not called;" another says, "You are
not converted." "Avaunt," says he, "avaunt! Christ died;"
and he just pleads the name of Christ as the power of God,
and the doubts flee apace, and he walks straight on. He comes
soon into the furnace of trouble; he is thrust into the innermost prison, and his feet are made fast in the stocks. God has
put his hand upon him. He is in deep trouble; at midnight
he begins to sing of Christ; and lo! the walls begin to totter,
and the foundation of the prison to shake; and the man's chains
are taken off, and he comes out free; for Christ hath delivered
him from trouble. Here is a hill to climb, on the road to
heaven. Wearily he pants up the side of that hill, and thinks
he must die ere he can reach the summit. The name of Jesus
is whispered in his ear; he leaps to his feet, and pursues his
way, with fresh courage, until the summit is gained, when he
cries, "Jesus Christ is the strength of my song; he also hath
become my salvation." See him again. He is on a sudden beset by many enemies; how shall he resist them? With this
true sword, this true Jerusalem blade, Christ, and him crucified. With this he keeps the devil at arm's length; with this
he fights against temptation, and against lust, against spiritual
wickedness in high places, and with this he resists. Now, he
has come to his last struggle; the river Death rolls black and
sullen before him; dark shapes rise upward from the flood,
and howl and fright him. How shall he cross the stream?
How shall he find a landing place on the other side? Dread
thoughts perplex him for a moment; he is alarmed; but he
remembers, Jesus died; and catching up that watchword he
ventures to the flood. Before his feet the Jordan flies apace;
like Israel of old, he walks through, dry shod, singing as he
goes to heaven, "Christ is with me, Christ is with me, passing
through the stream! Victory, victory, victory, to him that
oveth me!"

To the Christian in his own experience Christ is ever the
power of God. As for temptation he can meet that with Christ;
as for trouble he can endure that through Christ who strengthens him, yea, he can say with Paul, "I can do all things
through Christ who strengthens me." Have you never seen
a Christian in trouble, a true Christian? I have read a story

of a man who was converted to God by seeing the conduct of his wife in the hour of trouble. They had a lovely child, their only offspring. The father's heart doted on it perpetually, and the mother's soul was knit up in the heart of the little one. It lay sick upon its bed, and the parents watched it night and day. At last it died. The father had no God: he rent his hair, he rolled upon the floor in misery, wallowed upon the earth, cursing his being, and defying God in the utter casting down of his agony. There sat his wife, as fond of the child as ever he could be; and though tears would come, she gently said, "The Lord gave, and the Lord hath taken away; blessed be the name of the Lord." "What," said he, starting to his feet, "you love that child? I thought that when that child died you would break your heart. Here am I, a strong man; I am mad: here are you, a weak woman, and yet you are strong and bold; tell me what it is possesses you?" Said she, "Christ is my Lord, I trust in him; surely I can give this child to him who gave himself for me." From that instant the man became a believer. "There must," said he, "be some truth and some power in the gospel, which could lead you to believe in such a manner, under such a trial." Christians! try to exhibit that spirit wherever you are, and prove to the worldling that in your experience at least "Christ is the power of God and the wisdom of God."

And now the last point. In the *Christian's experience*, Christ is wisdom, as well as power. If you want to be a thoroughly learned man the best place to begin, is to begin at the Bible, to begin at Christ. It is said that even children learn to read more quickly from the Bible than from any other book; and this I am sure of, that we, who are but grown-up children, will learn better and learn faster by beginning with Christ, than we could by beginning with any thing else. I remember saying once, and as I can not say it better I will repeat it, that before I knew the gospel I gathered up a heterogeneous mass of all kinds of knowledge from here, there, and everywhere; a bit of chemistry, a bit of botany, a bit of astronomy, and a bit of this, that, and the other. I put them altogether, in one great confused chaos. When I learned the gospel, I got a shelf in my head to put every thing away upon just where it should be. It seemed to me as if, when I had discovered Christ and him crucified, I had got the center of the system, so that I could see every other science revolving around in order. From the earth, you know, the planets appear to move in a very irregular manner—they are progressive, retro grade, stationary; but if you could get upon the sun, you would see them marching round in their constant, uniform, circular motion. So with knowledge. Begin with any other science you like, and truth will seem to be awry. Begin with the science of Christ crucified, and you will begin with the sun, you will see every other science moving round it in complete harmony. The greatest mind in the world will be evolved by beginning at the right end. The old saying is, "Go from nature up to nature's God;" but it is hard work going up hill. The best thing is to go from nature's God down to nature; and if you once get to nature's God, and believe him and love him, it is surprising how easy it is to hear music in the waves, and songs in the wild whisperings of the winds; to see God everywhere, in the stones, in the rocks, in the rippling brooks, and hear him everywhere, in the lowing of cattle, in the rolling of thunder, and in the fury of tempests. Get Christ first, put him in the right place, and you will find him to be the wisdom of God in your own experience.

But wisdom is not knowledge; and we must not confound the two. Wisdom is the right use of knowledge; and Christ's gospel helps us, by teaching us the right use of knowl edge. It directs us. Yon Christian has lost his way in a dark wood; but God's Word is a compass to him, and a lantern too: he finds his way by Christ. He comes to a turn in the road. Which is right, and which is wrong? He can not tell. Christ is the great sign-post, telling him which way to go. He sees every day new straits attend; he knows not which way to steer. Christ is the great pilot who puts his hand on the tiller, and makes him wise to steer through the shoals of temptation and the rocks of sin. Get the gospel, and you are a wise man. "The fear of the Lord is the begin ning of wisdom, and right understanding have they who keep his commandments." Ah! Christian, you have had many doubts, but you have had them all unriddled, when you have come to the cross of Christ. You have had many difficulties; but they have been all explained in the light of Calvary. You have seen mysteries, when you have brought them to the face of Christ, made clear and manifest, which once you never could have known. Allow me to remark here, that some people make use of Christ's gospel to illuminate their heads, instead of making use of it to illuminate their hearts. They are like the farmer Rowland Hill once described. The farmer is sitting by the fire with his children; the cat is purring on the hearth, and they are all in great comfort. The plowman rushes in and cries, "Thieves! thieves! thieves!" The farmer rises up in a moment, grasps the candle, holds it up to his head, rushes after the thieves, and, says Rowland Hill, "he tumbles over a wheelbarrow, because he holds the light to his head, instead of holding it to his feet." So there are many who just hold religion up to illuminate their intellect, instead of holding it down to illuminate their practice; and so they make a sad tumble of it, and cast themselves into the mire, and do more hurt to their Christian profession in one hour than they will ever be able to retrieve. Take care that you make the wisdom of God, by God's Holy Spirit, a thing of true wisdom, directing your feet into his statutes, and keeping you in his ways.

And now a practical appeal, and we have done. I have been putting my arrow on the string; and if I have used any light similes, I have but done so just as the archer tips his arrow with a feather, to make it fly the better. I know that a rough quaint saying often sticks, when another thing is entirely forgotten. Now let us draw the bow, and send the arrow right at your hearts. Men, brethren, fathers, how many of you have felt in yourselves that Christ is the power of God, and the wisdom of God? Internal evidence is the best evidence in the world for the truth of the gospel. No Paley or Butler can prove the truth of the gospel so well as Mary, the servant girl yonder, that has got the gospel in her heart, and the power of it manifest in her life. Say, has Christ ever broken your bonds and set you free? Has he delivered you from your evil life, and from your sin? Has he given you "a good hope through grace," and can you now say, "On him I lean; or my beloved I stay myself?" If so, go away and rejoice : you are a saint ; for the apostle has said, " He is unto us who are saved, Christ the power of God and the wisdom of God." But if you can not say this, allow me affectionately to warn you. If you want not this power of Christ, and this wisdom of Christ now, you will want them in a few short moments, when God shall come to judge the quick and the dead, when you shall stand before his bar, and when all the deeds that you have done shall be read before an assembled world. You will want religion then. O that you had grace to tremble now ; grace to kiss the Son, lest he be angry, and you perish from the way, when his wrath is kindled but a little." Hear ye how to be saved, and I have done. Do you feel that you are a sinner ? Are you conscious that you have rebelled against God ? Are you willing to acknowledge your transgressions, and do you hate and abhor them, while at the same time you feel you can do nothing to atone for them ? Then hear this. Christ died for you ; and if he died for you, you can not be lost. Christ died in vain for no man for whom he died. If you are a penitent and a believer, he died for you, and you are safe ; go your way : rejoice " with joy unspeakable, and full of glory ;" for he who has taught you your need of a Saviour, will you give that Saviour's blood to be applied to your conscience, and you shall ere long, with yonder blood-washed host, praise God and the Lamb saying, " Hallelujah, for ever, Amen !" Only do you feel that you are a sinner ? If not, I have no gospel to preach to you ; I can but warn you. But if you feel your lost estate, and come to Christ, come, and welcome, for he will never cast you away.

SERMON XXVI

GOING HOME—A CHRISTMAS SERMON

" Go home to thy friends, and tell them how great things the Lord hath done for thee, and hath had compassion on thee."—MARK, v. 19

THE case of the man here referred to is a very extraordinary one: it occupies a place among the memorabilia of Christ's life, perhaps as high as any thing which is recorded by either of the evangelists. This poor wretch being possessed with a legion of evil spirits had been driven to something worse than madness. He fixed his home among the tombs, where he dwelt by night and day, and was the terror of all those who passed by. The authorities had attempted to curb him; he had been bound with fetters and chains, but in the paroxysms of his madness he had torn the chains in sunder, and broken the fetters in pieces. Attempts had been made to reclaim him; but no man could tame him. He was worse than the wild beasts, for they might be tamed; but his fierce nature would not yield. He was a misery to himself, for he would run upon the mountains by night and day, crying and howling fearfully, cutting himself with the sharp flints, and torturing his poor body in the most frightful manner. Jesus Christ passed by; he said to the devils, " Come out of him." The man was healed in a moment; he fell down at Jesus' feet; he became a rational being—an intelligent man, yea, what is more, a convert to the Saviour. Out of gratitude to his deliverer, he said, " Lord, I will follow thee whithersoever thou goest; I will be thy constant companion and thy servant; permit me so to be." " No," said Christ, " I esteem your motive; it is one of gratitude to me; but if you would show your gratitude, ' go home to thy friends, and tell them how great things the Lord hath done for thee, and hath had compassion on thee.' "

Now, this teaches us a very important fact, namely, this, true religion does not break in sunder the bonds of family relationship. True religion seldom encroaches upon that sacred, I had almost said divine institution called *home ;* it does not separate men from their families, and make them aliens to their flesh and blood. Superstition has done that; an awful superstition, which calls itself Christianity, has sundered men from their kind; but true religion has never done so. Why, if I might be allowed to do such a thing, I would seek out the hermit in his lonely cavern, and I would go to him and say, "Friend, if thou art what thou dost profess to be, a true servant of the living God, and not a hypocrite, as I guess thou art—if thou art a true believer in Christ, and would show forth what he has done for thee, upset that pitcher, eat the last piece of thy bread, leave this dreary cave, wash thy face, untie thy hempen girdle; and if thou wouldst show thy gratitude, go home to thy friends, and tell them what great things the Lord hath done for thee. Canst thou edify the sere leaves of the forest? Can the beasts learn to adore that God whom thy gratitude should strive to honor? Dost thou hope to convert these rocks, and wake the echoes into songs? Nay, go back: dwell with thy friends, reclaim thy kinship with men, and unite again with thy fellows, for this is Christ's approved way of showing gratitude." And I would go to every monastery and every nunnery, and say to the monks, "Come out, brethren, come out! If you are what you say you are, servants of God, go home to your friends. No more of this absurd discipline; it is not Christ's rule; you are acting differently from what he would have you; go home to your friends!" And to the Sisters of Mercy we would say, "Be sisters of mercy to your own sisters; go home to your friends; take care of your aged parents; turn your own houses into convents; do not sit here nursing your pride by a disobedience to Christ's rule, which says, ' go home to thy friends.' " " Go home to thy friends, and tell them how great things the Lord hath done for thee, and hath had compassion on thee." The love of a solitary and ascetic life, which is by some considered to be a divine virtue, is neither more nor less than a disease of the mind. In the ages when there was but little benevo ence, and consequently few hands to build lunatic asylums, superstition supplied the lack of charity, and silly men and women were allowed the indulgence of their fancies in secluded haunts or in easy laziness. Young has most truly said,

> " The first sure symptoms of a mind in health
> Are rest of heart and pleasure found at home."

Avoid, my friends, above all things, those romantic and absurd conceptions of virtue which are the offspring of superstition and the enemies of righteousness. Be not without natural affection, but love those who are knit to you by ties of nature.

True religion can not be inconsistent with nature. It never can demand that I should abstain from weeping when my friend is dead. " Jesus wept." It can not deny me the privilege of a smile, when Providence looks favorably upon me ; for once " Jesus rejoiced in spirit, and said, Father, I thank thee." It does not make a man say to his father and mother, "I am no longer your son." That is not Christianity, but something worse than what beasts would do, which would lead us to be entirely sundered from our fellows, to walk among them as if we had no kinship with them. To all who think a solitary life must be a life of piety, I would say, " It is the greatest delusion." To all who think that those must be good people who snap the ties of relationship, let us say, " Those are the best who maintain them." Christianity makes a husband a better husband, it makes a wife a better wife than she was before. It does not free me from my duties as a son ; it makes me a better son, and my parents better parents. Instead of weakening my love, it gives me fresh reason for my affection ; and he whom I loved before as my father, I now love as my brother and co-worker in Christ Jesus ; and she whom I reverenced as my mother, I now love as my sister in the covenant of grace, to be mine for ever in the state that is to come. O ! suppose not, any of you, that Christianity was ever meant to interfere with households ; it is intended to cement them, and to make them households which death itself shall never sever, for it binds them up in the bundle of life with the Lord their God, and reunites the several individuals on the other side of the flood.

Now, I will just tell you the reason why I selected my text, I thought within myself, there are a large number of young men who always come to hear me preach; they always crowd the aisles of my chapel, and many of them have been, converted to God. Now, here is Christmas day come round again, and they are going home to see their friends. When they get home they will want a Christmas carol in the evenin; I think I will suggest one to them—more especially to such of them as have been lately converted. I will give them a theme for their discourse on Christmas evening; it may not be quite so amusing as "The Wreck of the *Golden Mary*," but it will be quite as interesting to Christian people. It shall be this: "Go home and tell your friends what the Lord hath done for your souls, and how he hath had compassion on you." For my part I wish there were twenty Christmas days in the year. It is seldom that young men can meet with their friends; it is rarely they can all be united as happy families; and though I have no respect to the religious observance of the day, yet I love it as a family institution, as one of England's brightest days, the great Sabbath of the year, when the plow rests in its furrow, when the din of business is hushed, when the mechanic and the working-man go out to refresh themselves upon the green sward of the glad earth. If any of you are masters you will pardon me for the digression, when I most respectfully beg you to pay your servants the same wages on Christmas day as if they were at work. I am sure it will make their houses glad if you will do so. It is unfair for you to make them feast, or fast, unless you give them wherewithal to feast and make themselves glad on that day of joy.

But now to come to the subject. We are going home to see our friends, and here is the story some of us have to tell. "Go home to thy friends, and tell them how great things the Lord hath done for thee, and hath had compassion on thee." First, *here is what they are to tell;* then, secondly, *why they are to tell it;* and then, thirdly, *how they ought to tell it.*

I. First, then, HERE IS WHAT THEY ARE TO TELL. It is to be a story of *personal experience.* "Go home to thy friends, and tell them how great things the Lord hath done for thee, and hath had compassion on thee." You are not to repair to your houses, and forthwith begin to preach. That you are not commanded to do. You are not to begin to take up doctrinal subjects, and expatiate on them, and endeavor to bring persons to your peculiar views and sentiments. You are not to go home with sundry doctrines you have lately learned, and try to teach these. At least you are not commanded so to do; you may, if you please, and none shall hinder you; but you are to go home and tell not what you have believed, but what you have *felt*—what you really know to be your own; not what great things you have read, but what great things the Lord hath *done for you;* not alone what you have seen done in the great congregation, and how great sinners have turned to God, but what the Lord has done for *you*. And mark this: there is never a more interesting story than that which a man tells about himself. The Rhyme of the Ancient Mariner derives much of its interest because the man who told it was himself the mariner. He sat down, that man whose finger was skinny, like the finger of death, and began to tell that dismal story of the ship at sea in a great calm, when slimy things did crawl with legs over the shiny sea. The wedding guest sat still to listen, for the old man was himself a story. There is always a great deal of interest excited by a personal narrative. Virgil, the poet, knew this, and, therefore, he wisely makes Æneas tell his own story, and makes him begin it by saying, " In which I also had a great part myself." So if you would interest your friends, tell them what you felt yourself. Tell them how you were once a lost abandoned sinner, how the Lord met with you, how you bowed your knees, and poured out your soul before God, and how at last you leaped with joy, for you thought you heard him say within you, " I, even I, am he that blotteth out thy transgressions for my name's sake." Tell your friends a story of your own personal experience.

Note, next, it must be a story of *free grace*. It is not, "Tell thy friends how great things thou hast done thyself," but " how great things *the Lord* hath done for thee." The man who always dwells upon free will and the power of the creature, and denies the doctrines of grace, invariably mixes up a

great deal of what he has done himself in telling his experience; but the believer in free grace, who holds the great car-
dinal truths of the gospel, ignores this, and declares, "I will
tell what the Lord hath done for me. It is true I must tell
how I was first made to pray; but I will tell it thus—

> " 'Grace taught my soul to pray,
> Grace made my eyes o'erflow.'

It is true, I must tell in how many troubles and trials God has
been with me; but I will tell it thus—

> " ' 'Twas grace which kept me to this day,
> And will not let me go.' "

He says nothing about his own doings, or willings, or prayings,
or seekings, but he ascribes it all to the love and grace of the
great God who looks on sinners in love, and makes them his
children, heirs of everlasting life. Go home, young man, and
tell the poor sinner's story; go home, young woman, and open
your diary, and give your friends stories of grace. Tell them
of the mighty works of God's hand which he hath wrought in
you from his own free, sovereign, undeserved love. Make it
a free-grace story around your family fire.

In the next place, this poor man's tale was a *grateful* story.
I know it was grateful, because the man said, " I will tell thee
how great things the Lord hath done for me;" and (not meaning a pun in the least degree) I may observe, that a man who
is grateful is always full of the greatness of the mercy which
God has shown him; he always thinks that what God has done
for him is immensely good and supremely great. Perhaps
when you are telling the story one of your friends will say,
" And what of that?" And your answer will be, "It may
not be a great thing to you, but it is to me. You say it is
little to repent, but I have not found it so; it is a great and
precious thing to be brought to know myself to be a sinner,
and to confess it; do you say it is a little thing to have found
a Saviour?" Look them in the face, and say, " If you had
found him too you would not think it little. You think it little
I have lost the burden from my back; but if you had suffered
with it, and felt its weight as I have for many a long year, you

would think it no little thing to be emancipated and free, through a sight of the cross." Tell them it is a great story, and if they can not see its greatness, shed great tears and tell it to them with great earnestness, and I hope they may be brought to believe that you at least are grateful, if they are not. May God grant that you may tell a grateful story. No story is more worth hearing than a tale of gratitude.

And lastly, upon this point: it must be a tale told by a poor sinner who feels himself *not to have deserved* what he has received. "How he hath had *compassion* on thee." It was not a mere act of kindness, but an act of free compassion toward one who was in misery. O! I have heard men tell the story of their conversion and of their spiritual life in such a way that my heart hath loathed *them* and their story too, for they have told of their sins as if they did boast in the greatness of their crime, and they have mentioned the love of God not with a tear of gratitude, not with the simple thanksgiving of the really humble heart, but as if they as much exalted themselves as they exalted God. O! when we tell the story of our own conversion, I would have it done with deep sorrow, remembering what we used to be, and with great joy and gratitude, remembering how little we deserve these things. I was once preaching upon conversion and salvation, and I felt within myself, as preachers often do, that it was but dry work to tell this story, and a dull, dull tale it was to me; but on a sudden the thought crossed my mind, "Why, you are a poor lost ruined sinner yourself; tell it, tell it, as you received it: begin to tell of the grace of God as you trust you feel it yourself." When, then, my eyes began to be fountains of tears, those hearers who had nodded their heads began to brighten up, and they listened, because they were hearing something which the man felt himself, and which they recognized as being true to him, if it was not true to them. Tell your story, my hearers, as lost sinners. Do not go to your home, and walk into the house with a supercilious air, as much as to say, "Here's a saint come home to the poor sinners, to tell them a story;" but go home like a poor sinner yourself; and when you go in, your mother remembers what you used to be, you need not tell her there is a change—she will notice it, if it is only one day you are with her; and perhaps she will say, "John, what is this change that is in you?" and if she is a pious mother you will begin to tell her the story, and I know, man though you are, you will not blush when I say it, she will put her arms round your neck and kiss you as she never did before, for you are her twice-born son, hers from whom she shall never part, even though death itself shall divide you for a brief moment. Go home, then, and tell your friends what great things the Lord hath done for you, and how he hath had compassion on you.

II. But now, in the second place, WHY SHOULD WE TELL THIS STORY? For I hear many of my congregation say, "Sir, I could relate that story to any one sooner than I could to my friends; I could come to your vestry, and tell you something of what I have tasted and handled of the word of God; but I could not tell my father, nor my mother, nor my brethren, nor my sisters." Come, then; I will try and argue with you, to induce you to do so, that I may send you home this Christmas day, to be missionaries in the localities to which you belong, and to be real preachers, though you are not so by name Dear friends, do tell this story when you go home.

First, for *your Master's sake.* O! I know you love him; I am sure you do, if you have proof that he loved you. You can never think of Gethsemane and of its bloody sweat; of Gabbatha and of the mangled back of Christ, flayed by the whip; you can never think of Calvary and his pierced hands and feet, without loving him; and it is a strong argument when I say to you, for his dear sake who loved you so much, go home and tell it. What! do you think we can have so much done for us, and yet not tell it? Our children, if any thing should be done for them, do not stay many minutes before they are telling all the company, "such a one hath given me such a present, and bestowed on me such-and-such a favor." And should the children of God be backward in declaring how they were saved when their feet made haste to hell, and how redeeming mercy snatched them as brands from the burning? You love Jesus, young man! I put it to you, then, will you refuse to tell the tale of his love to you? Shall your lips be dumb, when his honor is concerned? Will you not, wherever you go, tell of the God who loved you and died for you? This poor man, we are told, "departed, and began to publish in Decapolis how great things Jesus had done for him, and all men did marvel." So with you. If Christ has done much for you, you can not help it—you must tell it. My esteemed friend, Mr. Oncken, a minister in Germany, told us last Monday evening that so soon as he was converted him self, the first impulse of his new-born soul was to do good to others. And where should he do that good? Well, he thought he would go to Germany. It was his own native land, and he thought the command was, "Go home to thy friends, and tell them." Well, there was not a single Baptist in all Germany, nor any with whom he could sympathize, for the Lutherans had swerved from the faith of Luther, and gone aside from the truth of God. But he went there and preached, and he has now seventy or eighty churches established on the Continent. What made him do it? Nothing but love for his Master, who had done so much for him, could have forced him to go and tell his kinsmen the marvelous tale of divine goodness.

But, in the next place, are your friends pious? Then go home and tell them, in order *to make their hearts glad.* I received last night a short epistle written with a trembling hand by one who is past the natural age of man, living in the county of Essex. His son, under God, had been converted by hearing the word preached, and the good man could not help writing to the minister, thanking *him,* and blessing most of all his God, that his son had been regenerated. "Sir," he begins, "an old rebel writes to thank you, and above all to thank his God, that his dear son has been converted." I shall treasure up that epistle. It goes on to say, "Go on! and the Lord bless you." And there was another case I heard some time ago, where a young woman went home to her parents, and when her mother saw her she said, "There! if the minister had made me a present of all London, I should not have thought so much of it as I do of this—to think that you have really become a changed character, and are living in the fear of God." O! if you want to make your mother's heart leap within her, and to make your father glad—if you would make that sister happy who sent you so many letters, which some times you read against a lamp-post, with your pipe in your mouth—go home and tell your mother that her wishes are all accomplished, that her prayers are heard, that you will no longer chaff her about her Sunday-school class, and no longer laugh at her because she loves the Lord, but that you will go with her to the house of God, for you love God, and you have said, "Your people shall be my people, and your God shall be my God, for I have a hope that your heaven shall be my heaven for ever." O! what a happy thing it would be if some here who had gone astray should thus go home! It was my privilege a little while ago to preach for a noble institution for the reception of women who had led abandoned lives—and before I preached the sermon I prayed to God to bless it, and in the printed sermon you will notice that at the end of it there is an account of two persons who were blessed by that sermon, and restored. Now, let me tell you a story of what once happened to Mr. Vanderkist, a city missionary, who toils all night long to do good in that great work. There had been a drunken broil in the street; he stepped between the men to part them, and said something to a woman who stood there concerning how dreadful a thing it was that men should thus be intemperate. She walked with him a little way, and he with her, and she began to tell him such a tale of woe and sin too, how she had been lured away from her parents' home in Somersetshire, and had been brought up here to her soul's eternal hurt. He took her home with him, and taught her the fear and love of Christ; and what was the first thing she did, when she returned to the paths of godliness, and found Christ to be the sinner's Saviour? She said, "Now I must go home to my friends." Her friends were written to; they came to meet her at the station at Bristol, and you can hardly conceive what a happy meeting it was. The father and mother had lost their daughter; they had never heard from her; and there she was, brought back by the agency of this Institution, and restored to the bosom of her family. Ah! if such a one be here! I know not; among such a multitude there may be such a one. Woman! hast thou strayed from thy family? Hast thou left them long? "Go home to thy friends," I beseech thee, ere thy father totters to his grave, and ere thy mother's gray hairs sleep on the snow-white pillow of her coffin. Go back, I beseech thee! Tell her thou art penitent; tell her that God hath met with thee—that the young minister said, "Go back to thy friends." And if so, I shall not blush to have said these things, though you may think I ought not to have mentioned them; for if I may but win one such soul, I will bless God to all eternity. "Go home to thy friends." Go home and tell them how great things the Lord hath done for thee. Can not you imagine the scene, when the poor demoniac mentioned in my text went home? He had been a raving madman; and when he came and knocked at the door, don't you think you see his friends calling to one another in affright, "O! there he is again," and the mother running up stairs and locking all the doors, because her son had come back that was raving mad; and the little ones crying, because they knew what he had been before—how he cut himself with stones, because he was possessed with devils. And can you picture their joy, when the man said, "Mother! Jesus Christ has healed me; let me in; I am no lunatic now?" And when the father opened the door, he said, "Father! I am not what I was; all the evil spirits are gone; I shall live in the tombs no longer. I want to tell you how the glorious man who wrought my deliverance accomplished the miracle—how he said to the devils, 'Get ye hence,' and they ran down a steep place into the sea, and I am come home healed and saved." O! if such a one, possessed with sin, were here this morning, and would go home to his friends, to tell them of his release, methinks the scene would be somewhat similar.

Once more, dear friends. I hear one of you say, "Ah! sir, would to God I could go home to pious friends! But when I go home I go into the worst of places; for my home is among those who never knew God themselves, and consequently never prayed for me, and never taught me any thing concerning heaven." Well, young man, go home to your friends. If they are ever so bad, they are your friends. I sometimes meet with young men wishing to join the church, who say, when I ask them about their father, "O, sir, I am parted from

my father." Then I say, " Young man, you may just go and
see your father before I have any thing to do with you; if
you are at ill-will with your father and mother I will not receive you into the church; if they are ever so bad they are
your parents." Go home to them, and tell them, not to make
them glad, for they will very likely be angry with you; but
tell them *for their soul's salvation.* I hope, when you are
telling the story of what God did for you, that they will be
led by the Spirit to desire the same mercy themselves. But I
will give you a piece of advice. Do not tell this story to your
ungodly friends when they are all together, for they will
laugh at you. Take them one by one, when you can get
them alone, and begin to tell it to them, and they will hear
you seriously. There was once a very pious lady who kept a
lodging-house for young men. All the young men were very
gay and giddy, and she wanted to say something to them concerning religion. She introduced the subject, and it was
passed off immediately with a laugh. She thought within
herself, " I have made a mistake." The next morning, after
breakfast, when they were all going, she said to one of them.
" Sir, I should like to speak with you a moment or two," and
taking him aside into another room she talked with him.
The next morning she took another, and the next morning
another, and it pleased God to bless her simple statement,
when it was given individually : but, without doubt, if she
had spoken to them all together they would have backed each
other up in laughing her to scorn. Reprove a man alone. A
verse may hit him whom a sermon flies. You may be the
means of bringing a man to Christ who has often heard the
Word and only laughed at it, but who can not resist a gentle
admonition. In one of the States of America there was an infidel who was a great despiser of God, a hater of the Sabbath
and all religious institutions. What to do with him the ministers did not know. They met together and prayed for him.
But among the rest, one Elder B—— resolved to spend a long
time in prayer for the man ; after that he got on horseback,
and rode down to the man's forge, for he was a blacksmith
He left his horse outside, and said, " Neighbor, I am under
very great concern about your soul's salvation ; I tell you I

pray day and night for your soul's salvation." He left him, and rode home on his horse. The man went inside to his house, after a minute or two, and said to one of his infidel friends, " Here's a new argument; here's Elder B—— been down here, he did not dispute, and never said a word to me except this, ' I say, I am under great concern about your soul; I can not bear you should be lost.' O! that fellow," he said, " I can not answer him ;" and the tears began to roll down his cheeks. He went to his wife, and said, " I can't make this out; I never cared about my soul, but here's an elder, that has no connection with me, but I have always laughed at him, and he has come five miles this morning on horseback just to tell me he is under concern about my salvation." After a little while he thought it was time he should be under concern about his salvation too. He went in, shut the door, began to pray, and the next day he was at the deacon's house, telling him that he too was under concern about his salvation, and asking him to tell him what he must do to be saved. O! that the everlasting God might make use of some of those now present in the same way, that they might be induced to

> " Tell to others round
> What a dear Saviour they have found;
> To point to his redeeming blood,
> And say, Behold the way to God!"

III. I shall not detain you much longer; but there is a third point, upon which we must be very brief. HOW IS THE STORY TO BE TOLD?

First, *tell it truthfully.* Do not tell more than you know; do not tell John Bunyan's experience, when you ought to tell your own. Do not tell your mother you have felt what only Rutherford felt. Tell her no more than the truth. Tell your experience truthfully; for mayhap one single fly in the pot of ointment will spoil it, and one statement you may make which is not true may ruin it all. Tell the story truthfully.

In the next place, *tell it very humbly.* I have said that before. Do not intrude yourselves upon those who are older, and know more; but tell your story humbly; not as a preacher not *ex-cathedra*, but as a friend and as a son.

Next, *tell it very earnestly.* Let them see you mean it.

Do not talk about religion flippantly; you will do no good if you do. Do not make puns on texts; do not quote Scripture by way of joke: if you do, you may talk till you are dumb, you will do no good, if you in the least degree give them oc casion to laugh by laughing at holy things yourself. Tell it very earnestly.

And then, *tell it very devoutly.* Do not try to tell your tale to man till you have told it first to God. When you are at home on Christmas day, let no one see your face till God has seen it. Be up in the morning, wrestle with God ; and if your friends are not converted, *wrestle with God for them ;* and then you will find it easy work to *wrestle with them for God.* Seek, if you can, to get them one by one, and tell them the story. Do not be afraid; only think of the good you may possibly do. Remember, he that saves a soul from death hath covered a multitude of sins, and he shall have stars in his crown for ever and ever. Seek to be, under God, saviours in your family, to be the means of leading your own beloved brethren and sisters to seek and to find the Lord Jesus Christ, and then one day, when you shall meet in Paradise, it will be a joy and blessedness to think that you are there, and that your friends are there too, whom God will have made you the instrument of saving. Let your reliance on the Holy Spirit be entire and honest. Trust not yourself, but fear not to trust him. He can give you words. He can apply those words to their hearts, and so enable you to "minister grace to the hearers."

To close up, by a short, and I think a pleasant turning of the text, to suggest another meaning to it. Soon, dear friends, very soon with some of us, the Master will say, "Go home to thy friends." You know where the home is. It is up above the stars,

> "Where our best friends, our kindred, dwell,
> Where God our Saviour reigns."

Yon gray-headed man has buried all his friends; he has said, "I shall go to them, but they will not return to me." Soon his Master will say, "Thou hast had enough tarrying here in this vale of tears: go home to thy friends!" O! happy hour. O! blessed moment, when that shall be the word— "Go home to thy friends! And when we go home to our

friends in Paradise, what shall we do? Why, first, we will
repair to that blest seat where Jesus sits, take off our crown
and cast it at his feet, and crown him Lord of all. And when
we have done that, what shall be our next employ? Why,
we will tell the blessed ones in heaven what the Lord hath
done for us, and how he hath had compassion on us. And
shall such a tale be told in heaven? Shall that be the Christ
mas carol of the angels? Yes, it shall be; it has been published there before—blush not to tell it yet again—for Jesus
has told it before, " When he cometh home, he calleth together
his friends and neighbors, saying unto them, Rejoice with me;
for I have found my sheep which was lost." And thou, poor
sheep, when thou shalt be gathered in, wilt thou not tell how
thy Shepherd sought thee, and how he found thee? Wilt
thou not sit in the grassy meads of heaven, and tell the story
of thine own redemption? Wilt thou not talk with thy brethren and thy sisters, and tell them how God loved thee and
hath brought thee there? Perhaps thou sayest, " It will be a
very short story." Ah! it would be if you could write now.
A little book might be the whole of your biography; but up
there, when your memory shall be enlarged, when your passions shall be purified and your understanding clear, you will
find that what was but a tract on earth will be a huge tome in
heaven. You will tell a long story there of God's sustaining,
restraining, constraining grace, and I think that when you
pause to let another tell his tale, and then another, and then
another, you will at last, when you have been in heaven a
thousand years, break out and exclaim, " O saints, I have
something else to say." Again they will tell their tales, and
again you will interrupt them with " O beloved, I have thought
of another case of God's delivering mercy." And so you will
go on, giving them themes for songs, finding them the material
for the warp and woof of heavenly sonnets. " Go home," he
will soon say, " go home to thy friends, and tell them how
great things the Lord hath done for thee, and hath had compassion on thee." Wait a while; tarry his leisure, and ye
shall soon be gathered to the land of the hereafter, to the
home of the blessed, where endless felicity shall be thy por
tion. God grant a blessing, for his name's sake !

SERMON XXVII

A MIGHTY SAVIOUR

"Mighty to save."—ISAIAH, lxiii. 1

This, of course, refers to our blessed Lord Jesus Christ, who is described as "coming from Edom with dyed garments from Bozrah," and who, when it is questioned who he is, replies, "I that speak in righteousness, mighty to save." It will be well, then, at the commencement of our discourse to make one or two remarks concerning the mysteriously complex person of the man and God whom we call our Redeemer, Jesus Christ our Saviour. It is one of the mysteries of the Christian religion, that we are taught to believe that Christ is God, and yet a man. According to Scripture, we hold that he is "*very God*," equal and co-eternal with the Father, possessing, as his Father doth, all divine attributes in an infinite degree. He participated with his Father in all the acts of his divine might; he was concerned in the decree of election, in the fashioning of the covenant; in the creation of the angels; in the making of the world, when it was wheeled from nothing into space, and in the ordering of this fair frame of nature. Before any of these acts the divine Redeemer was the eternal Son of God. "From everlasting to everlasting he is God." Nor did he cease to be God when he became man. He was equally "God over all, blessed for evermore," when he was "the man of sorrows, acquainted with grief," as before his incarnation. We have abundant proof of that in the constant affirmations of Scripture, and, indeed, also in the miracles which he wrought. The raising of the dead, the treading of the billows of the ocean, the hushing of the winds, and the rending of the rocks, with all those marvelous acts of his, which we have not time here to mention, were strong and potent proofs that he was

God, most truly God, even when he condescended to be man. And Scripture, most certainly, teaches us that he is God now, that he shares the throne of his Father—that he sits high above all " principalities and powers, and every name that is named," and is the true and proper object of the veneration, the worship, and the homage of all worlds. We are equally taught to believe that he is *man*. Scripture informs us that, on a day appointed, he came from heaven and did become man as well as God, taking upon himself the nature of a babe in the manger of Bethlehem. From that babe, we are told, he did grow to the stature of manhood, and became " bone of our bone, and flesh of our flesh," in every thing except our sin His sufferings, his hunger, above all, his death and burial, are strong proofs that he was man, most truly man; and yet it is demanded of us by the Christian religion, to believe, that while he was man, he was most truly God. We are taught that he was a " child born, a son given," and yet, at the same time, the " Wonderful, the Counselor, the mighty God, the everlasting Father." Whosoever would have clear and right views of Jesus, must not mingle his natures. We must not consider him as a God diluted into deified manhood, or as a mere man officially exalted to the Godhead, but as being two distinct natures in one person; not God melted into man, nor man made into God, but man and God taken into union together. Therefore, do we trust in him, as the Daysman, the Mediator, Son of God, and Son of Man. This is the person who is our Saviour. It is this glorious, yet mysterious being, of whom the text speaks, when it says, he is mighty—" mighty to save."

That he is mighty we need not inform you; for as readers of the Scriptures you all believe in the might and majesty of the incarnate Son of God. You believe him to be the Regent of providence, the King of death, the Conqueror of hell, the Lord of angels, the Master of storms, and the God of battles, and, therefore, you can need no proof that he is mighty. The subject of this morning is one part of his mightiness. He is " mighty to save." May God the Holy Spirit help us in briefly entering upon this subject, and make use of it to the salvation of our souls !

A MIGHTY SAVIOUR.

First, we shall consider *what is meant by the words " to save ;"* secondly, *how we prove the fact that he is " mighty to save ;"* thirdly, *the reason why he is " mighty to save ;"* and then, fourthly, *the inferences which are to be deduced from the doctrine that Jesus Christ is " mighty to save."*

I. First, then, WHAT ARE WE TO UNDERSTAND BY THE WORDS " TO SAVE ?"

Commonly, most men, when they read these words, consider them to mean salvation from hell. They are partially correct, but the notion is highly defective. It is true Christ does save men from the penalty of their guilt; he does take those to heaven who deserve the eternal wrath and displeasure of the Most High; it is true that he does blot out " iniquity, transgression, and sin," and that the iniquities of the remnant of his people are passed over for the sake of his blood and atonement. But that is not the whole meaning of the words " to save." This deficient explanation lies at the root of mistakes which many theologians have made, and by which they have surrounded their system of divinity with mist. They have said that to save is to pluck men as brands from the burning—to save them from destruction if they repent. Now, it means vastly, I had almost said infinitely more than this. " To save" means something more than just delivering penitents from going down to hell. By the words " to save" I understand the whole of the great work of salvation, from the first holy desire, the first spiritual conviction, onward to complete sanctification. All is done of God through Jesus Christ. Christ is not only mighty to save those who do repent, but he is able to make men repent; he is engaged not merely to carry those to heaven who believe, but he is mighty to give men new hearts and to work faith in them; he is mighty not merely to give heaven to one who wishes for it, but he is mighty to make the man who hates holiness love it, to constrain the despiser of his name to bend his knee before him, and to make the most abandoned reprobate turn from the error of his ways.

By the words " to save," I do not understand what some men say they mean. They tell us in their divinity that Christ came into the world to put all men into a salvable state—to make the salvation of all men possible by their own exertions

I believe that Christ came for no such thing—that he came into the world not to put men into a *salvable* state, but into a *saved* state ; not to put them where they could save them selves, but to do the work in them and for them, from the first even to the last. If I believed that Christ came only to put you, my hearers, and myself into a state where we might save ourselves, I should give up preaching henceforth and for ever ; for knowing a little of the wickedness of men's hearts, because I know something of my own—knowing how much men natu rally hate the religion of Christ—I should despair of any success in preaching a gospel which I had only to offer, its effects depending upon the voluntary acceptance of it by unrenewed and unregenerate men. If I did not believe that there was a might going forth with the word of Jesus, which makes men willing in the day of his power, and which turns them from the error of their ways by the mighty, overwhelming, constraining force of a divine and mysterious influence, I should cease to glory in the cross of Christ. Christ, we repeat, is mighty, not merely to put men into a salvable condition, but mighty absolutely and entirely to save them. This fact I regard as one of the grandest proofs of the divine character of the Bible revelation. I have many a time had doubts and fears, as most of you have had ; and where is the strong believer that has not sometimes wavered ? I have said, within myself, " Is this religion true, which, day after day, I incessantly preach to the people ? Is it the correct one ? Is it true that this religion has an influence upon mankind ?" And I will tell you how I have reassured myself. I have looked upon the hundreds, nay, upon the thousands whom I have around me, who were once the vilest of the vile—drunkards, swearers, and such like—and I now see them " clothed, and in their right mind," walking in holiness and in the fear of God ; and I have said within myself, " This must be the truth, then, because I see its marvelous effects. It is true, because it is efficient for purposes which error never could accomplish. It exerts an influence among the lowest order of mortals, and over the most abominable of our race. It is a power, an irresistible agent of good ; who, then, shall deny its truth? I take it that the highest proof of Christ's power is not that he offers salvation

not that he bids you take it if you will, but that when you reject it, when you hate it, when you despise it, he has a power
whereby he can change your mind, make you think differently
from your former thoughts, and turn you from the error of
your ways. This I conceive to be the meaning of the text.
"mighty to save."

But it is not all the meaning. Our Lord is not only mighty
to make men repent, to quicken the dead in sin, to turn them
from their follies and their iniquities. But he is exalted to do
more than that: he is mighty to keep them Christians after he
has made them so, and mighty to preserve them in his fear
and love, until he consummates their spiritual existence in
heaven. Christ's might doth not lie in making a believer, and
then leaving him to shift for himself afterward; but he who
begins the good work carries it on; he who imparts the first
germ of life which quickens the dead soul, gives afterward the
life which prolongs the divine existence, and bestows that
mighty power which at last bursts asunder every bond of sin,
and lands the soul perfected in glory. We hold and teach,
and, we believe, upon scriptural authority, that all men unto
whom Christ has given repentance, must infallibly hold on
their way. We do believe that God never begins a good
work in a man without finishing it; that he never makes a
man truly alive to spiritual things without carrying on that
work in his soul even to the end, by giving him a place among
the choirs of the sanctified. We do not think that Christ's
power dwells in merely bringing me one day into grace, and
then telling me to keep myself there, but in so putting me into
a gracious state, and giving me such an inward life, and such
a power within myself, that I can no more turn back than the
very sun in the heavens can stay itself in its course, or cease
to shine. Beloved, we regard this as signified by the terms
"mighty to save." This is commonly called Calvinistic doctrine; it is none other than Christian doctrine, the doctrine of
the holy Bible; for despite that it is now called Calvinism, it
could not be so called in Augustine's days; and yet in Augustine's works you find the very same things. And it is not to
be called Augustinism: it is to be found in the writings of the
Apostle Paul. And yet it was not called Paulism, simply for

this reason, that it is the expansion, the fullness of the gospel of our Lord Jesus Christ. To repeat what we have before said, we hold and boldly teach, that Jesus Christ is not merely able to save men who put themselves in his way, and who are willing to be saved, but that he is able to make men willing— that he is able to make the drunkard renounce his drunkenness and come to him—that he is able to make the despiser bend his knee, and make hard hearts melt before his love. Now, it is ours to show that he is able to do so.

II. How can we prove that Christ is "mighty to save?"

We will give you the strongest argument first; and we shall need but one. The argument is, that he *has* done it. We need no other; it were superfluous to add another. He *has* saved men. He has saved them, in the full extent and meaning of the word which we have endeavored to explain. But in order to set this truth in a clear light, we will suppose the worst of cases. It is very easy to imagine, say some, that when Christ's gospel is preached to some here who are amiable and lovely, and have always been trained up in the fear of God, they will receive the gospel in the love of it. Very well, then we will not take such a case. You see this South Sea Islander. He has just been eating a diabolical meal of human flesh ; he is a cannibal; at his belt are slung the scalps of men whom he has murdered, and in whose blood he glories. If you land on the coast he will eat you too, unless you mind what you are after. That man bows himself before a block of wood. He is a poor, ignorant, debased creature, but very little removed from the brute. Now, has Christ's gospel power to tame that man, to take the scalps from his girdle, to make him give up his bloody practices, renounce his gods, and become a civilized and Christian man ? You know, my dear friends, you talk about the power of education in England ; there may be a great deal in it ; education may do very much for some who are here, not in a spiritual, but in a natural way ; but what would education do with this savage : go and try. Send the best schoolmaster in England over to him ; he will eat him before the day is up. That will be all the good of it. But if the missionary goes with Christ's gospel, what will be come of him? Why, in multitudes of cases, he has been the pioneer of civilization, and, under the providence of God, has escaped a cruel death. He goes with love in his hands and in his eyes; he speaks to the savage. And, mark ye, we are telling facts now, not dreams. The savage drops his tomahawk. Says he, "It is marvelous; the things that this man tells me are wonderful; I will sit and listen." He listens, and the tears roll down his cheeks; a feeling of humanity which never burned within his soul before is kindled in him. He says, "I believe in the Lord Jesus Christ;" and soon he is "clothed, and in his right mind," and becomes in every respect a man—such a man as we could desire all men to be. Now, we say that this is a proof that Christ's gospel does not come to the mind that is prepared for it, but prepares the mind for itself; that Christ does not merely put the seed into the ground that has been prepared beforehand, but plows the ground too—ay, and harrows it, and does the whole of the work. He is able to do all this. Ask our missionaries who are in Africa, in the midst of the greatest barbarians in the world—ask them whether Christ's gospel is able to save, and they will point to the kraal of the Hottentot, and then they will point to the houses of the Kuraman, and they will say, "What has made this difference but the word of the gospel of Christ Jesus?" Yes, dear brethren, we have had proofs enough in heathen countries; and why need we say more, but merely to add this—we have had proofs enough at home. There are some who preach a gospel which is very well fitted to train man in morals, but utterly unfitted to save him—a gospel which does well enough to keep men sober when they are so, but not a gospel which makes men sober when they have become drunkards. It is a good thing enough to supply them with a kind of life when they have it already, but not to quicken the dead and save the soul, and it can give up to despair the very characters whom Christ's gospel was most of all intended to affect. I could a tale unfold of some who have plunged head-first into the blackest gulfs of sin, who would horrify you and me, if we could allow them to recount their guilt. I could tell you how they have come into God's house with their teeth set against the minister, determined that, say

what he would, they might listen, but it would be to scoff. **They**
stayed a moment; some word arrested their attention; **they**
thought within themselves, "I will hear that sentence." It
was some pointed, terse saying that entered into their souls.
They knew not how it was, but they were spell-bound, and
stood to listen a little longer; and by-and-by, unconsciously to
themselves, the tears began to fall, and when they went away,
they had a strange, mysterious feeling about them that led
them to their chambers. Down they fell on their knees; the
story of their life was all told before God; he gave them
peace through the blood of the Lamb, and they went to God's
house, many of them to say, " Come and hear what God hath
done for my soul," and to

> " Tell to sinners round
> What a dear Saviour they had found."

Remember the case of John Newton, the great and **mighty**
preacher of St. Mary, Woolnoth—an instance of the power **of**
God to change the heart, as well as to give peace when the
heart is changed.   Ah! dear hearers, I often think within
myself, " This is the greatest proof of the Saviour's power."
Let another doctrine be preached: will it do the same?   If it
will, why not let every man gather a crowd round him and
preach it?   Will it really do it?   If it will, then the blood
of men's souls must rest upon the man who does not boldly
proclaim it.   If he believes his gospel does save souls, how
does he account for it that he stands in his pulpit from the
first of January till the last of December, and never hears of a
harlot made honest, nor of a drunkard reclaimed?   Why?
For this reason, that it is a poor dilution of Christianity.   It is
something like it, but it is not the bold, broad Christianity of
the Bible; it is not the full gospel of the blessed God, for that
has power to save.   But if they do believe that theirs is the
gospel, let them come out to preach it, and let them strive
with all their might to win souls from sin, which is rife enough,
God knows.   We say again, that we have proof positive in
cases even here before us, that Christ is mighty to save **even**
the worst of men—to turn them from follies in which **they**

have too long indulged, and we believe that the same gospel preached elsewhere would produce the same results.

The best proof you can ever have of God's being mighty to save, dear hearers, is that he saved *you*. Ah! my dear hearer, it were a miracle if he should save thy fellow that stands by thy side; but it were more a miracle if he should save thee. What art thou this morning? Answer! "I am an infidel," says one, "I hate and despise Christ's religion." But suppose, sir, there should be such a power in that religion that one day thou'shouldst be brought to believe it! What wouldst thou say then? Ah! I know thou wouldst be in love with that gospel for ever; for thou wouldst say, "I above all men was the last to receive it; and yet here am I, I know not how, brought to love it." O! such a man, when constrained to believe, makes the most eloquent preacher in the world. "Ah! but," says another, "I have been a Sabbath-breaker upon principle; I despise the Sabbath, I hate utterly and entirely every thing religious." Well, I can never prove religion to you to be true, unless it should ever lay hold of you, and make you a new man. Then you will say there is something in it. "We speak that we do know, and testify that we have seen." When we have felt the change it works in ourselves, then we speak of facts, and not of fancies, and we speak very boldly too. We say again, then, he is "mighty to save."

III. But now it is asked, WHY IS CHRIST "MIGHTY TO SAVE?" To this there are sundry answers.

First, if we understand the word "save" in the popular acceptation of the word, which is not, after all, the full one, though a true one—if we understand salvation to mean the pardon of sin and salvation from hell, Christ is mighty to save, *because of the infinite efficacy of his atoning blood.* Sinner! black as thou art with sin, Christ this morning is able to make thee whiter than the driven snow. Thou askest why. I will tell thee. He is able to forgive, because he has been punished for thy sin. If thou dost know and feel thyself to be a sinner, if thou hast no hope or refuge before God but in Christ, then be it known that Christ is able to forgive, because he was once punished for the very sin which thou hast committed, and therefore he can freely remit, because the punish ment has been entirely paid by himself. Whenever I get on this subject I am tempted to tell a story; and though I have told it times enough in the hearing of many of you, others of you have never heard it, and it is the simplest way I know of setting out the belief I have in the atonement of Christ. Once a poor Irishman came to me in my vestry. He announced himself something in this way: "Your riverence, I'm come to ax you a question." "In the first place," said I, "I am not a reverend, nor do I claim the title; and in the next place, why don't you go and ask your priest that question?" Said he, "Well your riv—sir, I meant—I did go to him, but he did not answer me to my satisfaction exactly; so I have come to ask you, and if you will answer this you will set my mind at peace, for I am much disturbed about it." "What is the question?" said I. "Why, this. You say, and others say too, that God is able to forgive sin. Now, I can't see how he can be just, and yet forgive sin: for," said this poor man, "I have been so greatly guilty that if God Almighty does not punish me, *he ought ;* I feel that he would not be just if he were to suffer me to go without punishment. How, then, sir, can it be true that he can forgive, and still retain the title of just?" "Well," said I, "it is through the blood and merits of Jesus Christ." "Ah!" said he, "but then I do not understand what you mean by that. It is the kind of answer I got from the priest, but I wanted him to explain it to me more fully, how it was that the blood of Christ could make God just. You say it does, but I want to know how." "Well, then," said I, "I will tell you what I think to be the whole system of atonement, which I think is the sum and substance, the root, the marrow, and the essence of all the gospel. This is the way Christ is able to forgive. Suppose," said I, "you had killed some one. You were a murderer; you were condemned to die, and you deserved it." "Faith," said he, "yes, I should deserve it." "Well, her majesty is very desirous of saving your life, and yet at the same time universal justice demands that some one should die on account of the deed that is done. Now, how is she to manage?" Said he, "That is the question. I can not see how she can be inflexibly just, and yet suffer me to escape." "Well," said I, "suppose, Pat, I should go to her, and say, ' Here is this poor Irishman, he deserves to be hanged, your majesty; I don't want to quarrel with the sentence, because I think it just: but, if you please, I so love him that if you were to hang me instead of him I should be very willing.' Pat, suppose she should agree to it, and hang me instead of you: what then? would she be just in letting you go?" "Ay," said he, "I should think she would. Would she hang two for one thing? I should say not. I'd walk away, and there isn't a policeman that would touch me for it." "Ah," said I, "that is how Jesus saves. 'Father,' he said, I love these poor sinners: let me suffer instead of them!' ' Yes,' said God, 'thou shalt,' and on the tree he died, and suffered the punishment which all his elect people ought to have suffered; so that now all who believe on him, thus proving themselves to be his chosen, may conclude that he was punished for them, and that therefore they never can be punished." "Well," said he, looking me in the face once more, "I understand what you mean; but how is it, if Christ died for all men, that, notwithstanding, some men are punished again? For that is unjust." "Ah!" said I, "I never told you that. I say to you that he has died for all who believe in him, and all who repent, and that he was punished for their sins so absolutely and so really, that none of them shall ever be punished again." "Faith," said the man, clapping his hands, " that's the gospel; if it isn't, then I don't know anything, for no man could have made that up: it is so wonderful Ah!" he said, as he went down the stairs, "Pat's safe now; with all his sins about him he'll trust in the man that died for him, and so he shall be saved." Dear hearer, Christ is mighty to save, because God did not turn away the sword, but he sheathed it in his own Son's heart; he did not remit the debt, for it was paid in drops of precious blood; and now the great receipt is nailed to the cross, and our sins with it, so that we may go free if we are believers in him. For this reason he is " mighty to save," in the true sense of the word.

But in the large sense of the word, understanding it to mean all that I have said it does mean, he is " mighty to save." How is it that Christ is able to make men repent, to make men believe, and to make them turn to God? One answers,

" Why, by the eloquence of preachers." God forbid we should ever say that! It is "not by might nor by power." Others reply, "It is by the force of moral suasion." God forbid we should say "ay" to that; for moral suasion has been tried long enough on man, and yet it has failed of success. How does he do it? We answer, by something which some of you despise, but which nevertheless is a fact. He does it by the omnipotent influence of his divine Spirit. While men are hearing the word (in those whom God will save) the Holy Spirit works repentance; he changes the heart and renews the soul. True, the preaching is the instrument, but the Holy Spirit is the great agent. It is certain that the truth is the means of saving, but it is the Holy Ghost applying the truth which saves souls. Ah! and with this power of the Holy Ghost we may go to the most debased and degraded of men, and we need not be afraid but that God can save them. If God should please, the Holy Spirit could at this moment make every one of you fall on your knees, confess your sins, and turn to God. He is an Almighty Spirit, able to do wonders. In the life of Whitefield, we read that sometimes under one of his sermons two thousand persons would at once profess to be saved, and were really so, many of them. We ask why it was? At other times he preached just as powerfully, and not one soul was saved. Why? Because in the one case the Holy Spirit went with the word, and in the other case it did not. All the heavenly result of preaching is owing to the divine Spirit sent from above. I am nothing; my brethren in the ministry around are all nothing; it is God that doeth every thing. "Who is Paul, who is Apollos, and who is Cephas, but ministers by whom ye believed, even as God gave to every man." It must be "not by might, nor by power, but by my Spirit, saith the Lord." Go forth, poor minister! Thou hast no power to preach with polished diction and elegant refinement; go and preach as thou canst. The Spirit can make thy feeble words more mighty than the most ravishing eloquence. Alas! alas! for oratory! Alas! for elo-quence! It hath long enough been tried. We have had polished periods, and finely-turned sentences; but in what place have the people been saved by them? We have had

grand and gaudy language; but where have hearts been re‑
newed? But now, "by the foolishness of preaching," by the
simple utterance by a child of God's Word, he is pleased to
save them that believe, and to save sinners from the error of
their ways. May God prove his word again this morning!

IV. The fourth point was, WHAT ARE THE INFERENCES TO
BE DERIVED FROM THE FACT THAT JESUS CHRIST IS MIGHTY TO
SAVE?

Why, first, there is a fact for ministers to learn—that they
should endeavor to preach in faith, nothing wavering. "O
God," cries the minister at times, when he is on his knees, "I
am weak; I have preached to my hearers, and have wept over
them; I have groaned for them; but they will not turn to
thee. Their hearts are like the nether mill-stone; they will
not weep for sin, nor will they love the Saviour." Then I
think I see the angel standing at his elbow, and whispering in
his ear, "Thou art weak, but he is strong; thou canst do
nothing, but he is 'mighty to save.'" Bethink thyself of this.
It is not the instrument, but the God. It is not the pen
wherewith the author writes which is to have the praise of his
wisdom or the making of the volume, but it is the brain that
thinks it, and the hand that moves the pen. So in salvation.
It is not the minister, it is not the preacher, but the God who
first designs the salvation, and afterward uses the preacher to
work it out. Ah! poor disconsolate preacher, if thou hast had
but little fruit of thy ministry, go on still in faith, remember‑
ing it is written, "My word shall not return unto me void, but
it shall accomplish that which I please, and prosper in the
thing whereto I sent it." Go on; be of good courage; God
shall help thee; he shall help thee, and that right early.

Again, here is another encouragement for praying men and
women, who are praying to God for their friends. Mother,
you have been groaning for your son for many a year; he is
now grown up, and has left your roof, but your prayers have
not been heard. So you think. He is as gay as ever; not
yet has he made your breast rejoice. Sometimes you think he
will bring your gray hairs with sorrow to the grave. It was
but yesterday you said, "I will give him up, I will never pray
for him again." Stop, mother, stop! By all that is holy and

that is heavenly, stop! Utter not that resolution again; begin once more! Thou hast prayed over him; thou didst weep
over his infant forehead, when he lay in his cradle; thou didst
teach him when he came to years of understanding, and thou
hast often warned him since; but all of no avail. O! give not
up thy prayers; for remember, Christ is "mighty to save."
It may be that he waits to be gracious, and he keeps thee waiting, that thou mayest know more of his graciousness when the
mercy comes. But pray on. I have heard of mothers who
have prayed for their children twenty years; ay, and of some
who have died without seeing them converted, and then their
very death has been the means of saving their children, by
leading them to think. A father once had been a pious man
for many years, yet never had he the happiness of seeing one
of his sons converted. He had his children round his bed, and
he said to them when dying, "My sons, I could die in peace
if I could but believe you would follow me to heaven; but this
is the most sorrowful thing of all—not that I am dying, but
that I am leaving you to meet you no more." They looked
at him, but they would not weep, nor would they think on
their ways. They went away. Their father was sudden'y
overtaken with great clouds and darkness of mind; instead of
dying peacefully and happily, he died in great misery of soul,
but still trusting in Christ. He said, when he died, " O that
I had died a happy death, for that would have been a testimony to my sons; but now, O God, this darkness and these
clouds have in some degree taken away my power to witness
to the truth of thy religion." Well, he died, and was buried.
The sons came to the funeral. The day after, one of them
said to his brother, "Brother, I have been thinking, father
was always a pious man, and if his death was yet such a gloomy
one, how gloomy must ours be, without God and without
Christ." "Ah!" said the other, "that thought struck me
too." They went up to God's house, heard God's word, they
came home and bent their knee in prayer, and to their surprise
they found that the rest of the family had done the same, and
that the God who had never answered the father's prayer in
his life had answered it after his death, and by his death too,
and by such a death as would appear to be most unlikely to have

wrought the conversion of any. Pray on, then, my sister;
pray on, my brother! God shall yet bring thy sons and
daughters to his love and fear, and thou shalt rejoice over
them in heaven, if thou never dost on earth.

And finally, my dear hearers, there are many of you here
this morning who have no love to God, no love to Christ; but
you have a desire in your hearts to love him. You are saying, "O! can he save me? Can such a wretch as I be saved?"
In the thick of the crowd there you are standing, and you are
now saying within yourself, " May I one day sing among the
saints above? May I have all my sins blotted out by blood
divine?" Yes, sinner, he is "mighty to save;" and this is
comfort for thee. Dost thou think thyself the worst of men?
Does conscience smite thee as with a mailed fist, and does he
say it is all over with thee; thou wilt be lost; thy repentance
will be of no avail; thy prayers never will be heard; thou art
lost to all intents and purposes? My hearer, think not so.
He is "mighty to save." If thou canst not pray, he can help
thee to do it; if thou canst not repent, he can give thee repentance; if thou feelest it hard to believe, he can help thee
to believe, for he is exalted on high to give repentance, as
well as to give remission of sins. O poor sinner, trust in Jesus;
cast thyself on him. Cry, and may God help thee to do it
now. May he help thee this very day to cast thy soul on
Jesus; and this will be one of the best years of all thy life.
"Turn ye, turn ye; why will ye die, O house of Israel?"
Turn unto Jesus, ye wearied souls; come unto him, for lo! he
bids you come. " The Spirit and the bride say, Come; and let
him that heareth say, Come; and whosoever will, let him come
and take of the water of life," and have Christ's grace freely.
It is preached to you, and to all of you who are willing to receive it, it has been already given.

May God of his grace make you willing, and so save your
souls, through Jesus Christ our Lord and Saviour!   Amen.

SERMON XXVIII

ISRAEL IN EGYPT

"And they sing the song of Moses the servant of God, and the song of the Lamb, saying, Great and marvelous are thy works, Lord God Almighty; just and true are thy ways, thou King of saints."—REV., xv. 3

AT the outset, let us remark the carefulness of the Holy Spirit in guarding the honor of our blessed Lord. This verse is often quoted as if it runs thus—"They sing the song of Moses and the Lamb." This mistake has led many weak minds to wonder at the expression, for they have imagined that it divided the honor of the song of heaven between Moses and the Redeemer. The clause—"the servant of God"—is doubtless inserted by the Holy Spirit to prevent any error upon this point, and therefore it should be carefully included in the quotation. I take it that the song of Moses is here united with the song of the Lamb, because the one was a type and picture of the other. The glorious overthrow of Pharaoh in the Red Sea shadowed forth the total destruction of Satan and all his host in the day of the great battle of the Lord; and there was in the song of Moses the expression of the same feelings of triumph which will pervade the breasts of the redeemed when they shall triumph with their Captain.

May God the Holy Spirit enable me to *exhibit the parallel which exists between the condition of Israel when passing through the sea, and the position of the church of Christ at the present day.* Next, we shall *compare the triumph of the Lord at the Red Sea with the victory of the Lamb in the great and terrible day of the Lord.* And lastly, I shall *point out certain prominent features of the song of Moses, which will doubtless be as prominent in the song of the Lamb.*

I. First, it is our business to regard THE POSITION OF THE CHILDREN OF ISRAEL AS EMBLEMATICAL OF OUR OWN. And here we observe that, like the church of God, the vast host of Israel had been delivered from bondage. We, my brethren, who constitute a part of the Israel of God, were once the slaves of sin and Satan; we served with hard bondage and rigor while in our natural state; no bondage was ever more terrible than ours; we indeed made bricks without straw, and labored in the very fire; but by the strong hand of God we have been delivered. We have come forth from the prison-house; with joy we beheld ourselves emancipated—the Lord's free men. The iron yoke is taken from our necks; we no longer serve our lusts, and pay obedience to the tyrant sin. With a high hand and an outstretched arm, our God has led us forth from the place of our captivity, and joyfully we pursue our way through the wilderness.

But with the children of Israel it was not all joy; they were free, but their master was at their heels. Pharaoh was loth to lose so valuable a nation of servants; and therefore with his chosen captains, his horsemen, and his chariots, he pursued them in angry haste. Affrighted Israel beheld her infuriated oppressor close at her rear, and trembled for the issue —the hearts of the people failed them while they saw their hopes blighted and their joys ended by the approach of the oppressor; even so it is with some of you; you think you must be driven back again like dumb cattle, into Egypt, and once more become what you were. "Surely," you say, "I can not hold on my way with such a host seeking to drive me back; I must again become the slave of my iniquities." And thus dreading apostacy, and feeling that you would rather die than become what you were: you this morning are filled with trepidation. You are saying, "Alas for me! Better that I had died in Egypt than that I should have come out into this wilderness to be again captured." You have tasted for a moment the joys of holiness and the sweets of liberty; and now again to go back to endure the bondage of a spiritual Egypt, would be worse than before. This is the position of the sacramental host of God's elect; they have come out of Egypt, and they are pursuing their way to Canaan. But the world is against them ; the kings of the earth stand up, and the rulers take counsel together against the Lord and against his people saying, " Let us scatter them ; let us utterly destroy them." From the fiery days of the stakes of Smithfield even until now, the world's black heart has hated the church, and the world's cruel hand and laughing lip have been for ever against us. The host of the mighty are pursuing us, and are thirsty for our blood, and anxious to cut us off from the earth. Such is our position unto this hour, and such must it be until we are landed on the other side of Jordan, and until our Maker comes to reign on the earth.

But once more : the children of Israel were in a position more wonderful than this. They came to the edge of the Red Sea ; they feared their enemies behind ; they could not fly on either hand, for they were flanked by mountains and stupendous rocks; one course only was open to them, and that course was through the sea. God commands them to go forward. The rod of Moses is outstretched, and the affrighted waters divide ; a channel is left while the floods stand upright, and the waters are congealed in the heart of the sea. The priests, bearing the ark, march forward ; the whole host of Israel follow. And now behold the wondrous pilgrimage. A wall of alabaster is on either side, and myriads are in the pebbly depths. Like a wall of glass the sea stands on either side of them, frowning with beetling cliffs of foam ; but still on they march ; and until the last of God's Israel is safe the water stands still and firm, frozen by the lips of God. Such, my hearers, is the position of God's church now. You and I are marching through a sea, the floods of which are kept upright only by the sovereign power of God. This world is a world which is suddenly to be destroyed; and our position in it is just the position of the children of Israel, for whose sake the floods refused to meet until they were safely landed. O church of God ! thou art the salt of the earth : when thou art removed this earth must putrify and decay. O living army of the living God ! ye, like Israel, keep the floods of providence still standing fast ; but when the last of you shall be gone from this stage of action, God's fiery wrath and tremendous anger shall dash down upon the ground whereon you now are standing, and your enemies shall be overwhelmed in the place through which you now walk safely. Let me put my thoughts as plainly as I can. Naturally, according to the common order, the Red Sea should have flowed on in a level and even manner, constant in its waves, and unbroken in its surface. By the might of God the Red Sea was divided into two parts, and the floods stood back. Now mark. Naturally, according to the common course of justice, this world, which groaneth and travaileth until now, ought, if we only consider the wicked, to be utterly destroyed. The only reason why the Red Sea afforded a safe passage for the host was this—that Israel marched through it ; and the only reason why this world stands, and the only reason why it is not destroyed by fire, as it is to be at the last great day, is because God's Israel are in it ; but when once they shall have passed through, the parted floods shall meet their hands, and embrace with eager joy to clasp the adverse host within their arms. The day is coming when this world shall reel to and fro and stagger like a drunken man. Every Christian may say, with due reverence to God, "The earth is dissolved ; I bear up the pillars thereof." Let all the Christians that are in the world die, and the pillars of the earth would fall, and like a wreck and a vision all this universe of ours would pass away, never to be seen again. We are to-day, I say, passing through the floods, with enemies behind, pursuing us who are going out of Egypt up to Canaan.

II. And now the TRIUMPH OF MOSES was a picture of the ultimate triumph of the Lamb. Moses sang a song unto the Lord by the sea of Egypt. If you will turn to holy Scripture you will find that my text was sung by the holy spirits who had been preserved from sin and from the contamination of the beast ; and it is said that they sung this song upon "a sea of glass mingled with fire." Now the song of Moses was sung by the side of a sea, which was glassy, and still ; for a little season the floods had been disturbed, divided, separated, congealed, but in a few moments afterward, when Israel had safely passed the flood, they became as glassy as ever, for the enemy had sunken to the bottom like a stone, and the sea returned to its strength when the morning appeared. Is there ever a time, then, when this great sea of Providence, which now stands parted to give a passage to God's saints shall become a level surface ? Is there a day when the now divided dispensations of God, which are kept from following out their legitimate tendency to do justice upon sin—when the two seas of justice shall commingle, and the one sea of God's prov idence shall be " a sea of glass mingled with fire ?" Yes, the day is drawing nigh when God's enemies shall no longer make it necessary for God's providence to be apparently disturbed to save his people, when the great designs of God shall be accomplished, and therefore when the walls of water shall roll together, while in their inmost depths the everlasting burning fire shall still consume the wicked. O, the sea shall be calm upon the surface ; the sea upon which God's people shall walk shall seem to be a sea that is clear, without a weed, without an impurity ; while down in its hollow bosom, far beyond all mortal ken, shall be the horrid depths where the wicked must for ever dwell in the fire which is mingled with the glass

Well, I now want to show you why it was that Moses triumphed, and why it is that by-and-by we shall triumph. One reason why Moses sung his song was because *all* Israel were safe. They were all safely across the sea. Not a drop of spray fell from that solid wall until the last of God's Israel had safely planted his foot on the other side of the flood. That done, immediately the floods dissolved into their proper place again, but not till then. Part of that song was, " Thou hast led thy people like a flock through the wilderness." Now, in the last time, when Christ shall come upon earth, the great song will be—" Lord, thou hast saved thy people ; thou hast led them all safely through the paths of providence, and not one of them has fallen into the hands of the enemy." O, it is my strong belief, that in heaven there shall not be a vacant throne. I rejoice that all who love the Lord below must at last attain to heaven. I do not believe with some that men may start on the road to heaven, and be saved, and yet fall by the hand of the enemy. God forbid, my friends !

> " All the chosen race
> Shall meet around the throne,
> Shall bless the conduct of his grace,
> And make his glories known."

Part of the triumph of heaven will be, that there is not one throne that is unoccupied. As many as God hath chosen, as many as Christ hath redeemed, as many as the Spirit hath called, as many as believe, shall arrive safe across the stream. We are not all safely landed yet:

> "Part of the host have crossed the flood,
>   And part are crossing now."

The vanguard of the army have already reached the shore. I see them yonder;

> "I greet the blood-besprinkled bands
>   Upon th' eternal shore."

And you and I, my brethren, are marching through the depths. We are at this day following hard after Christ, and walking through the wilderness. Let us be of good cheer: the rearguard shall soon be where the vanguard already is; the last of the chosen shall soon have landed; the last of God's elect shall have crossed the sea, and then shall be heard the song of triumph, when all are secure. But O! if one were absent—O! if one of his chosen family should be cast away—it would make an everlasting discord in the song of the redeemed, and cut the strings of the harps of Paradise, so that music could never be distilled from them again.

But, perhaps, the major part of the joy of Moses lay in the destruction of *all* the enemies of God. He looked upon his people the day before.

> "He looked upon his people,
>   And the tear was in his eye;
> He looked upon the foeman,
>   And his glance was stern and high."

And now to-day he looks upon his people, and he says, " Blessed art thou, O Israel, safely landed on the shore;" and he looks not upon the foeman, but upon the foeman's tomb he looks where the living were protected by the shield of God from all their enemies; and he sees—what? A mighty sepulcher of water; a mighty tomb in which were engulfed princes, monarchs, potentates. " The horse and his rider hath he thrown into the sea." Pharaoh's chariots also are drowned therein. And soon, my hearers, you and I shall do the same. I say that now we have to look abroad on hosts of enemies. What with the wild beasts of Rome, what with the antichrist of Mohammed, what with the thousands of idolatries and false gods, what with infidelity in all its myriad shapes, many are the enemies of God, and mighty are the hosts of hell. Lo, you see them gathered together this day; horseman upon horseman, chariot upon chariot, gathered together against the Most High. I see the trembling church, fearing to be overthrown; I mark her leaders bending their knees in solemn prayer, and crying, "Lord, save thy people, and bless thy heritage." But mine eye looks through the future with telescopic glance, and I see the happy period of the latter days, when Christ shall reign triumphant. I shall ask them where is Babel? where is Rome? where is Mohammed? and the answer shall come—where? Why they have sunk into the depths; they have sunk to the bottom as a stone. Down there the horrid fire devours them, for the sea of glass is mingled with the fire of judgment. To-day I see a battle-field · the whole earth is torn by the hoofs of horses; there is the rumble of cannon and the roll of drum. "To arms! to arms!" both hosts are shouting. But you wait awhile, and you shall walk across this plain of battle, and say, "Seest thou that colosal system of error dead? There lies another, all frozen, in ghastly death, in motionless stupor. There lieth infidelity; there sleepeth secularism and the secularist; there lie those who defied God. I see all this vast host of rebels lying scattered upor the earth. "Sing unto the Lord, for he hath triumphed gloriously; Jehovah has gotten unto himself the victory, and the last of his enemies are destroyed." Then shall be the time when shall be sung "the song of Moses and of the Lamb."

III. Now, turning to the song of Moses, I shall conclude my address to you by noticing some interesting particulars in the song which will doubtless have a place in the everlasting orchestra of the redeemed, when they shall praise the Most High. O! my brethren, I could but wish that I had stood by the Red Sea, to have heard that mighty shout, and that tre-

mendous roar of acclamation!   Methinks one might well have
borne a servitude in Egypt, to have stood in that mighty host
who sung such mighty praise.   Music hath charms; but never
had it such charms as it had that day when fair Miriam led the
women, and Moses led the men, like some mighty leader, beating time with his hand.   "Sing unto the Lord, for he hath
done gloriously."   Methinks I see the scene; and I anticipate
the greater day, when the song shall be sung again, "as the
song of Moses and of the Lamb."

Now, just notice this song.   In the 15th chapter of Exodus
you find it, and in divers of the Psalms you will see it ampli-
fied.   The first thing I would have you notice in it is, that
from beginning to end it is *a praise of God*, and of nobody
else but God.   Moses, thou hast said nothing of thyself.   O
great lawgiver, mightiest of men, did not thine hand grasp the
mighty rod that split the sea—that burned its fair breast, and
left a scar for awhile upon its bosom?   Didst not thou lead
the hosts of Israel?   Didst not thou marshal their thousands
for battle, and like a mighty commander led them through
the depths?   Is there not a word for thee?   Not one.   The
whole strain of the song is, "I will sing unto the Lord," from
beginning to end.   It is all praise of Jehovah; there is not
one word about Moses, nor a single word in praise of the
children of Israel.   Dear friends, the last song in this world,
the song of triumph, shall be full of God, and of no one else
Here you praise the instrument; to-day you look on this man
and on that, and you say, "Thank God for this minister, and
for this man?"   To-day you say, "Blessed be God for Luther
who shook the Vatican, and thank God for Whitefield, who
stirred up a slumbering church;" but in that day you shall
not sing of Luther, nor of Whitefield, nor of any of the
mighty ones of God's hosts; forgotten shall their names be
for a season, even as the stars refuse to shine when the sun
himself appeareth.   The song shall be unto Jehovah, and
Jehovah only; we shall not have a word to say for preachers nor bishops, not a syllable to say for good men and
true; but the whole song from first to last shall be, "Unto
him that loved us, and hath washed us from our sins in his own
blood, unto him be glory for ever and ever.   Amen."

And next will you please to note, that this song celebrated something of *the fierceness of the enemy !* Do you observe how, when the songster describes the attack of Pharaoh, he says, "The enemy said, I will pursue, I will overtake, I will divide the spoil; my lust shall be satisfied upon them; I will draw my sword, my hand shall destroy them." A song is made out of the wrath of Pharaoh. And it shall be so at the last. The wrath of man shall praise God. I believe the last song of the redeemed, when they shall ultimately triumph, will celebrate in heavenly stanzas the wrath of man overcome by God. Sometimes after great battles, monuments are raised to the memory of the fight; and of what are they composed? They are composed of weapons of death and of instruments of war which have been taken from the enemy. Now, to use that illustration as I think it may be properly used, the day is coming when fury, and wrath, and hatred, and strife, shall all be woven into a song; and the weapons of our enemies, when taken from them, shall serve to make monuments to the praise of God. Rail on, rail on, blasphemer! Smite on, smite on, tyrant! Lift thy heavy hand, O despot; crush the truth, which yet thou canst not crush; knock from his head the crown—the crown that is far above thy reach—poor puny impotent mortal as thou art! Go on, go on! But all thou doest shall but increase his glories. For aught we care, we bid you still proceed with all your wrath and malice. Though it shall be worse for you, it shall be more glorious for our Master; the greater your preparations for war, the more splendid shall be his triumphal chariot, when he shall ride through the streets of heaven in pompous array. The more mighty your preparations for battle, the more rich the spoil which he shall divide with the strong. O! Christian, fear not the foe! Remember the harder his blows, the sweeter thy song; the greater his wrath, the more splendid thy triumph; the more he rages, the more shall Christ be honored in the day of his appearing. They sung the song of Moses and the Lamb.

And then will ye note, in the next place, how they sang *the total overthrow* of the enemy. There is one expression in this song, which ought to be and I believe is, when set to music,

very frequently repeated. It is that part of the song, as recorded in the Psalms, where it is declared that the whole host
of Pharaoh were utterly destroyed, and there was not one of
them left. When that great song was sung by the side of
the Red Sea, there was, no doubt, a special emphasis laid upon
that expression, "not one."   I think I hear the hosts of Israel
When the words were known by them, they began and they
proceeded thus—"There is not one of them left;" and then
in various parts the words were repeated, "Not one, not one."
And then the women with their sweet voices sang, "Not one,
not one." I believe that at the last, a part of our triumph
will be the fact, that there is not one left. We shall look
abroad throughout the earth, and see it all a level sea; and
not one foeman pursuing us—"not one, not one!" Raise
myself never so high, O thou deceiver, thou canst not live;
for not one shall escape. Lift thy head never so proudly, O
despot, thou canst not live; for not one shall escape. O heir
of heaven, not one sin shall cross the Jordan after thee; not
one shall pass the Red Sea to overtake thee; but this shall be
the summit of thy triumph—"Not one, not one! not one of
them is left."

Just let us note again, and I will not detain you too long,
lest I weary you. One part of the song of Moses consisted in
praising the ease with which God destroyed his enemies.
"Thou didst blow with thy wind, the sea covered them; they
sank as lead in the mighty waters." If *we* had gone to work
to destroy the hosts of Pharaoh, what a multitude of engines
of death should we have required. If the work had been committed to us, to cut off the hosts, what marvelous preparations,
what thunder, what noise, what great activity there would
have been. But mark the grandeur of the expression. God
did not even lift himself from his throne to do it: he saw
Pharaoh coming; he seemed to look upon him with a placid
smile; he did just blow with his lips, and the sea covered them.
You and I will marvel at the last how easy it has been to overthrow the enemies of the Lord. We have been tugging and
toiling all our life-time to be the means of overthrowing sys-
tems of error; it will astonish the church, when her Master
shall come, to see how, as the ice dissolveth before the fire, all

error and sin shall be utterly destroyed in the coming of the Most High. We must have our societies and our machinery, our preachings and our gatherings, and rightly too; but God will not require them at the last. The destruction of his enemies shall be as easy to him as the making of a world. In passive silence unmoved he sat; and he did but break the silence with "Let there be light; and light was." So shall he at the last, when his enemies are raging furiously, blow with his winds, and they shall be scattered; they shall melt even as wax, and shall be burned like tow; they shall be as the fat of rams; into smoke shall they consume, yea, into smoke shall they consume away.

Furthermore, in this song of Moses, you will notice there is one peculiar beauty. Moses not only rejoiced for what had been done, but for the future consequences of it. He says, "The people of Canaan, whom we are about to attack, will now be seized with sudden fear; by the greatness of thy arm they shall be as still as a stone." O! I think I hear them singing that too, sweetly and softly, "as still as a stone." How would the words come full, like gentle thunder heard in the distance, "as still as a stone!" And when we shall get on the other side the flood, see the triumph over our enemies, and behold our Master reigning, this will form a part of our song, that they must henceforth be "as still as a stone." There will be a hell, but it will not be a hell of roaring devils, as it now is. They shall be "as still as a stone." There will be legions of fallen angels, but they shall no longer have courage to attack us or defy God: they shall be "as still as a stone." O how grand will that sound, when the hosts of God's redeemed, looking down on the demons chained, bound, silenced, struck dumb with terror, shall sing exultingly over them! They must be "as still as a stone;" and there they must lie, and bite their iron bands. The fierce despiser of Christ can no more spit in his face; the proud tyrant can no more lift his hands to oppress the saints; even Satan can no more attempt to destroy. They shall be "as still as a stone."

And last of all, the song concludes by noticing *the eternity of God's reign;* and this will always make a part of the triumphant song. They sang, "The Lord shall reign for ever and ever." Then I can suppose the whole band broke out into their loudest strain of music. "The Lord shall reign for ever and ever." Part of the melody of heaven will be "The Lord shall reign for ever and ever." That song has cheered us here, "The Lord reigneth ; blessed be my Rock !" And that song shall be our exultation there. "The Lord reigneth for ever and ever." When we shall see the placid sea of providence, when we shall behold the world all fair and lovely, when we shall mark our enemies destroyed, and God Almighty triumphant, then we shall shout the song,

> "Hallelujah ! for the Lord
> God Omnipotent shall reign ;
> Hallelujah ! let the word
> Echo round the earth and main."

O ! may we be there to sing it !

I have one remark to make, and I have done. You know, my friends, that as there is something in the song of Moses which is typical of the song of the Lamb, there was another song sung by the waters of the Red Sea which is typical of the song of hell. "What mean you, sir, by that dread thought ?" O ! shall I use the word music ? Shall I profane the heavenly word so much as to say, 'twas doleful music which came from the lips of Pharaoh and his host ? Boldly and pompously, with roll of drum and blast of trumpet they had entered into the sea. On a sudden their martial music ceased ; and ah ! ye heavens and ye floods what was it ? The sea was coming down upon them, utterly to devour them. O ! may we never hear that shriek, that awful yell of hideous agony, that seemed to rend the sky, and then was hushed again, when Pharaoh and his mighty men were swallowed up, and went down quick into hell ! Ah ! stars, if ye had heard it, if the black pall of waters had not shut out the sound from you, ye might have continued trembling unto this hour, and mayhap ye are trembling now ; mayhap your twinklings by night are on account of that terrible shriek ye heard ; for sure it were enough to make you tremble on for ever. That dreadful shriek, that hideous moan, that horrible howl, when a whole army sank into hell at once, when the waters swallowed them up !

Take heed, my friends, take heed, lest you should have to join in that terrible *miserere ;* take heed, less that horrible howl should be yours, instead of the song of the redeemed. And remember, so must it be, unless ye be born again, unless ye believe in Christ, unless ye repent of sin and renounce it wholly, and with trembling hearts put your confidence in the man of sorrows, who is soon to be crowned the King of kings and Lord of lords. May God bless you, and give you all to taste of his salvation, that you may stand upon the sea of glass, and not have to feel the terrors of the mingled fire in the lower depths thereof! God Almighty bless this vast assembly, for Jesus' sake.

SERMON XXIX

PRESUMPTUOUS SINS

"**Keep** back thy servant also from presumptuous sins."—PSALM xix. 13

ALL sins are great sins, but yet some sins are greater than others. Every sin has in it the very venom of rebellion, and is full of the essential marrow of traitorous rejection of God. But there be some sins which have in them a greater development of the essential mischief of rebellion, and which wear upon their faces more of the brazen pride which defies the Most High. It is wrong to suppose that because all sins will condemn us, that therefore one sin is not greater than another. The fact is, that while all transgression is a greatly grievous sinful thing, yet there are some transgressions which have a deeper shade of blackness, and a more double scarlet-dyed hue of criminality than others. Now the presumptuous sins of our text are just the chief of all sins: they rank head and foremost in the list of iniquities. It is remarkable, that though an atonement was provided under the Jewish law for every kind of sin, there was this one exception: "But the soul that sinneth presumptuously shall have no atonement; it shall be cut off from the midst of my people." And now, under the Christian dispensation, although in the sacrifice of our blessed Lord there is a great and precious atonement for presumptuous sins, whereby sinners who have sinned in this manner are made clean, yet, without doubt, presumptuous sinners, dying without pardon, must expect to receive a double portion of the wrath of God, and a more wonderful manifestation of the unutterable anguish of the torment of eternal punishment in the pit that is digged for the wicked.

I shall this morning, first of all, endeavor to *describe presumptuous sins;* then, secondly, I shall try, if I can, to *show,*

*by some illustrations, why the presumptuous sin is mor. ein-
ous than any other;* and then thirdly, I shall try to *press the
prayer upon your notice*—the prayer, mark you, of the holy
man—the prayer of David : "Keep back thy servant also
from presumptuous sins "

I. First, then, WHAT IS A PRESUMPTUOUS SIN? Now, I think
there must be one of four things in a sin in order to make it
presumptuous.   It must either be a sin against light and
knowledge, or a sin committed with deliberation, or a sin
committed with a design of sinning, merely for sinning's sake,
or else it must be a sin committed through hardihood, from a
man's rash confidence in his own strength.   We will mark
these points one by one.

1. A sin that is *committed willfully against manifest light
and knowledge* is a presumptuous sin.   A sin of ignorance is
not presumptuous, unless that ignorance also be willful, in
which case the ignorance itself is a presumptuous sin.   But
when a man sins for want of knowing better—for want of
knowing the law, for want of instruction, reproof, advice, and
admonition, we say that his sin, so committed, does not partake to any great extent of the nature of a presumptuous sin.
But when a man knows better, and sins in the very teeth and
face of his increased light and knowledge, then his sin deserves
to be branded with this ignominious title of a presumptuous
sin.   Let me just dwell on this thought a moment.   *Conscience*
is often an inner light to men, whereby they are warned of
forbidden acts as being sinful.   Then if I sin against conscience,
though I have no greater light than conscience affords me,
still my sin is presumptuous, if I have presumed to go against
that voice of God in my heart, an enlightened conscience.
You, young man, were once tempted (and perhaps it was but
yesterday) to commit a certain act.   The very moment you
were tempted, conscience said, " It is wrong, it is wrong"—
it shouted *murder* in your heart, and told you the deed you
were about to commit was abominable in the sight of the
Lord.   Your fellow-apprentice committed the same sin without the warning of conscience ; in him it was guilt—guilt
which needs to be washed away with the Saviour's blood.   But
it was not such guilt in him as it was in you, beca se your

conscience checked you; your conscience told you of the danger, warned you of the punishment, and yet you dared to go astray against God, and therefore you sinned presumptuously. You have sinned very grievously in having done so. When a man shall trespass on my ground, he shall be a trespasser though he have no warning, but if straight before his face there stands a warning, and if he knowingly and willingly trespasses, then he is guilty of a presumptuous trespass, and is to be so far punished accordingly. So you, if you had not known better; if your conscience had been less enlightened, you might have committed the deed with far less of the criminality which now attaches to you, because you sinned against conscience, and consequently sinned presumptuously.

But, O! how much greater is the sin, when man not only has the light of conscience, but has also *the admonition of friends*, the advice of those who are wise and esteemed by him. If I have but one check, the check of my enlightened conscience, and I transgress against it, I am presumptuous; but if a mother with tearful eye warns me of the consequence of my guilt, and if a father with steady look, and with affectionate determined earnestness, tells me what will be the effect of my transgression—if friends who are dear to me counsel me to avoid the way of the wicked, and warn me what must be the inevitable result of continuing in it, then I am presumptuous, and my act in that very proportion becomes more guilty. I should have been presumptuous for having sinned against the light of nature, but I am more presumptuous when, added to that, I have the light of affectionate counsel and of kind advice, and therein I bring upon my head a double amount of divine wrath. And how much more is this the case, when the transgressor has been gifted with what is usually called a religious education; in childhood he has been lighted to his bed by the lamps of the sanctuary, the name of Jesus was mingled with the hush of lullaby, the music of the sanctuary woke him like a matin hymn at morning; he has been dandled on the knee of piety and has sucked the breasts of godliness; he has been tutored and trained in the way he should go; how much more fearful I say, is the guilt of such a man than that of those who have never had such training, but have been left to follow their own wayward lusts and pleasures without the restraint of a holy education and the restraints of an enlightened conscience!

But, my friends, even this may become worse still. A man sins yet more presumptuously, *when he has had most special warning from the voice of God against the sin.* "What mean you?" say you. Why, I mean this. You saw but yesterday a strong man in your neighborhood brought to the grave by sudden death; it is but a month ago that you heard the bell toll for one whom once you knew and loved, who procrastinated and procrastinated until he perished in procrastination. You have had strange things happen in your very street, and the voice of God has been spoken loudly through the lips of Death to you. Ay, and you have had warnings too in your own body; you have been sick with fever, you have been brought to the jaws of the grave, and you have looked down into the bottomless vault of destruction. It is not long ago since you were given up; all said they might prepare a coffin for you, for your breath could not long be in your body. Then you turned your face to the wall, and prayed; you vowed that if God would spare you you would live a godly life, that you would repent of your sins; but to your own confusion you are now just what you were. Ah! let me tell you, your guilt is more grievous than that of any other man, for you have sinned presumptuously, in the very highest sense in which you could have done so. You have sinned against reproofs, but what is worse still, you have sinned against your own solemn oaths and covenants, and against the promises that you made to God. He who plays with fire must be condemned as careless; but he who has been burned out once, and afterward plays with the destroying element, is worse than careless; and he who has himself been scorched in the flame, and has had his locks all hot and crisp with the burning, if he again should rush headlong into fire, I say he is worse than careless, he is worse than presumptuous, he is mad. But I have some such here. They have had warnings so terrible that they might have known better; they have gone into lusts which have brought their bodies into sickness, and perhaps this day they have crept up to this house, and they dare

not tell to their neighbor who stands by their side what is the
loathsomeness that even now doth breed upon their frame.
And yet they will go back to the same lusts; the fool will go
again to the stocks, the sheep will lick the knife that is to slay
him. You will go on in your lust and in your sins, despite
warnings, despite advice, until you perish in your guilt. How
worse than children are grown-up men! The child who goes
for a merry slide upon a pond, if he be told that the ice will
not bear him, starteth back affrighted, or if he daringly creep-
eth upon it how soon he leaves it, if he hears but a crack upon
the slender covering of the water! But you men have conscience, which tells you that your sins are vile, and that they
will be your ruin; you hear the crack of sin, as its thin sheet
of pleasure gives way beneath your feet; ay, and some of you
have seen your comrades sink in the flood, and lost; and yet
you go sliding on, worse than childish, worse than mad are
you, thus presumptuously to play with your own everlasting
state. O my God, how terrible is the presumption of some!
How fearful is presumption in any! O! that we might be enabled to cry, "Keep back thy servant also from presumptuous sins."

2. I said again, that another characteristic of a presumptuous sin was *deliberation*. A man, perhaps, may have a passionate spirit, and in a moment of hot haste he may utter an angry
word of which in a few short minutes he will sincerely repent.
A man may have a temper so hot that the least provocation
causes him at once to be full of wrath. But he may also have a
temperament which has this benefit to balance it, that he very
soon learns to forgive, and cools in a moment. Now, such a
man does not sin presumptuously, when suddenly overcome
by anger, though, without doubt, there is presumption in his
sin, unless he strives to correct that passion and keep it down.
A man, again, who is suddenly tempted and surprised into a
sin which is not his habit, but which he commits through the
force of some strong temptation, is guilty, but not guilty of
presumption, because he was taken unawares in the net and
caught in the snare. But there are other men who sin deliberately; there are some who can think of a lust for weeks
beforehand, and dote upon their darling crime with pleasure

They do, as it were, water the young seedling of lust until it grows to the maturity of desire, and then they go and commit the crime. There are some to whom lust is not a passer-by, but a lodger at home. They receive it, they house it, they feast it; and when they sin they sin deliberately, walk coolly to their lusts, and in cold blood commit the act which another might haply do in hot and furious haste. Now, such a sin has in it a great extent of sinfulness, it is a sin of high presumption. To be carried away, as by a whirlwind of passion, in a moment is wrong; but to sit down and deliberately resolve upon revenge is cursed and diabolical. To sit down and deliberately fashion schemes of wickedness is heinous, and I can find no other word fitly to express it. To deliberate carefully how the crime is to be done, and, Haman-like, to build the gallows, and to set to work to destroy one's neighbor, to get the pit digged that the friend may fall into it and be destroyed, to lay snares in secret, to plot wickedness upon one's bed—this is a high pitch of presumptuous sin. May God forgive any of us, if we have been so far guilty!

Again, *when a man continues long in sin, and has time to deliberate about it*, that also is a proof that it is a presumptuous sin. He that sins once, being overtaken in a fault, and then abhors the sin, has not sinned presumptuously; but he who transgresses to-day, to-morrow, and the next day, week after week, and year after year, until he has piled up a heap of sins that are high as a mountain, such a man, I say, sins presumptuously, because in a continued habit of sin there must be a deliberation to sin; there must be at least such a force and strength of mind as could not have come upon any man if his sin were but the hasty effect of sudden passion. Ah! take heed, ye that are sodden in sin, ye that drink it down as the greedy ox drinketh down water, ye who run to your lust as the rivers run to the sea, and ye who go to your passions as the sow to her wallowing in the mire. Take heed! your crimes are grievous, and the hand of God shall soon fall terribly on your heads, unless by divine grace it be granted to you to repent and turn unto him. Fearful must be your doom if, unpardoned, God should condemn you for presumptuous sin. O "Lord, keep back thy servant also from presumptuous sins."

3. Again: I said that a presumptuous sin must be a *matter of design*, and have been committed with the intention of sin. If at your leisure at home you will turn to that passage in the book of Numbers, where it says there is no pardon for a presumptuous sin under the Jewish dispensation, you will find immediately afterward a case recorded. A man went out on the Sabbath-day to gather sticks; he was taken in the act of Sabbath-breaking, and the law being very stringent under the Jewish dispensation, he was ordered at once to be put to death. Now, the reason why he was put to death was not because he gathered sticks on the Sabbath merely, but because the law had just then been proclaimed, "In it thou shalt do no manner of work." This man willfully, out of design, in order, as it were, to show that he despised God—to show that he did not care for God—without any necessity, without any hope of advantage, went straight out, in the very teeth of the law, to perform, not an act which he kept in his own house, which might perhaps have been overlooked, but an act which brought shame upon the whole congregation, because, infidel-like, he dared to brazen it out before God; as much as to say, "I care not for God. Has God just commanded, 'Ye shall do no manner of work?' Here am I; I do not want sticks to-day; I do not want to work; not for the sake of sticks, but with the design of showing that I despise God, I go out this day and gather sticks." "Now," says one, "surely there are no people in the world that have ever done such a thing as this." Yes, there are; and there are such in the Surrey Music Hall this day. They have sinned against God, not merely for the pleasure of it, but because they would show their want of reverence to God. That young man burned his Bible in the midst of his wicked companions—not because he hated his Bible, for he quivered and looked pale at the ashes on the hearth when he was doing it; but he did it out of pure bravado, in order to show them, as he thought, that he really was far gone from any thing like a profession of religion. That other man is accustomed sometimes to stand by the wayside, when the people are going to the house of God; and he swears

et them, not because he delights in swearing, but because he will show that he is irreligious, that he is ungodly. How many an infidel has done the same—not because he had any pleasure in the thing itself, but because out of the wickedness of his heart he would spit at God, if it were possible, having a design to let men know that though the sin itself was cheap enough, he was determined to do something which would be like spitting in the face of his Maker, and despising God who created him! Now, such a sin is a master-piece of iniquity. There is pardon for such a one—there is full pardon to those who are brought to repentance; but few of such men ever receive it; for when they are so far gone as to sin presumptuously, because they *will* do it—to sin merely for the sake of showing their disregard of God and of God's law, we say of such, there is pardon for them, but it is wondrous grace which brings them into such a condition that they are willing to accept it. O that God would keep back his servants here from presumptuous sins! And if any of us here have committed them, may he bring us back, to the praise of the glory of his grace!

4. But one more point, and I think I shall have explained these presumptuous sins. A presumptuous sin also is one that is committed *through a hardihood of fancied strength of mind.* Says one, " I intend to-morrow to go into such-and-such a society, because I believe, though it hurts other people, it does me no hurt." You turn round and say to some young man, " I could not advise you to frequent the Casino—it would be your ruin." But you go yourself, sir ? "Yes." But how do you justify yourself? Because I have such strength of principle that I know just how far to go, and no further. Thou liest, sir; against thyself thou liest; thou liest presumptuously in so doing. Thou art playing with bombshells that shall burst and destroy thee; thou art sitting over the mouth of hell, with a fancy that thou shalt not be burned Because thou hast gone to haunts of vice and come back tainted, much tainted, but because thou art so blind as not to see the taint, thou thinkest thyself secure. Thou art not so. Thy sin, in daring to think that thou art proof against sin, is a sin of presumption. " No, no," says one; " but I know that I can go

just so far in such-and-such a sin, and there I can stop." Presumption, sir; nothing but presumption. It would be presumption for any man to climb to the top of the spire of a
church, and stand upon his head. "Well, but he might come
down safe, if he were skilled in it." Yes, but it is presumptuous. I would no more think of subscribing a farthing to a
man's ascent in a balloon, than I would to a poor wretch cutting his own throat. I would no more think of standing and
gazing at any man who puts his life in a position of peril,
than I would of paying a man to blow his brains out. I think
such things, if not murders, are murderous. There is suicide
in men risking themselves in that way; and if there be suicide
in the risk of the body, how much more in the case of a man
who puts his own soul in jeopardy just because he thinks he
has strength of mind enough to prevent its being ruined and
destroyed. Sir, your sin is a sin of presumption; it is a great
and grievous one; it is one of the master-pieces of iniquity.

O! how many people there are who are sinning presumptuously to-day! You are sinning presumptuously in being to-
day what you are. You are saying, "In a little time I will
solemnly and seriously think of religion; in a few years, when
I am a little more settled in life, I intend to turn over a new
leaf, and think about the matters of godliness." Sir, you are
presumptuous. You are presuming that you shall live; you
are speculating upon a thing which is as frail as the bubble on
the breaker; you are staking your everlasting soul on the
deadly odds that you shall live for a few years, whereas, the
probabilities are, that you may be cut down ere the sun shall
set: and it is possible, that ere another year shall have passed
over your head, you may be in the land where repentance is
impossible, and useless were it possible. O! dear friends, procrastination is a presumptuous sin. The putting off a thing
which should be done to-day, because you hope to live to-
morrow, is a presumption. You have no right to do it—you
are, in so doing, sinning against God, and bringing on your
heads the guilt of presumptuous sin. I remember that striking
passage in Jonathan Edwards' wonderful sermon, which was
the means of a great revival, where he says, "Sinner, thou art
this moment standing over the mouth of hell, upon a single

plank, and that plank is rotten; thou art hanging over the jaws of perdition, by a solitary rope, and the strands of that rope are creaking now." It is a terrible thing to be in such a position as that, and yet to say, "to-morrow," and to procrastinate. You remind me, some of you, of that story of Dionysius the tyrant, who, wishing to punish one who had displeased him, invited him to a noble feast. Rich were the viands that were spread upon the table, and rare the wines of which he was invited to drink. A chair was placed at the head of the table, and the guest was seated within it. Horror of horrors! The feast might be rich, but the guest was miserable, dreadful beyond thought. However splendid might be the array of the servants, and however rich the danties, yet he who had been invited sat there in agony. For what reason? Because over his head, immediately over it, there hung a sword, a furbished sword, suspended by a single hair. He had to sit all the time with this sword above him, with nothing but a hair between him and death. You may conceive the poor man's misery. He could not escape; he must sit where he was. How could he feast? How could he rejoice! But O, my unconverted hearer, thou art there this morning, man, with all thy riches and thy wealth before thee, with the comforts of a home and the joys of a household; thou art there this day, in a place from which thou canst not escape; the sword of death above thee, prepared to descend; and woe unto thee, when it shall cleave thy soul from thy body! Canst thou yet make mirth, and yet procrastinate? If thou canst, then verily thy sin is presumptuous in a high degree. "Keep back thy servant also from presumptuous sins."

II. And now I come to the second part of the subject, with which I shall deal very briefly. I am to try and show WHY IT IS THAT THERE IS GREAT ENORMITY IN A PRESUMPTUOUS SIN.

Let me take any one of the sins; for instance, *the sin against light and knowledge*. There is greater enormity in such a presumptuous sin than in any other. In this our happy land it is just possible for a man to commit treason. I think it must be rather difficult for him to do it; for we are allowed to say words here which would have brought our necks beneath the guillotine if they had been spoken on the other side

the Channel; and we are allowed to do deeds here which
would have brought us long years of imprisonment if the deed
had been done in any other land. But I suppose it is just possible to commit treason here. Now, if two men should commit treason—if one of them should wantonly and wickedly
raise the standard of revolt to-morrow, should denounce the
rightful sovereign of this land in the strongest and most abominable language, should seek to entice the loyal subjects of
this country from their allegiance, and should draw some of
them astray, to the hurt and injury of the common weal; he
might have in his rebellious ranks one who had joined incau-
tiously, not knowing whereunto the matter might tend, who
might come into the midst of the rebels, not understanding
the intention of their unlawful assembling, not even knowing
the law which prohibited them from being banded together.
I can suppose these two men brought up upon a charge of
high treason: they have both, legally, been guilty of it; but
I can suppose that the one man who had sinned ignorantly
would be acquitted, because there was no malignant intent;
and I can suppose that the other man, who had willfully,
knowingly, maliciously and wickedly raised the standard of
revolt, would receive the highest punishment which the law
could demand. And why? Because in the one case it was a
sin of presumption, and in the other case it was not so. In
the one case the man dared to defy the sovereign, and defy
the law of the land, willfully, out of mere- presumption. In
the other case not so. Now, every man sees that it would be
just to make a distinction in the punishment, because there
is—conscience itself tells us—a distinction in the guilt.

Again: some men, I have said, sin *deliberately*, and others
do not do so. Now, in order to show that there is a distinction here, let me take a case. To-morrow the bench of magis-
trates are sitting. Two men are brought up. They are each
of them charged with stealing a loaf of bread. It is clearly
proved, in the one case, that the man was hungry, and that he
snatched the loaf of bread to satisfy his necessities. He is
sorry for his deed, he grieves that he has done this act; but
most manifestly he had a strong temptation to it. In the other
case the man was rich, and he wil'fully went into the sho;

merely because he would break the law and show that he was
a law-breaker. He said to the policeman outside, "Now, I
care neither for you nor the law; I intend to go in there, just
to see what you can do with me." I can suppose the magis-
trate would say to one man, "You are discharged; take care
not to do the like again; there is something for your present
necessities; seek to earn an honest living." But to the other
I can conceive him saying, "You are an infamous wretch;
you have committed the same deed as the other, but from
very different motives; I give you the longest term of imprisonment which the law allows me, and I can only regret
that I can not treat you worse than I have done." The pre
sumption of sin made the difference. So when you sin deliberately and knowingly, your sin against Almighty God is a
higher and a blacker sin than it would have been if you had
sinned ignorantly, or sinned in haste.

Now let us suppose one more case. In the heat of some
little dispute some one shall insult a man. You shall be insulted by a man of angry temper; you have not provoked him,
you gave him no just cause for it; but at the same time he
was of a hot and angry disposition; he was somewhat foiled
in the debate, and he insulted you, calling you by some name
which has left a stain upon your character, so far as epithets
can do it. I can suppose that you would ask no reparation
of him, if by to-morrow you saw that it was just a rash word
spoken in haste, of which he repented. But suppose another
person should waylay you in the street, should week after week
seek to meet you in the market-place, and should, after a great
deal of toil and trouble, at last meet you, and there, in the
center of a number of people, unprovoked, just out of sheer,
deliberate malice, come before you and call you a liar in the
street; I can suppose that, Christian as you are, you might find
it necessary to chastise such insolence, not with your hand, but
with the arm of that equitable law which protects us all from
insulting violence. In the other case I can suppose it would
be no trouble to forgive. You would say, "My dear fellow,
I know we are all hasty sometimes—there, now, I don't care
at all for it; you did not mean it." But in this case, where a
man has dared and defied you without any provocation what

ever, you would say to him, " Sir, you have endeavored to in. jure me in respectable society ; I can forgive you as a Chris. tian, but as a man and a citizen I shall demand that I am pro. tected against your insolence."

You see, therefore, in the cases that occur between man and man, how there is an excess of guilt added to a sin by pre- sumption. O ! ye that have sinned presumptuously—and who among us has not done so ?—bow your heads in silence, con- fess your guilt, and then open your mouths, and cry, " Lord have mercy upon me, a presumptuous sinner."

III. And now I have nearly done—not to weary you by too long a discourse—we shall notice THE APPROPRIATENESS OF THIS PRAYER—" Keep back thy servant also from presumptu- ous sins."

Will you just note, that this prayer was the *prayer of a saint*, the prayer of a holy man of God ? Did David need to pray thus ? Did the " man after God's own heart" need to cry, " Keep back thy servant ?" Yes, he did. And note the *beauty* of the prayer. If I might translate it into more meta- phorical style, it is like this: " Curb thy servant from pre- sumptuous sin." " Keep him back or he will wander to the edge of the precipice of sin. Hold him in, Lord ; he is apt to run away ; curb him ; put the bridle on him ; do not let him do it ; let thine overpowering grace keep him holy ; when he would do evil, then do thou draw him to good, and when his evil propensities would lead him astray, then do thou check him." " Check thy servant from presumptuous sins."

What then ? Is it true that the best of men may sin pre- sumptuously ? Ah ! it is true. It is a solemn thing to find the Apostle Paul warning saints against the most loathsome of sins. He says, " Mortify therefore your members which are upon the earth, fornication, uncleanness, idolatry, inordinate affection," and such like. What ! do saints want warning against such sins as these ? Yes, they do. The highest saints may sin the lowest sins, unless kept by divine grace. You old experienced Christians, boast not in your experience ; you may trip yet, unless you cry, " Hold thou me up, and I shall be safe." Ye whose love is fervent, whose faith is constant, whose hopes are bright, say not, " I shall never sin," but rather cry out, " Lord, lead me not into temptation, and when there leave me not there; for unless thou hold me fast I feel I must, I shall decline, and prove an apostate after all." There is enough tinder in the hearts of the best men in the world to light a fire that shall burn to the lowest hell, unless God should quench the sparks as they fall. There is enough cor- ruption, depravity, and wickedness in the heart of the most holy man that is now alive to damn his soul to all eternity, if free and sovereign grace does not prevent. O Christian, thou hast need to pray this prayer. But I think I hear you saying, " Is thy servant a dog, that I should do this thing ?" So said Hazael, when the prophet told him that he would slay his master; but he went home and took a wet cloth and spread it over his master's face and choked him, and did the next day the sin which he abhorred before. Think it not enough to abhor sin, you may yet fall into it. Say not, " I never can be drunken, for I have such an abhorrence of drunkenness ;" thou mayest fall where thou art most secure. Say not, " I can never blaspheme God, for I have never done so in my life ;" take care ; you may yet swear most profanely. Job might have said, " I will never curse the day of my birth ;" but he lived to do it. He was a patient man ; he might have said, " I will never murmur ; though he slay me, yet will I trust in him ;" and yet he lived to wish that the day were darkness wherein he was brought forth. Boast not, then, O Christian ; by faith thou standest. " Let him that thinketh he standeth take heed lest he fall."

But if this need to be the prayer of the best, how ought it to be the prayer of you and me ? If the highest saint must pray it, O mere moralist, thou hast good need to utter it. And ye who have begun to sin, who make no pretensions to piety, how much need is there for you to pray that you may be kept from presumptuously rebelling against God.

Instead, however, of enlarging upon that point, I shall close my few remarks this morning by just addressing myself most affectionately to such of you as are now under a sense of guilt by reason of presumptuous sins. God's Spirit has found some of you out this morning. I thought when I was describing presumptuous sin that I saw here and there an eye that was suffused with tears; I thought I saw here and ,here a head that was bowed down, as much as to say, "I am guilty there." I thought there were some hearts that palpitated with confession, when I described the guilt of presumption. I hope it was so. If it was, I am glad of it. If I hit your consciences, it was that I meant to do. Not to your ears do I speak, but to your hearts. I would not give the snap of this my finger to gratify you with mere words of oratory, with a mere flow of language. No, God is my witness. I never sought effect yet, except the effect of hitting your consciences. I would use the words that would be most rough and vulgar in all our language, if I could get at your heart better with them than with any other ; for I reckon that the chief matter with a minister is to touch the conscience. If any of you feel, then, that you have presumed against God in sinning, let me just bid you look at your sin, and weep over the blackness of it ; let me exhort you to go home and bow your heads with sorrow, and confess your guilt, and weep over it with many tears and sighs. You have greatly sinned, and if God should blast you into perdition now, he would be just; if now his fiery thunderbolt of vengeance should pierce you through, if the arrow that is now upon the string of the Almighty should find a target in your heart, he would be just. Go home and confess that, confess it with cries and sighs. And then what next wilt thou do ? Why, I bid thee remember that there was a man who was a God. That man suffered for presumptuous sin. I would bid thee this day, sinner, if thou knowest thy need of a Saviour, go up to thy chamber, cast thyself upon thy face, and weep for sin; and when thou hast done that, turn to the Scriptures, and read the story of that man whc suffered and died for sin. Think you see him in all his unut terable agonies, and griefs, and woes, ard say this—

> " My soul looks back to see
> The burdens thou didst bear
> When hanging on the accursed tree,
> And hopes her guilt was there."

Lift up your hand, and put it on his head whc bled, and say,

"My faith would lay its hand
On that dear head of thine,
While, like a penitent, I stand,
And there confess my sin."

Sit down at the foot of his cross, and watch him till your heart is moved, till the tears begin to flow again, until your heart breaks within you; and then you will rise and say,

"Dissolved by his mercy, I fall to the ground,
And weep to the praise of the mercy I found."

O sinner, thou canst never perish, if thou wilt cast thyself at the foot of the cross. If thou seekest to save thyself thou shalt die; if thou wilt come, just as thou art, all black, all filthy, all hell-deserving, all ill-deserving, I am my Master's hostage, I will be answerable at the day of judgment for this matter, if he does not save thee. I can preach on this subject now, for I trust I have tried my Master myself. As a youth I sinned, as a child I rebelled, as a young man I wandered into lusts and vanities: my Master made me feel how great a sinner I was, and I sought to reform, to mend the matter; but I grew worse. At last I heard it said, "Look unto me, and be ye saved, all the ends of the earth;" and I looked to Jesus. And O! my Saviour, thou hast eased my aching conscience, thou hast given me peace; thou hast enabled me to say,

"Now, freed from sin, I walk at large;
My Saviour's blood's a full discharge;
At his dear feet my soul I lay,
A sinner saved, and homage pay."

And O! my heart pants for you. O that you who never knew him could taste his love now. O that you who have never repented might now receive the Holy Ghost who is able to melt the heart! And O that you who are penitents would look to him now! And I repeat that solemn assertion—I am God's hostage this morning; ye shall feed me on bread and water to my life's end, ay, and I will bear the blame for ever, if any of you seek Christ, and Christ rejects you. It must not, it can not be. "Whosoever cometh," he says, "I will in nowise cast out." He is able to save to the uttermost them that come unto God by him." May God Almighty bless you; and may we meet again in yonder Paradise; and there will we sing more sweetly of redeeming love and dying blood, and of Jesus' power to save,

> "When this poor lisping, stammering tongue,
> Lies silent in the grave."

SPURGEON'S
SERMONS

SPURGEON'S SERMONS

Charles Haddon Spurgeon

Volume 4

PREFACE

To my American Readers—

Brethren, all hail! cordial greeting and a fervent blessing! I thank you heartily for the abundantly kind reception
which you have given to my Sermons. In preaching them I
had no idea that they would secure thousands of readers in
the great Republic. They are merely impromptu, extem-
pore discourses, and were never intended to be printed for
quiet reading. However, as the people would have them,
they were reported and printed, the author yielding his consent in the hope that the kindness which induced the demand
would overlook the unavoidable defects.

O, that some word of mine in this volume, might aid in
maintaining the great revival of which we have just heard on
this side of the Atlantic. Yours is a pleasant portion indeed; the Lord has greatly blessed you with his awakening
spirit. Make good use of your privileges. We, in England,
are panting for the like visitation. We beseech you, do not
neglect the grace given, but cherish the flame, that it may
increase until it shall overleap the dividing waters and burn
upon the shores of old England.

I have much evidence by letter, to prove that the former
volumes have been useful to many individuals in America,

and I humbly pray that a double blessing may rest upon this Fourth of the Series. I have much ground to hope it shall be so, for the present sermons have even exceeded the former in immediate fruits of conversion in my own congregation. To God be all the honor. I am free to confess all that my critics say against me; but the Lord is wiser than men, and be the sermons what they may, God has blessed them, and I am doubly content.

Accept the love of

Your brother in Jesus,

C. H. SPURGEON

London, April 1, 1858

CONTENTS

SERMON I

THE PARABLE OF THE ARK

"And they went in unto Noah into the ark, two and two of all flesh, wherein is the breath of life."—GENESIS vii. 15

CHRIST always taught by parables. Hence the popularity and the power of his teaching. The masses never were, and, perhaps, never will be, able to receive instruction in any other way than by parabolic illustrations. He who would be a successful minister must open his mouth in parables; he who would win the hearts of the multitude must closely imitate his Master, and preach in parables which all men can understand. I believe there are few living men who are able to devise a parable. Those who do possess this rare ability are very scarce indeed; nor do I myself profess to belong to the honorable confraternity. I have sometimes endeavored if it were possible to fashion a parable; and though I found it easy at times to manufacture a figure, yet a parable I can by no means make. I am happy to say it is not required of me to do so, for the book of God's word, if it be rightly used, is suggestive of a thousand parables; and I have no reason to fear that I shall be short of subjects for preaching, when I am able to find such mighty parables as I do in God's word. I shall preach to you this evening a parable. It shall be the parable of the ark. While I do so you must understand that the ark was a real thing— that it was really made to float upon the waters, and carry in it Noah and his family and two of all flesh. This is a fact, not a myth. But I shall take this real fact and use it as a parable. Making the ark represent salvation, I shall preach to all who are within sound of my voice the parable of the ark. The ark which saved from the floods of water is a beautiful picture of Jesus Christ as the means of salvation, by whom multitudes of all flesh are preserved, and saved from perishing in the floods of eternal perdition.

I. First, then, in working out this parable I shall remark, that there is BUT ONE MEANS OF SALVATION. The ark of gopher wood in the one case, and the person of Christ in the other case, sets forth the one only means that was ever planned or provided by God. The whole world was drowned except those happy ones who were found in the ark. The mightiest beast and the tiniest insect, the stately elephant and the loathsome reptile, the fleet horse and the creeping snail, the graceful antelope and the ugly toad—every living substance that was upon the face of the ground was involved in one common doom, save those only who were preserved alive in the ark. The noblest animals, endowed with the finest instincts, were all drowned, despite their powers of swimming (if they were not fish), save those only who were sheltered in the ark. The strongest winged fowls that ever cut the air were all wearied in their flight and fell into the water, save those only who were housed in the ark. The proudest tenants of the forest, those who ranged fearlessly in the broad light of day or those who prowled stealthily under the cover of night, the strongest, the mightiest, all were swallowed up in the vast abyss, save those only who were commanded by God to hide themselves within the shelter of the ark. Even so, in the application of my parable, there is only one way of salvation for all men living under heaven. There is only one name whereby they can be saved. Wouldst thou be saved, rich man ? There is no way but that whereby the poverty-stricken pauper is also to be saved. Wouldst thou be delivered, thou man of intelligence ? Thou shalt be saved in the same way as the most ignorant. There is none other name under heaven given among men whereby we must be saved, but Jesus Christ and him crucified. There were not two arks, but one ark : so there are not two Saviours, but one Saviour. There was no other means of salvation except the ark: so there is no plan of deliverance except by Jesus Christ, the Saviour of sinners. In vain you climb the lofty top of Sinai: fifteen cubits upwards shall the waters prevail. In vain you climb to the highest pinnacles of your self-conceit and your worldly merit: ye shall be drowned—drowned beyond the hope of salvation; for "other foundations can no man lay than that which is laid—Jesus Christ and him crucified." Would those of my congregation be saved? They must all be saved by one way. Do they object to Christ as the plan of salvation? Then they must be damned, for there is no other hope for them. Do they think this too hard? do they think the revealed plan of salvation too humbling? Then they must sink, even as the sons of Adam sank beneath the mighty flood, and all flesh was utterly consumed by the overwhelming billows. There is but one way. Enter into the ark: take refuge in Christ. Thus only can ye be saved. But, "how shall ye escape, if ye neglect so great salvation?" By what means shall ye secure your souls, or your bodies either? What plans can ye devise for your security? Your refuges shall prove to be refuges of lies; the winds, the rain, the hail, and the tempest shall destroy them. There is one Saviour, but there is only one. There is one Jesus who saves his people from their sins, but there is no other name and no other means of salvation. The ark stood alone, and even so doth Christ Jesus.

II. Proceeding with my parable, I must direct your attention to THE SIZE OF THIS ARK; this may be comforting to you. If you read the 15th verse of the 6th chapter, you will find that the ark was of immense size. "The length of the ark shall be three hundred cubits, the breadth of it fifty cubits, and the height of it thirty cubits." It is an old objection of infidels that there was not room enough in it for all kinds of creatures that lived on the face of the earth; but we know, on Divine authority, that if there were not room enough in it for all the different kinds of creatures which were then alive, they would have been drowned; yet of every kind some were safely housed, so that room enough was found for them all. This is not very logical, perhaps, you will say, but it is conclusive enough for us, if we believe in revelation. Yet there really is no reason for any one to make the objection, and we have no room to entertain it, since the most eminent calcu lators have proved to demonstration, that the vessel called the ark was of immense size, and was able not merely to hold all the creatures, but all the provender they would require for the year during which it floated on the water. I use this idea, without stopping to expound it further. Let me but trace its analogy as a beautiful picture of the plan of salvation —Oh! what a capacious plan! The ark was a great ark, which held all kinds of creatures; and our Christ is a great Refuge, who saves all kinds of sinners. The ark was an immense vessel—in it floated a multitude of animals who were saved; Christ's salvation is an immense salvation, and in it there shall be delivered a multitude which no man can number. The narrow-minded bigot limits salvation to his own contracted notions, and he still says, "There shall none be saved, except they walk arm-in-arm with me." Poor, little, miserable soul! he cuts his coat according to his own fashion, and declares, that if men do not all cut their coats in the same way they can not be saved. But not so the Bible. The Bible preaches a great salvation. It says there is a multitude that no man can number, who shall stand before the throne of God. Here is assembled a multitude of sinners; but if you all feel your need of a Saviour, there is room enough for you in heaven. Here is a multitude of hearers; but if every one of you this night should come to Christ with real penitence in your hearts, and belief in Him, you would not find that there was not room enough for you. That saying is still true, "And yet there is room." There is not room enough for a pharisee, for a man who does not feel himself a sinner, for a hypocrite, no, nor yet for a formalist; but there is room enough for every convinced sinner under God's heaven. There has been room enough hitherto, and we have never yet heard of saints complaining that they were cramped for room; but rather, I have heard them say in the words of David, "I called upon the Lord in distress; the Lord answered me, and set me in a large place." They have ever found abundance of room in Christ, and so shall you. Our Redeemer is able to save to the uttermost them that come unto him. He is able to save all of you. If the Father that hath sent him draw you, and you come unto him, doubt not there is room. Do not think, beloved, because we preach election, that we preach the election of a few. I find that this is a common mistake. Some one will say to me, "I don't like your Calvinism, sir because it says that there are a few elected, and that nobody else will be saved."

Nay, sir, but it does not say that there are a few elected, it says no such thing it says they are a multitude, that no man can number, that have been elected, and who knows but what you are one of them? It does not turn you out. It gives you ten thousand times more reason for hope than the Arminian preacher, who stands up and says, "There is room for everybody, but I do not think there is any special grace to make them come; if they won't come, they won't come, and there is an end of it; it is their own fault, and God will not make them come." The word of God says they cannot come, yet the Arminian says they can; the poor sinner feels that he cannot, yet the Arminian declares positively that he could if he liked; and though the poor sinner feels sometimes that he would if he could, and groans over his inability, this blind guide tells him that it is all nonsense; whereas, it is, in truth, God's own work to make a man feel that he is unable. You must feel it; and you may plead against yourself on account of it, but you shall *come* for all that. "He will not plead against you;" "no, but he will put strength in you." Ah! there is more hope for you in the pure Gospel of the blessed God, than there is in those fancies and fictions of men which are now-a-days preached everywhere, except in a few places where God hath reserved unto himself a people who have not bowed their knee to the Baal of the age. Nay, beloved, we do not preach that a few shall be saved; we preach that a mighty host, whom mortals cannot count, shall be the seed of Jesus. So shall he see of the travail of his soul, and be abundantly satisfied. Hear me, then, while out of this parable of the ark I draw encouragement concerning the capacity of the salvation of Christ.

III. In the third place, note that THE ARK WAS A SAFE REFUGE. Noah was commanded to make an ark of the best wood, gopher wood; and, lest there should be any leakage in it, he was commanded to "pitch it within and without with pitch," and we do not find that it ever sprung a leak while it was out at sea; she certainly never went into harbor to mend her bottom, for she had no harbor to go to. We never read that Noah called up Shem, Ham, and Japheth to work at the pumps, nor yet that they had any, for there was not a bit of leakage about her. No doubt there were storms during that year; but we do not hear that the ship was ever in danger of being wrecked. The rocks, it is true, were too low down to touch her bottom; for fifteen cubits upwards did the waters prevail, and the mountains were covered. Rising twenty-seven feet above the loftiest mountains, she had no quicksands to fear; they were too deep below her keel. But of course she was exposed to the winds; sometimes the hurricane might have rattled against her, and driven her along. Doubtless, at another time, the hail beat on her top, and the lightnings scarred the brow of night; but the ark sailed on, not one was cast out from her, nor were her sailors wearied with constant pumping to keep out the water, or frequent repairs to keep her secure. Though the world was inundated and ruined, that one ark sailed triumphantly above the waters. The ark was safe, and all who were in her were safe too.

Now, sinner, the Christ I preach to you is such a refuge as that. His Gospel has no flaw in it. As the ark never sank and the elements never prevailed against it, so Christ never failed, he can not fail; all the principalities and powers are subject unto him. Those who are in Christ are sheltered safely from every storm, they shall never perish, neither shall any pluck them out of his hands. Remember that God gave the pattern, and Noah perfected the work of the ark, ere a single fountain of the great deep was broken up, or one drop of the desolating storm fell from the vengeful clouds. And it is not less true that our glorious Lord was set up in the coun-sels of eternity a perfect Christ before the clouds of vindictive wrath began to brew on account of man's iniquity; and his mighty work of mediation was finished before thy poor soul was invited to take shelter in him. Oh, methinks as the angels looked out of the windows of heaven upon the swelling tide, and saw how securely the ark rode upon its surface, they never doubted that all who were inside were as safe as the ark itself. And is there any reason to doubt that those who are in Christ are as safe as Christ? Did he not say himself, " because I live, ye shall live also?" Were the sons of Noah commanded to take their tools into the ark to keep it in repair? And dost thou vainly think that thou canst make the matter of eternal salvation more perfect than it was when Jesus said "It is finished?" Oh, no; the work is done, the vessel is sea-worthy. " God can not mend it, the devil can not mar it." It is not an Arminian Gospel I preach to you, that tells of dangers, and sounds alarms in the ears of those who are within the ark of Christ. In him—in him—oh, hear it, poor trembling sinner! in him you are—

> " Beyond the reach of death's alarms,
>   The source of mortal woe."

" They that trust in the Lord shall be as mount Zion, which shall never be removed, which abideth forever." They that trust in the Lord are blessed. " They are like trees planted by rivers of water; their leaf shall not wither, and whatsoever they do shall prosper." If you once come unto Jesus, and trust in him, there is no fear of sinking. How sweet was the precious hymn we sang just now--

> " Firm as a rock Thy Gospel stands,
>   My Lord, my hope, my trust;
> If I am found in Jesus' hands
>   My soul can ne'er be lost."

Not but that there will be storms, and tempests will beat around you—these you will be sure to have; but you will be too high up ever to strike on the rocks. If you are once on board the good ship of salvation, you will be lifted up too high above the floods to be swallowed in the quicksands. With cheerful heart I can commend you to God, and the word of his testimony. Christ will preserve you.

> " Grace will preserve what grace begins,
> To save from sorrows and from sins;
> The work that wisdom undertakes
> Eternal mercy ne'er forsakes."

Believers! could you give up the doctrine of your security in Christ to any body? No, that I know you could not. Touch one of my brethren or sisters in the Lord who attends this chapel on that point, and you will soon get your answer. I have sometimes heard disputes outside the chapel door, when some who do not believe the truth have been disputing it, and I have felt confident that I might leave its defence in your hands. There be mighty men of valor among you, who are not ashamed to uphold the whole counsel of God, even as I am constantly anxious to declare it. Beloved, the ark is pitched within and without with pitch; it is made of good gopher wood; it can never sink so long as we are on board; if it were threescore years and ten, she will still preserve us. Salvation in Christ is a sure salvation.

IV. Now I go to another part of the parable. The creatures in the ark of course wanted light; but it is a singular thing that THERE WAS ONLY ONE WINDOW IN THE ARK. In the 16th verse of the 6th chapter we read—" A window shalt thou make to the ark." I have often wondered how all the creatures could see through one window; but I have not wondered what was meant by it, for I think it easy to point the moral. There is only one window whereby Christians ever get their light. All who come to Christ and receive salvation by him are illuminated in one way. That one window of the ark may fitly represent to us *the ministry of the Holy Ghost*. There is only one light which lighteneth every man who cometh into the world, if he be lightened at all. Christ is the light, and it is the Holy Spirit of truth by whom Christ is revealed. Thus we discern sin, righteousness, and judgment. No other conviction is of any real value. As we are brought under the teachings of the Spirit, we do perceive our guilt and misery, and our redemption and refuge in Christ. No other means exist. There is only one window to the ark. " Why," says one, " there are some of us who see light through one minister and some through another." True, my friend ; but still there is only one window. We ministers are only like panes of glass, and you can obtain no light through us but by the operations of the same Spirit that worketh in us. And even then the different panes of glass give different shades of light. There you have your fine polished preacher ; he is a bit of stained glass, not very transparent, made to keep the light out rather than to let it in. There is another pane ; he is a square cut diamond ; he seems an old-fashioned preacher, but still he is a bit of good glass, and lets the light through. Another one is cut after a more refined stile ; but still he is plain and simple, and the light shines through him. But there is only one light, and only one window. He who revealeth to us the light of the knowledge of the glory of God in the face of Jesus Christ is the Holy Spirit. We have only one instructor, if we preach the truth. One brother may be preaching this night in the Church of England, another may be holding forth the word of God amongst the Independents, and others amongst the Baptists ; but they have only one Spirit, if they are taught of God. There is only one window to the ark ; and though there were first, second, and third stories to the ark, all saw out of one window ; so that the little saint that is in the first story gets light through that window ; and the saint that has been brought up to the second story gets light through the same window ; and he who has been promoted to the loftiest story has to get light through the same window too. There is no other means of our seeing except through the one window made to the ark, the window of the Holy Spirit. Have we looked through that ? Have we seen the clear blue sky above us ? Or have we known that when our eye of faith was dim, and we could see nothing at all, still our Master was at the helm, and would preserve us through all our darkness and difficulties ? It is an instructive fact that the ark had only one window in it.

V. Now, if you will read the chapter attentively, you will find it said " ROOMS shalt thou make in the ark." When I read that I thought it would serve for a point in the parable, seeing it may teach my dear friends that they are not all to be put together ;—in the ark, rooms were made. Those who lived in one room did not stand or sit with those who lived in another ; but they were all in the same ark. So I have sometimes thought, There are our Wesleyan friends, some of them love the Lord ; I have no doubt they are in the ark, though they do not occupy the same apartment as we do. There are our Baptist friends, who love the Lord ; we welcome them in our room. Then there are our Independent friends, those also love the Lord ; they are in another room. And our Presbyterian and Episcopalian brethren,—in all these various sections are some who are called of God and brought into the ark, though they are in different rooms. But, beloved, they are all in one ark. There are not two Gospels. As long as I can find a man that holds the same Gospel, it does not matter what order of church government he adopts if he be in Chrst Jesus—it is of little consequence what room he is in so long as he is in the ark. If he belongs to those of whom it is written, " By grace are ye saved, through faith, and that not of your-selves, it is the gift of God," I will call him brother. We can not all expect to be in one room. The elephants did not live with the tigers, and the lions did not lie down with the sheep. There were different rooms for different classes of creatures ; and it is a good thing there are different denominations, for I am sure some of us would not get on very comfortably with certain denominations. We should want more liberty than we could get in the Church of England ; we should want more freedom than we could get with the Presbyterians ; we should want more soundness of doctrine than we could get with the Wesleyans ; and we should want a little more broth-erly love, perhaps, than we could get with some of the strict Baptists. We should not entirely agree with them all ; and happy is he who can sometimes put his head into one room and sometimes into another, and can say to all that love the Lord Jesus Christ, " Grace be with you all so long as you are in the ark." Do not let me condemn those that are taking refuge in the same vessel with myself. So long as you love Jesus, so long as you are attached to his person, so long as you are called by his grace, so long as you are partakers of his mercy, take heart. There were rooms in the ark, and there are rooms in the church. But one day you will be all associated together in one general assembly,

> "When He presents your souls,
> Unblemished and complete,
> Before the glory of His face,
> With joys divinely great."

VI. But though there were many rooms in the ark, I want you to notice one thing more, THERE WAS ONLY ONE DOOR. It is said, "And the door of the ark shalt thou set in the side thereof." And so, there is only one door into the ark of our salvation, and that is Christ. There are not two Christs preached, one in one chapel, and another in another. "If any man preach any other doctrine than that ye have received, let him be accursed." There is but one Gospel. We take in the righteous out of all sections, but we do not take in all sections. We pick out the godly from amongst them all, for we believe there is a remnant according to the election of grace in the vilest of them. But, still, there is only one door, and "he that cometh not in by the door, but climbeth up some other way, the same is a thief and a robber." There was only one door to the ark.

Some animals, like the camelopard, whose heads are higher than other animals, might have to bow their necks to go in by the same entrance as the waddling ducks, who naturally stoop, even as they enter a barn; and so, some of the lofty ones of this world must bend down their stiff necks, and bow their proud heads, if they would enter into the church by Christ. Thus, again, the swift horse and the slow-paced snail must enter by one door; so, too, the scribes and pharisees must come in the same way as the publicans and harlots, or be for ever excluded.

All the beasts God had chosen went in by the one door, and if any had stood without, and said, "We shall not come in that way," they would have been standing without till the flood overtook and destroyed them; for there was only one door. There is only one way of salvation, and there is only one means of getting into it. "Believe on the Lord Jesus Christ, and thou shalt be saved," but "he that believeth not," whoever he be, must "be damned." There is no hope of any other way of salvation. He that cometh in by the door shall be saved; and Jesus saith, "I am the door."

VII. Proceeding in the parable, you will notice, that THIS ARK HAD SUNDRY STORIES IN IT. They were not all of one height. There were lower, second, and third stories. Now, this is a figure to me of the different kinds of Christians who are carried to heaven. There is my poor mourning brother, who lives in the bottom story; he is always singing, "Lord, what a wretched land is this!" He lives just near the keel, on the bare ribs of the ark. He is never very happy. A little light reaches him from the window at times; but, generally, he is so far from the light that he walks in darkness, and sees very little indeed. His state is that of constant groaning; he loves to go and hear "*the corruption preachers;*" he revels with delight in the deep experience of the tried family of God; he likes to hear it said, "Through much tribulation you will enter the kingdom of heaven;" if you paint the Christian life as a very gloomy one, he will like your picture, for his is gloomy indeed; he is always poring over texts such as these, "Oh, wretched man that I am," or that other, "They that pass through the valley of Baca make it a well; the rain also filleth the pools." He is down in the lower story of the ark. But never mind; he is in the ark, so we will not scold him, though he has little faith, and very much doubt. "With lower, second, and third stories shalt thou make it." There is one of our brethren up a little higher, and he is saying, "I cannot exactly say I am safe; yet I have a hope that my head will be kept above the billows, though it goes hard with me at times. Now and then, too, the Lord bestows "some drops of heaven" upon me. Sometimes I am like the mountains of Hermon, where "the Lord commanded the blessing, even life for evermore." He is in the second story. Well, but he is no safer than the other one. He that is in the second story is no safer, though he is happier than the man on the ground floor. All are safe, so long as they are in the ark. For my part, I like the uppermost story best. I had rather live up there, where I can sing, "O God, my heart is fixed, I will sing and give praise, even with my glory."

I love the place where the saints are always admonishing and encouraging one another with psalms, and hymns, and spiritual songs,—

> " Children of the Heavenly King,
> As ye journey, sweetly sing;
> Sing your Saviour's worthy praise,
> Glorious in His works and ways."

I confess that I am obliged to go down to the lower story sometimes; but I like running up the ladder to the third deck, whenever I can, and there I can say—

> " Oh! how sweet to view the flowing
> Of His soul-redeeming blood ;
> With divine assurance knowing
> That He made my peace with God."

But I am no more safe when I am in the top story than I am when I am in the bottom. The same wave that would split the ship and drown me, were I in the lowest story, would drown me if I were in the highest. However high some of us, and however low others of us may be, the same vessel bears us all, for we are one crew in one boat, and there is no dividing us. Come, then, my poor desponding hearer, is that your place, somewhere down at the bottom of the hold, along with the ballast? Are you always in trials and troubles? Ah! well, fear not, so long as you are in the ark. Do not be afraid, Christ is your strength and righteousness. The ark was in each and every department a secure shelter to all who were shut in. "Ah!" says one, "but I am down there, sir, at the bottom always, and I am afraid the vessel will sink." Do not be so silly ; why should your heart beget such senseless fears ? I knew a man who went up the Monument, and when he had got half way, he declared it vibrated and was about to fall, and he would come down. But the Monument has not fallen; it is as safe as ever ; and if fifty like him, or fifty thousand, went up, the Monument would be just as firm. But some poor nervous Christians are afraid Christ will let them sink. A wave comes against the side of the ship, but it does not hurt the ship, it only drives the wedges in tighter. The Master is at the helm—will not that assure your heart? It has floated over so many billows—will not that increase your confidence? It must, indeed, be a strong billow that will sink it now; there never shall be such an one. And where, think you, is the power that could destroy the souls who are sheltered in the ark of our salvation? Who can lay anything to the charge of God's elect, since Christ hath died, and God the Father hath justified us? Happy assurance! We are all safe, so sure as we are in the covenant. The ark floated triumphantly on amidst all the dangers without, and when it finally rested on Mount Ararat, and God spake to Noah again, saying, "Go forth of the ark, thou, and thy wife, and thy sons, and thy sons' wives with thee. Bring forth with thee every living thing;" then the inventory was complete, all were safely landed. So, too, will Christ present the perfect number of all his people to the Father in the last day; not one shall perish. The ark of our salvation shall bring all its living freight into the haven of everlasting rest.

> "Truth is her compass, love her sail,
>   And heavenly grace her store;
> The Spirit's influence the gale
>   That wafts her to the shore.

> "Nor winds nor waves her progress check,
>   Her course she must pursue;
> And though you often fear a wreck,
>   She's saved with all her crew."

VIII. This brings me to notice, in the last place, THE DIFFERENT KINDS OF ANIMALS THAT ENTERED INTO THE ARK.— "Of every clean beast thou shalt take to thee by sevens: and of beasts that are not clean by two, the male and his female." Listen to the statement. This great ark was meant to save both clean and unclean beasts. In like manner, the great salvation of our Lord Jesus Christ is intended for sinners of all kinds, the clean and the unclean. There are some people in the world that we may well reckon in the former class. They are in every way respectable; their conduct in society is beyond reproach; exact in their commerce, they were never known to erase a figure in their account books; they would not defraud their neighbors, nor would they be so negligen of their fair fame as to do a disorderly action; their character is so amiable, that their mothers might regard them from childhood as almost without a fault; they have grown up to mature years without the hideous taint of immorality; their practice has been ever akin to piety; their zeal for the law of God has been truly commendable, so that Christ himself might have looked on them and loved them, although he tenderly and pitifully admonishes them, "One thing thou lackest." Ay, but the desolations of the flood are so universal, that there is no escape except in the ark. The clean beasts must go into the ark to be saved. There is not a soul among you so good, nor a character so clean, but ye have need of Christ, whether ye know your need or not. Ye may be never so good and excellent, but ye will want a Saviour. There is something about your character not clean. Your lives require purification, which ye can never find but in Christ.

> "The best performance of your hands,
> Dares not appear before his throne."

But, then, the unclean beasts went in likewise. Here is the opposite class. Are there not some of you (we know there are such) whose education from early childhood has been vicious—certainly not virtuous? From your earliest recollections you have gone into the paths of open profanity; you have dived into the kennel, and have steeped yourselves up to the very lips in the gall of bitterness. You have been drunkards, swearers, Sabbath-breakers, and injurious. You have indulged in all kinds of iniquities. You are just the sort of persons we should liken to unclean beasts. Ay! the ark was built for you—on purpose for you too. The most moral man will stand no better when he comes before God than you will. He must be saved just the same as you are. You **must** both be saved by the one common salvation, or not at all. There is but one Saviour for all who are saved—there is but one redemption for every one of you who really is redeemed. There is but one ark for the clean and the unclean. "Ah!" say some, "I suppose, then, you take the unclean beasts to come from the courts, the alleys, and the filthy slums of the metropolis." Oh! no, not particularly so. We can find the unclean as plentifully in St. James's as in St. Giles's. There be some of what you call the "higher circles," who from infancy have revelled in vice. Soon did ye learn to break the rule of your parents' authority. You laughed at your mother's tears, you sneered at your father's counsels; you drank up iniquity in your school-days as the greedy ox drinketh up water. You made a boast of your wild riots. You tell of your wickedness now with an air of impertinent triumph. You brag of having sowed your wild oats. So infamous has been your career, in spite of good example and education, that, I suppose, "Newgate" could hardly produce a class of unclean beasts more to be loathed than you are. Well, now, to each class of sinners I preach. If thou feelest and deplorest thine uncleanness, there is mercy for thee, unclean as thou art. I beseech thee, come into the ark, and thou wilt never be turned out. If God constrain thee to come, as he did those creatures, he will never, never drive thee away. The ark was for the unclean as well as for the clean—for the swine as well as for the sheep—for the poisonous asp as well as for the harmless dove—for the carnivorous raven as well as for the turtle. All creatures came in, some of every sort. Ah! thou swinish sinner, one of Satan's swine, come in; thou shalt be safe. And ah! thou lamb-like sinner, gentle and mild, come in thou, for there is no other ark for thee, and thou wilt be drowned unless thou comest in by the same door into the great ark of salvation.

Let us divide these creatures once more. There were *creeping things*, and there were *flying things*. On the morning when the ark door was opened, you might have seen in the sky a pair of eagles, a pair of sparrows, a pair of vultures, a pair of ravens, a pair of humming-birds, a pair of all kinds of birds that ever cut the azure, that ever floated on wing, or whispered their song to the evening gales. In they came. But if you had watched down on the earth, you would have seen come creeping along a pair of snails, a pair of snakes, and a pair of worms. There ran along a pair of mice there came a pair of lizards, and in there flew a pair of locusts There were pairs of creeping creatures, as well as pairs of flying creatures. Do you see what I mean by that? There are some of you that can fly so high in knowledge, that I should never be able to scan your great and extensive wisdom; and others of you so ignorant, that you can hardly read your Bibles. Never mind; the eagle must come down to the door, and you must go up to it. There is only one entrance for you all; and as God saved the birds that flew, so he saved the reptiles that crawled. Are you a poor, ignorant, crawling creature, that never was noticed—without intellect, without repute, without fame, without honor? Come along, crawling one! God will not exclude you. I have often wondered how the poor snail crawled in; but I dare say he started many a year before. And some of you have started for years, and still you keep crawling on. Ah! then, come along with thee, poor snail! If I could just pick thee up, and help thee on a yard or two, I would be glad to do it. It is strange how long you have been nigh to the ark, but not yet entered in; how long you have been near the portals of the church, but never joined it.

Remark again: they all got in. Oh! do not fear, if you are in your own esteem a crawling reptile: you may have the lowest possible opinion of yourself; still come; nobody forbids you to come, however mean you are; yea! and the meaner you are the more willing do I feel to invite you,—Christ came not to call the righteous but sinners to repentance. What a strange assemblage was there on that morn ing! But Noah was positively commanded to bring all sorts of creatures into the ark. He might have thought some too vile and worthless to preserve alive, yet his orders were to bring them in. When Peter was commanded to preach the

Gospel to the Gentiles, God showed him in a vision " all manner of four-footed beasts of the earth and wild beasts and
creeping things and fowls of the air." "Not so, Lord," said
Peter; and, lo! " the voice spake to him again a second time,
saying, What God hath cleansed, that call not thou common."
In Christ there be some out of every nation, every kindred,
and every tongue, who shall be saved to the praise of God
and the Lamb forever and ever. There may be some one
here who objects against himself, like Agur, "Surely I am
more brutish than any man, and have not the understanding
of a man." Thy vileness shall not disqualify thee from entering in. It does not prevent my urging you to come. Have
you not heard the words of my Master's commission, " *Of
every sort shalt thou bring into the ark to keep them alive with
thee ?*" Oh! I want to bring you in. The Lord will not reject thee if thou comest with a penitent believing heart; he
will not reproach *me* for having brought thee; he saith to his
ministers, " of every sort bring them in."

Moreover, it was a mysterious impulse by which God moved
the creatures to come. The sight must have been imposing;
the elephants, the camels, the dromedaries, the rhinoceroses,
and all the huge creatures walking in side by side (as it were)
with the timorous hares, the tiny mice, the lizards, ferrets,
squirrels, beetles, grasshoppers, and all such insignificant-look-
ing little creatures. So it hath been in the church, so it shall
be to the end of the chapter of her history : " As many as were
ordained unto eternal life believed," though their characters
by nature be various as this globe ever witnessed, rude as
barbarism's foulest sink, or polished as Grecian culture ever
knew.

Now, dear hearer, I do not care about asking you who you
are, or what you are. That has nothing to do with me. What
I ask you is, Are you in the ark, or are you not ? You are
saying, perhaps, "Sir, I do not care for you; why should you
inquire about my condition ?" But there will be a day when
you will be like those who spake to Noah, and said, "Go
along, greybeard; build your ark on the dry land, like a fool
as you are; build your ark there on the hill-side, where the

waters cannot come. As for us, we shall eat and drink, and if to-morrow we die, what heed, for we have eaten and drunk the merrier while we have had the opportunity."

In vain did Noah warn them that the waters would surely come; he seemed unto them as one that mocked, and they laughed at him. Even so, when I preached of the resurrection to you this morning, some of you may have mocked, and thought that I was but pursuing a wild reverie of imagination. Ah! but how different was their tune, when the rains fell, when "the fountains of the great deep were broken up!" They doubtless changed their notes, when the clouds began to empty themselves in fury, when the very earth did crack, and its bowels were dissolved, and the mighty fluid gushed up to devour them all. Did they think Noah was a fool, when the last man stood on the last mountain-top, and cried in vain for help? I saw some time ago, a master-picture, which I think time will never erase from my memory. It was a picture of a man who had been climbing up to the top of the last mountain, and the floods were coming around him. He had his old father on his back; his wife was clasping him round his waist, and he had one arm round her; she held one child at her breast, and with her other hand she grasped another. In the picture was represented one child just letting go, the wife dropping, and the father clinging to a tree on the top of the hill; the branches were breaking, and it was being torn up by the roots. Such a scene of agony I never saw depicted before; yet such a scene was likely enough to have been real when the waters entirely covered the earth. They had climbed up to the top of the last hill; and now they sank. False hopes gave place to fell despair. And so it will be with you, ye careless ones, unless ye take shelter in the ark.

You ask me, how can we do it? Ye look anxious, some of you. Hearken, then, while I finish, as I have often done before, with the simple statement which contains our authority to preach, and your admonition to believe. Jesus said, " Go ye into all the world, and preach the Gospel to every creature. He that believeth and is baptized shall be saved; but he that believeth not shall be damned."

What is it to believe, say you? It is with tny whole heart to rely simply on the Lord Jesus Christ; he is the only mediator—to look to his sufferings and his death for the forgiveness of thy sins. And what is it to be baptized? It is to be immersed in water on the profession of thy faith, " in the name of the Father, and of the Son, and of the Holy Ghost." " He that believeth and is baptized shall be saved." I cannot leave out one clause, nor yet the other. I dare not transpose or change their order, as some people do. I deliver unto you that which I have received, taking the text just as it stands. Let me ask once more, have you believed? have you been baptized? If not, you cannot say that those great promises written in the covenant are yours. On two grounds you have reason to doubt your salvation. " He that believeth not shall be damned." Where can I obtain faith, saith one? It is given by the Holy Spirit. " Every one that asketh, receiveth; and he that seeketh, findeth; and to him that knocketh, it shall be opened."

SERMON II

PROVING GOD

"Prove me now."—MALACHI, iii. 10

ACCORDING to the laws of our country, no man can be con
demned until his guilt is proved. It were well if we all carried out the same justice toward God which we expect from
our fellow-men; but how frequently will men condemn the
acts of their God as being hard and unkind! They do not
say so—they dare not; they scarcely avow that they think so;
but there is a kind of lurking imagination hardly amounting
to a deliberate thought, which leads them to fear that God
has forgotten to be gracious, and will be mindful of them no
more. Let us never, my friends, think hardly of our God,
till we can prove anything against him. He says to all his
unbelieving children who are doubtful of his goodness and his
grace, "Prove me now. Hast thou aught against me? Canst
thou prove aught that will be dishonorable to me? Wherein
have I ever broken my promise? In what have I ever failed
to fulfil my word? Ah, thou canst not say that. Prove me
now, if thou hast aught against me—if thou canst say anything
against my honor—if thou hast hitherto not received answers
to prayer and blessings according to promise. Set me not
down as false, I beseech thee, until thou hast so proved me."
"Prove me now," says the Lord to all his saints.

Moreover, not only is it unjust to think ill of any one,
until we can prove something against him, but it is extremely
unwise to be always suspicious of our fellow-creatures.
Though there is much folly in being over credulous, I question
if there is not far more in being over-suspicious. He who
believes every man, will soon be bitten; but he who suspects

every man, will not only be bitten, but devoured. He who lives in perpetual distrust of his fellow-creatures cannot be happy; he has defrauded himself of peace and happiness, and assumed a position in which he cannot enjoy the sweets of friendship or affection. I would rather be too credulous towards my fellow-creatures than too suspicious. I had rather they should impose upon me ·by making me believe them better than they are, than that I should impose upon them by thinking them worse than they are. It is better to be cheated sometimes ourselves than that we should cheat others; and it is cheating others to suspect those on whose characters there resteth no suspicion. We acknowledge such morality among men, but we act not so towards God; we believe any liar sooner than we believe him. When we are in trial and trouble we will believe the devil, when he says God will forsake us. The devil, who has been a liar from the beginning, we will credit; but if our God promises anything, we say, "Surely this is too good to be true," and we doubt the fulfilment, because it is not brought to pass exactly at the time and in the way we anticipate. Let us never harbor such suspicions of our God. If we say in our haste, "All men are liars," let us preserve this one truth, "God cannot lie." His counsel is immutable, and he hath confirmed it by an oath, that "we might have strong consolation, who have fled for refuge to lay hold of the hope set before us" in Christ Jesus; let not our faith then dally with a fear; let us rather seek grace, that we may confidently believe and assuredly rely on the words which the lips of God do speak. "Prove me now, if any of you are suspicious of my word." If you think my grace is not sweet, "taste and see that the Lord is gracious." If you think that I am not a rock, and that my work is not perfect, come now, tread upon the rock, and see if it be not firm; build on the rock, and see if it be not solid. If thou thinkest mine arm shortened that I cannot save, come, ask, and I will stretch it out to defend thee. If thou thinkest that mine ear is heavy that I cannot hear, come, try it; call upon me, and I will answer thee. If thou art suspicious, make proof of my promises, so shall thy suspicions be removed. But, oh, doubt me not, until thou hast found me unworthy of trust: "Prove me now."

In these words I find a *fact* couched, a *challenge* given, a *time* mentioned, and an *argument* suggested. Such are the four points I propose this morning to consider.

I. First, then, we have the FACT, that God allows himself to be proved—"Prove me now." In meditating on this subject it has occurred to me that all the works of creation are proofs of God; they evidence his eternal power and godhead. But inasmuch as he is not only the creator, but the sustainer of them all, they make continual proof of him, his goodness, his faithfulness, and his care. Methinks, when God launched the sun from his hand and sent him on his course, he said, " Prove me now ;" see, Oh sun, if I do not uphold thee till thou hast done thy work, and finished thy career; rejoice thou mayest, " as a strong man to run a race," but while thou fulfillest thy circuits, and nothing is hid from thy heat, thou shalt prove my glory and shed light upon my handiwork. When the Almighty whirled the earth in space, methinks he said, "Prove me now," O earth, see if I do not perpetuate thy seasons, and give thee " seed-time and harvest, cold and heat, summer and winter, day and night," refreshing thee with incessant providence. And to each creature he made, I can almost think the Almighty said, " Prove me now." Tiny gnat, thou art about to dance in the sunshine ; thou shalt prove my goodness. Huge leviathan, thou shalt stir up the deep, and make it frothy; go forth, and prove my power. Ye creatures, whom I have endowed with various instincts, wait on me ; I will give you your meat in due season. And you, ye mighty thunders and ye swift lightnings, go, teach the world reverence, and show forth my omnipotence. Thus, I think, all God's creatures are not merely proofs of his existence, but proofs of his manifold wisdom, his loving kindness, and his grace. The meanest and the mightiest of his created works, each and all, in some degree, prove his love, and teach us how marvelous is his nature ; but he has given to man this high prerogative above all the works of his hands, that he alone should make designed and intelligent proof. They do but prove him unin-

tentionally.   The things of earth prove God, yet they have no
intention of so doing.   The beasts praise God; the cattle on
a thousand hills low forth his honor, and the very lions roar
his praise; yet they do it not with intent, and judgment, and
will; and although the sun proveth the majesty and the
might of his Master, yet the sun hath neither mind nor
thought, and it is not his intention to glorify God.   But the
saint doth it intentionally.

It is a great fact, beloved, that God will have all his children proofs of the various attributes of his nature.   I do not
think any one of the children of God proves all of God, but
that they are all proving different parts of his one grand character, so that when the whole history of providence shall be
written, and the lives of all the saints shall be recorded, the
title of the book will be, "Proofs of God."   There will be one
compendious proof, that he is God, and changeth not; that
with him there "is no variableness, neither shadow of turning."
You will remember how one saint peculiarly proved the *long-
suffering* of God, in that he was permitted to pursue his career
to the utmost verge of destruction; while he hung on the
cross, the patience that had borne with him so long, brought
salvation to him at last.   He was "in the article of death,"
falling into the pit, when sovereign grace broke the fall, everlasting arms caught the soul, and Jesus himself conducted him
to paradise.   Then again, you will remember another saint
who plunged into a thousand sins, and indulged in the foulest
lust, but she was brought to Christ; out of her did he cast
seven evil spirits, and Mary Magdalene was made to prove
the richness of our Saviour's pardoning grace, as well as the
sweetness of a pardoned sinner's gratitude.   It is a fact that
the Lord is ready to forgive, and this woman is a great proof
of it.   There was Job, who was tortured with ulcers and made
to scrape himself with a potsherd; he proved the Lord, that
"he is very pitiful and of tender mercy;" from him we get
evidence that God is able to sustain us amidst unparalleled
sufferings.   Let me note how Solomon proved the bounty of
God.   When he asked wisdom and knowledge, the Lord not
only granted his request, but added riches and wealth and

honor to his store; and how did Solomon magnify this proof
of divine bounty as he translates the experience of his dream
into the counsel of his proverbs? While he advises us to get
wisdom, he assures us that, "length of days is in her right
hand, and in her left hand riches and honor." And then
once more, how great a proof of God's special providence in
maintaining in this world "a remnant according to the election of grace," do we derive from the history of Elijah. There
sat the venerable seer, beneath a juniper tree, in the lone
desert,—a great but grievous man,—an honored but a de-
jected prophet of the Most High. Do you mark him as he
comes to Horeb, takes up his lodging in a cave, and complains
in the awful solitude of his soul, "I, even I only, am left, and
they seek my life to take it away?" Oh, had his fears been
realized, what a blank would earth have been without a saint!
But Elijah proved from the mouth of God the impossibility.
He learnt for our sakes, as well as his own, what a reservation
God has made in seasons of direst persecution. It is proved
that there shall ever be still a church in the world while
earth's old pillars stand.

Nor need we suppose that the testimony of the witnesses is
closed. Each of God's saints is sent into the world to prove
some part of the divine character. Perhaps I may be one of
those who shall live in the valley of ease, having much rest,
and hearing sweet birds of promise singing in my ears. The
air is calm and balmy, the sheep are feeding round about me,
and all is still and quiet. Well, then, I shall prove the love of
God in sweet communings. Or, perhaps, I may be called to
stand where the thunder clouds brew, where the lightnings
play, and tempestuous winds are howling on the mountain
top. Well, then, I am born to prove the power and majesty
of our God; amid dangers he will inspire me with courage;
amid toils he will make me strong. Perhaps it shall be mine
to preserve an unblemished character, and so prove the power
of sanctifying grace in not being allowed to backslide from my
professed dedication to God. I shall then be a proof of the
omnipotent power of grace, which alone can save from the
power as well as the guilt of sin. The divers cases of all the

Lord's family are intended to illustrate different parts of his ways; and in heaven I do think one part of our blest employ will be to read the great book of the experience of all the saints, and gather from that book the whole of the divine character as having been proved and illustrated. Each Christian man is a manifestation and display of some position or other of God; a different part may belong to each of us, but when the whole shall be combined, when all the rays of evidence shall be brought, as it were, into one great sun, and shine forth with meridian splendor, we shall see in Christian experience a beautiful revelation of our God.

Let us remember, then, as an important fact, that God intends us to live in this world to prove him, and let us seek to do so, always endeavoring as much as we can to be finding out and proving the attributes of God. Remember, we have all the promises to prove in our lifetime; and it shall be found in the last great day that every one of them has been fulfilled. As the promises are read through now, it may be asked, " Who is a proof of such a promise ?" Peradventure the question relates to some promise of almost universal application, and millions of saints will rise and say, " I prove the truth of that." Or there may be a promise in the Bible that it will seldom fall to the lot of one of God's children to prove: it is so peculiar, and few shall have been able thoroughly to understand it. But mark, there will be some witnesses to attest it, and all the promises shall be fulfilled in the united experience of the church. Such, then, the fact—God allows his children to prove him.

II. And now, secondly, we have here a CHALLENGE given to us—" Prove me now." " You who have doubted me, prove me. You who mistrust me, prove me. You who tremble at the enemy, prove me. You who are afraid you cannot accomplish your work, believe my promise, and come and prove me."

Now, I must explain this challenge to you, as to the way in which it has to be carried out. There are different sorts of promises given in God's word, which have to be proved in different ways. In the Bible there are three kinds of promise,

In the first class I will place the conditional promises, such as are intended for certain characters, given alone to them, and them only on certain conditions. There is a second class, referring exclusively to the future, the fulfillment of which does not relate to us at the present time. While there is a third and most glorious class, called absolute promises, which have no conditions whatever, or which graciously supply the requirements that the conditional promises demand. Now, each class of these promises must be proved in a different and peculiar way. To begin with conditional promises: we can not prove a conditional promise in the same way as an absolute one. The manner of proving must accord with the character of the promise to be proved. Let me mention, for example—"Ask and ye shall receive." Here it is quite obvious that I must ask in order to verify the promise. I have a condition to fulfill in order to obtain a benefit. The way to test the faithfulness of the promiser, and the truth of the promise, is plainly this—comply with the stipulation. Very different is the promise, and equally different the proof, when God says, "I will put my spirit within you, and cause you to walk in my statutes." Here we have the simple—*will*—of the Almighty. Such a promise is to be proved in a very different manner from the fulfillment, on our part, of a condition; but of this more anon.

In order to prove conditional promises, then, it is necessary for us to fulfill the condition that God has annexed to them. He says, "Bring ye all the tithes into the storehouse, that there may be meat in mine house, and prove me now herewith." No man can prove God with reference to this promise, till he has brought all the tithes into the storehouse; for it is herewith this promise has to be proved. Suppose the Lord says, "Call upon me in the time of trouble, I will deliver thee and thou shalt glorify me;" the only way of proving him is by calling upon him in the time of trouble. We may stand as long as we like and say, "God will fulfill that promise;" ay, that he will, but we must fulfill the condition, and it behoves us to seek grace of him to enable us to do so; for we cannot prove such promises unless we fulfill the conditions appended to them. There are many very sweet conditional promises; one of them helped to set my soul at rest, it was this, "Look unto me, and be ye saved, all ye ends of the earth." The condition there is, "Look unto me;" but ye can not prove it, unless you do look unto Christ. Here is another, "He that calleth on the name of the Lord shall be saved." What a blessed promise that is! But then you can not prove the promise unless you call on the name of the Lord. So that whenever we see a promise to which a condition is attached, if we wish to prove it in our own experience, we must ask of God to give us grace to fulfill the condition. That is one way of proving God.

But some will say, do not these conditions restrict the liberality and graciousness of God's promises? Oh no, beloved! for first the conditions are often put to describe the persons to whom the promises are made. Hence, my brother, when it is written, "He forgetteth not the cry of the humble," the promise fits thy chastened soul. When it saith, "To this man will I look, even to him that is of a poor and contrite spirit, and trembleth at my word," thou canst perceive, as it were, a description of thine own state. And when it saith, "I will satisfy her poor with bread," ye can some of you take comfort that the promise finds you in the fit condition to receive the blessing. But again, if the condition be, not a state, but a duty; then, let it be prayer—he gives the spirit of prayer; let it be faith—he is the giver of faith; let it be meekness—he it is that clothes thee with meekness. Thus the conditions serve to commend the promises to God's own children, and to show the bounty of him who giveth grace for grace.

The second class of promises I will mention is *future*, and we cannot fully prove them yet, nor do we always wish it. Such a promise as this, "I know that my Redeemer liveth, and that he shall stand at the latter day upon the earth; and though after my skin worms destroy this body, yet in my flesh shall I see God." We cannot prove this yet, for Christ has not appeared. We are told, and we know there is laid up for us a crown of righteousness at that day; how can we prove that ? Depend upon it, we ought to prove it, for we are commanded to prove God, and we must prove each of his promises. We must prove it, then, by patient waiting for him. I must say in myself, "All the days of my appointed pilgrimage I will wait, till my change come;" and I doubt not he will give me victory in death, for he has promised that he will make us sing aloud upon our beds, and will cheer us when we are passing through the valley of the shadow of death. Christian, prove God's promise of future blessedness, by a firm belief in it, and a patient waiting for it! Does Christ say he will come again " a second time without sin unto salva tion?" Prove it by being among the number of those who look for his appearing, who patiently wait and hope for his advent. Does he say, that when we die we shall sleep in Jesus? We do prove this when we feel so confident of sleeping in Jesus that we are prepared to depart at any moment. You see that this kind of promise is to be proved in a different way from the conditional.

But then there is the absolute promise, and that is the largest and best promise of all, for if they were all conditional promises, and the conditions rested with us to fulfill, we should all be damned. If there were no absolute promises, there would not be a soul saved; if they were all made to characters, and no absolute promise were made that the characters should be given, we should perish, notwithstanding all God's promises. If he had simply said, " He that believeth shall be saved," we should all be lost, for we could not believe without strength; but when he says, " I have loved thee with an everlasting love, therefore with loving-kindness have I drawn thee," there is an absolute promise to back up the condition. If he hath told us that if we repent we shall be saved, there is the promise that he will give us a new heart—that he will draw us to himself and make us his people. Now, the absolute promise is not to be proved by doing any thing, but by believing in it. All I can do with an absolute promise is to believe. If I were to try to fulfill a condition, it would not be accepted by God, because no condition is appended to that kind of promise. He might well say to me, " If thou hast fulfilled the condition of another promise, thou shalt have it; but **stay,** I have put no condition to this. I have said, "I will put my Spirit within them, and they shall walk in my ways; I will be their God, and they shall be my people." There is a promise without any condition. Although the child of God may have sinned, yet the promise stands good, that he shall be brought to know his error, to repent, and be wholly forgiven. Such a promise we can only believe; we can not fulfill any condition relating to it. We must take it to God, and say, Hast thou said that Christ shall "see of the travail of his soul?" (Isa. liii. 11.) Lord, we believe; let him see of the travail of his soul. Dost thou say, "My word shall not return unto me void?" Lord, do as thou hast said. Thou hast said it; Lord, do it. Has he said, "Him that cometh unto me I will in no wise cast out?" Then go and say, "Lord, I come now; do as thou hast said." On an absolute promise, I can tell thee, faith gets good foothold. Conditional promises often cheer the soul; but it is the absolute promise which is the rock that faith delights to stand upon. It is the firm, unfailing—*shall*—which asks nothing, but which is irresistible, just as it was said, "Let there be light, and there was light," by his own omnipotent fiat.

Now, beloved friends, what promise has been laid this day to your hearts? Many of you have got one that God gave you when you arose from your beds. What is thy promise, then? Is it a conditional one?—Say, "Lord, I beseech thee, fulfill the condition;" and if the promise be applied to thy soul with a condition, he will give thee the condition and the promise both, for he never gives by halves. Has he put into thy soul, "Let the wicked man forsake his way, and the unrighteous man his thoughts?" He will give you grace to forsake your ways and your thoughts too He will not give you the conditional promise without in due time giving you the condition too. Is it laid on your heart? Well, ask of Him that ye may forsake your wicked ways and your unrighteous thoughts, and return to God. But hast thou an absolute promise laid to thy soul? Then thou art a happy man. Has God laid to thine inmost spirit some of those great and precious promises, such as this: "The mountains shall depart and the hills be removed, but my kindness shall not depart from thee, neither shall the covenant of my peace be removed"? Pause not to ask for conditions; take the promise just as it is. Go on thy knees and say, "Lord, thou hast said it." Again, hath the Lord promised, "I will never leave thee nor forsake thee;" plead it. Or art thou in trouble—search out the suitable promise, Thou hast said, "When thou passest through the waters I will be with thee, and through the rivers they shall not overflow thee." I believe thee, Lord! I am tried; but thou hast said I shall have no trial that I am not able to bear. Lord, give me all-sufficient grace, and make me more than conqueror. Go and prove God. Be not afraid with any amazement. If he gives a promise, he gives you an invitation to prove it. If he gives you a single word, he means that you should bring it to him and tell it to him again; for you know he has said, "I will yet for this be inquired of by the house of Israel, to do it for them." Do, I beseech you, put the Lord in mind of his own promises, and he will most assuredly fulfill them. Here is a challenge to all the redeemed —" Prove me now."

III. In the third place, there is a *season* mentioned— " Prove me *now*." Do you know what is the most perilous time in a Christian's life? I think I could hit upon it in a moment—"now." Many persons—I might well nigh say all Christians—are ever most apprehensive of the present hour. Suppose they are in trouble, though they may have had ten times worse troubles before, they forget all about them, and now is the most critical day they ever knew. Or, if they are at ease, they say—

> " Far more the treacherous calm I dread
> Than tempests rolling o'er my head;"

and they think no position in life more dangerous than "now.' The lions are before them—how great their danger! Anu when, a little while ago, they lost their roll in the arbor of ease, how dreadful it was then! And when they got to the slippery ground, going down hill, "now" seemed their greatest danger. When they get a little further, and Apollyon meets them, "Here," they say, "is the worst trial of all." Then comes the valley of the shadow of death, and they say, "Now this is the most serious period of my life." In fact it is right that we should feel in some degree that "now" is just the time we ought to be guarded; yesterdays and to-morrows we may leave, but, "now" is the time we must be watchful. God has made no promises for yesterdays and to-morrows; he only makes such promises as he applies to our hearts now. God never lays to-morrow's promise on my heart to-day, because I am not in immediate want of it; the promises are given in the *time*, in the *place*, and in the *manner* he has designed and intended they should be answered. But no doubt some of you will sympathize with me when I say that "now" is just the time when the Christian thinks he can trust God the least. "Oh!" says he, "if I were in the same state as I was before, I should be happy. I do believe that I could have trusted my Master better then; but just now I can not lay my head so confidently on the Saviour's breast I remember when I was sick how sweet the promises were. I could then say—

> " ' Sweet to lie passive in his hands,
>   And know no will but his.'

But now I am altered. Somehow or other a languor has come over me. I can not believe that I am a Christian." You compare yourself with some brother, and feel quite sure that if you were like him you would have faith. Go and speak to this brother, and he will say, "If I were like you I should be better off." And so they would change experiences, each failing to trust God under his own circumstances. But the Lord is pleased always to give us a word that suits the particular position we may be in: "Prove me now." To allegorize a moment. There is a ship upon the sea. It is the ship which the Lord has launched, and which he has said shall come to its desired haven. The sea is smooth; the waves ripple gently, and bear the bark steadily along. "Prove me now," says the Lord. The mariner stands on the deck and says, " Lord, I thank thee that thou hast given me such smooth sailing as this; but ah ! my Master, perhaps this very ease and comfort may destroy my grace." And a voice says, " Prove me now, and see if I can not keep thee amidst the storm." Anon the heavens have gathered blackness, the winds have begun to bluster, and the waves lift up their voice, while the poor ship is tossed to and fro on the yawning deep. Amid the screaming of the tempest and the howling of the winds, I hear a voice which says, " Prove me now." See, the ship is on the rock. She has been dashed upon it ; she has been broken well nigh in sunder, and the mariner sees her hold filling with water, while all his pumps can not keep her empty. The voice still cries, " Prove me now." Alas ! she well nigh sinks ; another wave will be enough to swamp her ; it seems as if one more drop would submerge her. Still the voice cries, " Prove me now." And the mariner does prove God, and he is delivered safely from all his distresses. " They reel to and fro," and " stagger like a drunken man, and are at their wits' end ;" but " so he bringeth them unto their desired haven." Now the ship is scudding merrily along before the wind, and, lo ! she cometh to the verge of the horizon. The mists have gathered round her ; strange phantoms dance to the waves of night; a lurid light flits through the shades ; and anon the darkness comes again. Something broods about the ship that the mariner hath never seen before. The water is black beneath his vessel's prow ; the air hangs damp and thick above him ; the very sweat is clammy on his face. Fresh fear has got hold of him that he never felt before. Just then, when he knows not what to do, a voice cries, " Prove me now ;" and so he does : he cries unto the Lord and is saved.

Ah, dear friends, I might give you a hundred illustrations. I think this old Bible speaks to me to-day. I have wielded it in your midst as God's soldier. This sword of the spirit hath been thrust into many of your hearts, and though they were hard as adamant, it has split them in sunder. Some of you have had sturdy spirits broken in pieces by this good old Jerusalem blade. Many a man has come during my ministrations, armed to his very teeth, and having on a coat of mail, yet hath this tried weapon cleft him in twain, and pierced to the dividing asunder of the joints and marrow. "Prove me now," says God, "go and prove me before blasphemers; go and prove me before reprobates, before the vilest of the vile, and the filthiest of the filthy; go and prove me now." Lift up that life-giving cross, and let it again be exhibited; into the regions of *death*, go and proclaim the word of *life;* into the most plague-smitten parts of the city, go and carry the waving censer of the incense of a Saviour's merits, and prove now whether he is not able to stay the plague and remove the disease. But what does God say to the church? "You have proved me aforetime, you have attempted great things; though some of you were faint-hearted, and said, we should not have ventured, others of you had faith and proved me. I say again, Prove me now." See what God can do, just when a cloud is falling on the head of him whom God has raised up to preach to you; go and prove him now—see if he will not pour out such a blessing as ye had not even dreamed of—see if he will not give you a Pentecostal blessing. "Prove me now." Why should we be unbelieving? Have we one thing to make us so? We are weak; what of that? Are we not strongest in our God when we are weakest in ourselves? We are fools, it is said, and so we are, we know it; but he maketh fools to confound the wise. We are base, but God has chosen the base things of the world. We are unlearned,—

"We know no schoolman's subtle art,"

yet we glory in infirmity when Christ's power doth rest upon us. Let them represent us as worse than we are; let them give us the most odious character that hath ever been given to man, we will bless them, and wish them good. What though the weapon be a stone, or even the jaw-bone of an ass, if the Lord direct it? Do you not know, say some, what wise men say? Yes, we do, but we can read their oracles backwards. Their words are the offspring of their wishes. We know *who* has instructed them, and we know *he* is a liar from the beginning. O fools, and slow of heart! do you shrink from the truth, or do ye shrink from obloquy and disgrace? In either case ye have not the love to your Master you should have. If ye be brave men and true, go on and conquer. Fear not, ye shall win the day yet; God's Holy Gospel shall yet shake the earth once more. The banner is lifted up, and multitudes are flocking to it—the Pharisees have taken counsel together—the learned stand confounded—the sages are baffled. They know not what to do. The little one God has made great, and he that was despised is exalted. Let us trust him, then. He will be with us even to the end, for he has said, "Lo, I will be with you always, even unto the end of the world."

IV. The last division of my subject is an ARGUMENT, and I have trenched on that already—"Prove me now." Why should we prove God? Because, beloved, it will glorify him if we do. Nothing glorifies God more than proving him. When a poor hungry child of God, without a crust in the cupboard, says, "Lord, thou hast said bread shall be given me, and water shall be sure; I will prove thee,"—more glory is given to God by that simple proof of him than by the hallelujahs of the archangels. When some poor despairing sinner, who has been fluttering round the word, in hopes that he may—

> "Light on some sweet promise there,
> Some sure defence against despair,"

when such a one giveth credence to God's promise, in the very teeth of evidence against him, staggering not at the promise through unbelief, then he glorifies God. If thou art this morning in thy own apprehension an almost damned sinner, and thou feelest thyself to be the vilest of all, if thou wilt believe this, that Christ loves thee, and that Christ came to save thee, sinner as thou art, thou wilt glorify God as much by doing that as thou wilt be able to do, when thy fingers shall sweep across the strings of the golden harps of Paradise. We glorify God by proving him. Try God. This is the way to bring out the glorious points of the Christian character. It

is in being singularly qualified for the duties of our holy
Christian warfare, in being singularly courageous, and singularly ready, with the martyr-spirit, to peril ourselves for his
service, that we may bring glory to God. God says, "Prove
me now." Saint, wilt thou rob him of his honor? Wilt thou
rob him of his honor? Wilt thou not do that which shall
crown him, in the estimation of the world, with many more
crowns? Oh, prove him, for by so doing thou wilt glorify his
name.

Prove him again, for thou hast proved him before. Canst
thou not remember that thou wast brought very low, and yet
thou canst say, "This poor man cried, and the Lord heard him
and saved him out of all his troubles." What! wilt thou not
prove him again? Mindest thou not the goodness thou hast
proved? When thou saidst, "My feet were almost gone, my
steps had well nigh slipped," did he not support thee, saying,
"Nevertheless, I am continually with thee; thou hast holden
me by my right hand?" Has thy foot slipped? Canst thou
not thus far witness to his mercy? then trust in it to hold
thee up still. If he had once failed thee, I should not advise
thee to trust him again; but since thou hast never found him
fail thee, therefore, I say, go and prove him once more.

Again, accept this challenge, prove God's word, as he has
called thee to do, and how much blessing it will give to thyself! Beloved brethren, we endure ten times as much anxiety
in this world as we need, because we confide not in divine
promise half as much as we might. If we were to live more
on God's promise, and less on creature feelings, we should be
happier men and women, all of us. If we were to get hold of
a promise, and say, "There, let me abide by this; though the
world says it is not true, I will believe it." Could we live
alway in faith on the promises, the shafts of the enemy could
never reach us. Let us constantly, then, seek to prove him.
How much good Mr. Müller has done by proving God. He is
called by God to a special work. What does he do? He
builds an asylum and trusts to God. He has no regular income; but he says, I will prove to the world that God hears
prayer. So he lives in the exercise of prayer; and though he

may at times be brought to his last shilling, yet there is never a meal that his children sit down to without sufficient bread. Our work may be different to his; but let us seek, whatever our work is, so to do it, that when any one reads of it he will say, he tried God in such and such a promise, and his life was a standing proof that that promise did not fail. Whatever your promise is, let your life be seen to be the working out of the problem which has to be proved, and like any one proposition of Euclid, which is stated at the beginning and proved at the end, so may we find a text put at the beginning of our lives as a promise to be fulfilled and seen at the close, demonstrated, proved, and carried out.

But, dear friends, I have really done. Let me just conclude by asking those here who have been brought to know their lost and ruined state, to remember this promise, " Prove me now." Thus saith my God unto thee, O sinner, " He that calleth on the name of the Lord shall be saved." My dear hearer, art thou lost and ruined? Prove God now. He says, " Call upon me, and I will answer thee;" come now, and call upon him. He hath said, " Seek, and ye shall find;" oh, seek him now. " Knock," he says, " and it shall be opened unto you;" lift up the knocker of heaven's door and sound it with all thy might; or, suppose thou art too weak to knock, let the knocker fall down of itself. He has said, " Ask, and ye shall receive; seek, and ye shall find; knock, and it shall be opened unto you." Go, and prove the promise now. Try to prove it. He has said, " Through this man is preached unto you the forgiveness of sins, and by him all that believe are freely justified." Oh, poor soul, prove it. Art thou a poor, sick, and wounded sinner? You are told that Jesus Christ is able and willing to heal your wounds, and extract the poison from your veins. Prove him, prove him, poor soul. Thou thinkest thyself to be a lost one; therefore, I urge thee in Christ's name to prove this promise, " I, even I, am he that blotteth out thy transgressions, and will not remember thy sins." Take this to him. Say, Thou hast said, O Lord, that " this is a faithful saying, and worthy of all acceptation, that Christ Jesus came into the world to save sinners, of whom I am chief." O God, I want faith to trust thy word ; I know thou dost mean what thou hast said ; thou hast said this morning by the mouth of thy minister, "Prove me now ;" Lord, I will prove thee now, this very day, even till nightfall if thou dost not answer me. I will still keep fast by thy promise—

> "Lo, I must maintain my hold ;
> 'Tis thy goodness makes me bold ;
> I can no denial take,
> Since I plead, for Jesus' sake."

Go, my beloved, and ye will not be gone long before you will be able to sing—

> "I'm forgiven, I'm forgiven ;
> I'm a miracle of grace."

Now, do not stand still and say, "God will not hear such an one as I ; my disease is too bad for him to cure." Go and see, put your hand on the hem of his garment, and then, if the blood does not stanch, go and tell the world that thou hast proved God, and proved him wrong. Go and tell it, if thou durst. But oh ! thou canst not. If thou dost touch the hem of his garment, I know what thou wilt say : "I have tasted that the Lord is gracious. He said, 'Trust in me, and I will deliver thee.' I have trusted in Him, and he has delivered me ;" for the promise will always have its fulfillment—"Prove me now." "Prove me now," says God.

SERMON III

MEDITATION ON GOD

"My meditation of him shall be sweet."—PSALM, civ. 34

DAVID, certainly, was not a melancholy man. Eminent as he was for his piety and for his religion, he was equally eminent for his joyfulness and gladness of heart. Read the verses that precede my text, "I will sing unto the Lord as long as I live: I will sing praise to my God while I have my being. My meditation of him shall be sweet: I will be glad in the Lord." It has often been insinuated, if it has not been openly said, that the contemplation of divine things has a tendency to depress the spirits. Religion, many thoughtful persons have supposed, doth not become the young; it checks the ardor of their youthful blood. It may be very well for men with gray heads, who need something to comfort and solace them as they descend the hill of life into the grave; it may be well enough for those who are in poverty and deep trial; but that it is at all congruous with the condition of a healthy, able-bodied, successful and happy man, this is generally said to be out of the question. Now, there is no greater falsehood. No man is so happy, but he would be happier still if he had religion. The man with a fullness of earthly pleasure, whose barns are full of store, and whose presses burst with new wine, would not lose any part of his happiness, had he the grace of God in his heart; rather, that joy would add sweetness to all his prosperity; it would strain off many of the bitter dregs from his cup; it would purify his heart, and freshen his taste for delights, and show him how to extract more honey from the honeycomb. Religion is a thing that can make the most melancholy joyful, at the same time that it can make the joyous ones more joyful still. It can make the gloomy bright, as it gives the oil of joy in the place of mourning, and the garment of praise for the spirit of heaviness. Moreover, it can light up the face that is joyous with a heavenly gladness; it can make the eye sparkle with tenfold more brilliance; and happy as the man may be, he shall find that there is sweeter nectar than he has ever drunk before, if he comes to the fountain of atoning mercy; if he knows that his name is registered in the book of everlasting life. Temporal mercies will then have the charm of redemption to enhance them. They will be no longer to him as shadowy phantoms which dance for a transient hour in the sunbeam. He will account them more precious because they are given to him, as it were, in some codicils of the divine testament, which hath promise of the life that now is, as well as of that which is to come. While goodness and mercy follow him all the days of his life, he will stretch forth his grateful anticipations to the future, when he shall dwell in the house of the Lord forever. He will be able to say, as our Psalmist does, "I will sing unto the Lord. I will sing praise to my God while I have my being. My meditation of him shall be sweet. I will be glad in the Lord."

Taking these few words as the motto of our sermon to-night, we shall speak, first, concerning a profitable exercise—*meditation*. Secondly, concerning the excellence of the subject—*my meditation of him*. Thirdly, concerning the desirable result—*my meditation of him shall be sweet*.

I. First, here is a very profitable exercise—MEDITATION.

Meditation is a word that more than half of you, I fear, do not know how to spell. You know how to repeat the letters of the word; but I mean to say, you can not spell it in the reality of life. You do not occupy yourselves with any meditation. What do many of you that are merchants know concerning this matter? You rise up in the morning, just in time to take your accustomed seat in the omnibus; you hasten to your counting-house for your letters, and there you continue all day long, for business when you are busy, or for gossip when business is dull, and at night you go home too tired and jaded for the wholesome recreation of your minds. Week by week, month by month, and year by year, it is still with you one everlasting grind, grind, grind. You nave no time for meditation; and you reckon, perhaps, that if you were to set apart half an hour in the day, to ponder the weighty matters of eternity, it would be to you a clear loss of time. It is very wise of you to economize your minutes, but I suppose if half an hour in a day could earn you a hundred pounds, you would not say you could not afford it, because you know how to estimate pecuniary profit. Now, if you really knew equally how to count the great profit of meditation, you would deem it a positive gain to yourselves to spend some time therein, for meditation is most profitable to the spirit; it is an extremely healthful and excellent occupation. Far from being idle time, it is judicious employment. Do not imagine that the meditative man is necessarily lazy; contrariwise, he lays the best foundation for useful works. He is not the best student who reads the most books, but he who meditates the most upon them; he shall not learn most of divinity who hears the greatest number of sermons, but he who meditates the most devoutly upon what he does hear; nor shall he be so profound a scholar who takes down ponderous volumes one after the other, as he who, reading little by little, precept upon precept, and line upon line, digests what he learns, and assimilates each sentiment to his heart by meditation—receiving the word first into his understanding, and afterwards receiving the spirit of the thing into his own soul. When he reads the letters with his eye it is merely mechanical, but that he may read them to his own heart he retires to meditate. Meditation is thus a very excellent employment; it is not the offspring of listlessness or lethargy, but it is a satisfactory mode of employing time, and very remunerative to the spirit. Let us for a moment or two tell you some of its uses.

First, I think meditation furnishes the mind somewhat with rest. It is the couch of the soul. The time that a man spends in necessary rest, he never reckons to be wasted, because he is refreshing and renovating himself for further exertion. Meditation, then, is the rest of the spirit. " Oh," says one, "I must have rest. Here have I been, fagging and toil-

ing incessantly for months; I must have a day's excursion; I
must do this thing, and the other." Yes, and such recreation, in its proper place, is desirable; we ought to have seasons of innocent recreation; but, at the same time, if many
of us knew how to spend a little time daily in the calm repose
of contemplative retirement, we should find ourselves less ex
hausted by the wear and tear of our worldly duties,—to
meditate, would be to us a salutary recreation, and instead
of running ourselves out of breath, and laboring till a respite
is compulsory, we should spread our intervals of ease and refreshing over the whole year, and secure a small portion
every day, by turning aside from the bustling crowd to meditate upon whatever subject we wish to occupy the most
honorable place in our mind. Just as a change of posture
relieves the weariness of the body, a change of thoughts will
prevent your spirits becoming languid. Sit down in a silent
chamber at eventide, throw the window up, and look at God's
bright stars, and count those eyes of heaven; or, if you like it
better, pause in the noon-tide heat, and look down upon the
busy crowd in the streets, and count the men like so many
ants, upon the ant-hill of this world; or, if you care not to
look about you, sit down and look within yourself, count the
pulses of your own heart, and examine the motions of your own
breast. At times, 'tis well to muse upon heaven; or if thou
art a man who lovest to revel in the prophetic future, turn
over the mystic page, and study the sacred visions recorded
in the Book of Daniel, or the Book of Revelation. As thou
dost enter into these hallowed intricacies, and dost meditate
upon these impressive symbols, thou wilt rise up from thy
study mightily refreshed. You will find it like a couch to
your mind. You will return to your business in a better
spirit; you may expect (other things being equal) to earn
more that day, than you ever earned before, by the painful
system of uninterrupted drudgery; for the diversion of
thought will rest, string up, and brace your nerves, and enable you to do more work, and do it better too. Meditation
is the couch of the mind.

Again, meditation is the machine in which the raw ma-

terial of knowledge is converted to the best uses. Let me
compare it to a wine-press. By reading, and research, and
study we gather the grapes; but it is by meditation we press
out the juice of those grapes, and obtain the wine. How is
it that many men who read very much know very little?
What a host of pedantic scholars we have, who can recount
book after book, from old Hesiod to the last volume in Ward's
catalogue, but they know little or nothing after all. The
reason is, they read tome upon tome, and stow away knowledge with lumbering confusion inside their heads, till they
have laid so much weight on their brain that it can not work.
Instead of putting facts into the press of meditation, and fer-
menting them till they can draw out inferences, they leave
them to rot and perish. They extract none of the sweet juice
of wisdom from the precious fruits of the vine-tree. A man
who reads only a tenth part as much, but who takes the grapes
of Eschol that he gathers, and squeezes them by meditation,
will learn more in a week than your pedant will in a year,
because he muses on what he reads. I like, when I have read
a book for about half an hour, to walk awhile, and think it
over. I shut up the volume, and say, "Now, Mr. Author,
you have made your speech, let me think over what you have
said. A little meditation will enable me to distinguish between what I knew before and the fresh subject you communicate to me—between your facts and your opinions—between your arguments and those I should make from the
same premises." Animals, after they have eaten, lie down
and ruminate; they first crop the grass, and afterwards di-
gest it. So meditation is the rumination of the soul; thereby
we get that nutriment which feeds and supports the mind.
When thou hast gathered flowers in the field or garden, ar-
range them and bind them together with the string of
memory; but take heed that thou dost put them into the
water of meditation, else they will soon fade, and be fit only
for the dunghill. When thou hast gathered pearls from the
sea, recollect that thou wilt have gathered with them many
worthless shells, and much mud; count them over, therefore,
and sort them in thy memory; keep what are worth preserv-

ing, and even then thou must open the oyster to extract the pearl, and polish it to make it appear more beautiful. Thou mayest not string it in the necklace of thy mind, until it has been rubbed and garnished by meditation. Thus, we need meditation to make use of what we have discovered. As it is the rest of the soul, so it is, at the same time, the means of naking the best use of what the soul has acquired.

Again, meditation is to the soul what oil was to the body of the wrestlers. When those old athletes went out to wrestle, they always took care before they went to oil themselves well—to make their joints supple and fit for labor. Now, meditation makes the soul supple—makes it so that it can use things when they come into the mind. Who are the men that can go into a controversy and get the mastery? Why, the men who meditate when they are alone. Who are the men that can preach? Not those who gad about and never commune with their own hearts alone; but those who think earnestly, as well when no one is near them as when there is a crowd around them. Who are the authors who write your books, and keep up the constant supply of literature? They are meditative men. They keep their bones supple and their limbs fit for exercise by continually bathing themselves in the oil of meditation. How important, therefore, is meditation as a mental exercise, to have our minds in constant readiness for any service.

I have thus pointed out to you that meditation is in itself useful to every man. But you did not come here to listen to a merely moral essay; you came to hear something about the Gospel of God; and what I have said already is but an introduction to what I have to say concerning the great necessity of meditation in religion. As meditation is good for the mind, even upon worldly topics and natural science, much more is it useful when we come to spiritual learning. The best and most saintly of men have been men of meditation. Isaac went out into the fields at eventide to meditate. David says, "As for me, I will meditate on thy statutes." Paul, who meditated continually, says to Timothy, "Give thyself to meditation." To the Christian meditation is most essential. I should almost question the being of a Christian, and I should positively deny his well-being who lived without habitual meditation. Meditation and prayer are twin sisters, and both of them appear to me equally necessary to a Christian life. I think meditation must exist where there is prayer, and prayer would be sure to exist where there is meditation. My brethren, there is nothing more wanting to make Christians grow in grace now-a-days than meditation. Most of you are painfully negligent in this matter. You remind me of a sermon that one of my quaint old friends in the country once preached from that text—" The slothful man roasteth not that which he took in hunting." He told us that many people who would hunt for a sermon, were too lazy to roast it by meditation. They knew not how to put the jack of memory through it, and then to twist it round by meditation before the fire of piety, and so to cook it and make it fit for your soul's food. So it is with many of you after you have caught the sermon : you allow it to run away. How often do you, through lack of meditation, miss the entire purpose for which the sermon was designed. Unless ye meditate upon the truths we declare unto you, ye will gather little sweetness, ye will acquire little profit, and, certainly, ye will be in no wise established therein to your edification. Can you get the honey from the comb until you squeeze it ! You may be refreshed by a few words while you listen to the sermon, but it is the meditation afterwards which extracts the honey, and gets the best and most luscious savor therefrom. Meditation, my friends, is a part of the life-blood of every true Christian, and we ought to abound therein.

Let me tell you that there ought to be times of meditation. I think every man should set apart a portion of time every day for this gracious exercise. But, then, again I am met with an apology ; you assure me that you have so much to do you cannot afford it. I generally treat with lightness the excuses of those who cannot afford time for obvious duties. If you have got no time you should make it. Let us see now, What time do you get up in the morning ? Could you not manage to get up a quarter of an hour earlier ? Well, yes ! How long do you take for your dinner ? So long. Then you read some trashy publication, possibly. Well, why could you not spend that time in tranquil communion with your own soul? The Christian will ever be in a lean state if he has no time for sacred musings before his God. Those men who know most of God are such as meditate most upon him. Those who realize most experimentally the doctrines of grace, are those who meditate and soar beyond the reach of all sublunary things. I think we shall never have much advancement in our churches until the members thereof begin to accept habitually the counsel, " Come, my people, enter into thy chambers;" or that other, " Commune with your own heart in your chamber, and be still." Till the din and noise of business somewhat abate, and we give ourselves to calmer thought, and in the solemn silence of the mind find at once our heaven and our God, we must still expect to have regiments of dwarfs, and only here and there a giant. Giant minds can not be nourished by casual hearing; gigantic souls must have meditation to support them. Would ye be strong? Would ye be mighty? Would ye be valiant for the Lord, and useful in his cause? Take care that ye follow the occupation of the Psalmist, David, and meditate. This is a happy occupation.

II. Now, secondly, let us consider a very precious *subject :* " My meditation of HIM shall be sweet."

Christian! thou needest no greater inducement to excite thee than the subject here proposed : " My meditation of him shall be sweet." Whom does that word " him" mean? I suppose it may refer to all the three persons of the glorious Trinity? My meditation upon Jehovah shall be sweet! And, verily, if you set down to meditate upon God the Father, and reflect on his sovereign, immutable, unchangeable love towards his elect people—if you think of God the Father as the great author and originator of the plan of salvation—if you think of him as the mighty being who has said that by two immutable things, wherein it is impossible for him to lie, he hath given us strong consolation who have fled for refuge to Christ Jesus —if you look to him as the giver of his only-begotten Son, and who, for the sake of that Son, his best gift, will, with him also, freely give us all things—if you consider him as having ratified the covenant, and pledged himself ultimately to complete all its stipulations, in the ingathering of every chosen ransomed soul, you will perceive that there is enough to engross your meditation for ever, even were your attention limited to the manner of the Father's love. Or, if you choose it, you shall think of God the Holy Spirit; you shall consider his marvellous operations on your own heart—how he quickened it when you were dead in trespasses and sins— how he brought you nigh to Jesus when you were a lost sheep, wandering far from the fold—how he called you with such a mighty efficacy that you could not resist his voice— how he drew you with the cords of love. If you think how often he has helped you in the hour of peril—how frequently he has comforted you with the promise in times of distress and trouble; and, if you think that, like holy oil, he will always supply your lamp, and until life's last hour he will always replenish you with his influences, proving himself still your teacher and your guide till you get up yonder, where you shall see your Saviour face to face, in the blessed presence of the Father, and of the Son, and of the Holy Ghost—in such revelation you might find a vast and infinite subject for your meditation. But rather to-night I prefer to confine this word " him" to the person of our adorable Saviour. " My meditation of him shall be sweet." Ah! if it be possible that the meditation upon one person of the Trinity can excel the meditation upon another, it is meditation upon Jesus Christ.

> "Till God in human flesh I see,
> My thoughts no comfort find;
> The holy, just, and sacred Three
> Are terrors to my mind.
>
> "But if Immanuel's face appear,
> My hope, my joy begins;
> His name forbids my slavish fear,
> His grace forgives my sins."

Thou precious Jesus! what can be a sweeter theme for me, than to think of thine exalted being—to conceive of thee as the Son of God, who with the golden compasses struck out a circle from space, and fashioned this round world? To think of thee as the God who holds this mighty orb upon thy shoulders, and art the King of Glory, before whom angels bow with modest homage; and yet to consider thee as likewise "bone of my bone, and flesh of my flesh"—

"In ties of blood with sinners one."

To conceive of thee as the Son of Mary, born of a Virgin, wearing flesh like men, clothed in garments of humanity like mortals of our feeble race; to picture thee in all thy suffering life, in all the anguish of thy death; to trace thee in all thy passion; to view thee in the agony of Gethsemane, enduring the bloody sweat, the sore amazement; and then to follow thee to the pavement, and thence up the steep side of Calvary, bearing the cross, braving the shame, when thy soul was made an offering for my sins, when thou didst die the reconciling death 'midst horrors still to all but God unknown. Verily, here is a meditation for my soul, which must be "sweet" for ever. I might begin, like the Psalmist David, and say, "My heart is inditing of a good matter; it bubbleth up, while I speak of things which I have made touching the king; my tongue is as the pen of a ready writer." "My meditation of him shall be sweet."

Christ! Consider Christ in any way you please, and your meditation of him will be sweet. Jesus may be compared to some of those lenses you have seen, which you may take up and hold one way, and you see one light, and another way, and you see another light, and whichever way you turn them you will always see some precious sparkling of light, and some new colors starting up to your view. Ah! take Jesus for your theme; sit down and consider him; think of his relation to your own soul, and you will never get through that one subject. Think of his eternal relationship with you; recollect that the saints of Jesus were from condemnation free, in union with the Lamb, before the world was made. Think of your everlasting union with the person of Jehovah Jesus before this planet was sent rolling through space, and how your guilty soul was accounted spotless and clean, even before you fell; and after that dire lapse, before you were restored, justification was imputed to you in the person of Jesus Christ. Think of your known and manifest relationship to him since you have been called by his grace. Think how he has become your brother; how his heart has beaten in sympathy with yours; how he has kissed you with the kisses of his love, and his love has been to you sweeter than wine. Look back upon some happy, sunny spots in your history, where Jesus has whispered, "I am yours," and you have said, "My beloved is mine." Think of some choice moments, when an angel has stooped from heaven, and taken you up on his wings, and carried you aloft, to sit in heavenly places where Jesus sits, that you might commune with him. Or think, if it please you, of some pensive moments, when you have had what Paul sets so much store by—fellowship with Christ in his sufferings. Think of seasons when the sweat has rolled from your brow, almost as it did from that of Jesus—yet not the sweat of blood—when you have knelt down, and felt that you could die with Christ, even as you had risen with him. And then, when you have exhausted that portion of the subject, think of your relationship in Christ, which is to be developed in heaven. Imagine the hour to have come when ye shall "greet the blood-besprinkled band on the eternal shore," and range the—

> "Sweet fields beyond the swelling flood,
>   Array'd in living green."

Picture to your mind that moment when Jesus Christ shall salute you as "more than a conqueror," and put a pearly crown upon your head, more glittering than stars. And think of that transporting hour, when you will take that crown from off your own brow, and climbing the steps of Jesus' throne, you shall put it on his head, and crown him once more Lord of your soul, as well as "Lord of all." Ah! if you come and tell me you have no subject for meditation, I will answer, Surely, you have not tried to meditate; for "My meditation of him shall be sweet."

Suppose you have done thinking of him as he is related to you; consider him next as he is related to the wide world. Recollect that Jesus Christ says he came into the world to save the world, and undoubtedly he will one day save the world, for he who redeemed it by price and by power will restore it and renew it from the effects of the fall. Oh! think of Jesus in this relationship as the repairer of the breach, the restorer of paths to dwell in. He will come again to our earth one day; and when he comes he will find this world defaced still with the old curse upon it—the primeval curse of Eden. He will find plague, and pestilence, and war here still; but when he comes, he shall bid men "beat their swords into plowshares, and their spears into pruning-hooks;" war shall be obliterated from among the sciences; he shall speak the word, and there shall be a company that will publish it. "The knowledge of the Lord shall cover the earth, as the waters cover the sea." Jesus Christ shall come! Christians! be ye waiting for the second coming of your Lord Jesus Christ! and whilst ye wait, meditate upon that coming. Think, O my soul, of that august day, when thou shalt see him with all his pompous train, coming to call the world to judgment, and to avenge himself upon his enemies. Think of all his triumphs when Satan shall be bound, and death shall be crushed, and hell shall be conquered, and when he shall be saluted as the universal Monarch, "Lord over all, blessed for ever. Amen." "My meditation of him shall be sweet."

Ah! Christian! you are not afraid to be alone a little while now, for want of subjects of meditation! Some persons say they cannot bear to be an hour in solitude; they have got nothing to do, nothing to think about. No Christian will ever talk so, surely; for if I can but give him one word to think of—Christ—let him spell that over for ever; let me give him the word Jesus, and only let him try to think it over, and he shall find that an hour is nought, and that eternity is not half enough to utter our glorious Saviour's praise. Yea, beloved, I believe when we get to heaven we shall want no subject for meditation there, except Jesus Christ. I know there are some great divines and learned philosophers who have been telling us that when we go to heaven we shall occupy our time in flying from star to star, and from one planet to another; that we shall go and see Jupiter, and Mercury, and Venus, and all the host of celestial bodies. We shall behold all the wonders of creation; we shall explore the depths of science, as they tell us, and there are no limits to the mysteries we shall understand. My reply to people who imagine thus of heaven, is, that I have no objection it should be so, if it will afford them any pleasure; I hope you will have, and I know my Father will let you have, whatsoever will make you happy. But, while you are viewing stars, I will sit down and look at Jesus; and if you told me you had seen the inhabitants of Saturn and Venus, and the man in the moon, I would say, Ah! yes—

> " But in His looks a wonder stands,
> The noblest glory of God's hands;
> God in the person of His Son
> Hath all His mightiest works outdone."

But you will say, You will become tired, surely, of looking at him. No, I should reply; I have been looking at but one of his hands, and I have not yet thoroughly examined the hole where one of the nails went in; and when I have lived ten thousand years more I will take his other hand, and sit down and look at each gaping wound, and then I may descend to his side and his feet :—

> " Millions of years my wond'ring eyes
> Shall o'er his beauties rove,
> And endless ages I'll adore
> The wonders of His love."

You may go flitting about as far as you like; I will sit there, and look at the God in human flesh, for I believe that I shall learn more of God and more of his works in the person of Jesus than you could with all the advantage of traveling on wings of light, though you should have the most elevated imaginations and the most gigantic intellects to help you in your search.   Brethren, our meditation of Christ will be sweet.   There will be little else we shall want of heaven besides Jesus Christ.   He will be our bread, our food, our beauty, and our glorious dress.   The atmosphere of heaven will be Christ; everything in heaven will be Christ-like: yea, Christ is the heaven of his people.   To be in Christ and to be with Christ is the essence of heaven :—

> " Not all the harps above
> Can make a heavenly place,
> Should Christ His residence remove,
> Or but conceal His face."

Here is the object of our meditation.   " Our meditation of him shall be sweet."

III. Let me proceed to point out a blessed result—" Our meditation of him shall be SWEET."   This depends upon the character very much.   Ah ! I know some persons come into chapel, who are very glad when they hear the minister pro- nounce the benediction, and dismiss the assembly ; they are very glad when all is over, and they would rather hear the parting doxology than the text. As for a meditation on Christ, instead of saying it is sweet, they would say, It is precious dry.   If they happen to hear an anecdote or a tale, they do not mind remembering that ; but a meditation which should be entirely on Christ, would be dry enough to them, and they would be glad to hear it brought to a close.   Ah ! that is be- cause of the taste you have in your mouth.   There is some- thing wrong about your palate.   You know, when we have been taking some kind of medicine, and our mouth has been impregnated with a strong flavor, whatever we eat acquires that taste.   So it is with you.   You have got your mouth out of taste with some of the world's poor dainties ; you have some of the powder of the apples of Sodom hanging on your lips, that spoils the glorious flavor of your meditation on Jesus.   In fact, it prevents your meditating on Christ at all. It is only a hearing of the meditation with your ears, not a receiving it with your hearts.   But here the Psalmist says, " My meditation of him shall be sweet."   What a mercy, dear

friends, that there is something sweet in this world for us! We
need it. For I am sure, as for most other things in the world,
they are very, very bitter. There is little here that seems
sweet at first, but what has some bitter flavor afterward; and
there are too many things that are actually bitter, and void
of any relish. Go through the great laboratory of this world
and how many will be the cases that you will see marked bitter! There are perhaps more of aloes put in our cup than of
any other ingredient. We have to take a great quantity of
bitters in the course of our lives. What a mercy then it is,
that there is one thing that is sweet! "My meditation of
him shall be sweet; so sweet, beloved, that all the other bitters are quite swallowed up in its sweetness. Have I not seen
the widow, when her husband has departed, and he who was
her strength, the stay of her life and her sustenance, has been
laid in the grave—have I not seen her hold up her hands, and
say, "Ah! though he is gone, still my Maker is my husband;
'The Lord gave, and the Lord hath taken away;' blessed be
his name!" What was the reason of her patient submission?
Because she had a sweet meditation to neutralize the bitterness of her reflections. And do I not remember, even now,
seeing a man, whose property had been washed away by the
tide, and his lands swallowed up, and become quicksands, instead of being any longer profitable to him? Beggared and
bankrupt, with streaming eyes, he held up his hands, and repeated Habbakuk's words, "Though the fig-tree shall not
blossom, &c., &c., yet will I rejoice in the Lord. I will joy
in the God of my salvation." Was it not because his meditation on Christ was so sweet that it absorbed the bitterness of
his trouble? And oh! how many, when they have come to
the dark waters of death, have found that surely their bitterness was past, for they perceived that death was swallowed up
in victory, through their meditation upon Jesus Christ! Now,
if any of you have come here with your mouths out of taste,
through affliction and trouble, if you have been saying with
Jeremiah, "Thou hast filled my mouth with gravel stones,
and made me drunken with worm-wood"—if so, take a little of
this choice cordial; I assure you it is sweet: *Lacrymœ Christi,*

as it is called. If thou wilt take these tears of Jesus and put them in thy mouth, they will take away all the unpleasant flavor. Or again, I bid you take this meditation upon Christ, as a piece of scented stuff that was perfumed in heaven. It matters not what thou hast in thy house ; this shall make it redolent of Paradise—shall make it smell like those breezes that once blew through Eden's garden, wafting the odor of flowers. Ah ! there is nothing that can so console your spirits, and relieve all your distresses and troubles, as the feeling that now you can meditate on the person of Jesus Christ. " My meditation of him shall be sweet."

But, my dear hearers, shall I send you away without asking you whether you have ever had such a meditation upon our Lord and Saviour Jesus Christ ? I do not like to preach a sermon, without pressing it home to the conscience of my hearers. I never like to bring you out a sword and show it you, and say, " There is a sword, and it is sharp ;" I always like to make you feel that it is sharp, by cutting you with it. Would to God the sword of the Spirit might penetrate many of your hearts now ! When I see so many gathered together even on a week-day, I am astonished. But wherefore have ye come, my brethren ? What went ye out for to see ? a reed shaken with the wind ? What have ye come out for to see ? a prophet ? Nay, but I say that you have come to see something more than a prophet. You have come to see and hear somewhat of Jesus Christ, our Saviour and our Lord. How many of you meditate on Christ ? Christian men and women, do you not live below your privileges, many of you ? Are you not living without having choice moments of communion with your Jesus ? Methinks, if you had a free pass to heaven's palace, you would use it very often ; if you might go there and hold communion with some person whom you dearly loved, you would often be found there. But here is your Jesus, the king of heaven, and he gives you that which can open the gates of heaven and let you in to hold company with him, and yet you live without meditating upon his work, meditating upon his person, meditating upon his offices, and meditating upon his glory Christian men and women ! I say to you, is it not time we should begin to live nearer to God? What is to become of our churches? I do not know what to think of Christendom at large. As I travel through the country and go here and there, I see the churches in a most awfully dwindled state. True, the Gospel is preached in most; but it is preached as it might be by humble-bees in pitchers— always the same monotonous sound, and no good is done. I fear that the fault lies in the pews, as well as in the pulpit. If hearers are meditative preachers must be meditative. It is very true that water does not run up-hill; but when you begin to meditate and pray over the word, your ministers will see that you have gone beyond them, and they will set to and meditate themselves, and give you the Gospel just as it comes fresh from their hearts, food for people's souls.

And for the rest of you—you who have never meditated on Jesus Christ—what do you think shall become of you when your bitterness shall be in your mouth? When you taste death, how do you hope to destroy its ill flavor? Yet "that last, that bttter cup which mortal man can taste" is but a dire presentiment. When you have to drink that gall in hell for ever—when the cup of torments which Jesus did *not* drain for you will have to be drained by yourself—what will you do then? The Christian can go to heaven, because Christ has drunk destruction dry for him; but the ungodly and unconverted man will have to drink the dregs of the wine of Gomorrah. What will you do then? The first drops are bad enough, when you sip here the drops of remorse on account of sin; but that future cup in hell—that terrific mixture which God deals out to the lost in the pit—what will you do when you have to drink that? when your meditation will be, that you rejected Jesus, that you despised his Gospel, that you scoffed at his word? What will you do in that dread extremity? Many of you business men! will you ledger serve you with a sweet meditation in hell? Lawyer! will it be sweet for you to meditate on your deeds when you go there? Laboring man! will it be a sweet meditation to thee, to think that thy wages were spent in drunkenness, or thy Sabbath profaned, and thy duties neglected? And thou, professor! will it be a sweet meditation to sit down and think of thine hypocrisy? And ah! ye carnally minded men, who are indulging the flesh, and pampering the appetite, and not serving the Lord, " whose God is your belly, and whose glory is in your shame," will your career furnish a sweet meditation to you at last? Be assured of this: your sins must be your meditation, then, if Christ is not 'your meditation now. May there be great searchings of heart this night! How often do your convictions disperse like the smoke from the chimney, or the chaff from the winnower's hand; they soon vanish. It will not profit you to live at this rate—hearing sermons and forgetting them. Take heed to the voice of warning, lest God should say, "He that being often reproved hardeneth his neck, shall be suddenly destroyed, and that without remedy." O wicked men! wicked men! one word to you, all of you who know not God, and ye shall go. I will give you a subject for your meditation to-night. It shall be a parable. A certain tyrant sent for one of his subjects, and said to him, "What is your employment?" He said, "I am a blacksmith." "Go home," said he, "and make me a chain of such a length." He went home; it occupied him several months, and he had no wages all the while he was making the chain, only the trouble and the pains of making it. Then he brought it to the monarch, and he said, "Go and make it twice as long." He gave him nothing to do it with, but sent him away. Again he worked on, and made it twice as long. He brought it up again, and the monarch said, "Go and make it longer still." Each time he brought it, there was nothing but the command to make it longer still. And when he brought it up at last, the monarch said, "Take it, bind him hand and foot with it, and cast him into a furnace of fire." There were his wages for making the chain. Here is a meditation for you to-night, ye servants of the devil! Your master the devil is telling you to make a chain. Some of you have been fifty years welding the links of the chain; and he says, "Go and make it longer still. Next Sunday morning you will open that shop of yours, and put another link on next Saturday night you will be drunk, and put another link on; next Monday you will do a dishonest action, and so you will keep on making fresh links to this chain; and when you have lived twenty more years, the devil will say, "More links on still!" And then, at last, it will be, "Take him, and bind him hand and foot, and cast him into a furnace of fire." "For the wages of sin is death." There is a subject for your meditation. I do not think it will be sweet; but if God makes it profitable, it will do good. You must have strong medicines sometimes, when the disease is bad. God apply it to your hearts!

SERMON IV

PARDON AND JUSTIFICATION

"Blessed is he whose transgression is forgiven, whose sin is covered."—
PSALM xxxii. 1

FEW men judge things aright. Most people measure by
appearances; few know the test of reality. We pronounce
the man blessed who grasps the scepter or wears the crown;
whereas, perhaps, no peasant in his dominions enjoys less happiness than he does. We pronounce that man blessed who
has uninterrupted and perpetual health; but we know not the
secret gnawings of the heart, devoured by its own anguish,
and embittered by a sorrow that a stranger can not perceive.
We call the wise man happy, because he understandeth all
things, from the hyssop on the wall to the cedar of Lebanon;
but he saith, "Of making many books there is no end," and
"much study is a weariness of the flesh." We are all for
pronouncing our neighbor's lot happier than our own. As
Young says of mortality, "All men think all men mortal but
themselves," we are apt to think all men happy but ourselves.
But oh! if we could see things as they are—if we were not
deceived by the masquerade of this poor life—if we were not
so easily taken in by the masks and dresses of those who act
in this great drama, be it comedy or tragedy—if we could
but see what the men are behind the scenes, penetrate their
hearts, watch the inner motions, and discern their secret feelings, we should find but few who could bear the name of
"blessed;" indeed, there are none except those who come
under the description of my text, "Blessed is he whose transgression is forgiven, whose sin is covered." He is blessed,
thrice blessed, blessed for evermore, blessed of heaven, blessed
of earth, blessed for time, blessed for eternity. The man

whose sin is not forgiven is not blessed,—the mouth of Jehovah hath said it, and God shall manifest that—cursed is every man whose transgression is not forgiven, whose sin is not covered.

Dearly beloved, we come to the consideration of that most excellent and choice blessing of God, which bespeaks our pardon and justification; and we trust that we shall be able to show you its extreme value.

And first, the blessedness of the person enjoying this mercy will appear, if we consider the exceeding value of it in its nature and its characteristics. Then if we notice the things that accompany it, and afterwards, if we muse upon the state of heart which a sense of forgiveness would engender, we shall see that indeed a man must be blessed whose sin is covered, and whose transgression is taken away. Let us first look at the blessing as it is. *It is an unpurchaseable blessing.* No one could purchase the pardon of his sin. What though we should each offer a hecatomb to our God ? the sacrifice would smoke in vain, for Lebanon is not sufficient to burn, nor the beasts thereof for a burnt offering. If we could make rivers of oil wide as the Amazon and long as the Mississippi, we could not offer them to God as an acceptable present, for he would be careless of its value. We might bring money in vain, for he saith the " Silver and gold are mine ;" no oblation can add to his wealth, for he saith " Every beast of the forest is mine, and the cattle on a thousand hills. If I were hungry, I would not tell thee, for the world is mine, and the fulness thereof." These are God's own creatures ; we could but offer to him what he did create. Nothing man can present by way of sacrifice can ever purchase the blessing.

Then consider, *the utter difficulty of procuring the blessing in any way.* Since it is not to be purchased, how can it be procured ? Here is a man to-night who has sinned against God, and he makes the inquiry, " How can I be pardoned ? How can I be forgiven ?" The first thought which starts up in his mind is this, " I will seek to amend my ways; in the virtue of the future I will endeavor to atone for the follies of the past, and I trust a merciful God will be disposed to forgive my sins, and spare my guilty but penitent soul." He then turns to Scripture to see if his hopes are warranted, and he reads there, " By the works of the law shall no flesh living be justified." " They sought salvation, not by faith, but by the works of the law. For they stumbled at that stumbling-stone; as it is written, Behold, I lay in Zion a stumbling-stone and rock of offence." He fancies that if he should reform and amend his life, he will be accepted, but there comes from the throne of God a voice which says, " The soul that sinneth, it shall die." " Having sinned, O man," says God, " I must inflict punishment for thy sin." God is so inflexibly just that he has never forgiven and never will forgive the sinner without having exacted the punishment for his sin. He is so strictly true to his threatenings, and so unutterably severe in his justice, that his Holy Law never relaxes its hold upon the sinner till the penalty is paid, and vengeance has exacted its utmost farthing. " Well," says the sinner, " I can not redeem the past: what must I do ? If I amend for the future, there is the dark catalogue of past offences still pursuing me. Even if I run up no other debts, there are the old accounts. How can I get them paid ? How can I get past sins forgiven ? How can I find my way to heaven ?" Then he thinks, " I will seek to humble myself before God ; I will cry and lament, and I hope, by deep penitence and heartfelt contrition, and by perpetual floods of tears, God may be induced to pardon me." O man ! Though thy tears drop on the black list of thy sins one by one, they will not blot out a single sin. Those sins are engraved in brass—these tears are not a liquid strong enough o burn out what God has thus inscribed. Thou mightest weep till thy very eyes were wept away, and until thy heart were all distilled in drops, and yet not remove one single stain from the brazen tablet of the memory of Jehovah.

> " Could thy tears for ever flow,
> 　Could thy zeal no respite know,
> 　All for sin could not atone :
> 　Christ must save and he alone."

There is no atonement in tears or repentance. God has not

said, " I will forgive you for the sake of your penitence."
What is there in thy penitence that can make you deserve
forgiveness ? If you deserved forgiveness you would have a
set-off against your guilt. This were to suppose some claims
upon God, and there would be no mercy in giving you what
you could claim. Repentance, of itself, is not an atonement
for sin. What, then, can be done? Justice says, " Blood for
blood ; a stroke for every sin, blood for every crime." Thus
saith the Lord, " I will by no means clear the guilty." The
sinner feels within his heart that the judgment is just; like
the man to whom I talked some time ago, who said, " If God
does not damn me, he ought. I have been so great a sinner
against his laws that his equity would be sullied by my
escape." The sinner, when convicted in his own conscience,
must own the righteousness of God in his condemnation. He
knows that he has been so wicked, he has sinned so much
against heaven, that God in justice must punish him. He
feels that God can not pass by his sin and his trangression.
Then there must be an atonement, in order to obtain pardon,
he thinks; who shall effect it? Speed your way up to
heaven. It is vain to ask it on earth. Go up there, where
cherubs stand around the throne of God. Ask one by one the
brilliant spirits, and say, " Can ye offer an atonement ? God
has said, man must die ; and the sentence can not be altered :
God himself can not reverse it, for it is like the laws of the
Medes and Persians, irrevocable. Punishment must follow
sin, and damnation must be the effect of iniquity. Thou
blazing seraph, wilt thou quench thy glories for a moment and
descend to hell ? But then it would not be for a moment ;
for thou shouldst tarry there for ever ; thou must be eternal
ages long in bearing the punishment of only one soul. Therefore, O seraph ! I would not ask thee. Besides, thou art not
a man ; and the Scripture says, ' *It* shall die.' No satisfaction
would it yield if thou didst die. Ye angels, I have no hope
from you." I must turn my eye in another direction. Where
shall I find help? Where shall I obtain deliverance ? Man
can not help me; angels can not. The greatest archangel can
do nought for us. Where shall we find forgiveness ? Where

is the priceless prize? The mine hath it not in its depths. Stars have it not in their brilliance. The floods can not tell me as they lift up their voice; nor can the hurricane's blast discover to me the mystery profound. It is hidden in the sacred counsels of the Most High. Where it is I know not, until from the throne of God I hear it said, "I am the substitute!" And looking up there, I see sitting on the throne a God and yet a man—a man who once was slain! I see his scarred hands and his yet open side. But he is a God, and, smiling benignantly, he says, "I have forgiveness, I have pardon; but I purchased it with blood. This heart was riven for it; this precious casket of divinity was broken open for your souls. I had to die—the just for the unjust. Excruciating agony, pains unutterable, and woes such as ye can not comprehend, I had to suffer for your sake." And can I say, this amazing grace is mine? Has he enrolled my worthless name in the covenant? Do I see the blood mark on the writ of my pardon? Do I know he purchased it with such a price? And shall I refuse to say, "Blessed is the man whose transgression is forgiven, whose sin is covered?" Nay; I must and will exult, for I have found this jewel, a jewel before which diadems do pale and lose their lustre. I have found this "pearl of great price;" and I must and will esteem all things but lost for Jesus' sake; for, having found this unpurchaseable mercy, this blessing which could not be bought except with blood, I must shout again, "Blessed is the man whose transgression is forgiven." It would be well for thee, Christian, if thou wouldst often review this mercy, and see how it was purchased for thee; if thou wouldst go to Gethsemane and see where the bloody clots lie thick upon the ground; if thou wouldst then take thy journey across that bitter brook of Kedron and go to Gabbatha, and see thy Saviour with his hair plucked by the persecutors, with his cheeks made moist with the spittle of his enemies, with his back lacerated by the deep ploughings of knotted whips, and himself in agony, emaciated, tormented; then, if thou wouldst stand at Calvary and see him dying, "the just for the unjust;" and having seen these bitter torments remember that these were but little

compared with his inward and soul-anguish; then thou
wouldst come away and say, "Blessed, yea, thrice blessed, is
the man who has thus been loved of Jesus, thus purchased
with his blood—'Blessed is he whose transgression is forgiven
whose sin is covered.'"

Another thing concerning this blessing of justification is
not only its immense value and its unpurchaseableness, but it
coming to us instantaneously. You know it is a doctrine that
has been taught by divines long enough, and taught in Scripture, that justification is an instantaneous act. I am perhaps
this moment unjustified. The moment God gives me faith, I
become justified; and being justified by faith I have peace
with God. It takes no time to accomplish it. Sanctification
is a lifelong work, continually effected by the Holy Ghost;
but justification is done in one instant. It is as complete the
moment a sinner believes as when he stands near the lamps
that smoke before the Eternal. Is it not a marvelous thing
that one moment should make thee clean? We love the physician who heals speedily. If you find a skillful physician who
can heal you of a sad disease even in years, you go to him,
and are thankful. But suppose some wondrous man who with
a touch could heal you, who with the very glance of his eyes
could make you well at once, and stanch that blood or stop
that disease, or turn aside that evil thing and make you well,
would you not go to him, and feel that he was a great physician indeed? So with Christ. There shall be a man standing
there with all his sins upon his head, and he may yet go down
these stairs just, complete in Christ, without a sin, freed from
its damning power, delivered from all his guilt and iniquity,
in one single instant! It is a marvelous thing, beyond our
power and comprehension. It is done in an instant. God
stamps it; the man is pardoned. He goes away in that same
instant justified, as the publican did when he said, "Lord,
have mercy upon me, a sinner," and received the mercy for
which he sued.

But one of the greatest things about it is, *that it is irreversible*. This is the sweetness of it. The irreversible nature
of justification is what makes it so lovely in the eyes of God's

people. We are justified and pardoned, and then the mercy is that we never can be unpardoned—we never can be condemned. Those who are opponents of this glorious doctrine may say what they please; but we know better than to suppose that God ever pardons a man, and punishes him afterward. We should not think Her gracious Majesty would have a criminal before her, and give him a free and full pardon, and then in the course of a few years bring him up and have him executed. "But," say you, "the man commits fresh crimes and iniquities; and though the pardon may suffice for the past, it will not do for the future." Well, if you have got that sort of pardon, you may go and rejoice in it. I thank God I have a different one. I can say, and all God's believing people can say,

> "Here's pardon for transgressions past;
> It matters not how black their cast:
> And, O my soul! with wonder view,
> For sins to come there's pardon too."

It is complete washing that Jesus gives—from that which is to come, as well as that which is past.

> "The moment a sinner believes,
> And trusts in his crucified God,
> His pardon at once he receives,
> Salvation in full through his blood."

God never did anything by halves. He speaks a man into a justified condition, and he will never speak him out of it again; nor can that man be cast away. Good God! and do any persons teach that men can be quickened by the Spirit, and yet that quickening Spirit has not power enough to keep them? Do they teach that God forgives, and then condemns? Do they teach that Christ stands surety for a man, and yet that man is damned himself on his own responsibility? Ah! let them teach it! We speak not thus; we have not so learned Christ. We can not use words so derogatory to divinity, so dishonorable to the blessed Saviour. We believe that if he stood our substitute, it was an actual, real, effectual deed; that we are positively delivered thereby; that if he did pay the penalty, God can not by any means exact it twice; that if he did discharge the debt, it is discharged, and can not be revived; that if the sin was imputed to Christ, he did suffer for it. We say before all men that heaven itself can not accuse the sons of God any more of sin. Who shall lay anything to the charge of God's elect, if God hath justified, and Christ hath died? Ah, Christian! thou mayest stand and wonder at this mighty justification, to think that thou art so pardoned that thou never canst be condemned, that all the powers in hell can not condemn thee, that nothing which can happen can destroy thee; but that thou hast a pardon that thou canst plead in the day of judgment, and that will stand as valid then as now. Oh, it is a glorious and gracious thing! Go, ye who believe in another gospel, and seek comfort. Yours is not the justification of the blessed God. When he justifies, he justifies for ever, and nothing can separate us from his love.

Well, this is the mercy itself. I have only made three remarks upon it, though there are some fifty that one might make, and each of them might be pregnant with meaning. Now we come to the second thing. "Blessed is he whose transgression is forgiven, whose sin is covered," BECAUSE THAT MERCY BRINGS EVERYTHING ELSE WITH it. When I know I am pardoned, then I can say all things are mine. I can look back to the dark past—all things are mine there! I can look at the present—all things are mine here! I can look into the deep future—all things are mine there! Back in eternity, I see God unrolling the mighty volume, and lo! in that volume I read my name. It must be there, for I am pardoned; for whom he calls, he had first predestinated, and whom he pardons, he had first elected. When I see that covenant roll, I say, It is mine! And all the great books of eternal purposes and infinite decrees, are mine! And what Christ did upon the cross is mine! The past is mine! The revolutions of past ages have worked for the good of me and of my brethren—all things are mine there! Standing in the present, I see Providence, and that is mine! Its various circumstances are working together for good. Its very wheels—though high and wonderful—are working, wheel within wheel, to produce some great and grand effect which shall be for the general good of the church. Afflictions are mine to sanctify me—a hot furnace where my dross is taken away. Prosperity is mine to comfort me—a sweet garden where I lie down to be refreshed in this weary journey. All the promises are mine. What though this Bible be the prince of books—what though each letter be a drop of honey, and it be filled with sweetness, there is not a precious text here which is not mine, if I am a believer; there is not a promise which I may not say is my own—all is mine! All these present things I may take without fear, for they are my Father's gift to me, a portion of my heritage! I rejoice also to know that all of the future is mine, whatever that future may be. I know that in the future there shall come an hour when at God's mandate the hot breasts of earth shall start up from between her brazen ribs—her mountains themselves shall be dissolved, and the earth shall pass away. But this great conflagration is mine! I know that on a certain day I shall stand before the judgment bar of Christ—that judgment day is mine! I fear it not, and dread it not. I know that soon I must die—but the river of death is mine! It is mine to wash me, that I may leave the dust of earth behind, and take my garments clean washed afterward, having swam through this glorious river; for it is a glorious river, though its waters may be tinged with blackness—it takes its rise in the mountains of love, hard by the throne of God. And then after death there comes a resurrection—and that resurrection is mine! With a bright body, clear as the sun, and fair as the moon, I shall live in paradise. And then, whatever there is in heaven is mine! If there be a city with azure light, with jasper wall—it is mine! What though there be palaces there of crystal and o gold, that sparkle so as to dim mortal eyes; what though there be delights above even the dream of the voluptuary · what though there be pleasures which heart and flesh could not conceive, and which even spirit itself can not fully enjoy,

the very intoxication of bliss; what though there be sublimities unlawful for us to utter, and wonders which mortal men
can not grasp; what though the Divinity hath spent itself in
heaven, and doth unravel his glory to make his people blessed
—all is mine! There is not a crown that is bright and glorious but it is mine! For I am pardoned! Though I may
have been the chief of sinners, and the vilest of the vile, if
God justify me to-night, all things in heaven are mine, however glorious, bright, majestic, and sublime. Oh! is not this
a mercy! Verily, "blessed is he whose transgression is for
given, whose sin is covered," as we consider what comes with
the mercy.

We would that time and bodily strength permitted us to
dilate upon this, for it is a wide subject; but we must pass on
to the next point. "Blessed is the man whose transgression
is forgiven, and whose sin is covered," BECAUSE IT MAKES HIM
BLESSED BY THE EFFECTS IT HAS UPON HIS MIND. What
glorious peace it brings to a man when he first knows himself
to be justified! The apostle Paul said, "Therefore being
justified by faith, we have peace with God." Some of you
do not know what peace means; you never had any real, satisfactory peace. "What," say ye, "never had any peace,
when we have been happy and merry and joyous?" Let me
ask you, when the morning has appeared after your evening
of mirth, could you look back upon it with joy? Could you
look upon it and say, "I rejoice in these unbridled revelings.
I always find laughter productive of a sweet calm to my
heart?" No; you could not, unless you are hardened. I
challenge you rather to tell me what fruit have ye ever
gathered from those things whereof ye are now ashamed?
Ye had not any peace. When alone in your chamber, a leaf
fell, or some little insect buzzed in the further corner: ye
trembled like the leaves of the aspen. Ye thought perhaps
the angel of death was there with a dreary omen. Or passing
from the haunts of fashion, ye have walked some lonely road
in solitude, and how then did your disordered fancy conjure
up all sorts of evil demons! Ye had no peace, and ye have
no peace even now. Some of you know not peace with God

Ye are at war with the Omnipotent; ye are lifting your puny hand against the Most High God. To-night ye are warriors against the King of Heaven, rebels to his government, and guilty of a great act of high treason against the Eternal Majesty. Oh! if ye did but know peace with God—that "peace which passeth all understanding." I compare not the peaceful mind to a lake without a ripple. Such a figure would be inadequate. The only comparison I can find is in that unbroken tranquility which seems to reign in the deep caverns and grottoes of the sea—far down where the sailor's body lies, where the sea-shells rest undisturbed, where there is nought but darkness, and where nothing can break the spell, for there are no currents there, and all is still—that is somewhat like the Christian's soul when God speaks to him. There may be billows on the surface, by these he may be sometimes ruffled, but inside the heart there will be no ebb or flow; he will have "eternal peace with God," a "peace that passeth all understanding," too deep to fathom, too perfect to conceive, for none but they who prove it know: such peace that you could to-night lay your head down to sleep with the knowledge that you would never wake again in this world as calmly as you could if you knew your days were like Hezekiah's, lengthened out for a certainty of fifteen years. When we have peace with God, we can lie down, and if an angel visited us to say, "Soul, your Master calls you," we could reply, "Tell my Master, I am ready. And if grim death were to come stalking to our bed-side, and were to say, "The pitcher is broken at the fountain, and the well is broken at the cistern: thou shalt die!" we might answer, "Die! we die willingly; we are prepared; we are not afraid; we have peace with God, through our Lord Jesus Christ; we have peace here, and we are willing to go and have that peace consummated up yonder in the better world." Could you say that, some of you? You know you could not. If I were to go round and ask you, you would have to say, "No; I am in an unsettled state of mind. I am afraid. I have no pardon, no forgiveness; I do not know that my sins are blotted out." Well, poor soul! at any rate you will say, "Blessed is

the man whose sin is covered." You know he is blessed,
though you are not blessed yourselves; you feel you would
be blessed indeed if you could once get your sins covered, and
your transgressions taken away.

But it not only gives peace, it gives joy; this is something
more. Peace is the flowing of the brook, but joy is the dash
ing of the cataract when the brook is filled, bursts its banks,
and rushes down the rocks. Joy is something that we can
know and esteem; and justification brings us joy. Oh! have
you ever seen the justified man when first he is justified? I
have often told you what I felt myself when first I realized
pardon through the blood of Christ. I had been sad and
miserable for months, and even years; but when I once received the message, "Look unto me and be ye saved, all ye
ends of the earth," verily, I could have leapt for joy of heart;
I felt that I understood that text, "The mountains and hills
shall break forth before you into singing, and all the trees of
the field shall clap their hands." I remember hearing Dr.
Alexander Fletcher, when speaking to children, tell them a
simple anecdote in order to illustrate the joy of a man when
he gets delivered from sin. He said, "I saw upon the pavement three or four little chimney-sweeps jumping about and
throwing up their heels in great delight. And I asked them,
'My boys, what are you making all this demonstration for?'
'Ah! said they, 'if you had been locked up for three months,
you would do the same when you once got out of prison.'"
I thought it a good illustration. We can not wonder that
people are joyous and glad when, after being long shut up in
the prison of the law, all sad and miserable, they have felt
their bonds broken, seen the door of the jail opened, and obtained a legal discharge. What heed they about trials and
troubles, or anything else? They could leap over the mountains: "By our God we leap over a wall," may they say.
"A troop may overcome, but we shall overcome at last."
The heart seems scarcely big enough to hold the joy, and it
bursts out, hardly knowing what to do or say. Thus it is at
that wondrous hour which comes but once in a Christian's
life, when he first feels himself delivered, when God for the

first time says to him, " I am he that blotteth out all **thy** transgressions for my name's sake !" I verily think that hour is a fragment of eternity cut off and given us here ; I am sure it is a foretaste of the happiness at God's right hand. It is a day of heaven upon earth, that splendid moment when God first gives us a knowledge of our own justification—Heaven's bliss itself can scarce exceed it ! We seem to drink of the very wine that saints in glory quaff ! We want nothing else —what can we desire more ? "Blessed is the man whose transgression is forgiven, and whose sin is covered ;" it gives him joy, it gives him peace.

And have you ever noticed one thing that I must mention here ? If you have ever had a great trouble, you have found that it has swallowed up all little troubles. Suppose a sailor has something on deck that is not quite right ; he fidgets and worries himself about this, that, and the other. A storm comes. Big clouds appear, and the winds begin to whistle through the cordage. The sails are rent, and now the ship is driving before the wind over mountains and into valleys of water ; he fears that the ship will be wrecked, and that he will be lost. What cares he now for the things on deck, for the cabin, or the furniture ? "Never mind about these," he says, "the ship is being lost !" And suppose the cook to run up and say, " I am afraid the dinner will be spoiled." What heeds he ? "The ship," he says, "may be lost, and that is of much more consequence than the dinner." So with you. If you once get into sore trouble on account of your souls, you will not fret much about the little troubles you have here, for they will all be swallowed up by the one giant alarm. And if you get this everlasting joy into your souls, it will be much the same ; it will consume all your smaller joys and griefs That joy will be like Moses' rod, which ate up all the serpents that the magicians threw down before Pharaoh—it will eat up all other joys. It will be enough if you can say—

> " I'm forgiven ! I'm forgiven !
> I'm a miracle of grace."

If you **can** but feel yourself justified ; if you **know that you**

are delivered, that you are indeed pardoned, that you are beyond the clutches of the law, you can rejoice that you know and feel the truth of the saying, "Blessed is the man whose transgression is forgiven, and whose sin is covered."

Now, let me ask in conclusion, How many such blessed men and women are there here to-night? How long shall I give you to answer the question? I wish preaching were done away with, and that we had a little more talking to one another. I wish to lay the formalities of the pulpit aside, and talk to you as if you were in your own houses. That, I believe, is the true kind of preaching. Let me inquire, then, how many of you, my friends, can claim the title of "blessed," because you are justified? Well, I think I can see one brother who puts his hands together and says—

> " 'A debtor to mercy alone—
> Of covenant mercy I sing.'

I know I am forgiven." My brother, I rejoice at it. I rejoice to hear thee speak thus confidently. But, I come to another, and I ask, What are you? "Ah! I cannot say as much as that brother did, but I hope I am justified." What ground have you for your hope? You know we cannot hope unless we have some grounds. We may wish, but we cannot hope. What are your grounds? Do **you** believe on the Lord Jesus Christ? "Yes," say you, "I do believe on him." What do you say "hope" for, then? Dear brother or sister, you *know* if you really believe in Christ, you have no need to talk about *hope* when you may be certain. And it is always better to use words of confidence when you can, and use little ones when you can't. Keep your head as high as you may, for you will find troubles enough to bring it down. But the next one replies:—Ah!

> "Tis a point I long to know,
> Oft it causes anxious thought.
> Do I love the Lord or no?
> Am I his, or am I not?"

I have heard a great deal said against that hymn. But I have

had occasion to sing it myself sometimes, so I cannot find
much fault with it. That state of mind is all very well if it
lasts a little while, though not if it lasts a long time. If a
man is always saying, "I long to know," or, "I am afraid,"
he never will know unless he gets a change. The Scripture
says, "He that is justified by faith has peace with God."
You would not have this distress always if you were brought
to realize your justification. You may have it sometimes
when the eye of faith is dim; but I do not like to see people
contenting themselves with any measure of faith short of that
which apprehends full redemption. Do not let me distress
the little ones, for be it known I often say—

> " Thousands in the fold of Jesus,
>   This attainment ne'er can boast:
>   To his name eternal praises,
>   None of them shall e'er be lost."

Their names were written in the Lamb's book of life before
the world was made; but if any of you are always in distress
and doubt, if you never did at any time feel confident, I
should begin to be apprehensive, for methinks you should now
and then get a little higher. You may pass through the valley of the shadow of death sometimes, but surely sometimes
also, the Spirit of God will carry you up to the top of the
mountain that is called "Clear." And yet, if you are still
dwelling on this point, "I long to know," are you not anxious
to settle the question? Suppose you do not belong to Christ.
Put it in that way—for in a doubtful case it is best to look at
the worst side—suppose you do not love the Lord. Nevertheless, you are a sinner; you feel you are a sinner, do you
not? God has convinced you that you are a sinner. Well,
as long as you can claim sinnership, you can go to his feet.
If you cannot go as a saint, you can go as a sinner. What a
mercy this is! It is enough to save us from despair. Even
if our evidence of saintship seems clean gone, we have not
lost our sinnership; and the Scripture still says, "This is a
faithful saying, and worthy of all acceptation, that Christ
Jesus came into the world to save sinners." And while it

says that, we will hang on it. But another one says, "I don't know whether I am justified, and I don't care much about it." Let me tell you, sir, when you will care. When you come near your end, young man, you will care then. You may think to live very well without Christ, but you cannot afford to die without him. You can stand very securely at present, but death will shake your confidence. Your tree may be fair now, but when the wind comes, if it has not its roots in the Rock of Ages, down it must come. You may think your worldly pleasures good, but they will then turn bitter as wormwood in your taste; worse than gall shall be the daintiest of your drinks, when you shall come to the bottom of your poisoned bowl. But there is another, who says, " I wish I were justified, but I feel I am too great a sinner." Now, I like to hear the first part, but the last is very bad. To say that you are bad is right; I know you are. You say you are vile, and that is true enough, I'm sure, and I hope you mean it. Do not be like some men I have read of. You know there was a monk who, on a certain occasion, described himself as being as great a hypocrite as Judas; and a gentleman at once said, " I knew it long ago; you are just the fellow I always thought." When up jumped the monk, and said, " Don't be saying such things as those of me!" His humility was feigned, not felt. Thus people may make such a general confession as this, " I am a great sinner," who would still resist any special charge brought home to their consciences, however true. Say to such a one, " You are a rogue," and he replies, " No, I'm not a rogue." " What are you, then? Are you a liar?" " Oh, no!" " Are you a Sabbath-breaker?" " No; nothing of the kind." And so, when you come to sift it, you find them sheltering themselves under the general term sinner, not to make confession, but to evade it. This is very different from a real conviction of sin. But if you feel yourself to be a real, actual sinner, remember you are not too bad to be saved, because it is written in Scripture that Christ came to save sinners; and that means that he came to save you, because you are a sinner. And I will preach it everywhere, without limitation, that if a man knows himself to be a sinner, Jesus Christ died for him, for that is the evidence that Christ came to save him. Let the sinner, then, believe on Jesus as his Savior; let the outcast come to Jesus, for it is said, "I will gather together the outcasts of Israel." There is an outcast here to night; there is a backslider over there who has been cut off from the church years ago. Behold his sad plight. As Achish said of David, "His own people Israel have utterly abhorred him. He shall be my servant for ever." But he shall escape yet. The prey shall not be taken from the mighty; the lawful captive shall not be taken from Jesus Christ. The Captain of our salvation conquered his soul once, and he will yet save it.

But another says, "I never was a member of a church, and I am afraid I never shall be. I am a hardened snner, a reprobate." Well, do you confess it? Then hear the word of the Lord: "He that believeth and is baptized shall be saved, and he that believeth not shall be damned." "He that believeth," —mark you, that is, he that believeth *on* Jesus and *in* Jesus; he that casts himself on Christ. Our hymn says, he who "ventures" on Christ, but that is not right. There is no venturing; it is all safe. He who puts himself on Christ—throws himself flat on sovereign mercy—"he that believeth;" notice what follows, "and is baptized;"—baptism is to come afterward, not for merit, but as a mode of profession—he that with his heart believeth, and with his mouth confesseth—he that believeth and is baptized—shall be saved; and he that believeth not shall be damned. I dare not leave any word out, whatever any of my brethren may do. Whether a man be baptized or not, if he does not believe he shall be damned. But the word "baptized," is not put into the last sentence, because the Holy Spirit saw there was no necessity for it For he knew, if the ordinance were correctly administered, that no person who did not believe would be baptized. So it was the same thing as putting it in, "He that believeth not shall be damned." Oh, may God grant that you may never know the meaning of that last dreadful word; but may you know what it is to be saved by grace divine!

SERMON V

THE GOOD SHEPHERD

"The Lord is my shepherd, I shall not want."—PSALM, XXIII. 1

DOES not this sound just like poetry or like singing? If you read the entire psalm through, it is written in such easy prose, that though it is not translated into meter, as it should have been, it reads just like it. "The Lord is my shepherd, I shall not want. He maketh me to lie down in green pastures; he leadeth me beside the still waters; he restoreth my soul, and leadeth me in the paths of righteousness for his name's sake." It sounds like music for this, among other reasons—because it came from David's heart. That which cometh from the heart always hath melody in it. When men speak of what they do know, and testify of what they have seen from the depths of their souls, they speak with what we call eloquence; for the meaning of the word eloquence is—speaking out of, speaking from the soul. Thus David spake of what he knew, what he had verified all his life long, and this rendered him truly eloquent. As "truth is stranger than fiction," so the truth that David spake is more sweet than even fancy could have sported with; and it hath more beauty than even the dream of the enthusiast could have pictured. "The Lord is my shepherd, I shall not want." How naturally it seems to strike on the ear as uttered by David, who had himself been a shepherd boy! He remembers how he had led his flock by the waters of Jordan in the warm summer, how he had made them lie down in shady nooks by the side of the river; how on sultry days he had led them on the high hills that they might feel the cool air; and how when the winter set in he had led them into the valleys that they might be hidden from the stormy blast; well could he remember the tender care with which he protected the lambs, and carried them; and how he had tended the wounded of the flock. And now, appropriating to himself the familiar figure of a sheep, he says, " The Lord is my shepherd, I shall not want." I will try to preach experimentally of this matter to-night, and I wonder how many of you will be able to follow the Psalmist with me while I attempt to do so ?

First of all, THERE ARE SOME PRELIMINARIES before a man can say this ; it is absolutely necessary he should feel himself to be like a sheep by nature; for he can not know that God is his shepherd, unless he feels in himself that he has the nature of a sheep. Secondly, THERE IS A SWEET ASSURANCE—a man must have had some testimony of Divine care and goodness in the past, otherwise he can not appropriate to himself this verse, " The Lord is my shepherd." And thirdly, THERE IS A HOLY CONFIDENCE. I wonder how many there are here who can place all the future in the hand of God, and can join with the last sentence, " The Lord is my Shepherd, I shall not want ;" if all the earth does, I shall not want.

I. First, then, we say there is a CERTAIN CONFESSION neces sary before a man can join in these words ; we must feel that there is something in us which is akin to the sheep ; we must acknowledge that in some measure we exactly resemble it, or else we can not call God our shepherd.

Well, I think the first apprehension we shall have, if the Lord has brought us into this condition, is this—*we shall be conscious of our own folly ; we shall feel how unwise we always are.* A sheep is one of the most unwise of creatures. It will go anywhere except in the right direction ; it will leave a fat pasture to wander into a barren one ; it will find out many ways but not the right way ; it would wander through a wood, and find its way through ravines into the wolf's jaws, but never by its wariness turn away from the wolf; it could wander near his den, but it would not instinct- ively turn aside from the place of danger ; it knoweth how to go astray, but it knoweth not how to come home again. The sheep is foolish. Left to itself, it would not know in what pasture to feed in summer, or whither to retire in winter.

Have we ever been brought to feel that in matters of providence, as well as in things of grace, we are truly and entirely foolish ? Methinks, no man can trust providence till he distrusts himself; and none can say, " The Lord is my shepherd, I shall not want," until he has given up every idle notion that he can control himself, or manage his own interests. Alas! we are most of us wise above that which is written, and we are too vain to acknowledge the wisdom of God. In our self-esteem we fancy our reason can rule our purposes, and we never doubt our own power to accomplish our own intentions, and then, by a little manœuvring, we think to extricate ourselves from the difficulty. Could we steer in such a direction as we have planned, we entertain not a doubt but we shall avoid at once the Scylla and the Charybdis, and have fair sailing all our life long. And too often, alas! we touch the forbidden thing, under the vain notion that the end will justify the means if we should be able entirely to clear our way. O beloved! surely it wants but little teaching in the school of grace to make out that we ourselves are fools. True wisdom is sure to set folly in a strong light. I have heard of a young man who went to college; and when he had been there one year, his parent said to him, " What do you know ? Do you know more than when you went ?" " Oh! yes," said he, " I do." Then he went the second year, and was asked the same question—" Do you know more than when you went ?" " Oh! no," said he, " I know a great deal less." " Well," said the father, " you are getting on." Then he went the third year, and was asked the same question—" What do you know now ?" " Oh !" said he, " I don't think I know anything." " That is right," said the father ; " you have now learnt to profit, since you say you know nothing." He who is convinced that he knows nothing of himself as he ought to know, gives up steering his ship, and lets God put his hand on the rudder. He lays aside his own wisdom, and cries, " O God! my little wisdom is cast at thy feet ; my little judgment is given to thee. Such as it is, I surrender it ; I am prepared to renounce it, for it hath caused me many an ill, and many a tear of regret, that I should have followed my own devices, but henceforth I

will delight in thy statutes. ' As the eyes of servants look
unto the hand of their masters, and as the eyes of a maiden
look unto the hand of her mistress, even so shall mine eyes
wait upon the Lord my God.' I will not trust in horses, ior
in chariots ; but the name of the God of Jacob shall be my
refuge. Too long, alas ! have I sought my own pleasure, and
labored to do everything for my own gratification. Now
would I ask, O Lord, thy help, that I may seek first the king
dom of God, and his glory, and leave all the rest to thee."
Do you, O my friends, feel persuaded that you are foolish ?
Have you been brought to confess the sheepishness of your
nature ? Or are you flattering your hearts with the fond conceit that you are wise ? If so, you are fools. But if brought
to see yourselves like Agur when he said, " I am more brutish than any man, and have not the understanding of a man,"
then even Solomon might pronounce thee wise. And if thou
art thus brought to confess, " I am a silly sheep," I hope thou
wilt be able to say, " The Lord is my shepherd, I can not have
any other, I want none other : he is enough for me."

Again, a sheep is not only a *foolish* but a *dependent* creature. The sheep, at least in its domesticated state, as we
know it, must ever be dependent. If we should take a horse,
we might turn him loose upon the prairie, and there he should
find sufficient scope for his powers ; and, years after, we might
see him in no worse condition than that in which we left him.
Even the ox might thus be treated and still be able to provide
for itself. But as for the silly sheep, set it alone in the wilderness, let it pursue its own course unheeded, and what
would be its fate ? Presently, if it did not wander into places
where it would be starved, it would ultimately come to ruin,
for assuredly some wild beast would lay hold upon it, and it
hath no means of defence for itself. Beloved, have we been
brought to feel that we have of ourselves no means of sub-
sistence, and no power of defence against our foes ? Do we
perceive the necessity for our dependence upon God ? If so,
then we have learnt another part of the great lesson, that the
Lord is our shepherd. Some of us have yet this lesson to
learn. Fain would we cater for ourselves and carve for our

selves; but, as the good old Puritan says, "No child of God ever carves for himself without cutting his fingers." We sometimes fancy that we can do a little. Ay, ay! but we shall have that conceit taken from us very soon. If we indeed be God's people, he will bring us to depend absolutely upon him, day by day. He will make us pray that prayer, "Give us *this* day our daily bread;" that we may make this acknowl edgment that he openeth his hand and giveth us our meat in due season. Sweet is the meal that we eat, as it were, out of his hand. Yet some will rebel against this dependence as very humiliating. Men like to vaunt their independence. Nothing is more respectable in their eyes than to live in independent circumstances. But it is no use for us to talk of being independent; we never can be. I remember a dear Christian man who prayed very sweetly on each Sunday morning at a certain prayer-meeting that I once attended— "O Lord, we are *independent* creatures upon thee." Except in such a sense as that, I never knew any independence worth having. Of course he put the syllable "*in*" too much. He meant "we are *de*pendent creatures," and "we are dependent creatures upon thee." So we must be. We cannot be independent even of one another, and certainly we are not independent of God: for, when we have health and strength we are dependent upon him for their continuance; and if we have them not, we are dependent on him to restore them to us. In all matters whatsoever it is sweet, it is blessed, to see the tokens of his watchful care. If I had a thing of which I could say, "God has not given me this," I hope, by Divine grace, I should turn it out of doors. Food, raiment, health, breath, strength, every thing, cometh from him, and we are constantly dependent upon him. As Huntingdon used to say, "My God gives me a hand-basket portion. He does not give me an abundance at once; but he gives it basket by basket, and I live from hand to mouth." Or, as old Hardy once said, "I am a gentleman commoner on the bounty of God; I live day by day upon morning commons and evening commons. And thus I am dependent upon him, independent of the world, but dependent upon God." The sheep is a dependent thing, always

needing some help; and so is the Christian; and he realizes
the blessedness of his dependence when he can say, in the
words of my text, "The Lord is my shepherd."

These are the two principal points upon which we view this
with regard to providence. I might wander from what I
wished to be the subject of this evening; and I might be
doing good if I were to show you some other points of comparison between the Christian and the sheep. O beloved!
there are some of you here present who know yourselves to
be sheep by reason of your frequent wanderings. How often
have we made this confession, "We have erred and strayed
from thy ways like lost sheep," and we do feel it this night,
bitterly rueing the waywardness of our hearts. But it is well to
be the sheep of God's pasture, even if we have been wandering
sheep. We do not read of wandering dogs, because dogs are
naturally wild, while sheep are always accounted to be some
one's property. The straying sheep has an owner, and however far it may stray from the fold, it ceases not to belong
to that owner. I believe that God will yet bring back into
the fold every one of his own sheep, and they shall all be
saved. It is something to feel our wanderings, for if we
feel ourselves to be lost, we shall certainly be saved; if we
feel ourselves to have wandered, we shall certainly be brought
back.

Again, we are just like sheep by reason of the perverseness
of our wills. People talk about free-will Christians, and tell
us of persons being saved and coming to God of their own free
will. It is a very curious thing, but though I have heard a
great many free-will sermons, I never heard any free-will
prayers. I have heard Arminianism in preaching and talking,
but I have never heard any Arminian devotion. In fact, I
do not think there can be any prayer of the sort. It is a
style that does not suit prayer. The theory may look very
nice in argument, and sound very proper in discourse, though
we somewhat differ from it; but for practical purposes it is
useless. The language will not suit in prayer, and this alone
would be sufficient reason to condemn it. If a man can not
pray in the spirit of his own convictions, it shows they are a

delusion from beginning to end, for if they were true he could pray in that language as well as in any other. Blessed be God! the doctrines of grace are as good to pray with as to preach with. We do not find ourselves out of order in any act of worship when once we have the old fundamental doctrines of the blessed gospel of grace. Persons talk about free-will Christians coming back to Jesus of themselves. I intend to believe them when they find me a free-will sheep that has come back of itself; when they have discovered some sheep after it has gone from its fold stand bleating at its master's door to be taken in again. You will not find such a thing, and you will not find a free-will Christian just yet, for they will all confess if you thoroughly probe the matter, that it was grace, grace alone that restored their souls—

> " Grace taught our souls to pray,
>   And made our eyes o'erflow;
> 'Tis grace that keeps us to this day,
>   And will not let us go."

Not to pause longer on the threshold, let us proceed to the text itself. The two things which I have explained to you we must feel before we can realize the pith of the matter are these—our own folly and our entire dependence upon the providence of God.

II. The next thing is, the ASSURANCE—how are we able to see that the Lord is our shepherd? It is very easy to say the Lord is *a* shepherd; but how shall we appropriate the blessedness to ourselves—the Lord is *our* shepherd? I answer that he hath had certain dealings with our souls in the past which have taught us that he is our shepherd. If every man and every woman in this assembly to-night should rise up and say, "The Lord is my shepherd," I feel convinced it would be in many instances the solemn utterance of an untruth; for there are, it is to be feared, many here who have not God for their shepherd. He is their guide, it is true, in some sense, because he overrules all the hearts and controls all the affairs of the children of men; but they are not the people of his pasture, they are not the sheep of his hand;

they do not believe, therefore they are not of his fold. And if some of you should say that you are, your own conscience would belie you. How, then, does a man come to know that the Lord is his Shepherd?

He knows it, *first*, because Jesus Christ has brought him back from his wanderings. If there be any one here who after a course of folly and sin has been brought from the mountains of error and the haunts of evil; if there be one here who has been stopped in a mad career of vice, and has been reclaimed by the power of Jehovah Jesus, such a one will know by a happy experience that the Lord is his shepherd. If I once wandered on yon mountain top, and Jesus climbed up and caught me, and put me on his shoulders, and carried me home, I can not and dare not doubt that he is my shepherd. If I had belonged to some other sheep-owner he would not have sought me. And from the fact that he did seek I learn that he must be my shepherd. Did I think any man convinced me of sin, or that any human power had converted me, I should fear I was that man's sheep and that he was my shepherd. Could I trace my deliverance to the hand of a creature, I should think that some creature might be my shepherd; but, since he who has been reclaimed of God must and will confess that God alone has done it, and will ascribe to his free grace, and to that alone, his deliverance from sin, such a one will feel persuaded that the Lord must be his shepherd, because he brought him, he delivered him, he snatched him out of the jaw of the lion and out of the paw of the bear. Such is the first token of the shepherd's care which we receive at the hand of the Lord.

We know still further, that like a shepherd he has supplied our wants. Some of you, beloved, know of a surety that God is your provider. You have been brought sometimes into such straits that if it had not been for an interposition of Heaven itself you never could have had deliverance. You have sunk so deep down into poverty, and lovers and acquaintance have stood so far aloof from you, that you know there is but one arm which could have fetched you up. You have been reduced perhaps to such straits that all you could do was to pray.

You have wrestled at the throne, and sought for an answer, but it has not come ; you have used every effort to extricate yourself, and still darkness has compassed your path. Again and again you have tried, till hope has well nigh vanished from your heart, and then, adding vows to your prayer, you have said in agony, " O God, if thou wilt deliver me this time I will never doubt thee again." Look back on the paths of your pilgrimage. Some of you can count as many Ebenezers as there are milestones from here to York ; Ebenezers piled up, with oil poured on the top of them ; places where you have said, " Hitherto the Lord hath helped me." Look through the pages of your diary, and you will see time after time, when your perils and exigencies were such as no earthly skill could relieve, and you felt constrained to witness what others among you have never felt—you felt that there is a God, that there is a Providence—" a God who compasseth your path," and " is acquainted with all your ways." You have received deliverance in so marvelous a way, from so unseen a hand, and so unlikely a source, under circumstances, perhaps, so foreign to your wishes, and yet the deliverance has been so perfect, so complete, and wonderful, that you have been obliged to say, " The Lord *is* my shepherd." Yes ; *he is.* The sheep, we know, fed day by day in good pasture, may forget its shepherd ; but if for a time it is taken from the pasture, and then brought home again, after having been nearly starved, it says, " Truly, he is my shepherd." If I had always been supplied with bread, without the pinch of anxiety, I might have doubted whether he had given it, and ascribed it to the ordinary course of passing events ; but, seeing that " everywhere and in all things I am instructed both to be full and to be hungry, both to abound and to suffer need," I own that it is " my God who supplies all my need ;" yea, and with gratitude I will write it down for a certainty, " The Lord is my shepherd."

But, beloved, do not be distressed, even though you should not have had these particular trials and deliverances, for there is a way whereby we can tell that the Lord is our shepherd without encountering so many rough and rugged passes, as I will show you presently. I have heard it said by some, that a man can not be a child of God unless he has gone through a certain set of trials and troubles. I recollect hearing a sermon from these words, "Passing through the valley of Baca, they make it a well." Certainly the preacher did not make his sermon a well, for it was as dry as a stick, and not worth hearing. There was nothing like cheerfulness in it; but a flood of declamation all the way through against hopeful Christians, against people going to heaven who are not always grumbling, and murmuring, and doubting; fumbling for their evidences amid the exercises of their own hearts; ever reading and striving to rival Job and Jeremiah in grief, taking the Lamentations as the fit expression of their own lips, troubling their poor brains, and vexing their poor hearts and smarting, and crying, and wearying themselves with the perpetual habit of complaining against God, saying, "My stroke is heavier than my groaning." Such persons measure themselves by their troubles, and trials, and distresses, and tribulations, and perplexities, and no end of these things that we will not stop to recount. WE believe, indeed, that such things will come to a child of God; we think every Christian will be corrected in due measure; we should be the last to deny that God's people are a tried people. They must all pass through the furnace of affliction, and he has chosen them there; but still we believe that religion is a blessed and a happy thing, and we love to sing that verse :—

> ' The men of grace have found
> Heaven begun below;
> Celestial fruits on earthly ground,
> From faith and hope do grow."

And what though some of my hearers have not yet had to swim through the rivers, though they may not have had to pass through the fiery furnace of providential trial—they have had trials enough, and trials that no heart has known except their own, sufferings which they could not tell to flesh and blood, which have gnawed their very souls and entered into the marrow of their spirits; bitter anguish and aching voids such as those who boast about their trials never felt, such as mere babbling troublers did never know, deep rushings of the stream of woe with which little bubbling narrow brooks could never compare. Such persons fear to murmur, they can not tell their sufferings, because they think it would be showing some want of trust in God ; they keep their trials to themselves, and only tell them into that ear which heareth and hath no lips to babble afterward. " But," you say, " how can you tell the Lord is your shepherd if you have not been tried in any of those great deeps ?" We know that he is, because he has fed us day by day in good pasture. And if he has not suffered us to wander so far away as others, we can lift up our eyes and say, " Lord, thou art my shepherd ; I can as fully prove that thou art my shepherd by thy keeping me in the grassy field, as by thy fetching me back when I have wandered ; I know thou art as much my shepherd when thou hast supplied my wants day by day as if thou hadst suffered me to go into poverty and given me bitterness ; I know thou art as much my shepherd when granting me a continual stream of mercy, as if that stream had stopped for a moment and then began again." Persons say if they have had an accident, and been nearly killed, or have narrowly escaped, " What a providence !" Why, it is as much a providence when you have no accident at all. A good man once went to a place to meet his son. Both his son and himself had ridden from some distance. When the son arrived he exclaimed, " O ! father, I had such a providence on the road." " Why, what was that ?" " My horse stumbled six times, and I was not thrown down and killed." " Dear me !" said his father, " but I have had a providence too." " And what was that ?" " Why, my horse never stumbled at all, and that is just as much a providence as if the horse had stumbled six times, and I had not been thrown down." Well, you know it is a great providence when you have lost your property, and God provides for you ; but it is quite as much a providence when you have no loss at all, and when you are still able to live above the depths of penury and so God provides for you. I say this to some of you whom God has blessed from your earliest youth, and continually provided for ; you, too, can say, " The Lord is my shepherd ;"

you can see it stamped on your mercies; though they come daily, they are given you of God; and you will say, by humble faith, the word "*my*" as loud as any one of them. "The Lord is *my* shepherd." Do not get despising the little ones because they have not had so many trials as you have. You great *standard* men, do not get cutting the children of G d in pieces because they have not been in such fights as you have. The master leads the sheep where he pleases, and be sure he will lead them rightly; and as long as they can say the word "my," do not trouble yourselves where they learned it—if they can say from their hearts, "The Lord is my shepherd, I shall not want."

III. Now, we finish up with the HOLY CONFIDENCE of the blessed Psalmist: "I shall not want—I am sure I shall not want." There poor unbelief says, "I am wanting in everything, I am wanting in spirituals, I am wanting in temporals; and I shall want. Ah! such distress as I had a little while ago. You can not tell what it was; it was enough to break one's heart. And it is coming again; I *shall* want." That is very good, unbelief, but you must write your own name at the bottom, and then I will repeat to you this, "The Lord is my shepherd, I shall not want." That is what David said, and I think David's faith rather preferable to your unbelief after all. I take your evidence in some matters, but I really would not take it before David's. I would accept your testimony as an honest man in some respects, but I think the words of inspiration are rather preferable to your words of apprehension. When I find it written, "The Lord is my shepherd, I shall not want," I would rather take one of David's affirmations than fifty of your negations. Methinks I hear some one saying, "I would bear the want of any temporal good, if I could but obtain spiritual blessings. I am in want this night of more faith, more love, more holiness, more communion with my Saviour." Well, beloved, the Lord is thy shepherd; thou shalt not want even these; if thou askest of him, he will give them to thee, though it may be by terrible things in righteousness that he will save thee. He often answers his people in an unexpected manner; most of God's answers to our letters come down in black envelopes; yet, mark you, they will come. If you want peace, joy, sanctification, and such like things, they shall be given to you, for God hath promised them. The Lord is your shepherd, you shall not want. I have often thought of the large promise written in the Bible—I do not know where there is a larger one—"No good thing will he withhold from them that walk uprightly." "No good thing!" It is a mercy that the word "good" was put in, for if it said, "nothing," we should have been asking for many things that would be bad for us; but it says, "no good thing!" Now, spiritual mercies are good things, and not only good things, but the best things, so that you may well ask for them; for if no good thing will be withholden, much more will none of the best things. Ask, then, Christian, for he is thy shepherd, and thou shalt not want; he will supply thy need; he will give thee whatever thou requirest; ask in faith, nothing doubting, and he shall give thee what thou wilt, according to thy desires. But still there are some who say, "The text applies to temporal matters," and persist in it. Well, then, I will accept this sense—the Lord is your shepherd, you shall not want. "Ah!" cries one, "I was once in affluence, and now I am brought down to penury. I once stood among the mighty and was rich, now I walk among the lowly and am poor." Well, it does not say, "The Lord is your shepherd, and you shall not come down in society;" it does not say, "The Lord is your shepherd, and therefore you shall have five hundred or a thousand pounds a year;" it does not say, "The Lord is your shepherd, and therefore you shall have whatsoever your soul lusteth after." All it says is, "The Lord is your shepherd, and you shall not want." There are different ways of wanting. There are many people whose foolish craving and restless anxiety make them always in want. If you gave them a house to live in, and fed them day by day, they would always be wanting. And after you had just relieved their necessities, they would want still. The fact is, theirs are not real wants, but simply fancied wants. It does not say, "The Lord is my shepherd, therefore I shall not fancy I want;" for, though God might promise it, it would need his omnipotence to carry it out: for his people often get fancying that they want, when they do not. It is real wants that are referred to. "The Lord is my shepherd, I shall not really want." There are many things we wish for that we do not want, but there is no promise given that we shall have all we wish for. God hath not said that he would give us anything more than the bread or the water: "Bread shall be given him; his waters shall be sure;" and he has not broken that promise yet, has he ? So, lift up thy head, and do not be afraid. Fear not, thy God is with thee; he shall prevent evil from hurting thee; he shall turn darkness into light, and bitter into sweet. All the way he hath led thee, and all the way he shall lead thee; this shall be thy constant joy. He is my shepherd, I shall not really want that which is absolutely necessary. Whatever I really require shall be given by the lavish hand of a tender father. Believer, here is thy jointure, here is thine inheritance, here is thine income, here is thy yearly living: "He•is thy shepherd, and thou shalt not want." What is thy income, believer ? "Why," you say, "it is different with some and others of us." Well, but a believer's income is still the same. This is it: "The Lord is my shepherd, I shall not want." That is my income, and it is yours, poor little one. That is the income of the poorest pauper in the workhouse who hath an interest in the grace of God. The Lord is her shepherd, she shall not want: that is the income of the poor foundling child that has to come to know the Lord in early life, and hath no other friend. The Lord is her shepherd, she shall not want: that is the widow's inheritance. The Lord is her shepherd, she shall not want: that is the orphan's fortune. The Lord is his shepherd, he shall not want: that is the believer's portion, his inheritance, his blessing.

"Well now," some may say, "but what is it worth ?" Beloved, if we could now change away this promise for a world of gold, we would not; we had rather live on this promise than live on the finest fortune in creation. We reckon that this is an inheritance that makes us rich indeed ! "The Lord is my shepherd, I shall not want." Give me ten thousand pounds, and one reverse of fortune may scatter it all away; but let me have a spiritual hold of this Divine assurance—"The Lord is my shepherd, I shall not want"—then I am all right—I am set up for life. I can not break with such stock as this in hand. I never can be a bankrupt. for I hold this security—"The Lord is my shepherd, I shall not want." Do not give me ready money now; give me a cheque-book, and let me draw what I like. This is what God does with the believer. He does not immediately transfer his inheritance to him, but lets him draw what he needs out of the riches of his fullness in Christ Jesus. The Lord is his shepherd, he shall not want. What a glorious inheritance! Walk up and down it, Christians; lie down upon it, it will do for thy pillow; it will be soft as down for thee to lie upon. "The Lord is my shepherd, I shall not want." Climb up that creaking staircase to the top of thy house, lie down on thy hard mattrass, wrap thyself round with a blanket, look out for the winter when hard times are coming, and say, "What shall I do?" But, then, just hum over to thyself these words, "The Lord is my shepherd, I shall not want." That will be like the hush of a lullaby to your poor soul, and you will soon sink to slumber. Go, thou business man, to thy counting-house again, after this little hour of recreation in God's house, again to cast up those wearisome books. Thou art saying, "How about business? These prices may be my ruin. What shall I do?" When thou hast cast up thine accounts, put this down against all thy fears, and see what a balance it will leave—"The Lord is my shepherd, I shall not want." There is another man. He does not lack anything, but still he feels that some great loss may injure him considerably. Go and write this down in thy cash-book. If thou hast made out thy cash-account truly, put this down: "The Lord is my shepherd, I shall not want;" put that down for something better than pounds, shillings and pence, something better than gold and silver. "The Lord is my shepherd, I shall not want." "Ah!" says the cold, calculating man, "your promise is not worth having, sir." No; it would not, if it were my promise. But fortunately it is not. It is God's promise. It is only my promise if God has given it to me. It has nothing to do with you. He that disregards it knows nothing about it, but he who apprehends it says, "Ah! yes! it is true, 'The Lord is my shepherd, I shall not want.' " He will find this promise like Chian wine of which the ancients said it was flavored to the lip of him that tasted it. The promise shall taste sweet to thee if thy palate is pure; yet it shall be worth nothing to thee but mere froth if thy taste is not healthy.

But, beloved, we must divide our congregation before we send you away, and remind you that there are some of you to whom this does not belong. Perhaps some of you professors of religion may want this promise badly enough; but it is not yours. The Lord is not your shepherd; you are not the sheep of his pasture, and the flock of his hand. You are not those who have gone astray; you are not sheep, but goats— unclean creatures, not harmless, and undefiled as sheep; but everything that is the very reverse. Oh! it is not only eternal loss, it is not only everlasting injury that you have to regret—it is present loss, it is present injury; the loss of a jointure on earth, the loss of an inheritance below. To lose this promise here on earth,—this were like a temporary hell. To be deprived of such a comfort and promise as this is a terrible privation. Oh! it is enough to make men long for religion if it were only for that sweet placidity and calm of mind which it giveth here below. Well might men wish for this heavenly oil to be cast on the troubled waters of this mortal life, even if they did not anoint their heads therewith, and enter into glory with the joy of their Lord upon their countenance. Beloved, there are some I know here—and your conscience tells you that I mean yourselves—who speak within your own hearts, and the voice now says, "I am none of his sheep." Well then, there is no promise for you that you shall not want; for you there is no help, there is no providence. The promise and the providence are for believers, and not for you. There is no word that all things shall work together for your good; but rather, cursed shalt thou be in thy basket and cursed in thy store, cursed in the field, cursed in thy house, and cursed in thy goings out, and cursed in thy comings in, for " the curse of the Lord is in the house of the wicked." It doth not peep in at his window, but it is in his house. Yet God "blesseth the habitation of the righteous." The curse shall follow you until your dying day; and not having him for your shepherd, you shall wander where that hungry wolf the devil shall at last seize upon your soul, and everlasting misery and destruction from the presence of Jeho- vah must be your inevitable, miserable, and inexpressibly awful doom. May the Lord in mercy deliver you from it! And this is the way of salvation : " He that believeth and is baptized shall be saved ; he that believeth not shall be damned." " He that believeth and is baptized"—we omit nothing that God has said. " He that believeth and is bap- tized"—not he that is baptized and believeth (which were to reverse God's order). " He that believeth and is baptized" —not he that is baptized without believing, but the two joined together. He that believeth with his heart and is baptized, confessing with his mouth—" he that believeth and is baptized shall be saved." Do you neglect one part of it ? It is at your peril, sir! " He that believeth and is baptized," says God. If any of you have neglected one portion of it, if you have believed and have not been baptized, God shall save you. Still this promise saith not so. " He that believeth and is baptized ;" it says the two together ; and " what God hath joined together let no man put asunder ;" what he hath ordered let no man disarrange. " He that believes"—that is, he that trusts in Jesus ; he that relies upon his blood, his merits, and his righteousness—" and is baptized, shall be saved ; he that believeth not shall be damned."

SERMON VI

THE GRACIOUS LIPS OF JESUS

" Grace is poured into thy lips."—Psalm, xlv. 2

It is marvellous what a never-ending theme there is in the
name and person of our blessed Lord and Savior Jesus Christ.
The poets of Scripture never mention his person but they fall
into rhapsodies at once; they never sing of his name or of his
glories but at once they seem to be so enchanted by the spirit
of poetry, that they soar up with ecstasies of joy, and their
love scarcely knows how to find language to express itself.
Love sometimes overleapeth language among sensitive men;
and so it does more palpably in sacred Scripture. Take, for
instance, the Canticles. There love hath strained language to
the uttermost, in order to embody its vehement passion : yea,
so strained it, that some of us *not so* filled with love to God
can scarcely appreciate its *glowing* utterance. Here, too, you
see our Psalmist no sooner begins to meditate on the person
of the Messiah, with harp in hand, than he cries, " My heart
bubbleth up with a good matter; I speak of the things which
I have made touching the king: my tongue is the pen of a
ready writer. Thou art fairer than the children of men;
grace is poured into thy lips." We shall have no time for
preface this morning, but we must proceed at once to the discussion of our text.

Grace is poured into the lips of Christ. Let us consider,
First, *the plenitude of this grace;* Secondly, *the nature of this
grace;* and Thirdly, endeavor to show you *in what offices
Jesus Christ proves that " grace is poured into his lips."*

I. We commence with the word "poured," as suggesting
the plenitude of "grace." "Grace is poured into thy
li] s." Others among the children of men have had " grace;"

mighty poets have spoken gracious words; and prophets of
old have uttered wondrous sayings, which were divinely inspired; so that it might be said, their doctrine " dropped" as
the rain, and that their speech "distilled" like the dew
Such imagery, however, is too faint to describe our Lord
Jesus. Not merely as the dew did he speak, nor did his
voice simply drop as the small rain: it was "POURED" from
his lips. Whenever he spoke, a copious stream of gracious
words flowed from him like a very cataract of eloquence
Jesus Christ had not a little grace, but it was " poured into"
him; not a phial of oil on his head, but he had a cruse and a
horn of oil emptied upon him. "Grace was poured into his
lips." I would remark that Calvin translates this: "Grace is
shed from thy lips." Not only did God give to his Son grace
on his lips, but the Son, whenever he speaks, whether he
addresses the people in doctrine and exhortation, or whether
he pleads with his Father on their behalf—whenever his lips
are open to speak to God for men, or from God to men, he
always has "grace shed from his lips." And when I turn to
the Septuagint translation of this passage, I find that it has
the idea of the very exhaustion of grace: "Grace is poured
from thy lips," as though emptied out till there is none left.
Jesus Christ had grace exhausted in his person. In him
"dwelt all the fullness of the Godhead bodily." All grace
was given to him; the very exhaustion of the inexhaustible
store: as much as to say that God could give no more, and
that Jesus Christ himself could not receive or possess more
grace. It was all poured into his person; and when he
speaks, he seems to exhaust grace itself. Imagination's utmost stretch cannot conceive of anything more gracious; and
the contemplation of the most devoted Christian cannot
think of any words more majestic in goodness, more tender
in sympathy, more full of honey, and more luscious in their
sweetness, than the gracious words that proceeded out of the
lips of Jesus Christ. "Grace is poured into his lips." Ah!
Christian, you may have some grace on your lips, but you
have not got it "poured" into them; you may have some
grace in your heart, but it is dropped there like small rain

from heaven—you have not got it " poured" theie , you may
be ever so full of grace, but Christ is more full than you are;
and when you are ever so reduced in grace, it is a consolation
that with him is plenteous grace—pienty that knows no lack,
for " grace is poured into his lips."   Be not afraid to go to
him in every time of need, nor think he will fail to comfort
you; his comforts are not like water spilled on the eaith, that
cannot be gathered up; they will yield perpetual streams, for
"grace is poured into his lips."   He has no stinted supply, no
short allowance to give you; but ask what you will, you shall
have as much as your faith can desire, and your heart can
hold, for " grace is poured into his lips" with the richest
plenitude.

II. Not to expatiate further on this, let us pass to the
second thought—THE KIND OF GRACE THAT JESUS CHRIST HAS,
WHICH IS THUS POURED INTO HIS LIPS, AND SHED FORTH FROM
HIS LIPS.   It is important to remark that Jesus Christ has what
none of the sons of men ever had—he has *inherent grace.*
Adam, when he was created of God, had some inherent grace,
which God gave to him ; yet not so much of God's grace as
to preserve the uprightness of his charater.   He had but the
grace of purity, as it could be displayed in the innocence of
his intelligent nature.   There must have been much grace in
the constitution of the man, seeing he was originally created
in the likeness of God; yet there could not have been perfect
grace in him, for he did not keep his first estate.   But Jesus
Christ had all the grace that Adam had, and all the grace
that any innocent man could have had, in the most sublime
perfection; and that grace was born in him.   You and I have
none of that ; it is all passed away and gone.   As for inherent
grace, where is it to be discovered ?   We have heard men say
that children are not born in sin, nor shapen in iniquity, but
that they have inherent grace; albeit we have not yet met
with the man whc has found so wonderful a child.   At any
rate, the children have been mightily spoiled in growing to
maturity, for they have not given much proof of grace afterwards.   No, beloved ; we are naturally graceless—a seed of
evil-doers; all our inherent grace was spoiled by Adam.

However full the pitcher might have been originally, it has been emptied out by the fall. Adam broke the earthen vessel, and spilt every drop of its contents, and we have none left. Jesus was born, not a sinful man, but begotten of the Holy Ghost, made of a pure virgin. In the conception of "that holy thing," there was no hereditary sin; his body was without taint or pollution, and his soul was impeccable. It was not possible he should sin, for in him there was no sin: he had inherent grace in himself.

And next, *he had grace which he derived from the constitution of his person, being God as well as man.* The manhood of Christ derived grace from the Godhead of Christ. I do not doubt but the two natures, though the distinction was not superseded, were so united in such wonderful union, that what the man did the God confirmed, and what the God willed, that the man did. Nor did the man Christ Jesus ever act without the God Christ Jesus. Nor did he ever speak without the God—the God within him—the God whom he is as truly as he is man. WE speak but as men, save when the Spirit of God speaks through us. The greatest and mightiest of all prophets have but spoken as men inspired; but Jesus spoke as man and God conjoined. "Grace" this unutterably Divine grace—his own grace of Godhead, "was poured into his lips," and "shed forth from his lips."

But more. I conceive that the Lord Jesus Christ, when he spoke, had also, as well as his ministers, *the assistance of God the Holy Spirit.* In fact, we are told that God gave the Spirit unto him without measure. It is a most remarkable fact, and I believe it is put in Scripture on purpose to make us honor the Holy Spirit, that Jesus Christ as a preacher—so far as we can judge from the Word of God—was not so successful in conversion as some of his followers have been. Now, if you turn over the life of Paul, you will notice how many thousands were brought through his preaching to know the Lord; and if you read the account of Peter's sermon, you will see that three thousand were converted in one day. You never hear of such an instance in the life of Christ. When he died, he left but three or four hundred disciples behind him; or if there were others, his success was not so manifest as that of many of his disciples. The reason was this, says Jesus: I will honor the Holy Spirit; I will let the world know that it is not by might, nor by power, but by my Spirit, saith the Lord. And though I speak as never man spake, and have more eloquence than mortal ever again can attain, yet I will in my sovereignty restrain myself from the exercise of that Spirit. The people's eyes shall be dull, and they shall slumber, their hearts shall wax fat, and they shall be gross. Then, in after years, I will speak more through an humble fisherman than I did myself. I will honor more the weakest instrument than I have done even my own self as a preacher. Ah! is it wonderful how God doth magnify the ministry of the Holy Ghost. We are so apt to forget his essential offices in the covenant, that God, as it were, says, Here is my own Son; although he preaches, I will show you that the preacher must rest on the Holy Spirit, and I will give him a congregation who shall take him to the brow of the hill to cast him down headlong ; while Paul, who is but a stammerer, I will clothe with such majesty, that wherever he goes his testimony shall be with the power of the Spirit to abase the gods of the heathens, and make their idols totter to the dust. But yet Jesus Christ has the Spirit without measure, for every sentence of his was instinct with energy Divine. "The words," said Jesus, "that I speak unto you, they are Spirit and they are life." Thus you see his words are not merely *of* the Spirit, but they *are* Spirit. It seems to me that, *as* " he that hath seen Christ hath seen the Father," so he that hath heard Christ hath heard the Holy Ghost. Still, the fruits of his ministry, like the homage due to his person, lay beyond the brief term of his sojourn on earth. He was rejected of his generation, but afterward " declared to be the Son of God, according to the Spirit of holiness by the resurrection from the dead." In like manner his words, though not seemingly productive at the time, were so full of the Spirit's quickening power, that they were after-wards the means of conversion to millions of millions, beyond the capacity of mortals to count. All conversions under Peter, Paul, and the other apostles, were by Christ Jesus. The words that I e spake in secret, they published far and wide. All conversions *now* are in his name, and by his word. The testimony of Jesus is the Spirit of prophecy. If an apostle spake of himself, it fell to the ground, but what their Master told them was rendered successful. Jesus Christ has the Spirit without measure; and herein is another kind of grace, of which it can be said, " Grace is poured into thy lips."

III. We have very hastily passed over these two divisions, that we may dilate on the third. We are now to consider THE VARIOUS OFFICES IN WHICH WE MAY DISCERN " GRACE" AS BEING "POURED INTO THE LIPS" OF CHRIST, AND SHED AGAIN FROM HIS LIPS.

First, let us regard our Saviour as *the eternal Surety of the covenant*, and we shall see that "grace was poured into his lips." When God the Father originally made the covenant, it stood somewhat in this form: " My Son, thou desirest, and I also agree with thee, to save a number, that no man can number, whom I have elected in thee. But in order to their salvation, that I may be just, and yet the justifier of the un-godly, it is necessary that some one should be their represen-tative, to stand responsible for their obedience to my laws and their substitute to suffer whatever penalties they incur. If thou, my Son, wilt stipulate to bear their punishment, and endure the penalty of their crimes, I on my part will stipulate that thou shalt see thy seed, shalt prolong thy days, and that the pleasure of the Lord shall prosper in thy hands. If thou to-day art prepared to promise that thou wilt bear the exact punishment of all the people whom thou wouldst save, I on my part am prepared to swear by myself, because I can swear by no greater, that all for whom thou shalt atone shall infallibly be delivered from death and hell, and that all for whom thou bearest the punishment shall hence go free, nor shall my wrath rise against them, however great may be their sins." Jesus spake the word, and he said, " My Father! lo, I come In the volume of the Book it is written of me, I delight to do thy will, O my God." Now, that was spoken in eternity, far back as faith on eagle wings can soar, and such grace was poured into the lips of Christ when he made that simple decla ration, that tens of thousands of saints entered heaven, simply on the ground of his solemn pledge. Long before our Saviour did come into the world and pay the penalty, God the Father rested on the words of Jesus, for "he sware to his own heart and changed not." Such grace truly was there shed from the lips of Jesus, that from the days of Adam, when one trans-gression involved the race in ruin, down to the times when the second Adam made reconciliation for iniquity, the saints all entered heaven upon the faith of Christ's promise alone. Not one drop of blood had been shed, not one agony suffered, the contract was not performed, the stipulation not yet fulfilled; but the Surety's oath was quite enough; in the Father's ears there needed no other confirmation. His heart was satisfied. Yea, more; in that self-same moment, when Jesus spake that word in his Father's ear, all the saints were in him justified and rendered complete; their salvation was secure. As soon as ever Jesus Christ said, "My Father, I will pay the penalty, they shall have my righteousness, and I will have their sin," their acceptance was an eternal fact.

> " In union with the Lamb,
>   From condemnation free,
>   The saints of God forever were
>   And shall for ever be."

Oh! was not grace poured into those lips! that one single promise could redeem all the people of God, and carry thou-sands to heaven, even without a single performance—because God the Father could so rely on him! He would never go back from his agreement, nor ever turn aside from his cove-nant. This is the first aspect in which we behold grace shed forth from Christ's lips.

Secondly, "Grace is poured into his lips" *as the greatest of all prophets and teachers*. The law was given by Moses, and there was some grace on his lips; for Moses, even when he preached the law, preached the gospel, privileged as he was to look steadfastly to the end of that which is abolished. When he taught the offering of the Lamb, the bullock, and the turtle-dove, there was gospel couched in the law itself, in the law of Levitical ceremonies. But Moses had but little grace. The beams that shone on the face of Moses were not the beams of grace, they were not " the glory as of the only begotten of the Father, full of grace and truth ;" they were the glory of justice, but not the glory of grace. And when other prophets rose at different periods of the first dispensation of the law, they each had some measure of grace. Whether we consider the heroic Elijah, or the plaintive Jeremiah, or Isaiah, that seraphic seer, who spoke more of Christ than all the rest —let us turn to any one of the prophets and we find that each and all had some grace in their lips ; what they preached was gracious doctrine, and well worthy to be received ; but who ever taught such doctrines as those of Jesus ? Where among the writings of the prophets and sages of antiquity, can we find such words as those which Jesus uttered ? Who ever taught the people that they should love all men, that God made of one flesh all nations that dwelt upon the face of the earth ? Who ever taught the people before Him that the poor were to have the gospel, while God would bring down the mighty from their seats, and would exalt the humble and the meek ? Who taught such wondrous doctrines as those which you will find in all his sermons ? Who could have been so great a teacher ? Who could so blessedly have prophesied to his people but Jesus Christ himself ? My soul, contemplate Jesus as the only rabbi of the Church ; view him as the only Lord and Master ; take thy doctrines and articles of faith from his lips, and his lips alone ; study his word and make that alone thy guide ; interpret all the rest by his light. When thou hast done so, thou wilt say, " O prophet of my salvation, thou teacher of Israel ! verily grace is poured into thy lips. No books afford me such instruction as thine, no ministers address me in such words as my Shepherd speaks. No learning hath in it such depths of wisdom as the wisdom of Christ. " More to be desired are his words than gold ; yea, than much fine gold." " Grace was poured into his lips" as the greatest of all prophets.

Thirdly, Christ had grace poured into his lips *as the most eloquent of all preachers.* One of the joys I anticipate in

heaven is to hear Christ speak to his people. I conceive that
there was a majesty about Jesus Christ when he spake on
earth—such a majesty as not Demosthenes, Cicero, nor Peri-
cles,—not all the orators of ancient or modern times could ever
approach. He had a voice, I suppose, more sweet than e'en
the songs which came from the harps of angels. He had an
eye expressive of sympathy with those whom he addressed.
He had a heart which animated every feature of his countenance. His was pathos which could break the stony heart;
his was sublimity which could elevate the sensual mind; each
word of his was a pearl, each sentence was of pure gold.
"Never man spake like this man." No poet in his most rapt
ecstacy could have grasped such conceptions as those the
Saviour delivered to his hearers; and when, stooping from his
flights, he condescends to speak in plain and simple words to
his fellows, there is naked, ungarnished simplicity in the familiar discourse of Christ to which man can not in the least
approach. Jesus Christ was the greatest and the plainest of
all preachers. We could put aside every other in comparison
with him. We have known men who could curb the restless
multitude, and hold them spell-bound. Some of us have listened
to some mighty man of God who chained our ears, held us
fast, and constrained our attention all the while he spoke.
Justice, sin, righteousness, and judgment to come have absorbed us while they enlisted our sympathies. But had you
heard the Saviour, you would have heard more wondrous
things than any man else could have spoken. Methinks if the
wild winds could have heard him, they would have ceased
their blustering; if the waves could have listened to him, they
would have hushed their tumult, and the rough back of ocean
would have been smoothed; if the stars could have heard him,
they would have stopped their hurried march; if the sun and
moon had heard Him whose voice is more potent than that of
Joshua, they would have stood still: if creation could have
heard him, then charmed, it would have stopped its ceaseless
motions, and the wheels of the universe would have stood still,
that all ears might listen, that all hearts might beat, and that
all eyes might glisten, and that so souls might be elevated,

while Jesus Christ spoke. It was fabled of Hercules, that he had golden chains in his mouth with which he chained the ears of men; it is true of Jesus that he had golden chains in his mouth, that chained men's ears and hearts too. He had no need to ask attention, for " grace was poured into his lips." Happy day ! happy day ! when I shall sit down at the feet of Jesus Christ and hear him preach. O beloved ! what we shall think of our poor preaching I can not tell. It is a mercy that Jesus Christ does not preach here now, for after hearing him, none of us would preach again, so ashamed should we be of ourselves. Sometimes when we try to preach, and afterward hear a more able minister, we feel so outdone that our preaching seems nothing,—we hardly dare try again. It is a mercy there is a veil between us and Christ. We can not hear him preach, or else we should all vacate our pulpits. But in heaven I hope to sit enchanted at his feet ; and if he will speak a million years, I would ask him to speak yet another million. And if he will still pursue, e'en then for the sweet redundance of that grace which is poured into his lips, my raptured soul would sit and love and smile itself away in ecstacies of joy to hear my Saviour speak. " Grace was poured into his lips" as the most eloquent of preachers.

Fourthly, " Grace was poured into the lips" of Christ *as the faithful Promiser*. I look upon all the promises of God's word as being the promises of Jesus as well as the promises of the Father and of the Holy Ghost. Every word that is spoken here to the Christian is spoken by Jesus Christ. All the promises, we are told, are yea and amen in Christ Jesus, to the glory of God ; and as the promises are all made IN him, so they are all spoken *by* him. Now, will you not concur with me when I say, that verily grace is poured into his lips as the faithful Promiser ? We have sometimes read his promises, we have heard them with our ears, and oh ! what grace there is in them ! Take, for instance, that great honeycomb promise, " The mountains shall depart, and the hills be removed ; but my kindness shall not depart from thee, neither shall the covenant of my peace be removed, saith the Lord that hath mercy on thee." Turn to another : " When thou passest through the rivers I will be with thee: the floods shall not overflow thee. When thou walkest through the fire thou shalt not be burned, neither shall the flame kindle upon thee." "Fear not, thou worm Jacob, and ye men of Israel: I will help thee, saith the Lord, and thy Redeemer, the Holy One of Israel." Listen to such sweet words as these: "Come unto me, all ye that labor and are heavy laden, and I will give you rest. Take my yoke upon you, and learn of me, for I am meek and lowly in heart." "Whosoever cometh unto me I will in no wise cast out." "He is able to save unto the uttermost them that come unto God by him." Beloved, you do not need that I tell you how beautiful these things are. The best way to preach of the faithful Promiser is to tell you some of the promises. I will not tell you what gold and silver there are in Christ's cabinet; I will break the door open, and let you look at some of the treasures for yourselves. "Can a woman forget her sucking child, that she should not have compassion on the son of her womb? Yea, they may forget; yet will I not forget thee. Behold, I have graven thee upon the palms of my hands; thy walls are continually before me." "I will never leave thee, I will never forsake thee." "Even to old age I am with thee, and even to hoar hairs will I carry thee." "He shall deliver thee in six troubles, yea, in seven there shall no evil touch thee." "He shall save thee from the pestilence that walketh in darkness, and from the destruction that wasteth at noonday."

> "He that hath made his refuge God
>   Shall find a most secure abode;
>   Shall walk all day beneath his shade,
>   And there at night shall rest his head."

"All that my Father hath given me shall come to me." "Having loved his own, he loveth them unto the end." "All his saints are in thy hand;" "No man shall pluck them out of my Father's hand." And then there is that great master-promise—"Whosoever believeth on the Son of God shall be saved." Is he not indeed full of grace as the faithful Promiser? You who have been drinking from he wells of promise well know his faithfulness and the grace therein. Poor souls! ye have come sick and weary oftentimes to this well, and your strength has been renewed till you were like giants refreshed with new wine. Your spirits have been depressed, and your souls have been melancholy; but when you have come here, you have tasted that wine which maketh glad the heart of man. O! did ever man speak like this man, when he speaks as the faithful Promiser? "Grace is poured into his lips."

Fifthly, "Grace is poured into his lips," *as the wooer and the winner of his people's hearts.* O beloved, Christ hath hard work to win his people's love! He sendeth out his messengers, but the messengers can not compel the people of God to love Jesus. He prepares his feast, the fatlings are killed, and those that are bidden will not come unless he says to his messengers, "Go out into the highways and hedges, and compel them to come in, that my house may be filled." But what a hard matter it is to bring poor souls to be in love with Jesus! In vain does the minister dilate upon his charms; in vain does he try to paint his features as well as he can. We are poor daubers, and we mar the beauty which we attempt to portray. Poor sinners say, "Is that Jesus? there is no beauty that we should desire him." They turn away and hide as it were their faces from him. With tears streaming from our eyes, we "seek to find out acceptable words," and we use the best language our hearts can dictate, but we can not win your souls. Sometimes we address you with rough words that we have borrowed from some ancient Boanerges; at other times, with smooth words such as a Chrysostom might approve, and they are alike in vain: the Lord is not there. But oh! when Jesus pleads his own cause, how sweetly does he plead it! Have you never watched the heart when Jesus Christ began to woo it—when he opens the ear and says, "Poor soul! I love thee, and because I love thee I will tell thee wha thou art. Thou art cast out into the open field; thou ar lying in thy blood; thou art dead in trespasses and sins. Yet I love thee. Wilt thou love me?" "Nay," saith the heart, "I will not." "But," saith Jesus, "my love is deep as hell; it is insatiable as the grave; will be thine, and thou shalt be mine." And have you noted how soon the soul begins to yield and the hard rock begins to flow like Niobe's tears, till at length the heart says, "O Jesus! love thee? Yes I do, because thou didst first love me." Why is it that some here have not given their hearts to Jesus? It is because perhaps Jesus has not revealed himself to them in person. But when he does, you can not deny him! I challenge any man to hold his heart back when Jesus comes for it: when he displays himself, when he takes the veil off our eyes and lets us look at his lovely face, shows us his wounded hands and his bleeding side, methinks there is no heart but must be drawn forth to him. Ah! Christian, do you not remember the hour when he pleaded with you? He knocked at the door, and you would not let him in; but your beloved put his hand at the hole of the door, and your bowels were moved toward him, and how sweetly did he tell you your sinnership, and with the next word made known your redemption; then told you of your death, and with the next word made you alive; then told you that you were powerless, and with the next word made you strong; then told you of your unbelief, and with the next sentence gave you faith. O! is he not filled with grace as he wins the hearts and affections of his people?

Sixthly, Jesus Christ hath his lips filled with grace, *as the great consolation of Israel, the comfort of all his people.* There is no comfort except that which cometh from the Lord Jesus. At no brook can ye slake the thirst of the soul, but at that stream of grace which floweth from Christ, and, never can run dry. Let us rehearse his mighty acts; let us go back our lifelong and see the various Ebenezers we have raised to his sovereign grace and mercy. Dost thou not remember how he appeared to thee in the solitude of the wilderness and said, "Yea, I have loved thee with an everlasting love?" Dost thou not remember, when, torn with the thorns and briars of this world, thou wast despairing and ready to die, how he came and touched thee and said, "Live?"—when he bid thee turn thine eye upward, and thou couldst then say, "Since Jesus is mine, I will fear nothing?" O ye who have tasted that the Lord is gracious, go ye to the banqueting house again, where the Saviour comforted you with flagons, and fed you with apples; where he gave you the sweet fruits of the kingdom, and took of the clusters of Eschol and squeezed them into your mouth. Do you not remember when he gave you some-thing better than angels' food at the Lord's table, or how he manifested himself to you in the use of the means while you were waiting upon him? And will you not say, "O Jesus! verily grace was poured into thy lips?" Desponding soul, if Jesus speaks to thee to-day, thou wilt not be desponding any longer. There is such a potency in the word "Jesus," that methinks it ought to be sung in all hospitals to charm away diseases; at least, in every lazar-house for souls. Wherever there are diseased hearts and troubled spirits, I would always go and sing, "Jesus!" There is no medicine able to heal melancholy like the body and blood of Jesus. When he draws near to comfort his people, midnight becomes noon, the thick-est darkness becomes a blaze of meridian splendor; for "grace is poured into his lips."

Seventhly, Grace is poured into Christ's lips *as the great Intercessor for his people before the throne.* Before Jesus ascended up on high, and led captivity captive, as Toplady says, "with prayers and groans he offered up his humble suit below;" but now Jesus Christ has gone up on high, "with authority he pleads before his Father." It must have been wonderful to hear the prayer of Jesus in the garden of Geth-semane, and especially to hear that sentence where he prayed for his people, "Father, I will that they also whom thou hast given me be with me where I am;" but oh, if we might see our blessed Lord this morning pleading in heaven! He stands before his Father's throne, points to his breast, and shows his bleeding hands. When our prayers rise to heaven, they always ask to be introduced by Jesus. They are broken prayers, but Jesus knows how to mend them. There are things in them that should not be—he corrects them, and so he takes an emended edition of our prayers, and says, "My Father! another petition I have come to lay before thee." Says the Father, "Who is it from?" "From one of my people." And should the Father hesitate a moment, Jesus

Christ says : " Father, I will—it must be done. Look here ! here is the price !" And he holds up his hands, and shows his side ; and then the Father says : " My Son ! it shall be done. Whatsoever thou askest in prayer, for thy sake it shall be bestowed." Do you see yon poor man ? his name is Peter. At no great distance is Satan, who wants to destroy his soul. He has got a large sieve, in which he desires to sift Peter. Can you imagine Satan presenting himself before the Lord, as in days of yore ? He says, " O Lord, let me have Peter in my sieve that I may sift him." Down goes Jesus before the throne, and says : " My Father ! I beseech thee let not this grain of wheat fall to the ground." Now Satan goes and catches Peter, and begins to sift him up and down. When Peter goes up the first time, he is a little frightened ; the second time he says, " Man, I know not what thou sayest ;" the third time he says, " I know not the Man ;" and at length he begins to curse and swear. How terrible that sieve ! But Christ looks at him, and out goes Peter : the prayer of Jesus availed for him—the look of Jesus prevailed with him : " he went out and wept bitterly," and his soul was saved. Oh ! the mighty power of intercession ! I do not think our prayers would ever be heard in heaven if it were not for Jesus Christ. He is the great Mediator by whom our prayers must be presented.

Eighthly, Jesus Christ has grace poured into his lips *as the Counsellor for his people.* You may have seen a special pleader rise with a brief in his hand : he shows the case against the prisoner to be a very bad one. Then witnesses are called. Afterwards another advocate gets up to plead the prisoner's cause—to rebut, if possible, the accusation, or to set forth extenuating circumstances in mitigation of punishment. Now, when we stand before the judgment bar of God, Satan will rise up—that old accuser of the brethren, and will gather together the evidences of our guilt, and the reasons why we must be condemned. Methinks I hear him say that we were born in sin and shapen in iniquity, and, therefore, we deserve to be lost ; that we have a corrupt nature, that we had the sin of Adam laid to us : and then, with malicious spleen, he will allege that we transgressed at such and such a time, when we were young; following up our career from youth to manhood, and even down to hoar hairs; clenching all his arguments by an appeal to our unbelief—that though we have professed to believe, we have doubted the promises, and could not, therefore, be children of God. Well might we, as transgressors, tremble when with a bad case the grounds of judgment against us are so maliciously stated. But there stands forth on our behalf "the Wonderful, the Counsellor;" he takes his brief in hand and begins to plead. Hark what he says, and see how all opinion is turned at once! "I confess," says he, "that every word is true that the last accuser has said. My client pleads guilty to every charge; but I have a full pardon signed by God's own hand, purchased by my own blood;" and, stripping himself, he shows his breast, and bares his arm, and says, "These were given to me of my Father before the foundation of the world. I bare their sins in my own body on the tree. My Father justified them; I pardoned them." And then, mounting to the highest point, he reaches the climax of grace as he exclaims, "Who shall lay anything to the charge of God's elect? Canst thou, O God? Hast thou not justified? I cannot, for I died." Then he sits down, in triumph, saying, "Whom he justified, them he also glorified. Nothing shall be able to separate them from the love of God." Shall not each ransomed sinner shout with joy? Oh! righteous Advocate, grace is poured into thy lips!

And now, lastly, Grace is poured into the lips of Jesus *as the great Judge of all at last.* That will be a gracious judgment which Jesus Christ shall dispense; it will be gracious, because it will be at once merciful and just. Sinners, ungodly men and women, now in this house of prayer, ye have never heard the voice of Jesus, and ye have never known what it is to confess that "grace was poured into his lips;" but let me tell you, in a few short years you will be made to confess that "grace is poured into his lips." You will stand there and hear him say to his own people, "Come, ye blessed of my Father, inherit the kingdom prepared for you from the foun-

dation of the world." When you hear it you will think with
in yourselves, "Never did such music break on our ears
before. Oh! what precious words." Ay, but you will fall
down and ask rocks to hide you, and mountains to cover you,
because the words were not spoken to you. You will tremble
as one by one the faithful soldiers of Jesus Christ come before
him. He will say to one, "Verily, thou hast been faithful in
a few things, I will make thee ruler over many things." To
another he will say, "Thou hast fought a good fight, thou
hast kept the faith: receive the crown laid up for thee from
the foundation of the world." You will then stand and say,
" Oh, what grace was poured into his lips! how graciously he
speaks!" And you all the while will feel that he is not speak
ing to you; you will stand there and know that your turn
will never come when he shall speak gracious words to you.
Oh! how you will stand fixed to the spot petrified as you
listen while you hear those matchless syllables. You laugh at
the saints now; you will envy them then. You despise them
now; but you will be ready to kiss the dust of their feet if
you might but get into heaven. You would not ask to sit on
a throne with them; but to lie at their feet would be enough
for you, if you might but hear Christ say to you, " Come, ye
blessed." But in a moment, instead of gracious words, my
hearers—I am not telling you a dream, but a reality –in a
moment—O believe me! for God speaketh it—instead of
words of grace there shall come words of terror, before the
sound of which heaven and earth shall flee away, and there
shall be found no blessed place for thee. These be the words:
" Depart, ye cursed, into everlasting fire in hell, prepared for
the devil and his angels." You would not wish to hear those
gracious lips utter such a sentence as that to you. I am sure
you are none of you anxious to make your bed in hell, and
find your abode in damnation; but, my hearers, I must warn
you faithfully. There are some of you who, if you die as you
are, will never go to heaven; there are many of you, my
regular attendants, and some of you who have just strayed in
here this morning, who know, and your heart confesses it,
that you are " in the gall of bitterness, and in the bonds of

iniquity." Weeping Christians! weep for them. Let your tears flow in rivers. It were a misery if they were sick, but this is worse, for they are sick unto the second death; it were painful if they were condemned to die by the law, but they are " condemned already." My beloved brethren and sisters, there are some of you now—start not—there are some sitting side by side with you in the pews, who are condemned criminals. How would you feel this morning if, as you sat in your pew, there was a man beside you who was to be hanged to-morrow? You would say, " O that God might bless the word to that poor creature's soul! O that God might send it into his heart, for he is a condemned man!" Do you not know it is so? There is a saint of God, and sitting by his side is a black child of hell; here is an heir of glory and immortality, and the neighbor who touches his arm this morning is dead in sins, and condemned to die! What! will ye not weep and feel for them? Will your hearts be like stone and steel? and will ye be worse than brutes, and let them perish without a sigh, without a prayer, without a tear? No; if we can pray, we will pray for them, that God in his mercy may yet give them grace to save them from the wrath to come. Poor sinners! do not despise my blessed Master, I beseech you. If you knew him you would love him, I know. O poor wicked sinner! thou who feelest self-condemned, conscience-stricken, hast thou no love to Jesus? Ah! if thou didst but know how much Jesus Christ loves thee, thou wouldst love him at once. I know a man who said he never was so struck by anything in all his life as when he heard—

" Jesus, lover of my soul!"

" Oh!" said he, " I did not recollect any thing in the sermon but those words at the beginning of a hymn—

" 'Jesus, lover of my soul!'"

He then went to a friend of mine, and he said—

" 'Jesus, lover of my soul!'"

Do you think Jesus Christ is the 'lover of *my* soul?' If I thought he was I think I could love him at once." The friend said, " Ah, well! if you feel like that, Jesus is the lover of your soul." Oh! beloved, what would you give if you might but call Jesus Christ your lover and your friend—if you could but know he loved you! Do you sigh for an interest in his love? Ah! then he does love you, for you would not have wanted him to love you if he had not set his heart upon you. Have you a desire for Jesus? then Jesus has a thousand times as much desire for you. I tell you Christ is more pleased to save poor sinners than poor sinners are to be saved. The shepherd is more ready to reclaim the lost sheep than the sheep is to be reclaimed. So let me tell thee, poor soul, Jesus has no pleasure in the death of him that dieth; but he has a pleasure deep as the sea, high as heaven, wide as the east is from the west, and as unsearchable as his own divinity, in saving souls. Only believe in his name, thou sinner—to thee I preach, thou sinner; thou actual, *bonâ fide* sinner; thou real sinner—to thee I preach: Jesus Christ says, " Whosoever liveth and believeth in me shall never die." Believest thou this? Wilt thou put thy trust in him? Wilt thou—

> " Renounce thy ways and works with grief,
> And fly to this most sure relief?"

Wilt thou drop into his arms, and let him carry thee? Wilt thou fall upon the Rock of Ages, and let that sustain thee? If thou dost it now, this moment, thou shalt become in this happy moment a changed man. Thou shalt be no longer an heir of wrath, but a child of grace; and thy salvation shall become as inevitably secure as if thou wast even now among the glorified.

SERMON VII

A TIME OF FINDING FOR LOST SHEEP

"I will seek that which was lost, and bring again that which was driven away, and will bind up that which was broken, and will strengthen that which was sick: but I will destroy the fat and the strong; I will feed them with judgment."—EZEK. xxxiv. 16

IT is a great mercy that God never leaves his church. He has not made a church as a watch-maker constructs a watch, which, after being wound up is left to depend upon the strength and fitness of the machinery; but he has made a church which, though fitted with the best of machinery, needs his hand every moment to keep it in motion;—he has lighted the lamps, but he walks among the golden candlesticks; he has placed the pillars of the temple, but his own mighty shoulders are the actual support thereof: he has not left the church to his ministers, but he himself is the great Bishop and Shepherd of souls. Even if, as some affirm, there were no immediate Divine interpositions in the works of Providence, we know that there are such interpositions constantly and every moment in the works of grace. We have direct experimental evidence of God's ever-watchful care over his church. He does not deal with his people only through instruments, but he himself takes the church in his own hands. It is his own declaration, "I the Lord do keep it; I will water it every moment, lest any hurt it: I will keep it night and day." Thus doth he speak of his vineyard. So, too, in this chapter. For awhile the shepherds had domineered over the flock; evil shepherds, who had crept into the office, fed themselves and not the sheep. It would have been an ill day for the church, if Divine interposition were not the rule of his government; but, because it is so, God said, "Away, ye shepherds! I am against you; I will require my flock at your hands. Behold I, even I, will both search my sheep and seek them out. Away, ye that have dispersed and scattered my family! I am about to make bare mine arm. As ye have proved unworthy servants, your **Ma**ster himself is coming; as ye have not fed the people of my pasture, and have not gathered together my flock, I myself will grasp the crook in my own hand." He speaks in his wrath to the foolish shepherds, yet he mingles his threats with pity for those he elsewhere calls "the flock of slaughter." "I will feed even you, O poor of the flock! I will seek that which was lost, and bring again that which was driven away, and will bind up that which was broken, and will strengthen that which was sick." Ah, beloved! if the Lord did not interfere in his church continually, the church would cease to exist; if the doctrines of his holy word had been left to man's teaching, they would by degrees have so degenerated that the church would not have had a particle of truth in its midst. If God had not stretched over his truth the broad ægis of his own omnipotence, truth would have ceased out of the land, and those who profess to be its ministers would have all prophesied lies in the name of the Lord. The preservation of truth in our midst is owing to the direct and immediate interposition of the Almighty. And mark it well: the inward witness of the truth in the heart of every individual believer is an instance and evidence of the same unceasing care, inasmuch as He only can apply it to the conscience with quickening power. There is not force enough in truth to convert souls, without the influence of the Holy Spirit. The minister may be a good under-shepherd—he may endeavor to feed the flock; but God's flock can not be fed, nor can God's wandering sheep be gathered home, unless the chief Shepherd, the great and mighty Archbishop, even Jesus Christ, shall interfere, and himself do the work. The Divine interposition of God in the midst of his church is her great bulwark, her hope, her shield, her stay. What we want just now is not so much more shepherds, perhaps, not other shepherds—albeit, when the Lord sends laborers into the field, it is because the crops are to be gathered in—but we want the great Master himself to visit us and say, "I will do my own work; since ye will not faithfully and fearlessly preach, I will come and interfere, that my word may be fully and boldly proclaimed."

Now notice what God has promised to do. In this text there is a character very graphically and minutely described; and we shall look at the four sentences as descriptive of that one character—" *that which was lost ; that which was driven away ; that which was broken ; and that which was sick.*" Then we shall look at the sentences one by one, as being very possibly *descriptions of four different characters.* We shall also endeavor to speak of the sweet promises appended to each character, and conclude with a solemn warning to " the fat and the strong."

I. First, then, notice the four features of character here : " that which was lost; that which was driven away; that which was broken; that which was sick." We say that some times all four of these meet in one individual.

To begin with " THAT WHICH WAS LOST." Doubtless there are some here who have felt in their hearts the solemn meaning of this wonderful word " lost." Not only have I no doubt, but I have strong hopes that some souls here present are really and actually lost in their own experience. It may seem a cruel thing that I should wish you to feel yourselves lost, but it is a well-intentioned cruelty ; because if you are lost, this promise is addressed to you, that God will seek that which was lost. I shall endeavor, therefore, to tell you how men feel when they are brought to know the dreadful word " lost" applicable to themselves.

A man is never lost until he is *devoid of all strength.* See you the mariner who has fallen from the ship ? As long as those brawny arms of his can stem the current, as long as he can buffet the waves and hurl them aside with the strong heart of resistance, he gives up nought for lost. Ay, and should his arms become weary, if he can float a little, and with one hand move himself amid the billows of the deep, he still thinks it is not all over yet. And while there is one particle of strength remaining his hopes are too buoyant to give himself up for a lost man. Suppose him to have grasped a spar ; as long as ever those hands of his can, with a death-clutch, keep

hold of that floating piece of timber, he does not consider him
self lost. Fond hope still whispers in his ear, "Hold on, thou
art not lost yet; some ship may cross this way, Providence
may guide its path hither, and thou mayest yet be delivered.
Hold on, thou art not lost while a sinew retains its might,
while there is any vital force in thy frame." So, soul, thou
canst never say thou art lost till thou feelest in thy heart an
utter departure of all thy strength. Hast thou been brought
to feel that there is nothing which of thyself thou canst do
apart from the strength of the Holy Spirit? There was a time
when thou couldst pray, when thou couldst repent, when thou
couldst believe after thine own fashion with thine own supposed
strength: is that time all passed over now? Art thou saying,
"I have no power to do any one of those things without grace
from on high! I would, but can not pray; I would, but can
not repent; this strong heart will not dissolve, although I
strive to melt it; this haughty mind will resist the Saviour,
although I wish to be led in chains of grace a willing captive
to my Lord?" Art thou brought to feel that if thy salvation
depended upon one motion of thy soul in the right direction
thou must be lost, for thou hast no spiritual strength? Art
thou lying down shorn of all thy might, bereft of all help and
hope in thyself; and dost thou confess, "I can do nothing
without thee?" Well, then, thou art one of those whom
Christ has come to save. This death unto the law is the pre-
cursor of thy being made alive to Christ, and a sure sign that
grace is at work in thy soul. So long as thou hast one particle of carnal strength, God will never show thee his salvation;
so long as thou thinkest to do one solitary good thing of thyself, or reliest upon one particle of good works for thy redemption, thou art under the ban and curse of the law, and art not
brought to know the covenant-plan of mercy. Oh! when thou
art stripped of all, when thou sayest, "Divinity must work, for
humanity hath failed; God's will must conquer my will, or
else I am lost,"—then rejoice, rejoice! though thou givest thyself up for lost, it is now that God writes thee saved. "I will
seek that which was lost."

Again, a man is never thoroughly lost until, not only his

strength has failed him, but *he hath come to his wit's end.*
You know, David describes the mariners at sea as rolling to
and fro, staggering like a drunken man, and at their wit's
end. While the captain could devise any scheme for scudding
before the wind, or evading the tempest, or nearing the harbor, or arriving at the haven, he gave not up his ship for
lost; but when every device had failed,—when, after suggesting twenty plans, all laid hold upon as sovereign remedies, but
which all failed, he was at his wit's end, or, as the margin
reads, " his wisdom is swallowed up," then he gave himself up
for being really lost. Have I one here who is at his wit's
end? Once he said, " I will do this, and then I shall be
saved; I will forego that lust, I will renounce that crime, I
will moderate my conduct, I will behave myself more Christian-like, and then I shall be saved." Hast thou tried these
high resolves, and have they failed thee? Perhaps thou hast
sought after ceremonies and said, " I will shelter myself in the
church, keep her ritual, and zealously obey her rubrics ;" yet
that has failed thee. Thou hast tried scheme after scheme,
only to discover each and all alike abortive. And now thou
dost anxiously inquire, " What must I do to be saved?" Do
you say, " I have done all that reason could dictate ; I have
followed every maxim I could learn, as I ran hither and thither
for counsel; I have strained every power mortal can exercise ;
I have taxed my poor brain till its fitful fancies bewilder me—
and, alas! all in vain : what must I do? what shall I do?
Let me tell thee. Thou art to-day like a traveler who has lost
his way in a wood. Thou thoughtest that there was a path,
and sorely hast thou been disappointed, until, entangled in the
brambles, thou hast rent thy clothes and torn thy flesh. How
sure thou didst make of some way of escape ; but lo! every
avenue was blocked up, and thou couldst not get out. Thou
hast climbed the highest tree in the forest, to see where the
end of the dark wood should be, but the further thou didst
look the more intricate did it appear. At length, thy hopes
extinguished, thy plans defeated, thy strength exhausted, thy
tongue parched, and thine eyes smarting, all that thou canst
do is, like the poor traveler in the desert, when the water is

spent and his power gone, to lay thee down in fell despair **and** die. Art thou such an one? Hast thou tried everything and has everything failed thee? Art thou now locked up in Despair's castle? If so, I commend to thee this sure promise: Christ came to seek the lost; and, oh! couldst thou believe it, what a joyous day this would be! Thou wouldst go out of his house dancing for joy of heart, saying, "I went there poor lost one, but the Shepherd of Israel has found me, **for** Christ came to seek that which was lost."

> "Depths of mercy! can there be
> Mercy yet reserved for me?"

Again, a man is not lost until *the door of hope is shut fast.* No man in the world ever gives himself up for lost as long as he hath a grain of hope. Tell the sick man that he must die, for the physician hath pronounced his case hopeless, and will he believe you? No; he will cherish the thought that he may yet rally. Has one case of recovery ever been known? Then he hopes his may not prove fatal. Has one miraculous cure been wrought? He thinks there may be another; or if not, perhaps that his case may be the first; and so he hopes on, and does not consider his condition desperate. The poor sinner, when lost, gives all up as hopeless; and he says, "I have no reason to hope that Christ will have mercy upon me. He might save all the rest of the world, but upon me he will never look with eyes of compassion. Here have I been lying for weeks and months by Bethesda's pool; the angel has often stirred the water; I have seen others step in, and they have been saved: my mother has been saved, my brother and my sister have found deliverance; yet here am I just the same as ever. I go to God's house, but I sit there as an alien—I am not like one of the family, and I know I am lost. It seems as if the ear of God were shut against my prayer; when I cry unto him, he answereth me not; when my sore runneth in the night season, he disregardeth the voice of my groaning. Alas! that my prayer is like the prayer of the wicked, an abomination to the Lord. I feel that he hath cast me out of his sight, and that I am condemned already!" What, then, I ask, is thy case too hard for him? "Nay," say you, "but he will not. I have called so long, I have cried so often, surely God hath forgotten to be gracious; I am not one of his elect; he hath shut up his bowels of compassion, and I never can be saved."

Hear this: Christ came to save thee. If thou feelest all that, let me solemnly assure thee, in God's name, that though lost in thyself, thou art saved in Christ. Would to God that all of you who hear me this day were either agonizing over your being lost, or rejoicing that ye are found. Ye were then equally safe, if not equally happy. I had rather, O ye careless sinners! that terrors took hold upon you, and fears compassed you about, than that ye should be dancing on the mountains of folly, and revelling in your sins, unconscious of danger. Know this, ye light-hearted, ye giddy and ye gay ones, the hour of your damnation draweth nigh. But as for you, who are broken in pieces, sighing and groaning, because ye think your case is hopeless, let me tell you, as God's ambassador, that your case is not *hopeless*, but *hopeful*. Ye may call to mind, like Jeremiah, "your affliction and your misery, the wormwood and the gall," and say with him, "Therefore have I hope." Have I faithfully described thee? Wilt thou answer to thy name, as a prodigal son, as a lost child? Then, lost as thou art, thou hast a Father. So lost as to need finding,—so lost as to need saving,—methinks I hear a Father's yearnings, "Is Ephraim my dear son? Is he a pleasant child? for since I spake against him, I do earnestly remember him still: therefore my bowels are troubled for him, I will surely have mercy upon him, saith the Lord." Methinks I hear the Saviour's voice saying, "The Son of man is come to seek and to save that which was lost." A vision flits before my eyes, I think I see the blessed Jesus in shepherd's garb, with staff in hand, bearing on his shoulders a lost sheep whom he has this morning recovered. Just now the poor thing was wandering in the wilderness in a solitary way; now he is laid on the everlasting shoulders, guarded by omnipotent power, and kept secure from harm. Happy soul!

the angels rejoice over thee, though thy heart hath not yet realized the sense of security which could give thee joy.

There is another characteristic of the man that feels himself lost more horrible than those I have mentioned. Waking to a consciousness that he is lost, not only does he behold the gate of hope shut, but *the gate of hell opened.* Ah! my friends, I speak now as one who should know, as one who hath felt in his own soul what his lips describe. I have passed through that experience which I have told you heretofore, and this have I likewise known. Well do I remember, after many a month of prayer without an answer from God, when faith I had none, and my hope had given up the ghost, I thought God would never save me; and just then I thought the gate of hell was opened before my soul; for if ever a soul did experience a foretaste of perdition I think I did; and I believe many of you experienced the same before you found peace with God. You knew you were not in hell, and yet you thought even that almost preferable to your condition, you were in such dread suspense. Sometimes there was a glimmer of hope, but that only made your darkness more visible. As John Bunyan hath it, the hell-drum was beating in your ears; you heard it from morning till night, and from night till morning—" Lost, lost, lost! thou wilt soon be in hell!" Dost thou not remember when thou didst walk the earth and think that every tuft of grass would be as the mouth of hell to open and swallow thee up—when thou couldst not sleep for frightful dreams, and didst wake and feel the very terror which haunted thee in thy night visions? Thy poor conscience was lashed by the whip of the law, and while thy wounds were smarting thou didst cry, " O God! what, wilt thou never save me? The sorrows of death have compassed me about, and all thy billows have gone over me." Dost thou not remember when, like David, all thy bones were out of joint, and thou saidst, " Create me a clean heart, O God, and renew a right spirit within me;" but there was no answer? And, moreover, Satan suggested a reply: " What! renew a right spirit in THEE! Thou art the worst wretch that ever lived; thy death-warrant is signed, the fagot is burning now that will consume thee, the chains are already forged to bind thee forever, and thou shalt be with me shut up under darkness unto the judgment of the great day." Now, is there such an one here—one to whom hell's gates are opened—upon whom fiends seem perpetually hissing; one who is brought to the black land of confusion, to the valley of the shadow of death, where not only is there no hope, but where the portending clouds seem to be gathered round him? Let him take heart: Christ has come to save such; and as surely as the devil is let loose upon thee in this way, Christ will bind him yet; he will break the teeth of the oppressor, and will take thee, his poor lost sheep, out of the jaw of the lion and the paw of the bear! Art thou so lost? Then here is thy promise, "I will seek that which was lost."

But thou sayest, "Sir, I have had too long a trial to think it possible; I have attended your ministry, and other ministries, for many a long year. Sometimes I have thought that surely I might be saved, but ah! it is of no use. You may speak of all the promises you like, they have nothing to do with me; I write my name down amongst the lost, and charm you never so wisely, I am like the deaf adder—never, never to be comforted! It is all over now, I am locked up in this iron cage of despair—lost, lost! beyond all hope; and I cannot believe what you say." Ah! poor soul, but just notice what the text says, "I will seek that which was lost." I have been seeking thee for many a Sabbath, and so have other ministers, but we have never found thee. Poor soul, God's seeking is very different from ours. Oh! if I could, I would come to thee with these weeping eyes of mine, and say, "Poor sinner, do take heart." I would go down upon my knees with thee, and offer my supplications for thee that thou mightest believe in Christ; but I know it would avail little, unless my Master sought thee. Oh! the shepherds have been after thee many a day, but they could not find thee; remember God knows, as we know not, where thou art. If thou art in the deepest pit in the forest, his almighty eye can see to the bottom. Ay, and in one of the favored moments of the day of salvation,—that time acepted,—he will send home a promise so sweetly that all thy fetters shall break off in an instant—thy night shall be scattered—thy dawn begin; and he will give thee the oil of joy for mourning, and the garment of praise for the spirit of heaviness. Believe now, and thou shalt be comforted now; for the time of faith is the time of comfort.

There is a second point which often meets in the same character: "I WILL BRING AGAIN THAT WHICH WAS DRIVEN AWAY." Souls there are, not only lost, but driven away. "I could tell you of a time," says one, "when I had a hope of heaven; or, at least, I thought I had; I groaned and prayed and strove, and one Sabbath day—I shall never forget it—I stepped into the house of God, and, during the reading of a chapter, or the singing of a hymn, I fondly thought that I had seen Christ, and had believed in him; but, oh! it was only for a moment: I was only permitted just to look into the well of living water; no one came to draw water for me, and give me to drink. I thought for a single second, 'Now is the hour of my salvation;' something said within my heart, 'Now is the appointed time, to-day is the day of salvation;' and I almost began to smile within myself at the thought that I had found the Lord. But, sir, I was driven away, and I dare not go again. If I were only lost, methinks I could believe what you have said. But, ah! I was once very near being a believer; I was just upon the edge of having faith in Christ—but it only makes the night darker to think I once saw a star; for I was driven away." Now there are different ways in which poor sinners are driven away, and in any case it is the devil's work. Sometimes unbelief does it: the sinner sees Christ on the cross, the blood flowing from his hands and feet, and he thinks,—

> "Oh! could I but believe,
> Then all would easy be."

He thinks of the happy effects that would follow faith in Christ, and something says within him, "Venture on him, venture wholly; let no other trust intrude." And he is just going to do it, when suddenly there comes a great black thought, "What, you! you have no right to come; away with you!" He has just pressed through the crowd, and is going to touch the hem of his Master's garment, but ere his finger reaches it, some one has pushed before him, and he goes away abashed; and, all the more so, to think that he should have ever had the presumption, as he deems it, to hope for salvation. Unbelief has pushed many a sinner away from Christ just when he was coming, and has kept him away for a long time.

Sometimes legal preachers drive souls away; they preach a gospel so much mixed up with law, so united with the doings of man, that the poor soul just coming to Christ gets driven away. And even some of God's true ministers—aye, the very best of them—sometimes drive poor sinners away from Christ. When they speak of the experience of the saint, they speak the truth, perhaps; but then there was something that was wanting; the poor soul takes what is said against him; he writes bitter things against himself, because he does not feel that he comes up to the experience which some of the Lord's children have had. Ah! we cannot always tell when we are driving poor souls away from Christ. Often, when we think we are wooing we are driving them away; when we would be winning to the Saviour, some harsh expression of ours frightens sinners away from him. Ah! poor soul, hast thou been driven away? Dost thou understand and sympathize with what I have said? Before I knew the Lord, I could declare that I was driven away. Once, under a powerful sermon, my heart shook within me, and was dissolved in the midst of my bowels; I thought I would seek the Lord, and I bowed my knee and wrestled, and poured out my heart before him. I ventured within his sanctuary to hear his word, hoping that in some favored hour he would send a precious promise to my consolation; but, ah! that wretched afternoon I heard a sermon wherein Christ was not; I had no longer any hope. I would have sipped at that fountain, but I was driven away; I felt that I would have believed in Christ, and I longed and sighed for him. But, ah! that dreadful sermon, and those dreadful things that were uttered; my poor soul knew not what was truth, or what was error; but I thought the man was surely preaching the truth, and I was driven back. I dared not go, I could not believe, I could not lay hold on Christ; I was shut out, if no one else was. Is there some one here who has been driven away? I may have done it, and I will weep before God in secret on account of it. But let me cheer you. Hear this: "I will bring again that which was driven away." As surely as you ever did come once you will be brought back again; that heavenly hour shall once more return; that blessed day shall dawn afresh; Christ shall appear, and his love and mercy shall be bestowed on you. He has drawn you once and he will draw you again, for God never fails. He may, for wise ends and purposes, suffer you to be driven away once; but he will ultimately bring you to himself, for he has said, "I will bring again that which was driven away."

The other two points have, I think, something to do with the driving away; "I WILL BIND UP THAT WHICH WAS BROKEN." This, I think, refers to those who have been broken by being driven away: the shepherds smote them so hard that they even broke their bones. How many have there been who, when they thought they had found Christ, but were driven away, have felt from that moment that they were broken—that they were more sorely wounded than ever they had been? They did entertain some little hope before, that Christ might look upon them with love, but now they are broken to pieces. And that breaking, together with the breaking of the Holy Spirit, which has ground them as in the mortar and pestle of conviction, has so broken them, that they feel utterly destroyed; besides the sickness of sin, they have upon them a sickness partly engendered by the strokes of those who drove them away. I may be taking an extreme case, when I suppose one character in whom those four points meet. Have I any one here in such a position—not only "lost," not only "driven away," but "broken" and "sick" likewise? Thy head has begun to whirl; thou knowest not how it is; but so strong have these convictions got hold of thee, that thy very mind seems to suffer from them;—a mystery to thyself, thou canst not tell where thou art. Some say that thou art mad, and thou thinkest within thyself that they have good ground for the suspicion. Thou art sick of thine existence, and almost ready to take away thy life; a terrible giddiness has seized thee, as if a hell were kindled in thy breast, to be the prelude of despair and irrevocable destruction, the first notes of the "Miserere" of eternal woe. Art thou reduced to such a terrible extremity? Art thou sick as well as broken and driven away and lost? Hear this, "I will seek that which was lost." Canst thou not believe God is true? "I will bring again that which was driven away." Dost thou think God's "*I will*" stands for nothing? "I will bind up that which was broken." Canst thou not implicitly believe what God so absolutely affirms? "I will strengthen that which was sick." O, sick one! God give thee grace to understand that he means what he says, and to believe that he will do what he promises. Come, now, is there one here in whom all these troubles meet? Let him lift up his head with joy from this moment, for Jesus Christ has come to save him, and his sighings shall, ere long, be exchanged for songs of thanksgiving.

II. Now very briefly let me hint at the four characters separately: First, "*that which was lost.*" This, of course, is the awakened sinner, who is made to know that in Adam he is lost, and by his own sins he is utterly ruined and destroyed Such an one has here the Divine authority for hope that God will seek him, and that he shall yet be saved.

"*I will bring again that which was driven away.*" This refers to the backslider, who has been driven away from God by sin. Strong temptations have goaded him to follow the propensities of his own wicked will. Poor backslider! God will restore thee. O! I could tell of some here who have greatly and grievously departed from the paths of righteousness; and their leanness will testify that they have been driven from the pastures. Let me speak to you in God's name: he will bring back "that which was driven away." "O! but," thou sayest, "six years ago I dishonored my profession, and

ever since I have been as one estranged from his people."
Ay, but if thou art the Lord's child, if it were sixty years, he
would bring thee back with weeping and lamentation unto
Zion. "O! sir, but I have so disgraced the cause." Turn
thee, turn thee at his bidding; God invites thee to come.
My backsliding brother, my backsliding sister, I will not condemn thee; I may become a backslider too, and the best ot
these who now stand fast by Jesus may be likewise "overtaken in a fault." Thou art condemned in thine own heart
enough; I would not that thou shouldst "be swallowed up
with overmuch sorrow." "Go and proclaim these words toward the north, and say, Return, thou backsliding Israel, saith
the Lord; and I will not cause mine anger to fall upon you."
'Tis even so with our God. "Yet doth he devise means that
his banished be not expelled from him." Come, Ephraim;
thou hast been a stubborn child, still thy father bids thee
come. Come, prodigal; thou hast wasted thy substance, yet
a father's loving eyes have beheld thee when thou wast a great
way off; come, his breast heaves with love for thee. Come,
thou driven away one, come to him; he loved thee before
thou lovedst him, and though thou didst rebel against him,
he has never ceased to love thee. Though thou hast sinned
much, his loving heart is immutably the same. O! believe in
his goodness in the teeth of thine own unworthiness, so shalt
thou be comforted, and the word on which he hath caused
thee to hope shall be fulfilled: "I will bring again that which
was driven away."

The next character is *the broken one.* The child of God is
often broken; especially if he has been a backslider, he is sure
to have broken bones, and he is likely to walk halting all the
rest of his days. Or the believer may be broken by trouble,
by affliction, by assaults of the enemy; he may be broken on
account of the inbred sin manifested to him by the Holy
Spirit. But, broken one, God will help thee, for he hath said,
"I will bind up that which was broken." Sweet thought!
Precious promises are the ligatures with which God himself
binds up broken bones. Marvelous surgeon! God Almighty
himself bowing down from heaven to put the heavenly link

ment and the fair white linen of a Saviour's righteousness round about the wounded spirit! Broken one, rejoice; God says, "I will heal thee."

Lastly, there are *the sick ones*, and many such there are among the Lord's people. Their faith is weak; their prayers are not so spiritual and fervent as they could desire; there is a chill about them, or else a heat of feverish anxiety—their hearts often palpitate with gloomy fears and sad forebodings; they are not so healthy as they desire to be before God; they long for that perfect love which casteth out fear. Ay, then, dost thou feel that sickness, poor saint, this morning? Say not, God will let thee die, because thou art sick. No, for he says, "I will strengthen that which was sick." So, then, saints in all your distresses, sinners in all your sins, here are exceedingly great promises ministered unto you this morning: and may the Holy Spirit show you their infinite value, and apply them to you with demonstration and with power.

How unspeakable the satisfaction of a poor sufferer when he hears the physician minutely describe all his ailments! But to hear him speak with confidence that, however painful, no symptom is beyond his skill, how the patient will brighten up. Thy case, my brother, is more cheering still. Have you not sometimes heard your doctor say, " When you recover from this sickness you will be better than you were before?" Well, now, think for one moment how far God's mercies exceed our miseries! how far his cure extends beyond our maladies! how sure he is to do for his people exceeding abundantly above all that we ask or think! Then, ho! despairing soul, what though thou hast all four maladies, thou shalt have all four promises! If so be thou art a member of his family, for every affliction and every chastisement thou shalt get so many peaceable fruits of righteousness, that thou wilt afterwards kiss the rod and subscribe to David's testimony, " Before I was afflicted I went astray, but now have I kept thy word." And mark you this— in the fulfillment of his promises ye shall receive *double* for all your distresses.

And, now, can I say aught more? Have I not gone to the uttermost case in the application of my text? Are there any

poor souls that I have not reached ? Then let me try once
again. My dear friends, do you know yourselves to be lost
and ruined by the fall ? Do you feel that you are utterly
undone, ruined, and lost without Christ ? Well, then, in his
name I solemnly declare this great truth of the gospel, that
all who know this and feel it may confidently believe that
there is salvation for them. The only proof that I can give
you that you shall be saints is, that you feel that you are now
sinners. Oh ! poor sin-sick soul, I thank God that thou art
afflicted with this sickness, for thou wilt have recourse to the
physician. Oh ! poor sinner, I thank God that thou knowest
thyself poor, for God will make thee rich.

But as for such of you as are " fat and strong," that boast
yourselves that you are good and have need of nothing, go your
way ; ye need no gospel and I have none to preach to you ; ye
who are so good and excellent, ye need no Christ to save you ;
ye will despise the man that comes in Christ's name to preach
free, unmerited, sovereign love. And what if ye do ? Doth he
care for your contempt ? Not one whit. Reproach will sit
lightly on him if he may but win souls to be found in Christ at
last. If ye need not the medicine, spurn it if you please ; but
you are fools for your pains. If ye want it not for yourselves
let others have it. If ye are so whole that ye need not the
physician, hoot him not while he goes to attend upon those
who feel their danger imminent. Grumble not that I preach
no gospel to you, for you want it not. You are as good as you
can be—in fact, rather better than most Christians, in your
own opinion ; you are no cants, no hypocrites. You may
want a patch or two of religion to make you all right at last.
Your garments are white and courtly, they only want a little
brushing to take the dust off. Alas ! for you, sirs, hell is
built for such good people as you are ; you shall find no place
in heaven ; its blessed mansions are prepared for sinners saved
by grace, and hell's dark dungeons remain for those who reject
Christ, despise mercy, and scorn to sue for pardon, because
they deem themselves too good, too holy, too excellent to need
a Saviour. I say again, as for you who are fat and strong, God
shall feed you with judgment. You think to stand by your

own works, and your best works will destroy you. You shall
appear before God in your own characters, and they shall ruin
you for ever. You think your own merits will suffice, and that
God will bestow on you a reward. Yes, and he will reward
you, and a terrible recompense it shall be, when you shall find
yourselves receiving what you have earned—tribulation, wrath,
and destruction from the presence of the Lord your God.
Your consciences tell you that what I speak is true. Despise
the warning now, but in the silent moments of your sober
thought this shall cling to you, this shall haunt you. When
your guilt recoils on your memory, when your heart and flesh
fail, and your reason totters at the prospect of a hereafter,
you will howl with misery and cry out, " Woe worth the day !"
Now, ye lost and ruined, come to Jesus ; ye broken sinners
believe in Jesus ; ye that are bruised and mangled by the fall,
come to Jesus.

> " With true belief and true repentance,
>   Every grace to bring you nigh,
>   Without money,
>   Come to Jesus Christ, and buy.

> " Let not conscience make you linger,
>   Nor of fitness fondly dream ;
>   All the fitness he requireth,
>   Is to feel your need of him.
>   This he gives you,
>   'Tis his Spirit's rising beam."

Lost souls, ye doubly lost, ye more than ruined, my Master
begs you to come ; he has sent me to you this morning. Just
as Abraham of old sent his servant to go wooing for his son,
so my God has sent me as his servant to bid you come to Jesus.
What sayest thou, lost sinner, wilt thou be made whole ? Does
thy heart leap into thy mouth, and dost thou answer, "Ay, with
joy I would be made whole ?"   Then that *willingness* God has
given thee ; the feeling of thy need he has bestowed on thee,
and he bids thee now believe.   Canst thou not believe Christ ?
See him there hanging on the cross ; on that bloody tree behold
him.   Sinner, wilt thou not believe him now ?   What ! dost

thou think he dost not love thee, when he gave up his body to death for thee? What! not love thee, and yet die for thee? "Ay," sayest thou, "I do not believe he did die for me." What! not believe what he himself has said? He said he came to save sinners: dost thou doubt whether thou art a sinner? "No, sir," you reply, "I know that." Well, then, wilt thou doubt my Master when he says he came to save sinners? Wilt thou not believe that he came to save thee? Or, if that be too bold for thy timid spirit, at least thou mayest say—

> "I can but perish if I go:
>   I am resolved to try:
> For if I stay away, I know
>   I must for ever die.
> But if I die, with mercy sought,
>   When I the King have tried,
> That were to die—delightful thought!—
>   As sinner never died!"

Sinner never did die so; try it, soul, and thou shalt find it true.

SERMON VIII

THE TWO TALENTS

"He also that had received two talents came and said, Lord, thou deliver edst unto me two talents: behold, I have gained two other talents beside them. His lord said unto him, Well done, good and faithful servant; thou hast been faithful over a few things, I will make thee ruler over many things: enter thou into the joy of thy Lord."—MATTHEW xxv. 22, 23

"Every good gift and every perfect gift is from above, and cometh down from the Father of lights." All that men have they must trace to the Great Fountain, the giver of all good. Hast thou talents? They were given thee by the God of talents. Hast thou time? hast thou wealth, influence, power? Hast thou powers of tongue? Hast thou powers of thought? Art thou poet, statesman, or philosopher? Whatever be thy position, and whatever be thy gifts, remember that they are not thine, but they are lent thee from on high. No man hath anything of his own, except his sins. We are but tenants at will. God hath put us into his estates, and he hath said, "Occupy till I come." Though our vineyards bear never so much fruit, yet the vineyard belongs to the King, and though we are to take the hundred for our hire, yet King Solomon must have his thousand. All the honor of our ability and the use of it must be unto God, because he is the Giver. The parable tells us this very pointedly; for it makes every person acknowledge that his talents come from the Lord. Even the man who digged in the earth and hid his Lord's money, did not deny that his talent belonged to his Master; for though his reply, "Lo, there thou hast that is thine," was exceedingly impertinent, yet it was not a denial of this fact. So that even this man was ahead of those who deny their obligations to God, who superciliously toss their heads at the very mention of obedience to their Creator, and spend their time and their

powers rather in rebellion against him than in his service.
Oh, that we were all wise to believe and to act upon this most
evident of all truths, that everything we have, we have received from the Most High.

Now, there are some men in the world who have but few
talents. Our parable says, "One had five, and another two."
To them I shall address myself this morning; and I pray that
the few pointed things I may say, may be blessed of God to
their edification or rebuke. First, I shall notice *the fact that
there are many persons who have but few talents*, and I will
try to account for God's dispensing but few to them. Secondly, I shall remind them that *even for these few talents they
must be brought to account*. And thirdly, I shall conclude by
making the comforting observation, that *if our few talents be
rightly used, neither our own conscience nor our Master's judgment shall condemn us for not having more.*

I. First, then, GOD HAS MADE SOME MEN WITH FEW TALENTS.
You very often hear men speak of one another as if God had
made no mental differences at all. One man finds himself
successful, and he supposes that if every one else could have
been as industrious and as persevering as himself, every one
must necessarily have been as successful. You will often hear
remarks against ministers who are godly and earnest men, but
who do not happen to have much attracting power, and they
are called drones and lazy persons, because they cannot make
much of a stir in the world, whereas the reason may be, that
they have but little talent, and are making the best use of
what they have, and therefore ought not to be rebuked for
the littleness of what they are able to accomplish. It is a
fact, which every man must see, that even in our birth there
is a difference. All children are not alike precocious, and all
men certainly are not alike capable of learning or of teaching
God hath made eminent and marvelous differences. We are
not to suppose that all the difference between a Milton and a
man who lives and dies without being able to read, has been
caused by education. There was doubtless a difference originally, and though education will do much, it cannot do everything. Fertile ground, when well-tilled will necessarily bring

forth more than the best tilled estate, the soil of which is hard and sterile. God has made great and decided differences; and we ought, in dealing with our fellow-men, to recollect this, lest we should say harsh things of those very men to whom God will afterwards say, "Well done, good and faithful servant."

But why is it that God has not given to all men like talents? My first answer shall be, because God is a Sovereign, and of all attributes, next to his love, God is the most fond of displaying his sovereignty. The Lord God will have men know that he has a right to do what he wills with his own. Hence it is, that in salvation he gives it to some and not to others; and his only reply to any accusation of injustice is, "Nay, but O man, who art thou that repliest against God? Shall the thing formed say to him that formed it, Why hast thou made me thus?" The worm is not to murmur because God did not make it an angel, and the fish that swims the sea must not complain because it hath not wings to fly into the highest heavens. God had a right to make his creatures just what he pleased, and though men may dispute his right, he will hold and keep it inviolate against all comers. That he may hedge his right about and make vain man acknowledge it, in all his gifts he continually reminds us of his sovereignty. "I will give to this man," he says, "a mind so acute that he shall pry into all secrets; I will make another so obtuse, that none but the plainest elements of knowledge shall ever be attainable by him. I will give to one man such a wealth of imagination, that he shall pile mountain upon mountain of imagery, till his language seems to reach to celestial majesty; I will give to another man a soul so dull, that he shall never be able to originate a poetic thought." Why this, O God? The answer comes back, "Shall I not do what I will with mine own?" "So, then, the children being not yet born, neither having done good or evil, that the purpose of God according to election might stand, it was written, the elder shall serve the younger." And so it is written concerning men, that one of them shall be greater than another; one shall bow his neck, and the other put his foot upon it, for the

Lord hath a right to dispose of places and of gifts, of talents and wealth, just as seemeth good in his sight.

Now, most men quarrel with this. But mark, the thing that you complain of in God, is the very thing that you love in yourselves. Every man likes to feel that he has a right to do with his own as he pleases. We all like to be little sovereigns. You will give your money freely and liberally to the poor; but if any man should impertinently urge that he had a claim upon your charity, would you give unto him? Certainly not; and who shall impeach the greatness of your generosity in so doing? It is even as that parable, that we have in one of the Evangelists, where, after the men had toiled, some of them twelve hours, some of them six, and some of them but one, the Lord gave every man a penny. Oh! I would meekly bow my head, and say, "My Lord, hast thou given me one talent? then I bless thee for it, and I pray thee bestow upon me grace to use it rightly. Hast thou given to my brother ten talents? I thank thee for the greatness of thy kindness towards him; but I neither envy him, nor complain of thee." Oh! for a spirit that bows always before the sovereignty of God.

Again: God gives to one five, and to another two talents, because the Creator is a lover of variety. It was said that order is heaven's first law; surely variety is the second; for in all God's works, there is the most beautiful diversity Look ye towards the heavens at night: all the stars shine not with the same brilliance, nor are they placed in straight lines, like the lamps of our streets. Then turn your eyes below: see in the vegetable world, how many great distinctions there are, ranging from the cedar of Lebanon to the hyssop on the wall, or the moss that is smaller still. See, how from the huge mammoth tree, that seems as if beneath its branches it might shade an army, down to the tiny lichen, God hath made everything beautiful, but everything full of variety. Look on any one tree, if you please: see how every leaf differs from its fellow—how even the little tiny buds that are at this hour bursting at the scent of the approaching perfume of spring, differ from each other—not two of them alike

Look again, upon the animated world: God hath not made every creature like unto another. How wide the range—from the colossal elephant, to the coney that burrows in the rock—from the whale, that makes the deep hoary with its lashings, to the tiny minnow that skims the brook; God hath made all things different, and we see variety everywhere. I doubt not it is the same, even in heaven, for there there are "thrones, and dominions, and principalities, and powers"—different ranks of angels, perhaps, rising tier upon tier. "One star differeth from another star in glory." And why should not the same rule stand good in manhood? Doth God cast us all in the same mold? It seems not so; for he hath not made our faces alike; no two countenances can be said to be exactly the same, for if there be some likeness, yet is there a manifest diversity. Should minds, then, be alike? Should souls all be cast in the same fashion? Should God's creation dwindle down into a great manufactory, in which everything is melted in the same fire and poured into the same mould? No, for variety's sake, he will have one man a renowned David, and another David's unknown armor bearer; he will have one man a Jeremy, who shall prophesy, and another a Baruch, who shall only read the prophesy; one shall be rich as Dives, another poor as Lazarus; one shall speak with a voice loud as thunder, another shall be dumb; one shall be mighty in word and doctrine, another shall be feeble in speech and slow in words. God will have variety, and the day will come when, looking down upon the world we shall see the beauty of its history to be mightily indebted to the variety of the characters that entered into it.

But a little further. God hath a deeper reason than this. God gives to some men but few talents, because he has many small spheres, and he would have these filled. There is a great ocean, and it needs inhabitants. O Lord, thou hast made Leviathan to swim therein. There is a secret grotto, a hidden cavern, far away in the depths of the sea; its entrance is but small; if there were naught but a Leviathan, it must remain untenanted for ever: a little fish is made, and that small place becomes an ocean unto it. There are a thousand sprays and twigs upon the trees of the forest; were all eagles, how would the forests be made glad with song, and how could each twig bear its songster? But because God would have each twig have its own music, he has made the little songster to sit upon it. Each sphere must have the creature to occupy it adapted to the size of the sphere. God always acts economically. Does he intend a man to be the pastor of some small parish with four or five hundred inhabitants? Of what use is it giving to that man the abilities of an apostle? Does he intend a woman to be a humble teacher of her own children at home, a quiet trainer of her own family? Would it not even disturb her and injure her if God should make her a poetess, and give her gifts that might electrify a nation? The littleness of her talents will to a degree fit her for the littleness of her sphere. There is some youth who is quite capable of assisting in a Ragged School: perhaps if he had a higher genius he might disdain the work, and so the Ragged School would be without its excellent teacher. There are little spheres, and God will have little men to occupy them. There are posts of important duty, and men shall be found with nerve and muscle fitted for the labor. He has made a statue for every niche, and a picture for every portion of the gallery; none shall be left vacant; but since some niches are small, so shall be the statuettes that occupy them. To some he gives two talents, because two are enough, and five would be too many.

Once more: God gives to men two talents, because in them very often he displays the greatness of his grace in saving souls. You have heard a minister who was deeply read in sacred lore; his wisdom was profound, and his speech graceful. Under his preaching many were converted. Have you never heard it not quite said, but almost hinted, that much of his success was traceable to his learning and to his graceful oratory? But, on the other hand, you have met with a man, rough in his dialect, uncouth in his manners, evidently without any great literary attainments; nevertheless, God has given that man the one talent of an earnest heart; he speaks like a son of thunder; with rough, stern language, he denounces sin and proclaims the gospel ; under him hundreds are converted. The world sneers at him. "I can see no reason for all this," says the scholar ; " it is all rubbish—cant ; the man knows nothing." The critic takes up his pen, nibs it afresh, dips it in the bitterest ink he can find, and writes a most delightful history of the man in which he goes so far as to say, not that he sees horns on his head, but almost everything but that. He is everything that is bad, and nothing that is good. He utterly denounces him. He is foolish, he is vain, he is base, he is proud, he is illiterate, he is vulgar. There was no word in the English language that was bad enough for him, but one must be coined. And now what says the church ? What says the man himself? " Even so, O Lord ; now must the glory be unto thee for ever, inasmuch as thou hast chosen the base things of this world, and the things that are not, to bring to naught the things that are." So it seemeth that out of the little God sometimes winneth more glory than he doth out of the great ; and I doubt not that he has made some of you with little power to do good, with little influence, and with a narrow sphere, that he may, in the last great day, manifest to angels how much he can do in a little space. You know, dear friends, there are two things that always will attract our attention. One is skill embodied in a stupendous mass. We see the huge ship, the Leviathan, and we wonder that man could have made it ; at another time we see an elegant piece of workmanship that will stand upon less than a square inch, and we say, " Well, I can understand how men can make a great ship, but I can not comprehend how an artist could have the patience and the skill to make so minute a thing as this." And ah ! my friends, it seems to me that God is not a greater God to our apprehension, when we see the boundless fields of ether and the unnumbered orbs swimming therein, than when we see a humble cottager, and behold God's perfect word carried out in her soul, and God's highest glory wrought from her little talent. Surely if in the little, man can honor himself as well as in the great, the Infinite, and the Eternal, can most of all glorify himself when he stoopeth to the littleness of mankind.

II. Our second proposition was, that even A FEW TALENTS MUST BE ACCOUNTED FOR. We are very apt when we think of the day of judgment, to imagine that certain characters will undergo a more trying process than others. I know I have often involuntarily said, when reading the history of Napoleon, "Here is a man of tremendous ability, the world's master; a dozen centuries might be required to produce such another man; but here is a man who prostitutes all his ability to ambition, carries his armies like a destroying deluge across every country, widows wives, and renders children fatherless, not by hundreds but by thousands, if not by millions. What must be his solemn account when he stands before the throne of God? Shall not the witnesses rise up from the fields of Spain, of Russia, of Italy, of Egypt, of Palestine, and accuse the man who, to gratify his own bold ambition, led them to death?" But will you please to remember that though Napoleon must be a prisoner at the bar, each of us must stand there also? And though our position is not very high, and we have not stood upon the pinnacle of fame, yet we have stood quite high enough to be borne under the observation of the Most High, and we have had just ability enough and power enough to have done mischief in the world, and to be accountable for it. "Oh!" said one, "I thought that surely in the day of judgment he would pass me by; I have been no Tom Paine; I have not been a leader among low and vulgar infidels; I have not been a murderer; I have not been a prince among sinners; I have not been a disturber of the public peace; what few sins I have committed have taken place quietly; nobody has heard of them; I don't think my bad example has gone far; perhaps my children have not been much blessed by my behavior, but, nevertheless, mine has been a very small quantum of mischief, too small to have poisoned any one beside myself. I have been, on the whole, so tolerably moral, that though I cannot say I have served God, yet my defalcations from the path of duty have been slight indeed!" Ah! truly friends! you may think yourselves never so little, but your making yourselves insignificant will not excuse you You have had but little entrusted to you! Then the les

trouble for you to make use of your talents. The man who has
many talents requires much hard labor to use them all. He might
make the excuse that he found five talents too many to put out
in the market at once ; you have only one ; anybody can lend
out his one talent to interest—it will cost you but little trouble
to supply that; and inasmuch as you live, and inasmuch as you
die, without having improved the one talent, your guilt will be
exceedingly increased by the very fact that your talent was
but little, and, consequently, the trouble of using it would
have been but little too. If you had but little, God required
but little of you ; why, then, did you not render that ? If
any man holds a house at a rental of a pound a year, let it be
never so small a house for the money, if he brings not his
rent there is not one half the excuse for him that there would
be if his rent had been a hundred pounds, and he had failed
to bring it. You shall be the more inexcusable on account of
the little that was required of you. Let me, then, address
you, and remind you that you must be brought to account.

Remember, my hearer, that in the day of judgment thy
account must be personal ; God will not ask you what your
church did—he will ask you what you did yourself. Now
there is a Sunday-school. If God should try all members of
the church in a body, they would each of them say, O Lord,
as a body we had an excellent Sunday-school, and had many
teachers, and so they would excuse themselves. But no ; one
by one, all professors must come before him. " What did
you do for the Sabbath-school ? I gave you a gift for teaching
children—what did you do ?" " O Lord, there was a Sabbath-school." That has nothing to do with it ? What did
you do ? You are not to account now for the company with
which you were united, but for yourself as an individual.
" O," says one, " there were a number of poor ministers ; I
was at the Surrey Hall, and so much was done for them."
No ; what did you do ? You must be held personally responsible for your own wealth, for your own ability. " Well,"
says one, " I am happy to say there is a great deal more
preaching now than there used to be ; the churches seem to
be roused." Yes, sir, and you seem to take part of the credit

to yourself. Do *you* preach more than you used to? You are a minister; do *you* make any greater efforts? Remember, it is not what your brethren are doing, but it is what *you* do that you will be called to account for at the bar of God; and each one of you will be asked this question, "What hast thou done with *thy* talent?" All your connection with churches will avail you nothing; it is your personal doings—your personal service towards God that is demanded of you as an evidence of saving grace. And if others are idle—if others pay not God his due—so much the more reason why you should have been more exceedingly diligent in doing so yourself.

Recollect, again, that your account will have to be particular. God will go into all the items of it. At the day of judgment you will not have to cast up a hurried account in the gross, but every item shall be read. Can you prove that? Yes. "For every idle word that man shall speak, he shall be brought unto account at the day of judgment." Now, it is in the items that men go astray "Well," says one, "If I look at my life in the bulk, I am not very much ashamed, but it is those items, those little items—they are the troublesome part of the account, that one does not care to meddle with." Do you know that all yesterday was made up of littles? And the things of to-day are all little, and what you do to-morrow will all be little things. Just as the tiny shells make up the chalk hills, and the chalk hills together make up the range, so the trifling actions make up the whole account, and each of these must be pulled asunder separately. You had an hour to spare the other day—what did you do? You had a voice —how did you use it? You had a pen—you could use that—how did you employ it? Each particular shall be brought out, and there shall be demanded an account for each one. Oh, that you were wise, that ye did not slur this matter, but would take every note in the music of your behavior, and seek to make each note in harmony with its fellow, lest, after all, the psalm of your life may prove to be a hideous discord. Oh, that ye who are without God would remember that your life is assuredly such, that the trial of the ast great day must end in your condemnation.

Again, that account will be very exact, and there will be no getting off without those little things. " Oh ! there were a few pecadillos, and very small matters indeed ; I never took stock of them at all." But they will all be taken stock of then. When God comes to look into our hearts at last, he will not only look at the great but at the little ; every th'ng will be seen into, the pence sins as well as the pound iniquities —all must be brought against us, and an exact account given.

Again, remember, in the last place, upon this point, that the account will be very impartial at the day of judgment, when all will be tried without any reference to their station. The prince will be summoned to give an account of his talents, and side by side must stand his courtier and his slave. The mightiest emperor must stand at God's bar, as well as the meanest cottager. And all must appear and be tried accord- ing to the deeds they have done in the body. As to our pro- fessions, they will avail us nothing. We may have been the proudest hypocrites that ever made the world sick with our pride, but we must be searched and examined, as much as if we had been the vilest sinners. We must take our own trial before God's eternal tribunal, and nothing can bias our judge, or give him an opinion for or against us, apart from the evi- dence. Oh, how solemn this will make the trial, especially if we have no blood of Christ to plead ! The great Advocate will get his people an acquittal, through his imputed merits, even though our sin in itself would condemn them. But re- member, that without him we shall never be able to stand the fiery ordeal of that last dread assize. " Well," said an old preacher, " when the law was given, Sinai was on a smoke, and it melted like wax ; but when the punishment of the law is given, the whole earth will quake and quail. For who shall be able to endure the day of the Lord, the day of God's fierce anger ?"

III. The last point is, IF BY DIVINE GRACE (and it is only by divine grace that this can ever be accomplished)—OUR TWO TALENTS BE RIGHTLY USED, THE FACT THAT WE HAD NOT FIVE, WILL BE NO INJURY TO US.

You say, when such a man dies, who stood in the midst of

the church, a triumphant warrior for the truth, the angels will crowd to heaven's gates to see him, for he has been a mighty hero, and done much for his Master. A Calvin or a Luther, with what plaudits shall they be received!—men with talents, who have been faithful to their trust. Yes, but know ye not, that there is many a humble village pastor whose flock scarcely numbers fifty, who toils for them as for his life, who spends hours in praying for their welfare, who uses all the little ability he has in his endeavor to win them to Christ; and do ye imagine that his entry into heaven shall be less triumphant than the entry of such a man as Luther? If so, ye know not how God dealeth with his people. He giveth them rewards, not according to the greatness of the goods with which they were entrusted, but according to their fidelity thereunto, and he that hath been faithful to the least, shall be as much rewarded, as he that hath been faithful in much. I want you briefly to turn to the chapter, to see this. You will note first, that the man with two talents came to his Lord with as great a confidence as the man that had five. "And he said, Lord, thou deliveredst unto me two talents; behold, I have gained two talents beside them." I will be bound to say, that while that poor man with the two talents was trading with them, he frequently looked upon his neighbor with the five talents, and said, "Oh, I wish I could do as much as he is doing! See now, he has five talents to put out, and how much interest he has coming every year; Oh, that I could do as much!" And as he went on he often prayed, "O my Lord, give me greater ability, and greater grace to serve thee, for I long to do more." And when he sat down to read his diary, he thought, "Ah, this diary does not tell much. There is no account of my journey through fifty counties; I can not tell how I have travelled from land to land, as Paul did, to preach the truth. No; I have just had to keep in this parish, and been pretty well starved to death, toiling for this people, and if I have added some ten or a dozen to the church, that has been a very great deal to me. Why, I hear that Mr. So-and-so, was privileged to add two or three hundred in a year, Oh, that I could do that! Surely when I go to heaven, I shall creep in at the door somehow, while he by grace will be enabled to go boldly in, bringing his sheaves with him." Now stop, poor little faith, stop; thy Master will not deal thus with thee. When thou shalt come to die, thou wilt through his grace feel as much confidence in dying with thy two well-used talents, as thy brother with his ten, for thou wilt, when thou comest there, have thy Lord's sweet presence, and thou wilt say, "I am complete in Christ. Christ's righteousness covers me from head to foot, and now in looking back upon my past life, I can say, Blessed be his holy name. It is little that I could do, but I have done as much as I could for him. I know that he will pardon my defects, and forgive my miscarriages, and I shall never look back upon my humble village charge without much joy, that the Lord allowed me to labor there." And, Oh, methinks, that man will have even a richer commendation in his own conscience, than the man who has been more publicly applauded, for he can say to himself, after putting all his trust in Christ, " Well, I am sure I did not do all this for fame, for I blushed unseen—I have lost my sweetness on the desert air. No one has ever read my deeds; what I did was between myself and my God, and I can render up my account to him and say, ' Lord, I did it for thee, and not to honor myself.' " Yes, friends, I might tell you now of many a score of earnest evangelists in this our land who are working harder than any one of us, and yet win far less honor. Yes, and I could bring you up many a score of city missionaries whose toil for Christ is beyond all measure of praise, who never get much reward here, nay, rather meet with slights and disrespect. You see the poor man start as soon as he goes from his place of worship to-day. He has got three hours this afternoon to go and spend among the sick, and then you will see him on Monday morning. He has to go from house to house, often with the door slammed in his face, often exposed to mobs and drunken men, sometimes jeered and scoffed at, meeting with persons of all religious persuasions and of no persuasion.

He toils on; he has his little evening meeting, and there he gets a little flock together and tries to pray with them, and he gets now and then a man or a woman converted; but he has no honor. He just takes him off to the minister, and he says, "Sir, here is a good man; I think he is impressed; will you baptize him and receive him into your church?" The minister gets all the credit of that, but as for the poor city missionary, there is little or nothing said of him. There is, perhaps, just his name, Mr. Brown, or Mr. Smith, mentioned sometimes in the report, but people do not think much of him, except, perhaps, as an object of charity they have to keep, whereas he is the man that gives them charity, giving all the sap and blood and marrow of his life for some poor sixty pounds a year, hardly enough to keep his family above want. But he, when he dies, my friend, shall have no less the approval of his conscience than the man who was permitted to stand before the multitudes and raised the nation into excitement on account of religion. He shall come before the Master clothed in the righteousness of Christ, and with unblushing face shall say, "I have received two talents; I have gained beside them two talents more."

Furthermore, and to conclude, you will notice there was no difference in his Master's commendation—none in the reward. In both cases, it was "Well done, good and faithful servant; thou hast been faithful in a few things, I will make thee ruler over many things; enter thou into the joy of thy Lord." Here comes Whitfield, the man who stood before twenty thousand at a time to preach the gospel, who in England, Scotland, Ireland, and America has testified the truth of God, and who could count his converts by thousands, even under one sermon! Here he comes, the man that endured persecution and scorn, and yet was not moved—the man of whom the world was not worthy, who lived for his fellow men, and died at last for their cause; stand by angels and admire, while the Master takes him by the hand and says, "Well done, well done, good and faithful servant; enter thou into the joy of thy Lord!" See how free grace honors the man whom it enabled to do valiantly. Hark! Who is this that comes there? a poor thin-looking creature, that on earth was a consumptive; there was a hectic flush now and then upon her cheek, and she lay three long years upon her bed of sickness. Was she a prince's daughter, for it seems heaven is making much stir about her? No, she was a poor girl that earned her living by her needle, and she worked herself to death!—Stitch, stitch, stitch, from morning to night! and here she comes. She went prematurely to her grave, but she is coming, like a shock of corn fully ripe, into heaven; and her Master says, "Well done, thou good and faithful servant, thou hast been faithful in a few things, I will make thee ruler over many things; enter thou into the joy of thy Lord." She takes her place by the side of Whitfield. Ask what she ever did, and you find out that she used to live in some back garret down some dark alley in London; and there used to be another poor girl come to work with her, and that poor girl, when she first came to work with her, was a gay and volatile creature, and this consumptive child told her about Christ; and they used, when she was well enough, to creep out of an evening to go to chapel or to church together. It was hard at first to get the other one to go, but she used to press her lovingly; and when the girl went wild a little, she never gave her up. She used to say, "O Jane, I wish you loved the Saviour;" and when Jane was not there she used to pray for her, and when she was there she prayed with her: and now and then when she was stitching away, read a page out of the Bible to her, for poor Jane could not read. And with many tears she tried to tell her about the Saviour who loved her and gave himself for her. At last, after many a day of hard persuasion, and many an hour of sad disappointment, and many a night of sleepless tearful prayer, at last she lived to see the girl profess her love to Christ; and she left her and took sick, and there she lay till she was taken to the hospital, where she died. When she was in the hospital she used to have a few tracts, and she used to give them to those who came to see her; she would try, if she could, to get the women to come round, and she would give them a tract. When she first went into the hospital, if she could creep out of bed, she used to get by the side of one who was dying, and the nurse used to let her do it; till at last she got too ill, and then she used to ask a poor woman on the other side of the ward, who was getting better, and was going out, if she would come and read a chapter to her ; not that she wanted her to read to her on her own account, but for her sake, for she thought it might strike her heart while she was reading it. At last this poor girl died and fell asleep in Jesus ; and the poor consumptive needle-woman had said to her, "Well done"—and what more could an archangel have said to her ?—" she hath done what she could."

See, then, the Master's commendation, and the last reward will be equal to all men who have used their talents well. Ah ! if there be degrees in glory, they will not be distributed according to our talents, but according to our faithfulness in using them. As to whether there are degrees or not, I know not ; but this I know, he that doeth his Lord's will, shall have said to him, "Well done, good and faithful servant."

SERMON IX

THE PRODIGAL'S RETURN

" But when he was yet a great way off, his father saw him, and had com
passion, and ran, and fell on his neck, and kissed him."—LUKE xv. 20

ALL persons engaged in education will tell you that they
find it far more difficult to make the mind unlearn its errors
than to make it receive truth. If we could suppose a man
totally ignorant of anything, we should have a fairer chance
of instructing him quickly and effectually than we should
have had if his mind had been previously stored with falsehood. I have no doubt you, each of you, find it harder to
unlearn than to learn. To get rid of old prejudices and pre-
conceived notions is a very hard struggle indeed. It has been
well said, that those few words, "I am mistaken," are the
hardest in all the English language to pronounce, and certainly it takes very much force to compel us to pronounce them:
and after having done so, it is even then difficult to wipe away
the slime which an old serpentine error has left upon the heart.
Better for us not to have known at all than to have known
the wrong thing. Now, I am sure that this truth is never
more true than when it applies to God. If I had been let
alone to form my notion of God, entirely from Holy Scripture, I feel, that with the assistance of his Holy Spirit it would
have been far more easy for me to understand what he is, and
how he governs the world, than to learn even the truths of
his own Word, after the mind had become perverted by th
opinions of others. Why, brethren, who is it that gives a fair
representation of God? The Arminian slanders God by
accusing him (not in his own intention, but really so) of unfaithfulness; for he teaches that God may promise what he
never performs; that he may give eternal life, and promise

that those who have it shall never perish, and yet they may perish after all. He speaks of God as if he were a mutable being, for he talks of his loving men one day, and hating them the next; of his writing their names in the Book of Life one hour, and then erasing their names in the next. And the influence of such an error as that, is very baneful. Many children of God, who have imbibed these errors in early youth, have had to drag along their poor wearied and broken frames for many a day, whereas they might have walked joyfully to heaven if they had known the truth from the beginning. On the other hand, those who hear the Calvinistic preacher, are very apt to misinterpret God. Although we trust we would never speak of God in any other sense than that in which we find him represented in sacred Scripture, yet are we well aware that many of our hearers, even through our assertions, when most guarded, are apt to get rather a caricature of God, than a true picture of him. They imagine that God is a severe being, angry and fierce, very easily to be moved to wrath, but not so easily to be induced to love; they are apt to think of him as one who sits in supreme and lofty state, either totally indifferent to the wishes of his creatures, or else determined to have his own way with them, as an arbitrary Sovereign, never listening to their desires, or compassionating their woes. O that we could unlearn all these fallacies, and believe God to be what he is! O that we could come to Scripture, and there look into that glass which reflects his sacred image, and then receive him as he is, the all-Wise, the all-Just, and yet the all-Gracious, and all-Loving Jehovah! J shall endeavor this morning, by the help of God's Holy Spirit, to represent the lovely character of Christ; and if I shall be happy enough to have some in my audience who are in the position of the prodigal son in the parable—coming to Christ, and yet a great way off from him—I shall trust that they will be led by the same Divine Spirit, to believe in the loving kindness of Jehovah, and so may find peace with God now, ere they leave this house of prayer.

"When he was yet a great way off, his father saw him, and had compassion, and ran, and fell on his neck, and kissed him."

First, I shall notice the *position* intended in the words, " a great way off ;" secondly, I shall notice the *peculiar troubles* which agitate the minds of those, who are in this condition ; and then, thirdly, I shall endeavor to teach *the great loving-kindness of our own adorable God*, inasmuch as when we are " a great way off," he runs to us, and embraces us in the arms of his love.

I. First, then, what is the POSITION signified by being ' a great way off ?" I must just notice what is *not* that position. It is not the position of the man who is careless and entirely regardless of God; for you notice that the prodigal is represented now as having come to himself, and as returning to his father's house. Though it be true that all sinners are a great way off from God, whether they know it or not, yet in this particular instance, the position of the poor prodigal is intended to signify the character of one, who has been aroused by conviction, who has been led to abhor his former life, and who sincerely desires to return to God. I shall not, then, this morning, specially address the blasphemer, and the profane. To him, there may be some incidental warning heard, but I shall not specially address such a character. It is another person for whom this text is intended : the man who has been a blasphemer, if you please, who may have been a drunkard, and a swearer, and what not, but who has now renounced these things, and is steadfastly seeking after Christ, that he may obtain eternal life. That is the man who is here said to be, though coming to the Lord, " a great way off."

Once again, there is another person who is not intended by this description, namely, the very great man, the Pharisee who thinks himself extremely righteous, and has never learned to confess his sin. You, sir, in your apprehension, are not a great way off. You are so really in the sight of God ; you are as far from him as light from darkness, as the east is from the west ; but you are not spoken of here. You are like the prodigal son, only that instead of spending your life righteously, you have run away from your Father, and hidden in the earth the gold which he gave you, and are able to feed upon the husks which swine do eat, whilst by a miserable economy of good works you are hoping to save enough of your fortune to support yourself here and in eternity. Your hope of self-salvation is a fallacy, and you are not addressed in the words of the text. It is the man who knows himself lost, but desires to be saved, who is here declared to be met by God, and received with affectionate embraces.

And now we come to the question, Who is the man, and why is he said to be a great way off? For he seems to be very near the kingdom, now that he knows his need and is seeking the Saviour. I reply, in the first place, he is a great way off in his own apprehensions. You are here this morning, and you have an idea that never was man so far from God as you are. You look back upon your past life, and you recollect how you have slighted God, despised his Sabbath, neglected his Book, trampled upon the blood of sprinkling, and rejected all the invitations of his mercy. You turn over the pages of your history, and you remember the sins which you have committed—the sins of your youth and your former transgressions, the crimes of your manhood, and the riper sins of your older years; like black waves dashing upon a dark shore, they roll in wave upon wave, upon your poor troubled memory. There comes a little wave of your childish folly, and over that there leaps one of your youthful transgressions, and over the head of this there comes a very Atlantic billow of your manhood's transgressions. At the sight of them you stand astonished and amazed. "O Lord my God, how deep is the gulf which divides me from thyself, and where is the power that can bridge it? I am separated from thee by leagues of sin, whole mountains of my guilt are piled upward between me and thyself. O God, shouldest thou destroy me now, thou wouldest be just; and if thou dost ever bring me to thyself, it must be nothing less than a power as Omnipotent as that which made the world, which can ever do it. O! how far am I from God!"

Some of you would be startled this morning, if your neighbors were to give you revelations of their own feelings. If yonder man standing there in the crowd could come into this pulpit, and tell you what he now feels, you might perhaps be

horrified at his description of his own heart. How many of
you have no notion of the way in which a soul is cut and
hacked about, when it is under the convictions of the law! If
you should hear the man tell out what he feels, you would say,
"Ah! he is a poor deluded enthusiast; men are not so bad as
that;" or else you would be apt to think he had committed
some nameless crime which he dare not mention, that was
preying on his conscience. Nay, sir, he has been as moral
and upright as you have been; but should he describe aimself
as he now discovers himself to be, he would shock you utterly. And yet you are the same, though you feel it not, and
would indignantly deny it. When the light of God's grace
comes into your heart, it is something like the opening of the
windows of an old cellar that has been shut up for many days.
Down in that cellar, which has not been opened for many
months, are all kinds of loathsome creatures, and a few sickly
plants blanched by the darkness. The walls are dark and
damp with the trail of reptiles; it is a horrid filthy place, in
which no one would willingly enter. You may walk there in
the dark very securely, and except now and then for the touch
of some slimy creature, you would not believe the place was
so bad and filthy. Open those shutters, clean a pane of glass,
let a little light in, and now see how a thousand noxious things
have made this place their habitation. Sure, 'twas not the
light that made this place so horrible, but it was the light that
showed how horrible it was before. So let God's grace just
open a window and let the light into a man's soul, and he will
stand astonished to see at what a distance he is from God.
Yes, sir, to-day you think yourself second to none but the
Eternal; you fancy that you can approach his throve with
steady step; it is but a little that you have to do to be saved;
you imagine that you can accomplish it at any hour, and save
yourself upon your dying bed as well as now. Ah! sir, if
you could but be touched by Ithuriel's wand, and made to
be in appearance what you are in reality, then you would see
that you are far enough from God even now, and so far from
him that unless the arms of his grace were stretched out to
bring you to himself, you must perish in your sin. Not I

turn my eye again with hope, and trust I have not a few in this large assembly who can say, " Sir, I feel I am far from God, and sometimes I fear I am so far from him that he will never have mercy upon me; I dare not lift so much as my eyes towards heaven; I smite on my breast, and say, ' Lord, have mercy upon me, a sinner.' " Oh! poor heart; here is a comforting passage for thee : " When he was yet a great way off, his father saw him, and had compassion on him."

But again, there is a second sense in which some now present may feel themselves to be far off from God. Conscience tells every man that if he would be saved he must get rid of his sin. The Antinomian may possibly pretend to believe that men can be saved while they live in sin; but conscience will never allow any man to swallow so egregious a lie as that. I have not one person in this congregation who is not perfectly assured that if he is to be saved he must leave off his drunkenness and his vices. Sure there is not one here so stupefied with the laudanum of hellish indifference as to imagine that he can revel in his lusts, and afterwards wear the white robe of the redeemed in paradise. If ye imagine ye can be partakers of the blood of Christ, and yet drink the cup of Belial ; if ye imagine that ye can be members of Satan and members of Christ at the same time, ye have less sense than one would give you credit for. No, you know that right arms must be cut off, and right eyes plucked out—that the most darling sins must be renounced, if ye would enter into the kingdom of God. And I have a man here who is convinced of the unholiness of his life, and he has striven to reform, not because he thinks reformation would save him, for he knows better than that, but because he knows that this is one of the first-fruits of grace—reformation from sin. Well, poor man, he has for many years been an inveterate drunkard, and he struggles now to overcome the passion. He has almost effected it ; but he never had such an Herculean labor to attempt before ; for now some temptation comes upon him so strongly that it is as much as he can do to stand against it ; and perhaps sometimes since his first conviction of sin he has even fallen into it. Or perhaps it is another vice, and you, my brother, have set your face against it; but there are many bonds and fetters that bind us to our vices, and you find that though it was easy enough to spin the warp and woo: of sin together, it is not so easy to unravel that which you have spun. You can not purge your house of your idols; you do not yet know how to give up all your lustful pleasures. Not yet can you renounce the company of the ungodly. You have cut off one by one your most intimate acquaintances, but it is very hard to do it completely, and you are struggling to accomplish it, and you often fall on your knees and cry, " O, Lord, how far I am from thee! what high steps these are which I have to climb! Oh! how can I be saved? Sure, if I can not purge myself from my old sins, I shall never be able to hold on my way; and even should I get rid of them, I should plunge into them once more." You are crying out, "Oh, how great my distance from God! Lord, bring me near!"

Let me present you with one other aspect of our distance from God. You have read your Bibles, and you believe that faith alone can unite the soul to Christ. You feel that unless you can believe in him who died upon the cross for your sins, you can never see the kingdom of God; but you can say this morning, " Sir, I have striven to believe; I have searched the Scriptures, not hours, but days together, to find a promise on which my weary foot might rest; I have been upon my knees many and many a time, earnestly supplicating a Divine blessing; but though I have pleaded, all in vain I have urged my plea, for until now no whisper have I had of grace, no token for good, no sign of mercy. Sir, I have striven to believe, and I have said,

> " O could I but believe
>   Then all would easy be;
>   I would, but can not—Lord, relieve,
>   My help must come from thee!"

I have used all the power I have, and have desperately striven to cast myself at the Saviour's feet and see my sins washed away in his blood. I have not been indifferent to the story of the cross; I have read it a hundred times, and even wept over it; but when I strive to put my hand upon the scape-goat's head, and labor to believe that my sins are transferred to him, some demon seems to stop the breath that would breathe itself forth in adoration, and something checks the hand that would lay itself upon the head that died for me." Well, poor soul, thou art indeed far from God. I will repeat the words of the text to thee. May the Holy Spirit repeat them in thine ear! "When he was yet a great way off, his father saw him, and had compassion, and ran, and fell on his neck, and kissed him." So shall it be with thee if thou hast come thus far, though great may be the distance, thy feet shall not have to travel it, but God, the Eternal One, shall from his throne look down and visit thy poor heart, though now thou tarriest by the way, afraid to approach him.

II. Our second point is the PECULIAR TROUBLES which agitate the breasts of those who are in this position. Let us introduce to you the poor ragged prodigal. After a life of ease, he is, by his own vice, plunged into penury and labor. After feeding swine for a time, and being almost starved, he sets about returning to his father's house. It is a long and weary journey. He walks many a mile, until his feet are sore, and at last, from the summit of a mountain, he views his father's house far away in the plain. There are yet many miles between him and his father whom he has neglected. Can you conceive his emotions when, for the first time after so long an absence, he sees the old house at home? He remembers it well in the distance, for though it is long since he trod its floors, he has never ceased to recollect it; and the remembrance of his father's kindness, and of his own prosperity when he was with him, has never yet been erased from his consciousness. You would imagine that for one moment he feels a flash of joy, like some flash of lightning in the midst of the tempest, but anon a black darkness comes over his spirit. In the first place, it is probable he will think, "Oh! suppose I could reach my home, will my father receive me? Will he not shut the door in my face and tell me begone and spend the rest of my life where I have been spending the first of it?"

Then another suggestion might arise: "Surely, the demon that led me first astray may lead me back again, before I salute my parent." "Or mayhap," thought he, "I may even die upon the road, and so, before I have received my father's blessing, my soul may stand before its God." I doubt not each of these three thoughts has crossed your mind if you are now in the position of one who is seeking Christ, but mourns to feel himself far away from him.

First, you have been afraid lest you should die before Christ has appeared to you. You have been for months seeking the Saviour without finding him, and now the black thought comes, "And what if I should die with all these prayers unanswered? Oh! if he would but hear me ere I departed this world I would be content, though he should keep me waiting in anguish for many years. But what, if before to-morrow morning I should be a corpse? At my bed I kneel to-night and cry for mercy. Oh! if he should not send the pardon before to-morrow morning, and in the night my spirit should stand before his bar!—What then?" It is singular that other men think they shall live for ever, but men convinced of sin, who seek a Saviour, are afraid they shall not live another moment. You have known the time, dear Christian brethren, when you dared not shut your eyes for fear you should not open them again on earth; when you dreaded the shadows of the night lest they should darken for ever the light of the sun, and you should dwell in outer darkness throughout eternity. You have mourned as each day has entered, and you have wept as it has departed, because you fancied that your next step might precipitate you into your eternal doom. I have known what it is to tread the earth and fear lest every tuft of grass should but cover a door to hell; trembling, lest every particle, and every atom, and every stone, should be so at league with God against me, as to destroy me. John Bunyan says, that at one time in his experience, he felt that he had rather have been born a dog or a toad than a man; he felt so unutterably wretched on account of sin; and his great point of wretchedness was the fact, that though he had been three years seeking Christ, he might after

all die without finding him. And in truth, this is no needless
alarm. It may be perhaps too alarming to some who already
feel their need of Christ, but the mass of us need perpetually
to be startled with the thought of death. How few of you
ever indulge that thought! Because ye live and are in health,
and eat, and drink, and sleep, ye think ye shall not die. Do
ye ever soberly look at your last end? Do ye ever, when ye
come to your beds at night, think how one day ye shall un-
dress for the last slumber? And when ye wake in the morning, do ye never think that the trump of the archangel shall
startle you to appear before God in the last day of the great
assize, wherein an universe shall stand before the Judge?
No. "All men think all men mortal but themselves;" and
thoughts of death we still push off, until at last we shall find
ourselves waking up in torment, where to wake is to wake too
late. But thou to whom I specially speak this morning, thou
who feelest that thou art a great way off from Christ, thou
shalt never die, but live, and declare the works of the Lord;
if thou hast really sought him, thou shalt never die until thou
hast found him. There was never a soul yet, that sincerely
sought the Saviour, who perished before he found him. No;
the gates of death shall never shut on thee till the gates of
grace have opened for thee; till Christ has washed thy sins
away thou shalt never be baptized in Jordan's flood. Thy life
is secure, for this is God's constant plan—he keeps his own
elect alive till the day of his grace, and then he takes them to
himself. And inasmuch as thou knowest thy need of a
Saviour, thou art one of his, and thou shalt never die until
thou hast found him.

Your second fear is, "Ah, sir! I am not afraid of dying
before I find Christ, I have a worse fear than that; I have had
convictions before, and they have often passed away; my
greatest fear to-day is, that these will be the same." I have
heard of a poor collier, who on one occasion, having been
deeply impressed under a sermon, was led to repent of sin and
forsake his former life; but he felt so great horror of ever
returning to his former conversation, that one day he knelt
down and cried thus unto God, "O Lord, let me die on this

spot, rather than ever deny the religion which I have espoused, and turn back to my former conversation :" and we are credibly told, that he died on that very spot, and so his prayer was answered. God had rather take him home to heaven than suffer him to bear the brunt of temptation on earth. Now, when men come to Christ, they feel that they had rather suffer anything than lose their convictions. Scores of times have you and I been drawn to Christ under the preaching of the Word. We can look back upon dozens of occasions on which it seemed just the turning point with us. Something said in our hearts, "Now, believe in Christ, now is the accepted time, now is the day of salvation." But we said, "To-morrow, to-morrow ;" and when to-morrow came our convictions were gone. We thought what we said yesterday would be the deed of to-day ; but instead of it, the procrastination of yesterday became the hardened wickedness of to-day : we wandered farther from God and forgot him. Now you are crying to him for fear, lest he should give you up again. You have this morning prayed before you came here, and you said, "Father, suffer not my companions to laugh me out of my religion ; let not my worldly business so engross my thoughts, as to prevent my due attention to the matters of another world. Oh, let not the trifles of to-day so absorb my thoughts that I may not be preparing myself to meet my God—

'Deeply on my thoughtful heart,
Eternal things impress,'

and make this a real saving work that shall never die out, nor be taken from me." Is that your earnest prayer ? O poor prodigal, it shall be heard, it shall be answered. Thou shalt not have time to go back. To-day thy Father views thee from his throne in heaven ; to-day he runs to thee in the message of his gospel ; to-day he falls upon thy neck and weeps for joy ; to-day he says to thee, "Thy sins, which are many, are all forgiven ;" to-day, by the preaching of the Word, he bids thee come and reason with him, " for though thy sins be as scarlet, they shall be as wool, though they be red like crimson, they shall be whiter than snow,"

But the last and the most prominent thought which I suppose the prodigal would have, would be, that when he did get
to his father, he would say to him, "Get along with you, I
will have nothing more to do with you." "Ah!" thought he
to himself, "I recollect the morning, when I rose up before
day-break, because I knew I could not stand my mother's
tears; I remember how I crept down the back staircase and
took all the money with me, how I stole down the yard and
ran away into the land where I spent my all. Oh! what will
the old gentlemen say of me when I come back? Why, there
he is! he is running to me. But he has got a horsewhip with
him, to be sure, to whip me away. It is not at all possible
that if he comes he will have a kind word for me. The most
I can expect is that he will say, 'Well John, you have wasted
all your money, you can not expect me to do anything for
you again. I won't let you starve; you shall be one of my
servants: there, come, I will take you as footman;' and if he
will do that I will be obliged to him; nay, that is the very
thing I will ask of him; I will say, 'Make me as one of thy
hired servants.'" "Oh," said the devil within him, "your
father will never speak comfortably to you: you had better
run away again. I tell you if he gets near you, you will
have such a dressing as you never received in your life. You
will die with a broken heart; you will very likely fall dead
here; the old man will never bury you; the carrion crows
will eat you. There is no hope for you: see how you have
treated him. Put yourself in his place: what would you do
if you had a son that had run away with half your living, and
spent it upon harlots?" And the son thought if he were in
his father's place he should be very harsh and severe; and
possibly, he almost turned upon his heel to run away. But
he had not time to do that. When he was just thinking
about running away, on a sudden his father's arms were about
his neck, and he had received the paternal kiss. Nay, before
he could get his whole prayer finished, he was arrayed in a
white robe, the best in the house; and they had brought him
to the table, and the fatted calf was being killed for his repast.
And poor soul, it shall be so with you. Thou sayest, "If I

go to God, he will never receive me. I am too vile and wretched : others he may have pressed to his heart, but he will not me. If my brother should go, he might be saved ; but there are such aggravations in my crime ; I have grown so old since ; I have done such a deal of mischief; I have so often blasphemed him, so frequently broken his Sabbaths; ah ! and I have so often deceived him ; I have promised I would repent, and when I got well I have lied to God, and gone back to my old sin. Oh, if he would but let me creep inside the door of heaven ! I will not ask to be one of his children ; I will only ask that he will let me be where the Syro-Phœni-cian woman desired to be—to be a dog, to eat the crumbs that fall from the Master's table. That is all I ask ; and oh ! if he will but grant it to me, he shall never hear the last of it, for as long as I live I will sing his praise ; and when the world doth fade away, and the sun grow dim with age, my grati-tude, immortal as my soul, shall never cease to sing his love, who pardoned my grossest sins and washed me in his blood." It shall be so. Come and try. Now, sinners, dry your tears ; let hopeless sorrows cease ; look to the wounds of Christ, who died ; let all your griefs now be removed, there is no further cause for them ; your Father loves you ; he accepts and receives you to his heart.

III. Now, in conclusion, I may notice HOW THESE FEARS WERE MET IN THE PRODIGAL'S CASE, and how they shall be met in ours if we are in the same condition.

The text says, " The Father saw him." Yes, and God saw thee just now. That tear which was wiped away so hastily— as if thou wast ashamed of it—God saw it, and he stored it in his bottle. That prayer which thou didst breathe just a few moments ago, so faintly, and with such little faith—God heard it. The other day thou wast in thy chamber, where no ear heard thee ; but God was there. Sinner, let this be thy com-fort, that God sees thee when thou beginnest to repent. He does not see thee with his usual gaze, with which he looks on all men ; but he sees thee with an eye of intense interest. He has been looking on thee in all thy sin, and in all thy sorrow, hoping that thou wouldst repent ; and now he sees the first gleam of grace, and he beholds it with joy. Never warder on the lonely castle top saw the first grey light of morning with more joy than that with which God beholds the first desire in thy heart. Never physician rejoiced more when he saw the first heaving of the lungs in one that was supposed to be dead, than God doth rejoice over thee, now that he sees the first token for good. Think not that thou art despised, and unknown, and forgotten. He is marking thee from his high throne in glory, and rejoicing in what he sees. He saw thee pray, he heard thee groan; he marked thy tear; he looked upon thee and rejoiced to see that these were the first seeds of grace in thine heart.

And then, the text says, "he had compassion on him." He did not merely see him, but he wept within himself to think he should be in such a condition. The old father had a very long range of eye-sight; and though the prodigal could not see him in the distance, he could see the prodigal. And the father's first thought when he saw him was this—"O my poor son, O my poor boy! that ever he should have brought himself into such a state as this!" He looked through his telescope of love, and he saw him, and said, "Ah! he did not go out of my house in such trim as that. Poor creature, his feet are bleeding; he has come a long way, I'll be bound. Look at his face, he doesn't look like the same boy he was when he left me. His eye that was so bright, is now sunken in its socket; his cheeks that once stood out with fatness, have now become hollow with famine. Poor wretch, I can tell all his bones, he is so emaciated." Instead of feeling any anger in his heart, he felt just the contrary; he felt such pity for his poor son. And so the Lord feels for you—you that are groaning and moaning on account of sin. He forgets your sins; he only weeps to think you should have brought yourself to be what you are: "Why didst thou rebel against me, and bring thyself into such a state as this?" It was just like that day when Adam sinned. God walked in the garden, and he missed Adam. He did not cry out, "Adam, come here and be judged!" No; with a soft, sorrowful, and plaintive voice, he said, "Adam, where art thou? Oh, my fair Adam, thou whom

I made so happy, where art thou now? Oh, Adam! thou didst think to become a God; where art thou now? Thou hast walked with me: dost thou hide thyself from thy friend? Little dost thou know, O Adam, what woes thou hast brought on thyself, and thine offspring. Adam, where art thou?" And Jehovah's bowels yearn to-day over you. He is not angry with you; his anger is passed away, and his hands are stretched out still. Inasmuch as he has brought you to feel that you have sinned against him, and to desire reconciliation with him, there is no wrath in his heart. The only sorrow that he feels is sorrow that you should have brought yourself into a state so mournful as that in which you now are found.

But he did not stop in mere compassion. Having had compassion, " he ran, and fell on his neck, and kissed him." This you do not understand yet; but you shall. As sure as God is God, if you this day are seeking him aright through Christ, the day shall come when the kiss of full assurance shall be on your lip, when the arms of sovereign love shall embrace you, and you shall know it to be so. Thou mayest have despised nim, but thou shalt know him yet to be thy Father and thy Friend. Thou mayest have scoffed his name: thou shait one day come to rejoice in it as better than pure gold. Thou mayest have broken his Sabbaths and despised his Word; the day is coming when the Sabbath shall be thy delight, and his Word thy treasure. Yes, marvel not; thou mayest have plunged into the kennel of sin, and made thy clothes black with iniquity; but thou shalt one day stand before his throne white as the angels be; and that tongue that once cursed him shall yet sing his praise. If thou be a real seeker, the hands that have been stained with lust shall one day grasp the harp of gold, and the head that has plotted against the Most High shall yet be girt with gold. Seemeth it not a strange thing that God should do so much for sinners? But strange though it seem, it shall be strangely true. Look at the staggering drunkard in the ale-house. Is there a possibility that one day he shall stand among the fairest sons of light? Possibility! ay, certainty, if he repents and turns from the error of his ways. Hear you yon curser and swearer? See you the man who labels himself as a servant of hell, and is not ashamed to do so? Is it possible that he shall one day share the bliss of the redeemed? Possible! ay, more, it is sure, if he turneth from his evil ways. O sovereign grace, turn men that they may repent! "Turn ye, turn ye, why will ye die, O house of Israel?"

> "Lord, do thou the sinner turn,
> For thy tender mercy's sake."

SERMON X

GOD, THE ALL-SEEING ONE

"Hell and destruction are before the Lord: how much more then the nearts of the children of men?"—PROVERBS xv. 11

You have often smiled at the ignorance of heathens who bow themselves before gods of wood and stone. You have quoted the words of Scripture, and you have said, "Eyes have they, but they see not; ears have they, but they hear not." You have therefore argued that they could not be gods at all, because they could neither see nor hear, and you have smiled contemptuously at the men who could so debase their understandings as to make such things objects of adoration. May I ask you one question—but one? Your God can both see and hear: would your conduct be in any respect different, if you had a god such as those that the heathen worship? Suppose for one minute, that Jehovah, who is nominally adored in this land, could be (though it is almost blasphemy to suppose it) smitten with such a blindness, that he could not see the works and know the thoughts of man: would you then become more careless concerning him than you are now? I trow not. In nine cases out of ten, and perhaps in a far larger and sadder proportion, the doctrine of Divine Omniscience, although it is received and believed, has no practical effect upon our lives at all. The mass of mankind forget God: whole nations who know his existence and believe that he beholds them, live as if they had no God at all. Merchants, farmers, men in their shops, and in their fields, husbands in their families, and wives in the midst of their households, live as if there were no God; no eye inspecting them; no ear listening to the voice of their lips, and no eternal mind always treasuring up the recollection of their acts.

Ah! we are practical Atheists, the mass of us; yea, all but those that have been born again, and have passed from death unto life, be their creeds what they may, are Atheists, after all, in life; for if there were no God, and no hereafter, multitudes of men would never be affected by the change; they would live the same as they do now—their lives being so full of disregard of God and his ways, that the absence of a God could not affect them in any great degree. Permit me, then, this morning, as God shall help me, to stir up your hearts; and may God grant that something I may say, may drive some of your practical Atheism out of you. I would endeavor to set before you, God, the all-seeing one, and press upon your solemn consideration the tremendous fact, that in all our acts, in all our ways, and in all our thoughts, we are continually under his observing eye.

We have in our text, first of all, *a great fact declared,*— "Hell and destruction are before the Lord;" we have, secondly, *a great fact inferred,*—"How much more then the hearts of the children of men?"

I. We will begin with THE GREAT FACT WHICH IS DECLARED —a fact which furnishes us with premises from which we deduce the practical conclusion of the second sentence—"How much more then the hearts of the children of men?" The best interpretation that you can give of those two words, "hell" and "destruction," is, I think, comprehended in a sentence something like this,—"*Death and hell are before the Lord.*" The separate state of departed spirits, and destruction, *Abaddon,* as the Hebrew has it, the place of torment, are both of them, although solemnly mysterious to us, manifest enough to God.

1. First, then, the word here translated "hell," might just as well be translated "death," or the state of departed spirits. Now, death, with all its solemn consequences, is visible before the Lord. Between us and the hereafter of departed spirits a great black cloud is hanging. Here and there, the Holy Spirit hath made chinks, as it were, in the black wall of separation, through which, by faith we can see; for he hath "revealed unto us by the Spirit" the things which "eye hath

not seen nor ear heard," and which the human intellect could never compass. Yet, what we know is but very little. When men die, they pass beyond the realm of our knowledge: both in body and in soul, they go beyond our understandings. But God understands all the secrets of death. Let us divide these into several heads, and enumerate them.

God knows the burial-places of all his people. He notes as well the resting-place of the man who is buried tombless and alone, as the man over whom a mighty mausoleum has been raised. The traveler who fell in the barren desert, whose body became the prey of the vulture, and whose bones were bleached in the sun—the mariner, who was wrecked far out at sea, and over whose corpse no dirge was ever wailed, except the howling of the winds, and the murmuring of the wild waves—the thousands who have perished in battle, unnumbered and unnoticed—the many who have died alone, amid dreary forests, frozen seas, and devouring snow-storms—all these, and the places of their sepulchre, are known to God. That silent grot within the sea, where pearls lie deep, where now the shipwrecked one is sleeping, is marked by God as the death-place of one of his redeemed; that place upon the mountain-side, the deep ravine into which the traveler fell and was buried in a snow-drift, is marked in the memory of God as the tomb of one of the human race. No body of man, however it may have been interred or uninterred, has passed beyond the range of God's knowledge. Blessed be his name, if I shall die, and lie where the rude forefathers of the hamlet sleep, in some neglected corner of the churchyard, I shall be known as well, and rise as well recognized by my glorious Father, as if interred in the cathedral, where forests of gothic pillars proudly stand erect, and where the songs of myriads perpetually salute high heaven. I shall be known as well as if I had been buried there in solemn pomp, and had been interred with music and with dread solemnities, and I shall be recognised as well as if the marble trophy and the famous pillar had been raised to my remembrance; for God knoweth no such thing as forgetfulness of the burying-places of his children. Moses sleeps in some spot that eye hath not seen

God kissed away his soul, and he buried him where Israel could never find him, though they may have searched for him. But God knoweth where Moses sleeps; and if he knows that, he understands where all his children are hidden. Ye cannot tell me where is the tomb of Adam; ye could not point out to me the sleeping place of Abel. Is any man able to discover the tomb of Methuselah and those long-lived dwellers in the time before the flood? Who shall tell where the once-treasured body of Joseph now sleeps in faith? Can any of you discover the tombs of the kings, and mark the exact spot where David and Solomon rest in solitary grandeur? No, those things have passed from human recollection, and we know not where the great and mighty of the past are buried; but God knoweth, for death and Hades are open before the Lord.

And again, further, not only does he know the place where they were buried, but he is cognizant of the history of all their bodies after sepulture or after death. It has often been asked by the infidel, " How can the body of man be restored, when it may have been eaten by the cannibal, or devoured by wild beasts?" Our simple reply is, that God can track every atom of it if he pleases. We do not think it necessary to resurrection that he should do so, but if he so willed it, he could bring every atom of every body that hath ever died: although it hath passed through the most complicated machinery of nature, and become entangled in its passage with plants and beasts, yea, and with the bodies of other men, God hath it still within the range of his knowledge to know where every atom is, and it is within the might of his Omnipotence to call every atom from its wandering, and restore it to its proper sphere, and rebuild the body of which it was a part. It is true, we could not track the dust that long since has moldered. Buried with exactest care, preserved with the most scrupulous reverence, years passed away, and the body of the monarch, which had long slept well guarded and protected, was at last reached by the careless hand. The coffin had moldered, and the metal was broken for the sake of its own value; a handful of dust was discovered, the last relics of one who was master of many nations. That dust by sacrilegious hand was cast in the aisle of the church, or thrown into the churchyard and blown by the winds into the neighboring field. It was impossible for ever to preserve it; the greatest care was defeated; and at last the monarch was on a level with his slave, "alike unknowing and unknown." But God knows where every particle of the hand-ful of dust has gone: he has marked in his book the wander-ing of every one of its atoms. He hath death so open before his view, that he can bring all these together, bone to bone, and clothe them with the very flesh that robed them in the days of yore, and make them live again. Death is open be-fore the Lord.

And as the body, so the soul when separated from the body is before the Lord. We look upon the countenance of our dying friend, and on a sudden a mysterious change passes over his frame. "His soul has fled," we say. But have we any idea of what his soul is? Can we form even a conjecture of what the flying of that soul may be, and what the august presence into which it is ushered when it is disentangled from its earthly coil? Is it possible for us to guess what is that state where spirits without bodies, perpetually blest, behold their God? It is possible for us to compass some imagination of what heaven is to be, when bodies and souls, reunited, shall before God's throne enjoy the highest bliss; but I do think, that so gross are our conceptions, whilst we are in our bodies, that it is almost, if not quite, impossible for any of us to form any idea whatever as to the position of souls, whilst in the disembodied state, between the hour of death and the time of resurrection.

> "This much, and this is all, we know,
>   They are supremely blest:
> Have done with sin, and care, and woe,
>   And with their Saviour rest."

But the best of the saints can tell us nothing more than this. They are blest, and in paradise they are reigning with their Lord. Brethren, these things are known to God. The separate state of the dead, the heaven of disembodied spirits, is within the gaze of the Most High, and at this hour, if so he pleased, he could reveal to us the condition of every man that is dead—whether he has mounted to Elysian fields, to dwell for ever in the sunlight of his Master's countenance, or has been plunged into hell, dragged down by iron chains, to wait in dreary woe the result of the awful trial, when "Depart ye cursed," must be the re-affirmation of a sentence once pronounced, and already in part endured.   God understands the separate doom of every man's spirit before the great tribunal day—before the last sentence shall have been pronounced, death is open before the Lord.

2. The next word, "*destruction*," signifies hell, or the place of the damned.   That also is open before the Lord.   Where hell is, and what its miseries, we know not; except "through a glass darkly," we have never seen the invisible things of horror.   That land of terror is a land unknown.   We have much reason to thank God that he has put it so far off from the habitations of living mortals, that the pains, the groans, the shrieks, the yells, are not to be heard here, or else earth itself would have become a hell, the solemn prelude and the ante-past of unutterable torment.   God has put somewhere, far on the edge of his dominions, a fearful lake that burneth with fire and brimstone; into that he cast the rebel angels, who (though by a license they are now allowed to walk the earth) do carry a hell within their bosoms, and are by-and-by to be bound with chains, reserved in blackness and darkness for ever for them that kept not their first estate, but lifted the arm of their rebellion against God.   Into that place we dare not look.   Perhaps it would not be possible for any man to get a fair idea of the torments of the lost, without at once becoming mad.   Reason would reel at such a sight of horror. One moment of listening to the shrill screams of spirits tortured, might forever drive us into the depths of despair, and make us only fit to be bound in chains whilst we lived on earth.   Raving lunatics surely we must become.   But whilst God has mercifully covered all these things from us, they are all known to him; he looks upon them; yea, it is his look that

makes hell what it is. His eyes, full of fury, flash the light-nings that scathe his enemies; his lips, full of dreadful thun-ders, make the thunders that now affright the wicked. O! could they escape the eye of God, could they shut out that dreary vision of the face of the incensed Majesty of heaven, then might hell be quenched; then might the wheels of Ixion stand still; then might doomed Tantalus quench his thirst and eat to his very full. But there, whilst they lie in their chains, they look upward, and they see ever that fearful vision of the Most High; the dreadful hands that grasp the thun-derbolts, the dreadful lips that speak the thunders, and the fearful eyes that flash the flames that burn their souls, with horrors deeper than despair. Yes, hell, horrible as it is, and veiled in many clouds, and covered over with darkness, is naked before the vision of the Most High.

There is the grand fact stated—"Hell and destruction are before the Lord." After this the inference seems to be easy —"How much more then the hearts of the children of men?"

II. We now come to the GREAT FACT INFERRED.

In briefly entering upon this second part I will discuss the subject thus: You notice there an argument—"How much more then the hearts of the children of men?" I will there-fore begin by asking, why does it follow that the hearts of men are seen by God? *Why—how—what—when*—shall be four questions into which we shall divide what we have now to say.

1. *Why* is it so clear, that "if hell and destruction are open before the Lord," the hearts of men must be very plainly viewed by him?

We answer, because the hearts of men are not so extensive as the realms of death and torment. What is man's heart? what is man's self? Is he not in Scripture compared to a grasshopper? Does not God declare that he "takes up the isles"—whole islands full of men—"as a very little thing And the nations before him are but as the drop of a bucket?" If, then, the all-seeing eye of God takes in at one glance the wide regions of death—and wide they are, wide enough to startle any man who shall try to range them through—if, I say, with one glance God seeth death and seeth hell through, with all its bottomless depths, with all its boundlessness of misery, surely, then, he is quite able to behold all the actions of the little thing called man's heart. Suppose a man so wise as to be able to know the wants of a nation and to remember the feelings of myriads of men, you can not suppose it difficult for him to know the actions of his own family and to understand the emotions of his own household. If the man is able to stretch his arm over a great sphere, and to say, "I am monarch of all this," surely he shall be able to control the less. He who in his wisdom can walk through centuries shall not say that he is ignorant of the history of a year; he who can dive into the depths of science, and understand the history of the whole world from its creation, is not to be alarmed by some small riddle that happens at his own door. No, the God who seeth death and hell seeth our hearts, for they are far less extensive.

Reflect again, that they are far less aged too. Death is an ancient monarch; he is the only king whose dynasty stands fast. Ever since the days of Adam he has never been succeeded by another, and has never had an interregnum in his reign. His black ebon sceptre hath swept away generation after generation; his scythe hath mowed the fair fields of this earth a hundred times, and is sharp to mow us down, and when another crop shall succeed us he is still ready to devour the multitudes, and sweep the earth clean again. The regions of death are old domains; his pillars of black granite are ancient as the eternal hills. Death made his prey on earth long ere Adam was here. Those mighty creatures that made the deep hoary with their strength, and stirred the earth with their tramplings—those elder born of nature's sons, the mighty creatures that lived here long ere Adam walked in Eden— death made them his prey: like a mighty hunter he speared the mighty lizard and laid it low, and now we dig it from the stony tomb, and wonder at it. He is our ancient monarch; but ancient as he is, his whole monarchy is in the records of God, and until death itself is dead, and swallowed up in victory, death shall be open before the Lord. How old, too, is

Hell! –old as the first sin. In that day when Satan tempted the angels, and led astray the third part of the stars of heaven, then hell was digged; then was that bottomless pit first struck out of solid rocks of vengeance, that it might stand a marvellous record of what God's wrath can do. The fires of hell are not the kindlings of yesterday : they are ancient flames that burned long ere Vesuvius cast forth its lurid flame. Long ere the first charred ashes fell upon the plain from earth's red volcanoes, hell's flames were burning; for "Tophet is prepared of old, the pile thereof is wood and much smoke; the breath of the Lord like a stream of brimstone, doth kindle it. If, then, the ancient things, these old ones, death and hell, have been observed by God, and if their total history is known to him, how much more then shall he know the history of those mere animalculæ, those ephemera of an hour, that we call men ! You are here to-day, and gone to-morrow ; born yesterday— the next hour shall see our tomb prepared, and another minute shall hear, "ashes to ashes, dust to dust," and the falling of the clod upon the coffin lid. We are the creatures of a day, and know nothing. We are scarcely here ; we are only living and dead. "Gone !" is the greatest part of our history. Scarcely have we time enough to tell the story, ere it comes to its finis. Surely, then, God may easily understand the history of a beast, when he knows the history of the monarchies of death and hell.

This is the *why*. I need not give further arguments, though there be abundance deducible from the text. "How much more then the hearts of the children of men ?"

2. But now, *how* does God know the heart ? I mean to what degree and to what extent does he understand and know that which is in man ? I answer, Holy Scripture in divers places gives us most precise information. God knows the heart so well that he is said to "search" it. We all understand the figure of a search. There is a search-warrant out against some man who is supposed to be harboring a traitor in his house. The officer goes into the lower room, opens the door of every cupboard, looks into every closet, peers into every cranny, takes the key, descends into the cellar, turns over the

coals, disturbs the wood, lest any one should be hidden there
Up stairs he goes: there is an old room that has not been
open for years,—it is opened. There is a huge chest: the
lock is forced, and it is broken open. The very top of the
house is searched, lest upon the slates or upon the tiles some
one should be concealed. At last, when the search has been
complete, the officer says, "It is impossible that there can be
anybody here, for, from the tiles to the foundation, I have
searched the house thoroughly through; I know the very
spiders well, for I have seen the house completely." Now, it
is just so that God knows our heart. He searches it—
searches into every nook, corner, crevice, and secret part;
and the figure of the Lord is pushed further still. "The can·
dle of the Lord," we are told, "searches the secret parts of
the belly." As when we wish to find something, we take a
candle, and look down upon the ground with great care, and
turn up the dust. If it is some little piece of money we de·
sire to find, we light a candle and sweep the house, and search
diligently till we find it. Even so it is with God. He searches
Jerusalem with candles, and pulls every thing to day-light.
No partial search, like that of Laban, when he went into
Rachel's tent to look for his idols. She put them in the
camel's furniture, and sat upon them; but God looks into the
camel's furniture, and all. "Can any hide himself in secret
places, that I shall not see him? saith the Lord." His eye
searches the heart, and looks into every part of it.

In another passage we are told that God tries the reins.
That is even more than searching. The goldsmith when he
takes gold, looks at it, and examines it carefully. "Ah!"
says he, "but I don't understand this gold yet: I must try
it." He thrusts it into the furnace; there coals are heaped
upon it, and it is fused and melted, till he knows what there
is of dross, and what there is of gold. Now, God knows to
the very carat how much there is of sound gold in us, and
how much of dross. There is no deceiving him. He has put
our hearts into the furnace of his Omniscience; the furnace—
his knowledge—tries us as completely as the goldsmith's cru
cible doth try the gold—how much there is of hypocrisy, how

much of truth—how much of sham, how much of real—how much of ignorance, how much of knowledge—how much of devotion, how much of blasphemy—how much of carefulness, how much of carelessness. God knows the ingredients of the heart; he reduces the soul to its pristine metals; he divides it asunder—so much of quartz, so much of gold, so much of dung, of dross, of wood, of hay, of stubble, so much of gold, silver, and precious stones. " The Lord trieth the hearts and searcheth the reins of the children of men."

Here is another description of God's knowledge of the heart. In one place of Sacred Writ—(it will be well if you set your children to find out these places at home)—God is said to ponder the heart. Now, you know, the Latin word *ponder* means *weigh*. The Lord weighs the heart. Old Master Quarles has got a picture of a great one putting a heart into one scale, and then putting the law, the Bible, into the other scale, to weigh it. This is what God does with men's hearts. They are often great, puffed-up, blown-out things, and people say, " What a great-hearted man that is !' But God does not judge by the appearance of a man's great heart, nor the outside appearance of a good heart; but he puts it in the scales and weighs it—puts his own Word in one scale and the heart in the other. He knows the exact weight —knows whether we have grace in the heart, which makes us good weight, or only pretence in the heart, which makes us weigh light weight when put into the scale. He searches the heart in every possible way, he puts it into the fire, and then thrusts it into the balances. Oh, might not God say of many of you, " I have searched your heart, and I have found vanity therein ? Reprobate silver shall men call you ; for God has put you in the furnace and rejected you." And then he might conclude his verdict by saying, " *Mene, mene, tekel* --thou art weighed in the balances and found wanting." This, then, is the answer to the question, *How ?*

The next question was, *What ?* What is it that God sees in man's heart ? God sees in man's heart a great deal more than we think of. God sees, and has seen in our hearts, lust, and blasphemy, and murder, and adultery, and malice and wrath, and all uncharitableness.   The heart never can be painted too black, unless you daub it with something blacker than the devil himself.   It is as base as it can be.   You have never committed murder, but yet you have had murder in your heart; you may never have stained your hands with lusts and the aspersions of uncleanness, but still it is in the heart   Have you never imagined an evil thing?   Has your soul never for a moment doted on a pleasure which you were too chaste to indulge in, but which for a moment you surveyed with at least some little complacency and delight?   Has not imagination often pictured, even to the solitary monk in his cell, greater vice than men in public life have ever dreamed of?   And may not even the divine in his closet be conscious that blasphemies, and murders, and lusts of the vilest class, can find a ready harbor even in the heart which he hopes is dedicated to God?   Oh! beloved, it is a sight that no human eye could endure: the sight of a heart really laid bare before one's own inspection would startle us almost into insanity: but God sees the heart in all its bestial sensuousness, in all its wanderings and rebellions, in all its highmindedness and pride; God has searched and knows it altogether.

God sees all the heart's imaginations, and what they are let us not presume to tell.   O children of God, these have made you cry and groan full many a time, and though the worldling groans not over them, yet he hath them.   Oh, what a filthy stye of Stygian imaginations is the heart; all full of every thing that is hideous, when it once begins to dance and make carnival and revelry concerning sin.   But God sees the heart's imaginations.

Again, God sees the heart's devices.   You, perhaps, O sinner, have determined to curse God; you have not done so, but you intend to do it.   He knows your devices—reads them all.   You perhaps will not be permitted to run into the excess of riotousness into which you purpose to go; but your very purpose is now undergoing the inspection of the Most High.   There is never a design forged in the fires of the heart, before it is beaten on the anvil of resolve, that is not known, and seen, and noted by Jehovah our God.

He knows, next, the resolves of the heart. He knows, O sinner, how many times you have resolved to repent, and have resolved and re-resolved, and then have continued the same. He knows, O thou that hast been sick, how thou didst resolve to seek God, but how thou didst despise thine own resolution, when good health had put thee beyond the temporary danger. Thy resolves have been filed in heaven, and thy broken promises, and thy vows despised, shall be brought out in their order as swift witnesses for thy condemnation. All these things are known of God. We have often had very clear proof of God's knowing what is in man's heart, even in the ministry. Some months ago, whilst standing here preach-ing, I deliberately pointed to a man in the midst of the crowd, and said these words—"There is a man sitting there that is a shoemaker, keeps his shop open on Sunday, had his shop open last Sabbath morning, took ninepence, and there was four-pence profit out of it. His soul is sold to Satan for fourpence." A City Missionary, when going round the West end of the town, met with a poor man, of whom he asked this question: "Do you know Mr. Spurgeon?" He found him reading a sermon. "Yes," he said, "I have every reason to know him; I have been to hear him, and under God's grace I have be-come a new man. But," said he, "shall I tell you how it was? I went to the Music Hall, and took my seat in the middle of the place, and the man looked at me as if he knew me, and deliberately told the congregation that I was a shoe-maker, and that I sold shoes on a Sunday; and I did, sir. But, sir, I should not have minded that; but he said I took ninepence the Sunday before, and that there was fourpence profit; and so I did take ninepence, and fourpence was just the profit, and how he should know that I'm sure I can not tell. It struck me it was God had spoken to my soul through him; and I shut my shop last Sunday, and was afraid to open it and go there, lest he should split about me again." I could tell as many as a dozen authentic stories of cases that have hap-pened in this Hall, where I have deliberately pointed at some-body, without the slightest knowledge of the person, or ever having in the least degree any inkling or idea that what I said was right, except that I believed I was moved thereto by the Spirit; and so striking has been the description, that the persons have gone away and said, " Come, see a man that told me all things that ever I did : he was sent of God to my soul, beyond a doubt, or else he could not have painted my case so clearly."

And not only so, but we have known cases in which the thoughts of men have been revealed from the pulpit. I have sometimes seen persons nudge with their elbows, because they have got a smart hit, and I have heard them say, when they went out, " That is just what I said to you when I went in at the door." " Ah!" says the other, "I was thinking of the very thing he said, and he told me of it." Now, if God thus proves his own Omniscience by helping his poor, ignorant servant, to state the very thing, thought and done, when he did not know it, then it must remain decisively proved that God does know everything that is secret, because we see he tells it to men, and enables them to tell it to others. Oh, ye may endeavor as much as ye can to hide your faults from God, but beyond a doubt he shall discover you. He discovers you this day. His Word is " a discerner of the thoughts and intents of the heart," and " pierces to the dividing asunder of the joints and of the marrow;" and in that last day, when the book shall be opened, and he shall give to every man his sentence, then shall it be seen how exact, how careful, how precious, how personal was God's knowledge of the heart of every man whom he had made.

4. And now the last question : *When?* When does God see us ? The answer is, he sees us everywhere and in every place. O foolish man, who thinks to hide himself from the Most High! It is night! no human eye sees thee; the curtain is drawn, and thou art hidden. There are his eyes lowering at thee through the gloom. It is a far-off country; no one knows thee ; parents and friends have been left behind, restraints are cast off. There is a Father near thee, who looks upon thee even now. It is a lone spot, and if the deed be done, no tongue shall tell it. There is a tongue in heaven that shall tell it ; yea, the beam out of the wall, and the stones in

the field, shall raise up themselves as witnesses against thee. Canst thou hide thyself anywhere where God shall not detect thee ? Is not this whole world like a glass hive, wherein we put our bees ? and does not God stand and see all our motions when we think we are hidden ? Ah, it is but a glass hiding-place. He looketh from heaven, and through stone walls and rocks ; yea, to the very centre itself, does his eye pierce, and in the thickest darkness he beholds our deeds.

Come, then, let me make a personal application of the matter, and I have done. If this be true, hypocrite, what a fool thou art ! If God can read the heart, O man, what a sorry, sorry thing thy fair pretence must be ! Ah ! ah ! ah ! what a change will come over some of you ! This world is a masquerade, and ye, many of you, wear the mask of religion. Ye dance your giddy hours, and men think you to be the saints of God. How changed will you be, when, at the door of eternity, you must drop the vizor, and must announce the theatricals in which you live ! How you will blush when the paint is washed from off your cheek—when you stand before God naked to your own shame, a hypocrite, unclean, diseased, covered up before with the gew-gaws and the trickery of pretended formality in religion, but now standing there, base, vile, and hideous ! There is many a man that bears about him a cancer that would make one sick to see. Oh, how shall hypocrites look when their cancerous hearts are laid bare ! Deacon ! how you will tremble when your old heart is torn open, and your vile pretences rent away ! Minister ! how black you will look when your surplice is off, and when your grand pretensions are cast to the dogs ! How will you tremble ! There will be no sermonizing others then. You yourself will be preached to, and the sermon shall be from that text, " Depart ye cursed." O brethren, above all things shun hypocrisy. If ye mean to be damned, make up your minds to it, and be damned like hones* men ; but do not, I beseech you, pretend to go to heaven while all the time you are going to hell. If ye mean to mak your abodes in torment forever, then serve the devil, and do not be ashamed of it ; stand it right out, and let the world know what you are. But oh ! never put on the cloak of relig ion. I beseech you, do not add to your eternal misery by being a wolf in sheep's clothing. Show the cloven foot; do not hide it. If you mean to go to hell, say so. "If God be God, serve him. If Baal be God, serve him." Do not serve Baal and then pretend to be serving God.

One other practical conclusion. If God sees and knows everything, how this ought to make you tremble—you that have lived in sin for many years! I have known a man who was once stopped from an act of sin by the fact of there being a cat in the room. He could not bear even the eyes of that poor creature to see him. Oh, I would ye could carry about with you the recollection of those eyes that are always on you. Swearer! could you swear if you could see God's eye looking at you? Thief! drunkard! harlot! could ye indulge in your sins, if ye saw his eyes on you? Oh, methinks they would startle you and bid you pause, before ye did in God's own sight rebel against his law. There is a story told of the American War, that one of the prisoners taken by the Americans was subjected to a torture of the most refined character. He says, "I was put into a narrow dungeon; I was comfortably provided for with all I needed; but there was a round slit in the wall, and through that, both night and day, a soldier always looked at me." He says, "I could not rest, I could not eat nor drink, nor do anything in comfort, because there was always that eye—an eye that seemed never to be turned away, and never shut—always following me round that little apartment. Nothing ever hidden from it." Now take home that figure. Recollect that is your position; you are shut in by the narrow walls of time, when ye eat, and when ye drink, when ye rise, and when ye lie upon your beds; when ye walk the streets, or when ye sit at home, that eye is always fixed upon you. Go home now and sin against God, if ye dare; go home now and break his laws to his face, and despise him, and set him at nought! Rush on your own destruction; dash yourselves against the buckler of Jehovah, and destroy yourselves upon his own sword! Nay, rather, "turn ye, turn ye." Turn ye, ye that have followed the ways of sin, turn ye to Christ, and live; and then the same Omniscience which is now your horror, shall be your pleasure.   Sinner! if thou now dost pray, he seeth thee ; if thou now dost weep he seeth thee. " When he was yet a great way off his father saw him, and ran, and fell on his neck and kissed him."   It shall be even so with thee, if now thou turnest to God and dost believe in his Son Jesus Christ.

SERMON XI

THE IMMUTABILITY OF CHRIST

"Jesus Christ the same yesterday, and to-day, and for ever."—HEBREWS xiii. 8

IT is well that there is one person who is the same. It is well that there is one stable rock amidst the changing billows of this sea of life; for how many and how grievous have been the changes of this year? How many of you who commenced in affluence, have by the panic, which has shaken nations, been reduced almost to poverty? How many of you, who in strong health marched into this place on the first Sabbath of last year, have had to come tottering here, feeling that the breath of man is in his nostrils, and wherein is he to be accounted of? Many of you came to this hall with a numerous family, leaning upon the arm of a choice and much-loved friend. Alas! for love, if thou wert all and naught beside, O earth! For ye have buried those ye loved the best. Some of you have come here childless, or widows, or fatherless, still weeping your recent affliction. Changes have taken place in your estate that have made your heart full of misery. Your cups of sweetness have been dashed with draughts of gall; your golden harvests have had tares cast into the midst of them, and you have had to reap the noxious weed along with the precious grain. Your much fine gold has become dim, and your glory has departed; the sweet frames at the commencement of last year became bitter ones at the end. Your raptures and your ecstacies were turned into depression and forebodings. Alas! for our changes, and hallelujah to him that hath no change.

But greater things have changed than we; for kingdoms have trembled in the balances. We have seen a peninsula

deluged with blood, and mutiny raising its bloody war whoop.
Nay, the whole world hath changed; earth hath doffed its
green, and put on its somber garment of Autumn, and soon
expects to wear its ermine robe of snow. All things have
changed. We believe that not only in appearance but in
reality, the world is growing old. The sun itself must soon
grow dim with age; the folding up of the worn-out vesture
has commenced; the changing of the heavens and the earth
has certainly begun. They shall perish; they all shall wax
old as doth a garment; but for ever blessed be him who is
the same, and of whose years there is no end. The satisfaction that the mariner feels, when, after having been tossed
about for many a day, he puts his foot upon the solid shore, is
just the satisfaction of a Christian when, amidst all the
changes of this troublous life, he plants the foot of his faith
upon such a text as this—"the same yesterday, and to-day,
and for ever." The same stability that the anchor gives the
ship, when it hath at last got the grip of some immovable
rock, that same stability doth our hope give to our spirits,
when, like an anchor, it fixes itself in a truth so glorious as this
—"Jesus Christ the same yesterday, and to-day, and for ever."

I shall first try this morning to open the text by a little
explanation; then I shall try to *answer a few objections,*
which our wicked unbelief will be quite sure to raise against
it; and afterward I shall try to *draw a few useful, consoling,
and practical lessons* from the great truth of the immutability
of Jesus Christ.

I. First, then, we open the text by a little EXPLANATION—
"Jesus Christ the same yesterday, and to-day, and for ever."
He is the same *in his person.* *We* change perpetually; the
bloom of youth gives place to the strength of manhood, and
the maturity of manhood fades away into the weakness of old
age. But "Thou hast the dew of thy youth." Christ Jesus,
whom we adore, thou art as young as ever! We came into
this world with the ignorance of infancy; we grow up searching, studying, and learning with the diligence of youth; we
attain to some little knowledge in our riper years; and then
in our old age we totter back to the imbecility of our child-

hood. But O, our Master! thou didst perfectly foreknow all mortal or eternal things from before the foundations of the world, and thou knowest all things now, and for ever thou shalt be the same in thine omniscience. We are one day strong, and the next day weak—one day resolved, and the next day wavering—one hour constant, and the next hour unstable as water. We are one moment holy, kept by the power of God; we are the next moment sinning, led astray by our own lusts; but our Master is for ever the same; pure, and never spotted; firm, and never changing—everlastingly Omnipotent, unchangeably Omniscient. From him no attribute doth pass away; to him no parallax, no tropic, ever comes; without variableness or shadow of a turning, he abideth fast and firm. Did Solomon sing concerning his best beloved, "His head is as the most fine gold: his locks are bushy and black as a raven. His eyes are as the eyes of doves by the rivers of waters, washed with milk, and fitly set. His cheeks are as a bed of spices, as sweet flowers: his lips like lilies, dropping sweet smelling myrrh. His hands are as gold rings set with the beryl: his belly is as bright ivory overlaid with sapphires. His legs are as pillars of marble, set upon sockets of fine gold: his countenance is as Lebanon, excellent as the cedars?" Surely we can even now conclude the description from our own experience of him; and while we endorse every word which went before, we can end the description by saying, "His mouth is most sweet, yea he is altogether lovely. His matchless beauty is unimpaired; he is still 'the chief among ten thousand'—fairest of the sons of men." Did the divine John talk of him when he said—"His head and his hairs were white like wool, as white as snow; and his eyes were as a flame of fire; and his feet like unto fine brass, as if they burned in a furnace; and his voice as the sound of many waters. And he had in his right hand seven stars; and out of his mouth went a sharp two-edged sword; and his countenance was as the sun shineth in his strength." He is the same; upon his brow there is ne'er a furrow; his locks are gray with reverence, but not with age; his feet stand as firm as when they trod the everlasting mountains in the years before the world was made—his eyes as piercing as when, for the first time he looked upon a new-born world. Christ's person never changes. Should he come on earth to visit us again, as sure he will, we should find him the same Jesus; as loving, as approachable, as generous, as kind, and though arrayed in nobler garments than he wore when first he visited earth, though no more the Man of Sorrows and grief's acquaintance, yet he would be the same person, unchanged by all his glories, his triumphs, and his joys. We bless Christ that amid his heavenly splendors his person is just the same, and his nature unaffected. "Jesus Christ the same yesterday, to-day, and for ever."

Again: Jesus Christ is the same with regard *to his Father* as ever. He was his Father's well-beloved Son before all worlds; he was his well-beloved in the stream of baptism; he was his well-beloved on the cross; he was his well-beloved when he led captivity captive, and he is not less the object of his Father's infinite affection now than he was then. Yesterday he lay in Jehovah's bosom, God, having all power with his Father—to-day he stands on earth, man, with us, but still the same, for ever—he ascends on high, and still he is his Father's son—still by inheritance, having a more excellent name than angels—still sitting far above all principalities and powers, and every name that is named. O Christian, give him thy cause to plead; the Father will answer him as well now as he did aforetime. Doubt not the Father's grace. Go to thine Advocate. He is as near to Jehovah's heart as ever—as prevalent in his intercession. Trust him, then, and in trusting him thou mayest be sure of the Father's love to thee.

But now there is a yet sweeter thought. Jesus Christ is *the same to his people* as ever. We have delighted, in our happier moments, in days that have rolled away, to think of him that loved us when we had no being; we have often sung with rapture of him that loved us when we loved not him.

> "Jesus sought me when a stranger,
>   Wandering from the fold of God;
>   He to save my soul from danger
>   Interposed his precious blood"

We have looked back, too, upon the years of our troubles and our trials; and we can bear our solemn though humble witness that he has been true to us in all our exigencies, and has never failed us once. Come, then, let us comfort ourselves with this thought—that though to-day he may distress us with a sense of sin, yet his heart is just the same to us as ever. Christ may wear masks that look black to his people, but his face is always the same; Christ may sometimes take a rod in his hand instead of a golden scepter, but the name of his saints is as much engraved upon the hand that grasps the rod as upon the palm that clasps the scepter. And oh, sweet thought that now bursts upon our mind! Beloved, can you conceive how much Christ will love you when you are in heaven? Have you ever tried to fathom that bottomless sea of affection in which you shall swim, when you shall bathe yourself in seas of heavenly rest? Did you ever think of the love which Christ will manifest to you, when he shall present you without spot, or blemish, or any such thing before his Father's throne? Well, pause and remember that he loves you at this hour as much as he will love you then; for he will be the same for ever as he is to-day, and he is the same to-day as he will be for ever. This one thing I know: if Jesus' heart is set on me he will not love me one atom better when this head wears a crown, and when this hand shall, with joyous fingers, touch the strings of golden harps, than he does now, amid all my sin and care and woe. I believe that saying which is written—"As the Father hath loved me, even so have I loved you;" and a higher degree of love we can not imagine. The Father loves his Son infinitely, and even so to day, believer, doth the Son of God love thee. All his heart flows out to thee. All his life is thine; all his person is thine. He can not love thee more; he will not love thee less. The same yesterday, to-day, and for ever.

But let us here recollect that Jesus Christ is *the same to sinners* to-day as he was yesterday. It is now eight years ago since I first went to Jesus Christ. Come the sixth of this month, I shall then be eight years old in the gospel of the grace of Jesus; a child, a little child therein as yet. I recall that

ιour when I heard that exhortation—"Look unto me and be
ye saved, all the ends of the earth, for I am God, and beside
me there is none else." And I remember, how with much
trembling and with a little faith I ventured to approach the
Saviour's feet. I thought he would spurn me from him
"Sure," said my heart, "if thou shouldst presume to put thy
trust in him as thy Saviour, it would be a presumption more
damnable than all thy sins put together. Go not to him; he
will spurn thee." However, I put the rope about my neck,
feeling that if God destroyed me for ever, he would be just ·
I cast the ashes on my head, and with many a sigh I did con
fess my sin; and then, when I ventured to draw nigh to him,
when I expected that he would frown, he stretched out his
hand and said, " I, even I, am he that blotteth out thy transgressions for mine own sake, and will not remember thy sins."
I came like the prodigal, because I was forced to come. I
was starved out of that foreign country where, in riotous living I had spent my substance, and I saw my Father's house
a great way off; little did I know that my Father's heart was
beating high with love to me. O rapturous hour, when Jesus
whispered I was his, and when my soul could say, "Jesus
Christ is my salvation." And now I would refresh my own
memory by reminding myself that what my Master was to
me yesterday that he is to-day; and if I know that as a sinner
I went to him then and he received me, if I have never so
many doubts about my saintship I can not doubt but what I
am a sinner; so to thy cross, O Jesus, I go again, and if thou
didst receive me then, thou wilt receive me now; and believing that to be true, I turn round to my fellow-immortals, and
I say, "He that received me, he that received Manasseh, he
that received the thief upon the cross, is the same to-day as
he was then. Oh! come and try him! Come and try him!
Oh! ye that know your need of him, come ye to him; ye that
have sold for nought your heritage above may have it back un-
bought, the gift of Jesus' love. Ye that are empty, Christ is
as full to-day as ever. Come! fill yourselves here. Ye that
are thirsty, the stream is flowing; ye that are black, the fountain
still can purify; ye that are naked, the wardrobe is not empty.

" Come, guilty souls, and flee away,
  To Christ, and heal your wounds;
Still 'tis the gospel's gracious day,
  And now free grace abounds."

I can not pretend to enter into the fullness of my text as I could desire, but one more thought. Jesus Christ is the same to-day as he was yesterday *in the teachings of his Word.* They tell us in these times that the improvements of the age require improvements in theology. Why, I have heard it said that the way Luther preached would not suit this age. We are too polite! The style of preaching, they say, that did in John Bunyan's day, is not the style now. True, they honor these men; they are like the Pharisees; they build the sepulchers of the prophets that their fathers slew, and so they do confess that they are their father's own sons, and like their parents. And men that stand up to preach as those men did, with honest tongues, and know not how to use polished courtly phrases, are as much condemned now as those men were in their time; because, say they, the world is marching on, and the gospel must march on too. No, sirs, the old gospel is the same; not one of her stakes must be removed, not one of her cords must be loosened. " Hold fast the form of sound words, which thou hast heard of me, in faith and love which is in Christ Jesus." Theology hath nothing new in it except that which is false. The preaching of Paul must be the preaching of the minister to-day. There is no advancement here. We may advance in our knowledge of it; but it stands the same, for this good reason, that it is perfect, and perfection can not be any better. The old truth that Calvin preached, that Chrysostom preached, that Paul preached, is the truth that I must preach to-day, or else be a liar to my conscience and my God. I can not shape the truth. I know of no such thing as the paring off the rough edges of a doctrine. John Knox's gospel is my gospel. That which thundered through Scotland must thunder through England again. The great mass of our ministers are sound enough in the faith, but not sound enough in the way they preach it. Election is not mentioned once in the year in many a pulpit; final perseverance is kept back; the great things of God's law are forgotten, and a kind of mongrel mixture of Arminianism and Calvinism is the delight of the present age. And hence the Lord hath forsaken many of his tabernacles and left the house of his covenant ; and he will leave it till again the trumpet gives a certain sound. For wherever there is not the old gospel we shall find " Ichabod" written upon the church walls ere long. The old truth of the Covenanters, the old truth of the Puritans, the old truth of the Apostles, is the only truth that will stand the test of time, and never need to be altered to suit a wicked and ungodly generation. Christ Jesus preaches to-day the same as when he preached upon the mount; he hath not changed his doctrines; men may ridicule and laugh, but still they stand the same—*semper idem* written upon every one of them. They shall not be removed or altered.

Let the Christian remember that this is equally true of the *promises.* Let the sinner remember this is just as true of the *threatenings.* Let us each recollect that not one word can be added to this Sacred Book, nor one letter taken away from it; for as Christ Jesus is yet the same, so is his Gospel, the same yesterday, to-day and for ever.

I have thus briefly opened the text, not in its fullest meanings, but still enough to enable the Christian at his own leisure to see into that depth without a bottom—the immutability of Christ Jesus the Lord.

II. And now comes in one of crooked gait, with hideous aspect—one that hath as many lives as a cat, and that can not be killed any how, though many a great gun hath been shot against him. His name is old Mr. Incredulity—unbelief; and he begins his miserable oration by declaring, " How can that be true ? ' Jesus Christ the same yesterday, and to-day, and for ever.' Why, yesterday Christ was all sunshine to me— to-day I am in distress !" Stop, Mr. Unbelief, I beg you to remember that Christ is not changed. You have changed yourself, for you have said in your very accusation that yesterday you rejoiced, but to-day you are in distress. All that may happen, and yet there may be no change in Christ. The

sun may be the same always, though one hour may be cloudy
and the next bright with golden light; yet there is no proo
that the sun has changed.   'Tis even so with Christ.

> " If to-day he deigns to bless us
>   With a sense of pardoned sin,
>   He to-morrow may distress us,
>   Make us feel the plague within.
>   All to make us,
>   Sick of self and fond of him."

There is no change in him.

> " Immutable his will,
>   Though dark may be my frame,
>   His loving heart is still
>   Unchangeably the same.
>   My soul through many changes goes,
>   His love no variation knows."

Your frames are no proof that Christ changes: they are only
proof that you change.

But saith old Unbelief again—" Surely God has changed:
you look at the old saints of ancient times. What happy men
they were! How highly favored of their God! How well
God provided for them! But now, sir, when I am hungry,
no ravens come and bring me bread and meat in the morning,
and bread and meat in the evening. When I am thirsty, no
water leaps out of the rock to supply my thirst. It is said of
the children of Israel that their clothes waxed not old; but I
have a hole in my coat to-day, and where I shall get another
garment I know not. When they marched through the desert he suffered no man to hurt them; but, sir, I am continually beset by enemies. It is true of me as it says in the Scriptures, ' And the Ammonites distressed Israel at the coming in
of the year;' for they are distressing me. Why, sir, I see my
friends die in clouds; there are no fiery chariots to carry
God's Elijahs to heaven now. I lost my son; no prophet lay
upon him and gave him life again; no Jesus met me at the
city gates, to give me back my son from the gloomy grave.
No, sir, these are evil times; the light of Jesus Christ has

become dim ; if he walks among the golden candlesticks, yet, still it is not as he used to do. And worse than that, sir, I have heard my father talk of the great men that were in the age gone by : I have heard the names of Romaine, and Top-lady, and Scott; I have heard of Whitfields and of Bunyans; and even but a few years ago I heard talk of such men as Joseph Irons—solemn and earnest preachers of a full gospel. But where are those men now ? Sir, we have fallen upon an age of drivellings ; *men* have died out, and we have only a few dwarfs left us; there are none that walk with the giant tramp and the colossal tread of the mighty fathers, like Owen, and Howe, and Baxter, and Charnock. We are all little men. Jesus Christ is not dealing with us as he did with our fathers. Stop, Unbelief, a minute : let me remind thee that the ancient people of God had their trials too. Know ye not what the apostle Paul says ? "For thy sake we are killed all the day long." Now, if there be any change it is a change for the better ; for you have not yet "resisted unto blood, striving against sin."

But remember *that* does not affect Christ; for neither nakedness, nor famine, nor sword, has separated us from the love of God, which is in Christ Jesus our Lord. It is true that you have no fiery chariot; but then the angels carry you to Jesus' bosom, and that is as well. It is true no ravens bring you food ; it is quite as true you get your food somehow or other. It is quite certain that no rock gushes out with water ; but still your water has been sure. It is true your child has not been raised from the dead ; but you remember that David had a child that was not raised any more than yours. You have the same consolation that he had : " I shall go to him ; he shall not return to me." You say that you have more heart-rendings than the saints had of old. It is your ignor-ance that makes you say so. Holy men of old said, " Why art thou cast down, O my soul ? Why art thou disquieted within me ?" Even prophets had to say—" Thou hast made me drunken with wormwood, and broken my teeth with gravel stones." O, you are mistaken : your days are not more full of trouble than the days of Job ; you are not more vexed by the wicked than was Lot of old, you have not moie temptations to make you angry than had Moses; and certainly your way is not half so rough as the way of your blessed Lord. The very fact that you have troubles is a proof of his faithfulness; for you have got one half of his legacy, and you will have the other half. You know that Christ's last will and testament has two portions in it. "In the world ye shall have tribulation:" you have got that. The next clause is—"In me ye shall have peace." You have that too. "Be of good cheer; I have overcome the world." That is yours also.

And then you say that you have fallen upon a bad age with regard to ministers. It may be so; but remember, the promise is true still. "Though I take away from thee bread and water, yet will I never take away thy pastors." You have still such as you have—still some that are faithful to God and to his covenant, and who do not forsake the truth, and though the day may be dark, yet it is not so dark as days have been; and besides remember, what you say to-day is just what your forefathers said. Men in the days of Toplady looked back to the days of Whitfield; men in the days of Whitfield looked back to the days of Bunyan; men in the days of Bunyan wept because of the days of Wycliffe, and Calvin, and Luther; and men then wept for the days of Augustine and Chrysostom. Men in those days wept for the days of the Apostles; and doubtless men in the days of the Apostles wept for the days of Jesus Christ; and no doubt some in the days of Jesus Christ were so blind as to wish to return to the days of prophesy, and thought more of the days of Elijah than they did of the most glorious day of Christ. Some men look more to the past than the present. Rest assured, that Jesus Christ is the same to-day as he was yesterday, and he will be the same for ever.

Mourner, be glad! I have heard of a little girl who, when her father died, saw her mother weeping immoderately. Day after day, and week after week, her mother refused to be comforted; and the little girl stepped up to her mother, and putting her little hand inside her mother's hand, looked up in her face, and said, "Mamma, is God dead? Is God dead, mam·

ma?" And her mother thought, "Surely, no." The child
seemed to say, "Thy maker is thy husband; the Lord of hosts
is his name. So you may dry your tears, I have a father in
heaven, and you have a husband still." O! ye saints that
have lost your gold and your silver; ye have got treasure in
heaven, where no moth nor rust doth corrupt, where no
thieves break through and steal! Ye that are sick to-day, ye
that have lost health, remember the day is coming when all
that shall be made up to you, and when ye shall find that the
flame has not hurt you, it has but consumed your dross and
refined your gold. Remember, Jesus Christ is " the same to-
day, yesterday, and for ever."

III. And now I must be brief in drawing one or two sweet
conclusions from that part of the text.

First, then, if he be the same to-day as yesterday, my soul,
set not thine affections upon these changing things, but set
thine heart upon him. O my heart, build not thine house
upon the sandy pillars of a world that soon must pass away,
but build thy hopes upon this rock, which, when the rain
descends, and floods shall come, shall stand immovably secure.
O my soul, I charge thee, lay up thy treasure in this secure
granary. O my heart, I bid thee now put thy treasure where
thou canst never lose it. Put it in Christ; put all thine affections in his person, all thy hope in his glory, all thy trust in
his efficacious blood, all thy joy in his presence, and then thou
wilt have put thyself and put thine all where thou canst never
lose anything, because it is secure. Remember, O my heart,
that the time is coming when all things must fade, and when
thou must part with all. Death's gloomy night must soon
put out thy sunshine; the dark flood must soon roll between
thee and all thou hast. Then put thine heart with him who
will never leave thee; trust thyself with him who will go with
thee through the black and surging current of death's stream,
and who will walk with thee up the steep hills of heaven and
make thee sit together with him in heavenly places for ever.
Go, tell thy secrets to that friend that sticketh closer than a
brother. My heart, I charge thee, trust all thy concerns with
him who never can be taken from thee, who will never leave

thee, and who will never let thee leave him, even "Jesus Christ, the same yesterday, and to-day, and for ever." That is one lesson.

Well, then, the next. If Jesus Christ be always the same, then, my soul, endeavor to imitate him. Be thou the same, too. Remember that if thou hadst more faith, thou wouldst be as happy in the furnace, as on the mountain of enjoyment. Thou wouldst be as glad in famine, as in plenty; thou wouldst rejoice in the Lord when the olive yielded no oil, as well as when the vat was bursting and overflowing its brim. If thou hadst more confidence in thy God, thou wouldst have far less of tossings up and down; and if thou hadst greater nearness to Christ thou wouldst have less vacillation. Yesterday thou couldst pray with all the power of prayer; perhaps if thou didst always live near thy Master, thou mightest always have the same power on thy knees. One time thou canst bid defiance to the rage of Satan, and thou canst face a frowning world; to-morrow thou wilt run away like a craven. But if thou didst always remember him who endured such contradiction of sinners against himself, thou mightest always be firm and stedfast in thy mind. Beware of being like a weathercock. Seek of God, that his law may be written on your hearts as if it were written on stone, and not as if it were written in sand. Seek, that his grace may come to you like a river, and not like a brook that fails. Seek, that you may keep your conversation always holy; that your course may be like the shining light that tarries not, but that burneth brighter and brighter, until the fullness of the day. Be ye like Christ—ever the same.

Again: if Christ be always the same, Christian, rejoice! Come what may, thou art secure.

> "Let mountains from their seats be hurled
> Down to the deeps, and buried there;
> Convulsions shake the solid world;
> Our faith shall never need to fear."

If kingdoms should go to rack, the Christian need not tremble! Just, for a minute, imagine a scene like this. Suppose for the next three days the sun should not rise; suppose the moon should be turned into a clot of blood, and shine no more upon the world; imagine that a darkness that might be felt, brooded over all men; imagine, next, that all the world did tremble in an earthquake, till every tower, and house, and hut fell down: imagine, next, that the sea forgot its place, and leaped upon the earth; and that the mountains ceased to stand, and began to tremble from their pedestals; conceive after that, that a blazing comet streamed across the sky—that the thunder bellowed incessantly—that the lightnings, without a moment's pause, followed one the other; conceive, then, that thou didst behold divers terrible sights, fiendish ghosts, and grim spirits; imagine, next, that a trumpet, waxing exceeding loud, did blow; that there were heard the shrieks of men dying and perishing; imagine, that in the midst of all this confusion, there was to be a found a saint. My friend, "Jesus Christ, the same yesterday, to-day, and for ever," would keep him as secure amidst all these horrors, as we are to-day. Oh! rejoice! I have pictured the worst that can come. *Then* you would be secure. Come what may then, you are safe, while Jesus Christ is the same.

And now, last of all, if Jesus Christ be "the same yesterday, to-day, and for ever," what sad work this is for the ungodly! Ah! sinner, when he was on earth, he said, "Their worm dieth not, and their fire is not quenched." When he stood upon the mount, he said, "It were better to enter life halt or maimed, than having two hands, and two eyes to be cast into hell-fire." As a man on earth, he said that the goats should be on the left, and that he would say to them, "Depart, ye cursed." Sinner, he will be as good as his word. He has said, "He that believeth not shall be damned." He will damn you if you believe not, depend upon it. He has never broken a promise yet; he will never break a threatening. That same truth which makes us confident to-day that the righteous shall go away into everlasting life, should make you quite as confident that unbelievers shall go into eternal misery. If he had broken his promise, he might break his threatening; but as he has kept one, he will keep the other.

Do not hope that he will change, for change he will not. Think not that the fire which he said was unquenchable, will, after all, be extinguished. No, within a few more years, my hearer, if thou dost not repent, thou wilt find that every jot and every letter of the threatenings of Jesus will be fulfilled; and, mark thee, fulfilled in *thee*. Liar, he said, "All liars shall have their portion in the lake that burns with fire and brimstone." He will not deceive you. Drunkard, he has said, "Ye know that no drunkard hath eternal life." He will not belie his word. You shall not have eternal life. He has said, "The nations that forget God shall be cast into hell." All ye that forget religion, moral people you may be, he will keep his word to you; he will cast you into hell. O "kiss the Son lest he be angry, and ye perish from the way, when his wrath is kindled but a little; blessed are all they that put their trust in him." Come, sinner, bow thy knee; confess thy sin and leave it; and then come to him; ask him to have mercy upon thee. He will not forget his promise—"Him that cometh unto me I will in no wise cast out." Come and try him. With all your sins about you, come to him *now*. "Believe on the Lord Jesus, and thou shalt be saved;" for this is my Master's gospel, and I now declare it—"He that believeth and is immersed shall be saved; he that believeth not shall be damned." God grant you grace to believe, through Jesus Christ our Lord. Amen.

SERMON XII

PAUL'S SERMON BEFORE FELIX

" And as he reasoned of righteousness, temperance, and judgment to come, Felix trembled, and answered, Go thy way for this time; when I have a convenient season, I will call for thee."—ACTS, xxiv. 25

THE power of the gospel appears in marvelous grandeur when we see its hold upon hearts devoted to it, when subjected to trouble, persecution, and sorrow. How mighty must that gospel be, which, when it gained an entrance into the heart of Paul, could never be driven out of it! For it he suffered the loss of all things, and as for them, he counted them but dung, that he might win Christ. To spread the truth, he encountered hardships, shipwrecks, perils on the land, and perils by sea; but none of these things moved him, neither did he count his life dear unto him, that he might win Christ and be found in him. Persecution followed persecution; of the Jews was he beaten with rods; he was dragged from one tribunal to another; scarce in any city did he find anything but bonds and imprisonment awaiting him. Attacked in his own country—he is accused at Jerusalem, and arraigned at Cesarea; he is taken from one tribunal to another to be tried for his life. But mark how he always maintains the prominent passion of his soul. Put him where you may, he seems to be like John Bunyan, who says, " If you let me out of prison to-day, I will preach the gospel again to-morrow, by the grace of God." Nay, more than that, he preached it in prison, before his judges he proclaimed it. Standing up before the Sanhedrim, he cries, " As touching the resurrection of the dead I am called in question." When brought to stand before Agrippa, he tells out his conversion, and so sweetly speaks of the grace of God, that the king himself cries, " Almost thou persuadest me to be a Christian ;" and here in our text when he stands before the Roman Procurator, to be tried for life or death, instead of entering into a defence of himself, he reasons " of righteousness, continence, and judgment to come," until his judge trembles, and he that sits upon the throne takes the prisoner's place, while the prisoner judges him, in anticipation of that time when the saints shall judge the angels, as assessors with Christ Jesus. Why, once let a man believe the gospel, and determine to spread it, and it makes him a grand man. If he be a man destitute of power, intellect, and talent, it makes him grandly earnest in his arduous desire to serve Christ, in the little measure in which he can do it ; but if he be a gifted man, it sets his whole soul on fire, brings out all his powers, develops everything that lies hidden, digs up every talent that had been buried in its napkin, and spreads out all the gold and silver of man's intellectual wealth, displaying it all to the honor of that Christ who has bought it all with his blood.

We might stay a little while and dilate on this thought, and show you how, in all ages, this has been the truth, that the power of the gospel has been eminently proved in its influence over men's hearts, proving the truth of that utterance of Paul, when he said, that neither tribulation, or distress, or persecution, or famine, or nakedness, or peril, or sword, shall separate them from the love of God, which is in Jesus Christ their Lord. But instead of so doing, I invite you to contemplate the text more closely. We have before us a picture containing three characters : Felix and Drusilla, sitting side by side upon the judgment-seat ; Paul, the prisoner, brought in bound in chains, to explain to Drusilla and Felix the doctrines of the Christian religion, in order that he might either be acquitted or condemned to die. You have a judge extremely willing to put the prisoner to death, because he desired to please the Jews ; you have, on the other hand, a prisoner, unabashed, who comes before the judge, and without any debate, begins to unfold the gospel, selecting a certain part of it, described in our text as reasoning concerning " righteousness, temperance, and judgment to come." The judge trembles, dismisses the prisoner in haste, and promises to attend to him at a convenient season

Note, first then, *the appropriate sermon ;* note, secondly, *the affected audience*—for the audience was certainly moved— "Felix trembled !" Note, then, thirdly, the *lamentable disappointment.* Instead of attending to the message, " Go thy way" was all that Paul had.

I. First, then, we have an APPROPRIATE SERMON. Just hear for a moment or two the history of Felix. Felix was orig inally a slave ; he was freed by Claudius, and became one of the infamous favorites of the emperor. Of course in that capacity he pandered to his master's vices, and was at all times prepared to indulge the Emperor in every lustful wish of his abominable l eart. Through this he became promoted, and ran through the stages of Roman preferment, until he obtained the Governorship of Judea. Whilst he was Governor there, he committed every act of extortion which it was possible for him to commit, and went so far at last, that the Emperor Nero was obliged to recall him, and he would have been severely punished for his crimes, had it not been for the influence of his brother Pallas, another freedman, with the Emperor, through whom he obtained a release, after a sharp rebuke. The Roman historian, Tacitus, says, " He exercised, in Judea, the imperial functions with a mercenary soul." You may easily see, then, how appropriate was the discourse, when the apostle Paul reasoned concerning righteousness. Felix had been an unjust extortioner, and the apostle purposely selected righteousness to be a topic of his discourse. By the side of Felix sat Drusilla; in the verse preceding our text she is called his wife. It is said she was a Jewess. This Drusilla was a daughter of Herod Agrippa, the great—a woman noted in that age for her superlative charms, and for her unbridled voluptuousness. She had been once affianced to Antiochus, who, upon the death of Herod, refused to marry her. She was afterward married to Azizus, the king of the Amesenes, who, although a heathen, was so fond of her, that he submitted to the most rigorous rites of the Jewish religion in order to obtain her in marriage. His love was but ill-requited, for in a little time she deserted him at the instigation of Felix, and was, at the time of Paul's address, living as the wife of tha lascivious Felix. We may easily understand then, why the apostle Paul, fixing his stern eye on Drusilla, reasoned concerning continence, and publicly rebuked both Felix and Drusilla for the shameless lust in which they were publicly living. And then you may imagine since there was now a court sitting, and Felix himself was the judge, and Paul the prisoner how strikingly appropriate was the last theme—"judgment to come."

I think, my brethren, it would not be very hard for us to imagine how well the apostle handled this subject. I can conceive that Felix expected to have a grand disquisition upon some recondite themes of the gospel. Possibly he expected that the apostle Paul would reason concerning the resurrection of the dead. He thought perhaps that predestination, election, and free will would be the topics of the apostle's discourse. " Surely," thought he, " he will tell me those deep and hidden matters in which the gospel of Jesus differs from Judaism." Not so. In another place, on Mar's Hill, the apostle would speak of resurrection ; in another place he could speak of election, and declare that God was the potter, and man was but the clay. This was not the place for that ; and this was not the time for such subjects; this was the time for preaching the plain precepts of the gospel, and for dealing sternly with a wicked man who sat in eminent power. Conceive then, the pointed manner of his opening discourse—How he would address Felix concerning righteousness. I can imagine how he would bring before the mind of Felix, the widow who had been defrauded of inheritance, the fatherless children, who, cast from affluence, were led to beg their bread. I can suppose how he brought before the mind of that base man the many bribes that he had taken, when he sat upon his judgment-seat. He would recall to him the false decisions that he had given ; he would remind him how the Jews, as a nation, had been oppressed—how, by taxation, they had been ground to the earth ; he would bring before him one scene after another, where avarice had overridden equity, boldly and sternly depicting the exact character of the man ; and then, at the end, declaring that such men could have no in heritance in the kingdom of God—bidding him repent of this his wickedness, that his sins might be forgiven him. Then gently and delicately turning to the other subject, I can imagine how he would fix his eyes upon Drusilla, and remind her that she had lost everything for which a woman ought to live, and solemnly bring the most powerful motives to bear upon her lascivious heart; and then turning to Felix, would remind him that adulterers, fornicators, and unclean persons, have no inheritance in the kingdom of God—reminding him how the vices of a ruler would tend to pollute a nation, and how the iniquities of the nation of the Jews must, in a great measure, be laid to his charge. I can conceive how, for a moment, Felix would bite his lips. Paul gave him no time for anger and passion; for in a moment, in a fury of impassioned eloquence, he introduced the "judgment to come." He made Felix think he saw the great white throne, the books opened, and himself arraigned before his judge: he made him hear the voices of the trumpet—the "Come ye blessed"—the "Depart ye cursed." He petrified him, nailed him to his seat, opened his ears, and made them listen, while with stern and impassioned earnestness, though his hands were bound with chains, he used the liberty of the gospel in upbraiding him. Well do I conceive that then Felix began to tremble. He that had been base, and mean, and perfidious, trembled like a coward slave, as he really was; and though sitting on throne, he pictured himself already damned. What he next would have done we can not tell, if the devil had not then suggested to him that it was time to rise; for in hot haste he and Drusilla left the throne. "Go thy way for this time; when I have convenient season, I will call for thee."

Hear me, then, brethren! What the apostle Paul did, every minister ought to do. He selected a topic appropriate to his audience. It is ours ever to do the same. But are there not to be found many ministers who, if they addressed kings and princes, would pour out before them the vilest adulation and flattery that ever came from mortal lips? Are there not many who, when they are aware the great and mighty ones are listening to them, trim their doctrine, cut the edges of their speech, and endeavor in some way or other to make themselves pleasing to their audience? Can there not be found many ministers who, if addressing an Antinomian audience, would confine themselves strictly to predestination and reprobation? and ministers who, if they addressed an audience of philosophers, would just talk about morality but never mention such words as the covenant of grace and salvation by blood? Are there not some to be found, who think the highest object of the minister is to attract the multitude and then to please them? O my God! how solemnly ought each of us to bewail our sin, if we feel that we have been guilty in this matter. What is it to have pleased men? Is there aught in it that can make our head lie easy on the pillow of our death? Is there aught in it that can give us boldness in the day of judgment, or cause us happiness when we face thy tribunal, O Judge of quick and dead? No, my brethren, we must always take our texts so that we may bear upon our hearers with all our might. I hope I may never preach *before* a congregation—I desire always to preach *to* you; nor do I wish to exhibit powers of eloquence, nor would I even pretend to exhibit any depth of learning. I would simply say, " Hear me, my fellow men, for God doth send me unto you. There are some things that concern you; I will tell you of them. You are dying; many of you when you die must perish for ever; it is not for me to be amusing you with some deep things that may instruct your intellect but do not enter your hearts; it is for me to fit the arrow to the string and send it home—to unsheathe the sword—be the scabbard never so glittering, to cast it aside, and let the majesty of naked truth smite at your hearts; for in the day of judgment aught beside personal home-speaking will be consumed as wood, and hay, and stubble; but these shall abide, like the gold and silver and precious stones that can not be consumed.

But some men will say, " Sir, ministers ought not to be personal." Ministers ought to be personal, and they will never be true to their Master till they are. I admire John Knox for going, Bible in hand, to Queen Mary, and sternly upbraid ing her. I admit I do not exactly love the way in which he did it; but the thing itself I love. The woman had been a sinner, and he told her so flat to her face But now we poor craven sons of nobodies have to stand and talk about general-ities; we are afraid to point you out and tell you of your sins personally. But, blessed be God, from that fear I have been delivered long ago. There walketh not a man on the surface of this earth whom I dare not reprove. There are none of you, however connected with me by ties of profession or in any other respect, that I would blush to speak person-ally to, as to the things of the kingdom of God; and it is only by being bold, courageous, and sending home the truth, that we shall at last be free from the blood of our hearers. May God grant us the power of Paul, that we may reason on appropriate subjects, and not select generalities, when we ought to be pushing home truths to the consciences of our hearers. After all, the apostle Paul needs no eulogy. The best eulogy that could be passed on the apostle was the fact that "Felix trembled." And that brings us to the second part of our discourse."

II. "FELIX TREMBLED." Yes, the poor prisoner, having nought wherewith to assist him in the delivery of the truth but having everything to his disadvantage—the chain, the prison dress, the character of one that had stirred up sedition in a nation—this poor prisoner, with believing hand, laid hold on the sword of truth, and with this he did divide in sunder the joints and marrow. He did beard the lion in his den. Even now I see him look the governor sternly in the face, at-tack him in his heart, drive him from his excuses, push the word home at the point of the bayonet of truth, drive him from every refuge of lies, and make him tremble! O marvel-lous power of a preached gospel! O mighty truth that God is with the ministry, when the kings of the earth that take counsel together are yet dismayed by it. Who is he that doth not see here something more than human eloquence, when prisoner becomes the judge and the prince upon the throne becomes the criminal? "Felix trembled." Have I not some here who have experienced the same feelings as Felix? Some plain-spoken minister has told you something that was rather too plain for you. At first you were angry; on second thoughts, and as the man moved on in his discourse, you became chagrined that you gave him the opportunity of thus exposing you, as you imagined. A better thought struck you, and you saw at once that the man could have no intention personally to insult you; and then your feelings changed. Thunderbolt after thunderbolt fell from his lips; he seemed a very Jupiter Tonans sitting upon his throne, casting lightnings from his lips. Ye began to tremble. "Verily here is a man that has told me all things that ever I did; is not this man sent from Christ?" Ah! and thus you have borne your witness to the truth of the gospel. Though you have not felt its power to your salvation, yet you have been an unwilling witness that the gospel has been true; for you have felt its power when it made your knees knock together, and your eyes run down with tears.

But what is it that makes men tremble under the sound of the Gospel? Some say it is their conscience. Yes, and doubtless it is in some sense. The poet said, "Conscience makes cowards of us all;" and certainly, when the minister's exposition is faithful and pertinent to our own case, conscience, if it be not thoroughly seared and dead, will make the blush mantle on our cheeks. But I take it that conscience of itself is so thoroughly corrupt, together with all the other powers of manhood, that it would never even make a man go so far as trembling, if there were not something at work upon the conscience, besides being left to its own natural force. My brethren, I believe that what some people call natural conviction is, after all, the work of the Spirit. Some very profound divines are so fond of the doctrine that the Holy Spirit always works efficaciously, that they think that the Spirit never can work a transitory emotion in a man's soul; they impute such things to conscience. And if they see a man like Felix trembling, they say 'tis all natural conscience! Now, do they not see that they are in this touching on another doctrine eqially dear to them—the doctrine of total depravity?--for if men be totally depraved by nature, then, as trembling is a good thing, they are not capable even of that without some influence of the Holy Spirit. The fact is, my hearers, the Holy Spirit works in two ways. In some men's hearts he works with restraining Grace only, and the restraining Grace, though it will not save them, is enough to keep them from breaking out into the open and corrupt vices in which some men indulge who are totally left by the restraints of the Spirit. Now, there was in Felix some little portion of this restraining Grace; and when the Apostle laid the Gospel open to him, this restraining Grace quickened the conscience, and compelled Felix to tremble. Mark you, this Grace man may resist and does resist; for albeit that the Holy Spirit is Omnipotent and never can be resisted when he works Omnipotently, yet as a strong man may sometimes not put out all his strength, but work with his finger, for instance, so that he may permit even a gnat or an ant to overcome him, even so the Holy Spirit sometimes works but temporarily and but for good and excellent purposes, which he always accomplishes; but he allows men to quench and resist his influences, so that salvation is not so much as approached thereby. God the Holy Spirit may work in men some good desires and feelings, and yet have no design of saving them. But mark, none of these feelings are things that accompany sure salvation, for if so, they would be continued. But he does not work Omnipotently to save, except in the persons of his own elect, whom he assuredly bringeth to himself. I believe, then, that the trembling of Felix is to be accounted for by the restraining grace of the Spirit quickening his conscience and making him tremble.

But what shall be said of some of you who never tremble? Thou hast come hither this morning with thy brazen face, and with thine impudent and arrogant heart. Thou hast been mouthing high heaven with thy blasphemies; and now thou standest all unmoved and unabashed in the house of God. Though a Baxter should rise from the dead, and with moving sighs and tears should preach the Gospel, you would laugh and scoff; though Boanerges with a tongue of thunder should come and preach to you, you would turn up your lip and find some fault with his oratory, and his words would never reach your heart. O ungodly generation! how hath God given you up, and how hath hell bewitched you? O race of evil doers! children that are corrupters! how are ye seared. My soul reads with prophetic glance the handwriting on the wall! You are condemned already; you are past hope, "trees plucked up by the roots, twice dead." For in the fact that ye tremble not, tnere is proof not only of your death but of your positive corruption. Ye shall die as ye are, without hope, without trust or refuge; for he that hath lost feeling hath lost hope; he that is past conscience God the Holy Spirit hath given up, and he will no more strive with him for ever.

III. And now, passing rapidly over this point of the trembling audience, we come in the next place to the LAMENTABLE DISAPPOINTMENT which Paul experienced, when he saw Felix rise in haste, and dismiss him from his presence. "It is wonderful," said a good man once to a minister, "it is wonderful to see a whole congregation moved to tears by the preaching of the Word." "Yes," said that minister, "it is wonderful; but I know a wonder ten times greater than that: the wonder is, that those people should so soon wipe away their tears and forget what they have heard." 'Tis wonderful that Felix trembled before Paul; 'tis more wonderful that Felix should say, "Go thy way." "'Tis strange, 'tis passing strange," that when the word touches the conscience, even then sin hath such power over men, that the truth can be repulsed and driven out of the heart. Felix, unhappy Felix! why is it that thou dost rise from thy judgment-seat? Is it that thou hast much business to do? Stop, Felix; let Paul speak to thee a minute longer. Thou hast business: but hast thou no business for thy soul? Stop, unhappy man! Art thou about again to be extortionate, again to make thy personal riches greater! Oh! stop: canst thou not spare another minute for thy poor soul? It is to live for ever: hast thou naught laid up for it—no hope in heaven, no blood of Christ, no pardon of sin, no sanctifying Spirit, no imputed righteousness? Ah! man there will be a time when the business that seems so important to thee will prove to have been but a day-dream, a poor substitute for the solid realities thou hast forgotten. Dost thou reply, " Nay, the king has sent me an urgent commission ; I must attend to Cæsar." Ah ! Felix, but thou hast a greater monarch than Cæsar : there is one who is Emperor of heaven and Lord of earth ; canst thou spare no time to attend to his commands ? Before his presence Cæsar is but a worm. Man ! wilt thou obey the one, and wilt thou despise the other ? Ah ! no ; I know what thou durst not say. Felix, thou art turning aside again to indulge in thy lascivious pleasures. Go, and Drusilla with thee ! But stop ! Darest thou do that, with that last word ringing in thy ears, " Judgment to come." What ! wilt thou repeat that wanton dalliance that hath damned thee already, and wilt thou go again to imbrue thy hands in lust, and doubly damn thy spirit, after warnings heard and felt ? O man ! I could weep o'er thee, to think that as the bullock goeth to the slaughter, and as the lamb licks the knife, so dost thou go back to the sin that destroys thee, and to the lust that ruins thee. You, too, many of you, have often been impressed under the ministry. I know what you have said on the Monday morning, after deep searchings of heart on the Sabbath : you have said, " I must attend to business, I must see after the things of this world." Ah ! you will say that one day, when hell shall laugh you in the face for your folly. Think of men that are dying every day saying, " We must live," and forgetting that they must die. O poor soul ! to be caring about that house, thy body, and neglecting the tenant within ! Another replies, " I must have a little more pleasure." Pleasure dost thou call it ? What ! can there be pleasure in turning suicide to thine own soul—pleasure in defying thy Maker, trampling on his laws, despising his grace ? If this be pleasure, 'tis a pleasure over which angels might weep. What, man, wilt thou count this pleasure when thou comest to die ? Above all, wilt thou count this pleasure when thou dost stand before thy Maker's bar at last ? It is a strange delusion that causes thee to believe a lie. There is no pleasure in that which brings wrath upon thy soul, even to the uttermost.

But the usual reply is, "There is time enough yet." The young man says, "Let me alone till I grow old." And you old men, what do you say ? I can suppose that the youth looks forward to life, and expects to find a future time more convenient. But there are some of you o'er whose heads seventy winters have blown. When do you hope to find a convenient season ? You are within a few days' march of the tomb : if you do but it open your poor dull eyes, you may see death but a slight distance in advance. The young *may* die ; the old *must !* To sleep in youth is to sleep in a siege ; to sleep in old age is to slumber during the attack. What ! man, wilt thou that art so near thy Maker's bar still put him off with a " Go thy way ?" What ! procrastinate now, when the knife is at thy throat—when the worm is at the heart of the tree, and the branches have begun to wither—when the grinders fail even now, because they are few, and they that look out of the windows are darkened ? The sere and yellow leaf has come upon thee, and thou art still unready for thy doom ! O man ' of all fools, a fool with a gray head is the worst fool anywhere. With one foot in the grave, and another foot on a sandy foundation, how shall I depict you, but by saying to you, as God said to the rich man, " Thou fool ! a few more nights and thy soul shall be required of thee ;" and then where art thou ?

But still the common cry is, " There is time enough." Even the worldly moralist said, " Time enough is always little enough." Time enough, man ! What for ? Surely you have spent time enough in sin : the time past may " suffice you to have wrought the will of the Gentiles." What ! time enough to serve a God that laid down his life for you ? No ! eternity will not be too long to utter his praise, and therefore it can not be too long to love him here, and serve him the few remaining days that you are to live on earth.

But stop ! I will reason with you. Come, Felix ! thou shalt not go away this morning till my whole soul hath poured itself out over thee, not until I have cast mine arms round thee, and tried to stop thee this time from turning from the face of him that bids thee live. Thou sayest, " Another time."

How knowest thou that thou wilt ever feel again as thou feelest now? This morning, perhaps, a voice is saying in thine heart, "Prepare to meet thy God." To-morrow that voice will be hushed. The gayeties of the ball-room and the theater will put out that voice that warns thee now, and perhaps thou wilt never hear it again. Men all have their warnings, and all men who perish have had a *last warning*. Perhaps this is your last warning. You are told to-day, that except ye repent, ye must perish, except ye put your trust in Christ, ye must be cast away forever. Perhaps no honest lip will again warn you; perhaps no tearful eye will ever look on you affectionately again; God to-day is pulling the reins tight to check you from your lust; perhaps, if to day you spurn the bit, and rush madly on, he will throw the reins upon your back, saying, "Let him alone;" and then it is a dark steeple-chase between earth and hell, and you will run it in mad confusion, never thinking of a hell till you find yourself past warning, past repentance, past faith, past hope.

But again: how knowest thou, if thou shouldst ever have these feelings again, God will accept thee then? "To-day," he says, "to-day, if ye will hear his voice, harden not your hearts." This hour his love weepeth over you, and his bowels yearn for you. To-day he says, "Come, let us reason together; though your sins be as scarlet, they shall be as wool; and though they be red like crimson, they shall be whiter than snow." Do you to-day turn a deaf ear to him? Do you to-day forego his invitation and despise his warning? Take heed! You may one day need what now you despise, and you may then cry to him, but he will not hear you; you may then pray to him, but he will shut out your prayer, and his only answer will be, "*I called!*" "*I called, and you refused.* You stood against that pillar under the gallery; *I called and you refused! I stretched out my hands*, as if I would bring you to my bosom, *and no man regarded* me You were there in the gallery; you listened, but it was as though you heard not; therefore"—and oh! the dreadful conclusion!—"*I also will laugh at your calamity, I will mock when your fear cometh.*" Stay! those are not my words;

they are God's words. Turn ye to the book of Proverbs, and find them there. It were a harsh thing for me to say of God; but God says it of himself, and God is true, though every man be a liar; and if he be true, how know ye that he may not despise your prayer one day, shut out your cry, and banish you forever?

But again, how do you know that you shall live to be warned again? Said a minister once, when I gently hinted to him that he had not preached the gospel that morning, "No, I did not mean to preach to sinners in the morning; but I will preach to them in the evening." "Ah!" said I, "but what if some of your congregation of the morning should be in hell before the evening." So may I say to you. You have promised to go to a friend's house to-day, you think you can not break that promise; you wish you could. You wish you could go home and fall on your knees and pray; but no, you can not, because your promise binds you. You will have a convenient season one of these days! And so God Almighty is to wait man's convenience! How do you know you will live till that convenience comes? A little too much heat or too much cold within the brain—a little too fast flowing of the blood, or a little too slow circulation thereof—some little turning of the fluids of the body in a wrong direction, and you are dead!

> " Dangers stand thick through all the ground,
>   To bear you to the tomb,
>   And fierce diseases wait around,
>   To hurry mortals home."

Oh! why will you then dare to procrastinate, and say, "Time enough yet?" Will your soul ever be saved by your saying "Time enough yet?" Archbishop Tillotson well says, "A man might say I resolve to eat, but the resolve to eat would never feed his body. A man might say, I am resolved to drink, but the resolve to drink would never slake his thirst." And you may say, "I am resolved by-and-by to seek God;' but your resolve will not save you. It is not the forgetful hearer, but the doer of the word that shall be blessed therein.

Oh that ye might now say—To-day, my God, to-day I confess my sin; to-day I ask thee to manifest thy grace; to-day receive my guilty soul, and show me a Saviour's blood; to-day I renounce my follies, my vices, and my sins, constrained by Sovereign Grace; to-day I cast away my good works as my ground of trust; to-day I cry,

> "Nothing in my hands I bring,
> Simply to thy cross I cling!"

Oh! happy minister who shall have such an audience!—happier than Paul, if he should know that his congregation had said this! Come, O Holy Spirit, and draw unwilling hearts, and make them bow before the scepter of sovereign grace.

Preaching, you see, takes away my voice. Ah! it is not that. It is not the preaching, but the sighing over your souls that is the hard work. I could preach forever: I could stand here day and night to tell my Master's love, and warn poor souls; but 'tis the after-thought that will follow me when I descend these pulpit steps, that many of you, my hearers, will neglect this warning. You will go; you will walk into the street; you will joke; you will laugh. My Master says, "Son of man, hast thou heard what the children of Israel say concerning thee? Behold, thou art as one that playeth a tune upon an instrument; they make merry with thee, and they go their ways." Yes, but that were little. To be laughed at is no great hardship to me. I can delight in scoffs and jeers; caricatures, lampoons, and slanders, are my glory; of these things I boast, yea, in these I will rejoice. But that you should turn from your own mercy, this is my sorrow. Spit on me, but oh! repent! Laugh at me: but oh! believe in my Master! Make my body as the dirt of the streets, if you will: but damn not your own souls! Oh! do not despise your own mercies. Put not away from you the gospel of Christ. There are many other ways of playing fool beside that. Carry coals in your bosom: knock your head against a wall: but do not damn your souls for the mere sake of being a fool, for fools to laugh at.   Oh! be in earnest upon an earnest subject.   If there be no hereafter, live as you like; if there be no heaven, if there be no hell, laugh at me!   But if these things be true, and you believe them, I charge you, as I shall face you at the judgment bar of the Lord Jesus in the day of judgment—I charge you, by your own immortal welfare, lay these things to heart.   Prepare to meet your God, O sons of Israel!   And the Lord help you in this thing; for Jesus' sake.   Amen.

SERMON XIII

THE DEATH OF CHRIST

" Yet it pleased the Lord to bruise him; he hath put him to grief. when thou shalt make his soul an offering for sin, he shall see his seed, he shall prolong his days, and the pleasure of the Lord shall prosper in his hand.— ISAIAH, liii. 10.

WHAT myriads of eyes are casting their glances at the sun! What multitudes of men lift up their eyes, and behold the starry orbs of heaven! They are continually watched by thousands—but there is one great transaction in the world's history, which every day commands far more spectators than that sun which goeth forth like a bridegroom, strong to run his race. There is one great event, which every day attracts more admiration than do the sun, and moon, and stars, when they march in their courses. That event is, the death of our Lord Jesus Christ. To it, the eyes of all the saints who lived before the Christian era were always directed; and backwards, through the thousand years of history, the eyes of all modern saints are looking. Upon Christ, the angels in heaven perpetually gaze. " Which things the angels desire to look into," said the apostle. Upon Christ, the myriad eyes of the redeemed are perpetually fixed; and thousands of pilgrims, through this world of tears, have no higher object for their faith, and no better desire for their vision, than to see Christ as he is in heaven, and in communion to behold his person. Beloved, we shall have many with us, whilst this morning we turn our face to the Mount of Calvary. We shall not be solitary spectators of the fearful tragedy of our Saviour's death: we shall but dart our eyes to that place which is the focus of heaven's joy and delight, the cross of our Lord and Saviour Jesus Christ.

Taking our text, then, as a guide, we propose to visit Cal

vary, hoping to have the help of the Holy Spirit whilst we look upon him who died upon the cross. I would have you notice this morning, first of all, *the cause of Christ's death*— "It pleased the Lord to bruise him." "It pleased *Jehovah* to bruise him," saith the original; "*he* hath put him to grief." Secondly, *the reason of Christ's death*—"When thou shalt make his soul an offering for sin." Christ died because he was an offering for sin. And then, thirdly, *the effects and consequences of Christ's death.* "He shall see his seed, he shall prolong his days, and the pleasure of the Lord shall prosper in his hand." Come, Sacred Spirit, now, whilst we attempt to speak on these matchless themes.

I. First, we have here THE ORIGIN OF CHRIST'S DEATH. "It pleased Jehovah to bruise him; he hath put him to grief." He who reads Christ's life, as a mere history, traces the death of Christ to the enmity of the Jews, and to the fickle character of the Roman governor. In this he acteth justly, for the crime and sin of the Saviour's death must lay at the door of manhood. This race of ours became a deicide and slew the Lord, and nailed its Saviour to a tree. But he who reads the Bible with the eye of faith, desiring to discover its hidden secrets, sees something more in the Saviour's death than Roman cruelty, or Jewish malice: he sees the solemn decree of God fulfilled by men, who were the ignorant, but guilty instruments of its accomplishment. He looks beyond the Roman spear and nail, beyond the Jewish taunt and jeer, up to the Sacred Fount, whence all things flow, and traces the crucifixion of Christ to the breast of Deity. He believes with Peter—"Him, being delivered by the determinate counsel and foreknowledge of God, ye have taken, and by wicked hands have crucified and slain." We dare not impute to God the sin, but at the same time the fact, with all its marvelous effects in the world's redemption, we must ever trace to the Sacred Fountain of divine love. So doth our prophet. He says, "It pleased Jehovah to bruise him." He overlooks both Pilate and Herod, and traces it to the heavenly Father, the first Person in the Divine Trinity. "It pleased the Lord to bruise him, *he* hath put him to grief."

Now, beloved, there be many who think that God the Father is at best but an indifferent spectator of salvation. Others do belie him still more. They look upon Him as an unloving, severe Being, who had no love to the human race, and could only be made loving by the death and agonies of our Saviour. Now, this is a foul libel upon the fair and glorious grace of God the Father, to whom for ever be honor: for Jesus Christ did not die to make God loving, but he died because God *was* loving.

> " Twas not to make Jehovah's love
> Toward his people flame,
> That Jesus from the throne above,
> A suffering man became.

> " Twas not the death which he endured,
> Nor all the pangs he bore,
> That God's eternal love procured,
> For God was love before."

Christ was sent into the world by his Father, as the consequence of the Father's affection for his people. Yea, he " so loved the world, that he gave his only begotten Son that whosoever believeth in him should not perish, but have everlasting life." The fact is, that the Father as much decreed salvation, as much effected it, and as much delighted in it, as did either God the Son, or God the Holy Spirit. And when we speak of the Saviour of the world, we must always include in that word, if we speak in a large sense, God the Father, God the Son, and God the Holy Ghost, for all these three, as one God, do save us from our sins. The text puts away every hard thought concerning the Father, by telling us that it pleased Jehovah to bruise Jesus Christ. The death of Christ is traceable to God the Father. Let us try if we can see it is so.

1. First it is traceable in decree. God, the one God of heaven and earth, hath the book of destiny entirely in his power. In that book there is nothing written by a stranger's hand. The penmanship of the solemn book of predestination is from beginning to end entirely divine.

> " Chained to his throne a volume lies
>   With all the fates of men,
>   With every angel's form and size
>   *Drawn by th' eternal pen.*

No inferior hand hath sketched even so much as the most minute parts of providence. It was all, from its Alpha to its Omega, from its divine preface to its solemn finis, marked out, designed, sketched, and planned by the mind of the all-wise, all-knowing God. Hence, not even Christ's death was exempt from it. He that wings an angel and guides a sparrow, he that protects the hairs of our head from falling prematurely to the ground, was not likely, when he took notice of such little things, to omit in his solemn decrees the greatest wonder of earth's miracles, the death of Christ. No ; the blood-stained page of that book, the page which makes both past and future glorious with golden words,—that blood-stained page, I say, was as much written of Jehovah, as any other. He determined that Christ should be born of the Virgin Mary, that he should suffer under Pontius Pilate, that he should descend into Hades, that thence he should rise again, leading captivity captive, and then should reign for ever at the right hand of the Majesty on high. Nay, I know not but that I shall have Scripture for my warrant when I say, that this is the very core of predestination, and that the death of Christ is the very center and main-spring by which God did fashion all his other decrees, making this the bottom and foundation-stone upon which the sacred architecture should be builded. Christ was put to death by the absolute foreknowledge and solemn decree of God the Father, and in this sense " it pleased the Lord to bruise him ; he hath put him to grief."

2. But a little further, Christ's coming into the world to die was the effect of the Father's will and pleasure. Christ came not into this world unsent. He had laid in Jehovah's bosom from before all worlds, eternally delighting himself in his Father, and being himself his Father's eternal joy. " In the fullness of time" God did rend his Son from his bosom, his only-begotten Son, and freely delivered him up for *us* all. Herein was matchless, peerless love, that the offended judge

should permit his co-equal Son to suffer the pains of death for the redemption of a rebellious people. I want your imagination for one minute to picture a scene of olden times. There is a bearded patriarch, who rises early in the morning and awakes his son, a young man full of strength, and bids him arise and follow him. They hurry from the house silently and noiselessly, before the mother is awake. They go three days' journey with their men; until they come to the Mount, of which the Lord hath spoken. You know the patriarch. The name of Abraham is always fresh in our memories. On the way, that patriarch speaks not one solitary word to his son. His heart is too full for utterance. He is overwhelmed with grief. God has commanded him to take his son, his only son, and slay him upon the mountain as a sacrifice. They go together; and who shall paint the unutterable anguish of the father's soul, whilst he walks side by side with that beloved son, of whom he is to be the executioner? The third day has arrived; the servants are bidden to stay at the foot of the hill, whilst they go to worship God yonder. Now, can any mind imagine how the father's grief must overflow all the banks of his soul, when, as he walked up that hill-side, his son said to him, "Father, behold the fire and the wood; but where is the lamb for a burnt-offering?" Can you conceive how he stifled his emotions, and, with sobs, exclaimed, "My son, God will provide himself a lamb?" See! the father has communicated to his son the fact that God has demanded his life. Isaac, who might have struggled and escaped from his father, declares that he is willing to die, if God hath decreed it. The father takes his son, binds his hands behind his back, piles up the stones, makes an altar, lays the wood, and has his fire ready. And now where is the artist that can depict the anguish of the father's countenance, when the knife is unsheathed, and he holds it up, ready to slay his son? But here the curtain falls. Now the black scene vanishes at the sound of a voice from heaven. The ram caught in the thicket supplies the substitute, and faith's obedience need go no further. Ah! my brethren, I want to take you from this scene to a far greater one. What faith and obedience made man do, that love constrained God himself to do. He had but one son, that son his own heart's delight: he covenanted to yield him up for our redemption, nor did he violate his promise; for, when the fullness of time was come, he sent his Son to be born of the Virgin Mary, that he might suffer for the sins of man. O! can ye tell the greatness of that love, which made the everlasting God not only put his Son upon the altar, but actually do the deed, and thrust the sacrificial knife into his Son's heart? Can you think how overwhelming must have been the love of God toward the human race, when he completed in act what Abraham only did in intention? Look ye there, and see the place where his only Son hung dead upon the cross, the bleeding victim of awakened justice! Here is love indeed; and here we see how it was, that it pleased the Father to bruise him.

3. This allows me to push my text just one point further. Beloved, it is not only true that God did design and did permit with willingness the death of Christ; it is moreover, true that the unutterable agonies that clothed the death of the Saviour with superhuman terror, were the effect of the Father's bruising of Christ in very act and deed. There is a martyr in prison: the chains are on his wrists, and yet he sings. It has been announced to him that to-morrow is his burning day. He claps his hands right merrily, and smiles while he says, "It will be sharp work to-morrow, I shall breakfast below on fiery tribulations, but afterward I will sup with Christ. To-morrow is my wedding-day, the day for which I have long panted, when I shall sign the testimony of my life by a glorious death." The time is come; the men with the halberts precede him through the streets. Mark the serenity of the martyr's countenance. He turns to some who look upon him, and exclaims, "I value these iron chains far more than if they had been of gold; it is a sweet thing to die for Christ." There are a few of the boldest of the saints gathered round the stake, and as he unrobes himself, ere he stands upon the fagots to receive his doom, he tells them that it is a joyous thing to be a soldier of Christ, to be allowed to give his body to be burned; and he shakes hands with them, and bids them

"Good by" with merry cheer. One would think he were going to a bridal, rather than to be burned. He steps upon the fagots; the chain is put about his middle; and after a brief word of prayer, as soon as the fire begins to ascend, he speaks to the people with manful boldness. But hark! he sings whilst the fagots are crackling and the smoke is blowing upward. He sings, and when his nether parts are burned, he still goes on chanting sweetly some psalm of old. "God is our refuge and strength, a very present help in trouble; there fore will we not fear, though the earth be removed and the mountains be carried into the midst of the sea."

Picture another scene. There is the Saviour going to his cross, all weak and wan with suffering; his soul is sick and sad within him. There is no divine composure there. So sad is his heart, that he faints in the streets. The Son of God faints beneath a cross that many a criminal might have carried. They nail him to the tree. There is no song of praise. He is lifted up in the air, and there he hangs preparatory to his death. You hear no shout of exultation. There is a stern compression of his face, as if unutterable agony were tearing his heart—as if over again Gethsemane were being acted on the cross—as if his soul were still saying, "If it be possible let this cross pass from me; nevertheless, not as I will, but as thou wilt." Hark! he speaks. Will he not sing sweeter songs than ever came from martyr's lips? Ah! no; it is an awful wail of woe that can never be imitated. "My God, my God, why hast thou forsaken me?" The martyrs said not that: God was with them. Confessors of old cried not so, when they came to die. They shouted in their fires, and praised God on their racks. Why this? Why doth the Saviour suffer so? Why, beloved, it was because the Father bruised him. That sunshine of God's countenance that has cheered many a dying saint, was withdrawn from Christ; the consciousness of acceptance with God, which has made many a holy man espouse the cross with joy, was not afforded to our Redeemer, and therefore he suffered in thick darkness of mental agony. Read the 22nd Psalm, and learn how Jesus suffered. Pause over the solemn words in the 1st, 2nd, 6th, and following verses. Underneath the Church are the ever lasting arms; but underneath Christ there were no arms at all, but his Father's hand pressed heavily against him; the upper and the nether mill-stones of divine wrath pressed and bruised him; and not one drop of joy or consolation was afforded to him. "It pleased Jehovah to bruise him; *he* hath put him to grief." This, my brethren, was the climax of the Saviour's woe, that his Father turned away from him, and put him to grief.

Thus have I expounded the first part of the subject—the origin of our Saviour's worst sufferings, the Father's pleasure.

II. Our second head must explain the first, or otherwise it is an insolvable mystery how God should bruise his Son, who was perfect innocence, while poor fallible confessors and martyrs have had no such bruising from him in the time of their trial. WHAT WAS THE REASON OF THE SAVIOUR'S SUFFERING? We are told here, "Thou shalt make his soul an offering for sin." Christ was thus troubled, because his soul was an offering for sin. Now, I am going to be as plain as I can, while I preach over again the precious doctrine of the atonement of Christ Jesus our Lord. Christ was an offering for sin, in the sense of a substitute. God longed to save; but, if such a word may be allowed, Justice tied his hands. "I must be just," said God; "that is a necessity of my nature. Stern as fate, and fast as immutability, is the truth that I must be just. But then my heart desires to forgive—to pass by man's transgressions and pardon them. How can it be done? Wisdom stepped in, and said, "It shall be done thus;" and Love agreed with Wisdom. "Christ Jesus, the Son of God, shall stand *in man's place*, and he shall be offered upon Mount Calvary *instead of man*. Now, mark: when you see Christ going up the Mount of Doom, you see man going there: when you see Christ hurled upon his back, upon the wooden cross, you see the whole company of his elect there; and when you see the nails driven through his blessed hands and feet, it is the whole body of his Church who there, in their substitute, are nailed to the tree. And now the soldiers lift the cross, and

dash it down into the socket prepared for it. His bones are
every one of them dislocated, and his body is thus torn with
agonies which can not be described. 'Tis manhood suffering
there ; 'tis the Church suffering there, in the substitute. And
when Christ dies, you are to look upon the death of Christ,
not as his own dying merely, but as the dying of all those for
whom he stood as the scape-goat and the substitute. It is
true, Christ died really himself; it is equally true that he did
not die for himself, but died as the substitute, in the room, place,
and stead of all believers. When you die you will die for yourselves ; when Christ died, he died for you, if you be a believer in
him. When you pass through the gates of the grave, you go
there solitary and alone ; you are not the representative of a
body of men, but you pass through the gates of death as an individual ; but, remember, when Christ went through the sufferings of death, he was the representative Head of all his people.

Understand, then, the sense in which Christ was made a
sacrifice for sin. But here lies the glory of this matter. It
was as a substitute for sin that he did actually and literally
suffer punishment for the sin of all his elect. When I say this,
I am not to be understood as using any figure whatever, but
as saying actually what I mean. Man for his sin was condemned to eternal fire ; when God took Christ to be the substitute, it is true, he did not send Christ into eternal fire, but
he poured upon him grief so desperate, that it was a valid
payment for even an eternity of fire. Man was condemned to
live forever in hell. God did not send Christ forever into
hell ; but he put on Christ, punishment that was equivalent for
that. Although he did not give Christ to drink the actual
hells of believers, yet he gave him a *quid pro quo*—something
that was equivalent thereunto. He took the cup of Christ's
agony, and he put in there, suffering, misery, and anguish
such as only God can imagine or dream of, that was the exact
equivalent for all the suffering, all the woe, and all the eternal
tortures of every one that shall at last stand in heaven, bought
with the blood of Christ. And you say, " Did Christ drink
it all to its dregs ?" Did he suffer it all ? Yes, my brethren,
he took the cup, and

> " At one triumphant draught of love,
> He drank damnation dry."

He suffered all the horror of hell : in one pelting shower of iron wrath it fell upon him, with hail-stones bigger than a talent ; and he stood until the black cloud had emptied itself completely.   There was our debt, huge and immense ; he paid the utmost farthing of whatever his people owed ; and now there is not so much as a doit or a farthing due to the justice of God in the way of punishment from any believer ; and though we owe God gratitude, though we owe much to his love, we owe nothing to his justice ; for Christ in that hour took all our sins, past, present, and to come, and was punished for them all there and then, that we might never be punished, because he suffered in our stead.   Do you see, then, how it was that God the Father bruised him ?   Unless he had so done the agonies of Christ could not have been an equivalent for our sufferings ; for hell consists in the hiding of God's face from sinners, and if God had not hidden his face from Christ, Christ could not—I see not how he could—have endured any suffering that could have been accepted as an equivalent for the woes and agonies of his people.

Methinks I heard some one say, " Do you mean us to understand this atonement that you have now preached as being a literal fact ?"   I say, most solemnly, I do.   There are in the world many theories of atonement ; but I can not see any atonement in any one, except in this doctrine of substitution. Many divines say that Christ did something when he died that enabled God to be just, and yet the Justifier of the ungodly. What that something is they do not tell us.   They believe in an atonement made for every body ; but then, their atonement is just this.   They believe that Judas was atoned for just as much as Peter ; they believe that the damned in hell were as much an object of Jesus Christ's satisfaction as the saved in heaven ; and though they do not say it in proper words, yet they must mean it, for it is a fair inference, that in the case of multitudes, Christ died in vain, for he died for them all, they say , and yet so ineffectual was his dying for them, that though he died for them they are damned afterward. Now, such an atonement I despise—I reject it. I may be called Antino mian or Calvinist for preaching a limited atonement; but I had rather believe a limited atonement that is efficacious for all men for whom it was intended, than an universal atonement that is not efficacious for anybody, except the will of man be joined with it. Why, my brethren, if we were only so far atoned for by the death of Christ that any one of us might afterward save himself, Christ's atonement were not worth a farthing, for there is no man of us can save himself—no, not under the gospel; for if I am to be saved by faith, if that faith is to be my own act, unassisted by the Holy Spirit, I am as unable to save myself by faith as to save myself by good works. And after all, though men call this a limited atonement, it is as effectual as their own fallacious and rotten redemptions can pretend to be. But do you know the limit of it? Christ hath bought a "multitude that no man can number." The limit of it is just this: *He hath died for sinners;* whoever in this congregation inwardly and sorrowfully knows himself to be a sinner, Christ died for him; whoever seeks Christ, shall know Christ died for him; for our sense of need of Christ, and our seeking after Christ, are infallible proofs that Christ died for us. And, mark, here is something substantial. The Arminian says Christ died for him; and then, poor man, he has but small consolation therefrom, for he says, "Ah! Christ died for me; that does not prove much. It only proves I may be saved if I mind what I am after. I may perhaps forget myself; I may run into sin and I may perish. Christ has done a good deal for me, but not quite enough, unless I do something." But the man who receives the Bible as it is, he says, "Christ died for me, then my eternal life is sure. I know," says he, "that Christ can not be punished in a man's stead, and the man be punished afterwards. No," says he, "I believe in a just God, and if God be just, he will not punish Christ first, and then punish men afterwards. No; my Saviour died, and now I am free from every demand of God's vengeance, and I can walk through this world secure; no thunderbolt can smite me, and I can die absolutely certain that for me there is no flame of hell, and no pit digged; for Christ, my ransom, suffered in my stead, and, therefore, am I clean delivered. Oh! glorious doctrine! I would wish to die preaching it! What better testimony can we bear to the love and faithfulness of God than the testimony of a substitution eminently satisfactory for all them that believe on Christ? I will here quote the testimony of that pre-eminently profound divine, Dr. John Owen:—"Redemption is the freeing of a man from misery by the intervention of a ransom. Now, when a ransom is paid for the liberty of a prisoner, does not justice demand that he should have and enjoy the liberty so purchased for him by a valuable consideration? If I should pay a thousand pounds for a man's deliverance from bondage to him that retains him, who hath power to set him free, and is contented with the price I give, were it not injurious to me and the poor prisoner that his deliverance be not accomplished? Can it possibly be conceived that there should be a redemption of men, and those men not redeemed? That a price should be paid and the ransom not consummated? Yet all this must be made true, and innumerable other absurdities, if universal redemption be asserted. A price is paid for all, yet few delivered; the redemption of all consummated, yet few of them redeemed; the judge satisfied, the jailer conquered, and yet the prisoners inthralled! Doubtless 'universal,' and 'redemption,' where the greatest part of men perish, are as irreconcilable as 'Roman' and 'Catholic.' If there be a universal redemption of all, then all men are redeemed. If they are redeemed, then are they delivered from all misery, virtually or actually, whereunto they were inthralled, and that by the intervention of a ransom. Why, then, are not all saved? In a word, the redemption wrought by Christ being the full deliverance of the persons redeemed from all misery, wherein they were inwrapped, by the price of his blood, it can not possibly be conceived to be universal unless all be saved: so that the opinion of the Universalists is unsuitable to redemption."

I pause once more; for I hear some timid soul say—"But, sir, I am afraid I am not elect, and if so, Christ did not die for me." Stop, sir! Are you a sinner? Do you feel it?

Has God, the Holy Spirit, made you feel that you are a lost sinner? Do you want salvation? If you do not want it it is no hardship that it is not provided for you; but if you really feel that you want it, you are God's elect. If you have a desire to be saved, a desire given you by the Holy Spirit, that desire is a token for good. If you have begun believingly to pray for salvation, you have therein a sure evidence that you are saved. Christ was punished for you. And if now you can say,

> "Nothing in my hands I bring,
> Simply to the cross I cling,"

you may be as sure you are God's elect as you are sure of your own existence; for this is the infallible proof of election—a sense of need and a thirst after Christ.

III. And now I have just to conclude by noticing the BLESSED EFFECTS of the Saviour's death. On this I shall be very brief.

The *first* effect of the Saviour's death is, "He shall see his seed." Men shall be saved by Christ. Men have offspring by life; Christ had an offspring by death. Men die and leave their children, and they see not their seed; Christ lives, and every day sees his seed brought into the unity of the faith. One effect of Christ's death is the salvation of multitudes. Mark, not a chance salvation. When Christ died the angel did not say, as some have represented him, "Now by his death many *may* be saved;" the word of prophecy had quenched all "buts" and "peradventures;" "By his righteousness he *shall* justify many." There was not so much as an atom of chance-work in the Saviour's death. Christ knew what he bought when he died; and what he bought he will have—that, and no more, and no less. There is no effect of Christ's death that is left to peradventure. "Shalls" and "wills" made the covenant fast: Christ's bloody death shall effect its solemn purpose. Every heir of grace shall meet around the throne,

> "Shall bless the wonders of his grace,
> And make his glories known."

The *second* effect of Christ's death is, " He shall prolong s days." Yes, bless his name, when he died he did not end s life. He could not long be held a prisoner in the tomb. ' .ie third morning came, and the conqueror, rising from his sl.(p burst the iron bonds of death, and came forth from his prison-house, no more to die. He waited his forty days, and then, with shouts of sacred song, he " led captivity captive, and ascended up on high." " In that he died he died unto sin once ; but in that he liveth he liveth unto God,'' no more to die.

> " Now by his Father's side he sits,
> And there triumphant reigns,"

the conqueror over death and hell.

And, *last* of all, by Christ's death the Father's good pleasure was effected and prospered. God's good pleasure is, that that this world shall one day be totally redeemed from sin ; God's good pleasure is, that this poor planet, so long swathed in darkness, shall soon shine out in brightness, like a new-born sun. Christ's death hath done it. The stream that flowed from his side on Calvary shall cleanse the world from all its blackness. That hour of mid-day darkness was the rising of a new sun of righteousness, which shall never cease to shine upon the earth. Yes, the hour is coming when swords and spears shall be forgotten things—when the harness of war and the pageantry of pomp shall all be laid aside for the food of the worm or the contemplation of the curious. The hour approacheth when old Rome shall shake upon her seven hills, when Mahommed's crescent shall wane to wax no more, when all the gods of the heathens shall lose their thrones and be cast out to the moles and the bats ; and then, when from the equator to the poles Christ shall be honored, the Lord paramount of earth, when from land to land, from the river even to the ends of the earth, one King shall reign, one shout shall be raised, " Hallelujah, hallelujah, the Lord God Omnipotent reigneth." Then, my brethren, shall it be seen what Christ's death has accomplished, for " the pleasure of the Lord shall prosper in his hand."

SERMON XIV

A CALL TO THE UNCONVERTED

" For as many as are of the works of the law are under the curse: for it is written, Cursed is every one that continueth not in all things which are written in the book of the law to do them."—GALATIANS iii. 10

My hearer, art thou a believer, or no? for, according to thine answer to that question, must be the style in which I shall address thee to-night. I would ask thee as a great favor to thine own soul, this evening to divest thyself of the thought that thou art sitting in a chapel, and hearing a minister who is preaching to a large congregation. Think thou art sitting in thine own house, in thine own chair, and think that I am standing by thee, with thy hand in mine, and am speaking personally to thee, and to thee alone; for that is how I desire to preach this night to each of my hearers—one by one. I want thee, then, in the sight of God, to answer me this all-important and solemn question before I begin—Art thou in Christ, or art thou not? Hast thou fled for refuge to him who is the only hope for sinners? or art thou yet a stranger to the commonwealth of Israel, ignorant of God, and of his holy Gospel? Come—be honest with thine own heart, and let thy conscience say yes, or no, for one of these two things thou art to-night—thou art either under the wrath of God, or thou art delivered from it. Thou art to-night either an heir of wrath, or an inheritor of the kingdom of grace. Which of these two? Make no " ifs" or " ahs" in your answer Answer straight forward to thine own soul; and if there be any doubt whatever about it, I beseech thee rest not till that doubt be resolved. Do not take advantage of that doubt to thyself, but rather take a disadvantage from it. Depend upon it, thou art more likely to be wrong than thou art to be right;

and now put thyself in the scale, and if thou dost not kick the beam entirely, but if thou hangest between the two, and thou sayest, "I know not which," better that thou shouldst decide for the worst, though it should grieve thyself, than that thou shouldst decide for the better, and be deceived, and so go on presumptuously until the pit of hell shall wake thee from thy self-deception. Canst thou, then, with one hand upon God's holy word, and the other upon thine own heart, lift thine eye to heaven, and say, "One thing I know, that whereas I was blind, now I see; I know that I have passed from death unto life; I am not now what I once was; 'I the chief of sinners am, but Jesus died for me.' And if I be not awfully deceived, I am this night "A sinner saved by blood, a monument of grace?'" My brother, God speed you; the blessing of the Most High be with you. My text has no thunders in it for you. Instead of this verse, turn to the 13th, and there read your inheritance—"Christ hath redeemed us from the curse of the law, being made a curse for us: for it is written, Cursed is every one that hangetn on a tree." So Christ was cursed in the stead of you, and you are secure, if you are truly converted, and really a regenerated child of God

But my hearer, I am solemnly convinced that a large proportion of this assembly dare not say so; and thou to-night (for I am speaking personally to thee), remember that thou art one of those who dare not say this, for thou art a stranger to the grace of God. Thou durst not lie before God, and thine own conscience, therefore thou dost honestly say, "I know I was never regenerated; I am now what I always was, and that is the most I can say." Now, with you I have to deal, and I charge you by him who shall judge the quick and the dead, before whom you and I must soon appear, listen to the words I speak, for they may be the last warning you shall ever hear, and I charge my own soul also, be thou faithful to these dying men, lest haply on thy skirts at last should be found the blood of souls, and thou thyself shouldst be a castaway. O God, make us faithful this night and give the hearing ear, and the retentive memory, and the conscience touched by the Spirit, for Jesus' sake.

First, to-night we shall *try the prisoner ;* secondly, we shall *declare his sentence ;* and thirdly, if we find him confessing and penitent, we shall *proclaim his deliverance ;* but not unless we find him so.

I. First, then, we are about to TRY THE PRISONER.

The text says—" Cursed is every one that continueth not in all things which are written in the book of the law to do them." Unconverted man, are you guilty, or not guilty ? Have you continued " in all things that are written in the book of the law to do them ?" Methinks you will not dare to plead, " Not guilty." But I will suppose for one moment that you are bold enough to do so. So, then, sir, you mean to assert that you have continued " in all things which are written in the book of the law." Surely the very reading of the law would be enough to convince thee that thou art in error. Dost thou know what the law is ? Why, I will give thee what I may call the outside of it, but remember that within it there is a broader spirit than the mere words. Hear thou these words of the law—" *Thou shalt have no other gods before me.*" What ! hast thou never loved anything better than God ? Hast thou never made a god of thy belly, or of thy business, or of thy family, or of thine own person ? Oh ! surely thou durst not say thou art guiltless here. " *Thou shalt not make unto thee any graven image, or any likeness of anything that is in heaven above, or that is in the earth beneath, or that is in the water under the earth.*" What ! hast thou never in thy life set up anything in the place of God ? If thou hast not, I have, full many a time. And I wot, if conscience would speak truly, it would say, " Man, thou hast been a mammon worshiper, thou hast been a belly worshiper, thou hast bowed down before gold and silver; thou hast cast thyself down before honor, thou hast bowed before pleasure, thou hast made a god of thy drunkenness, a god of thy lust, a god of thy uncleanness, a god of thy pleasures !" Wilt thou dare to say that thou hast never taken *the name of the Lord thy God in vain ?* If thou hast never sworn profanely, yet surely in common conversation thou hast sometimes made use of God's name when thou oughtest not to have done so. Say, hast thou always hallowed that most holy name? Hast thou never called upon God without necessity? Hast thou never read his book with a trifling spirit? Hast thou never heard his gospel without paying reverence to it? Surely thou art guilty here. And as for that fourth commandment, which relates to the keeping of the Sabbath— "*Remember the Sabbath day to keep it holy*,"—hast thou never broken it? Oh, shut thy mouth and plead guilty, for these four commandments were enough to condemn thee! "*Honor thy father and thy mother*." What! wilt thou say thou has kept that? Hast thou never been disobedient in thy youth? Hast thou never kicked against a mother's love, and striven against a father's rebuke? Turn over a page of your history till you come to your childhood; see if you cannot find it written there; ay, and your manhood too may confess that you have not always spoken to your parents as you should, or always treated them with that honor they deserved, and which God commanded you to give unto them. "*Thou shalt not kill;*" you may never have killed any, but have you never been angry? He that is angry with his brother is a murderer; thou art guilty here. "*Thou shalt not commit adultery*." Mayhap thou hast committed unclean things, and art here this very day stained with lust; but if thou hast been never so chaste, I am sure thou hast not been quite guiltless, when the Master says, "He that looketh on a woman to lust after her, hath committed adultery already with her in his heart." Has no lascivious thought crossed thy mind? Has no impurity ever stirred thy imagination? Surely if thou shouldest dare to say so, thou wouldest be brazen-faced with impudence. And hast thou never stolen? "*Thou shalt not steal;*" you are here in the crowd to-night with the product of your theft mayhap, you have done the deed, you have committed robbery; but if you have been never so honest, yet surely there have been times in which you have felt an inclination to defraud your neighbor, and there may have been some petty, or mayhap some gross frauds which you have secretly and silently committed, on which the law of the land could not lay its hand, but which nevertheless, was a breach of this law. And who dare say he has not borne *false witness against his neighbor ?* Have we never repeated a story to our neighbor's disadvantage, which was untrue ? Have we never misconstrued his motives ? Have we never misinterpreted his designs ? And who among us can dare to say that he is guiltless of the last—" *Thou shalt not covet ?*" for we have all desired to have more than God has given us ; and at times our wandering heart has lusted after things which God has not bestowed upon us. Why, to plead not guilty, is to plead your own folly ; for verily, my brethren, the very reading of the law is enough, when blessed by the Spirit, to make us cry, " Guilty, O Lord, guilty."

But one cries, " I shall not plead guilty, for though I am well aware that I have not continued ' in all things which are written in the book of the law,' yet I have done the best I could." That is a lie—before God a falsehood. You have not ! You have not done the best you could. There have been many occasions upon which you might have done better. Will that young man dare to tell me that he is doing the best he can *now ?* that he cannot refrain from laughter in the house of God ? It may be possible that it is hard for him to do so, but it is just possible he could, if he pleased, refrain from insulting his Maker to his face. Surely we have none of us done the best we could. At every period, at every time, there have been opportunities of escape from temptation. If we had had no freedom to escape from the sin, there might have been some excuse for it ; but there have been turning points in our history when we might have decided for right or for wrong, but when we have chosen the evil and have eschewed the good, and have turned into that path which leadeth unto hell.

" Ah, but," saith another, " I declare, sir, that while I have broken that law, without a doubt, I have been no worse than ny fellow-creatures." And a sorry argument is that, for what availeth it thee ? To be damned in a crowd is no more comfortable than to be damned alone. It is true, thou hast been no worse than thy fellow-creatures, but this will be of very poor service to thee. When the wicked are cast into hell, it will be very little comfort to thee that God shall say, "Depart ye cursed" to a thousand with thee. Remember, God's curse, when it shall sweep a nation into hell, shall be as much felt by every individual of the crowd, as if there were but that one man to be punished. God is not like our earthly judges. If their courts were glutted with prisoners, they might be inclined to pass over many a case lightly; but not so with Jehovah. He is so infinite in his mind, that the abundance of criminals will not seem to be any difficulty with him. He will deal with thee as severely and as justly as if there were ne'er another sinner in all the world. And pray, what hast thou to do with other men's sins? Thou art not responsible for them. God made thee to stand or fall by thyself. According to thine own deeds thou shalt be judged. The harlot's sin may be grosser than thine, but thou wilt not be condemned for her iniquities. The murderer's guilt may far exceed thy transgressions, but thou wilt not be damned for the murderer. Religion is a thing between God and thine own soul, O man; and therefore, I do beseech thee, do not look upon thy neighbor's, but upon thine own heart.

"Ay, but," cries another, "I have very many times striven to keep the law, and I think I have done so for a little." Hear ye the sentence read again—"Cursed is every one that *continueth* not in all things which are written in the book of the law to do them." Oh! sirs; it is not some hectic flush upon the cheek of consumptive irresolution that God counts to be the health of obedience. It is not some slight obedience for an hour that God will accept at the day of judgment. He saith "continueth;" and unless from my early childhood to the day when my gray hairs descend into the tomb, I shall have continued to be obedient to God, I must be condemned. Unless I have from the first dawn of reason, when I first began to be responsible, obediently served God, until, like a shock of corn, I am gathered into my Master's garner, salvation by works must be impossible to me, and I must (standing on my own footing), be condemned. It is not, I say, some slight obedience that will save the soul. Thou hast not continued " in all things which are written in the book of the law," and therefore thou art condemned.

" But," says another, " there are many things I have not done, but still I have been very virtuous." Poor excuse that, also. Suppose thou hast been virtuous ; suppose thou hast avoided many vices : turn to my text. It is not my word, but God's—turn to it—" *all things*." It does not say " *some things*."—" Cursed is every one that continueth not in *all things* which are written in the book of the law to do them." Now, hast thou performed all virtues ? Hast thou shunned all vices ? Dost thou stand up and plead, " I never was a drunkard ?"—Yet shalt thou be damned, if thou hast been a fornicator. Dost thou reply, " I never was unclean ?" Yet thou hast broken the Sabbath. Dost thou plead guiltless of that charge ? Dost thou declare thou hast never broken the Sabbath ? Thou hast taken God's name in vain, hast thou not ? Somewhere or other God's law can smite thee. It is certain (let thy conscience now speak and affirm what I assert)—it is certain thou hast not continued " in *all things* which are written in the book of the law." Nay, more, I do not believe thou hast even continued in any one commandment of God to the full, for the commandment is exceeding broad. It is not the overt act, merely, that will damn a man ; it is the thought, the imagination, the conception of sin, that is sufficient to ruin a soul. Remember, my dear hearers, I am speaking now God's own word, not a harsh doctrine of my own. If you had never committed one single act of sin, yet the thought of sin, the imagination of it would be enough to sweep your soul to hell for ever. If you had been born in a cell, and had never been able to come out into the world, either to commit acts of lasciviousness, murder, or robbery, yet the thought of evil in that lone cell might be enough to cast your soul for ever from the face of God. Oh ! there is no man here that can hope to escape. We must every one of us bow our heads before God, and cry, " Guilty, Lord, guilty—every one of as guilty—' Cursed is *every one* that continueth not in *all things* which are written in the book of the law to do them.' " When I look into thy face, O law, my spirit shudders. When I hear thy thunders, my heart is melted like wax in the midst of my bowels. How can I endure thee? If I am to be tried at last for my life, surely I shall need no judge, for I shall be mine own swift accuser, and my conscience shall be a witness to condemn.

I think I need not enlarge further on this point. O thou that art out of Christ, and without God, dost thou not stand condemned before him? Off with all thy masks, and away with all excuses; let every one of us turn our idle pretences to the wind. Unless we have the blood and righteousness of Jesus Christ to cover us, we must every one of us acknowledge that this sentence shuts the gates of heaven against us, and only prepares us for the flames of perdition.

II. Thus have I singled out the charater, and he is found guilty; now I have TO DECLARE THE SENTENCE.

God's ministers love not such work as this. I would rather stand in this pulpit and preach twenty sermons on the love of Jesus, than one like this. It is very seldom that I meddle with the theme, because I do not know that it is often necessary; but I feel that if these things were kept altogether in the background, and the law were not preached, the Master would not own the gospel; for he will have both preached in their measure, and each must have its proper prominence. Now, therefore, hear me whilst I sorrowfully tell you what is the sentence passed upon all of you who this night are out of Christ. Sinner, thou art cursed to-night. *Thou art cursed*, not by some wizard whose fancied spell can only frighten the ignorant. Thou art cursed—not cursed by some earthly monarch who could turn his troops against thee, and swallow up thy house and thy patrimony quick. Cursed! Oh! what a thing a curse is anyhow! What an awful thing is the curse of a father. We have heard of fathers, driven to madness by the undutiful and ungracious conduct of their children, who have lifted their hands to heaven, and have implored a curse, a withering curse upon their children. We can not excuse the parent's mad and rash act. God forbid we should exempt him from sin; but oh, a father's curse must be awful. I can not think what it must be to be cursed by him that did beget me. Sure, it would put out the sunlight of my history for ever, if it were deserved. But to be cursed of God—I have no words with which to tell what that must be. "Oh, no," you say, "that is a thing of the future; we do not care about the curse of God; it does not fall upon us now." Nay, soul, but it does. The wrath of God *abideth* on you even now. You have not yet come to know the fullness of that curse, but you are cursed this very hour. You are not yet in hell; not yet has God been pleased to shut up the bowels of his compassion, and cast you for ever from his presence; but notwithstanding all that, you are cursed. Turn to the passage in the book of Deuteronomy, and see how the curse is a present thing upon the sinner.

In the 28th chapter of Deuteronomy, at the 15th verse, we read all this as the sentence of the sinner: "Cursed shalt thou be in the city"—where you carry on your business God will curse you. "Cursed shalt thou be in the fields"—where you take your recreation; where you walk abroad, there shall the curse reach you. "Cursed shall be thy basket and thy store. Cursed shall be the fruit of thy body, and the fruit of thy land, the increase of thy kine, and the flocks of thy sheep. Cursed shalt thou be when thou comest in, and cursed shalt thou be when thou goest out." There are some men upon whom this curse is very visible. Whatever they do is cursed. They get riches, but there is God's curse with the riches. I would not have some men's gold for all the stars, though they were gold: and if I might have all the wealth of the world, if I must have the miser's greed with it, I would rather be poor than have it. There are some men who are visibly cursed. Don't you see the drunkard? He is cursed, let him go where he may. When he goes into his house, his little children run up stairs to bed, for they are afraid to see their own father; and when they grow a little older, they begin to drink just as he did, and they will stand and imitate him; and they too will begin to swear, so that he is cursed in the fruit of his body. He thought it was not so bad for him to be drunk and to swear; but O what a pang shoots through the father's conscience, if he has a conscience at all, when he sees his child following his footsteps. Drunkenness brings such a curse upon a man, that he can not enjoy what he eats. He is cursed in his basket, cursed in his store. And truly, though one vice may seem to develop the curse more than others, all sin brings the curse, though we can not always see it. O! thou that art out of God, and out of Christ, and a stranger to Jesus, thou art cursed where thou sittest, cursed where thou standest; cursed is the bed thou liest on; cursed is the bread thou eatest; cursed is the air thou breathest. All is cursed to thee. Go where thou mayest, thou art a cursed man. Ah! that is a fearful thought. O! there are some of you that are cursed to-night. O, that a man should say that of his brethren! but we must say it, or be unfaithful to your poor dying souls. O! would to God that some poor soul in this place would say, " Then I am cursed to-night; I am cursed of God, and cursed of his holy angels—cursed! cursed! cursed!—for I am under the law." I do think, God the Spirit blessing it, it wants nothing more to slay our carelessness than that one word—" cursed!" " Cursed is every one that continueth not in all things which are written in the book of the law to do them."

But now, my hearer, thou that art in this state, impenitent and unbelieving, I have more work to do before I close. Remember, the curse that men have in this life is as nothing compared with the curse that is to come upon them hereafter. In a few short years, you and I must die. Come, friend, I will talk to you personally again—young man, we shall soon grow old, or, perhaps, we shall die before that time, and we shall lie upon our bed—the last bed upon which we shall ever sleep—we shall wake from our last slumber to hear the doleful tidings that there is no hope; the physician will feel our pulse, and solemnly assure our relatives that it is all over! And we shall lie in that still room, where all is hushed except the ticking of the clock, and the weeping of our wife and children; and we must die. O! how solemn will it be that hour when we must struggle with that enemy, Death! The death-rattle is in our throat—we can scarce articulate— we try to speak; the death-glaze is on the eye: Death hath put his fingers on those windows of the body, and shut out the light for ever; the hands well-nigh refuse to lift them selves, and there we are, close on the borders of the grave! Ah! that moment, when the Spirit sees its destiny; that moment, of all moments the most solemn, when the soul looks through the bars of its cage, upon the world to come! No, I can not tell you how the spirit feels, if it be an ungodly spirit, when it sees a fiery throne of judgment, and hears the thunders of Almighty wrath, while there is but a moment between it and hell. I can not picture to you what must be the fright which men will feel, when they realize what they often heard of! Ah! it is a fine thing for you to laugh at me to-night. When you go away, it will be a very fine thing to crack a joke concerning what the preacher said; to talk to one another, and make merry with all this. But when you are lying on your death-bed, you will not laugh. Now, the curtain is drawn, you can not see the things of the future, it s a very fine thing to be merry. When God has removed that curtain, and you learn the solemn reality, you will not find it in your hearts to trifle. Ahab, on his throne laughed at Micaiah. You never read that Ahab laughed at Micaiah when the arrow was sticking between the joints of his harness. In Noah's time, they laughed at the old man; they called him a grey-headed fool, I doubt not, because he told them that God was about to destroy the earth with a flood. But ah! ye scorners, ye did not laugh in that day when the cataracts were falling from heaven, and when God had unloosed the doors of the great deep, and bidden all the hidden waters leap upon the surface; then ye knew that Noah was right. And when ye come to die, mayhap ye will not laugh at me. You will say, when you lie there, "I remember such-and-such a night I strolled into Park street; I heard a man talk very solemnly; I thought at the time I did not like it, but I knew he was in earnest, I am quite certain that he meant good for me; oh, that I had hearkened to his advice; oh, that I had regarded his words! What would I give to hear him again!" Ah! it was not long ago that a man who had laughed and mocked at me full many a time, went down one Sabbath day to Brighton, to spend his day in the excursion—he came back that night to die! On Monday morning, when he was dying, who do you suppose he wanted ? He wanted Mr. Spurgeon! the man he had laughed at always; he wanted him to come and tell him the way to heaven, and point him to the Saviour. And although I was glad enough to go, it was doleful work to talk to a man who had just been Sabbath-breaking, spending his time in the service of Satan, and had come home to die. And die he did, without a Bible in his house, without having one prayer offered for him except that prayer which I alone did offer at his bedside. Ah! it is strange how the sight of a death-bed may be blessed to the stimulating of our zeal. I stood some year or so ago, by the bedside of a poor boy, about sixteen years of age, who had been drinking himself to death, in a drinking bout, about a week before, and when I talked to him about sin and right eousness, and judgmeet to come, I knew he trembled, and I thought that he had laid hold on Jesus. When I came down from those stairs, after praying for him many a time, and try-ing to point him to Jesus, and having but a faint hope of his ultimate salvation, I thought to myself, O God! I would that I might preach every hour, and every moment of the day, the unsearchable riches of Christ; for what an awful thing it is to die without a Saviour. And then, I thought how many a time I had stood in the pulpit, and had not preached in earnest as I ought to have done; how I have coldly told out the tale of the Saviour, when I ought to have wept very showers of tears, in overwhelming emotion. I have gone to my bed full many a season, and have wept myself to sleep, because I have not preached as I have desired, and it will be even so to-night. But, oh, the wrath to come! the wrath to come! the wrath to come!

My hearers, the matters I now talk of are no dreams, no frauds, no whims, no old wives' stories. These are realities, and you will soon know them. O sinner, thou that hast not continued in all things written in the book of the law; thou that hast no Christ; the day is coming when these things will stand before thee, as dread, solemn, real things. And then; ah! then; ah! then; ah! then what wilt thou do ?—"**And** after death *the judgment*."—O, can ye picture—

"The pomp of that tremendous day,
When Christ with clouds shall come."

I think I see that terrible day. The bell of time has tolled the last day. Now comes the funeral of damned souls. Your body has just started up from the grave, and you unwind your cerements, and you look up. What is that I see? O! what is that I hear? I hear one dread, tremendous blast, that shakes the pillars of heaven, and makes the firmament reel with affright; the trump, the trump, the trump of the arch-angel shakes creation's utmost bound. You look and wonder. Suddenly a voice is heard, and shrieks from some, and songs from others—he comes—he comes—he comes; and every eye must see him. There he is; the throne is set upon a cloud, which is white as alabaster. There he sits. 'Tis He, the Man that died on Calvary—I see his pierced hands—but ah, how changed! No thorn-crown now. He stood at Pilate's bar, but now the whole earth must stand at his bar. But hark! the trumpet sounds again: the Judge opens the book, there is silence in heaven, a solemn silence: the universe is still. "Gather mine elect together, and my redeemed from the four winds of heaven." Swiftly they are gathered. As with a lightning flash, the angel's wing divides the crowd. Here are the righteous all in-gathered; and sinner, there art thou on the left hand, left out, left to abide the burning sentence of eternal wrath.

Hark! the harps of heaven play sweet melodies; but to you they bring no joy, though the angels are repeating the Saviour's welcome to his saints. "Come ye blessed, inherit the kingdom prepared for you from the foundations of the world." You have had that moment's respite, and now his face is gathering clouds of wrath, the thunder is on his brow; he looks on you that have despised him, you that scoffed his grace, that scorned his mercy, you that broke his Sabbath, you that mocked his cross, you that would not have him to reign over you; and with a voice louder than ten thousand thunders, he cries, "Depart, ye cursed." And then——No, I will not follow you. I will not tell of quenchless flames: I will not talk of miseries of the body, and tortures for the spirit. But hell is terrible; damnation is doleful. Oh, escape! escape! Escape, lest haply, being where you are, you should have to learn what the horrors of eternity must mean, in the gulf of everlasting perdition. "Cursed is the man that hath not continued in *all things* that are written in the book of the law to do them."

III. DELIVERANCE PROCLAIMED.

"You have condemned us all," cries one. Yes, but not I —God has done it. Are you condemned? Do you feel you are to-night? Come, again, let me take thee by the hand, my brother: yes, I can look round upon the whole of this assembly, and I can say, there is not one now in this place whom I do not love as a brother. If I speak severely unto any of you, it is that you may know the right. My heart, and my whole spirit are stirred for you. My harshest words are far more full of love than the smooth words of soft-speaking ministers, who say, "Peace, peace," where there is no peace. Do you think it is any pleasure to me to preach like this? Oh? I had far rather be preaching of Jesus; his sweet, his glorious person, and his all-sufficient righteousness. Now, come, we will have a sweet word before we have done. Do you feel you are condemned? Do you say, "O God, I confess thou wouldest be just, if thou shouldest do all this to me?" Dost thou feel thou canst never be saved by thine own works, but that thou art utterly condemned through sin? Dost thou hate sin? Dost thou sincerely repent? Then, let me tell thee how thou mayest escape.

Men and brethren, Jesus Christ, of the seed of David, was crucified, dead, and buried; he is now risen, and he sitteth on the right hand of God, where he also maketh intercession for us. He came into this world to save sinners, by his death. He saw that poor sinners were cursed: he took the curse on his own shoulders, and he delivered us from it. Now, if God has cursed Christ for any man, he will not curse that man again. You ask me, then, "Was Christ cursed for me?" Answer me this question, and I will tell you—Has God the Spirit taught you that you are accursed? Has he made you feel the bitterness of sin? Has he made you cry, "Lord, have mercy upon me, a sinner?" Then, my dear friend, Christ was cursed for you; and you are not cursed. You are not cursed now. Christ was cursed for you. Be of good cheer; if Christ was cursed for you, you can not be cursed again "Oh!" says one, "if I could but think he was cursed for me." Do you see him bleeding on the tree? Do you see his hands and feet all dripping gore? Look unto him, poor sinner. Look no longer at thyself, nor at thy sin; look unto him, and be saved. All he asks thee to do is to look, and even that he will help thee to do. Come to him, trust him, believe on him. God the Holy Spirit has taught you that you are a condemned sinner. Now, I beseech you, hear this word and believe it: "This is a faithful saying, and worthy of all acceptation, that Jesus Christ came into the world to save sinners." Oh, can you say, "I believe this Word—it is true—blessed be his dear name; it is true to me, for whatever I may not be, I know that I am a sinner; the sermon of this night convinces me of that, if there were nothing else; and, good Lord, thou knowest when I say I am a sinner, I do not mean what I used to mean by that word. I mean that I am a real sinner. I mean that if thou shouldest damn me, I deserve it; if thou shouldest cast me from thy presence forever, it is only what I have merited richly. O my Lord I am a sinner; I am a hopeless sinner, unless thou savest me; I am a helpless sinner, unless thou dost deliver me. I have no hope in my self-righteousness; and Lord, I bless thy name, there is one thing else, I am a sorrowful sinner, for sin grieves me; I can not rest, I am troubled. Oh, if I could get rid of sin, I would be holy, even as God is holy. Lord, I believe." But I hear an objector cry out, "What, sir, believe that Christ died for me simply because I am a sinner!" Yes; even so. "No, sir; but if I had a little righteousness; if I could pray well, I should then think Christ died for me." No, that would not be faith at all, that would be self-confidence. Faith believes in Christ when it sees sin to be black, and trusts in him to remove it all. Now, poor sinner, with all thy sin about thee, take this promise in thy hands, go home to-night, or if thou canst, do it before thou gettest home—go home, I say, up stairs, alone, down by the bed-side, and pour out thine heart, " O Lord, it is all true that that man said ; I am condemned, and Lord, I deserve it. O Lord, I have tried to be better, and I have done nothing with it all, but have only grown worse. O Lord, I have slighted thy grace, I have despised thy gospel : I wonder thou hast not damned me years ago ; Lord, I marvel at myself, that thou sufferest such a base wretch as I am to live at all. I have despised a mother's teaching, I have forgotten a father's prayers. Lord, I have forgotten thee ; I have broken thy Sabbath, taken thy name in vain. I have done everything that is wrong ; and if thou dost condemn me, what can I say ? Lord, I am dumb before thy presence. I have nothing to plead. But Lord, I come to tell thee to-night, thou hast said in the Word of God, " Him that cometh unto me, I will in no wise cast out." Lord, I come : my only plea is that thou hast said, ' This is a faithful saying, and worthy of all acceptation, that Jesus Christ came into the world to save sinners.' Lord, I am a sinner ; he came to save *me ;* I trust in it—sink or swim—Lord, this is my only hope : I cast away every other, and hate myself to think I ever should have had any other. Lord, I rely on Jesus only. Do but save me, and though I can not hope by my future life to blot out my past sin, O Lord, I will ask of thee to give me a new heart and a right spirit, that from this time forth even for ever I may run in the way of thy commandments : for, Lord, I desire nothing so much as to be thy child. Thou knowest, O Lord, I would give all, if thou wouldest but love me ; and I am encouraged to think that thou dost love me ; for my heart feels so. I am guilty, but I should never have known that I was guilty, if thou hadst not taught it to me. I am vile, but I never should have known my vileness, unless thou hadst revealed it. Surely, thou wilt not destroy me, O God, after having taught me this. If thou dost, thou art just, but,

> ' Save a trembling sinner, Lord,
> Whose hopes still hovering round thy Word,
> Would light on some sweet promise there ;
> Some sure support against despair."

If you can not pray such a long prayer as that, I tell you what to go home and say. Say this, "Lord Jesus, I know I am nothing at all; be thou my precious all in all."

Oh, I trust in God there will be some to-night that will be able to pray like that, and if it be so, ring, the bells of heaven; sing, ye seraphim; shout, ye redeemed; for the Lord hath done it, and glory be unto his name, for ever and ever.

SERMON XV

THE WARNING NEGLECTED

'He heard the sound of the trumpet, and took not warning; his blood shall be upon him.—EZEKIEL, xxxiii. 5

IN all worldly things, men are always enough awake to understand their own interests. There is scarce a merchant who reads the paper, who does not read it in some way or other, with a view to his own personal concerns. If he finds that by the rise or fall of the markets, he will be either a gainer or loser, that part of the day's news will be the most important to him. In politics, in everything, in fact, that concerns temporal affairs, personal interest usually leads the van. Men will always be looking out for themselves, and personal and home interests will generally engross the major part of their thoughts. But in religion, it is otherwise. In religion men love far rather to believe abstract doctrines, and to talk of general truths, than the searching inquiries which examine their own personal interest in it. You will hear many men admire the preacher who deals in generalities, but when he comes to press home searching questions, by-and-by they are offended. If we stand and declare general facts, such as the universal sinnership of mankind, or the need of a Saviour, they will give an assent to our doctrine, and possibly they may retire greatly delighted with the discourse, because it has not affected them; but how often will our audience gnash their teeth, and go away in a rage, because, like the Pharisees with Jesus, they perceive, concerning a faithful minister, that he spoke of *them*. And yet, my brethren, how foolish this is. If in all other matters we like personalities—if in everything else we look to our own concerns, how much more should we do so in religion? for, surely, every man must give an account for himself, at the day of judgment We must die alone; we must rise at the day of resurrection one by one, and each one for himself must appear before the bar of God; and each one must either have said to him, as an individual, "Come ye blessed;" or else, he must be appalled with the thundering sentence, "Depart, ye cursed." If there were such a thing as national salvation; if it could be possible that we could be saved in the gross and in the bulk, that so, like the sheaves of corn, the few weeds that may grow with the stubble, would be gathered in for the sake of the wheat, then, indeed, it might not be so foolish for us to neglect our own personal interests; but if the sheep must, every one of them, pass under the hand of him that telleth them, if every man must stand in his own person before God, to be tried for his own acts—by everything that is rational, by everything that conscience would dictate, and self-interest would command, let us each of us look to our own selves, that we be not deceived, and that we find not ourselves, at last, miserably cast away.

Now, this morning, by God's help, I shall labor to be personal, and whilst I pray for the rich assistance of the Divine Spirit, I will also ask one thing of each person here present— I would ask of every Christian that he would lift up a prayer to God, that the service may be blessed; and I ask of every other person that he will please to understand that I am preaching *to him,* and *at him ;* and if there be anything that is personal and pertinent to his own case, I beseech him, as for life and death, to let it have its full weight with him, and not begin to think of his neighbor, to whom perhaps it may be even more pertinent, but whose business certainly does not concern him.

The text is a solemn one—"He heard the sound of the trumpet, and took not warning: his blood shall be upon him." The first head is this—*the warning was all that could be desired*—" he heard the sound of the trumpet." Secondly, *the excuses for not attending to the startling warning are all of them both frivolous and wicked:* and therefore, in the third place, *the consequences of inattention must be terrible, because man's blood must then be on his own head.*

I. First, then, THE WARNING WAS ALL THAT COULD BE

DESIRED. When in time of war an army is attacked in the night, and cut off and destroyed whilst asleep, if it were impossible for them to be aware of the attack, and if they had made all diligence in placing their sentinels, but nevertheless the foe were so wary as to destroy them, we should weep; we should attach no blame to any one, but should deeply regret, and should give to that host our fullest pity. But if, on the other hand, they had posted their sentinels, and the sentinels were wide awake, and gave to the sleepy soldiers every warning that could be desired, but nevertheless, the army were cut off, although we might for common humanity regret the loss thereof, yet at the same time we should be obliged to say, if they were foolish enough to sleep when the sentinels had warned them; if they folded their arms in presumptuous sloth, after they had sufficient and timely notice of the progress of their blood-thirsty enemy, then in their dying, we cannot pity them: their blood must rest upon their own heads. So, it is with you. If men perish under an unfaithful ministry, and have not been sufficiently warned to escape from the wrath to come, the Christian may pity them, yea, and methinks, even when they stand before the bar of God, although the fact of their not having been warned will not fully excuse them, yet it will go far to diminish their eternal miseries, which otherwise might have fallen upon their heads; for we know it is more tolerable for unwarned Tyre and Sidon in the day of judgment, than it is for any city, or any nation that has had the Gospel proclaimed in its ears. My brethren, if on the other hand, we have been warned, if our ministers have been faithful, if they have aroused our conscience, and have constantly and earnestly called our attention to the fact of the wrath to come, if we have not attended to their message, if we have despised the voice of God, if we have turned a deaf ear to their earnest exhortation, if we perish, we shall die warned—die under the sound of the Gospel, and our damnation must be an unpitied one, for our blood must fall upon our own heads. Permit me then, to try, if I can, to enlarge upon this thought, that the warning has been, in the case of many of you, all that could have been needed.

In the first place, the warnings of the ministry have been to most of you warnings that have been *heard*—"He heard the sound of the trumpet." In far off lands, the trumpet sound of warning is not heard. Alas! there are myriads of our fellow-creatures who have never been warned by God's embassadors, who know not that wrath abideth on them, and who do not yet understand the only way and method of salvation In your case it is very different. You have heard the Word of God preached to you. You cannot say, when you come before God, "Lord, I knew no better." There is not a man or a woman within this place who will dare then to plead ignorance. And moreover, you have not only heard with your ears, but some of you have been obliged to hear it in your consciences. I have before me many of my hearers whom I have had the pleasure of seeing now for some years. It has not been once, or twice, but many a time, I have seen the tear guttering their cheeks when I have spoken earnestly, faithfully, and affectionately to you. I have seen your whole soul moved within you; and yet, to my sorrow, you are now what you were: your goodness has been as the early cloud, and as the morning dew that passeth away. You have heard the Gospel. You wept under it, and you loved the sound of it, and you came again, and wept again, and many marveled that you did weep, but the greatest marvel was, that after having wept so well, you wiped away your tears so easily Oh, yes, God is my witness, there are some of you not an inch nearer heaven, but ye have sealed your own damnation doubly sure, unless ye repent: for ye have heard the Gospel, ye have despised prophesyings, ye have rejected the counsel of God against yourself; and, therefore, when you shall die, ye must die pitied by your friends, but at the same time with your blood on your own heads.

The trumpet was not only *heard*, but, more than that, *its warning was understood*. When the man, supposed in the text, heard the trumpet, he understood by it that the enemy was at hand, and yet he took not warning. Now, my brethren, in your case, the sound of the Gospel warning has been understood. A thousand faults your minister may have but there is one fault from which he is entirely free, and that is, he is free from all attempts to use fine language in the expression of his thoughts; ye are all my witnesses, that if there be a Saxon word, or a homely phrase, a sentence that is rough and market-like, that will tell you the truth, I always use that first. I can say solemnly, as in the sight of God, that I never went out of my pulpit, except with the firm belief, that whatever might have happened, I was perfectly understood. I had sought, at least, so to gather wise words, that no man might mistake my meaning; gnash his teeth he might, but he could not say, "The preacher was misty and cloudy, talking to me of metaphysics, beyond my comprehension; he has been obliged to say, "Well, I know what he meant, he spoke plainly enough to me." Well, sirs, then if it be so, and if ye have heard warnings that ye could understand, so much the more guilty are ye, if ye are living this day in rejection of them. If I have preached to you in a style above comprehension, then on my head must be your blood, because I ought to have made you understand; but if I come down to men of low estate, and pick even vulgar phrases to suit common people, then if you understood the warning, and if ye then risked it, mark you, my hands are clean of your blood. If ye be damned, I am innocent of your damnation, for I have told you plainly, that except ye repent, ye must perish, and that except ye put your trust in the Lord Jesus Christ, there is for you no hope of salvation.

Again, this trumpet sound was *startling*. The trumpet's sound is ever considered to be the most startling in the world. 'Tis that which shall be used on the resurrection morning to startle the myriads of sleepers, and make them rise from their tombs. Ay, and ye have had a startling ministry. Ye have sat, some of you, under ministers that might have made the devil himself tremble, so earnest have they been; and they have made you tremble sometimes, so much, that you could not sleep. The hair of your head was well nigh moved to stand upright. They spake as though they ne'er might speak again: as dying men to dying men. They spoke as if they had been in hell, and knew the vengeance of the Almighty, and anon, they spoke as if they had entered into the heart of Jesus, and read his love to sinners. They had brows of brass; they knew not how to flinch. They laid your iniquity bare before your face, and with rough language that was unmistakeable, they made you feel that there was a man there who told you all things that ever you did. They so declared it, that you could not help feeling under it. You always retained a veneration for that minister, because you felt that he at least was honest with you; and you have sometimes thought that you would even go and hear him again, because there at least your soul was moved, and you were made to hear the truth. Yes, you have had a startling ministry, some of you. Then, sirs, if ye have heard the cry of fire, if ye are burned in your beds, your charred ashes shall not accuse me. If I have warned you that he that believeth not must be damned, if you are damned, your miserable souls shall not accuse me. If I have startled you sometimes from your slumbers, and made your balls and your pleasure parties uneasy, because I have sometimes warned you of these things, then sirs, if after all you put away these warnings, and you reject these counsels, you will be obliged to say, " My blood is on my own head."

In many of your cases the warning has been *very frequent*. If the man heard the trumpet sound once and did not regard it, possibly we might excuse him; but how many of my audience have heard the trumpet sound of the gospel very frequently. There you are, young man. You have had many years of a pious mother's teaching, many years of a pious minister's exhortations. Wagon loads of sermons have been exhausted upon you. You have had many sharp providences, many terrible sicknesses. Often when the death-bell has tolled for your friend, your conscience has been aroused. To you warnings are not unusual things; they are very common. Oh! my hearers, if a man should hear the gospel but once, his blood would be upon his own head for rejecting it; but of how much sorer punishment shall you be thought worthy who have heard it many and many a time. Ah! I may well weep, when I think how many sermons you have listened to,

many of you, how many times you have been put to the heart
A hundred times every year you have gone up to the house
of God, and far oftener than that, and you have just added a
hundred billets to the eternal pile. A hundred times the
trumpet has sounded in your ears, and a hundred times you
have turned away to sin again, to despise Christ, to neglect
your eternal interests, and to pursue the pleasures and the
concerns of this world. Oh! how mad is this, how mad
Oh, sirs, if a man had but once poured out his heart before
you concerning your eternal interests, and if he had spoken
to you earnestly, and you had rejected his message, then, even
then, ye had been guilty. But what shall we say to you
upon whom the shafts of the Almighty have been exhausted?
Oh, what shall be done unto this barren ground that hath been
watered with shower after shower, and that hath been quickened with sunshine after sunshine? What shall be done unto
him who being often rebuked, still hardeneth his neck? Shall
he not be suddenly destroyed, and that without remedy, and
shall it not then be said, " His blood lieth at his own door,
his guilt is on his own head?"

And I would just have you recollect one thing more. This
warning that you have had so often has come to you *in time*.
" Ah," said an infidel once, " God never regards man. If there
be a God, he would never take notice of men." Said a Christian minister, who was sitting opposite to him in the carriage,
" The day may come, sir, when you will learn the truth of what
you have just said." " I do not understand your allusion,
sir," said he. " Well, sir, the day may come, when you may
call, and he will refuse; when you may stretch out your hands
and he will not regard you, but as he has said in the book of
Proverbs, so will he do, ' Because I called, and ye refused;
because I stretched out my hands, and no man regarded, I
also will mock at your calamity, I will laugh when your fear
cometh.' " But oh, sirs, your warning has not come too late.
You are not warned on a sick bed, at the eleventh hour, when
there is but a bare possibility of salvation, but you are warned
in time, you are warned to-day, you have been warned for
these many years that are now past. If God should send a

preacher to the damned in hell, that were an unnecessary ad
dition to their misery. Surely, if one could go and preach
the gospel through the fields of Gehenna, and tell them of a
Saviour they had despised, and of a gospel that is now beyond
their reach, that were taunting poor souls with a vain attempt
to increase their unutterable woe; but O my brethren, to
preach the gospel now is to preach in a hopeful period; for
"now is the accepted time: now is the day of salvation."
Warn the boatman before he enters the current, and then,
if he is swept down the rapids, he destroys himself. Warn
the man before he drinks the cup of poison, tell him it is
deadly: and then, if he drinks it, his death lies at his own
door. And so, let us warn you before you depart this life;
let us preach to you while as yet your bones are full of marrow, and the sinews of your joints are not loosed. We have
then warned you in time, and so much the more shall your
guilt be increased, because the warning was timely; it was
frequent, it was earnest, it was appropriate, it was arousing,
it was continually given to you, and yet you sought not to
escape from the wrath to come.

And so even this morning would I say to you, if ye perish,
my skirts are white of your blood; if ye are damned, it is
not for want of calling after, nor for want of praying for, nor
for want of weeping over. Your blood must be on your own
heads; for the warning is all that is needed.

II. And now we come to the second point. MEN MAKE
EXCUSES WHY THEY DO NOT ATTEND TO THE GOSPEL WARNING,
BUT THESE EXCUSES ARE ALL FRIVOLOUS AND WICKED. I will
just go over one or two of the excuses that people make. Some
of them say, "Well, I did not attend to the warning because
I did not believe there was any necessity for it." Ah! You
were told that after death there was a judgment, and you did
not believe there was any necessity that you should be prepared for that judgment. You were told that by the works
of the law there shall no flesh living be justified, and that only
through Christ can sinners be saved; and you did not think
there was any necessity for Christ. Well, sir, you ought to
have thought there was a necessity. You know there was a

necessity in your inner consciousness. You talked very large things when you stood up as an unbeliever, a professed unbeliever: but you know there was a still small voice that while you spake belied your tongue. You are well aware that in the silent watches of the night you have often trembled; in a storm at sea you have been on your knees to pray to a God whom on the land you have laughed at; and when you have been sick nigh unto death, you have said, "Lord, have mercy upon me;" and so you have prayed, that you have believed it after all. But if you did not believe it, you ought to have believed it. There was enough in reason to have taught you that there was an hereafter; the Book of God's revelation was plain enough to have taught it to you, and if you have rejected God's Book, and rejected the voice of reason and of conscience, your blood is on your own head. Your excuse is idle. It is worse than that, it is profane and wicked, and still on your own head be your everlasting torment.

"But," cries another, "I did not like the trumpet. I did not like the Gospel that was preached." Says one, "I did not like certain doctrines in the Bible. I thought the minister preached too harsh doctrines sometimes, I did not agree with the Gospel; I thought the Gospel ought to have been altered, and not to have been just what it was." You did not like the trumpet, did you? Well, but God made the trumpet, God made the Gospel; and inasmuch as ye did not like what God made, it is an idle excuse. What was that to you what the trumpet was, so long as it warned you? And surely, if it had been time of war, and you had heard a trumpet sounded to warn you of the coming of the enemy, you would not have sat still, and said, "now I believe that is a brass trumpet, I would like to have had it made of silver." No, but the sound would have been enough for you, and up you would have been to escape from the danger. And so it must be now with you. It is an idle pretence that you did not like it. You ought to have liked it, for 'God made the Gospel what it is.

But you say, "I did not like the man that blew it." Well, if you did not like one messenger of God, there are many in this city. Could you not find one you did like? You did not like one man's manner; it was too theatrical; you did not like another's: it was too doctrinal; you did not like another's: it was too practical—there are plenty of them, you may take which you do like, but if God has sent the men, and told them how to blow, and if they blow to the best of their ability, it is all in vain for you to reject their warnings, because they do not blow the way you like. Ah, my brethren, we do not find fault with the way a man speaks, if we are in a house that is on fire. If the man calls, "Fire! Fire!" we are not particular what note he takes, we do not think what a harsh voice he has got. You would think any one a fool, who should lie in his bed, to be burned, because he said he did not like the way the man cried, "Fire." Why his business was to have been out of bed and down the stairs at once, as soon as he heard it.

But another says, "I did not like the man himself; I did not like the minister; I did not like the man that blew the trumpet; I could hear him preach very well, but I had a personal dislike to him, and so I did not take any notice of what the trumpet said." Verily, God will say to thee at last, "Thou fool, what hadst thou to do with that man; to his own master he stands or falls; thy business was with thyself." What would you think of a man? A man has fallen overboard from a ship, and when he is drowning, some sailor throws him a rope, and there it is. Well, he says, in the first place, "I do not like that rope; I don't think that rope was made at the best manufactory; there is some tar on it too, I do not like it; and in the next place, I do not like that sailor that threw the rope over, I am sure he is not a kind-hearted man, I do not like the look of him at all;" and then comes a gurgle and a groan, and down he is in the bottom of the sea; and when he was drowned, they said, that it served him right, if he would not lay hold of the rope, but would be making such foolish and absurd objections, when it was a matter of life and death. Then on his own head be his blood. And so shall it be with you at last. You are so busy with criticising the minister, and his style, and his doctrine, that your own soul perishes. Remember you may get into hell by criticism, but you will never criticise your soul out of it. You may there make the most you can of it. You may be there and say, "I did not like the minister, I did not like his manner, I did not like his matter;" but all your dislikings will not get one drop of water to cool your burning tongue, nor serve to mitigate the unalleviated torments of that world of agony.

There are many other people who say, "Ah, well, I did none of those things, but I had a notion that the trumpet sound ought to be blown to everybody else, but not to me." Ah! that is a very common notion. "All men think all men mortal, but themselves," said a good poet; and all men think all men need the Gospel, but not themselves. Let each of us recollect that the Gospel has a message to each one of us. What saith the Gospel to *thee* my hearer? What saith the Word to *thee?* Forget thy neighbors, and ask this question. Doth it condemn *thee?* or doth it assure *thee* of *thy* pardon? for recollect, all thou hast to do in the hearing of the Word, is to hear with thine own ears for thine own soul, and it will be idle for any one to say "I did not think it applied to me," when we know that it is to be preached to every creature under heaven, and therefore there must be something in it for every creature or else it would not be preached to every creature.

Well, says another, "But I was so busy, I had so much to do, that I could not possibly attend to my soul's concerns. What will you say of the man who had so much to do that he could not get out of the burning house, but was burnt to ashes? What will you say of the man that had so much to do, that when he was dying, he had not time to send for a physician? Why, you will say, then he ought not to have so much to do. And if any man in the world has a business which causes him to lose his own soul for want of time, let him lay this question to his heart, "What shall it profit a man, if he gain the whole world, and lose his own soul?" But it is false—it is false—men have got time. It is the want of will, not want of way. You have time, sir, have you not, despite all your business, to spend in pleasure? You have time to read your newspaper—have you no time to read your Bible? You have time to sing a song—have you no time to pray a prayer? Why, you know when farmer Brown met farmer Smith in the market one day, he said to him, "Farmer Smith, I can't think how it is you find time for hunting. Why, man, what with sowing and mowing and reaping and plowing, and all that, my time is so fully occupied on my farm, and I have no time for hunting." "Ah," said he, "Brown, if you liked hunting as much as I do, if you could not find time, you'd make it." And so it is with religion, the reason why men can not find time for it is, because they do not like it well enough. If they liked it, they would find time. And besides, what time does it want? What time does it require? Can I not pray to God over my ledger? Can I not snatch a text at my very breakfast, and think over it all day? May I not even when I am busy in the affairs of the world, be thinking of my soul, and casting myself upon a Redeemer's blood and atonement? It wants no time. There may be some time required some time for my private devotions, and for communion with Christ, but when I grow in grace, I shall think it right to have more and more time, the more I can possibly get, the happier I shall be, and I shall never make the excuse that I have no time.

"Well," says another, "but I thought I had time enough; you do not want me, sir, to be religious in my youth, do you? I am a lad, and may I not have a little frolic and sow my wild oats as well as anybody else?" Well—yes, yes; but at the same time the best place for pleasure that I know of, is where a Christian lives; the finest happiness in all the world is the happiness of a child of God. You may have your pleasures— oh, yes! you shall have them doubled and trebled, if you are a Christian. You shall not have things that worldlings call pleasures, but you shall have some that are a thousand times better. But only look at that sorrowful picture. There, far away in the dark gulf of woe, lies a young man, and he cries, "Ah! I meant to have repented when I was out of my apprenticeship, and I died before my time was up." "Ah!"

says another by his side, "and I thought, whilst I was a journeyman, that when I came to be a master, I would then think of the things of Christ, but I died before I had got money enough to start for myself." And then a merchant behind wails with bitter woe, and says, "Ah! I thought I would be religious when I had got enough to retire on, and live in the country; then I should have time to think of God, when I had got all my children married out, and my concerns settled about me, but here I am shut up in hell; and now what are all my delays worth, and what is all the time I gained for all the paltry pleasures in the world? Now I have lost my soul over them." We experience great vexation if we are unpunctual in many places; but we can not conceive what must be the horror and dismay of men who find themselves too late in the next world! Ah! friends, if I knew there was one here who said, "I shall repent next Wednesday," I would have him feel in a dreadful state till that Wednesday came; for what if he should die? Oh! what if he should die? Would his promise of a Wednesday's repentance save him from a Tuesday damnation?

Ah, these are all idle excuses. Men make not such when their bodily life is concerned. Would God that we were wise, that we would not make such pitiful pretences to apology, when our soul, our own soul, is the matter at stake. If they take not warning, whatever their excuse, their blood must be upon their own head.

III. And now, I come most solemnly to conclude with all the power of earnestness; the warning has been sufficient, the excuse for not attending to it has been proved profane then the last thought is "HIS BLOOD SHALL BE ON HIS OWN HEAD." Briefly thus—he shall perish; he shall perish *certainly*; he shall perish *inexcusably*. He shall *perish*. And what does that mean? There is no human mind, however capacious, that can ever guess the thought of a soul eternally cast away from God. The wrath to come is as inexpressible as the glory that shall be revealed hereafter. Our Saviour labored for words with which to express the horrors of a future state of the ungodly. You remember he talked of worms that die not, and fires that are never quenched, of a pit without a bottom, of weeping, and wailing and gnashing of teeth in the outer darkness.

No preacher was ever so loving as Christ, but no man ever spoke so horribly about hell; and yet even when the Saviour had said his best and said his worst, he had not told us what are the horrors of a future state. Ye have seen sicknesses, ye have heard the shrieks of men and women when their pangs have been upon them. We, at least, have stood by the bed-sides even of some dear to us, and we have seen to what an extent agony may be carried in the human body, but none of us know how much the body is capable of suffering. Certainly the body will have to suffer forever—"He is able to cast both body and soul into hell." We have heard of exquisite torments, but we have never dreamt of any like unto this. Again, we have seen something of the miseries of the soul. Have we never marked the man that we used to know in our childhood who was depressed in spirits. All that ever could be done for him never could evoke a smile from him—never did the light of cheerfulness light up his eye —he was mournfully depressed. Ay, and it was my unhappy lot to live with one who was not only depressed in spirits, but whose mind had gone so far amiss, that it did brood fancies so mournful and dismal, that the very sight of him was enough to turn the sunlight of summer into the very darkness of a dreary winter. He had nothing to say but dark, groaning words. His thoughts always had a sombre appearance about them. It was midnight in his soul—a darkness that might be felt. Have you never seen yourselves what power the mind has over us to make us full of misery? Ah, brethren and sisters, if ye could go to many of our asylums, and to our sick wards—ay, and dying beds, too, you may know what acute anguish the mind may feel. And remember that the mind, as well as the mortal frame, is to endure damnation. Yes, we must not shirk that word, the Scripture saith it, and we must use it. Oh! men and women, except we repent, except we do each of us cry for mercy to him that is able to save, we must perish. All that is meant by that word "hell," must be realized in me, except I be a believer; and so all that is meant by " Depart, ye cursed," must be thine, unless thou dost turn unto God with full purpose of heart.

But again, he that turneth not at the rebuke of the minister shall die, and he shall die *certainly*. This is not a matter of perhaps or chance. The things we preach, and that are taught in Scripture, are matters of solemn certainty. It may be that death is that bourne from which no traveller returns, but it is not true that we know nothing of it. It is as certain as that there are men, and a world in which they live, that there is another world to come, and that if they die impenitent, that world will be to them one of misery. And mark you—there is no chance of escape, die without Christ, and there is no gate out of which you can escape—forever, oh, forever lost, and not one hope of mercy—cast away, and not one outlet for escape, not one solitary chance of ransom. Oh, if there were hope that in the world to come, men might escape, we need not be so earnest; but since once lost, lost for aye—once cast away, cast away without hope, without any prospect of a hope, we must be earnest. Oh, my God, when I remember that I have to-day some here present who in all probability must be dead before next Sabbath, I must be earnest. Out of so large an assembly, the chances are that we shall not all of us be found pilgrims in this world within another seven days. It is not only possible, but probable, that some one out of this vast audience will have been launched upon a world unknown. Shall it be myself, and shall I sail to the port of bliss, or must I sail over fiery waves forever, lost, shipwrecked, stranded, on the rocks of woe? Soul, which shall it be with thee? It may be thou shalt die, my grey-headed hearer, or thou young lad, thou boy, thou mayest die—I know not which, nor can we tell—God only knoweth. Then let each one ask himself—Am I prepared, should I be called to die? Yes, you may die where you are, on the benches where you are sitting—you may now die—and whither would you go? for recollect that whither ye go, ye go forever. Oh! eternity—eternity—eternity—must I climb thy topless steeps forever, and never reach the summit, and must my path be ever misery or joy. Oh! eternity, thou depth without a bottom, thou sea without a shore, must I sail over thy boundless waves forever in one undeviating track— and must I either plough through seas of bliss, or else be driven by the stormy winds of vengeance, over gulfs of misery? "Then what am I?" "My soul awake and an impartial survey take." Am I prepared? Am I prepared. Am I prepared? For, prepared or not, death admits of no delay, and if he is at my door, he will take me where I must go forever, prepared or not.

Now, the last thing is, *the sinner will perish*—he will perish certainly, but, last of all, he will perish *without excuse*—his blood shall be on his own head. When a man is bankrupt, if he can say, "It is not through reckless trading—it has been entirely through the dishonesty of one I trusted that I am what I am;" he takes some consolation, and he says, "I can not help it." But oh, my hearers, if you make bankrupts of your own souls, after you have been warned, then your own eternal bankruptcy shall lie at your own door. Should never so great a misfortune come upon us, if we can trace it to the providence of God, we bear it cheerfully; but if we have inflicted it upon ourselves, then how fearful is it! And let every man remember that if he perish after having heard the Gospel, he will be his own murderer. Sinner, thou wilt drive the dagger into thine heart thyself. If thou despisest the Gospel, thou art preparing fuel for thine own bed of flames, thou art hammering out the chain for thine own everlasting binding; and when damned, thy mournful reflection will be this:—I have damned myself, I cast myself into this pit; for I rejected the Gospel; I despised the message; I trod under foot the Son of Man; I would have none of his rebukes; I despised his Sabbaths; I would not hearken to his exhortations, and now I perish by mine own hand, the miserable suicide of my own soul."

And now a sweet reflection strikes me. A good writer says, "There are, doubless, spots in the world that would be barren forever, if we recollected what had happened there." Says he, "I was once in St. Paul's cathedral, just under the dome, and a friend just touched me gently and said, 'Do you see that little chisel mark? and I said 'Yes.' He said, 'That is where a man threw himself down, and there he fell, and was dashed to atoms.'" The writer says, "We all started aside from that little spot, where a fellow-creature's blood had been shed. It seemed an awful place when we remembered that." Now, there is many a street, there is many a way-side, there is many a house of God, where men have taken the last decision, and damned their own souls. I doubt not, there are some here this morning, standing or sitting, to whom the voice of conscience says, "Decide for God," and now Satan and the evil heart together are saying, "Reject the message; laugh it off; forget it: take a ticket for the theater to-morrow: do not let this man alarm us: it is his very profession to talk to us like this; let us go away, and laugh it off; and let us spend the rest of this day in merriment." Yes, that is the last warning thou wilt ever have. It is so with some of you. There are some of you that will this hour decide to damn yourselves, and you will look forever throughout eternity, to that place under the gallery, and you will say, "Alas! woe was the day I heard that man, I was half impressed—almost he persuaded me to be a Christian, but I decided for hell." And that will be a solemn spot to angels where you are standing, or where you are sitting, for angels will say to one another, "Stand aside; that is a spot where a man ruined his own soul for ever and ever." But the sweet thought is, that there are some places just the reverse.

Why, you are sitting, my friend, this morning, on a spot where some three weeks ago one sat who was converted to God; and that place where you are sitting you ought to venerate, for in that place there sat one who was one of the chiefest of sinners like yourself, and there the Gospel message met him. And far back there, behind the door, many a soul has been brought to Christ. Many a piece of good news have I heard from some in yonder upper gallery. "I could not see your face, sir, all the sermon through, but the arrow of the Lord found its way round the corner, and reached my heart notwithstanding that, and I was saved." Ah, well, may

God so bless this place, that every seat of it this day may be solemnized by his own grace, and a spot to be remembered in your future history by reason of the beginning of your blessedness, the dawn of your salvation. " Believe on the Lord Jesus, and be baptized, and thou shalt be saved." This is the gospel we are told to preach to every creature—" He that believeth, and is immersed, shall be saved, he that believeth not shall be damned."

SERMON XVII

"WHAT HAVE I DONE?"

"What have I done?"—JEREMIAH viii. 6

PERHAPS no figure represents God in a more gracious light than those figures of speech, which represent him as stooping from his throne, and as coming down from heaven to attend to the wants and to behold the woes of mankind. We must have love for that God, who, when Sodom and Gomorrah were reeking with iniquity, would not destroy those cities, although he knew their guilt and their wickedness, until he had made an actual visitation to them and had sojourned for awhile in their streets. Methinks we can not help pouring out our heart in affection to that God, of whom we are told that he inclines his ear from the highest glory, and puts it to the lip of the faintest that breathes out the true desire. How can we resist feeling that he is a God whom we must love, when we know that he regards everything that concerns us, numbers the very hairs of our heads, bids his angels protect our footsteps lest we dash our feet against stones, marks our path and ordereth our ways. But especially is this great truth brought near to man's heart, when we recollect how attentive God is, not merely to the temporal interests of his creatures, but to their spiritual concerns. God is represented in Scripture as waiting to be gracious, or, in the language of the parable, when his prodigals are yet a great way off he sees them; he runs and falls upon their neck and kisses them. He is so attentive to everything that is good, even in the poor sinner's heart, that to him there is music in a sigh, and beauty in a tear; and in this verse that I have just read, he represents himself as looking upon man's heart and listening—listening, if possibly he may hear something that is good. "I hearkened and heard; I listened; I stood still, and I attended to them." And how amiable does God appear, when he is represented as turning aside, and as it were with grief in his heart, exclaiming, "I *did* listen, I *did* hearken, but they spake not aright; no man repented of his wickedness, saying, "What shall I do?" Ah! my hearer, thou never hast a desire toward God which does not excite God's hope; thou dost never breathe a prayer toward heaven which he does not notice; and though thou hast very often uttered prayers which have been as the morning cloud and as the early dew that soon passeth away, yet all these things have moved Jehovah's bowels; for he has been hearkening to thy cry and noticing the breathing of thy soul, and though it all hath passed away, yet it did not pass away unnoticed, for he remembers it even now. And oh! thou that art this day seeking a Saviour, remember, that Saviour's eyes are on thy seeking soul to-day. Thou art not looking after one who can not see thee; thou art coming to thy Father, but thy Father sees thee even in the distance. It was but one tear that trickled down thy cheek, but thy Father noticed that as a hopeful sign; it was but one throb that went through thy heart just now during the singing of the hymn, but God, the Loving, noticed even that, and thought upon it as at least some omen that thou wast not yet quite hardened by sin, nor yet given up by love and mercy.

The text is "What have I done?" I shall just introduce that by a *few words of affectionate persuasion*, urging all now present to ask that question: secondly, I shall give them a *few words of assistance in trying to answer it;* and when I have so done, I shall finish by a *few sentences of solemn admonition to those who have had to answer the question against themselves.*

I. First, then, a few words of EARNEST PERSUASION, requesting every one now present, and more especially every unconverted person, to ask this question of himself, and answer it solemnly: "What have I done?"

Few men like to take the trouble to review their own lives; most men are so near bankruptcy that they are ashamed to look at their own books. The great mass of mankind are like the silly ostrich, which, when hard pressed by the hunters, buries its head in the sand and shuts its eyes, and then thinks, because it does not see its pursuers, that therefore it is safe. The great mass of mankind, I repeat, are ashamed to review their own biographies; and if conscience and memory together could turn joint authors of a history of their lives throughout, they would buy a huge iron clasp and a padlock to it, and lock the volume up, for they dare not read it. They know it to be a book full of lamentation and woe, which they dare not read, and still go on in their iniquities. I have therefore a hard task in endeavoring to persuade you one and all to take down that book, and be its pages few or many, be they white or be they black, I have some difficulty in getting you to read them through. But may the Holy Spirit persuade you now, so that you may answer this question, "What have I done?" For remember, my dear friend, that searching yourself can do you no hurt. No tradesman ever gets the poorer by looking to his books; he may find himself to be poorer than he thought he was, but it is not the looking to the books that hath hurt him; he hath hurt himself by some ill trading before. Better, my friend, for you to know the past whilst there is yet time for repairing it, than that you should go blindfolded, hoping to enter the gates of Paradise and find out your mistake when alas! it is too late, because the door is shut. There is nothing to be lost by taking stock; you can not be any the worse for a little self examination. This of itself shall be one strong argument to induce you to do it; but remember you may be a great deal the better; for suppose your affairs are all right with God, why then you may make good cheer and comfort yourself, for he that is right with his God has no cause to be sad. But ah! remember there are many probabilities that you are wrong. There are so many in this world that are deceived, that there are many chances that you are deceived too. You may have a name to live and yet be dead; you may be like John Bunyan's tree, of which he said " 'twas fair to look upon and green outside, but the inside of it was rotten enough to be tinder for the devil's tinder box." You may this day thus stand before yourself your fellow creatures well whitewashed, and exceeding fair, but you may be like that Pharisee of whom Christ said, "Thou art a whited sepulcher, for inwardly thou art full of rottenness and dead men's bones." Now, man, however thou mayest wish to be self-deceived, for my own part I feel that I would a thousand times rather know my own state really than have the most pleasing conceptions about it and find myself deceived. Many a time have I solemnly prayed that prayer, "Lord, help me to know the worst of my own case; if I be still an apostate from thee, without God and without Christ, at least let me be honest to myself and know what I am." Remember, my friend, that the time you have for self-examination is, after all, very short. Soon thou wilt know the great secret. I perhaps may not say words rough enough to rend off the mask which thou now hast upon thee, but there is one called Death who will stand no compliment. You may masquerade it out to-day in the dress of the saint, but death will soon strip you, and you must stand before the judgment seat after death has discovered you in all your nakedness, be that naked innocence or naked guilt. Remember, too, though you may deceive yourself, you will not deceive your God. You may have light weights, and the beam of the scale in which you weigh yourself may not be honest, and may not therefore tell the truth; but when God shall try you he will make no allowances; when the everlasting Jehovah grasps the balances of justice and puts his law into one scale, ah, sinner, how wilt thou tremble when he shall put thee into the other; for unless Christ be thy Christ thou wilt be found light weight—thou wilt be weighed in the balances and found wanting, and be cast away for ever.

O! what words shall I adopt to induce every one of you now to search yourselves! I know the various excuses that some of you will make. Some of you will plead that you are members of churches, and that, therefore, all is right with you. Perhaps you look across from the gallery, and you say to me, "Mr. Spurgeon, your hands baptized me but this year into the Lord Jesus, and you have often passed to me the sacramental bread and wine. Ah, my hearer, I know that, and I have baptized, I fear, many of you that the Lord hath never bap tized; and some of you have been received into the church fellowship on earth who were never received by God. If Jesus Christ had one hypocrite in his twelve, how many hypocrites must I have here in nearly twelve hundred? Ah! my hearers, in this age it is a very easy thing to make a profession of religion: many churches receive candidates into their fellowship without examination at all; I have had such come to me, and I have told them, "I must treat you just the same as if you came from the world," because they said, "I never saw the minister; I wrote a note to the Church, and they took me in." Verily, in this age of profession, a man may make the highest profession in the world, and yet be at last found with damned apostates. Do not put off the question for that; and do not say, "I am too busy to attend to my spiritual concerns; there is time enough yet." Many have said that, and before their "time enough" has come, they have found themselves where time shall be no more. O! thou that sayest thou hast time enough, how little dost thou know how near death is to thee. There are some present that will not see New Year's Day; there is every probability that a very large number will never see another year. O, may the Lord our God prepare us each for death and for judgment, and bless this morning's exhortation to our preparation, by leading us to ask the question—"What have I done?"

II. Now, then, I am to help you to answer the question— "What have I done?"

Christian, true Christian, I have little to say to thee this morning. I will not multiply words, but leave the inquiry with thine own conscience. What hast thou done? I hear thee reply, "I have done nothing to save myself; for that was done for me in the eternal covenant, from before the foundation of the world. I have done nothing to make a righteousness for myself, for Christ said, 'It is finished;' I have done nothing to procure heaven by my merits, for all that Jesus did for me before I was born." But, say, brother, what hast thou done for him who died to save thy wretched soul? What hast thou done for his church? What hast

thou done for the salvation of the world ? What hast thou
done to promote thine own spiritual growth in grace ? Ah ! I
might hit some of you that are true Christians very hard
here; but I will leave you with your God. God will chastise
his own children. I will, however, put a pointed question.
Are there not many Christians now present who can not recollect that they have been the means of the salvation of one
oul during this year. Come, now ; turn back. Have you
any reason to believe that directly or indirectly you have been
made the means this year of the salvation of a soul ? I will go
further. There are some of you who are old Christians, and
I will ask you this question : Have you any reason to believe
that ever since you were converted you have evèr been the
means of the salvation of a soul ? It was reckoned in the
East, in the time of the patriarchs, to be a disgrace to a woman
that she had no children ; but what disgrace it is to a Christian to have no spiritual children—to have none born unto
God through his instrumentality ! And yet, there are some
of you here that have been spiritually barren, and have never
brought one convert to Christ ; you have not one star in your
crown of glory, and must wear a starless crown in heaven.
Oh ! I think I see the joy and gladness with which a good
child of God looked upon me last week, when we had heard
some one who had been converted to God by her instrumentality. I took her by the hand and said, " Well, now, you
have reason to thank God." " Yes, sir," she said, " I feel a
happy and an honored woman now. I have never, that I know
of, before been the means of bringing a soul to Christ." And
the good woman looked so happy ; the tears were in her eyes
for gladness. How many have you brought during this
year ? Come, Christian, what have you done ? Alas ! alas !
you have not been barren fig-trees, but still your fruit is such
that it can not be seen. You may be alive unto God but
how many of you have been very unprofitable and exceedingly unfruitful ? And do not think that while I thus deal
hardly with you I would escape myself. No, I ask myself the
question, " What have I done ?" And when I think of the
zeal of Whitfield, and of the earnestness of many of those

great evangelists of former times, I stand here astounded at myself, and I ask myself the question, "What have I done?" And I can only answer it with some confusion of face. How often have I preached to you, my hearers, the Word of God, and yet how seldom have I wept over you as a pastor should? How often ought I to have warned you of the wrath to come, when I have forgotten to be so earnest as I might have been. I fear lest the blood of souls should lie at my door, when I come to be judged of my God at last. I beseech you, pray for your minister in this thing, that he may be forgiven, if there has ever been a lack of earnestness, and energy, and prayerfulness, and pray that during the next year I may always preach as though I ne'er might preach again.

"A dying man to dying men."

I heard the moralist whilst I was questioning the Christian, say, "What have I done? Sir, I have done all I ought to have done. You may, as a Gospeller, stand there and talk to me about sins; but I tell you, Sir, I have done all that was my duty; I have always attended my church or chapel regularly every Sunday as ever a man or woman could; I have always read prayers in the family, and I always say prayers before I go to bed and when I get up in the morning. I don't know that I owe anybody anything, or that I have been unkind to anybody; I give a fair share to the poor, and I think if good works have any merit I certainly have done a great deal." Quite right, my friend, very right, indeed, *if* good works have any merit; but then it is very unfortunate that they have not any; for our good works, if we do them to save ourselves by them, are no better than our sins. You might as well hope to go to heaven by cursing and swearing, as by the merits of your own good works; for although good works are infinitely preferable to cursing and swearing in a moral point of view, yet there is no more merit in one than there is in the other, though there is less sin in one than in the other. Will you please to remember, then, that all you have been doing all these years is good for nothing? "Well, but, sir, I have trusted in Christ." Now, stop! Let me ask you a question. Do you mean to say, that you have trusted partly in Christ, and partly in your own good works? "Yes, sir." Well, then, let me tell you, the Lord Jesus Christ will never be a make weight; you must take Christ wholly, or else no Christ at all, for Christ will never go shares with you in the work of salvation. So, I repeat, all you have ever done is good for nothing. You have been building a card-house, and the tempest will blow it down; you have been building a house upon the sand, and when the rains descend and the floods come, the last vestige of it will be swept away forever. Hear ye the word of the Lord! "By the works of the law shall no flesh living be justified." "Cursed is every one that continueth not in *all* things that are written in the book of the law to do them;" and in as much as you have not continued in all things that are written in the law you are transgressors of the law, and you are under the curse, and all that the law has to say to you is, "Cursed, cursed, cursed! Your morality is of no help to you whatever, as to eternal things."

I turn to another character. He says, "Well, I don't trust in my morality nor in anything else; I say,

'Begone dull care, I pray thee begone from me.'

I have nothing to do with talking about eternity, as you would have me. But, sir, I am not a bad fellow after all. It is a very little that I ever do amiss; now and then a peccadillo, just a little folly, but neither my country, nor my friends, nor my own conscience, can say anything against me. True, I am none of your saints; I don't profess to be too strict; I may go a little too far sometimes, but it is only a little; and I dare say we shall be able to set all matters straight before the end comes." Well, friend, but I wish you had asked yourself the question, "What have I done?"——it strikes me that if each of you would just take off that film, that films your heart and your life over, you might see a grievous leprosy lurking behind what you have done. "Well, for the matter of that," says one, "perhaps I may have taken a glass or two too much

sometimes." Stop a bit! What is the name of .hat? Statter
as much as you like! Out with it! What is the name of it?
"Why, it is just a little mirth, sir." Stop, let us have the
right name of it. What do you call it in any one else?
"Drunkenness, I suppose." Says another, "I have been a little
loose in my talk sometimes." What is that? "It has been
just a merry spree." Yes, but please to call it what it ought
to be called—lascivious conversation. Write that down.
"Oh! no, sir; things are looking serious." Yes, they are
indeed; but they do not look any more serious than they really are. Sometimes you have been out on the Sabbath day
haven't you? "Oh! yes; but that has been only now and
then—just sometimes." Yes, but let us put it down what it
is, and we will see what the list comes to. Sabbath-breaking!
"Stop," you say, "I have gone no further, sir; certainly I
have gone no further." I suppose in your conversation, sometimes during your life, you have quoted texts of Scripture to
make jokes of them, haven't you? And sometimes you have
cried out, when you have been a little surprised, "Lord, have
mercy upon me!" and such things. I don't venture to say
you swear; though there is a Christian way of swearing that
some people get into, and they think it is not quite swearing,
but what it is besides nobody knows, and so we will put it
down as swearing—cursing and swearing. "Oh! sir, it was
only when somebody trod on my toes, or I was angry."
Never mind, put it down by its right name: we shall get a
pretty good list against you by and by. I suppose that in
trade you never adulterate your articles. "Well that is a
matter of business in which you ought not to interfere."
Well, it so happens I am going to interfere—and if you please
we will call it by its right name—stealing. We will put that
down. I suppose you have never been hard with a debtor,
have you? You have never at any time wished that you were
richer, and sometimes half wished that your opposite neighbor would lose part of his custom, so that you might have it?
Well, we will call it by its right name: that is "covetousness,
which is idolatry." Now, the list seems to be getting black
indeed. Besides that, how have you spent all this year; and

though you have pretended sometimes to say prayers, have you ever really prayed? No, you have not. Well, then there is prayerlessness to put down. You have sometimes read the Bible, you have sometimes listened to the ministry but have you not, after all, let all these things pass away? Then I want to know whether that is not despising God, and whether we must not put that down under that name. Truly we need go but very little further; for the list already when summed up is most fearful, and few of us can escape from sins so great as these, if our conscience be but a little awake.

But there is one man here who has grown very careless and indifferent to every point of morality, and he says, "Ah! young man, I could tell you what I have done during the year." Stop, sir, I don't particularly wish to know just now; you may as well tell it to yourself when you get home. There are young people here: it would not do them much good to know what you have done perhaps. You are no better than you should be, some people say; which means, you are so bad they would not like to say what you are. Do you suppose in all this congregation we have no debauched men—none that indulge in the vilest sin and lust? Why, God's angel seems even now to be flying through our midst, and touching the conscience of some, to let them know in what iniquities they have indulged during the year. I pray God that my just simply alluding to them may be the means of startling your conscience. Ah! ye may hide your sins; the coverlet of darkness may be your shelter; you may think they shall never be discovered; but remember, every sin that you have done shall be read before the sun, and men and angels shall hear it in the day of final account. Ah! my hearer, be thou moral or be thou dissolute, I beseech thee, answer this question solemnly to-day: "What have I done?" It would be as well if you took a piece of paper when you went home, and just wrote down what you have done from last January to December; and if some of you do not get frightened at it I must say you have got pretty strong nerves, and are not likely to be frightened at much yet.

Now I specially address myself to the unconverted man

and I would help him to answer this question in another point of view. " What have I done ?" Ah! man, thou that livest in sin, thou that art a lover of pleasure more than a lover of God, what hast thou done? Dost thou not know that one sin is enough to damn a soul for ever? Hast thou never read in Holy Scripture that cursed is he that sins but once? How damned then, art thou by the myriad sins of this one year! Recall, I beseech thee, the sins of thy youth and thy former transgressions up till now; and if one sin would ruin thee for ever, how ruined art thou now! Why, man, one wave of sin may swamp thee. What will these oceans of thy guilt do? One witness against thee will be enough to condemn thee: behold the crowds of follies and of crimes now gathered round the judgment-seat that have gone before thee into judgment. How wilt thou escape from their testimonies, when God shall call thee to his bar. What hast thou done? Come, man, answer this question. There are many consequences involved in thy sin, and in order to answer this question rightly thou must reply to every consequence, what hast thou done to thine own soul? Why, thou hast destroyed it; thou hast done thy best to ruin it for ever. For thine own poor soul thou hast been digging dungeons; thou hast been piling fagots; thou hast been forging chains of iron —fagots with which to burn it, and fetters with which to bind it for ever.

Remember, thy sins are like sowing for a harvest. What a harvest is that which thou hast sown for thy poor soul! Thou hast sown the wind, thou shalt reap the whirlwind; thou hast sown iniquity, thou shalt reap damnation. But what hast thou done against the gospel? Remember, how many times this year thou hast heard it preached? Why, since thy birth there have been wagon-loads of sermons wasted on thee. Thy parents prayed for thee in thy youth; thy friends instructed thee till thou didst come to manhood. Since then how many a tear has been wept by the minister for thee! How many an earnest appeal has been shot into thine heart! But thou hast rent out the arrow. Ministers have been concerned to save thee, and thou hast never been concerned about thyself. What hast thou done against Christ ? Remember, Christ has been a good Christ to sinners here; but as there is nothing that burns so well as that soft substance, oil, so there is nothing that will be so furious as that gentle-hearted Saviour, when he comes to be your Judge. Fiercer than a lion on his prey is rejected love. Despise Christ on the cross, and it will be a terrible thing to be judged by Christ on his hrone.

But again: what have you done for your children this year ? Oh! there be some here present that have been doing all they could to ruin their children's souls. 'Tis solemn what responsibility rests upon a father; and what shall be said of a drunken father ?—the father that sets his children an example of drunkenness. Swearer, what have you done for your family ? Haven't you, too, been twisting the rope for their eternal destruction ? Will they not be sure to do as you do ? Mother, you have several children, but this year you have never prayed for one of them, never put your arms round their necks as they kneeled at their little chair at night, and said, " Our Father;" you have never told them of Jesus that loved children, and once became a child like them. Ah, then, you too have neglected your children. I remember a mother who was converted to God in her old age, and she said to me—and I shall never forget the woman's grief— " God has forgiven me, but I shall never forgive myself. · For sir," she said, "I have nourished and brought up children but I have done it without any respect to religion." And then she burst into tears, and said, "I have been a cruel mother, sir; I have been a wretch!" "Why," said I, "my good woman, you have brought your children up." " Yes," said she, " my husband died when they were young, and left me with six of them, and these hands have earned their bread and found them clothes; no one," she said, " can accuse me of being unkind to them in anything but this; but this is the worst of all; I have been a cruel mother to them, for while I fed their bodies I neglected their souls." But some have gone further than this. Ah, young man, you have not only done your best this year to damn yourself, but you have done your best to damn others! Remember, last January, when you took that young man into the tavern for the first time, and laughed at all his boyish scruples, as you called them, and told him to drink away, as you did. Remember, when in the darkness of night you first led astray one young man whose principles were virtuous, and who had not known lust unless you had revealed it to him; you said at the time, "Come with me; I'll show you London life, I'll let you see pleasure!" That young man, when he first came to your shop, used to go to the house of God on Sunday, and seemed to bid fair for heaven—"Ah," you say, "I have laughed religion out of Jackson, he doesn't go any where on a Sunday now except for a spree, and he is just as merry as any of us." Ah! sir, and you will have two hells when you are damned; you will have your own hell and his too, for he will look through the lurid flames upon you, and say, " Mayhap, I had never been here if you had not brought me here!" And ah! seducer, what eyes will be those that will glare at you through hell's horror?—The eyes of one whom you led into iniquity! what double hells they will be to you as they glare on you like two stars, whose light is fury, and wither your blood for ever! Pause, ye that have led others astray, and tremble now. I paused myself, and prayed to God when I first knew a Saviour, that he would help me to lead those to Christ that I had ever in any way led astray. And I remember George Whitfield says when he began to pray, his first prayer was that God would convert those with whom he used to play at cards and waste his Sundays. "And blessed be God," he says, "I got every one of them."

O my God, can I not detect in some face here astonishment and terror. Doth no man's knees knock together? Doth no man's heart quail within him because of his iniquity? Surely it cannot be so, else were your hearts turned to steel, and your bowels become as iron in the midst of you. Surely, if it be so, the words of God are most certainly true, wherein he saith, in the seventh verse of this chapter—"The stork in the heaven knoweth her appointed times; and the turtle, and the crane, and the swallow, observe the time of their coming;

but my people know not the judgment of the Lord;" and certainly that prophet was true who said, "The ox knoweth its owner, and the ass his master's crib; but my people doth not know, Israel doth not consider." Oh, are ye so brutish as to let the reflections of that guilt pass over you without causing astonishment and terror? Then, surely we who feel our guilt have need to bend our knees for you, and pray that God might yet bring you to know yourselves; for, living and dying as you are, hardened and without hope, your lot must be horrible in the extreme.

How happy should I be if I might hope that the great mass of you could accompany me in this humble confession of our faith; may I speak as if I were speaking for each one of you? It shall be at your option, either to accept what I say, or to reject it; but, I trust, the great multitude of you will follow me. "Oh, Lord! I this morning confess that my sins are greater than I can bear; I have deserved thy hottest wrath, and thine infinite displeasure; and I hardly dare to hope that thou canst have mercy upon me; but inasmuch as thou didst give thy Son to die upon the cross for sinners, thou hast also said, 'Look unto me and be ye saved all the ends of the earth,' Lord, I look to thee this morning, though I never looked before, yet I look now; though I have been a slave of sin to this moment, yet Lord, accept me, sinner though I be, through the blood and righteousness of thy Son, Jesus Christ. Oh Father, frown not on me; thou mayest well do so, but I plead that promise which says, 'Whosoever cometh unto me, I will in no wise cast out. Lord, I come—

> Just as I am, without one plea,
> But that thy blood was shed for me,
> And that thou bid'st me come to thee,
>   O Lamb of God, I come.
>
> My faith doth lay its hand,
>   On that dear head of thine,
> While like a penitent I stand,
>   And there confess my sin.

Lord accept me, Lord pardon me, and take me as I am, from this time forth and for ever, to be thy servant whilst I live, to be thy redeemed when I die." Can you say that? Did not many a heart say it? Did I not hear many a lip in silence utter it? Be of good cheer, my brother, my sister, that if that came from your heart, you are as safe as the angels of heaven, for you are a child of God, and you shall never perish.

III. Now I have to address a few words of AFFECTIONATE ADMONITION, and then I have done. It is a very solemn thing to think how years roll away. I never spent a shorter year in my life than this one, and the older I grow, the shorter the years get; and you, old men, I dare say, look back on your sixty and seventy years, and you say, " Ah, young man, they will seem shorter, soon !" No doubt, they will. " So teach us to number our days, O God, that we may apply our hearts unto wisdom." But, is it not a solemn thing, that there is another year nearly gone; and yet many of you are unsaved? You are just where you were last year. No, you are not, you are nearer death, and you are nearer hell, except you repent; and, perhaps, even what I have said this morning will have no effect upon you. You are not altogether hardened, for you have had many serious impressions. Scores of times you have wept under discourses, and yet all has been in vain, for you are what you were. I beseech you, answer this question, " What have I done?" for, remember, there will be a time when you will ask this question, but it will be too late. When is that—say you—on the death bed? No, it is not too late there.

> " While the lamp holds out to burn,
> The vilest sinner may return."

But it will be too late to ask, " What have I done?" when the breath has gone out of your body. Just suppose the monument as it used to be, before they caged it round. Suppose a man going up the winding staircase to the top, with a full determination to destroy himself. He has got on the outside of the railings. Can you imagine him for a moment saying, " What have I done ?" just after he has taken his leap. Why, methinks some spirit in the air might whisper, " Done ? you have done what you can never undo. You are lost—lost—lost !" Now, remember that you that have not Christ, are to-day going up that spiral stair-case ; perhaps, to-morrow you will be standing in the article of death upon the palisading, and when death has gotten you, and you are just leaping from that monument of life down to the gulf of despair, that question will be full of horror to you. " What have you done ?" But the answer for it will not be profitable, but full of terror. Methinks, I see a spirit launched upon the sea of eternity. I hear it say, " What have I done ?" It is plunged in flaming waves, and cries, " What have I done ?" It sees before it a long eternity ; but it asks the question again, " What have I done ?" The dread answer comes ; thou hast earned all this for thyself. Thou knewest thy duty, but thou didst it not ; Thou wast warned, but thou didst despise the warning." Ah ! hear the doleful soliloquy of such a spirit. The last great day is come ; the flaming throne is set, and the great book is opened. I hear the leaves as with terrible rustle they are turned over. I see men motioned to the right or to the left, according to the result of that great book. And what have I done ? I know that to me sin will be destruction, for I have never sought a Saviour. What is that ? The Judge has fixed his eye on me. Now, it is on me turned. Will he say, " Depart ye cursed," unto me ? Oh ! let me be crushed for ever, rather than bear that sight. There is no noise, but the finger is lifted, and I am dragged out of the crowd, and singly I stand before the Judge. He turns to my page, and. before he reads it, my heart quakes within me. " Be it so," says he, " it has never been blotted with my blood. You despised my calls ; you laughed at my people ; you would have none of my mercy ; you said that you would take the wages of unrighteousness. You shall have them, the wages of sin is death." Ah ! me, and is he about to say, " Depart, ye cursed ?" Yes, with a voice louder than a thousand thunders, he says, " Depart, ye cursed, into everlasting fire, prepared for the devil and his angels." Ah !

it is all true now. I laughed at the minister, because he preached about hell; and here am I in hell, myself. Ah! I used to wonder why he wanted to frighten us so. Ah! I would to God he had frightened me more, if he might but have frightened me out of this place. But now, here am I lost, and there is no escape. I am in darkness so dark, there is not a ray of light can ever reach me. I am shut up so close, that not one of the bolts and bars can ever be removed. I am damned for ever. Ah! that is a dreary soliloquy. I cannot tell it to you. Oh! if you were there, yourselves, if you could only know what they feel, and see what they endure, then would you wonder that I am not more earnest in preaching the Gospel, and you would marvel, not that I wish to make you weep, but that I did not weep far more myself, and preach more solemnly. Ah! my hearers, as the Lord my God liveth, before whom I stand, I shall one day stand acknowledged by our conscience as having been a true witness unto you this morning; for there is not one of you here to-day, but will be without excuse, if you perish. You have been warned, I have warned you as earnestly as I can. I have no more powers to spend, no more arts to try, no more persuasion that I can use. I can only conclude by saying, I beseech you, fly to Jesus. I entreat you, as immortal spirits that are bound for endless weal or woe, fly ye to Christ; seek for mercy at his hands; trust in him, and be saved; and, at your peril, reject my solemn warning. Remember, ye may reject it, but ye reject not me, but him that sent me. Ye may despise it, but ye despise not me, but a greater than Moses, even Jesus Christ the Lord; and when ye come before his bar, piercing will be his language, and terrible his words, when he condemns you for ever, for ever, for ever, without hope, for ever, for ever, for ever. May God deliver us from that, for Jesus' sake. Amen.

SERMON XVII

LIGHT AT EVENING TIME

"It shall come to pass that at evening time it shall be light."—ZECHARIAH xiv. 7.

I SHALL not stay to notice the particular occasion upon which these words were uttered, or to discover the time to which they more especially refer; I shall rather take the sentence as a rule of the kingdom, as one of the great laws of God's dispensation of grace, " that at evening time it shall be light." Whenever philosophers wish to establish a general law, they think it necessary to collect a considerable number of individual instances; these being put together, they then infer from them a general rule. Happily, this need not be done with regard to God. We have no need, when we look abroad in providence, to collect a great number of incidents, and then from them infer the truth; for since God is immutable, one act of his grace is enough to teach us the rule of his conduct. Now, I find in this one place it is recorded that on a certain occasion, during a certain adverse condition of a nation, God promised that " at evening time it should be light." If I found that in any human writing, I should suppose that the thing might have occurred once, that a blessing was conferred in emergency on a certain occasion, but I could not from it deduce a rule; but when I find this written in the book of God, that on a certain occasion when it was evening time with his people God was pleased to give them light, I feel myself more than justified in deducing from it the rule, that always to his people at evening time there shall be light.

This, then, shall be the subject of my present discourse. There are different evening times that happen to the church and to God's people, and as a rule we may rest quite certain that at evening time there shall be light.

God very frequently acts in grace in such a manner that we can find a parallel in nature. For instance, God says, " As the rain cometh down and the snow from heaven, and return eth not thither, even so shall my word be, it shall not return unto me void, it shall accomplish that which I please, it shall prosper in the thing whereto I have sent it." We find him speaking concerning the coming of Christ, " He shall come down like rain upon the mown grass, as showers that water the earth." We find him liking the covenant of grace to the covenant which he made with Noah concerning the seasons, and with man concerning the different revolutions of the year —" Seed-time and harvest, and cold and heat, and summer and winter, and day and night shall not cease." We find that the works of creation are very frequently the mirror of the works of grace, and that we can draw figures from the world of Nature to illustrate the great acts of God in the world of his grace toward his people. But sometimes God oversteps nature. In nature after evening time there cometh night. The sun hath had its hours of journeying; the fiery steeds are weary; they must rest. Lo, they descend the azure steeps and plunge their burning fetlocks in the western sea, while night in her ebon chariot follows at their heels. God, however, oversteps the rule of nature. He is pleased to send to his people times when the eye of reason expects to see no more day, but fears that the glorious landscape of God's mercies will be shrouded in the darkness of his forget- fulness. But instead thereof God overleapeth nature, and declares that at evening time instead of darkness there shall be light.

It is now my business to illustrate this general rule by dif- ferent particulars. I shall dwell most largely upon the last, that being the principal object of my sermon this morning.

I. To begin, then, " At evening time it shall be light." The first illustration we take from *the history of the church at large.* The church at large has had many evening-times. If I might derive a figure to describe her history from anyth

In this lower world, I should describe her as being like a sea At times the abundance of grace has been gloriously manifest. Wave upon wave has triumphantly rolled in upon the land, covering the mire of sin, and claiming the earth for the Lord of Hosts. So rapid has been its progress that its course could scarce be obstructed by the rocks of sin and vice. Complete conquest seemed to be foretold by the continual spread of the truth. The happy church thought that the day of her ultimate triumph had certainly arrived, so potent was her word by her ministers, so glorious was the Lord in the midst of her armies, that nothing could stand against her. She was "fair as the moon, clear as the sun, and terrible as an army with banners." Heresies and schisms were swept away, false gods and idols lost their thrones; Jehovah Omnipotent was in the midst of his church, and he upon the white horse rode forth conquering and to conquer. Before long, however, if you read history, you find it always has happened that there came an ebb-tide. Again the stream of grace seemed to recede, the poor church was driven back either by persecution or by internal decay; instead of gaining upon man's corruptions it seemed as if man's corruptions gained on her; and where once there had been righteousness like the waves of the sea, there was the black mud and mire of the filthiness of mankind. Mournful tunes the church had to sing, when by the rivers of Babylon she sat down and wept, remembering her former glories, and weeping her present desolation. So has it always been—progressing, retrograding, standing still awhile, and then progressing once more, and falling back again. The whole history of the church has been a history of onward marches, and then of quick retreats—a history which I believe is, on the whole, a history of advance and growth, but which read chapter by chapter, is a mixture of success and repulse, conquest and discouragement. And so I think it will be even to the last. We shall have our sunrises, our meridian noon, and then the sinking in the west; we shall have our sweet dawnings of better days, our Reformations, our Luthers and our Calvins; we shall have our bright full noon-tide, when the gospel is fully preached, and the power of God is

known; we shall have our sunset of ecclesiastical weakness
and decay. But just as sure as the evening-tide seems to be
drawing over the church, "at evening time it shall be light."
Mark well that truth all through the sacred history of the
church. In the day when every lamp of prophesy seemed to
have ceased, when he who once thundered in the streets of
Rome was burned at the stake and strangled; when Savana-
rola had departed, and his followers had been put to confusion, and the black clouds of Popery seemed to have quenched
the sunlight of God's love and grace upon the world; in those
dark dim ages when the gospel seemed to have died out, no
doubt Satan whispered in himself, "The church's sunset is
now come." It is evening time with her. Only a few rays
are struggling from the sun of righteousness to cheer the
darkness. Satan thought mayhap the world should lie for
ever beneath the darkness of his dragon wing. But lo! at
evening time it was light. God brought forth the solitary
monk that shook the world; he raised up men to be his coad-
jutors and helpers; the sun rose in Germany; it shone in
every land, nor have we ever had an even-tide so near to
darkness since that auspicious time. Yet there have been
other seasons of dark foreboding. There was a time when
the church of England was sound asleep, when the various
bodies of Dissenters were quite as bad, when religion degenerated into a dead formality, when no life and no power could
be found in any pulpit throughout the land, but when an earnest man was so rare that he was almost a miracle. Good
men stood over the ruins of our Zion, and said, "Alas, alas,
for the slain of the daughter of my people! Where, where
are the days of the mighty puritans who with the banner of
the truth in their hand crushed a lie beneath their feet? O
'ruth! thou hast departed; thou hast died." "No," says
God, "it is evening time; and now it shall be light." There
were six young men at Oxford who met together to pray
those six young men were expelled for being too godly; they
went abroad throughout our land, and the little leaven leav-
ened the whole lump. Whitfield, Wesley, and their immediate successors flashed o'er the land like lightning in a dark

night, making all men wonder whence they came and who they were; and working so great a work, that both in and out of the Establishment, the gospel came to be preached with power and vigor. At evening time God has always been pleased to send light to his church.

We may expect to see darker evening times than have ever been beheld. Let us not imagine that our civilization shal be more enduring than any other that has gone before it, unless the Lord shall preserve it. It may be that the suggestion will be realized which has so often been laughed at as folly, that one day men should sit upon the broken arches of London Bridge, and marvel at the civilization that has departed, just as men walk over the mounds of Nimroud, and marvel at cities buried there. It is just possible that all the civilization of this country may die out in blackest night; it may be that God will repeat again the great story which has been so often told—" I looked, and lo, in the vision I saw a great and terrible beast, and it ruled the nations, but lo, it passed away and was not." But if ever such things should be—if the world ever should have to return to barbarism and darkness—if instead of what we sometimes hope for, a constant progress to the brightest day, all our hopes should be blasted, let us rest quite satisfied that " at evening time there shall be light," that the ends of the world's history shall be an end of glory. However red with blood, however black with sin the world may yet be, she shall one day be as pure and perfect as when she was created. The day shall come when this poor planet shall find herself unrobed of those swaddling bands of darkness that have kept her luster from breaking forth. God shall yet cause his name to be known from the rising of the sun to the going down thereof,

> "And the shouts of jubilee,
>   Loud as mighty thunders roar,
> Or the fullness of the sea,
>   When it breaks upon the shore,
> Shall yet be heard the wide world o'er."

"At evening time it shall be light."

II. This rule holds equally good *in the little*, as well as *in the great*. We know that in nature the very same law that rules the atom, governs also the starry orbs.

> " The very law that molds a tear,
>   And bids it trickle from its source,
>   That law preserves the earth a sphere,
>   And guides the planets in their course."

It is even so with the laws of grace. "At evening time it shall be light" to the church; "at evening time it shall be light" *to every individual.* Christian let us descend to lowly things. Thou hast had thy bright days *in temporal matters :* thou hast sometimes been greatly blessed : thou canst remember the day when the calf was in the stall, when the olive yielded its fruit, and the fig-tree did not deny its harvest ; thou canst recollect the years when the barn was almost bursting with the corn, and when the vat overflowed with the oil ; thou rememberest when the stream of thy life was deep, and thy ship floated softly on, without one disturbing billow of trouble to molest it. Thou saidst in those days, " I shall see no sorrow ; God hath hedged me about ; he hath preserved me ; he hath kept me ; I am the darling of his providence ; I know that all things work together for my good, for I can see it is plainly so." Well, Christian, thou hast after that had a sunset ; the sun which shone so brightly, began to cast his rays in a more oblique manner every moment, until at last the shadows were long, for the sun was setting, and the clouds began to gather ; and though the light of God's countenance tinged those clouds with glory, yet it was waxing dark. Then troubles lowered o'er thee ; thy family sickened, thy wife was dead, thy crops were meager, and thy daily income was diminished, thy cupboard was no more full, thou wast wondering for thy daily bread ; thou didst not know what should become of thee, mayhap thou wast brought very low ; the keel of thy vessel did grate upon the rocks ; there was not enough of bounty to float thy ship above the rocks of poverty. " I sink in deep mire," thou saidst, " where there is no standing ; all thy waves and thy billows have gone over me." What to do you could not tell ; strive as you might, your strivings did but make you worse. "Except the Lord build the house, they labor in vain that build it." You used both industry and economy, and you added thereunto perseverance ; but all in vain. It was in vain that you rose up early, and sat up late, and ate the bread of carefulness ; nothing could you do to deliver yourself, for all attempts failed. You were ready to die in despair. You thought the night of your life had gathered with eternal blackness. You would not live always, but had rather depart from this vale of tears. Christian ! bear witness to the truth of the maxim of the text ! Was it not light with thee at evening time ? The time of thine extremity was just the moment of God's opportunity. When the tide had run out to its very furthest, then it began to turn ; thine ebb had its flow ; thy winter had its summer ; thy sunset had its sunrise ; "at evening time it was light." On a sudden by some strange work of God, as thou didst think it then, thou wast completely delivered. He brought out thy righteousness like the light, and thy glory as the noon-day. The Lord appeared for thee in the days of old : he stretched out his hand from above ; he drew thee out of deep waters ; he set thee upon a rock and established thy goings. Mark, thou then, O heir of heaven ! what hath been true to thee in the years that are past, shall be true to thee even till the last. Art thou this day exercised with woe, and care, and misery ? Be of good cheer ! In thine "evening time it shall be light." If God chooseth to prolong thy sorrow, he shall multiply thy patience ; but the rather, it may be, he will bring thee into the deeps, and thence will he lead thee up again. Remember thy Saviour descended that he might ascend : so must thou also stoop to conquer ; and if God bids thee stoop, should it be to the very lowest hell, remember, if he bade thee stoop, he will bring thee up again. Remember what Jonah said—"Out of the belly of hell cried I, and thou heardest me." Oh ! exclaim with him of old, who trusted his God when he had nothing else to trust · "Although the fig-tree shall not blossom, neither shall fruit be in the vines ; the labor of the olive shall fail, and the fields shall yield no meat; the flock shall be cut off from the fold, and there shall be no herd in the stalls: Yet I will rejoice in the Lord, I will joy in the God of my salvation." Do thou so, and be blessed; for " at evening time it shall be light."

III. But now we seek a third illustration from *the spiritual sorrows of God's own people.* God's children have two kinds of trials, trials temporal and trials spiritual. I shall be brief on this point, and shall borrow an illustration from good John Bunyan. You remember John Bunyan's description of Apollyon meeting Christian. Bunyan tells it figuratively, but it is no figure: he that hath ever met Apollyon will tell you that there is no mistake about the matter, but that there is a dread reality in it. Our Christian met Apollyon when he was in the valley of humiliation, and the dragon did most fiercely beset him; with fiery darts he sought to destroy him, and take away his life. The brave Christian stood to him with all his might, and used his sword and shield right manfully, till his shield became studded with a forest of darts, and his hand did cleave unto his sword. You remember how for many an hour that man and that dragon fought together, till at last the dragon gave Christian a horrible fall, and down he went upon the ground; and woe worth the day! at the moment when he fell he dropped his sword! You have but to picture the scene: the dragon drawing up all his might, planting his foot upon Christian's neck, and about to hurl the fiery dart into his heart. " Aha! I have thee now," saith he, " thou art in my power."

Strange to say, " at evening time it was light." At the very moment when the dragon's foot was enough to crush the very life out of poor Christian, it is said, he did stretch out his hand; he grasped his sword, and giving a desperate thrust at the dragon, he cried, " Rejoice not over me, O mine enemy; for when I fall I shall arise again ;" and so desperately did he cut the dragon that he spread his wings and flew away and Christian went on his journey rejoicing in his victory. Now, the Christian understands all that! it is no dream to him. He has been under the dragon's foot many a time. Ah! and all the world put on a man's heart at once is not equal in weight to one foot of the devil. When Satan once gets the upper hand of the spirit, he neither wants strength, nor will nor malice, to torment it. Hard is that man's lot, that has fallen beneath the hoof of the evil one in his fight with him. But blessed be God, the child of God is ever safe, as safe beneath the dragon's foot as he shall be before the throne of God in heaven. "At evening time it shall be light." And let all the powers of earth and hell, and all the doubts and fears that the Christian ever knew, conspire together to molest a saint, in that darkest moment, lo, God shall arise and his enemies shall be scattered, and he shall get unto himself the victory. O for faith to believe that. O! for confidence in God never to doubt him, but in the darkest moment of our sorrows, still to feel all is well with us! "At evening time it shall be light."

IV. Bear with me whilst I just hint at one more particular, and then I will come to that upon which I intend to dwell mainly at the last. To *the sinner when coming to Christ* this is also a truth. "At evening time it shall be light." Very often when I am sitting to see inquirers, persons have come to me to tell me the story of their spiritual history; and they tell me their little tale with an air of the greatest possible wonder, and ask me as soon as they have told it whether it is not extremely strange. "Do you know, sir, I used to be so happy in the things of the world, but conviction entered into my heart, and I began to seek the Saviour; and do you know that for a long time, sir, when I was seeking the Saviour I was so miserable that I could not bear myself? Surely sir, this is a strange thing." And when I have looked them in the face, and said, "No, it is not strange; do you know I have had a dozen to-night, and they have all told me the same; that is the way all God's people go to heaven," they have stared at me as if they did not think I would tell them an untruth, but as if they thought it the strangest thing in all the world that anybody else should have felt as they have felt. "Now, sit down," I say sometimes, "and I will tell you what were my feelings when I first sought the Saviour." "Why, sir," they say, "that is just how I felt; but I did not think any one ever went the same path that I have gone." Ah! well, it is no wonder that when we hold little acquaintance with each other in spiritual things our path should seem to be solitary; but he who knows much of the dealings of God with poor seeking sinners, will know that their experience is always very much alike, and you can generally tell one by another, while they are coming to Christ. Now, whenever the soul is truly seeking Christ it will have to seek him in the dark. When poor Lot ran out of Sodom, he had to run all the way in the twilight. The sun did not rise upon him until he got into Zoar. And so when sinners are running from their sins to the Saviour they have to run in the dark. They get no comfort and no peace, till they are enabled by simple faith to look for all to him who died upon the cross. I have in my presence this morning many poor souls under great distress. Poor heart! my text is a comfort to thee. "At evening time it shall be light." You had a little light once, the light of morality; you thought you could do something for yourself. That is all put out now. Then you had another light: you had the wax taper of ceremonies, and you thought full sure that it would light you; but that is all out now. Still you thought you could grope your way a little by the remaining twilight of your good works, but all that seems to have gone now. You think "God will utterly destroy such a wretch as I am! O sir! O sir!

'I the chief of sinners am.'"

There never lived a wretch so vile; or if there ever lived such an one, surely God must have cast him into hell at once; I am certain there is no hope for me. Why, sir, do what I may, I can not make myself any better. When I try to pray I find I can't pray as I should like; when I read the Bible it is all black against me; it is no use, when I go to the house of God the minister seems to be like Moses, only preaching the law to me—he never seems to have a word of comfort to my soul. Well, I am glad of it, poor heart, I am glad of it; far be it from me to rejoice in thy miseries as such, but I am glad thou art where thou art. I remember what the Countess of Hunt

ingdon once said to Mr. Whitfield's brother. Mr. Whitfield's
brother was under great distress of mind, and one day when
sitting at tea, talking of spiritual things, he said, " Your ladyship, I know I am lost, I am certain I am!" Well, they talked
to him, and they tried to rally him; but he persisted in it, that
he was absolutely undone, that he was a lost man. Her lady
ship clapped her hands, and said, "I am glad of it, Mr. Whitfield, I'm glad of it." He thought it was a cruel thing for
her to say. He knew better when she explained herself by
saying, "For the Son of man came to seek and to save that
which was lost; so then, he came to seek and to save you."
Now, if there be any here who are lost, I can only say, I am
glad of it too, for such the mighty Shepherd came to rescue.
If there are any of you who feel that you are condemned by
God's law, I thank God you are; for those who are condemned
by the law in their consciences shall yet be pardoned by the
gospel.

> " Come, guilty souls, and flee away
>   To Christ, and heal your wounds;
>   This is the glorious gospel day,
>   Wherein free grace abounds."

Nay, this very hour, when you have no day in your heart,
when you think the evening time has come, and you must perish for ever—now is the time when God will reveal himself to
you. Whilst thou hast a rag of thine own thou shalt never
have Christ; whilst thou hast a farthing of thine own righteousness, thou shalt never have him; but when thou art nothing, Christ is thine; when thou hast nothing of thyself to trust
to, Jesus Christ in the gospel is thy complete Saviour; he bids
me tell thee he came to seek and to save such as thou art.

V. And now I am about to close, dwelling rather more
largely upon the last particular—"At evening time it shall be
light." If our sun do not go down ere it be noon, we may
all of us expect to have an evening time of life. Either we
shall be taken from this world by death, or else, if God should
spare us, ere long we shall get to the evening of life. In a few
more years, the sere and yellow leaf will be the fit companion

of every man and every woman. Is there anything melan choly in that? I think not. The time of old age, with all its infirmities, seems to me to be a time of peculiar blessedness and privilege to the Christian. To the worldly sinner, whose zest for pleasure has been removed by the debility of his powers and the decay of his strength, old age must be a season of tedium and pain; but to the veteran soldier of the cross, old age must assuredly be a time of great joy and blessedness.

I was thinking, the other evening, whilst riding in a delightful country, how like to evening time old age is. The sun of hot care has gone down; that sun which shone upon that early piety of ours, which had not much depth of root, and which scorched it so that it died—that sun which scorched our next true godliness, and often made it well nigh wither, and would have withered it had it not been planted by the rivers of water—that sun is now set. The good old man has no particular care now in all the world. He says to business, to the hum and noise and strife of the age in which he lives, "Thou art nought to me; to make my calling and election sure, to hold firmly this my confidence, and wait until my change comes, this is all my employment; with all your worldly pleasures and cares I have no connection." The toil of his life is all done, he has no more now to be sweating and toiling, as he had in his youth and manhood; his family have grown up, and are now no more dependent upon him; it may be, God has blessed him, and he has sufficient for the wants of his old age, or it may be that in some rustic alms-house he breathes out the last few years of his existence. How calm and quiet! Like the laborer, who, when he returns from the field at evening time casts himself upon his couch, so does the old man rest from his labors. And at evening time we gather into families, the fire is kindled, the curtains are drawn, and we sit around the family fire, to think no more of the things of the great rumbling world; and even so in old age, the family and not the world are the engrossing topic.

Did you ever notice how venerable grandsires, when they write a letter, fill it full of intelligence concerning their children? "John is ill," "Mary is well," "all our family are in health." Very likely some business friend writes to say "Stocks are down," or, "the rate of interest is raised," but you never find *that* in any good old man's letters; he writes about his family, his lately married daughters, and all that. Just what we do at evening time; we only think of the family circle and forget the world. That is what the gray-headed old man does. He thinks of his children, and forgets all beside. Well, then, how sweet it is to think that for such an old man there is light in the darkness! "At evening time it shall be light." Dread not thy days of weariness, dread not thine hours of decay, O soldier of the cross; new lights shall burn when the old lights are quenched; new candles shall be lit when the lamps of life are dim. Fear not! The night of thy decay may be coming on, but "at evening time it shall be light." At evening time the Christian has many lights that he never had before; lit by the Holy Spirit and shining by his light. There is the light of bright experience. He can look back, and he can raise his Ebenezer, saying, "Hither, by thy help I've come." He can look back at his old Bible, the light of his youth, and he can say, "This promise has been proved to me, this covenant has been proved true. I have thumbed my Bible many a year; I have never yet thumbed a broken promise. The promises have all been kept to me; 'not one good thing has failed.'" And then, if he has served God he has another light to cheer him: he has the light of the remembrance of what good God has enabled him to do. Some of his spiritual children come in and talk of times when God blessed his conversation to their souls. He looks upon his children, and his children's children, rising up to call the Redeemer blessed; at evening time he has a light. But at the last the night comes in real earnest; he has lived long enough, and he must die. The old man is on his bed; the sun is going down, and he has no more light. "Throw up the windows, let me look for the last time into the open sky," says the old man. The sun has gone down; I can not see the mountains yonder; they are all a mass of mist; my eyes are dim, and the world is dim too. Suddenly a light shoots across his face, and he cries, "O daughter! daughter, here!]

can see another sun rising. Did you not tell me that the sun went down just now? Lo, I see another; and where those hills used to be in the landscape, those hills that were lost in the darkness, daughter, I can see hills that seem like burning brass; and methinks upon that summit I can see a city bright as jasper. Yes, and I see a gate opening, and spirits coming forth. What is that they say? O they sing! they sing! Is this death?" And ere he has asked the question, he hath gone where he needs not to answer it, for death is all unknown. Yes, he has passed the gates of pearl; his feet are on the streets of gold; his head is bedecked with a crown of immortality; the palm-branch of eternal victory is in his hand. God hath accepted him in the beloved.

> "Far from the world of grief and sin,
>   With God eternally shut in,"

he is numbered with the saints in light, and the promise is ful filled, " At evening time it shall be light."

And now, my gray-headed hearer, will it be so with thee? I remember the venerable Mr. Jay once in Cambridge, when preaching, reaching out his hand to an old man who sat just as some of you are sitting there, and saying, "I wonder whether those gray hairs are a crown of glory, or a fool's cap; they are one or else the other." For a man to be unconverted at the age to which some of you have attained is indeed to have a fool's cap made of gray hairs; but if you have a heart consecrated to Christ, to be his children now, with the full belief that you shall be his for ever, is to have a crown of glory upon your brows.

And now, young men and maidens, we shall soon be old. In a little time our youthful frame shall totter; we shall need a staff by-and-by. Years are short things; they seem to us to get shorter, as each one of them runs o'er our head. My brother, thou art young as I am; say, hast thou a hope that thine even-tide shall be light? No, thou hast begun in drunkenness; and the drunkard's eventide is darkness made more dark, and after it damnation No, young man; thou hast begun thy life with profanity, and the swearer's even-tide hath no light, except the lurid flame of hell. Beware thou of such an even-tide as that! No; thou hast begun in gayety; take care lest that which begins in gayety ends in eternal sadness. Would God ye had all begun with Christ! Would that ye would choose wisdom; for " her ways are ways of pleasantness, and all her paths are peace." Some religious men are miserable; but religion does not make them so. True religion is a happy thing. I never knew what the hearty laugh and what the happy face meant, till I knew Christ; but knowing him I trust I can live in this world like one who is not of it, but who is happy in it. Keeping my eye upward to the Saviour, I can say with David, " Bless the Lord, O my soul, and all that is within me bless his holy name." and bless him most of all for this, that I know how to bless him. Ah! and if ye in your prime, in the days of your youth, have been enabled by the Holy Spirit to consecrate yourselves to God, you will, when you come to the end, look back with some degree of sorrow upon your infirmities, but with a far greater degree of joy upon the grace which began with you in childhood, which preserved you in manhood, which matured you for your old age, and which at last gathered you like a shock of corn fully ripe into the garner. May the great God and Master bless these words to us each, through Jesus Christ our Lord. Amen.

SERMON XVIII

THY REDEEMER

"And thy redeemer, the Holy One of Israel."—ISAIAH, xli. 14

AND why does it say, "and thy Redeemer?" What was the use of appending the Redeemer's name to this precious exhortation? By God's help it shall be the business of this evening to show why there is a peculiar blessedness in the fact that God hath not only said, "I will help thee, saith the LORD," but has added, "and thy redeemer, the Holy One of Israel."

You will please to notice that it looks as if this were a repetition by three different persons. Israel was cast down, and Jehovah, for that is the first word—(you will notice that the word "LORD" is in capitals, and should be translated "Jehovah")—says to his poor, tried, desponding servant, "I will help thee." No sooner is that uttered than we think we shall not be straining the text if we surmise that God the Holy Spirit, the Holy One of Israel, adds his solemn affidavit also; and declares by oath and covenant, "I will help thee." Does not this, we say, look somewhat like repetition? Was it not sufficient that Jehovah the Father should declare that he would help his people! Why did the other persons of the divine Trinity unite in this solemn declaration? We think we shall be able, if God shall help us, to show great usefulness therein, especially dwelling to-night upon that word; "thy Redeemer," and marking how the repetition of the word by our Lord Jesus Christ, our Redeemer, adds a peculiar blessedness to the exhortation—"Fear not, thou worm Jacob."

First, methinks this was added *for amplification;* secondly *for sweetness;* thirdly, *for confirmation.*

I. First, when it says, "and thy redeemer, the Holy One of Israel," it was added FOR AMPLIFICATION. There are some preachers from whom you will never learn anything; not because they do not say much which is instructive, but because they just mention the instructive thought once, and immediately pass on to another thought, never expanding upon the second thought, but immediately passing on, almost without connection, to a third—just casting forth, as it were, bare thoughts, without opening them up, and explaining them to the people. Such preachers are generally complained of as being very unprofitable to the hearers. " Why," said the hearer, " it made no impression upon me; it was good, but there was so much of it that I could not recollect it. I had nothing to bring away." Other preachers, on the other hand, follow a better method. Having given one idea, they endeavor to amplify it, so that their hearers, if they are not able to receive the idea in the abstract, at least are able to lay hold upon some of its points, when they come to the amplification of it. Now, God, the great Author of the great book, God, the preacher of the truth by his prophets, when he would preach it, and when he would write it, so amplifies a fact, so extends a truth, and enlarges upon a doctrine, says, " I will help thee, saith Jehovah." That means Father, Son, and Holy Ghost. " Ah! but," said God, " my people will forget that, unless I amplify the thought; so I will even break it up; I will remind them of my Trinity. They understand my Unity; I will bid them recollect that there are Three in One, though these Three be One ;" and he adds, " thy Redeemer, the Holy One of Israel." Jehovah—Redeemer—Holy One of Israel—three persons, all included, indeed, in the word Jehovah, but very likely to be forgotten unless they had been distinctly enumerated.

Now, ·brethren, suffer your thoughts for a moment to enlarge upon the fact, that the promise contained in this verse, "Fear not, I will help thee" (*I* will help thee), is a promise from Three Divine Persons. Hear Jehovah, the everlasting Father, saying, " I will help thee." " Mine are the ages: before the ages began, when there were no worlds, when nought had been created, from everlasting I am thy God. I am the God of election. the God of the decree, the God of the covenant; by my strength I did set fast the mountains, by my skill I laid the pillars of the earth; and the beams of the firmament of heaven; I spread out the skies as a curtain, and as a tent for man to dwell in; I the Lord made all these things, '*I* will help thee.'" Then comes Jehovah the Son. "And I, also, am thy Redeemer, I am eternal; my name is wisdom. I was with God, when there were no depths, before he had digged the rivers, I was there as one brought up with him. I am Jesus, the God of ages; I am Jesus, the man of sorrows; 'I am he that liveth and was dead, I am alive for evermore.' I am the High Priest of your profession, the Intercessor before the throne, the Representative of my people. I have power with God. '*I* will help thee.'" Poor worm, thy Redeemer vows to help thee; by his bleeding hands he covenants to give thee aid. And then in comes the Holy Spirit. "And I," saith the Spirit, "am also God—not an influence, but a person —I, eternal and everlasting, co-existent with the Father and the Son—I, who did brood over chaos, when as yet the world was not brought into form and fashion, and did sow the earth with the seeds of life when I did brood over it,—I, that brought again from the dead your Lord Jesus Christ, the Shepherd of the sheep—I, who am the Eternal Spirit, by whose power the Lord Jesus did arise from the thraldom of his tomb —I, by whom souls are quickened, by whom the elect are called out of darkness into light—I, who have the power to maintain my children and preserve them to the end—'*I* will help thee.'" Now, soul, gather up these three, and dost thou want more help than they can afford? What! dost thou need more strength than the omnipotence of the United Trinity? Dost thou want more wisdom than exists in the Father, more love than displays itself in the Son, and more power than is manifest in the influences of the Spirit? Bring hither thine empty pitcher! Sure this well will fill it. Haste! gather up thy wants, and bring them here—thine emptiness, thy woes, thy needs. Behold, this river of God is full for thy supply. What canst thou want beside? Stand up, Christian, in this thy might. Jehovah Father, Jehovah Jesus, Jehovah Spirit,—these are with thee to help thee. This is the first thing. It is an *amplification.*

II. And now, secondly, concerning that word, "thy Redeemer," it is a SWEETENING OF THE PROMISE. Did you never notice that a promise always seems all the sweeter for having Jesus in it? All the promises are yea and amen in him; but when a promise mentions the name of the Redeemer, it imparts a peculiar blessedness to it. Brethren, it is something like, if I may represent it by such a figure, the beautiful effect of certain decorations of stained glass. There are some persons whose eyes are so weak that the light seems to be injurious to them, especially the red rays of the sun, and a glass has been invented, which rejects the rays that are injurious, and allows only those to pass which are softened and modified to the weakness of the eye. It seems as if the Lord Jesus were some such a glass as this. The grace of God the Trinity, shining through the man Christ Jesus, becomes a mellow, soft light, so that mortal eye can bear it. My God, I could not drink from thy well, if thou hadst not put there the earthen pitcher of my Saviour; but with him living waters from thy sacred well I draw. Heaven! thou art too bright; I could not bear thine insufferable light, if I had not this shade with which I cover thee; but through it, as through a mist, I do behold the halo of thy glory, undiminished in its effulgence, but somewhat diminished in their potency which would be my destruction. The Saviour seems to calm his glory, to tone it down to our poor feeble frame. His name put into this wine of heaven, does not diminish in the least degree its sparkling and its exhilirating power; but it takes out of it that deep strength which might upset an angel's brain, if he could drink to his full. It takes away the profundity of mystery, which would make the deep old wine of the kingdom intoxicating rather than cheering. Christ Jesus cast into the river of God, makes all the streams more sweet; and when the believer sees God in the person of the Saviour, he then sees the God whom he can love, and to whom with boldness he can approach. Surely I love this promise all the better, because I think I see my Saviour, with his hand all bleeding, stamping his hand upon it, and saying, "And thy Redeemer," and there is the blood-mark left upon the promise. It does seem to me as if when

God uttered that promise to the poor worm Jacob, Jesus Christ could not be still. He heard his Father say, "Fear not, worm Jacob;" and he saw the poor worm, with his head on one side, with his eyes all flowing with tears, with his heart palpitating with terror, and his arms folded in dismay; and when his Father had said, "Fear not," he stepped from behind, and whispered in a voice more soft than the voice of his Father, "Fear not, worm Jacob, it is God that speaks;" and then the soft voice says, "And it is thy Redeemer that speaks too." *He* says, "Fear not." He who loves thee, who knows thee, who has felt what thou feelest, who has passed through the woes which thou art now enduring—he who is thy Kinsman and thy Brother, he also says "Fear not, worm Jacob." Oh, it is sweet, it is precious to look upon that word, as spoken by our Redeemer.

III. And now we come to the other point. I think this is put in by way of CONFIRMATION. "In the mouth of two or three witnesses surely the whole shall be established."

"Blind unbelief is sure to err."

It needs many witnesses to make such unbelieving souls as we are, believe the promises. "Now," says God, "I will help thee." Unbelief! wilt thou doubt Jehovah? Can the "I Am that I Am" lie? Can the God of faithfulness and truth deceive thee? O unbelief! infamous traitor! wilt thou dare to doubt him? Yes, and Christ knew it would; and so he comes in and he says, "and thy Redeemer," as a second witness; whilst the Spirit is the third. "Thy Redeemer," volunteers to be the second guarantee, the other security to the faithfulness of this promise. The Father will lose his honor if he breaks his word; and I too do give as the security for the fulfillment of this promise, my troth and honor also. "Thy Redeemer" engages that he will help thee, O thou worm!

And now, I want you to read the promise, recollecting that t says, "Thy Redeemer;" and then, as you read it through, you will see how the word "Redeemer" seems to confirm it all. Now begin. "*I* will help thee:" lay a stress on that word. If you read it so, there is one blow at your unbelief. "*I* will help thee," saith the Redeemer. "Others may not, but I have loved thee with an everlasting love, and by the bands of my lovingkindness have I drawn thee. '*I* will help thee,' though the earth forsake thee; though thy father and thy mother forsake thee, *I* will take thee up. Wilt thou doubt me? I have proved my love to thee. Behold this gash, this spear thrust in my side. Look hither at my hands: wilt thou but believe me? ''Tis I.' I said that on the waters, and I said to my people, 'Be not afraid; it is I.' I say to thee, now thou art on the waters, 'Be not afraid; *I* will help thee.' Sure thou needst not fear that I shall ever forget thee. 'Can a woman forget her sucking child, that she should not have compassion on the son of her womb? Yea, they may forget, yet will I not forget thee.' 'I have graven thee on my hands; thy walls are ever before me.' '*I* will help thee.'" Now, you must just suppose the Saviour standing here—that Man whose garments are red with blood; you must suppose him standing where I stand to-night, and saying to you, personally, "Fear not, *I* will help you." O my Lord, I have ungratefully doubted thy promise many a time; but methinks, if I could see thee in all thy woe and sorrow for me, if I could hear thee say, "*I* will help thee," I should cast myself at thy feet, and say, "Lord, I believe, help thou mine unbelief." But though he is not here to speak it, though the lips that utter it are but the lips of man, remember that he speaks through me to-night, and through his word, as truly as if he spoke himself. If some great man should by a servant, or by a letter send to you this message, "I will keep you," though you had not heard his own lips declare it, yet if you saw his own hand writing, you would say, "It is enough, I believe it; there is the master's hand writing; it is his own autograph, it is written by himself; behold the bloody signature!" It is stamped with his cross, and I his messenger am sent to-night to myself and to you, and I say to my own heart and to you, "Why art thou cast down, O my soul? Why art thou disquieted within me? Hope thou in God; for I shall yet praise him;'

for the Redeemer says, *I* will help thee," and if he saith " *I* will help thee," who can doubt him ? who dare distrust him ?

And now let us read the promise again, and lay the stress on the " will." Oh, the " wills" and the " shalls :" they are the sweetest words in the Bible. " I *will* help thee." When God says " I will," there is something in it, brethren. The will of God started worlds into existence ; the will of God made nature leap from chaos ; the will of God sustains all worlds, " bears the earth's huge pillars up," and establishes creation. It is God's " I will." He lets the world live ; they live on the " will " of God ; and if he willed that they should die, they must sink as the bubble into the breaker, when its moment has arrived. And if the " will " of God is so strong as that, may we not lay a great stress upon it here—" I *will* help thee ?" There is no doubt about it. I do not say I may help thee peradventure. No ; I *will*. I do not say, that possibly I may be persuaded to help thee. No ; I voluntarily *will* to help thee. " I *will* help thee." I do not say that, in all probability, ninety-nine chances out of a hundred, it is likely I may help thee. No ; but without allowing any peradventure, or so much as a jot or tittle of hap or hazard, I *will*. Now, is there not strength in that ? Indeed, my brethren, this is enough to cheer any man's spirit, however much he may be cast down, if God the Holy Spirit does but breathe upon the text, and let its spices flow abroad into our poor souls, " Fear not, I *will* help thee."

And now we lay stress on another word : " I will *help* thee." That is very little for me to do, to *help* thee. Consider what I have done already. What ! not help thee ? Why, I bought thee with my blood. What ! not help thee ? I have died for thee ; and if I have done the greater, will I not do the less ? *Help* thee, my beloved ! It is the least thing I will ever do for thee. I have done more, and I will do more. Before the day-star first began to shine I chose thee. " I will *help* thee." I made the covenant for thee, and exercised all the wisdom of my eternal mind in the scheming of the plan of salvation. " I will *help* thee." I became a man for thee; I doffed my diadem, and laid aside my robe; I laid the purple of the universe aside to become a man for thee. If I did this, I will *help* thee. I gave my life, my soul, for thee; I slumbered in the grave, I descended into Hades, all for thee; I will *help* thee. It will cost me nothing. Redeeming thee cost me much, but I have all and abound. In helping thee, I am giving thee what I have bought for thee already. It is no new thing. I can do it easily. "Help thee?" Thou needst never fear that. If thou needest a thousand times as much help as thou dost need, I would give it thee; but it is little that thou dost require compared with what I have to give. 'Tis great for thee to need, but it is nothing for me to bestow. "*Help* thee?" Fear not. If there were an ant at the door of thy granary asking for help, it would not ruin thee to give him a handful of thy wheat; and thou art nothing but a tiny insect at the door of my all-sufficiency. All that thou couldst ever eat, all that thou couldst ever take, if thou wert to take on to all eternity, would no more diminish my all-sufficiency, than the drinking of the fish would diminish the sea. No; "I will *help* thee." If I have died for thee, I will not leave thee.

And now, just take the last word—"I will help *thee*." Lay the stress there. "Fear not, thou worm Jacob; I will help *thee*." If I let the stars fall, I will help *thee*; if I let all nature run to rack and ruin, I will help *thee*. If I permit the teeth of time to devour the solid pillars upon which the earth doth stand, yet I will help *thee*. I have made a covenant with the earth, "that seed-time and harvest, summer and winter, shall never cease;" but that covenant, though true, is not so great as the covenant that I have made concerning thee. And if I keep my covenant with the earth, I will certainly keep my covenant with my Son. "Fear not; I will help *thee*." Yes, thee! Thou sayest, "I am too little for help;" but I will help thee, to magnify my power; thou sayest, "I am too vile to be helped," but I will help thee to manifest my grace. Thou sayest, "I have been ungrateful for former help;" but I will help thee to manifest my faithfulness. Thou sayest "But I shall still rebel, I shall still turn aside." "I will help *thee*," to show forth my long suffering : let it be known, "I will help *thee*."

And now just conceive my Master on his cross bleeding there, looking down on you and on me. Picture him, whilst his voice falters with love and misery conjoined ; and hear him. He has just now spoken to the thief, and he has said to him, "To-day, shalt thou be with me in Paradise." And after he has said that, he catches a sight of you and of me, poor and depressed, and he says, "Fear not, worm Jacob ; I will help *thee ;* I helped the thief—I will help *thee*. I promised him that he should be with me in paradise ; I may well promise thee that thou shalt be helped. I will help thee. O Master! may thy love that prompts thee thus to speak, prompt us to believe thee.

And now hear Him again. He is exalted on high ; he hath "led captivity captive and received gifts for men ;"—now hear him, as in the midst of the solemn pomp of heaven he is not unmindful of his poor relations. He looks down, and he sees us in this world still struggling with sin and care and woe ; he hears us claiming kingship with himself ; and he says, "Worm Jacob! thou I now do reign exalted high, my love is still as great. I *will* help *thee*." I pray the Lord apply the sweetness of that pronoun to your hearts, my brethren, and to mine. "I will help *thee*." O surely when the husband speaks to the wife in the hour of darkness and sorrow, and comforts her, you can easily understand what arguments he uses, when he says, "Wife of my youth! my joy, my delight, I will help *thee !*" You can easily conceive how he enumerates times of love, seasons when he stood by her in the hour of trouble ; you can easily think how he reminds her of the days of their espousals, and tells her of their struggles, and of their joys ; and he says, "Wife, canst thou doubt me ? No ; as I am a husband I *will* help *thee !*" And now you hear the Saviour speaking of his church. "Betrothed to me ere time began, I have taken thee into union with my adorable person ; and O my bride, though my palace stand in ruins, and heaven itself should shake, I *will* help thee. Forget thee ? Forget my bride ? Be false to my troth ? Forsake my covenant? No; never. I *will* help *thee*." Hear the mother speaking to her little child in great danger; "Child," she says, "I will help *thee ;*" and then she reminds that child that she is its mother, that from her breast the child drew its needed nourishment in the days of weakness; she reminds it how she has nursed it, and dandled it upon her knee, and how in every way she has been its solace and support. 'Child!" says she, and her heart runs over—"I will help *thee!*" Why, the child never doubts it, it says, "Yes, mother, I know you will; I am sure of that, I do not need to be told it, I was certain you would; for I have had such proofs of your love." And now ought not we who love the Saviour just to let our eyes run with tears, and say, "O thou blest Redeemer! thou needst not tell us thou wilt help us, for we know thou wilt. Oh do not suppose that we doubt thee so much as to want to be told of it again; we know thou wilt help us; we are sure of it; thy former love, thine ancient love, the love of thine espousals, thy deeds of kindness, thine everlasting drawings, all these declare that thou never canst forsake us." No, no; "I *will* help *thee*."

And now, brethren, we are coming to eat the body of Christ and drink his blood in a spiritual manner; and I hope whilst we are partaking of that bread and wine, the emblems of the Saviour, we shall think we hear every mouthful of bread and every sip of wine saying out in the Master's behalf, "I *will* help *thee*, I *will* help *thee*." And then let us just frighten Satan, by cheering up our spirits through the power of the Holy Ghost, and buckling on our armor, let us go forth into the world to-morrow, to show what the Redeemer can do, when his promise is applied by the Spirit. "Fear not, thou worm Jacob, and ye men of Israel; I will help thee." Come, bring your fears out to-night, and serve them in the worst way you can. Hang them here upon the scaffold this night. Come now, and blow them away at the great guns of the promises, let them be destroyed forever. They are renegade mutineers; let them be cut off, let them be utterly destroyed, and let us go and sing, "Therefore will we not fear, though the earth be removed, and though the mountains be carried into the midst of the sea; though the waters thereof roar and be troubled, though the mountains shake with the swelling thereof." "I *will* help *thee*," saith the Redeemer.

O sinners, I pity you, that this is not your promise. If this were all that you did lose by being out of Christ, it were enough to lose indeed. May God call you, and help you to trust in the Redeemer's blood. Amen.

SERMON XIX

THE FIRST AND GREAT COMMANDMENT

"Thou shalt love the Lord thy God with all thy heart, and with all thy soul, and with all thy mind, and with all thy strength: this is the first commandment."—MARK xii. 30

OUR Saviour said, "This is the first and great commandment." It is "*the first*" commandment—the first for *antiquity*, for this is older than even the ten commandments of the written law. Before God said, "Thou shalt not commit adultery, thou shalt not steal," this law was one of the commands of his universe; for this was binding upon the angels when man was not created. It was not necessary for God to say to the angels, "Thou shalt do no murder, thou shalt not steal;" for such things to them were very probably impossible; but he did doubtless say to them, "Thou shalt love the Lord thy God with all thy heart;" and when first Gabriel sprang out of his native nothingness at the fiat of God, this command was binding on him. This is "the first commandment," then, for antiquity. It was binding upon Adam in the garden; even before the creation of Eve, his wife, God had commanded this; before there was a necessity for any other command this was written upon the very tablets of his heart—"Thou shalt love the Lord thy God."

It is "the first commandment," again, not only for antiquity, but for *dignity*. This command, which deals with God the Almighty must ever take precedence of every other. Other commandments deal with man and man, but *this* with man and his Creator. Other commands of a ceremonial kind, when disobeyed, may involve but slight consequences upon the person who may happen to offend, but this disobeyed provokes the wrath of God, and brings his ire at once upon the sinner's head. He that stealeth committeth a gross offence, inasmuch as he hath also violated this command; but if it were possible for us to separate the two, and to suppose an offence of one command without an offence of this, then we must put the violation of this commandment in the first rank of offences. This is the king of commandments; this is the emperor of the law; it must take precedence of all those princely commands that God afterwards gave to men.

Again, it is "the first commandment," for its *justice*. If men can not see the justice of that law which says, "Love thy neighbor," if there be some difficulty to understand how I can be bound to love the man that hurts and injures me, there can be no difficulty here. "Thou shalt love thy God" comes to us with so much Divine authority, and is so ratified by the dictates of nature and our own conscience, that, verily, this command must take the first place for the justice of its demand. It is "the first" of commandments. Whichever law thou dost break, take care to keep this. If thou breakest the commandments of the ceremonial law, if thou dost violate the ritual of thy church, thine offence might be propitiated by the priest, but who can escape when this is his offence? This mandate standeth fast. Man's law thou mayest break, and bear the penalty; but if thou breakest this the penalty is too heavy for thy soul to endure; it will sink thee, man, it will sink thee like a mill-stone lower than the lowest hell. Take heed of this command above every other, to tremble at it and obey it, for it is "the first commandment."

But the Saviour said it was a "*great* commandment," and so also it is. It is "great," for it containeth in its bowels every other. When God said, "Remember to keep holy the Sabbath-day;" when he said, "Thou shalt not bow down unto the idols nor worship them,"—when he said, "Thou shalt not take the name of the Lord thy God in vain," he did not instance particulars which are all contained in this general mandate. This is the sum and substance of the law; and indeed even the second commandment lies within the folds of the first. 'Thou shalt love thy neighbor," is actually to be found within the center of this command, "Thou shalt love the Lord thy

God;" for the loving of God would necessarily produce the loving of our neighbor.

It is a great command, then, for its *comprehensiveness*, and it is a great command for the immense demand which it makes upon us. It demands all our mind, all our soul, all our heart, and all our strength. Who is he that can keep it, when there is no power of manhood which is exempt from its sway? And to him that violateth this law it shall be proven that it is a great command in the greatness of its condemning power, for it shall be like a great sword having two edges, wherewith God shall slay him. It shall be like a great thunderbolt from God, wherewith he shall cast down and utterly destroy the man that goeth on in his willful breaking thereof. Hear ye, then, O Gentiles, and O house of Israel, hear ye, then, this day, this first and great commandment: "Thou shalt love the Lord thy God with all thy heart, and with all thy soul, and with all thy mind, and with all thy strength."

I shall divide my discourse thus—first, *What saith this commandment unto us*, secondly, *What say we unto it?*

I. And in discussing the first point, WHAT SAITH THIS COMMANDMENT UNTO US? we shall divide it thus. Here is, first, the duty—"Thou shalt love the Lord thy God;" here is, secondly, the measure of the duty—"Thou shalt love him with all thy heart, mind, soul, strength;" here is, thirdly, the ground of the claim, enforcing the duty—because he is "thy God." God demandeth of us to obey, simply upon the ground that he is our God.

1. To begin, then. This command *demands a duty*. That duty is, that we should love God. How many men do break this? One class of men do break it willfully and grievously; for they *hate* God. There is the infidel, who gnashes his teeth against the Almighty; the atheist, who spits the venom of his blasphemy against the person of his Maker. You will find those who rail at the very being of a God, though in their consciences they know there is a God, yet with their lips will blasphemously deny his existence. These men say there is no God, because they wish there were none. The wish is father to the thought, and the thought demands great grossness of

heart, and grievous hardness of spirit before they dare to express it in words; and even when they express it in words, it needeth much practice ere they can do it with a bold, unblushing countenance. Now this command beareth hard on all them that hate, that despise, that blaspheme, that malign God, or that deny his being, or impugn his character. O sinner! God says thou shalt love him with all thy heart; and inasmuch as thou hatest him, thou standest this day condemned to the sentence of the law.

Another class of men know there is a God, but they *neglec.* him; they go through the world with indifference, "caring for none of these things." "Well," they say, "It does not signify to me whether there is a God or not." They have no particular care about him; they do not pay one half so much respect to his commands as they would to the proclamation of the Queen. They are very willing to reverence all powers that be, but he who ordained them is to be passed by and to be forgotten. They would not be bold enough and honest enough to come straight out, and despise God, and join the ranks of his open enemies, but they forget God; he is not in all their thoughts. They rise in the morning without a prayer, they rest at night without bending the knee, they go through the week's business and they never acknowledge a God. Sometimes they talk about good luck and chance, strange deities of their own brain; but God, the over-ruling God of Providence, they never talk of, though sometimes they may mention his name in flippancy, and so increase their transgressions against him. O ye despisers and neglecters of God! this command speaks to you—"Thou shalt love the Lord thy God with all thy heart and with all thy soul."

But I hear one of these gentlemen reply, "Well, sir, I make no pretensions to religion, but still I believe I am quite as good as those that do; I am quite as upright, quite as moral and benevolent. True, I do not often darken the door of a church or chapel, I do not think it necessary, but I am a right good sort; there are many, many hypocrites in the church, and therefore I shall not think of being religious." Now, my dear friend, allow me just to say one word—what business is that of yours? Religion is a personal matter between you and your Maker. Your Maker says—"Thou shalt love me with all thine heart:" it is of no use for you to point your finger across the street, and point at a minister whose life is inconsistent, or at a deacon who is unholy, or to a member of the church who does not live up to his profession. You have just nothing to do with that. When your Maker speaks to you, he appeals to you personally; and if you should tell him, "My Lord, I will not love thee, because there are hypocrites," would not your own conscience convince you of the absurdity of your reasoning? Ought not your better judgment to whisper "Inasmuch, then, as so many are hypocrites, take heed that thou art not; and if there be so many pretenders who injure the Lord's cause by their lying pretensions, so much the more reason why thou shouldst have the real thing and help to make the church sound and honest." But no , the merchants of our cities, the tradesmen of our streets, our artisans and our workmen, the great mass of them, live in total forgetfulness of God. I do not believe that the heart of England is infidel. I do not believe that there is any vast extent of deism or atheism throughout England: the great fault of our time is the fault of indifference; people do not care whether the thing is right or not. What is it to them? They never take the trouble to search between the different professors of religion to see where the truth lies; they do not think to pay their reverence to God with all their hearts. Oh, no; they forget what God demands, and so rob him of his due. To you, to you, great masses of the population, this law doth speak with iron tongue—"Thou shalt love the Lord thy God with all thy heart, and with all thy soul, and with all thy mind."

There are a class of men who are a great deal nobler than the herd of simpletons who allow the sublimities of the Godhead to be concealed by their carking care for mere sensual good. There are some who do not forget that there is a God; no, they are astronomers, and they turn their eyes to heaven, and they view the stars, and they marvel at the majesty of the Creator. Or they dig into the bowels of the earth, and they are astonished at the magnificence of God's works of yore. Or they examine the animal, and marvel at the wisdom of God in the construction of its anatomy. They, whenever they think of God, think of him with the deepest awe, with the profoundest reverence. You never hear them curse or swear: you will find that their souls are possessed of a deep awe of the great Creator. But ah! my friends, this is not enough: this is not obedience to the command. God does not say thou shalt wonder at him, thou shalt have awe of him. He asks more than that; he says, "Thou shalt love me!" Oh! thou that seest the orbs of heaven floating in the far expanse, it is something to lift thine eye to heaven, and say—

> " These are thy glorious works, Parent of good,
>   Almighty, thine this universal frame.
>   Thus wondrous fair; thyself, how wondrous then!
>   Unspeakable, who sitt'st above these Heavens
>   To us invisible, or dimly seen
>   In these thy lowest works; yet these declare
>   Thy goodness beyond thought, and power divine."

'Tis something thus to adore the great Creator, but 'tis not all he asks. Oh! if thou couldst add to this—" He that made these orbs, that leadeth them out by their hosts, is my Father, and my heart beats with affection towards him." Then wouldst thou be obedient, but not till then. God asks not thine admiration, but thine affection. " Thou shalt *love* the Lord thy God with all thine heart."

There are others, too, who delight to spend time in contemplation. They believe in Jesus, in the Father, in the Spirit; they believe that there is but one God, and that these three are one. It is their delight to turn over the pages of revelation, as well as the pages of history. They contemplate God; he is to them a matter of curious study; they like to meditate upon him; the doctrines of his Word they could hear all day long. And they are very sound in the faith, extremely orthodox, and very knowing; they can fight about doctrines, they can dispute about the things of God with all their hearts; but, alas! their religion is like a dead fish, cold and stiff, and when you take it into your hand, you say there is no life in it; their souls were never stirred with it; their hearts were never thrown into it. They can contemplate, but they cannot love; they can meditate, but they cannot commune; they can think of God, but they can never throw up their souls to him, and clasp him in the arms of their affections. Ah, to you, cold-blooded thinkers—to you, this text speaks. Oh! thou that canst contemplate, but canst not love,—" Thou shalt love the Lord thy God with all thy heart."

Another man starts up, and he says, "Well, this command does not bear on me; I attend my place of worship twice every Sunday; I have family prayer. I am very careful not to get up of a morning without saying a form of prayer; I sometimes read my Bible; I subscribe to many charities." Ah! my friend, and you may do all that, without loving God. Why, some of you go to your churches and chapels as if you were going to be horsewhipped. It is a dull and dreary thing to you. You dare not break the Sabbath, but you would, if you could. You know very well, that if it were not for a mere matter of fashion and custom, you would sooner by half be anywhere else, than in God's house. And as for prayer, why, it is no delight to you; you do it, because you think you ought to do it. Some indefinable sense of duty rests upon you; but you have no delight in it. You talk of God with great propriety, but you never talk of him with love. Your heart never bounds at the mention of his name; your eyes never glisten at the thought of his attributes; your soul never leapeth when you meditate on his works, for your heart is all untouched, and while you are honoring God with your lips, your heart is far from him, and you are still disobedient to this commandment, "Thou shalt love the Lord thy God."

And now, my hearers, do you understand this command ment? Do I not see many of you seeking to look for loop holes through which to escape? Do I not think I see some of you striving to make a breach in this divine wall which girds us all. You say, "I never do anything against God." Nay, my friend, that is not it: it is not what thou dost not do—it is this, "Dost thou *love* him?" "Well, sir, but I never violate any of the proprieties of religion." No, that is not it; the command is, "Thou shalt *love* him." "Well, sir, but I do a great deal for God; I teach in a Sunday school, and so on." Ah! I know; but dost thou *love* him? It is the heart he wants, and he will not be content without it. "Thou shalt ove the Lord thy God." That is the law, and though no man can keep it since Adam's fall, yet the law is as much binding upon every son of Adam this day, as when God first of all pronounced it. "Thou shalt love the Lord thy God."

2. That brings us to the second point—*the measure of this law.* How much am I to love God? Where shall I fix the point? I am to love my neighbor as I love myself. Am I to love my God more than that? Yes, certainly. The measure is even greater. We are not bound to love ourselves with all our mind, and soul, and strength, and therefore we are not bound to love our neighbor so. The measure is a greater one. We are bound to love God with all our heart, soul, mind, and strength.

And, we deduce from that, first, that we are to love God *supremely.* Thou art to love thy wife, O husband. Thou canst not love her too much, except in one case, if thou shouldst love her before God, and prefer her pleasure to the pleasure of the Most High. Then wouldst thou be an idolater. Child! thou art to love thy parents; thou canst not love him too much who begat thee, nor her too much who brought thee forth; but remember, there is one law that doth override that. Thou art to love thy God more than thy father or thy mother. He demands thy first, and thy highest affection; thou art to love him "with all thy heart." We are allowed to love our relatives: we are taught to do so. He that doth not love his own family is worse than a heathen man and a publican. But we are not to love the dearest object of our hearts, so much as we love God. Ye may erect little thrones for those whom ye rightly love; but God's throne must be a glorious high throne; you may set them upon the steps, but God must sit on the very seat itself. He is to be enthroned, the royal One within your heart, the king of your affections.

Say, say hearer, hast thou kept this commandment? I know I have not; I must plead guilty before God; I must cast myself before him, and acknowledge my transgression. But, nevertheless, there standeth the commandment—" Thou shalt love God with all thy heart"—that is, thou shalt love him *supremely.*

Note, again, that from the text we may deduce that a man is bound to love God *heartily:* that is plain enough, for it says, " Thou shalt love the Lord thy God with all thy heart." Yes, there is to be in our love to God a heartiness. We are to throw our whole selves into the love that we give to him. Not the kind of love that some people give to their fellows, when they say, " Be ye warmed and filled," and nothing more. No: our heart is to have its whole being absorbed into God, so that God is the hearty object of its pursuit and its most mighty love. See how the word " all" is repeated again and again. The whole going forth of the being, the whole stirring up of the soul, is to be for God only. " With *all* thy heart."

Again : as we are to love God heartily, we are to love him with *all our souls.* Then we are to love him with all our life ; for that is the meaning of it. If we are called to die for God, we are to prefer God before our own life. We shall never reach the fullness of this commandment, till we get as far as the martyrs, who rather than disobey God would be cast into the furnace, or devoured by wild beasts. We must be ready to give up house, home, liberty, friends, comfort, joy, and life, at the command of God, or else we have not carried out this commandment, " Thou shalt love him with all thy heart and with all thy life."

And, next we are to love God with all our *mind.* That is, the intellect is to love God. Now, many men believe in the existence of a God, but they do not love that belief. They know there is a God, but they greatly wish there were none. Some of you to-day would be very pleased, ye would set the bells a-ringing, if ye believed there were no God. Why, if there were no God, then you might live just as you liked ; if there were no God, then you might run riot and have no fear of future consequences. It would be to you the greatest joy that could be, if you heard that the eternal God had ceased to be. But the Christian never wishes any such a thing as that. The thought that there is a God is the sunshine of his existence. His intellect bows before the Most High; not like a slave who bends his body because he must, but like the angel who prostrates himself because he loves to adore his Maker. His intellect is as fond of God as his imagination. "Oh!" he saith, "My God, I bless thee that thou art; for thou art my highest treasure, my richest and my rarest delight. I love thee with all my intellect; I have neither thought, nor judgment, nor conviction, nor reason, which I do not lay at thy feet, and consecrate to thine honor.

And, once again, this love to God is to be characterized by *activity;* for we are to love Him with all our heart, heartily —with all our soul, that is, to the laying down of our life— with all our mind, that is mentally; and we are to love him with all our *strength*, that is, *actively*. I am to throw my whole soul into the worship and adoration of God. I am not to keep back a single hour, or a single farthing of my wealth, or a single talent that I have, or a single atom of strength, bodily or mental, from the worship of God. I am to love him with all my strength.

Now, what man ever kept this commandment? Surely, none; and no man ever can keep it. Hence, then, the necessity of a Saviour. O! that we might by this commandment be smitten to the earth, that our self-righteousness may be broken in pieces by this great hammer of "the first and great commandment!" But oh! my brethren, how may we wish that we could keep it! for, could we keep this command intact, unbroken, it would be a heaven below. The happiest of creatures are those that are the most holy, and that unreservedly love God.

3. And now, very briefly, I have just to state *God's claim* upon which he bases this commandment. "Thou shalt love him with all thy heart, soul, mind, strength." Why? First, because he is the Lord—that is, Jehovah; and secondly, because he is thy God.

Man, the creature of a day, thou oughtest to love Jehovah *for what he is.* Behold, him whom thou canst not behold! Lift up thine eyes to the seventh heaven; see where in dreadful majesty, the brightness of his skirts makes the angels veil their faces, lest the light, too strong for even them, should smite them with eternal blindness. See ye him, who stretched the heavens like a tent to dwell in, and then did weave into their tapestry, with golden needle, stars that glitter in the darkness. Mark ye him who spread the earth, and created man upon it. And hear ye what he is. He is all-sufficient, eternal, self-existent, unchangeable, omnipotent, omniscient! Wilt thou not reverence him? He is good, he is loving, he is kind, he is gracious. See the bounties of his providence; behold the plenitude of his grace! Wilt thou not love Jehovah, because he is Jehovah?

But thou art most of all bound to love him *because he is thy God.* He is thy God *by creation.* He made thee; thou didst not make thyself. God, the Almighty, though he might use instruments, was nevertheless the sole creator of man. Though he is pleased to bring us into the world by the agency of our progenitors, yet is he as much our Creator as he was the Creator of Adam, when he formed him of clay and made him man. Look at this marvelous body of thine: see how God hath put the bones together, so as to be of the greatest service and use to thee. See how he hath arranged thy nerves and blood vessels: mark the marvelous machinery which he has employed to keep thee in life! O thing of an hour! wilt thou not love him that made thee? Is it possible that thou canst think of him who formed thee in his hand, and molded thee by his will, and yet wilt thou not love him who hath fashioned thee?

Again, consider, he is *thy* God, for *he preserves thee.* Thy table is spread, but he spread it for thee. The air that thou dost breathe is a gift of his charity; the clothes that thou hast on thy back are gifts of his love; thy life depends on him One wish of his infinite will would have brought thee to the grave, and given thy body to the worms; and at this moment, though thou art strong and hearty, thy life is absolutely dependent upon him. Thou mayest die where thou art, in stanter: thou art out of hell only as the result of his good ness. Thou wouldst be at this hour sweltering in flames unquenchable, had not his sovereign love preserved thee. Traitor though thou mayest be to him, an enemy to his cross and cause, yet he is thy God, so far as this, for he made thee and he keeps thee alive. Surely, thou mayest wonder that he should keep thee alive, when thou refusest to love him. Man! thou wouldst not keep a horse that did not work for thee. Would you keep a servant in your house who insulted you? Would you spread bread upon his table, and find livery for his back, if instead of doing your will and good pleasure he would be his own master, and would run counter to you? Certainly you would not. And yet here is God feeding you, and you are rebelling against him. Swearer! the lip with which you cursed your Maker is sustained by him; the very lungs that you employ in blasphemy are inspired by him with the breath of life, else you had ceased to be. O! strange that you should eat God's bread, and then lift up your heel against him; O! marvelous that ye should sit at the table of his prov- idence and be clothed in the livery of his bounty, and yet that you should turn round and spit against high heaven, and lift the puny hand of your rebellion against the God that made you, and that preserves you in being. O, if instead of our God we had one like unto ourselves to deal with, my breth- ren, we should not have patience with our fellow-creatures for an hour. I marvel at God's long-suffering toward men. I see the foul-mouthed blasphemer curse his God. O God! how canst thou endure it? Why dost thou not smite him to the ground? If a gnat should torment me, should I not in one moment crush it? And what is man compared with his Maker? Not one half so great as an emmet compared with man. O! my brethren, we may well be astonished that God hath mercy upon us, after all our violations of this high com- mand. But I stand here to-day his servant, and from myself and from you I claim for God, because he is God, because he is our God and our Creator—I claim the love of all hearts, I claim the obedience of all souls and of all minds, and the con- secration of all our strength.

O people of God, I need not speak to you. You know that God is your God in a special sense; therefore you ought to love him with a special love.

II. This is what the commandment says to us. I shall be very short indeed upon the second head, which is, WHAT HAVE WE TO SAY TO IT?

What hast thou to say to this command, O man? Have I one here so profoundly brainless as to reply, "I intend to keep it, and I believe I can perfectly obey it, and I think I can get to heaven by obedience to it?" Man, thou art either a fool, or else willfully ignorant; for sure, if thou dost understand this commandment, thou wilt at once hang down thine hands, and say, "Obedience to that is quite impossible; thorough and perfect obedience to that no man can hope to reach to! Some of you think you will go to heaven by your good works, do you? This is the first stone that you are to step upon—I am sure it is too high for your reach. You might as well try to climb to heaven by the mountains of earth, and take the Himalayas to be your first step; for surely when you had stepped from the ground to the summit of Chimborazo you might even then despair of ever stepping to the height of this great commandment; for to obey this must ever be an impossibility. But remember, you can not be saved by your works, if you can not obey this entirely, perfectly, constantly, for ever.

"Well," says one, "I dare say if I try and obey it as well as I can, that will do." No, sir, it will not. God demands that you perfectly obey this, and if you do not perfectly obey it he will condemn you. "Oh!" cries one, "who then can be saved?" Ah! that is the point to which I wish to bring you. Who, then, can be saved by this law? Why, no one in the world. Salvation by the works of the law is proved to be a clean impossibility. None of you, therefore, will say you will try to obey it, and so hope to be saved. I hear the best Christian in the world groan out his thoughts—"O God," saith he, "I am guilty; and shouldst thou cast me into hell I dare not say otherwise. I have broken this command from my youth up, even since my conversion; I have violated it every day; I know that if thou shouldst lay justice to the line, and righteousness to the plummet, I must be swept away for ever. Lord, I renounce my trust in the law; for by it I know I can never see thy face and be accepted." But hark! I hear the Christian say another thing. "Oh!" saith he to the commandment, "Commandment I can not keep thee, but my Saviour kept thee, and what my Saviour did, he did for all them that believe; and now, O law, what Jesus did is mine. Hast thou any question to bring against me? Thou demand-est that I should keep this commandment wholly: lo, my Saviour kept it wholly for me, and he is my substitute; what I can not do myself my Saviour has done for me; thou canst not reject the work of the substitute, for God accepted it in the day when he raised him from the dead. O law! shut thy mouth for ever; thou canst never condemn me; though I break thee a thousand times, I put my simple trust in Jesus only; his righteousness is mine, and with it I pay the debt and satisfy thy hungry mouth."

"Oh '" ries one, "I wish I could say that I could thus escape the wrath of the law! Oh that I knew that Christ did keep the law for me!" Stop, then, and I will tell you. Do you feel to-day that you are guilty, lost, and ruined? Do you with tears in your eyes confess that none but Jesus can do you good? Are you willing to give up all trusts, and cast yourself alone on him who died upon the cross? Can you look to Calvary, and see the bleeding sufferer, all crimson with streams of gore? Can you say

> "A guilty, weak, and helpless worm,
>   Into thine arms I fall;
> Jesus, be thou my righteousness,
>   My Saviour and my all!"

Canst say that? Then he kept the law for you, and the law can not condemn whom Christ has absolved. If Law comes to you and says, "I will damn you because you did not keep the law," tell him that he dares not touch a hair of your head, for though you did not keep it, Christ kept it for you, and Christ's righteousness is yours; tell him there is the money and though you did not coin it Christ did; and tell him, when you have paid him all he asks for, he dares not touch you; you must be free, for Christ has satisfied the law.

And after that—and here I conclude—O child of God I know what thou wilt say; after thou hast seen the law satisfied by Jesus thou wilt fall on thy knees and say, "Lord, I thank thee that this law can not condemn me, for I believe in Jesus. But now, Lord, help me from this time forth for ever to keep it. Lord, give me a new heart, for this old heart never will love thee! Lord, give me a new life, for this old life is too vile. Lord, give me a new understanding; wash my mind with the clean water of the Spirit; come and dwell in my judgment, my memory, my thought; and then give me the new strength of thy Spirit, and then will I love thee with all my new heart, with all my new life, with all my renewed mind, and with all my spiritual strength, from this time forth, even for evermore."

May the Lord convince you of sin, by the energy of his divine Spirit, and bless this simple sermon, for Jesus's sake! Amen.

SERMON XX

AWAKE! AWAKE!

"Therefore let us not sleep as do others but let us watch and be sober."
—1 THESS., v. 6.

WHAT sad things sin hath done. This fair world of ours was once a glorious temple, every pillar of which reflected the goodness of God, and every part of which was a symbol of good, but sin has spoiled and marred all the metaphors and figures that might be drawn from earth. It has so deranged the divine economy of nature, that those things which were inimitable pictures of virtue, goodness, and divine plenitude of blessing, have now become the figures and representatives of sin. 'Tis strange to say, but it is strangely true, that the very best gifts of God have by the sin of man become the worst pictures of man's guilt. Behold the flood! breaking forth from its fountains, it rushes across the fields, bearing plenty on its bosom; it covers them awhile, and anon it doth subside and leaves upon the plain a fertile deposit, into which the farmer shall cast his seed and reap an abundant harvest. One would have called the breaking forth of water a fine picture of the plenitude of providence, the magnificence of God's goodness to the human race; but we find that sin has appropriated that figure to itself. The beginning of sin is like the breaking forth of waters. See the fire! how kindly God hath bestowed upon us that element, to cheer us in the midst of winter's frosts. Fresh from the snow and from the cold we rush to our household fire, and there by our hearth we warm our hands, and glad are we. Fire is a rich picture of the divine influences of the Spirit, a holy emblem of the zeal of the Christian; but, alas! sin hath touched this, and the tongue is called "a fire;" "it is set on fire of hell," we are told, and

It is so evidently full often, when it uttereth blasphemy and slanders; and Jude lifts up his hand and exclaims, when he looks upon the evils caused by sin, "Behold how great a matter a little fire kindleth." And then there is sleep, one of the sweetest of God's gifts, fair sleep

"Tired nature's sweet restorer, balmy sleep."

Sleep God hath selected as the very figure for the repose of the blessed. "They that sleep in Jesus," saith the Scripture. David puts it amongst the peculiar gifts of grace: "So he giveth his beloved sleep." But alas! sin could not let even this alone. Sin did over-ride even this celestial metaphor; and though God himself had employed sleep to express the excellence of the state of the blessed, yet sin must have even this profaned, ere itself can be expressed. Sleep is employed in our text as a picture of a sinful condition. "Therefore let us not sleep as do others; but let us watch and be sober."

With that introduction, I shall proceed at once to the text. The "sleep" of the text is *an evil to be avoided.* In the second place, the word "therefore" is employed to show us that there are *certain reasons for the avoiding of this sleep.* And since the apostle speaks of this sleep with sorrow, it is to teach us that there are some, whom he calls " others," *over whom it is our business to lament,* because they sleep, and do not watch, and are not sober.

I. We commence, then, in the first place, by endeavoring to point out the EVIL WHICH THE APOSTLE INTENDS TO DESCRIBE UNDER THE TERM SLEEP. The apostle speaks of " others" who are asleep. If you turn to the original you will find that the word translated " others" has a more emphatic meaning. It might be rendered (and Horne so renders it) "the refuse," —" Let us not sleep as do *the refuse,*" the common herd, the ignoble spirits, those who have no mind above the troubles of earth. "Let us not sleep as do the others," the base ignoble multitude who are not alive to the high and celestial calling of a Christian. "Let us not sleep as do the refuse of mankind." And you will find that the word " sleep," in the original, has also a more emphatic sense. It signifies a deep sleep, a profound slumber; and the apostle intimates, that the refuse of mankind are now in a profound slumber. We will now try if we can explain what he meant by it.

First, the apostle meant, that the refuse of mankind *are in a state of deplorable ignorance.* They that sleep know nothing. There may be merriment in the house, but the sluggard shareth not in its gladness; there may be death in the family but no tear bedeweth the cheek of the sleeper. Great events may have transpired in the world's history, but he wots not of them. An earthquake may have tumbled a city from its greatness, or war may have devastated a nation, or the banner of triumph may be waving in the gale, and the clarions of his country may be saluting us with victory, but he knoweth nothing.

> "Their labor and their love are lost,
> Alike unknowing and unknown."

The sleeper knoweth not anything. Behold how the refuse of mankind are alike in this! Of some things they know much, but of spiritual things they know nothing; of the divine person of the adorable Redeemer they have no idea; of the sweet enjoyments of a life of piety they can not even make a guess; toward the high enthusiasms and the inward raptures of the Christian they can not mount. Talk to them of divine doctrines, and they are to them a riddle; tell them of sublime experiences, and they seem to them to be enthusiastic fancies. They know nothing of the joys that are to come; and alas! for them, they are oblivious of the evils which shall happen to them if they go on in their iniquity. The mass of mankind are ignorant; they know not; they have not the knowledge of God, they have no fear of Jehovah before their eyes; but, blind-folded by the ignorance of this world, they march on through the paths of lust to that sure and dreadful end, the everlasting ruin of their souls. Brethren, if we be saints, let us not be ignorant as are others. Let us search the Scriptures, for in them we have eternal life, for they lo testify of Jesus. Let us be diligent; let not the Word depart out of our hearts; let us meditate therein both by day and night, that we may be as the tree planted by the rivers of water. " Let us not sleep as do others."

Again, sleep pictures *a state of insensibility.* There may be much knowledge in the sleeper, hidden, stored away in his mind, which might be well developed, if he could but be awakened. But he hath no sensibility, he knoweth nothing. The burglar hath broken into the house; the gold and silver are both in the robber's hands; the child is being murdered by the cruelty of him that hath broken in; but the father slumbereth, though all the gold and silver that he hath, and his most precious child, are in the hands of the destroyer. He is unconscious, how can he feel, when sleep had utterly sealed his senses! Lo! in the street there is mourning. A fire hath just now burned down the habitation of the poor, and houseless beggars are in the street. They are crying at his window, and asking him for help. But he sleeps, and what wots he, though the night be cold, and though the poor are shivering in the blast? He hath no consciousness; he feeleth not for them. There! take the title-deed of his estate, and burn the document. There! set light to his farm-yard! burn up all that he hath in the field; kill his horse and destroy his cattle; let now the fire of God descend and burn up his sheep; let the enemy fall upon all that he hath and devour it. He sleeps as soundly as if he were guarded by the angel of the Lord.

Such are the refuse of mankind. But alas! that we should have to include in that word "refuse" the great bulk thereof! How few there are that feel spiritually! They feel acutely enough any injury to their body, or to their estate; but alas! for their spiritual concerns they have no sensation whatever! They are standing on the brink of hell, but they tremble not; the anger of God is burning against them, but they fear not the sword of Jehovah is unsheathed, but terror doth not seize upon them. They proceed with the merry dance; they drink the bowl of intoxicating pleasure; they revel and they riot still do they sing the lascivious song; yea, they do more than this; in their vain dreams they do defy the Most High

whereas, if they were once awakened to the consciousness of
their state, the marrow of their bones would melt, and their
heart would dissolve like wax in the midst of their bowels.
They are asleep, indifferent and unconscious. Do what you
may to them; let every thing be swept away that is hopeful,
that might give them cheer when they come to die, yet they
feel it not; for how should a sleeper feel anything? But,
" Therefore let us not sleep, as do others; but let us watch
and be sober."

Again: the sleeper *can not defend himself.* Behold yonder
prince, he is a strong man, ay, and a strong man armed. He
hath entered into the tent. He is wearied. He hath drunken
the woman's milk; he hath eaten her "butter in a lordly
dish;" he casteth himself down upon the floor, and he slumbereth. And now she draweth nigh. She hath with her her
hammer and her nail. Warrior! thou couldst break her into
atoms with one blow of thy mighty arm; but thou canst not
now defend thyself. The nail is at his ear, the woman's hand
is on the hammer, and the nail hath pierced his skull; for when
he slept he was defenceless. The banner of Sisera had waved
victoriously over mighty foes; but now it is stained by a woman. Tell it, tell it, tell it! The man, who when he was
awake, made nations tremble, dies by the hand of a feeble
woman when he sleepeth.

Such are the refuse of mankind. They are asleep; they
have no power to resist temptation. Their moral strength is
departed, for God is departed from them. There is the temptation to lust. They are men of sound principle in business
matters, and nothing could make them swerve from honesty;
but lasciviousness destroyeth them; they are taken like a bird
in the snare; they are caught in a trap; they are utterly subdued. Or, mayhap, it is another way that they are conquered.
They are men that would not do an unchaste act, or even
think a lascivious thought, they scorn it. But they have another weak point, they are entrapped by the glass. They are
taken and they are destroyed by drunkenness. Or, if they can
resist these things, and are inclined neither to looseness of life
nor to excess in living, yet mayhap covetousness entereth into

them; by the name of prudence it slideth into their hearts, and they are led to grasp after treasure and to heap up gold, even though that gold be wrung out of the veins of the poor, and though they do suck the blood of the orphan. They seem to be unable to resist their passion. How many times have I been told by men, "I can not help it, sir, do what I may; I resolve, I re-resolve, but I do the same; I am defenceless; I can not resist the temptation!" Oh, of course you can not, while you are asleep. O Spirit of the living God! wake up the sleeper! Let sinful sloth and presumption both be startled, lest haply Moses should come their way, and finding them asleep should hang them on the gallows of infamy for ever.

Now, I come to give another meaning to the word "sleep." I hope there have been some of my congregation who have been tolerable easy whilst I have described the first three things, because they have thought that they were exempt in those matters. But sleep signifies also *inactivity*. The farmer can not plow his field in his sleep, neither can he cast the grain into the furrows, nor watch the clouds, nor reap his harvest. The sailor can not reef his sail, nor direct his ship across the ocean, whilst he slumbereth. It is not possible that on the Exchange, or the mart, or in the house of business, men should transact their affairs with their eyes fast closed in slumber. It would be a singular thing to see a nation of sleepers; for they would be a nation of idle men. They must all starve; they would produce no wealth from the soil; they would have nothing for their backs, nought for clothing and nought for food. But how many we have in the world that are inactive through sleep! Yes, I say inactive. I mean by that, that they are active enough in one direction, but they are inactive in the right. Oh how many men there are that are totally inactive in anything that is for God's glory, or for the welfare of their fellow creatures! For themselves, they can "rise up early, and sit up late, and eat the bread of carefulness;"—for their children, which is an alias for themselves, they can toil until their fingers ache—they can weary themselves until their eyes are red in their sockets, till the brain whirls, and they can do no more. But for God they can do nothing. Some say they have no time, others frankly confess that they have no will: for God's church they would not spend an hour, whilst for this world's pleasure they could lay out a month. For the poor they can not spend their time and attention. They may haply have time to spare for themselves and for their own amusment; but for holy works, for deeds of charity, and for pious acts they declare they have no leisure; whereas, the fact is, they have no will.

Behold ye, how many professing Christians there are that are asleep in this sense! They are inactive. Sinners are dying in the street by hundreds; men are sinking into the flames of eternal wrath, but they fold their arms, they pity the poor perishing sinner, but they do nothing to show that their pity is real. They go to their places of worship; they occupy their well-cushioned easy pew; they wish the minister to feed them every Sabbath; but there is never a child taught in the Sunday-school by them; there is never a tract distributed at the poor man's honse; there is never a deed done which might be the means of saving souls. We call them good men; some of them we even elect to the office of deacons; and no doubt good men they are; they are as good as Anthony meant to say that Brutus was honorable, when he said, "So are we all, all honorable men." So are we all, all good, · if they be good. But these are good, and in some sense—good for nothing; for they just sit and eat the bread, but they do not plow the field; they drink the wine, but they will not raise the vine that doth produce it. They think that they are to live unto themselves, forgetting that "no man liveth unto himself, and no man dieth unto himself." Oh, what a vast amount of sleeping we have in all our churches and chapels; for truly if our churches were once awake, so far as material is concerned, there are enough converted men and women, and there is enough talent with them, and enough money with them, and enough time with them, God granting the abundance of His Holy Spirit, which he would be sure to do if they were all zealous—there is enough to preach the gospel in every corner of the earth. The church does not need to stop for want of instruments, or for want of agencies; we have everything now except the will; we have all that we may expect God to give for the conversion of the world, except just a heart for the work, and the Spirit of God poured out into our midst. Oh! brethren, "let us not sleep as do others." You will find the "others" in the church and in the world: "the refuse" of both are sound asleep.

Ere, however, I can dismiss this first point of explanation, it is necessary for me just to say that the apostle himself furnishes us with part of an exposition; for the second sentence, "let us watch and be sober," implies that the reverse of these things is the sleep, which he means. "Let us watch." There are many that never watch. They never watch against sin; they never watch against the temptations of the enemy; they do not watch against themselves, nor against "the lusts of the flesh, the lusts of the eye, and the pride of life." They do not watch for opportunities to do good; they do not watch for opportunities to instruct the-ignorant, to confirm the weak, to comfort the afflicted, to succor them that are in need; they do not watch for opportunities of glorifying Jesus, or for times of communion; they do not watch for the promises; they do not watch for answers to their prayers; they do not watch for the second coming of our Lord Jesus. These are the refuse of the world: they watch not because they are asleep. But let us *watch:* so shall we prove that we are not slumberers.

Again: let us "*be sober.*" Albert Barnes says, this most of all refers to abstinence, or temperance in eating and drinking, Calvin says, not so; this refers more especially to the spirit of moderation in the things of the world. Both are right; it refers to both. There be many that are not sober; they sleep because they are not so; for insobriety leadeth to sleep. They are not sober—they are drunkards, they are gluttons. They are not sober—they can not be content to do a little business—they want to do a great deal. They are not sober—they can not carry on a trade that is sure—they must speculate. They are not sober—if they lose their property, their spirit is cast down within them, and they are like men that are drunken with wormwood. If on the other hand, they get rich, they are not sober: they so set their affections upon things on earth that they become intoxicated with pride, because of their riches—become purse-proud, and need to have the heavens lifted up higher, lest their heads should dash against the stars. How many people there are that are not sober! Oh! I might especially urge this precept upon you at this time, my dear friends. We have hard times coming, and the times are hard enough now. Let us be sober. The fearful panic in America has mainly risen from disobedience to this command—" Be sober ;,' and if the professors of America had obeyed this commandment, and had been sober, the panic might at any rate have been mitigated, if not totally avoided. Now, in a little time, you who have any money laid by will be rushing to the bank to have it drawn out, because you fear that the bank is tottering. You will not be sober enough to have a little trust in your fellow-men, and help them through their difficulty, and so be a blessing to the commonwealth. And you who think there is anything to be got by lending your money at usury will not be content with lending what you have, but you will be extorting and squeezing your poor debtors, that you may get the more to lend. Men are seldom content to get rich slowly, but he that hasteth to be rich shall not be innocent. Take care, my brethren—if any hard times should come, if commercial houses should smash, and banks be broken—take care to be sober. There is nothing will get us over a panic so well as every one of us trying to keep our spirits up—just rising in the morning and saying, " Times are very hard, and to-day I may lose my all; but fretting will not help it; so just let me set a bold heart against hard sorrow, and go to my business. The wheels of trade may stop; I bless God, my treasure is in heaven; I can not be bankrupt. I have set my affections on the things of God ; I can not lose those things. There is my jewel; there is my heart !" Why, if all men could do that, it would tend to create public confidence; but the cause of the great ruin of many men is the covetousness of all men, and the fear of some. If we could all go through the world with confidence, and with boldness, and with courage, there is nothing in the world that could avert the shock so well. Come, I suppose, the shock must; and there are many men now present, who are very respectable, who may expect to be beggars ere long. Your business is, so to put your trust in Jehovah that you may be able to say, "Though the earth be removed, and though the mountains be carried into the midst of the sea, God is my refuge and strength, a very present help in trouble; therefore will I not fear;" and doing that, you will be creating more probabilities for the avoidance of your own destruction than by any other means which the wisdom of man can dictate to you. "Let us not be intemperate in business, as are others; but let us awake. "Let us not sleep"—not be carried away by the somnambulism of the world, for what it is better than that?—activity and greed in sleep; "but let us watch and be sober." Oh, Holy Spirit, help us to watch and be sober.

II. Thus I have occupied a great deal of time in explaining the first point—What was the sleep which the apostle meant? And now you will notice that the word "therefore" implies that there are CERTAIN REASONS FOR THIS. I shall give you these reasons; and if I should cast them somewhat into a dramatic form, you must not wonder; they will the better perhaps, be remembered. "Therefore," says the apostle, "let us not sleep."

We shall first look at the chapter itself for our reasons. The first reason precedes the text. The apostle tells us that "we are all the children of *the light* and of the day; *therefore* let us not sleep as do others." I marvel not when, as I walk through the streets after nightfall, I see every shop closed, and every window-blind drawn down; and I see the light in the upper room significant of retirement to rest. I wonder not that a half an hour later my footfall startles me, and I find none in the streets. Should I ascend the staircase, and look into the sleeper's placid countenances, I should not wonder; for it is night, the proper time for sleep. But if, some morning, at eleven or twelve o'clock, I should walk down the streets and find myself alone, and notice every shop closed, and every house straitly shut up, and hearken to no noise, I should say, "'Tis strange, 'tis passing strange, 'tis wonderful

What are these people at? 'Tis day-time, and yet they are all asleep. I should be inclined to seize the first rapper I could find, and give a double knock, and rush to the next door, and ring the bell, and so all the way down the street, or go to the police station, and wake up what men I found there, and bid them make a noise in the street; or go for the fire-engine, and bid the firemen rattle down the road and try to wake these people up. For I should say to myself, " There is some pestilence here; the angel of death must have flown through these streets during the night and killed all these people, or else they would have been sure to have been awake." Sleep in the daytime is utterly incongruous. " Well, now," says the apostle Paul, " ye people of God, it is day-time with you; the sun of righteousness has risen upon you with healing in his wings; the light of God's Spirit is in your conscience; ye have been brought out of darkness into marvelous light; for you to be asleep, for a church to slumber, is like a city a-bed in the day, like a whole town slumbering when the sun is shining. It is untimely and unseemly."

And now, if you look to the text again, you will find there is another argument. " Let us, who are of the day, be sober, putting on the breastplate of faith and love." So, then, it seems, it is *war-time;* and therefore, again, it is unseemly to slumber. There is a fortress, yonder, far away in India. A troop of those abominable Sepoys have surrounded it. Blood-thirsty hell-hounds, if they once gain admission, they will rend the mother and her children, and cut the strong man in pieces. They are at the gates: their cannon are loaded, their bayonets thirst for blood, and their swords are hungry to slay. Go through the fortress, and the people are all asleep. There is the warder on the tower, nodding on his bayonet. There is the captain in his tent, with his pen in his hand, and his dispatches before him, asleep at the table. There are soldiers lying down in their tents, ready for the war, but all slumbering. There is not a man to be seen keeping watch there is not a sentry there. All are asleep. Why, my friends, you would say, " Whatever is the matter here? What can it be? Has some great wizard been waving his

wand, and put a spell upon them all? Or are they all
mad? Have their minds fled? Sure, to be asleep in war-
time is indeed outrageous. Here! take down that trumpet;
go close up to the captain's ear, and blow a blast, and see if
it does not awake him in a moment. Just take away that bayonet from the soldier that is asleep on the walls, and give him
a sharp prick with it, and see if he does not awake." But
surely, surely, nobody can have patience with people asleep,
when the enemy surround the walls and are thundering at the
gates.

Now, Christians, this is your case. Your life is a life of
warfare; the world, the flesh, and the devil; that hellish trinity, and your poor flesh is a wretched mudwork behind which
to be intrenched. Are you asleep? Asleep, when Satan has
fire-balls of lust to hurl into the windows of your eyes—when
he has arrows of temptation to shoot into your heart—when
he has snares into which to trap your feet? Asleep, when he
has undermined your very existence, and when he is about to
apply the match with which to destroy you, unless sovereign
grace prevents? Oh! sleep not, soldier of the cross! To
sleep in war-time is utterly inconsistent. Great Spirit of God
forbid that we should slumber.

But now, leaving the chapter itself, I will give you one or
two other reasons that will, I trust, move Christian people to
awake out of their sleep. " *Bring out your dead! Bring
out your dead! Bring out your dead!*" Then comes the
ringing of a bell. What is this? Here is a door marked with
a great white cross. Lord, have mercy upon us! All the
houses down that street seem to be marked with that white
death cross. What is this? Here is the grass growing in the
streets; here are Cornhill and Cheapside deserted; no one is
found treading the solitary pavement; there is not a sound to
be heard but those horse-hoofs like the hoofs of death's pale
horse upon the stones, the ringing of that bell that sounds the
death-knell to many, and the rumbling of the wheels of that
cart, and the dreadful cry, " Bring out your dead! Bring
out your dead! Bring out your dead!" Do you see that
house? A physician lives there. He is a man who has great

skill, and God has lent him wisdom. But a little while ago, whilst in his study, God was pleased to guide his mind, and he discovered the secret of the plague. He was plague-smitten himself, and ready to die; but he lifted the blessed phial to his lips, and he drank a draught and cured himself. Do you believe what I am about to tell you? Can you imagine it? That man has the prescription that will heal all these people; he has it in his pocket. He has the medicine which, if once distributed in those streets, would make the sick rejoice, and put that dead man's bell away. And he is asleep! he is asleep! He is asleep! O ye heavens! why do ye not fall and crush the wretch? O earth! how couldst thou bear this demon upon thy bosom? Why not swallow him up quick? He has the medicine; he is too lazy to go and tell forth the remedy. He has the cure, and is too idle to go out and administer it to the sick and the dying! No, my friends, such an inhuman wretch could not exist! But I can see him here to-day. There are you! You know the world is sick with the plague of sin, and you yourself have been cured by the remedy which has been provided. You are asleep, inactive, loitering. You do not go forth to

> "Tell to others round,
> What a dear Saviour you have found."

There is the precious gospel; you do not go and put it to the lips of a sinner. There is the all-precious blood of Christ; you never go to tell the dying what they must do to be saved. The world is perishing with worse than plague: and you are idle! And you are a minister of the gospel; and you have taken that holy office upon yourself; and you are content to preach twice on a Sunday, and once on a week-day, and there is no remonstrance within you. You never desire to attract the multitudes to hear you preach; you had rather keep your empty benches, and study propriety, than you would once, at the risk of appearing over-zealous, draw the multitude and preach the word to them. You are a writer; you have great power in writing; you devote your talents alone to light literature, or to the production of other things which may furnish amusement, but which can not benefit the soul. You know the truth, but you do not tell it out. Yonder mother is a converted woman: you have children, and you forget to instruct them in the way to heaven. You, yonder, are a young man, having nothing to do on the Sabbath-day, and there is the Sunday school; you do not go to tell those children the sovereign remedy that God has provided for the cure of sick souls. The death-bell is ringing e'en now; hell is crying out, howling with hunger for the souls of men. " Bring out the sinner! Bring out the sinner! Bring out the sinner! Let him die and be damned!" And there are you, professing to be a Christian, and doing nothing which might make you the instrument of saving souls—never putting out your hand to be the means in the hand of the Lord, of plucking sinners as brands from the burning! Oh! May the blessing of God rest on you, to turn you from such an evil way, that you may not sleep as do others, but may watch and be sober. The world's eminent danger demands that we should be active and not be slumbering.

Hark how the mast creaks! See the sails there, rent to ribbons. Breakers ahead! She will be on the rocks directly. Where is the captain? Where is the boatswain? Where are the sailors? Ahoy there! Where are you? Here's a storm come on. Where are you? You are down in the cabin. And there is the captain in a soft sweet slumber. There is the man at the wheel, as sound asleep as ever he can be; and there are all the sailors in their hammocks. What! and the breakers ahead? What! the lives of two hundred passengers in danger, and here are these brutes asleep? Kick them out. What is the good of letting such men as these be sailors, in such a time as this especially? Why, out with you! If you had gone to sleep in fine weather we might have forgiven you. Up with you, captain! What have you been at? Are you mad? But hark! the ship has struck; she will be down in a moment. Now you will work, will you? Now you will work, when it is of no use, and when the shrieks of drowning women shall toll you into hell for your most accursed negligence, in not having taken care of them. Well, that is very much like a great many of us, in these times too.

This proud ship of our commonwealth is reeling in a storm of sin; the very mast of this great nation is creaking under the hurricane of vice that sweeps across the noble vessel; every timber is strained, and God help the good ship, or alas! none can save her. And who are her captain and her sailors, but ministers of God, the professors of religion? These are they to whom God gives grace to steer the ship. "Ye are the salt of the earth;" ye preserve and keep it alive, O children of God. Are ye asleep in the storm? Are ye slumbering now? If there were no dens of vice, if there were no harlots, if there were no houses of profanity, if there were no murders and no crimes, oh! ye that are the salt of the earth, ye might sleep; but to-day the sin of London crieth in the ears of God. This behemoth city is covered with crime, and God is vexed with her. And are we asleep, doing nothing? Then God forgive us! But sure of all the sins he ever doth forgive, this is the greatest, the sin of slumbering when a world is damning—the sin of being idle when Satan is busy, devouring the souls of men. "Brethren, let us not sleep" in such times as these; for if we do, a curse must fall upon us, horrible to bear.

There is a poor prisoner in a cell. His hair is all matted, over his eyes. A few weeks ago the judge put on the black cap, and commanded that he should be taken to the place from whence he came, and hung by the neck until dead. The poor wretch has his heart broken within him, whilst he thinks of the pinion, of the gallows, and of the drop, and of after-death. O! who can tell how his heart is rent and racked, whilst he thinks of leaving all, and going he knoweth not where! There is a man there, sound asleep upon a bed. He has been asleep there these two days, and under his pillow he has that prisoner's free pardon. I would horsewhip that scoundrel, horsewhip him soundly, for making that poor man have two days of extra misery. Why, if I had had that man's pardon, I would have been there, if I rode on the wings of lightning to get at him, and I should have thought the fastest train that ever run but slow, if I had so sweet a message to carry, and such a poor heavy heart to carry it to. But that man, that brute, is sound asleep, with a free pardon under his pillow, whilst that poor wretch's heart is breaking with dismay! Ah.! do not be too hard with him: he is here to-day. Side by side with you this morning there is sitting a poor penitent sinner; God has pardoned him, and intends that you should tell him that good news. He sat by your side last Sunday, and he wept all the sermon through, for he felt his guilt. If you had spoken to him then, who can tell? He might have had comfort; but there he is now—you do not tell him the good news. Do you leave that to me to do? Ah! sirs, but you can not serve God by proxy; what the minister does is nought to you; you have your own personal duty to do, and God has given you a precious promise. It is now on your heart. Will you not turn round to your next neighbor, and tell him that promise? O! there is many an aching heart that aches because of our idleness in telling the good news of this salvation. "Yes," says one of my members, who always comes to this place on a Sunday, and looks out for young men and young women whom he has seen in tears the Sunday before, and who brings many into the church, "yes, I could tell you a story." He looks a young man in the face, and says, "Hav'nt I seen you here a great many times?" "Yes." "I think you take a deep interest in the service, do you not?" "Yes, I do: what makes you ask me that question?" "Because I looked at your face last Sunday, and I thought there was something at work with you." "O! sir," he says, "nobody has spoken to me ever since I have been here till now, and I want to say a word to you. When I was at home with my mother, I used to think I had some idea of religion; but I came away, and was bound apprentice with an ungodly lot of youths, and have done everything I ought not to have done. And now, sir, I begin to weep, I begin to repent. I wish to God that I knew how I might be saved! I hear the word preached, sir, but I want something spoken personally to me by somebody." And he turns round; he takes him by the hand and says, "My dear young brother, I am so glad I spoke to you; it makes my poor old heart rejoice to think that the Lord is doing something here still. Now, do not be cast down; for you know, "This is a faithful saying, and worthy of all acceptation, that Christ Jesus came into the world to save sinners.'" The young man puts his handkerchief to his eyes, and after a minute, he says, "I wish you would let me call and see you, sir." "O! you may," he says. He talks with him, he leads him onward, and at last by God's grace the happy youth comes forward and declares what God has done for his soul, and owes his salvation as much to the humble instrumentality of the man that helped him as he could do to the preaching of the minister.

Beloved brethren, the bridegroom cometh! Awake! Awake! The earth must soon be dissolved, and the heavens must melt! Awake! Awake! O Holy Spirit arouse us all, and keep us awake.

III. And now I have no time for the last point, and therefore I shall not detain you. Suffice me to say in warning, there is AN EVIL HERE LAMENTED. There are some that are asleep, and the apostle mourns it.

My fellow sinner, thou that art this day unconverted, let me say six or seven sentences to thee, and thou shalt depart. Unconverted man! unconverted woman! you are asleep today, as they that sleep on the top of the mast in time of storm; you are asleep, as he that sleeps when the water-floods are out, and when his house is undermined, and being carried down the stream far out to sea; you are asleep, as he who in the upper chamber, when his house is burning and his own locks are singeing in the fire, knows not the devastation around him; you are asleep—asleep as he that lies upon the edge of a precipice, with death and destruction beneath him. One single start in his sleep would send him over, but he knows it not. Thou art asleep this day; and the place where thou sleepest has so frail a support that when once it breaks thou shalt fall into hell: and if thou wakest not till then, what a waking it will be! "In hell he lifted up his eyes, being in torment;" and he cried for a drop of water, but it was denied him. "He that believeth in the Lord Jesus Christ, and is baptized shall be saved; he that believeth not shall be damned." This is the gospel. Believe ye in Jesus, and ye shall "rejoice with joy unspeakable and full of glory."

SERMON XXI

THE LOVED ONES CHASTENED

"As many as I love, I rebuke and chasten: be zealous therefore, and repent."—REVELATION, iii. 19.

THE dealings of God towards the sons of men have always puzzled the wise men of the earth who have tried to understand them. Apart from the revelation of God the dealings of Jehovah towards his creatures in this world seem to be utterly inexplicable. Who can understand how it is that the wicked flourish and are in great power? The ungodly man flourishes like a green bay tree; behold, he stretcheth out his roots by the river: he knoweth not the year of drought; his leaf withereth not; and his fruit doth not fall in an untimely season. Lo, these are the ungodly that flourish in the world; they are filled with riches; they heap up gold like dust; they leave the rest of their substance to their babes; they add field to field, and acre to acre, and they become the princes of the earth. On the other hand, see how the righteous are cast down. How often is virtue dressed in the rags of poverty! How frequently is the most pious spirit made to suffer from hunger, and thirst, and nakedness! We have sometimes heard the Christian say, when he has contemplated these things, "Surely, I have served God in vain; it is for nothing that I have chastened myself every morning and vexed my soul with fasting; for lo, God hath cast me down, and he lifteth up the sinner. How can this be?" The sages of the heathen could not answer this question, and they therefore adopted the expedient of cutting the gordian knot. "We can not tell how it is," they might have said; therefore they flew at the fact itself, and denied it. "The man that prospers is favored of the gods; the man who is unsuccessful is obnoxious to the Most High." So said the heathen, and they knew no better. Those more enlightened easterns, who talked with Job in the days of his affliction, got but little further; for they believed that all who served God would have a hedge about them; God would multiply their wealth and increase their happiness; while they saw in Job's affliction, as they conceived, a certain sign that he was a hypocrite, and therefore God had quenched his candle and put out his light in darkness. And alas! even Christians have fallen into the same error. They have been apt to think, that if God lifts a man up there must be some excellence in him; and if he chastens and afflicts, they are generally led to think that it must be an exhibition of wrath. Now hear ye the text, and the riddle is all unriddled; listen ye to the words of Jesus, speaking to his servant John, and the mystery is all unmysteried. "As many as I love, I rebuke and chasten: be zealous therefore, and repent."

The fact is, that this world is not the place of punishment. There may now and then be eminent judgments; but as a rule God does not in the present state fully punish any man for sin. He allows the wicked to go on in their wickedness; he throws the reins upon their necks; he lets them go on unbridled in their lusts; some checks of conscience there may be; but these are rather as monitions than as punishments. And, on the other hand, he casts the Christian down; he gives the most afflictions to the most pious; perhaps he makes more waves of trouble roll over the breast of the most sanctified Christian than over the heart of any other man living So, then, we must remember that as this world is not the place of punishment, we are to expect punishment and reward in the world to come; and we must believe that the only reason, then, why God afflicts his people must be this:—

> " In love I correct thee, thy gold to refine,
> To make thee at length in my likeness to shine."

I shall try this morning to notice, first, *what it is in his children that God corrects;* secondly, *why God corrects them;*

and thirdly, *what is our comfort, when we are laboring under the rebukes and correctings of our God.* Our comfort must be the fact that he loves us even then. "As many as I love, I rebuke and chasten."

I. First, then, beloved, WHAT IS IT IN THE CHRISTIAN THAT GOD REBUKES? One of the Articles of the Church of England saith right truly, that, naturally, "man is very far gone from original righteousness, and is of his own nature inclined to evil, so that the flesh lusteth always contrary to the spirit; and therefore in every person born into this world, it deserveth God's wrath and damnation. And this infection of nature doth remain, yea in them that are regenerated; whereby the lust of the flesh, called in the Greek, φρόνημα σαρκὸς, which some do expound the wisdom, some sensuality, some the affection, some the desire, of the flesh, is not subject to the Law of God. And although there is no condemnation for them that believe and are baptized, yet the Apostle doth confess, that concupiscence and lust hath of itself the nature of sin," and because evil remains in the regenerate there is therefore a necessity that that evil should be upbraided. Ay, and a necessity that when that upbraiding is not sufficient, God should go to severer measures, and after having failed in his rebukes, adopt the expedient of chastening. "I rebuke and chasten." Hence God has provided means for the chastisement and the rebuking of his people. Sometimes God rebukes his children under the ministry. The minister of the gospel is not always to be a minister of consolation. The same Spirit that is the Comforter is he who convinces the world of sin, of righteousness, and of judgment; and the same minister who is to be as the angel of God unto our souls, uttering sweet words that are full of honey, is to be at times the rod of God, the staff in the hand of the Almighty, with which to smite us on account of our transgressions. And ah! beloved, how often under the ministry ought we to have been checked when we were not? Perhaps the minister's words were very forcible, and they were uttered with true earnestness, and they applied to our case; but alas! we shut our ear to them, and applied them to our brother instead of to ourselves. I have often marveled

when I have been preaching. I have thought that I have de-
cribed the cases of some of my most prominent members.
I have marked in them diverse sins, and as Christ's faithful
pastor, I have not shunned to picture their case in the pulpit,
that they might receive a well-deserved rebuke; but I have
marveled when I have spoken to them afterward, that they
have thanked me for what I have said, because they thought
it so applicable to such another brother in the church, whilst
I had intended it wholly for them, and had, as I thought, so
made the description accurate, and so brought it out in all its
little points, that it must have been received by them. But
alas! you know, my friends, that we sit under the sound of
the Word, and we seldom think how much it belongs to us,
especially if we hold an office in the Church. It is hard for a
minister when he is hearing a brother minister preach, to
think, it may be, he has a word of rebuke to me. If exalted
to the office of elder or deacon, there groweth sometimes
with that office a callousness to the Word when spoken to
himself; and the man in office is apt to think of the hundreds
of inquirers unto whom that may be found applicable, and of
the multitudes of the babes in grace to whom such a word
comes in season. Ay, friends, if we did but listen more to
the rebukes of God in the ministry, if we hearkened more to
his Word as he speaks to us every Sabbath day, we might be
spared many corrections, for we are not corrected until we
have despised rebukes, and after we have rejected those, then
out comes the rod.

Sometimes, again, God rebukes his children *in their consciences*, without any visible means whatever. Ye that are
the people of God will acknowledge that there are certain
times, when, apparently without any instrumentality, your
sins are brought to remembrance; your soul is cast down
within you, and your spirit is sore vexed. God the Holy
Spirit is himself making inquisition for sin; he is searching
Jerusalem with candles; he is so punishing you because you
are settled on your lees. If you look around you there is nothing that could cause your spirits to sink. The family are
not sick; your business prospers; your body is in good

health; why then this sinking of spirit? You are not conscious at the time, perhaps, that you have committed any
gross act of sin; still this dark depression continues, and at
last you discover that you had been living in a sin which you
did not know—some sin of ignorance, hidden and unper-
ceived, and therefore God did withdraw from you the joy of
his salvation, till you had searched your heart, and discovered
wherein the evil lay. We have much reason to bless God
that he does adopt this way sometimes of rebuking us before
he chastens.

At other seasons, the rebuke is *quite indirect.* How often
have I met rebuke, where it never was intended to be given!
But God overruled the circumstance for good. Have you
never been rebuked by a child? The innocent little prattler
uttered something quite unwittingly, which cut you to your
heart, and manifested your sin. You walked the street, may
hap, and you heard some man swear; and the thought perhaps struck your mind, "How little am I doing for the
reclaiming of those who are abandoned!" And so, the very
sight of sin accused you of negligence, and the very hearing
of evil was made use of by God to convince you of another
evil. Oh! if we kept our eyes open, there is not an ox in the
meadow, nor a sparrow in the tree, which might not sometimes suggest a rebuke. There is not a star in midnight, there
is not a ray in the noon-day, but what might suggest to us
some evil that is hidden in our hearts, and lead us to investigate our inner man, if we were but awake to the soft whispers
of Jehovah's rebukes. You know, our Saviour made use of
little things to rebuke his disciples. He said, "Consider the
lilies of the field, how they grow. Behold the fowls of the
air, how they are fed!" So he made lilies and ravens speak
to his disciples, to upbraid their discontent. Earth is full of
monitors: all that we need, are ears to hear. However, when
these rebukes all fail, God proceeds from rebuke to correction.
He will not always chide; but, if his rebukes are unheeded,
then he grasps the rod, and he uses it. I need not tell you
how it is that God uses the rod. My brethren, you have all
been made to tingle with it. He has sometimes smitten you

in your persons, sometimes in your families, frequently in your estates, oftentimes in your prospects. He has smitten you in your nearest and dearest friend; or, worse still, it may be he has given you "a thorn in the flesh, a messenger of Satan to buffet you." But you all understand, if you know anything of the life of a Christian, what the rod, and the staff, and the covenant are; and what it is to be corrected by God. Let me just particularize for a few minutes, and show what it is that God corrects in us.

Very frequently, God corrects *inordinate affection*. It is right of us to love our relatives—it is wrong of us to love them more than God. You, perhaps, are yourselves to-day guilty of this sin. At any rate, beloved, we may most of us look at home when we come to dwell on this point. Have we not some favored one—perhaps, the partner of our heart, or the offspring of our bosom, more dear to us than life itself? Have I not heard some man whose life is bound up in the life of the lad, his child?—some mother, whose soul is knit into the soul of her babe—some wife, some husband, to whom the loss of the partner would be the loss of life? Oh, there are many of us who are guilty of inordinate affection toward relations. Mark you, God will rebuke us for that. He will rebuke us in this way. Sometimes he will rebuke us by the minister; if that is not enough, he will rebuke us by sending sickness or disease to those very persons upon whom we have set our hearts; and if that rebuke us not, and if we are not zealous to repent, he will chasten us: the sickness shall yet be unto death. The disease shall break forth with more fearful violence, and the thing which we have made our idol shall be smitten, and shall become the food of worms. There never was an idol, that God either did not, or will not pull out of its place. "I am the Lord thy God; I am a jealous God;" and if we put any, however good and excellent their characters may be, and however deserving of our affection, upon God's throne, God will cry, "Down with it," and we shall have to weep many tears; but if we had not done so, we might have preserved the treasure, and have enjoyed it far better, without having lost it.

But other men are baser than this. One can easily overlook the fault of making too much of children, and wife, and friends, although very grievous in the sight of God; but alas! there are some that are too sordid to love flesh and blood; they love dirt, mere dirty earth, yellow gold. It is that on which they set their hearts. Their purse, they tell us, is dross; but when we come to take aught from it, we find they do not think it is so. "Oh," said a man once, "if you want a subscription from me, Sir, you must get at my heart, and then you will get at my purse." "Yes," said I, "I have no doubt I shall, for I believe that is where your purse lies, and I shall not be very far off from it." And how many there are who call themselves Christians, who make a god out of their wealth! Their park, their mansion, their estate, their warehouses, their large ledgers, their many clerks, their expanding business, or if not these, their opportunity to retire, their money in the Three per Cents. All these things are their idols and their gods; and we take them into our churches, and the world finds no fault with them. They are prudent men. You know many of them; they are very respectable people, they hold many respectable positions, and they are so prudent, only that the love of money, which is the root of all evil, is in their hearts too plainly to be denied. Every one may see it, though, perhaps, they see it not themselves. "Covetousness, which is idolatry," reigns very much in the church of the living God. Well, mark you, God will chasten for that. Whosoever loveth mammon among God's people, shall first be rebuked for it, as he is rebuked by me this day, and if that rebuke be not taken, there shall be a chastisement given. It may be, that the gold shall melt like the snow-flake before the sun; or if it be preserved, it shall be said, "Your gold and silver are cankered; the moth shall eat up your garments, and destroy your glory." Or else, the Lord will bring leanness into their souls, and cause them to go down to their graves with few honors on their heads, and with little comfort in their hearts; because they loved their gold more than their God, and valued earthly riches more than the riches that are eternal. The Lord save us from that, or else he will surely correct us

But this is not the only sin: we are all subject to another crime which God abhors exceedingly. It is the sin of *pride*. If the Lord gives us a little comfort, we grow so big that we hardly know what to do with ourselves. Like Jeshurun of old, of whom it is said, "Jeshurun waxed fat and kicked." Let us for a little time enjoy the full assurance of faith; self-conceit whispers, "You will retain the savor of that all your days;" and there is not quite a whisper, but something even fainter than that—"You have no need to depend upon the influence of the Holy Spirit now. See what a great man you have grown. You have become one of the Lord's most valued people; you are a Samson; you may pull down the very gates of hell and fear not. You have no need to cry, 'Lord, have mercy upon me.'" Or at other times, it takes a different turn. He gives us temporal mercies, and then we presumptuously say, "My mountain standeth firm; I shall never be moved." We meet with the poor saints, and we begin to hector over them, as if we were something, and they were nothing. We find some in trouble; we have no sympathy with them; we are bluff and blunt with them, as we talk with them about their troubles; yea, we are even savage and cruel with them. We meet with some who are in deep distress and faint-hearted; we begin to forget when we were faint-hearted too, and because they cannot run as fast as we can, we run far ahead, and turn back and look at them, call them sluggards, and say they are idle and lazy. And perhaps even in the pulpit, if we are preachers, we have got hard words to say against those who are not quite so advanced as we are. Well, mark, there never was a saint yet, that grew proud of his fine feathers, but what the Lord plucked them out by-and-by. There never yet was an angel that had pride in his heart, but he lost his wings, and fell into Gehenna, as Satan and those fallen angels did; and there shall never be a saint who indulges self-conceit, and pride, and self-confidence, but the Lord will spoil his glories, and trample his honors in the mire, and make him cry out yet again, "Lord, have mercy upon me," less than the least of all saints, and the "very chief of sinners."

Another sin that God rebukes, is *sloth*. Now I need not stop to picture that. How many of you are the finest specimens of sloth that can be discovered! I mean not in a business sense, for you are "not slothful in business;" but with regard to the things of God, and the cause of truth, why, nine out of ten of all the professors of religion, I do hazard the assertion, are as full of sloth as they can be. Take our churches all around, and there is not a corporation in the world, however corrupt, that is less attentive to its professed interest, than the church of Christ. There certainly are many societies and establishments in the world that deserve much blame for not attending to those interests which they ought to promote; but I do think the Church of God is the hugest culprit of all. She says that she is the preacher of the gospel to the poor: does she preach it to them? Yes, here and there: now and then there is a spasmodic effort: but how many are there that have got tongues to speak, and ability to utter God's Word that are content to be still! She professes to be the educator of the ignorant, and she is so in a measure: there are many of you who have no business to be here this morning—you ought to have been teaching in the Sabbath-school, or instructing the young, and teaching others. Ye have no need of teachers just now; ye have learned the truth, and should have been teaching it to other people. The church professes that she is yet to cast the light of the gospel throughout the world. She does a little in missionary enterprise; but ah! how little! how little! how little compared with what her Master did for her and the claims of Jesus upon her! We are a lazy set. Take the church all round, we are as idle as we can be; and we need to have some whipping times of persecution, to whip a little more earnestness and zeal into us. We thank God this is not so much the case now, as it was even twelve months ago. We hope the church may progress in her zeal; for if not, she, as a whole, and each of us as members, will be first rebuked, and if we take not the rebuke, we shall afterwards be chastened for this our great sin.

I have no time to enter into all the other reasons for which God will rebuke and chasten. Suffice it to say that every sin has one twig in God's rod appropriated to itself. Suffice it to say, that in God's hand there are punishments for each particular transgression; and it is very singular to notice how in Bible history almost every saint has been chastened for the sin he has committed by the sin itself falling upon his own head. Transgression has been first a pleasure, and afterward it has been a scourge. "The backslider in heart shall be filled with his own ways," and that is the severest punishment in all the world.

Thus I have tried to open the first head—*it is that God rebukes and chastens.*

II. Now, secondly, WHY DOES GOD REBUKE AND CHASTEN? "Why," says one, "God rebukes his children because they are his children; and he chastens them because they are his children." Well; I will not go the length of saying that is false, but I will go the length of saying it is not true. If any one should say to a father, after he had chastened his child, "Why is it you have chastened the child?" he would not say, it is because I am his father. It is true in one sense; but he would say, "I have chastened the child because he has done wrong." Because the proximate reason why he had chastened his child would not be that he was his father, though that would have something to do with it as a primary reason; but the absolute and primary cause would be, "I have chastened him because he has done wrong, because I wish to correct him for it, that he might not do so again." Now, God, when he chastens his children, never does it absolutely; because he is his father; but he does it for a wise reason. He has some other reason besides his fatherhood. At the same time, one reason why God afflicts his children and not others, is because he is their Father. If you were to go home to-day and see a dozen boys in the streets throwing stones and breaking windows it is very likely you would start the whole lot of them; but if there is one boy that would get a sweet knock on the head it would be your own; for you would say, "What are you at, John? What business have you here?" You might not be justified, perhaps, in meddling with the others—you would let their own fathers attend to them; but because you

were his father, you would try to make him remember it.
Certain special chastisements are inflicted on God's children,
because they are his children ; but it is not because they are
his children that he chastens them at any one time, but be
cause they have been doing something wrong. Now, if you
are under chastisement, let this truth be certain to you. Are
the consolations of God small with thee ? Is there any secret
thing with thee ? Art thou chastened in thy business ? Then
what sin hast thou committed ? Art thou cast down in thy
spirit ? Then what transgression has brought this on thee ?
Remember, it is not fair to say, " I am chastened because I
am his child ;" the right way to say it is, " I am his child, and
therefore when he chastens me he has a reason for it." Now,
what is it ? I will help you to judge.

Sometimes God chastens and afflicts us, *to prevent sin*. He
sees that the embryo of lust is in our hearts ; he sees that
that little egg of mischief is beginning to hatch and to produce sin, and he comes and crushes it at once—nips the sin in
the bud. Ah ! we can not tell how much guilt Christians have
been saved from by their afflictions. We are running on
madly to our destruction, and then some dark apparition of
trouble comes, and stretches itself across the way, and in great
fright we fly back astonished. We ask, why this trouble ?
Oh ! if we knew the danger into which we were rushing we
should only say, " Lord, I thank thee that by that direful trouble thou didst save me from a sin, that would have been far
more troublous and infinitely more dangerous."

At other times God chastens us for sins already committed.
We perhaps have forgotten them ; but God has not. I think
that sometimes years elapse between a sin and the chastisement for it. The sins of our youth may be punished in our
gray old age ; the transgression you did twenty years ago,
those of you who have grown old, may this very day be found
in your bones. God chastens his children, but he sometimes
lays the rod by. The time would not be seasonable perhaps ;
they are not strong enough to bear it : so he lays the rod by
and he says, as surely as he is my child, though I lay the rod
by, I will make him smart for it, that I may at last deliver him

from his sin, and make him like unto myself. But mark, ye people of God, in all these chastisments for sin there is no punishment. When God chastises you he does not punish as a judge does, but he chastens as a father. When he lays the rod on, with many blows and smart ones, there is not one thought of anger in his heart—there is not one look of displeasure in his eye; he means it all for your good; his heaviest blows are as much tokens of his affection as his sweetest caresses. He has no motive but your profit and his own glory. Be of good cheer, then, if these be the reasons. But take care that thou dost fulfil the command—" Be zealous, therefore, and repent."

I read in an old Puritan author the other day a very pretty figure. He says, " A full wind is not so favorable to a ship when it is fully fair as a side wind. It is strange," says he, " that when the wind blows in an exact direction to blow a ship into port, she will not go near so well as if she had a cross wind sideways upon her." And he explains it thus : " The mariners say that when the wind blows exactly fair it only fills a part of the sails, and it can not reach the sails that are ahead, because the sail, bellying out with the wind, prevents the wind from reaching that which is further ahead. But when the wind sweeps sideways, then every sail is full, and she is driven on swiftly in her course with the full force of the wind. Ah !" says the old Puritan, " there is nothing like a side wind to drive God's people to heaven. A fair wind only fills a part of their sails; that is, fills their joy, fills their delight ; but," says he, " the side wind fills them all ; it fills their caution, fills their prayerfulness, fills every part of the spiritual man, and so the ship speeds onward toward its haven." It is with this design that God sends affliction, to chasten us on account of our transgressions.

III. And now I am to conclude by noting WHAT IS OUR COMFORT WHEN GOD REBUKES AND CHASTENS US ?

Our great comfort is, that he *loves* us still. Oh ! what a precious thing faith is, when we are enabled to believe our God, and how easy then it is to endure and to surmount all trouble . Hear the old man in the garret, with a crust of bread and a cup of cold water. Sickness has confined him these years within that narrow room. He is too poor to maintain an attendant. Some woman comes in to look to him in the morning and in the evening, and there he sits, in the depths of poverty. And you will suppose he sits and groans. No, brethren; he may sometimes groan when the body is weak, but usually he sits and sings; and when the visitor climbs the creaking staircase of that old house, where human beings scarcely ought to be allowed to live; and when he goes into that poor cramped up room that is more fit to accommodate swine than men, he sits down upon that bottomless chair, and when he has seated himself as well as he can upon the four cross pieces of it he begins to talk to him, and he finds him full of heaven. "Oh! sir," he says, "my God is very kind to me." Propped up he is with pillows, and full of pain in every member of his body, but he says, "Blessed be his name, he has not left me. Oh! sir, I have enjoyed more peace and happiness in this room, out of which I have not gone for years,"—(the case is real that I am now describing) "I have enjoyed more happiness here than I ever did in all my life. My pains are great, sir, but they will not be for long; I am going home soon." Ay, were he more troubled still, had he such rich consolation poured into his heart, he might endure all with a smile and sing in the furnace. Now, child of God, thou art to do the same. Remember, all thou hast to suffer is sent in love. It is hard work for a child, when his father has been chastening it, to look at the rod as a picture of love. You can not make your children do that: but when they grow up to be men and women how thankful they are to you then! "O father," says the son, "I know now why it was I was so often chastened; I had a proud hot spirit; it would have been the ruin of me if thou hadst not whipped it out of me. Now, I thank thee, my father, for it."

So, while we are here below we are nothing but little children; we can not prize the rod: when we come of age, and we go into our estates in Paradise, we shall look back upon the rod of the Covenant as being better than Aaron's rod, for it blossoms with mercy. We shall say to it, "Thou art the most wondrous thing in all the list of my treasures. Lord, i thank thee that thou didst not leave me unafflicted, or else I had not been where I am, and what I am, a child of God in Paradise." " I have this week," says one, " sustained so serious a loss in my business, that I am afraid I shall be utterly broken up." There is love in that. "I came here this morning," says one, " and I left a dead child in the house—dear to my heart." There is love in that. That coffin and that shroud will both be full of love ; and when your child is taken away, it shall not be in anger. " Ah !" cries another, " but I have been exceedingly sick, and even now I feel I ought not to have ventured out ; I must return to my bed." Ah ! he makes your bed in your affliction. There is love in every pain, in every twitch of the nerve ; in every pang that shoots through the members, there is love. " Ah !" says one, "it is not myself, but I have got a dear one that is sick." There is love there, too. Do what God may, he can not do an unloving act toward his people. O Lord ! thou art Omnipotent ; thou canst do all things ; but thou canst not lie, and thou canst not be unkind to thine elect. No, Omnipotence may build a thousand worlds, and fill them with bounties ; Omnipotence may powder mountains into dust, and burn the sea, and consume the sky, but Omnipotence can not do an unloving thing toward a believer. Oh ! rest quite sure, Christian, a hard thing, an unloving thing from God toward one of his own people is quite impossible. He is kind to you when he casts you into prison as when he takes you into a palace ; He is as good when he sends famine into your house as when he fills your barns with plenty. The only question is, Art thou his child ? If so, he hath rebuked thee in affection, and there is love in his chastisement.

I have now done, but not until I have made my last appeal. I have now to turn from God's people to the rest of you. Ah ! my hearers, there are some of you that have no God ; you have no Christ on whom to cast your troubles. I see some of you to-day dressed in the habiliments of mourning ; I suppose you have lost some one dear unto you. Oh ! ye that are robed in black, is God your God ? Or are you mourning now, without God to wipe every tear from your eye? I know that many of you are struggling now in your business with very sharp and hard times. Can you tell your troubles to Jesus, or have you to bear them all yourself—friendless and helpless? Many men have been driven mad, because they had no one to whom to communicate their sorrow; and how many others had been driven worse than mad, because when they told their sorrows their confidence was betrayed. O poor mourning spirit, if thou hadst, as thou mightest have done, gone and told him all thy woes, he would not have laughed at thee, and he would never have told it out again. Oh I remember when once my young heart ached in boyhood, when I first loved the Saviour. I was far away from father and mother, and all I loved, and I thought my soul would burst; for I was an usher in a school, in a place where I could meet with no sympathy or help. Well, I went to my chamber, and told my little griefs into the ears of Jesus. They were great griefs to me then, though they are nothing now. When I just whispered them on my knees into the ear of him who had loved me with an everlasting love, oh! it was so sweet, none can tell. If I had told them to somebody else, they would have told them again; but he, my blessed confidant, he knows my secrets, and he never tells them. Oh! what can you do that have got no Jesus to tell your troubles to? And the worst of it is, you have got more troubles to come. Times may be hard now, but they will be harder one day—they will be harder when they come to an end. They say it is hard to live, but it is very hard to die. When one comes to die and has Jesus with him, even then dying is hard work; but to die without a Saviour! Oh! my friends, are you inclined to risk it? Will you face the grim monarch, and no Saviour with you? Remember, you must do it; you must die soon. The chamber shall soon be hushed in silence no sound shall be heard except the babbling watch that ever tells the flight of time. The physician shall "Hush!" and hold up his finger, and whisper in a suppressed voice, "He can not last many minutes longer." And the wife and the children, or the father and the mother, will stand around your bed and look at you, as I have looked at some, with a sad, sad heart. They will look at you a little while, till at last the death-change will pass o'er your face. "He is gone!" it shall be said; and the hand uplifted shall be dropped down again, and the eye shall be glazed in darkness, and then the mother will turn away and say, "O my child, I could have borne all this if there had been hope in thine end!" And when the minister comes in to comfort the family, he will ask the question of the father, " Do you think your son had an interest in the blood of Christ?" The reply will be, "O sir, we must not judge, but I never saw anything like it; I never had any reason to hope: that is my greatest sorrow." There, there! I could bury every friend without a tear, compared with the burial of an ungodly friend. Oh! it seems such an awful thing, to have one allied to you by ties of blood, dead and in hell.

We generally speak very softly about the dead. We say, "Well, we hope." Sometimes we tell great lies, for we know we do not hope at all. We wish it may be so, but we can not hope it; we never saw any grounds that should lead us to hope. But would it not be an awful thing if we were honest enough to look the dread reality in its face—if the husband were simply to look at it, and say, " There was my wife; she was an ungodly, careless woman. I know at least, she never said anything concerning repentance and faith; and if she died so, and I have every reason to fear she did, then she is cast away from God." It would be unkind to say it; but it is only honest for us to know it—to look dread truth in the face. Oh! my fellow-men and brethren! oh! ye that are partners with me of an immortal life! We shall one day meet again before the throne of God; but ere that time comes, we shall each of us be separated, and go our divers ways down the shelving banks of the river of death. My fellow-man, art thou prepared to die alone? I ask thee this question again— Art thou prepared to arise in the day of judgment without a Saviour? Art thou willing to run all risks and face thy Maker, when he comes to judge thee, without an advocate to plead thy cause? Art thou prepared to hear him say, "Depart ye cursed!" Are ye ready now to endure the everlasting ire of him who smites, and smiting once, doth smite forever? Oh! if ye will make your bed in hell, if you are prepared to be damned, if you are willing to be so, then live in sin and indulge in pleasures;—you will get your wish. But if ye would not; if ye would enter heaven, and ye would be saved, "Turn thee, turn thee, why will ye die, O house of Israel?" May God the Holy Spirit, enable you to repent of sin and to believe on Jesus; and then you shall have a portion among them that are sanctified: but unrepenting and unbelieving, if ye die so, ye must be driven from his presence, never to have life, and joy, and liberty, as long as eternity shall last.

The Lord prevent this, for Jesus' sake.

SERMON XXII

FEAR NOT

" Fear not, thou worm Jacob, *and* ye men of Israel ; I will help thee, saith the LORD, and thy redeemer the Holy One of Israel."—ISAIAH, xli. 14

I SHALL speak this morning to those that are discouraged, depressed in spirit, and sore troubled in the Christian life. There are certain nights of exceeding great darkness, through which the spirit has to grope in much pain and misery, and during which much of the comfort of the Word is particu- larly needed. Those seasons occur in this manner. Fre- quently they occur at the outset of a religious life. A young man, deeply impressed under the ministry, has been led to feel the weight of sin ; he trusts also he has been led to look for salvation to the Christ who is preached in the gospel. In the young ardor of his spirit he devotes himself wholly to Christ ; with the most solemn vows he dedicates body, soul, time, talents, all that he has, to the great work of serving God ; he thinks it easy to fulfill his vow ; he doth not count the cost ; he reckons it will be easy to forsake gay compan- ions, to renounce old established habits, and to become a Christian. Alas ! before many days he finds out his mistake, if he did not reckon without his host he certainly reckoned without his heart, for his evil heart of unbelief had deceived him, he knew not how hard would be the struggle, and how desperate the wrestling between his old evil nature and the new-born principle of grace within him. He finds it to be like the rending off of right arms to give up old and cherished habits ; he discovers it to be painful to renounce his former pursuits, as painful as it would be to pluck out his right eye. He sits down then, and he says, " If this be the trouble at the outset what may I expect as I proceed. O my soul, thou wast too fast in dedicating thyself to God; thou hast undertaken a warfare which thy prowess can never accomplish; thou hast started on a journey for which thy strength is not adequate; let me again return unto the world;" and if the Spirit saith, "Nay, thou canst not," then the poor soul sits itself down in deep misery, and cries, "I can not go back and I can not g forward; what must I do? I am exceedingly discouraged be cause of the way." The same feeling often overcomes the most valiant Christian veteran. He who has been long expe-rienced in the things of the divine life will sometimes be over-taken with a dark night and a stormy tempest; so dark will be the night, that he will not know his right hand from his left, and so horrible the tempest, that he can not hear the sweet words of his Master, saying, "Fear not, I am with thee." Periodical tornadoes and hurricanes will sweep o'er the Chris-tian; he will be subjected to as many trials in his spirit as trials in his flesh. This much I know, if it be not so with all of you it is so with me. I have to speak to-day to myself; and whilst I shall be endeavoring to encourage those who are distressed and down-hearted, I shall be preaching, I trust to myself, for I need something which shall cheer my heart—why I can not tell, wherefore I do not know, but I have a thorn in the flesh, a messenger of Satan to buffet me; my soul is cast down within me, I feel as if I had rather die than live; all that God hath done by me seems to be forgotten, and my spirit flags and my courage breaks down with the thought of that which is to come. I need your prayers; I need God's Holy Spirit; and I felt that I could not preach to-day, unless I should preach in such a way as to encourage you and to en-courage myself in the good work and labor of the Lord Jesus Christ.

What a precious promise to the young Christian, or to the old Christian attacked by lowness of spirits and distress of mind! "Fear not, thou worm Jacob, and ye men of Israel; I will help thee, saith the LORD, and thy redeemer the Holy One of Israel." Christian brethren, there are some in this congregation, I hope many, who have solemnly devoted them-selves to the cause and service of the Lord Jesus Christ: let them hear, then, the preparation which is necessary for this service set forth in the word of our text. First, *before we can do any great things for Christ there must be a sense of weakness:* "Worm Jacob." Secondly, *there must be trust in promised strength;* and thirdly, *there must be fear removed by that promise:* "Fear not, for I will help thee."

I. In the first place, the first qualification for serving God with any amount of success, and for doing God's work well and triumphantly, is A SENSE OF OUR OWN WEAKNESS. When God's warrior marches forth to battle with plumed helmet, and with mail about his loins, strong in his own majesty— when he says, "I know that I shall conquer, my own right arm and my mighty sword shall get unto me the victory," defeat is not far distant. God will not go forth with that man who goeth forth in his own strength. He who reckoneth on victory having first calculated his own might, has reckoned wrongly, for "it is not by might, nor by power, but by my Spirit, saith the Lord of hosts." They that go forth to fight, boasting that they can do it, shall return with their banners trailed in the dust, and with their armor stained with defeat; for God will not go forth with the man who goeth forth in his own strength. God hath said it; men must serve him, they·must serve him in his own way, and they must serve him in his own strength too, or he will never accept their service. That which man doth, unaided by divine strength, God never can accept. The mere fruits of the earth he casteth away; he will only have that, the seed of which was sown from heaven, sprinkled in the heart, and harvested by the sun of grace. There must be a consciousness of weakness, before there can be any victory.

I think I hear many saying to-day, "Well, sir, if that be a qualification for doing much, I have it to a very large extent." Well, do not marvel, do not wonder. Depend on this: God will empty out all that thou hast before he will ever put his own into thee; he will first empty out all thy granaries, before he will fill them with the finest of the wheat. The river of God is full of water; but there is not one drop of it that takes its rise in earthly springs. God will have no strength used in his own battles but the strength which he himself imparts, and I would not have you that are now distressed in the least discouraged by it. Your emptiness is but the preparation for your being filled, and your casting down is but the making ready for your lifting up.

Are there others of you that would almost desire to be cast down that they might be prepared to serve God? Let me tell you, then, how you can promote in yourself a sense of your own nothingness. The text addresses us as worms. Now, the mere rationalist, the man who boasts of the dignity of human nature, will never subscribe his name to such a title as this. "Worm," says he, "I am no worm: I am a man; a man is the most glorious thing that God has made; I am not going to be called a worm; I am a man—I can do anything; I want not your revelations; they may be fit for children, for men of childish minds that only learn by believing: I am a man: I can think out truth; I will make my own Bible, fashion my own ladder, and mount on it to heaven, if there be a heaven, or make a heaven, if that be all, and dwell in it myself." Not so, however, he who is wise and understandeth; he knows that he is a worm, and he knows it in this way:

First, he knows it by *contemplation*. He that thinks, will always think himself little. Men who have no brains are always great men; but those who think, must think their pride down—if God is with them in their thinking. Lift up now your eyes, behold the heavens, the work of God's fingers; behold the sun guided in his daily march; go ye forth at midnight, and behold the heavens; consider the stars and the moon; look ye upon these works of God's hands, and if ye be men of sense, and your souls are attuned to the high music of the spheres, ye will say, "What is man that thou art mindful of him, and the son of man that thou visitest him?" My God! when I survey the boundless fields of ether, and see those ponderous orbs rolling therein—when I consider how vast are thy dominions—so wide that an angel's wing might flap to all eternity and never reach a boundary—I marvel that thou shouldst look on insects so obscure as man. I have taken to myself the microscope and seen the ephemera upon the

leaf, and I have called him small. I will not call him so
again; compared with me he is great, if I put myself in comparison with God. I am so little that I shrink into nothingness when I behold the Almightiness of Jehovah—so little,
that the difference between the animalculæ and man dwindles
into nothing, when compared with the infinite chasm between
God and man. Let your mind rove upon the great doctrines
of the Godhead; consider the existence of God from before
the foundations of the world; behold Him who is, and was,
and is to come, the Almighty; let your soul comprehend as
much as it can of the Infinite, and grasp as much as possible
of the Eternal, and I am sure if you have minds at all, they
will shrink with awe. The tall archangel bows himself before
his Master's throne, and we shall cast ourselves into the lowest
dust when we feel what base nothings, what insignificant
specks we are when compared with our all-adorable Creator.
Labor, O soul, to know thy nothingness, and learn it *by con-
templating God's greatness.*

Again, if you want to know your own nothingness, consider
what you are in suffering. I was thinking, the other evening,
how small a matter it must be with God to cast any man into
the most unutterable agony. We are well and in good spirits; we know not why, but it seems as if God's finger had
touched one nerve, but one poor nerve, and we are so miserable that we could sit down and weep; we do not know how
to bear ourselves. But half an hour ago we could have
"smiled at Satan's rage, and faced a frowning world;" and
God does but put his hand on our hearts, and just let one of
the strings run loose, and what discord there is in our spirits;
we are annoyed at the slightest matter; we wish to be continually alone; the very promises yield us no comfort; our days
are nights, and our nights are black as Gehenna. We know
not how to endure ourselves. How easily, then, can God cast
us into misery! O man, what a little thing thou art, if so
little a thing can overthrow thee. Ye have heard men talk
big words when they have been prosperous; did you ever
hear them talk so when they were in deep distress, and great
anguish and sorrow? No, then they say, "Am I a seal or a

whale, that thou settest a watch upon me? What am I, that
thou shouldst visit me every morning, and chasten me every
night? Let me alone, until I swallow down my spittle. Why
am I sore vexed? What am I, that thou shouldst make me a
butt for thine arrows, and a target for thy wrath? Spare me,
O my God, for I am less than nothing; I am but a shadow
that passeth away and declineth. Oh deal not hardly with thy
servant, for thy mercies' sake." Great sorrow will always
make a man think little of himself, if God blesseth it to him.

Again: if you would know your own weakness, *try some
great labor for Christ.* I can understand how some minister
who preaches to his hundred-and-fifty on a Sabbath-day, and
regards himself as having a large congregation, should be
very precise about the color of his cravat, and about the respect that is paid to his dignity in his little church; I can
well comprehend how he should be as big as my Lord Archbishop—because he does nothing; he has nothing at all to try
him; but I can not imagine Martin Luther standing before
the Diet at Worms, being proud because he had to do such a
deed as that. I can not conceive John Calvin, in his incessant labors for Christ, leading on the reformation, and teaching the truth of God with power, saying to himself, "Lo! this
great Babylon that I have builded." I can suppose the man
that has nothing to do and that is doing nothing, sitting
down in devout complacency with his own adorable self; but
I can not conceive, if you nerve yourselves to great labors,
but what you will have to say, "Lord, what a worm am I
that thou shouldst call me to such work as this!" Turn, if
you please, to the history of all men who have done great
deeds for God, and you will find them saying, "I marvel that
God should use me thus!" "This day my mind was exceedingly cast down," says one of them, "for God had called me
to a great labor, and I never felt so much of my own insuffi-
ciency as I did to-day." Says another, "I have to-morrow to
do such-and-such an eminent service for my Master, and I can
say that when I was in my low estate, I was often exalted
above measure, but this day my God has cast me into the
lowest depths at the recollection of the work for which he has

engaged me." Go and do something, some of you, and I will be bound to say it will be the means of pricking that fair bubble of your pride, and letting some of it blow away. If you would understand what is meant by being a worm, go and do what the 15th verse says the worm should do—go and thrash the mountains, and beat them small; make the hills as chaff fanned by the wind, scatter them, and then rejoice in God: and if you can do that,

> " The more God's glories strike your eyes,
> The humbler you will lie."

Devout contemplation, sharp suffering, hard labor—all these will teach us what little creatures we are. Oh! may God by all means and every means keep us, well understanding and knowing that we are nothing more and nothing better than worms!

How easy it is, my brethren, for you and I to fly up! How hard to keep down! That demon of pride was born with us, and it will not die one hour before us. It is so woven into the very warp and woof of our nature, that till we are wrapped in our winding-sheets we shall never hear the last of it. If any man telleth me that he is humble, I know him to be profoundly proud; and if any man will not acknowledge this truth, that he is desperately inclined to self-exaltation, let him know that his denial of this truth is the best proof of it. Do you know what is the sweetest flattery in all the world? It is that flattery that Cæsar's courtiers of old gave to him, when they said Cæsar hated flattery, being then most highly flattered. We do not hate flattery, any one of us; we all like it. We do not like it if it is labeled flattery; but we like it if it is given in a little underhand fashion. We all love praise.

> " The proud to gain it toils on toils endure,
> The modest shun it, but to make it sure."

We all love it, every soul of us, and it is right and meet that we should all bow before God, and acknowledge that pride which is woven into our nature, and ask him to teach us what little things we are, that we may claim this promise—"Fear not, thou worm Jacob."

II. Now the next point. Before devoting ourselves to Christ, or doing any great labor for the Saviour, it is necessary THERE SHOULD BE TRUST IN THE PROMISED STRENGTH. "I will help thee, saith the LORD, and thy Redeemer, the Holy One of Israel." It is a certain fact, that though men be worms, they do what worms never could do; although men be nothing they do accomplish deeds which need even the power of the Infinite to rival them. How shall we account for this? Certainly it is not the worms; it must be some secret energy which gives them might. The mystery is unravelled in the text. "I will help thee, saith the LORD." In ancient history there is a story told of a valiant captain whose banner was always foremost in the fight, whose sword was dreaded by his enemies, for it was the herald of slaughter and of victory. His monarch once demanded of him that he should send this potent sword to him to be examined. The monarch took the sword, quietly criticised it, and sent it back with this message—"I see nothing wonderful in the sword; I can not understand why any man should be afraid of it." The captain sent back in the most respectful manner a message of this kind: "Your Majesty has been pleased to examine the sword, but I did not send the arm that wielded it; if you had examined that, and the heart that guided the arm, you would have understood the mystery." And now we look at men, and see what men have done, and we say, "I can not understand this; how was it done?" "Why, we are only seeing the sword; if we could see the heart of infinite love that guided that man in his onward course, we should not wonder that he, as God's sword, gained the victory. Now, the Christian may remember, that little though he be, God is with him; God will help him, and that right early. Brethren, I like a man who, when he begins to do anything, is afraid of himself, and says, "It is of no use; I can not do it." Let him alone: he will do it. He is all right. The man who says, "Oh there is nothing in it, I can do it," will break down to a dead certainty. But let him begin, by saying, " I know what I am at, and I feel confident I can not do it unless I have something more given to me than I feel to-day;" that man will come back with flying banners, the trumpets proclaiming that he has been victorious. But it must be because he puts reliance upon help promised. Now, Christian, I see you this morning ready to run away from the battle; you have been so dispirited this last week, through divers adverse circumstances, that you are ready to give up your religion. Now, man, here is a brother comrade that is passing through just the same; he comes here this morning, half inclined to run off to Tarshish, like Jonah did of old, only he could not find a boat, or else he might have sailed away; and he has come here to pat you on the shoulder and say, " Brother, do not let you and I play deserters, after all; let us up to arms, and still fight for our Master; for the promise says, " I will help thee." Brother, what an all-sufficient promise that is— " *I* will help thee." Why, it matters not what God has given us to do; if he helps us we can do it. Give me God to help me, and I will split the world in halves, and shiver it till it shall be smaller than the dust of the threshing floor; ay, and if God be with me, this breath could blow whole worlds about, as the child bloweth a bubble. There is no saying what man can do when God is with him. Give God to a man, and he can do all things. Put God into a man's arm, and he may have only the jawbone of an ass to fight with, but he will lay the Philistines in heaps: put God into a man's hand, and he may have a giant to deal with, and nothing but a sling and a stone; but he will lodge the stone in the giant's brow before long; put God into a man's eye, and he will flash defiance on kings and princes; put God into a man's lip, and he will speak right honestly, though his death should be the wages of his speech. There is no fear of a man who has got God with him; he is all-sufficient; there is nothing beyond his power. And my brethren, what an opportune help God's is! God's help always comes in at the right time.

We are often making a fuss because God does not help us when we do not want to be helped. " O !" says one, " I do not think that I could die for Christ; I feel I could not; ⅰ wish I felt that I had strength enough to die." Well, you just won't feel that, because you are not going to die, and God will not give you strength to die with, to lay up till the dying time comes. Wait till ye are dying, and then he will give you strength to die. " O !" says another, "I wish I felt as strong in prayer as so-and-so." But you do not want so much strength in prayer, and you shall not have it. You shall have what you want, and you shall have it when you want it; but you shall not have it before. Ah, I have often cried to God and desired that I might feel happy before I began to preach—that I might feel I could preach to the people. I could never get it at all. And yet sometimes God hath been pleased to cheer me as I have gone along, and given me strength that has been equal to my day. So it must be with you. God will come in when you want him—not one minute before, nor yet one minute later. "I will help thee." I will help thee when thou needest help ! And oh ! brethren, what an ennobling thing it is to be helped by God ! To be helped by a fellow man is no disgrace, but it is no honor; but to be helped by God, what an honor that is ! When the Christian prophet preacheth his Master's word, and feels that he has girded about his loins the belt of the Almighty, to strengthen him for his day's work, that he may not fear the people, what a noble being he is then ! When the Christian philanthropist goes into the prison, in the midst of reeking disease and death, and feels that God has put the wing of the angel over him, to shield him in the day of pestilence, how it ennobles and honors him to have God with him ! To have his strength girding his loins and nerving his arm, is just the highest thing to which man can attain. I thought but yesterday, " O, if I were a cherub I would stand with wings outstretched, and I would bless God for opportunities for serving him ;" but I thought within myself, " I have an opportunity of serving God, but I am too weak for it. O my God, I wish thou hadst not put the load on me." And then it struck me, " Do the cherubim and seraphim ever say that ?" Do they ever for a moment say, 'I have not strength enough to do it !'" No, if a cherub had a work to do which was beyond his might, he would meekly bow his head and say, "My Lord; I fly, I fly! He that commanded the deed will enable me to perform it." And so must the Christian say; "My God, dost thou command? It is enough: 'tis done. Thou never didst send us to a warfare at our own charges, and thou wilt never do so; thou wilt help us, and be with us to the end."

Before we can do much, then, we must *know our own weakness; and believe God's strength.*

III. And now comes the last point, upon which I shall be brief. We must, then, LABOR TO GET RID, AS MUCH AS POSSIBLE, OF FEAR. The prophet says, "Fear not;" thou art a worm, but do not fear; God will help thee; why shouldst thou fear? Let us labor to get rid of fear, when we are not certain we are serving our Master. And let these be our reasons :

Get rid of fear, *because fear is painful.* How it torments the spirit! When the Christian trusts, he is happy; when he doubts, he is miserable. When the believer looks to his Master and relies upon him, he can sing; when he doubts his Master, he can only groan. What miserable wretches the most faithful Christians are when they once begin doubting and fearing! It is a trade I never like to meddle with, because it never pays the expenses, and never brings in any profit —the trade of doubting. Why, the soul is broken in pieces, lanced, pricked with knives, dissolved, racked, pained. It knoweth not how to exist when it gives way to fear. Up, Christian! thou art of a sorrowful countenance; up, and chase thy fears. Why wouldst thou be for ever groaning in thy dungeon? Why should the Giant Despair for ever beat thee with his crabtree cudgel? Up! drive him away! touch the key of the promises; be of good cheer! Fear never helped thee yet, and it never will.

Fear, too, is *weakening.* Make a man afraid—he will run at his own shadow; make a man brave, and he will stand before an army and overcome them. He will never do much good in the world who is afraid of men. The fear of God bringeth blessings, but the fear of men bringeth a snare, and *such* a snare that many feet have been tripped by it. No man shall be faithful to God, if he is fearful of man; no man shall find his arm sufficient for him, and his might equal to his emergencies unless he can confidently believe, and quietly wait. We must not fear; for fear is weakening.

Again; we must not fear; for fear *dishonors God.* Doubt the Eternal, distrust the Omnipotent? O, traitorous fear! thinkest thou that the arm which piled the heavens, and sustains the pillars of the earth shall ever be palsied? Shall the brow which eternal ages have rolled over without scathing it, at last be furrowed by old age? What! shall the Eternal fail thee? Shall the faithful Promiser break his oath? Thou dishonorest God, O unbelief! Get thee hence! God is too wise to err, too good to be unkind; leave off doubting him, and begin to trust him, for in so doing, thou wilt put a crown on his head, but in doubting him thou dost trample his crown beneath thy feet.

And lastly, doubt not the Lord, O Christian; for in so doing *thou dost lower thyself.* The more thou believest, the greater thou art; but the more thou doubtest, the less thou becomest. It was said of the world's conqueror, that when he was sick, he puled like a child. "Give me some drink," cried one, like a sick girl, it was said to his dishonor. And is it not to the dishonor of a Christian, who lives in secret on his God, and professes to trust alone in him, that he can not trust him; that a little child will overcome his faith? O, poor cockle-shell boat, that is upset by a rain-drop! O poor puny Christian that is overcome by every straw, that stumbles at every stone! Then, Christian men, behave like men! It is childish to doubt; it is manhood's glory to trust. Plant your foot upon the immoveable Rock of Ages; lift your eye to heaven; scorn the world; never play craven; bend your fist in the world's face, and bid defiance to it and hell, and you are a man, and noble. But crouch, and cringe, and dread, and doubt, and you have lost your Christian dignity and are no longer what you should be. You do not honor God. "Fear not, thou worm Jacob; I will help thee, saith the LORD." Then why shouldst thou fear?"

I feel that my voice fails me, and with it my very powers of thought too, and therefore I can only turn to my comrades in arms, in the good war of Christ, and I say to them, brethren, you and I can do nothing of ourselves; we are poor puny things; but let us attempt great things, for God is with us; let us dare great things, for God will not leave us. Remember what he has done aforetime; and remember what he has done of old he will do again. Remember David the shepherd-boy. Think ye well of Shamgar, with his ox-goad. Forget ye not the jawbone of the ass, and the stone from the sling. If these worked wonders, why should not we? If little things have done great things, let us try to do great things also. You know not, ye atoms, but that your destiny is sublime. Try and make it so by faith; and the least of you may be mighty through the strength of God. O for grace to trust God, and there is no telling what ye can do. Worms, ye are nothing, but ye have eaten princes; worms ye are nothing, but ye have devoured the roots of cedars, and laid them level with the earth; worms, ye are nothing, but ye have piled rocks in the deep, deep sea, and wrecked mighty navies; worms, ye have eaten through the keel of the proudest ship that ever sailed the ocean. If ye have done this yourselves, what can not we do? your strength lies in your mouths; our strength lies in ours too. We will use our mouths in prayer, and in constant adoration, and we shall conquer yet, for God is with us, and victory is sure.

> Ye trembling souls! dismiss your fears;
>   Be mercy all your theme:
> Mercy, which, like a river, flows
>   In one continued stream.
>
> Fear not the powers of earth and hell;
>   GOD will these powers restrain;
> His mighty arm their rage repel,
>   And make their efforts vain.
>
> Fear not the want of outward good;
>   He will for his provide,
> Grant them supplies of daily food,
>   And all they need beside.

Fear not that he will e'er forsake,
  Or leave his work undone;
He's faithful to his promises—
  And faithful to his Son.

Fear not the terrors of the grave,
  Or death's tremendous sting;
He will from endless wrath preserve—
  To endless glory bring.

SERMON XXIII

THE CONDESCENSION OF CHRIST

"For ye know the grace of our Lord Jesus Christ, that, though he was rich, yet for your sakes he became poor, that ye through his poverty might be rich."—2 COR. viii. 9.

THE apostle, in this chapter, was endeavoring to stir up the Corinthians to liberality. He desired them to contribute something for those who were the poor of the flock, that he might be able to minister to their necessities. He tells them, that the churches of Macedonia, though very much poorer than the church at Corinth, had done even beyond their means for the relief of the Lord's family, and he exhorts the Corinthians to do the same. But suddenly recollecting that examples taken from inferiors seldom have a powerful effect he lays aside his argument drawn from the church of Macedonia, and he holds before them a reason for liberality which the hardest heart can scarcely resist, if once that reason be applied by the Spirit. "My brethren," said he, "there is One above, by whom you hope you have been saved, One whom you call Master and Lord, now if you will but imitate him, you can not be ungenerous or illiberal. For, my brethren, I tell you a thing which is an old thing with you and an undisputed truth—'For ye know the grace of our Lord Jesus Christ, that, though he was rich, yet for your sakes he became poor, that ye through his poverty might be rich.' Let this constrain you to benevolence." O Christian, whenever thou art inclined to an avaricious withholding from the church of God, think of thy Saviour giving up all that he had to serve thee, and canst thou then, when thou beholdest self-denial so noble, —canst thou then be selfish, and regard thyself, when the claims of the poor of the flock are pressed upon thee?

Remember Jesus; think thou seest him look thee in the face and say to thee, "I gave myself for thee, and dost thou withhold thyself from me? For if thou dost so, thou knowest not my love in all its heights and depths and lengths and breadths."

And now, dear friends, the argument of the apostle shall be our subject to-day. It divides itself in an extremely simple manner. We have first, *the pristine condition of our Saviour* —" He was rich." We have next, *his condescension*—" He became poor." And then we have *the effect and result of his poverty*—" That we might be made rich." We shall then close by giving you a doctrine, a question, and an exhortation. May God bless all these, and help us to tell them aright.

I. First, then, our text tells us THAT JESUS CHRIST WAS RICH. Think not that our Saviour began to live when he was born of the Virgin Mary; imagine not that he dates his existence from the manger at Bethlehem; remember he is the Eternal, he is before all things, and by him all things consist. There was never a time in which there was not God. And just so, there was never a period in which there was not Christ Jesus our Lord. He is self-existent, hath no beginning of days, neither end of years; he is the immortal, invisible, the only wise God, our Saviour. Now, in the past eternity which had elapsed before his mission to this world, we are told that Jesus Christ was rich; and to those of us who believe his glories and trust in his divinity, it is not hard to see how he was so. Jesus was rich *in possessions*. Lift up thine eye, believer, and for a moment review the riches of my Lord Jesus, before he condescended to become poor for thee. Behold him, sitting upon his throne and declaring his own allsufficiency. " If I were hungry, I would not tell thee, for the cattle on a thousand hills are mine. Mine are the hidden treasures of gold; mine are the pearls that the diver can not reach; mine every precious thing that earth hath seen." The Lord Jesus might have said, " I can stretch my scepter from the east even to the west, and all is mine; the whole of this world, and yon worlds that glitter in far off space, all are mine. The illimitable expanse of unmeasured space, filled as it is with worlds that I have made, all this is mine. Fly upward, and thou canst not reach the summit of the hill of my dominions; dive downward, and thou canst not enter into the innermost depths of my sway. From the highest throne in glory to the lowest pit of hell, all, all is mine without exception. I can put the broad arrow of my kingdom upon every thing that I have made."

But he had besides that which makes men richer still. We have heard of kings in olden times who were fabulously rich, and when their riches were summed up, we read in the old romances, " And this man was possessed of the philosopher's stone, whereby he turned all things into gold." Surely all the treasures that he had before were as nothing compared with this precious stone that brought up the rear. Now, whatever might be the wealth of Christ in things created, he had the *power of creation*, and therein lay his boundless wealth. If he had pleased he could have spoken worlds into existence; he had but to lift his finger, and a new universe as boundless as the present would have leaped into existence. At the will of his mind, millions of angels would have stood before him, legions of bright spirits would have flashed into being. He spake, and it was done; he commanded, and it stood fast. He who said, " Light, be," and light was, had power to say to all things, " Be," and they should be. Herein then, lay his riches; this creating power was one of the brightest jewels of his crown.

We call men rich, too, who have *honor*, and though men have never so much wealth, yet if they be in disgrace and shame, they must not reckon themselves among the rich. But our Lord Jesus had honor, honor such as none but a divine being could receive. When he sat upon his throne, before he relinquished the glorious mantle of his sovereignty to become a man, all earth was filled with his glory. He could look both beneath and all around him, and the inscription, " Glory be unto God," was written over all space; day and night the smoking incense of praise ascended before him from golden viols held by spirits who bowed in reverence the harps of myriads of cherubim and seraphim continually thrilled with his praise, and the voices of all those mighty hosts were ever eloquent in adoration. It may be, that on set days the princes from the far off realms, the kings, the mighty ones of his boundless realms, came to the court of Christ, and brought each his annual revenue. Oh, who can tell but that in the vast eternity, at certain grand eras, the great bell was rung, and all the mighty hosts that were created gathered together in solemn review before his throne? Who can tell the high holiday that was kept in the court of heaven when these bright spirits bowed before his throne in joy and gladness, and, all united, raised their voices in shouts and hallelujahs such as mortal ear hath never heard. Oh, can ye tell the depths of the rivers of praise that flowed hard by the city of God? Can ye imagine to yourselves the sweetness of that harmony that perpetually poured into the ear of Jesus, Messias, King, Eternal, equal with God his Father? No; at the thought of the glory of his kingdom, and the riches and majesty of his power, our souls are spent within us, our words fail, we can not utter the tithe of his glories.

Nor was he poor in any other sense. He that hath wealth on earth, and honor too, is poor if he hath not *love*. I would rather be the pauper, dependent upon charity, and have love, than I would be the prince, despised and hated, whose death is looked for as a boon. Without love, man is poor—give him all the diamonds, and pearls, and gold that mortal hath conceived. But Jesus was not poor in love. When he came to earth, he did not come to get our love because his soul was solitary. Oh no, his Father had a full delight in him from all eternity. The heart of Jehovah, the first person of the Sacred Trinity, was divinely, immutably linked to him; he was beloved of the Father and of the Holy Spirit; the three persons took a sacred complacency and delight in each other And besides that, how was he loved by those bright spirits who had not fallen. I can not tell what countless orders and creatures there are created who still stand fast in obedience to God. It is not possible for us to know whether there are, or not, as many races of created beings as we know there are created men on earth. We can not tell but that in the boundless regions of space, there are worlds inhabited by beings infinitely superior to us : but certain it is, there were the holy angels, and they loved our Saviour ; they stood day and night with wings outstretched, waiting for his commands, hearkening to the voice of his word ; and when he bade them fly, there was love in their countenance, and joy in their hearts. They loved to serve him, and it is not all fiction that when there was war in heaven, and when God cast out the devil and his legions, then the elect angels showed their love to him, being valiant in fight and strong in power.   H wanted not our love to make him happy, he was rich enough in love without us.

Now, though a spirit from the upper world should come to tell you of the riches of Jesus he could not do it. Gabriel, in thy flights thou hast mounted higher than my imagination dares to follow thee, but thou hast never gained the summit of the throne of God.

" Dark with insufferable light thy skirts appear."

Jesus, who is he that could look upon the brow of thy Majesty, who is he that could comprehend the strength of the arm of thy might ? Thou art God, thou art infinite, and we poor finite things, are lost in thee. The insect of an hour can not comprehend thyself. We bow before thee, we adore thee ; thou art God over all, blessed for ever. But as for the comprehension of thy boundless riches, as for being able to tell thy treasures, or to reckon up thy wealth, that were impossible. All we know is, that the wealth of God, that the treasures of the infinite, that the riches of eternity, were all thine own : thou wast rich beyond all thought.

II. The Lord Jesus Christ, then, was rich. We all believe that, though none of us can truly speak it forth. Oh, how surprised angels were, when they were first informed that Jesus Christ, the Prince of Light and Majesty, intended to shroud himself in clay and become a babe, and live and die ! We know not how it was first mentioned to the angels, but when the rumor first began to get afloat among the sacred hosts, you may imagine what strange wonderment there was. What! was it true that he whose crown was all bedight with stars, would lay that crown aside? What! was it certain that he about whose shoulders was cast the purple of the universe, would become a man dressed in a peasant's garment? Could it be true that he who was everlasting and immortal would one day be nailed to a cross? Oh! how their wonderment increased! They desired to look into it. And when he descended from on high, they followed him; for Jesus was "seen of angels," and seen in a special sense, for they looked upon him in rapturous amazement, wondering what it all could mean. "He for our sakes became poor." Do you see him as on that day of heaven's eclipse he did ungird his majesty? Oh, can ye conceive the yet increasing wonder of the heavenly hosts when the deed was actually done, when they saw the tiara taken off, when they saw him unbind his girdle of stars, and cast away his sandals of gold? Can ye conceive it, when he said to them, "I do not disdain the womb of the virgin; I am going down to earth to become a man?" Can ye picture them as they declared they would follow him! Yes, they followed him as near as the world would permit them. And when they came to earth they began to sing, "Glory to God in the highest, on earth peace, good will toward men." Nor would they go away till they had made the shepherds wonder, and till heaven had hung out new stars in honor of the new-born King. And now wonder, ye angels, the Infinite has become an infant; he, upon whose shoulders the universe doth hang, hangs at his mother's breast; he who created all things, and bears up the pillars of creation, hath now become so weak that he must be carried by a woman! And oh, wonder, ye that knew him in his riches, whilst ye admire his poverty! Where sleeps the new-born King? Had he the best room in Cæsar's palace? hath a cradle of gold been prepared for him, and pillows of down, on which to rest his head? No, where the ox fed, in the dilapidated stable, in the manger, there the Saviour lies, swathed in the swaddling bands of the children of poverty! Nor there doth he

rest long; on a sudden his mother must carry him to Egypt
he goeth there, and becometh a stranger in a strange land.
When he comes back, see him that made the worlds handle
the hammer and the nails, assisting his father in the trade of
a carpenter! Mark him who has put the stars on high, and
made them glisten in the night; mark him without one star
of glory upon his brow—a simple child, as other children.
Yet, leave for a while the scenes of his childhood and his earlier life; see him when he becomes a man, and now ye may
say, indeed, that for our sakes he did become poor. Never
was there a poorer man than Christ; he was the prince of
poverty. He was the reverse of Crœsus—*he* might be on the
top of the hill of riches, *Christ* stood in the lowest vale of
poverty. Look at his dress, it is woven from the top through
out, the garment of the poor! As for his food, he oftentimes
did hunger; and always was dependent upon the charity of
of others for the relief of his wants! He who scattered the
harvest o'er the broad acres of the world, had not sometimes
wherewithal to stay the pangs of hunger? He who digged
the springs of the ocean, sat upon a well and said to a Samaritan woman, "Give me to drink!" He rode in no chariot, he
he walked his weary way, foot sore, o'er the flints of Galilee!
He had not where to lay his head. He looked upon the fox
as it hurried to its burrow, and the fowl as it went to its resting-place, and he said, "Foxes have holes, and the birds of
the air have nests; but I, the Son of man, have not where to
lay my head." He who had once been waited on by angels,
becomes the servant of servants, takes a towel, girds himself,
and washes his disciples' feet! He who was once honored
with the hallelujahs of ages, is now spit upon and despised!
He who was loved by his Father, and had abundance of the
wealth of affection, could say, "He that eateth bread with me
hath lifted up his heel against me." Oh, for words to picture
the humiliation of Christ! What leagues of distance between
him that sat upon the throne, and him that died upon the
cross! Oh, who can tell the mighty chasm between yon
heights of glory, and the cross of deepest woe! Trace him,
Christian, he has left thee his manger to show thee how God

came down to man. He hath bequeathed thee his cross, to show thee how man can ascend to God. Follow him, follow him, all his journey through; begin with him in the wilderness of temptation, see him fasting there, and hungering with the wild beasts around him; trace him along his weary way, as the Man of Sorrows, and acquainted with grief. He is the by-word of the drunkard, he is the song of the scorner, and he is hooted at by the malicious; see him as they point their finger at him, and call him "drunken man and wine-bibber!" Follow him along his *via dolorosa*, until at last you meet him among the olives of Gethsemane; see him sweating great drops of blood! Follow him to the pavement of Gabbatha; see him pouring out rivers of gore beneath the cruel whips of Roman soldiers! With weeping eye follow him to the cross of Calvary, see him nailed there! Mark his poverty, so poor that they have stripped him naked from head to foot, and exposed him to the face of the sun! So poor, that when he asked them for water they gave him vinegar to drink! So poor that his unpillowed head is girt with thorns in death! Oh, Son of Man, I know not which to admire most, thine height of glory, or thy depths of misery! Oh, Man, slain for us, shall we not exalt thee? God over all, blessed for ever, shall we not give thee the loudest song? "He was rich, yet for our sakes he became poor." If I had a tale to tell you this day, of some king, who, out of love to some fair maiden, left his kingdom and became a peasant like herself, ye would stand and wonder, and would listen to the charming tale; but when I tell of God concealing his dignity to become our Saviour, our hearts are scarcely touched. Ah, my friends, we know the tale so well, we have heard it so often; and, alas, some of us tell it so badly that we cannot expect that you would be as interested in it as the subject doth demand. But surely, as it is said of some great works of architecture, that though they be seen every morning, there is always something fresh to wonder at; so we may say of Christ, that though we saw him every day, we should always see fresh reason to love, and wonder, and adore. "He was rich, yet for your sakes he became poor."

I have thought that there is one peculiarity about the poverty of Christ, that ought not to be forgotten by us. Those who were nursed upon the lap of want feel less the woes of their condition. But I have met with others whose poverty I could pity. They were once rich; their very dress which now hangs about them in tatters, tells you that they once stood foremost in the ranks of life. You meet them amongst the poorest of the poor; you pity them more than those who have been born and bred to poverty, because they have known something better. Amongst all those who are poor, I have always found the greatest amount of suffering in those who had seen better days.

I can remember, even now, the look of some who have said to me when they have received assistance—and I have given it as delicately as I could, lest it should look like charity— "Ah, sir, I have known better days." And the tear stood in the eye, and the heart was smitten at bitter recollections. The least slight to such a person, or even too unmasked a kindness, becomes like a knife cutting the heart. "I have known better days," sounds like a knell over their joys. And verily our Lord Jesus might have said in all his sorrows, "I have known better days than these." Methinks when he was tempted of the devil in the wilderness, it must have been hard in him to have restrained himself from dashing the devil into pieces. If I had been the Son of God, methinks, feeling as I do now, if that devil had tempted me, I should have dashed him into the nethermost hell, in the twinkling of an eye! And then conceive the patience our Lord must have had, standing on the pinnacle of the temple, when the devil said, "Fall down and worship me." He would not touch him, the vile deceiver, but let him do what he pleased. Oh! what might of misery and love there must have been in the Saviour's heart when he was spit upon by the men he had created; when the eyes he himself had filled with vision looked on him with scorn, and when the tongues, to which he himself had given utterance, hissed and blasphemed him! Oh, my friends, if the Saviour had felt as we do, and I doubt not he did feel in some measure as we do—only by great patience he curbed himself—me thinks he might have swept them all away ; and, as they said, he might have come down from the cross, and delivered him-self, and destroyed them utterly. It was mighty patience that could bear to tread this world beneath his feet, and not to crush it, when it so ill-treated its Redeemer. You marvel at the patience which restrained him ; you marvel also at the pov-erty he must have felt, the poverty of spirit, when they re-buked him and he reviled them not again ; when they scoffed him, and yet he said, " Father, forgive them, for they know not what they do." He had seen brighter days ; that made his misery more bitter, and his poverty more poor.

III. Well, now we come to the third point—why DID THE SAVIOUR COME TO DIE AND BE POOR ? Hear this, ye sons of Adam—the Scripture says, " For your sakes he became poor, that ye through his poverty might be made rich." For *your* sakes. Now, when I address you as a great congregation, you will not feel the beauty of this expression, " For *your* sake." Husband and wife, walking in the fear of God, let me take you by the hand and look you in the face, let me repeat those words, " for *your* sakes he became poor." Young man, let a brother of thine own age, look on thee and repeat these words, " Though he was rich, yet for your sake he became poor." Gray-headed believer, let me look on you and say the same, " For *your* sake he became poor." Brethren, take the word home, and see if it does not melt you—" Though he was rich, yet for *my* sake he became poor." Beg for the influences of the Spirit upon that truth, and it will make your heart de-vout and your spirit loving—" I the chief of sinners am, yet for my sake he died." Come, let me hear you speak; let us bring the sinner here, and let him soliloquize—" I cursed him, I blasphemed, and yet for my sake he was made poor; I scoffed at his ministers, I broke his Sabbath, yet for my sake was he made poor. What ! Jesus, couldst thou die for one who was not worth thy having ? Couldst thou shed thy blood for one who would have shed thy blood, if it had been in his power ? What ! couldst thou die for one so worthless, so vile ?" " Yes, yes," says Jesus, " I shed that blood for thee." Now let the saint speak: " I," he may say, " have professed to love him, but how cold my love, how little have I served him! How far have I lived from him; I have not had sweet communion with him as I ought to have had. When have I been spending and spent in his service? And yet, my Lord thou dost say, 'for *thy* sake I was made poor.' " " Yes," saith Jesus, " see me in my miseries; see me in my agonies; see me in my death—all these I suffered for *thy* sake." Wilt thou not love him who loved thee to this great excess, and became poor for thy sake?

That, however, is not the point to which we wish to bring you, just now; the point is this, *the reason why Christ died* was, " that we through his poverty might be rich." He became poor from his riches, that our poverty might become rich out of his poverty. Brethren, we have now a joyful theme before us—those who are partakers of the Saviour's blood are rich. All those for whom the Saviour died, having believed in his name and given themselves to him, are this day rich. And yet I have some of you here who can not call a foot of land your own. You have nothing to call your own to-day, you know not how you will be supported through another week; you are poor, and yet if you be a child of God, I do know that Christ's end is answered in you; *you are rich*. No, I did not mock you when I said you were rich: I did not taunt you—you are. You are really rich; you are *rich in possessions;* you have in your possession now things more costly than gems, more valuable than gold and silver. Silver and gold, have I none, thou mayest say; but if thou canst say afterward, " Christ is all," thou hast outspoken all that the man can say who had piles of gold and silver. " But," thou sayest, " I have nothing." Man, thou hast all things. Knowest thou not what Paul said? He declares that " things present and things to come, and this world, and life and death, all are yours and ye are Christ's, and Christ is God's." The great machinery of providence has no wheel which does not revolve for you. The great economy of grace with all its fullness, is yours. Remember that adoption, justification, sanctification, all are yours. Thou hast everything that heart can wish in spiritual things; and thou hast everything that is necessary

THE CONDESCENSION OF CHRIST.

for this life ; for you know who hath said, "having food and raiment, let us therewith be content." You are rich; rich with true riches, and not with the riches of a dream. There are times when men by night do scrape gold and silver together, like shells upon the sea shore ; but when they wake in the morning they find themselves penniless. But, yours are everlasting treasures ; yours are solid riches. When the sun of eternity shall have melted the rich man's gold away, yours shall endure. A rich man has a *cistern* full of riches, but a poor saint has got a *fountain* of mercy, and he is the richest who has a fountain. Now, if my neighbor be a rich man, he may have as much wealth as ever he pleases, it is only a cistern full, it will soon be exhausted ; but a Christian has a fountain that ever flows, and let him draw, draw on forever, the fountain will still keep on flowing. However large may be the stagnant pool, if it be stagnant, it is but of little worth ; but the flowing stream, though it seem to be but small, needs but time, and it will have produced an immense volume of precious water. Thou art never to have a great pool of riches, they are always to keep on flowing to thee; "Thy bread shall be given thee, and thy water shall be sure." As old William Huntingdon says, "The Christian has a hand-basket portion. Many a man, when his daughter marries, does not give her much, but he says to her, ' I shall send you a sack of flour one day, and so-and-so the next day, and now and then a sum of gold ; and as long as I live I will always send you something. " Says he, " She will get a great deal more than her sister, who has had a thousand pounds down. That is how my God deals with me ; he gives to the rich man all at once, but to me day by day." Ah, Egypt, thou wert rich when thy granaries were full, but those granaries might be emptied; Israel was far richer when they could not see their granaries, but only saw the manna drop from heaven, day by day. Now, Christian, that is thy portion—the portion of the fountain always flowing, and not of the cistern-full, and soon to be emptied.

But remember, O saint, that thy wealth does not all lie in thy possession just now ; remember thou art rich in *promises*. Let a man be never so poor as to the metal that he hath, let him have in his possession promissory notes from rich and true men, and he says, " I have no gold in my purse, but here is a note for such-and-such a sum—I know the signature—I can trust the firm—I am rich, though I have no metal in hand." And so the Christian can say, " If I have no riches in possession, I have the promise of them; my God hath said, ' No good thing will I withhold from them that walk uprightly,'—that is a promise that makes me rich. He has told me, ' My bread shall be given me, and my water shall be sure.' I can not doubt his signature, I know his word to be authentic; and as for his faithfulness, I would not so dishonor him as to think he would break his promise. No, the promise is as good as the thing itself. If it be God's promise, it is just as sure that I shall have it, as if I had it."

But then the Christian is very rich in *reversion*. When a certain old man dies that I know of, I believe that I shall be so immensely rich that I shall dwell in a place that is paved with gold, the walls of which are builded with precious stones. But, my friends, you have all got an old man to die, and when he is dead, if you are followers of Jesus, you will come in for your inheritance. You know who that old man is, he is very often spoken of in Scripture; may the old man in you die daily, and may the new man be strengthened in you. When that old man of corruption, your old nature, shall totter into its grave, then you will come in for your property. Christians are like heirs, they have not much in their minority, and they are minors now; but when they come of age, they shall have the whole of their estate. If I meet a minor, he says, " That is my property." " You can not sell it, sir; you can not lay hold of it." " No," says he, " I know I can not; but it is mine when I am one-and-twenty, I shall then have complete control; but at the same time, it is as really mine now as it ever will be. I have a legal right to it, and though my guardians take care of it for me, it is mine, not theirs." And now, Christian, in heaven there is a crown of gold which is thine to-day; it will be no more thine when thou hast it on thy head than it is now.

I remember to have heard it reported that I once spoke in

metaphor, and bade Christians look at all the crowns hanging in rows in heaven—very likely I did say it—but if not, I will say it now. Up, Christian, see the crowns all ready, and mark thine own; stand thou and wonder at it; see with what pearls it is bedight, and how heavy it is with gold! And that is for thy head, thy poor aching head; thy poor tortured brain shall yet have that crown for its arraying! And see that garment, it is stiff with gems, and white like snow; and that is for thee! When thy week-day garment shall be done with, this shall be the raiment of thy everlasting Sabbath. When thou hast worn out this poor body, there remaineth for thee, "A house not made with hands, eternal in the heavens." Up to the summit, Christian, and survey thine inheritance; and when thou hast surveyed it all, when thou hast seen thy present possessions, thy promised possessions, thine entailed possessions, then remember that all these were bought by the poverty of thy Saviour! Look thou upon all thou hast, and say, "Christ bought them for me." Look thou on every promise, and see the bloodstains on it; yea, look too, on the harps and crowns of heaven, and read the bloody purchase! Remember, thou couldst never have been anything but a damned sinner, unless Christ had bought thee! Remember, if he had remained in heaven, thou wouldst for ever have remained in hell; unless he had shrouded and eclipsed his own honor, thou wouldst never have had a ray of light to shine upon thee. Therefore, bless his dear name, extol him, trace every stream to the fountain; and bless him who is the source, and the fountain of everything thou hast. Brethren, "Ye know the grace of our Lord Jesus Christ, that, though he was rich, yet for your sakes he became poor, that ye through his poverty might be rich."

IV. I have not done, I have three things now to say, and I shall say them as briefly as possible.

The first *is a doctrine;* the doctrine is this: If Christ in his poverty made us rich, what will he do now that he is glorified If the Man of Sorrows saved my soul, will the man now exalted suffer it to perish? If the dying Saviour availed for our salvation, should not the living, interceding Saviour, abundant ly secure it?

"He lived, he lives and sits above,
    For ever interceding there;
What shall divide us from his love,
    Or what shall sink us in despair?"

If when the nail was in thine hand, O Jesus, thou didst rout all hell, canst thou be defeated now that thou hast grasped the scepter? If, when the thorn crown was put about thy brow, thou didst prostrate the dragon, canst thou be overcome and conquered now that the acclamations of angels are ascending to thee? No, my brethren, we can trust the glorified Jesus; we can repose ourselves on his bosom; if he was so strong in poverty, what must he be in riches?

The next thing was *a question*, that question was a simple one. My hearer, hast thou been made rich by Christ's poverty? Thou sayest, "I am good enough without Christ; I want no Saviour." Ah, thou art like her of old, who said, "I am rich and increased in goods, and have need of nothing, whereas, saith the Lord, 'Thou art naked, and poor, and miserable.'" O ye that live by good works, and think that ye shall go to heaven because you are as good as others; all the merits you can ever earn yourselves, are good for nothing. All that human nature ever made, turns to a blot and a curse. If those are your riches, you are no saints. But can you say this morning, my hearers, "I am by nature without anything, and God has by the power of his Spirit taught me my nothingness."

My brother, my sister, hast thou taken Christ to be thine all in all? Canst thou say this day, with an unfaltering tongue, "My Lord, my God, I have nothing; but thou art my all?" Come, I beseech thee, do not shirk the question. Thou art careless, heedless; answer it, then, in the negative. But when thou hast answered it, I beseech thee, beware of what thou hast said. Thou art sinful, thou feelest it. Come I beseech thee, and lay hold on Jesus. Remember, Christ came to make those rich, that have nothing of their own. My Saviour is a physician; if you can heal yourself, he will have nothing to do with you. Remember, my Saviour came to clothe the naked. He will clothe you, if you have not a rag of your own; but unless you let him do it from head to foot, he will have nothing to do with you. Christ says he will never have a partner; he will do all, or none. Come then, hast thou given up all to Christ? Hast thou no reliance and trust save in the cross of Jesus? Then thou hast answered the question well. Be happy, be joyous; if death should surprise thee the next hour, thou art secure. Go on thy way, and rejoice in the hope of the glory of God.

And now I close with the third thing, which was *an exhortation.* Sinner, dost thou this morning feel thy poverty? Then look to Christ's poverty. O ye that are to-day troubled on account of sin—and there are many such here—God has not let you alone; he has been plowing your heart with the sharp plowshare of conviction; you are this day saying, "What must I do to be saved?" You would give all you have, to have an interest in Jesus Christ. Your soul is this day sore broken and tormented. O sinner, if thou wouldst find salvation, thou must find it in the veins of Jesus. Now, wipe that tear from thine eye a moment, and look here. Dost thou see him high, where the cross rears its terrible tree? There he is. Dost see him? Mark his head. See the thorn-crown, and the beaded drops still standing on his temples. Mark his eyes; they are just closing in death. Canst see the lines of agony, so desperate in woe? Dost see his hands? See the streamlets of blood flowing down them. Hark, he is about to speak. "My God, my God, why hast thou forsaken me!" Didst hear that, sinner? Pause a moment longer, take another survey of his person; how emaciated his body, and how sick his spirit! Look at him. But hark, he is about to speak again—"It is finished." What means he by that? He means, that he has finished thy salvation. Look thou to him, and find salvation there. Remember, to be saved, all that God wants of a penitent, is to look to Jesus. My life for this—if you will risk your all on Christ, you shall be saved. I will be Christ's bondsman to-day, to be bound for ever, if he break his promise. He has said, "Look unto me, and be ye saved, all the ends of the earth." It is not your hands that will save you; it must be your eyes. Look from those works whereby you hope to be saved.   No longer strive to weave a garment that will not hide your sin, throw away that shuttle; it is only filled with cobwebs.   What garment can you weave with that?   Look thou to him, and thou art saved.   Never sinner looked, and was lost.   Dost mark that eye there?   One glance will save thee, one glance will set thee free.   Dost thou say, "I am a guilty sinner?"   Thy guilt is the reason why I bid thee look.   Dost thou say, "I cannot look?"   Oh, may God help thee to look now.   Remember, Christ will not reject thee; thou mayest reject him.   Remember now, there is the cup of mercy put to thy lip by the hand of Jesus.   I know, if thou feelest thy need, Satan may tempt thee not to drink, but he will not prevail; thou wilt put thy lip feebly and faintly, perhaps, to it.   But oh, do but sip it; and the first draught shall give thee bliss; and the deeper thou shalt drink, the more of heaven shalt thou know.   Sinner, believe on Jesus Christ; hear the whole gospel preached to thee.   It is written in God's Word, "He that believeth and is baptized shall be saved."   Hear me translate it—He that believeth and is *immersed* shall be saved.   Believe thou, trust thyself on the Saviour, make a profession of thy faith in baptism, and then thou mayest rejoice in Jesus, that he hath saved thee.   But remember not to make a profession till thou hast believed: remember, baptism is nothing, until thou hast faith.   Remember, it is a farce and a falsehood, until thou hast first believed; and afterwards, it is nothing but the profession of thy faith.   Oh, believe that; cast thyself upon Christ, and thou art saved for ever!   The Lord add his blessing, for the Saviour's sake.   Amen.

SERMON XXIV

THE GREAT RESERVOIR

"**Keep** thy heart with all diligence; for out of it are the issues of life."—
PROVERBS, iv. 23.

IF I should vainly attempt to fashion my discourse after lofty
models, I should this morning compare the human heart to the
ancient city of Thebes, out of whose hundred gates multitudes
of warriors were wont to march. As was the city such were
her armies, as was her inward strength, such were they who
came forth of her. I might then urge the necessity of keeping the heart, because it is the metropolis of our manhood, the
citadel and armory of our humanity. Let the chief fortress
surrender to the enemy, and the occupation of the rest must
be an easy task. Let the principal stronghold be possessed by
evil, the whole land must be overrun thereby. Instead, however, of doing this, I shall attempt what possibly I may be
able to perform, by a humble metaphor and a simple figure,
which will be easily understood; I shall endeavor to set forth
the wise man's doctrine, that our life issues from the heart,
and thus I shall labor to show the absolute necessity of keeping the heart with all diligence.

You have seen the great reservoirs provided by our water
companies, in which the water which is to supply hundreds
of streets and thousands of houses is kept. Now, the heart is
just the reservoir of man, and our life is allowed to flow in its
proper season. That life may flow through different pipes—
the mouth, the hand, the eye; but still all the issues of hand,
of eye, of lip, derive their source from the great fountain and
central reservoir, the heart; and hence there is no difficulty
in showing the great necessity that exists for keeping this
reservoir, the heart, in a proper state and condition, since

otherwise that which flows through the pipes must be tainted and corrupt. May the Holy Spirit now direct our meditations.

Mere moralists very often forget the heart, and deal exclusively with the lesser powers. Some of them say, " If a man's life be wrong, it is better to alter the *principles* upon which his conduct is modeled : we had better adopt another scheme of living ; society must be re-modeled, so that man may have an opportunity for the display of virtues, and less temptation to indulge in vice." It is as if, when the reservoir was filled with poisonous or polluted fluid, some sage counsellor should propose that all the piping had better be taken up, and fresh pipes laid down, so that the water might run through fresh channels ; but who does not perceive that it would be all in vain, if the fountain-head were polluted, however good the channels. So in vain the rules by which men hope to fashion their lives ; in vain the regimen by which we seek to constrain ourselves to the semblance of goodness, unless the heart be right, the very best scheme of life shall fall to the ground, and fail to effect its design. Others say, " Well, if the life be wrong, it would be better to set the understanding right : you must inform man's judgment, educate him, teach him better, and when his head is well informed, then his life will be improved." Now, *understanding* is, if I may use such a figure, the stop-cock which controls the emotions, lets them flow on, or stops them ; and it is as if some very wise man, when a reservoir had been poisoned, proposed that there should be a new person employed to turn the water off or on, in hope that the whole difficulty would thus be obviated. If we followed his advice, if we found the wisest man in the world to have control of the fountain, Mr. Understanding would still be incapable of supplying us with healthy streams, until we had first of all purged the cistern whence they flowed. The Arminian divine, too, sometimes suggests another way of improving man's life. He deals with the *will*. He says, the will must first of all be conquered, and if the will be right, then every thing will be in order. Now, *will* is like the great engine which forces the water out of the fountain-head along the pipes, so that it is made to flow into our dwellings. The learned counsellor proposes that there should be a new steam-engine employed to force the water along the pipes. " If," says he, " we had the proper machinery for forcing the fluid, then all would be well." No, sir, if the stream be poisonous, you may have axles to turn on diamonds, and you may have a machine that is made of gold, and a force as potent as Omnipotence, but even then you have not accompilshed your purpose until you have cleansed the polluted fountain, and purged the issues of life which flow therefrom. The wise man in our text seems to say, " Beware of misapplying your energies, be careful to begin in the right place." It is very necessary the understanding should be right; it is quite needful the will should have its proper predominance ; it is very necessary that you should keep every part of man in a healthy condition ; but," says he, " if you want to promote true holiness, you must begin with the heart, for out of it are the issues of life ; and when you have purged *it*, when you have made its waters pure and limpid, then shall the current flow and bless the inhabitants with clear water; but not till then." Here let us pause and ask the solemn and vital question, " Is my heart right in the sight of God?" For unless the inner man has been renewed by the grace of God, through the Holy Spirit, our heart is full of rottenness, filth, and abominations. And if so, here must all our cleansing begin, if it be real and satisfactory. Unrenewed men, I beseech you ponder the words of an ancient Christian which I here repeat in thine ear :—" It is no matter what is the sign, though an angel, that hangs without, if the devil and sin dwell therein. New trimmings upon an old garment will not make it new, only give it a new appearance ; and truly it is no good husbandry to bestow a great deal of cost in mending up an old suit, that will soon drop to tatters and rags, when a little more might purchase a new one that is lasting. And is it not better to labor to get a new heart, that all thou dost may be accepted, and thou saved, than to lose all the pains thou takest in religion, and thyself also for want of it ?"

Now, ye who love the Lord, let me take you to the reservoir of your heart, and let me urge upon you the great neces sity of keeping the heart right, if you would have the stream of your life happy for yourselves and beneficial to others.

I. First, keep the heart *full*. However pure the water may be in the central reservoir, it will not be possible for the company to provide us with an abundant supply of water, unless the reservoir itself be full. An empty fountain will most assuredly beget empty pipes; and let the machinery be never so accurate, let every thing else be well ordered, yet if that reservoir be dry, we may wait in vain for any of the water that we require. Now, you know many people—(you are sure to meet with them in your own society, and your own circle; for I know of no one so happy as to be without such acquaintances)—whose lives are just dry, good-for-nothing emptiness. They never accomplish anything; they have no mental force; they have no moral power; what they say, nobody thinks of noticing; what they do is scarcely ever imitated.

We have known fathers whose moral force has been so despicable, that even their children have scarcely been able to imitate them. Though imitation was strong enough in them, yet have they unconsciously felt, even in their childhood, that their father was, after all, but a child like themselves, and had not grown to be a man. Do you not know many people, who if they were to espouse a cause, and it were entrusted to them, would most certainly pilot it to shipwreck. Failure would be the total result. You could not use them as clerks in your office, without feeling certain that your business would be nearly murdered. If you were to employ them to manage a concern for you, you would be sure they would manage to spend all the money, but could never produce a doit. If they were placed in comfortable circumstances for a few months, they would go on carelessly till all was gone. They are just the flats, preyed on by the sharpers in the world; they have no manly strength, no power at all. See these people in religion: it does not matter much what are their doctrinal sentiments, it is quite certain they will never affect the minds of others. Put them in the pulpit: they are the slaves of the deacons, or else they are over-ridden by the church; they never have an opinion of their own, can not come out with a thing; they have not the heart to say, " Such a thing is, and I know it is." These men just live on, but as far as any utility to the world is concerned, they might almost as well never have been created, except it were to be fed upon by other people. Now, some say that this is the fault of men's heads: " Such a one," they say, " could not get on; he had a small head; it was clean impossible for him to prosper, his head was small, he could not do anything; he had not enough force." Now, that may be true; but I know what was truer still—he had got a small heart and that heart was empty. For, mark you, a man's force in the world, other things being equal, is just in the ratio of the force and strength of his heart. A full-hearted man is always a powerful man: if he be erroneous, then he is powerful for error; if the thing is in his heart, he is sure to make it notorious, even though it may be a downright falsehood. Let a man be never so ignorant, still if his heart be full of love to a cause, he becomes a powerful man for that object, because he has got heart-power, heart force. A man may be deficient in many of the advantages of education, in many of those niceties which are so much looked upon in society; but once give him a good strong heart, that beats hard, and there is no mistake about his power. Let him have a heart that is right full up to the brim with an object, and that man will do the thing, or else he will die gloriously defeated, and will glory in his defeat. HEART IS POWER. It is the emptiness of men's hearts that makes them so feeble. Men do not feel what they are at. Now, the man in business that goes heart and soul into his business, is more likely to prosper than anybody else. That is the preacher we want, the man that has a full soul. Let him have a head—the more he knows the better; but, after all, give him a big heart; and when his heart beats, if his heart be full, it will, under God, either make the hearts of his congregation beat after him; or else make them conscious that he is laboring hard to compel them to follow. O! if we had more heart in our Master's service, how much more labor we could endure. You are a Sunday-school teacher, young man, and you are complaining that you can not get on in' the Sunday-school. Sir, the serv ice-pipe would give out plenty of water if the heart were full. Perhaps you do not love your work. O, strive to love your work more, and then when your heart is full, you will go on well enough. "O," saith the preacher, "I am weary of my work in preaching; I have little success; I find it a hard toil." The answer to that question is, "Your heart is not full of it, for if you loved preaching, you would breathe preaching, feed upon preaching, and find a compulsion upon you to follow preaching; and your heart being full of the thing, you would be happy in the employment. O for a heart that is full, and deep, and broad! Find the man that hath such a soul as that, and that is the man from whom the living waters shall flow, to make the world glad with their refreshing streams.

Learn, then, the necessity of keeping the heart full; and let the necessity make you ask this question—"But how can I keep my heart full? How can my emotions be strong? How can I keep my desires burning and my zeal inflamed?" Christian! there is one text which will explain all this. "All my springs are in thee," said David. If thou hast all thy springs in God, thy heart will be full enough. If thou dost go to the foot of Calvary, there will thy heart be bathed in love and gratitude. If thou dost frequent the vale of retire· ment, and there talk with thy God, it is there that thy heart· shall be full of calm resolve. If thou goest out with thy Mas· ter to the hill of Olivet, and dost with him look down upon a wicked Jerusalem, and weep over it with him, then will thy heart be full of love for never-dying souls. If thou dost con· tinually draw thine impulse, thy life, the whole of thy being from the Holy Spirit, without whom thou canst do nothing; and if thou dost live in close communion with Christ, there will be no fear of thy having a dry heart. He who lives with· out prayer—he who lives with little prayer—he who seldom reads the Word—he who seldom looks up to heaven for a fresh influence from on high—he will be the man whose heart will become dry and barren; but he who calls in secret on his God—who spends much time in holy re· tirement--who delights to meditate on the words of the

Most High—whose soul is given up to Christ—who delights in his fullness, rejoices in his all-sufficiency, prays for his second coming, and delights in the thought of his glorious advent—such a man, I say, must have an overflowing heart; and as his heart is, such will his life be. It will be a full life; it will be a life that will speak from the sepulcher, and wake the echoes of the future. "Keep thine heart with all diligence," and entreat the Holy Spirit to keep it full; for, otherwise, the issues of thy life will be feeble, shallow, and superficial; and thou mayest as well not have lived at all.

2. Secondly, it would be of little use for our water companies to keep their reservoirs full, if they did not also keep them *pure.* I remember to have read a complaint in the newspaper of a certain provincial town, that a tradesman had been frequently supplied with fish from the water company, large eels having crept down the pipe, and sometimes creatures a little more loathsome. We have known such a thing as water companies supplying us with solids when they ought to have given us nothing but pure crystal. Now, no one likes that. The reservoir should be kept pure and clean; and unless the water comes 'from a pure spring, and is not impregnated with deleterious substances, however full the reservoir may be, the company will fail of satisfying or of benefiting its customers. Now it is essential for us to do with our hearts as the company must do with its reservoir. We must keep our hearts pure; for if the heart be not pure, the life can not be pure. It is quite impossible that it should be so. You see a man whose whole conversation is impure and unholy; when he speaks he lards his language with oaths; his mind is low and groveling; none but the things of unrighteousness are sweet to him, for he has no soul above the kennel and the dunghill. You meet with another man who understands enough to avoid violating the decencies of life; but still, at the same time he likes filthiness; any low joke, anything that will in some way stir unholy thoughts is just the thing that he desires. For the ways of God he has no relish; in God's house he finds no pleasure, in his Word no delight. What is the cause of this? Say some, it is because of his family connections—because of

the situation in which he stands—because of his early educa
tion, and all that. No, no; the simple answer to that is the
answer we gave to the other inquiry; the heart is not right;
for, if the heart were pure, the life would be pure too. The
unclean stream betrays the fountain. A valuable book of
German parables, by old Christian Scriver, contains the following homely metaphor:—" A drink was brought to Gotthold,
which tasted of the vessel in which it had been contained; and
this led him to observe. We have here an emblem of our
thoughts, words, and works. Our heart is defiled by sin, and
hence a taint of sinfulness cleaves unfortunately to everything
we take in hand; and although, from the force of habit, this
may be imperceptible to us, it does not escape the eye of the
omniscient, holy, and righteous God." Whence come our
carnality, covetuousness, pride, sloth and unbelief? Are they
not all to be traced to the corruption of our hearts? When
the hands of a clock move in an irregular manner, and when
the bell strikes the wrong hour, be assured there is something
wrong within. O how needful that the main-spring of our motives be in proper order, and the wheels in a right condition.

Ah! Christian keep thy heart pure. Thou sayest, "How
can I do this?" Well, there was of old a stream of Marah,
to which the thirsty pilgrims in the desert came to drink;
and when they came to taste of it, it was so brackish that though
their tongues were like torches, and the roofs of their mouths
were parched with heat, yet they could not drink of that bitter
water. Do you remember the remedy which Moses pre-
scribed? It is the remedy which we prescribe to you this
morning. He took a certain tree, and he cast it into the
waters, and they became sweet and clear. Your heart is by
nature like Marah's water, bitter and impure. There is a
certain tree, you know its name, that tree on which the Saviour hung, *the cross*. Take that tree, put it into your heart,
and though it were even more impure than it is, that sweet
cross, applied by the Holy Spirit, would soon transform it
into its own nature, and make it pure. Christ Jesus in the
heart is the sweet purification. He is made unto us *sanctifi.
cation*. Elijah cast salt into the waters; but we must cast

the blood of Jesus there. Once let us know and love Jesus, once let his cross become the object of our adoration and the theme of our delight, the heart will begin its cleansing, and the life will become pure also. Oh! that we all did learn the sacred lesson of fixing the cross in the heart! Christian man! love thy Saviour more; cry to the Holy Spirit that thou mayest have more affection for Jesus; and then, however gainful may be thy sin, thou wilt say with the poet,

> "Now for the love I bear his name,
>   What was my gain I count my loss;
> My former pride I call my shame,
>   And nail my glory to his cross."

The cross in the heart is the purifier of the soul; it purges and it cleanses the chambers of the mind. Christian! keep thy heart pure, "for out of it are the issues of life."

3. In the third place, there is one thing to which our water companies need never pay much attention; that is to say, if their water be pure, and the reservoir be full, they need not care to keep it *peaceable* and quiet, for let it be stirred to a storm, we should receive our water in the same condition as usual. It is not so, however, with the heart. Unless the heart be kept peaceable, the life will not be happy. If calm doth not reign over that inner lake within the soul which feeds the rivers of our life, the rivers themselves will always be in storm. Our outward acts will always tell that they were born in tempests, by rolling in tempests themselves. Let us just understand this, *first*, with regard to ourselves. We all desire to lead a joyous life; the bright eye and the elastic foot are things which we each of us desire; to carry about a contented mind is that to which most men are continually aspiring. Let us all remember, that the only way to keep our life peaceful and happy is to keep the heart at rest; for come poverty, come wealth, come honor, come shame, come plenty, or come scarcity, if the heart be quiet there will be happiness anywhere. But whatever the sunshine and the brightness, if the heart be troubled the whole life must be troubled too. There is a sweet story told in one of the German martyrologies well worth both my telling and your remembering. A

holy martyr who had been kept for a long time in prison, and had there exhibited, to the wonderment of all who saw him, the strongest constancy and patience, was at last, upon the day of execution, brought out, and tied to the stake preparatory to the lighting of the fire. While in this position "he craved permission to speak once more to the judge, who, according to the Swiss custom, was required to be also present at the execution. After repeatedly refusing, the judge at last came forward, when the peasant addressed him thus: You have this day condemned me to death. Now, I freely admit that I am a poor sinner, but positively deny that I am a heretic,' because from my heart I believe and confess all that is contained in the Apostles' Creed (which he thereupon repeated from beginning to end). Now, then, sir, he proceeded to say, I have but one last request to make, which is, that you will approach and place your hand, first upon my breast and then upon your own, and afterwards frankly and truthfully declare, before this assembled multitude, which of the two, mine or yours, is beating most violently with fear and anxiety. For my part, I quit the world with alacrity and joy, to go and be with Christ, in whom I have always believed; what your feelings are at this moment is best known to yourself. The judge could make no answer, and commanded them instantly to light the pile. It was evident, however, from his looks, that he was more afraid than the martyr."

Now, keep your heart right. Do not let it smite you. The Holy Spirit says of David, "David's heart smote him." The smiting of the heart is more painful to a good man than the rough blows of the fist. It is a blow that can be felt; it is iron that enters into the soul. Keep your heart in good temper. Do not let that get fighting with you. Seek that the peace of God which passeth all understanding, may keep your heart and mind through Christ Jesus. Bend your knee at night, and with a full confession of sin, express your faith in Christ, then you may "dread the grave as little as your bed." Rise in the morning and give your heart to God, and put the sweet angels of perfect love and holy faith therein, and you may go into the world, and were it full of lions and of tigers, you would no more need to dread it than Daniel when he was cast into the lion's den. Keep the heart peaceable and your life will be happy.

Remember, in the *second* place, that it is just the same with regard to other men. I should hope we all wish to lead quiet lives, and as much as lieth in us to live peaceably with all men. There is a particular breed of men—I do not know where they come from, but they are mixed up now with the English ¬ace and to be met with here and there—men who seem to be born for no other reason whatever but to fight—always quarreling, and never pleased. They say that all Englishmen are a little that way—that we are never happy unless we have something to grumble at, and that the worst thing that ever could be done with us would be to give us some entertainment at which we could not grumble, because we should be mortally offended, because we had not the opportunity of displaying our English propensities. I do not know whether that is true of all of us, but it is of some. You can not sit with them in a room but they introduce a topic upon which you are quite certain to disagree with them. You could not walk with them half a mile along the public streets but they would be sure to make an observation against every body and every thing they saw. They talk about ministers: one man's doctrine is too high, another's is too low; one man they think is a great deal too effeminate and precise, another they say is so vulgar they would not hear him at all. They say of another man that they do not think he attends to visiting his people; of another, that he visits so much that he never prepares for the pulpit. No one can be right for them.

Why is this? Whence arises this continual snarling? The heart must again supply the answer, they are morose and sullen in the inward parts, and hence their speech betrayeth them. They have not had their hearts brought to feel that God hath made of one blood all nations that dwell upon the face of the earth, or if they have felt that, they have never been brought to spell in their hearts—" By this shall all men know that ye are my disciples, if ye love one another." Whichever may have been put there of the other ten, the eleventh commandment was never written there. "A new commandment give I unto you, that ye love one another." That they forgot. Oh! dear Christian people, seek to have your hearts full of love, and if you have had little hearts till now that could not hold love enough for more than your own denomination, get your hearts enlarged, so that you may have enough to send out service-pipes to all God's people throughout the habitable globe; so that whenever you meet a man who is a true-born heir of heaven, he has nothing to do but to turn to the tap, and out of your loving heart will begin to flow issues of true, fervent, unconstrained, willing, living love. Keep thine heart peaceable, that thy life may be so; for out of the heart are the issues of life.

How is this to be done? We reply again, we must ask the Holy Spirit to pacify the heart. No voice but that which on Galilee's lake said to the storm "Be still," can ever lay the troubled waters of a stormy heart. No strength but Omnipotence can still the tempest of human nature. Cry out mightily unto him. He still sleeps in the vessel with his church. Ask him to awake, lest your piety should perish in the waters of contention. Cry unto him that he may give your heart peace and happiness. Then shall your life be peaceful; spend ye it where ye may, in trouble or in joy.

4. A little further. When the water-works company have gathered an abundance of water in the reservoir, there is one thing they must always attend to, and that is, they must take care they do not attempt too much, or otherwise they will fail. Suppose they lay on a great main pipe in one place to serve one city, and another main pipe to serve another, and the supply which was intended to fill one channel is diverted into a score of streams, what would be the result? Why nothing would be done well, but everyone would have cause to complain. Now, man's heart is after all so little, that there is only one great direction in which its living water can ever flow; and my fourth piece of advice to you from this text is, Keep your heart *undivided*. Suppose you see a lake, and there are twenty or thirty streamlets running from it: why, there will not be one strong river in the whole country; there

will be a number of little brooks which will be dried up in the summer, and will be temporary torrents in the winter. They will every one of them be useless for any great purposes, because there is not water enough in the lake to feed more than one great stream. Now, a man's heart has only enough life in it to pursue one object fully. Ye must not give half your love to Christ, and the other half to the world. No man can serve God and mammon because there is not enough life in the heart to serve the two. Alas! many people try this, and they fail both ways. I have known a man who has tried to let some of his heart run into the world, and another part he allowed to drip into the church, and the effect has been this: when he came into the church he was suspected of hypocrisy. " Why," they said, " if he were truly with us, could he have done yesterday what he did, and then come and profess so much to-day?" The church looks upon him as a suspicious one : or if he deceive them they feel he is not of much use to them, because they have not got all his heart. What is the effect of his conduct in the world ? Why, his religion is a fetter to him there. The world will not have him, and the church will not have him ; he wants to go between the two, and both despise him. I never saw anybody try to walk on both sides of the street but a drunken man : *he* tried it, and it was very awkward work indeed ; but I have seen many people in a moral point of view try to walk on both sides of the street, and I thought there was some kind of intoxication in them, or else they would have given it up as a very foolish thing. Now, if I thought this world and the pleasures thereof worth my seeking, I would just seek them and go after them, and I would not pretend to be religious ; but if Christ be Christ, and if God be God, let us give our whole hearts to him, and not go shares with the world. Many a church member manages to walk on both sides of the street in the following manner : His sun is very low indeed—it has not much light, not much heat, and is come almost to its setting. Now sinking suns cast long shadows, and this man stands on the world's side of the street, and casts a long shadow right across the road, to the opposite side of the wall just across the pave ment. Ay, it is all we get with many of you. You come and you take the sacramental bread and wine; you are baptized; you join the church; and what we get is just your shadow; there is your substance on the other side of the street, after all. What is the good of the empty chrysalis of a man? And yet many of our church members are little better. They just do as the snake does that leaves its slough behind. They give us their slough, their skin, the chrysalis case in which life once was, and then they go themselves hither and thither after their own wanton wills; they give us the outward, and then give the world the inward. O how foolish this, Christian! Thy master gave himself wholly for thee; give thyself unreservedly to him. Keep not back part of the price. Make a full surrender of every motion of thy heart; labor to have but one object, and one aim. And for this purpose give God the keeping of thine heart. Cry out for more of the divine influences of the Holy Spirit, that so when thy soul is preserved and protected by him, it may be directed into one channel, and one only, that thy life may run deep and pure, and clear and peaceful; its only banks being God's will, its only channel the love of Christ and a desire to please him. Thus wrote Spencer in days long gone by: "Indeed, by nature, man's heart is a very divided, broken thing, scattered and parceled out, a piece to this creature, and a piece to that lust. One while this vanity hires him (as Leah did Jacob of Rachel), anon when he hath done some drudgery for that, he lets out himself to another: thus divided is man and his affections. Now the elect, whom God hath decreed to be vessels of honor, consecrated for his holy use and service, he throws into the fire of his word, that being there softened and melted, he may by his transforming Spirit cast them anew, as it were, into a holy oneness; so that he who before was divided from God, and lost among the creatures, and his lusts, that shared him among them, now, his heart is gathered into God from them all; it looks with a single eye on God, and acts for him in all that he doth: if therefore thou wouldest know whether thy heart be sincere, inquire whether it be thus made anew."

5. Now, my last point is rather a strange one perhaps. Once upon a time, when one of our kings came back from a captivity, old historians tell us that there were fountains in Cheapside that did run with wine. So bounteous was the king, and so glad the people, that instead of water, they made wine flow free to everybody. There is a way of making our life so rich, so full, so blessed to our fellow men, that the metaphor may be applicable to us, and men may say, that our life flows with wine when other men's lives flow with water. Ye have known some such men. There was a Howard. John Howard's life was not like our poor common lives; he was so benevolent, his sympathy with the race so self-denying, that the streams of his life were like generous wine. You have known another, an eminent saint, one who lived very near to Jesus: when you talked yourself, you felt your conversation was poor watery stuff; but when he talked to you, there was an unction and a savor about his words, a solidity, and a strength about his utterances, which you could appreciate, though you could not attain unto it. You have sometimes said, " I wish my words were as full, as sweet, as mellow, and as unctuous as the words of such an one ! Oh ! I wish my actions were just as rich, had as deep a color, and as pure a taste as the acts of so-and-so. All I can do seems but little and empty when compared with his high attainments. Oh, that I could do more ! Oh, that I could send streams of pure gold into every house, instead of my poor dross." Well, Christian, this should teach thee to keep thine heart full of rich things. Never, never neglect the Word of God; that will make thy heart rich with precept, rich with understanding; and then thy conversation, when it flows from thy mouth, will be like thine heart, rich, unctuous, and savory. Make thy heart full of rich, generous love, and then the stream that flows from thy hand will be just as rich and generous as thine heart. Above all, get Jesus to live in thine heart, and then out of thy belly shall flow rivers of living water, more rich, more satisfying than the water of the well of Sychar of which Jacob drank. Oh ! go, Christians, to the great mine of riches, and cry unto the Holy Spirit to make thy heart rich unto salvation. So shall thy life and conversation be a boon to thy fellows; and when they see thee, thy face shall be as the angel of God. Thou shalt wash thy feet in butter and thy steps in oil; they that sit in the gate shall rise up when they see thee, and men shall do thee reverence.

But one single sentence, and we have done. Some of your hearts are not worth keeping. The sooner you get rid of them the better. They are hearts of stone. Do you feel to-day that you have a stony heart? Go home, and I pray the Lord hear my desire that thy polluted heart may be removed. Cry unto God and say, " Take away my heart of stone, and give me a heart of flesh;" for a stony heart is an impure heart, a divided heart, an unpeaceful heart. It is a heart that is poor and poverty-stricken, a heart that is void of all good-ness, and thou canst neither bless thyself nor others, if thy heart be such. O Lord Jesus! wilt thou be pleased this day to renew many hearts? Wilt thou break the rock in pieces, and put flesh instead of stone, and thou shalt have the glory, world without end!

SERMON XXV

HOW TO KEEP THE HEART

"The peace of God, which passeth all understanding, shall keep your hearts and minds, through Christ Jesus."—PHILLIPIANS, iv. 7

It is remarkable, that when we find an exhortation given to God's people in one part of the Holy Scripture, we almost invariably find the very thing which they are exhorted to do guaranteed to them, and provided for them, in some other part of the same blessed volume. This morning, my text was, "Keep the heart with all diligence, for out of it are the issues of life." Now, this evening we have the promise upon which we must rest, if we desire to fulfill the precept:—"The peace of God, which passeth all understanding, shall keep your hearts and minds, through Christ Jesus."

This evening we shall use another figure, distinct from the one used in the morning, of *the reservoir*. We shall use the figure of *a fortress*, which is to be kept. And the promise saith that it shall be kept—kept by "the peace of God, which passeth all understanding, through Christ Jesus."

Inasmuch as the heart is the most important part of man—for out of it are the issues of life—it would be natural to expect that Satan, when he intended to do mischief to manhood, would be sure to make his strongest and most perpetual attacks upon the heart. What we might have guessed in wisdom, is certainly true in experience; for although Satan will tempt and try us in every way, though every gate of the town of Mansoul may be battered, though, against every part of the walls thereof he will be sure to bring out his great guns, yet the place against which he levels his deadliest malice, and his most furious strength, is the heart. Into the heart, already of itself evil enough, he thrusts the seeds of every evil thing, and doth his utmost to make it a den of un‧ clean birds, a garden of poisonous trees, a river flowing with destructive water. Hence, again, arises the second necessity that we should be doubly cautious in keeping the heart with all diligence; for if, on the one hand, it be the most important, and, on the other hand, Satan, knowing this, makes his most furious and determined attacks against it, then, with double force the exhortation comes, "Keep thy heart with all diligence." And the promise also becomes doubly sweet, from the very fact of the double danger—the promise which says, "The peace of God shall keep your hearts and minds through Christ Jesus our Lord."

We shall notice, first of all, *that which keeps the heart and mind.* Secondly, we shall note *how to obtain it*—for we are to understand this promise as connected with certain precepts which come before it. And then, when we have had this, we shall try to show *how it is true that the peace of God does keep the mind free from the attacks of Satan, or delivers it from those attacks when they are made.*

I. First, then, beloved, the preservation which God in this promise confers upon the saints, is "THE PEACE OF GOD WHICH PASSETH ALL UNDERSTANDING," to keep us through Jesus Christ. It is called PEACE; and we are to understand this in a double sense. There is a peace of God which exists between the child of God, and God his Judge, a peace which may be truly said to pass all understanding. Jesus Christ has offered so all-sufficient a satisfaction for all the claims of injured justice, that now God hath no fault to find with his children. "He seeth no sin in Jacob, nor iniquity in Israel;" nor is he angry with them on account of their sins—a peace unbroken, and unspeakable being established by the atonement which Christ hath made on their behalf.

Hence flows a peace experienced in the conscience, which is the second part of this peace of God : for, when the conscience sees that God is satisfied, and is no longer at war with it, then it also becomes satisfied with man ; and conscience, which was wont to be a great disturber of the peace of the heart, now gives its verdict of acquittal, and the heart sleeps in the arms of conscience, and finds a quiet resting-place there. Against the child of God conscience brings no accusation, or if it brings the accusation, it is but a gentle one—a gentle chiding of a loving friend, who hints that we have done amiss; and that we had better change, but doth not afterward thunde' in our ears the threat of a penalty. Conscience knows full well that peace is made betwixt the soul and God, and, therefore, it does not hint that there is anything else but joy and peace to be looked forward to by the believer. Do we understand anything of this double peace? Let us pause here, and ask ourselves a question upon this doctrinal part of the matter—Let us make it an experimental question with our own hearts :—" Come, my soul, art thou at peace with God? Hast thou seen thy pardon signed and sealed with the Redeemer's blood? Come, answer this, my heart; hast thou cast thy sins upon the head of Christ, and hast thou seen them all washed away in the crimson streams of blood? Canst thou feel that now there is a lasting peace between thyself and God, so that, come what may, God shall not be angry with thee—shall not condemn thee—shall not consume thee in his wrath, nor crush thee in his hot displeasure? If it be so, then, my heart, thou canst scarcely need to stop and ask the second question—Is my conscience at peace? For, if my heart condemn me not, God is greater than my heart, and doth know all things; if my conscience bears witness with me, that I am a partaker of the precious grace of salvation, then happy am I ! I am one of those to whom God hath given the peace which passeth all understanding. Now, why is this called " the peace of God?" We suppose it is because it comes from God—because it was planned by God—because God gave his Son to make the peace—because God gives his Spirit to give the peace in the conscience—because, indeed, it is God himself in the soul, reconciled to man, whose is the peace. And while it is true that this man shall have the peace—even the Man-Christ, yet we know it is because he was the God-Christ that he was our peace. And hence we may clearly perceive how Godhead is mixed up with the peace which we enjoy with our Maker, and with our conscience.

Then, we are told that it is "the peace of God which passeth all understanding." What does he mean by this? He
means such a peace, that the understanding can never understand it, can never attain to it. The understanding of mere
carnal man can never comprehend this peace. He who tries
with a philosophic look to discover the secret of the Christian's
peace, finds himself in a maze. "I know not how it is, nor
why it is," saith he; "I see these men hunted through the
earth; I turn the pages of history, and I find them hunted to
their graves. They wandered about in sheepskins and goat-
skins, destitute, afflicted, and tormented; yet, I also see upon
the Christian's brow a calm serenity. I can not understanc
this; I do not know what it is. I know that I myself, even
in my merriest moments, am disturbed; that when my enjoy
ments run the highest, still there are waves of doubt and fear
across my mind. Then why is this? How is it that the
Christian can attain a rest so calm, so peaceful, and so quiet?"
Understanding can never get to that peace which the Christian hath attained. The philosopher may teach us much; he
can never give us rules whereby to reach the peace that
Christians have in their conscience. Diogenes may tell us to
do without everything, and may live in his tub, and then
think himself happier than Alexander, and that he enjoys
peace; but we look upon the poor creature after all, and
though we may be astonished at his courage, yet we are
obliged to despise his folly. We do not believe that even
when he had dispensed with everything, he possessed a quiet
of mind, a total and entire peace, such as the true believer can
enjoy. We find the greatest philosophers of old laying down
maxims for life, which they thought would certainly promote
happiness. We find that they were not always able to prac
tise them themselves, and many of their disciples, when they
labored hard to put them in execution, found themselves en-
cumbered with impossible rules to accomplish impossible objects. But the Christian man does with faith what a man can
never do himself. While the poor understanding is climbing
up the craigs, faith stands on the summit; while the poor understanding is getting into a calm atmosphere, faith flies aloft

and mounts higher than the storm, and then looks down on the valley, and smiles while the tempest blows beneath its feet. Faith goes further than understanding, and the peace which the Christian enjoys is one which the worldling can not comprehend, and can not himself attain. "The peace of God, which passeth all understanding."

And this peace is said to "keep the mind through Christ Jesus." Without Christ Jesus this peace would not exist; without Christ Jesus this peace, even where it has existed, can not be maintained. Daily visits from the Saviour, continual lookings by the eye of faith to him who bled upon the cross, continual drawings from his ever-flowing fountain, make this peace broad, and long, and enduring. But take Jesus Christ, the channel of our peace away, and it fades and dies, and droops, and comes to naught. A Christian hath no peace with God except through the atonement of his Lord Jesus Christ.

I have thus gone over what some will call the dry doctrinal part of the subject—"The peace of God, which passeth all understanding, shall keep your hearts and minds through Christ Jesus." I can not show you what that peace is, if you have never felt it ; but yet I think I could tell you where to look for it, for I have sometimes seen it. I have seen the Christian man in the depths of poverty, when he lived from hand to mouth, and scarcely knew where he should find the next meal, still with his mind unruffled, calm, and quiet. If he had been as rich as an Indian prince, yet could he not have had less care ; if he had been told that his bread should always come to his door, and the stream which ran hard by should never dry—if he had been quite sure that ravens would bring him bread and meat in the morning, and again in the evening, he would not have been one whit more calm. There is his neighbor on the other side of the street not half so poor, but wearied from morning to night, working his fingers to the bone, bringing himself to the grave with anxiety ; but this poor good man, after having industriously labored, though he found he had gained little with all his toil, yet hath sanctified his little by prayer, and hath thanked his Father for what

he had ; and though he doth not know whether he will have
more, still he trusted in God, and declared that his faith should
not fail him, though providence should run to a lower ebb
than he had ever seen.   There is " the peace of God which
passeth all understanding."   I have seen that peace, too, in
the case of those who have lost their friends.   There is a
widow—her much-loved husband lies in the coffin ; she is soon
to part with him.   Parted with him she has before : but now,
of his poor clay-cold corpse—even of that she has to be be
reaved.   She looks upon it for the last time, and her heart is
heavy.   For herself and her children, she thinks how they
shall be provided for.   That broad tree that once sheltered
them from the sunbeam has been cut down.   Now, she thinks
there is a broad heaven above her head, and her Maker is her
husband ; the fatherless children are left with God for their
father, and the widow is trusting in him.   With tears in her
eyes she still looks up, and she says, " Lord, thou hast given
and thou hast taken away, blessed be thy name."   Her husband is carried to the tomb ; she doth not smile, but though
she weeps, there is a calm composure on her brow, and she
tells you she would not have it otherwise, even if she could,
for Jehovah's will is right.   There, again, is " the peace of
God that passeth all understanding."   Picture another man.
There is Martin Luther standing up in the midst of the Diet
of Worms ; there are the kings and the princes, and there are
the bloodhounds of Rome with their tongues thirsting for
his blood—there is Martin rising in the morning as comfortable as possible, and he goes to the Diet, and delivers himself
of the truth, solemnly declares that the things which he has
spoken are the things which he believes, and God helping him,
he will stand by them till the last.   There is his life in his
hands ; they have him entirely in their power.   The smell of
John Huss's corpse has not yet passed away, and he recollects
that princes before this have violated their words ; but there
he stands, calm and quiet ; he fears no man, for he has naught
to fear ; " the peace of God which passeth all understanding"
keeps his heart and mind through Jesus Christ.   There is another scene : there is John Bradford in Newgate.   He is to

be burned the next morning in Smithfield, and he swings himself on the bedpost in very glee, and delights, for to-morrow is his wedding-day; and he says to another, "Fine shining we shall make to-morrow, when the flame is kindled." And he smiles and laughs, and enjoys the very thought that he is about to wear the blood-red crown of martyrdom. Is Bradford mad? Ah, no; but he has got the peace of God that passeth all understanding. But perhaps the most beautiful, as well as the most common illustration of this sweet peace, is the dying bed of the believer. Oh, brethren, you have seen this sometimes—that calm, quiet serenity; you have said, Lord, let us die with him. It has been so good to be in that solitary chamber where all was quiet and so still, all the world shut out, and heaven shut in, and the poor heart nearing its God, and far away from all its past burdens and griefs—now nearing the portals of eternal bliss. And ye have said, "How is this? Is not death a black and grim thing? Are not the terrors of the grave things which make the strong man tremble?" Oh yes, they are; but, then, this one has the "peace of God which passeth all understanding." However, if you want to know about this, you must be a child of God, and possess it yourselves; and when you have once felt it, when you can stand calm amid the bewildering cry, confident of victory, when you can sing in the midst of the storm, when you can smile when surrounded by adversity, and can trust your God, be your way ne'er so rough, ne'er so stormy; when you can always repose confidence in the wisdom and goodness of Jehovah, then it is you will have "the peace of God which passeth all understanding."

II. Thus we have discussed the first point, what is this peace? Now the second thing was, HOW IS THIS PEACE TO BE OBTAINED? You will note that although this is a promise, it hath precepts preceding, and it is only by the practice of the precepts that we can get the promise. Turn now to the fourth verse, and you will see the first rule and regulation for getting peace. Christian, would you enjoy "the peace of God which passeth all understanding?"

The first thing you have to do is to "rejoice evermore."

The man who never rejoices, but who is always sorrowing, and groaning, and crying, who forgets his God, who forgets the fullness of Jehovah, and is always murmuring concerning the trials of the road and the infirmities of the flesh, that man will lose the prospect of enjoying a peace that passeth all understanding. Cultivate, my friends, a cheerful disposition; endeavor, as much as lieth in you, always to bear a smile about with you; recollect that this is as much a command of God as that one which says, "Thou shalt love the Lord with all thy heart." "Rejoice evermore," is one of God's commands; and it is your duty, as well as your privilege, to try and practice it. Not to rejoice, remember, is a sin. To rejoice is a duty, and such a duty that the richest fruits and the best rewards are appended to it. Rejoice always, and then the peace of God shall keep your hearts and minds. Many of us, by giving way to disastrous doubts, spoil our peace. It is as I once remember to have heard a woman say, when I was passing down a lane; a child stood crying at the door, and I heard her calling out, "Ah, you are crying for nothing; I will give you something to cry for." Brethren, it is often so with God's children. They get crying for nothing. They have a miserable disposition, or a turn of mind always making miseries for themselves, and thus they have something to cry for. Their peace is disturbed, some sad trouble comes, God hides his face, and then they lose their peace. But keep on singing, even when the sun does not keep on shining; keep a song for all weathers; get a joy that will stand clouds and storms; and then, when you know how always to rejoice, you shall have this peace.

The next precept is, "Let your moderation be known unto all men." If you would have peace of mind, be moderate. Merchant, you can not push that speculation too far, and then have peace of mind. Young man, you can not be so fast in trying to rise in the world, and yet have the peace of God which passeth all understanding. You must be moderate, and when you have got a moderation in your desires, then you shall have peace. Sir, you with the red cheek, you must be moderate in your anger. You must not be quite so fast in flying into a passion with your fellows, and not quite so long in getting cool again; because the angry man can not have peace in his conscience. Be moderate in that; let your vengeance stay itself; for if you give way to wrath, if you are angry, " be ye angry and sin not." Be moderate in this; be moderate in all things which thou undertakest, Christian; moderate in your expectations. Blessed is he who expects little, for he shall have but little disappointment. Remember never to set thy desires very high. He that has aspirations to the moon, will be disappointed if he only reaches half as high; whereas, if he had aspired lower, he would be agreeably disappointed when he found himself mounting higher than he first expected. Keep moderation, whatsoever you do, in all things, but in your desires after God; and so shall you obey the second precept, and get the glimpse of this promise, "The peace of God shall keep your hearts and minds through Jesus Christ."

The last precept that you have to obey is, " be careful for nothing, but in every thing by prayer and supplication make known your requests unto God." You can not have peace unless you turn your troubles up. You have no place in which to pour your troubles except the ear of God. If you tell them to your friends, you but put your troubles out a moment, and they will return again. If you tell them to God, you put your troubles into the grave; they will never rise again when you have committed them to him. If you roll your burden anywhere else it will roll back again, just like the stone of Sysiphus; but just roll your burden unto God, and you have rolled it into a great deep, out of which it will never by any possibility rise. Cast your troubles where you have cast your sins; you have cast your sins into the depth of the sea, there cast your troubles also. Never keep a trouble half an hour on your own mind before you tell it to God. As soon as the trouble comes, quick, the first thing, tell it to your father. Remember, that the longer you take telling your trouble to God, the more your peace will be impaired. The longer the frost lasts, the more likely the ponds will be frozen. Your frost will last till you go to the sun; and when you go to God—

the sun, then your frost will soon become a thaw, and your troubles will melt away. But do not be long, because the longer you are in waiting, the longer will your trouble be in thawing afterwards. Wait a long time till your troubles gets frozen thick and firm, and it will take many a day of prayer to get your trouble thawed again. Away to the throne as quick as ever you can. Do as the child did, when he ran and told his mother as soon as his little trouble happened to him ; run and tell your Father the first moment you are in affliction. Do this in every thing, in every little thing—" in every thing by prayer and supplication make known your wants unto God." Take your husband's head-ache, take your children's sicknesses, take all things, little family troubles as well as great commercial trials—take them all to God ; pour them all out at once. And so by an obedient practice of this command in every thing making known your wants unto God, you shall preserve that peace " which shall keep your heart and mind through Jesus Christ."

These, then, are the precepts. May God the Holy Spirit enable us to obey them, and we shall then have the continual peace of God.

III. Now, the third thing, was to show HOW THE PEACE, which I attempted to describe in the first place, KEEPS THE HEART. You will clearly see how this peace will keep the heart full. That man who has continued peace with God, will not have an empty heart. He feels that God has done so much for him that he must love his God. The eternal basis of his peace lays in divine election—the solid pillars of his peace, the incarnation of Christ, his righteousness, his death— the climax of his peace, the heaven hereafter where his joy and his peace shall be consummated ; all these are subjects for grateful reflection, and will, when meditated upon, cause more love. Now, where much love is, there is a large heart and a full one. Keep, then, this peace with God, and thou wilt keep thy heart full to the brim. And, remember, that in proportion to the fullness of thine heart will be the fullness of thy life. Be empty-hearted and thy life will be a meager, skeleton existence. Be full hearted, and thy life will be full, fleshy, gigantic, strong, a thing that will tell upon the world. Keep, then, thy peace with God firm within thee. Keep thou close to this, that Jesus Christ hath made peace between thee and God. And keep thy conscience still; then shall thy heart be full and thy soul strong to do thy Master's work. Keep thy peace with God. This will keep thy heart pure. Thou wilt say if temptation comes, "What dost thou offer me? Thou offerest me pleasure; lo! I have got it. Thou offerest me gold; lo! I have got it; all things are mine, the gift of God; I have a city that hands have not made, 'a house not made with hands, eternal in the heavens.' I will not barter this for your poor gold." "I will give you honor," saith Satan. "I have honor enough," says the peaceful heart; "God will honor me in the last great day of his account." "I will give thee everything that thou canst desire," saith Satan. "I have everything that I can desire," says the Christian

> "I nothing want on earth;
> Happy in my Saviour's love,
> I am at peace with God."

Avaunt, then, Satan! While I am at peace with God, I am a match for all thy temptations. Thou offerest me silver; I have gold. Thou bringest before me the riches of the earth; I have something more substantial than these. Avaunt, tempter of human kind! Avaunt, thou fiend! Your temptations and blandishments are lost on one who has peace with God. This peace, too, will keep the heart undivided. He who has peace with God will set his whole heart on God. "Oh!" says he, "why should I go to seek anything else on earth, now that I have found my rest in God? As the bird by wandering, so should I be if I went elsewhere. I have found a fountain; why should I go and drink at the broken cistern that will hold no water? I lean on the arm of my beloved; why should I rest on the arm of another? I know that religion is a thing worth my following; why should I leave the pure snows of Lebanon to follow something else? I know and feel that religion is rich when it brings forth to me a hundredfold the fruits of peace; why should I go and sow elsewhere? I will be like the maiden Ruth, I will stop in the fields of Boaz. Here will I ever stay and never wander."

Again, this peace keeps the heart rich. My hearers will notice that I am passing over the heads of the morning's discourse, and showing how this peace fulfills the requisites that we thought necessary in the morning. Peace with God keeps the heart rich. The man who doubts and is distressed has got a poor heart; it is a heart that has nothing in it. But when a man has peace with God, his heart is rich. If I am at peace with God I am enabled to go where I can get riches. The throne is the place where God gives riches. If I am at peace with him, then I can have access with boldness. Meditation is a great and another field of enrichment. When my heart is at peace with God, then I can enjoy meditation; but if I have not peace with God, then I can not meditate profitably; for "the birds come down on the sacrifice," and I can not drive them away, except my soul is at peace with God. Hearing the word is another way of getting rich. If my mind is disturbed I can not hear the word with profit. If I have to bring my family into the chapel; if I have to bring my business, my ships, or my horses, I can not hear. When I have cows, and dogs, and horses in the pew, I can not hear the Gospel preached. When I have got a whole week's business, and a ledger on my heart, I can not hear then; but when I have peace, peace concerning all things, and rest in my Father's will, then I can hear with pleasure, and every word of the gospel is profitable to me; for my mouth is empty, and I can fill it with the heavenly treasures of his Word. So you see the peace of God is a soul-enriching thing. And because it keeps the heart rich, thus it is it keeps the heart and mind through Jesus Christ our Lord. I need hardly say that the peace of God fulfills the only other requisite which I did not mention, because it was unnecessary to do so. It keeps the heart always peaceable. Of course, peace makes it full of peace—peace like a river, and righteousness like the waves of the sea.

Now, then, brother and sister, it is of the first importance

that you keep your heart aright. You can not keep your
heart right but by one way. That one way is by getting,
maintaining, and enjoying peace of God to your own conscience. I beseech you then, you that are professors of religion, do not let this night pass over your heads till you have a
confident assurance that you are now the possessor of the
peace of God. For let me tell you, if you go out to the
world next Monday morning without first having peace with
God in your own conscience, you will not be able to keep
your heart during the week. If this night, ere you rest, you
could say that with God as well as all the world you are at
peace, you may go out to-morrow, and whatever your business, I am not afraid for you. You are more than a match
for all the temptations to false doctrine, to false living, or to
false speech that may meet you. For he that has peace with
God is armed *cap-à-pié ;* he is covered from head to foot in a
panoply. The arrow may fly against it, but it can not pierce
it, for peace with God is a mail so strong that the broad sword
of Satan itself may be broken in twain ere it can pierce the
flesh. O ! take care that you are at peace with God ; for if you
are not, you ride forth to to-morrow's fight unarmed, naked ;
and God help the man that is unarmed when he has to fight
with hell and earth. O, be not foolish, but " put on the whole
armor of God," and then be confident for you need not fear.

As for the rest of you, you can not have peace with God,
because " there is no peace, saith my God, to the wicked."
How shall I address you. As I said this morning, I can not
exhort you to keep your hearts. My best advice to you is,
to get rid of your hearts, and as soon as you can, to get new
ones. Your prayer should be, " Lord, take away my stony
heart, and give me a heart of flesh." But though I can not
address you from this text, I may address you from another.
Though your heart is bad, there is another heart that is good ;
and the goodness of that heart is a ground of exhortation to
you. You remember Christ said, " Come unto me all ye that
are weary and heavy laden ;" and then his argument would
come to this, " for I am meek and lowly of heart, and ye shall
find rest to your souls." Your heart is proud, and high, and

black, and lustful; but look at Christ's heart, it is meek and lowly. There is your encouragement. Do you feel to-night your sin? Christ is meek; if you come to him he will not spurn you. Do you feel your insignificance and worthlessness? Christ is lowly; he will not despise you. If Christ's heart were like your heart, you would be damned to a certainty. But Christ's heart is not as your heart, nor his ways like your ways. I can see no hope for you when I look into your hearts, but I can see plenty of hope when I look into Christ's heart.

O, think of his blessed heart; and if you go home to-night sad and sorrowful, under a sense of sin, when you go to your chamber, shut to your door—you need not be afraid—and talk to that heart so meek and lowly; and though your words be ungrammatical, and your sentences incoherent, he will hear and answer you from heaven, his dwelling place; and when he hears, he will forgive and accept, for his own name's sake.

SERMON XXVI

HUMAN INABILITY

"No man can come to me, except the Father which hath sent me draw him."—JOHN, vi. 44.

"COMING to Christ" is a very common phrase in Holy Scripture. It is used to express those acts of the soul wherein, leaving at once our self-righteousness and our sins, we fly unto the Lord Jesus Christ, and receive his righteousness to be our covering, and his blood to be our atonement. Coming to Christ, then, embraces in it repentance, self-negation, and faith in the Lord Jesus Christ, and it sums within itself all those things which are the necessary attendants of these great states of heart, such as the belief of the truth, earnestness of prayer to God, the submission of the soul to the precepts of God's gospel, and all those things which accompany the dawn of salvation in the soul. Coming to Christ is just the one essential thing for a sinner's salvation. He that cometh not to Christ, do what he may, or think what he may, is yet in "the gall of bitterness and in the bonds of iniquity." Coming to Christ is the very first effect of regeneration. No sooner is the soul quickened than it at once discovers its lost estate, is horrified thereat, looks out for a refuge, and believing Christ to be a suitable one, flies to him and reposes in him. Where there is not this coming to Christ, it is certain that there is as yet no quickening; where there is no quickening, the soul is dead in trespasses and sins, and being dead it can not enter into the kingdom of heaven. We have before us now an announcement very startling, some say very obnoxious. Coming to Christ, though described by some people as being the very easiest thing in all the world, is in our text declared to be a thing utterly and entirely impossible to any man, unless the Father shall draw him to Christ. It shall be our business, then, to enlarge upon this declaration. We doubt not that it will always be offensive to carnal nature, but, nevertheless, the offending of human nature is sometimes the first step towards bringing it to bow itself before God. And if this be the effect of a painful process, we can forget the pain and rejoice in the glorious consequences.

I shall endeavor this morning, first of all, to notice *man's inability*, wherein it consists. Secondly, *the Father's drawings*—what these are, and how they are exerted upon the soul. And then I shall conclude by noticing *a sweet consolation* which may be derived from this seemingly barren and terrible text.

I. First, then, MAN'S INABILITY. The text says, "No man can come to me, except the Father which hath sent me, draw him." Wherein does this inability lie?

First, it does not lie in any *physical* defect. If in coming to Christ, moving the body, or walking with the feet should be of any assistance, certainly man has all physical power to come to Christ in that sense. I remember to have heard a very foolish Antinomian declare, that he did not believe any man had the power to walk to the house of God unless the Father drew him. Now the man was plainly foolish, because he must have seen that as long as a man was alive and had legs, it was as easy for him to walk to the house of God as to the house of Satan. If coming to Christ includes the utterance of a prayer, man has no physical defect in that respect, if he be not dumb, he can say a prayer as easily as he can utter blasphemy. It is as easy for a man to sing one of the songs of Zion as to sing a profane and libidinous song. There is no lack of physical power in coming to Christ. All that can be wanted with regard to the bodily strength man most assuredly has, and any part of salvation which consists in that is totally and entirely in the power of man without any assistance from the Spirit of God. Nor, again, does this inability lie in any *mental* lack. I can believe this Bible to be true just as easily as I can believe any other book to be true. So far as believing on Christ is an act of the mind, I am just as able to believe on Christ as I am to believe on any body else. Let his statement be but true, it is idle to tell me I can not believe it. I can believe the statement that Christ makes as well as I can believe the statement of any other person. There is no deficiency of faculty in the mind: it is as capable of appreciating as a mere mental act the guilt of sin, as it is of appreciating the guilt of assassination. It is just as possible for me to exercise the mental idea of seeking God, as it is to exercise the thought of ambition. I have all the mental strength and power that can possibly be needed, so far as mental power is needed in salvation at all. Nay, there is not any man so ignorant that he can plead a lack of intellect as an excuse for rejecting the gospel. The defect, then, does not lie either in the body, or, what we are bound to call, speaking theologically, the mind. It is not any lack or deficiency there, although it is the vitiation of the mind, the corruption or the ruin of it, which, after all, is the very essence of man's inability.

Permit me to show you wherein this inability of man really does lie. It lies deep *in his nature.* Through the fall, and through our own sin, the nature of man has become so debased, and depraved, and corrupt, that it is impossible for him to come to Christ without the assistance of God the Holy Spirit. Now, in trying to exhibit how the nature of man thus renders him unable to come to Christ, you must allow me just to take this figure. You see a sheep; how willingly it feeds upon the herbage! You never knew a sheep sigh after carrion; it could not live on lion's food. Now bring me a wolf; and you ask me whether a wolf can not eat grass, whether it can not be just as docile and just as domesticated as the sheep. I answer no; because its nature is contrary thereunto. You say, " Well, it has ears and legs; can it not hear the shepherd's voice, and follow him whithersoever he leadeth it?" I answer, certainly, there is no physical cause why it can not do so, but its nature forbids, and therefore I say it *can not* do so. Can it not be tamed? can not its ferocity be removed? Probably it may so far be subdued that it may become apparently tame, but there will always be a marked distinction be

tween it and the sheep, because there is a distinction in nature
Now, the reason why man can not come to Christ, is not because he can not come, so far as his body or his mere power
of mind is concerned, but because his nature is so corrupt
that he has neither the will nor the power to come to Christ.
unless drawn by the Spirit. But let me give you a better illustration. You see a mother with a babe in her arms. You
put a knife into her hand, and tell her to stab that babe to the
heart. She replies, and very truthfully, "I can not." Now,
so far as her bodily power is concerned, she can, if she
pleases; there is the knife, and there is the child. The child
can not resist, and she has quite sufficient strength in her
hand immediately to stab it to its heart. But she is quite
correct when she says she can not do it. As a mere act of
the mind, it is quite possible she might think of such a thing
as killing the child, and yet she says she can not think of such
a thing; and she does not say falsely, for her nature as a
mother forbids her doing a thing from which her soul revolts.
Simply because she is that child's parent she feels she can not
kill it. It is even so with a sinner. Coming to Christ is so
obnoxious to human nature that, although, so far as physical
and mental forces are concerned (and these have but a very
narrow sphere in salvation) men could come if they would:
it is strictly correct to say that they can not and will not unless the Father who hath sent Christ doth draw them. Let
us enter a little more deeply into the subject, and try to show
you wherein this inability of man consists, in its more minute
particulars.

1. First, it lies in the *obstinacy of the human will*. "Oh !"
saith the Arminian, "men may be saved if they will." We
reply, "My dear sir, we all believe that; but it is just the
if they will that is the difficulty. We assert that no man *will*
come to Christ unless he be drawn; nay, *we* do not assert it,
but *Christ* himself declares it—'*Ye will not come unto me that
ye might have life ;*' and as long as that '*ye will not come*'
stands on record in Holy Scripture, we shall not be brought
to believe in any doctrine of the freedom of the human will."
It is strange how people, when talking about free-will, talk of

things which they do not at all understand. "Now," says one, "I believe men can be saved if they will." My dear sir, that is not the question at all. The question is, are men ever found naturally willing to submit to the humbling terms of the gospel of Christ? We declare, upon Scriptural authority, that the human will is so desperately set on mischief, so depraved, and so inclined to everything that is evil, and so disinclined to everything that is good, that without the powerful, supernatural, irresistible influence of the Holy Spirit, no human will will ever be constrained toward Christ. You reply, that men sometimes are willing, without the help of the Holy Spirit. I answer—Did you ever meet with any person who was? Scores and hundreds, nay, thousands of Christians have I conversed with, of different opinions, young and old, but it has never been my lot to meet with one who could affirm that he came to Christ of himself, without being drawn. The universal confession of all true believers is this—"I know that unless Jesus Christ had sought me when a stranger wandering from the fold of God, I would to this very hour have been wandering far from him, at a distance from him, and loving that distance well." With common consent, all believers affirm the truth, that men will not come to Christ till the Father who hath sent Christ doth draw them.

2. Again, not only is the will obstinate, but the *understanding is darkened*. Of that we have abundant Scriptural proof. I am not now making mere assertions, but stating doctrines authoritatively taught in the Holy Scriptures, and known in the conscience of every Christian man—that the understanding of man is so dark, that he can not by any means understand the things of God until his understanding has been opened. Man is by nature blind within. The cross of Christ, so laden with glories, and glittering with attractions, never attracts him, because he is blind and can not see its beauties Talk to him of the wonders of the creation, show to him th many-colored arch that spans the sky, let him behold the glories of a landscape, he is well able to see all these things ; but talk to him of the wonders of the covenant of grace, speak to him of the security of the believer in Christ, tell him of

the beauties of the person of the Redeemer, he is quite deaf to all your description; you are as one that playeth a goodly tune, it is true; but he regards not, he is deaf, he has no comprehension. Or, to return to the verse which we so specially marked in our reading, "The natural man receiveth not the things of the Spirit of God, for they are foolishness unto him: neither can he know them because they are spiritually discerned;" and inasmuch as he is a natural man, it is not in his power to discern the things of God. "Well," says one, "I think I have arrived at a very tolerable judgment in matters of theology; I think I understand almost every point." True, that you may do in the letter of it; but in the spirit of it, in the true reception thereof into the soul, and in the actual understanding of it, it is impossible for you to have attained, unless you have been drawn by the Spirit. For as long as that Scripture stands true, that carnal men can not receive spiritual things, it must be true that you have not received them, unless you have been renewed and made a spiritual man in Christ Jesus. The will, then, and the understanding, are two great doors, both blocked up against our coming to Christ, and until these are opened by the sweet influences of the Divine Spirit, they must be for ever closed to anything like coming to Christ.

3. Again, *the affections*, which constitute a very great part of man, are depraved. Man, as he is, before he receives the grace of God, loves anything and everything above spiritual things. If ye want proof of this, look around you. There needs no monument to the depravity of the human affections. Cast your eyes everywhere—there is not a street, nor a house, nay, nor a heart, which doth not bear upon it sad evidence of this dreadful truth. Why is it that men are not found on the Sabbath Day universally flocking to the house of God? Why are we not more constantly found reading our Bibles? How is it that prayer is a duty almost universally neglected? Why is it that Christ Jesus is so little beloved? Why are even his professed followers so cold in their affections to him? Whence arise these things? Assuredly, dear brethren, we can trace them to no other source than this, the cor

ruption and vitiation of the affections. We love that which we ought to hate, and we hate that which we ought to love. It is but human nature, fallen human nature, that man should love this present life better than the life to come. It is but the effect of the fall, that man should love sin better than righteousness, and the ways of this world better than the ways of God. And again, we repeat it, until these affections be renewed, and turned into a fresh channel by the gracious drawings of the Father, it is not possible for any man to love the Lord Jesus Christ.

4. Yet once more—*conscience*, too, has been overpowered by the fall. I believe there is no more egregious mistake made by the divines, than when they tell people that conscience is the vicegerent of God within the soul, and that it is one of those powers which retains its ancient dignity, and stands erect amidst the fall of its compeers. My brethren, when man fell in the garden, manhood fell entirely; there was not one single pillar in the temple of manhood that stood erect. It is true, conscience was not destroyed. The pillar was not shattered; it fell, and it fell in one piece, and there it lies along, the mightiest remnant of God's once perfect work in man. But that conscience is fallen, I am sure. Look at men. Who among them is the possessor of a " good conscience toward God," but the regenerated man ? Do you imagine that if men's consciences always spoke loudly and clearly to them, they would live in the daily commission of acts, which are as opposed to the right as darkness to light ? No, beloved; conscience can tell me that I am a sinner, but conscience can not make me *feel* that I am one. Conscience may tell me that such and such a thing is wrong, but how wrong it is conscience itself does not know. Did any man's conscience, unenlightened by the Spirit, ever tell him that his sins deserved damnation ? Or if conscience did do that, did it ever lead any man to feel an abhorrence of sin as sin ? In fact, did conscience ever bring a man to such a self-renunciation, that he did totally abhor himself and all his works and come to Christ ? No, conscience, although it is not dead, is ruined, its power is impaired, it hath not that clearness of eye

and that strength of hand, and that thunder of voice, which it had before the fall; but hath ceased to a great degree, to exert its supremacy in the town of Mansoul. Then, beloved, it becomes necessary for this very reason, because conscience is depraved, that the Holy Spirit should step in, to show us our need of a Saviour, and draw us to the Lord Jesus Christ.

"Still," says one, "as far as you have hitherto gone, it appears to me that you consider that the reason why men do not come to Christ is that they will not, rather than they can not." True, most true. I believe the greatest reason of man's inability is the obstinacy of his will. That once overcome, I think the great stone is rolled away from the sepulchre, and the hardest part of the battle is already won. But allow me to go a little further. My text does not say, "No man will come," but it says, "No man can come." Now, many interpreters believe that the *can* here, is but a strong expression conveying no more meaning than the word *will*. I feel assured that this is not correct. There is in man, not only unwillingness to be saved, but there is a spiritual powerlessness to come to Christ; and this I will prove to every Christian at any rate. Beloved, I speak to you who have already been quickened by the divine grace, does not your experience teach you that there are times when you have a will to serve God, and yet have not the power? Have you not sometimes been obliged to say that you have wished to believe, but you have had to pray, "Lord, help mine unbelief?" Because, although willing enough to receive God's testimony, your own carnal nature was too strong for you, and you felt you needed supernatural help. Are you able to go into your room at any hour you choose, and to fall upon your knees and say, "Now, it is my will that I should be very earnest in prayer, and that I should draw near unto God?" I ask, do you find your power equal to your will? You could say, even at the bar of God himself, that you are sure you are not mistaken in your willingness; you are willing to be wrapt up in devotion, it is your will that your soul should not wander from a pure contemplation of the Lord Jesus Christ, but you find that you can not do that, even when you are willing, without the help of the Spirit. Now, if the quickened child of God finds a spiritual inability, how much more the sinner who is dead in trespasses and sin? If even the advanced Christian, after thirty or forty years, finds himself sometimes willing and yet powerless—if such be his experience—does it not seem more than likely that the poor sinner who has not yet believed, should find a need of strength as well as a want of will?

But, again, there is another argument. If the sinner has strength to come to Christ, I should like to know how we are to understand those continual descriptions of the sinner's state which we meet with in God's holy Word? Now, a sinner is said to be dead in trespasses and sins. Will you affirm that death implies nothing more than the absence of a will? Surely a corpse is quite as unable as unwilling. Or again, do not all men see that there is a distinction between *will* and *power:* might not that corpse be sufficiently quickened to get a will and yet be so powerless that it could not lift as much as its hand or foot? Have we never seen cases in which persons have been just sufficiently re-animated to give evidence of life, and have yet been so near death that they could not have performed the slightest action? Is there not a clear difference between the giving of the will and the giving of power? It is quite certain, however, that where the will is given, the power will follow. Make a man willing, and he shall be made powerful; for when God gives the will, he does not tantalize man by giving him to wish for that which he is unable to do; nevertheless he makes such a division between the will and the power, that it shall be seen that both things are quite distinct gifts of the Lord God.

Then I must ask one more question : if all that were needed were to make a man willing, do you not at once degrade the Holy Spirit? Are we not in the habit of giving all the glory of salvation wrought in us to God the Spirit? But now, if all that God the Spirit does for me is to make me willing to do these things for myself, am I not in a great measure a sharer with the Holy Spirit in the glory? and may I not boldly stand up and say, "It is true the Spirit gave me the will to do it, but still I did it myself, and therein will I glory; for if I did these things myself without assistance from on high, I will not cast my crown at his feet; it is my own crown, I earned it, and I will keep it." Inasmuch as the Holy Spirit is evermore in Scripture set forth as the person who worketh in us to will and to do of his own good pleasure, we hold it to be a legitimate inference that he must do something more for us than the mere making of us willing, and that therefore there must be another thing besides want of will in a sinner—there must be absolute and actual want of power.

Now, before I leave this statement, let me address myself to you for a moment. I am often charged with preaching doctrines that may do a great deal of hurt. Well, I shall not deny the charge, for I am not careful to answer in this matter. I have my witnesses here present to prove that the things which I have preached have done a great deal of hurt, but they have not done hurt either to morality or to God's church; the hurt has been on the side of Satan. There are not ones or twos, but many hundreds who this morning rejoice that they have been brought near to God; from having been profane Sabbath-breakers, drunkards, or worldly persons, they have been brought to know and love the Lord Jesus Christ; and if this be any hurt, may God of his infinite mercy send us a thousand times as much. But further, what truth is there in the world which will not hurt a man who chooses to make hurt of it? You who preach general redemption, are very fond of proclaiming the great truth of God's mercy to the last moment. But how dare you preach that? Many people make hurt of it by putting off the day of grace, and thinking that the last hour may do as well as the first. Why, if we never preached anything which man could misuse, and abuse, we must hold our tongues forever. Still says one, "Well, then, if I can not save myself, and can not come to Christ, I must sit still and do nothing." If men do say so, on their own heads shall be their doom. We have very plainly told you that there are many things you can do. To be found continually in the house of God is in your power; to study the Word of God with diligence is in your power; to renounce your outward sin, to forsake the vices in which you indulge, to make your life honest, sober, and right-eous, is in your power. For this you need no help from the Holy Spirit; all this you can do yourself; but to come to Christ truly is not in your power, until you are renewed by the Holy Ghost. But mark you, your want of power is no excuse, seeing that you have no desire to come, and are liv-ing in willful rebellion against God. Your want of power lies mainly in the obstinacy of nature. Suppose a liar says that it is not in his power to speak the truth, that he has been a liar so long, that he can not leave it off; is that an ex-cuse for him? Suppose a man who has long indulged in lust should tell you that he finds his lusts have so girt about him like a great iron net that he can not get rid of them, would you take that as an excuse? Truly it is none at all. If a drunkard has become so foully a drunkard, that he finds it impossible to pass a public-house without stepping in, do you therefore excuse him? No, because his inability to reform lies in his nature, which he has no desire to restrain or con-quer. The thing that is done, and the thing that causes the thing that is done, being both from the root of sin, are two evils which can not excuse each other. What though the Ethiopian can not change his skin, nor the leopard his spots? It is because you have learned to do evil that you can not now learn to do well; and instead, therefore, of letting you sit down to excuse yourselves, let me put a thunderbolt beneath the seat of your sloth, that you may be startled by it and aroused. Remember, that to sit still is to be damned to all eternity. Oh! that God the Holy Spirit might make use of this truth in a very different manner! Before I have done I trust that I shall be enabled to show you how it is that this truth, which apparently condemns men and shuts them out, is, after all, the great truth, which has been blessed to the con-version of men.

II. Our second point is THE FATHER'S DRAWINGS. "No man can come to me, except the Father which hath sent me draw him." How then does the Father draw men? Ar

minian divines generally say that God draws men by the
preaching of the gospel. Very true; the preaching of the
gospel is the instrument of drawing men, but there must be
something more than this. Let me ask to whom did Christ
address these words? Why, to the people of Capernaum,
where he had often preached, where he had uttered mournfully and plaintively the woes of the law and the invitations
of the gospel. In that city he had done many mighty works
and worked many miracles. In fact, such teaching and such
miraculous attestation had he given to them, that he declared
that Tyre and Sidon would have repented long ago in sack-
cloth and ashes, if they had been blessed with such privileges.
Now, if the preaching of Christ himself did not avail to the
enabling these men to come to Christ, it can not be possible
that all that was intended by the drawing of the Father was
simply preaching. No, brethren, you must note again, he
does not say no man can come except the *minister* draw him,
but except the *Father* draw him. Now there is such a thing
as being drawn by the gospel, and drawn by the minister,
without being drawn by God. Clearly, it is a divine drawing
that is meant, a drawing by the Most High God—the First
Person of the most glorious Trinity sending out the Third
Person, the Holy Spirit, to induce men to come to Christ.
Another person turns round and says with a sneer, " Then do
you think that Christ drags men to himself, seeing that they
are unwilling!" I remember meeting once with a man
who said to me, " Sir, you preach that Christ takes people
by the hair of their heads, and drags them to himself." I
asked him whether he could refer to the date of the sermon
wherein I preached that extraordinary doctrine, for if he
could, I should be very much obliged. However, he could
not. But said I, while Christ does not drag people to himself by the hair of their heads, I believe that he draws them
by the heart quite as powerfully as your caricature would
suggest. Mark that in the Father's drawing there is no compulsion whatever; Christ never compelled any man to come
to him against his will. If a man be unwilling to be saved,
Christ does not save him against his will. How, then, does

the Holy Spirit draw him ? Why, by making him willing. It is true he does not use " moral suasion ;" he knows a nearer method of reaching the heart. He goes to the secret fountain of the heart, and he knows how, by some mysterious operation, to turn the will in an opposite direction, so that, as Ralph Erskine paradoxically puts it, the man is saved " with full consent against his will ;" that is, against his old will he is saved. But he is saved with full consent, for he is made willing in the day of God's power. Do not imagine that any man will go to heaven kicking and struggling all the way against the hand that draws him. Do not conceive that any man will be plunged in the bath of a Saviour's blood while he is striving to run away from the Saviour. Oh, no. It is quite true that first of all man is unwilling to be saved. When the Holy Spirit hath put his influence into the heart, the text is fulfilled—" draw me and I will run after thee." We follow on while he draws us, glad to obey the voice which once we had despised. But the gist of the matter lies in the turning of the will. How that is done no flesh knoweth ; it is one of those mysteries that is clearly perceived as a fact, but the cause of which no tongue can tell, and no heart can guess. The apparent way, however, in which the Holy Spirit operates, we can tell. The first thing the Holy Spirit does when he comes into a man's heart is this : he finds him with a very good opinion of himself: and there is nothing which prevents a man coming to Christ like a good opinion of himself. Why, says man, " I don't want to come to Christ. I have as good a righteousness as anybody can desire. I feel I can walk into heaven on my own rights." The Holy Spirit lays bare his heart, lets him see the loathsome cancer that is there eating away his life, uncovers to him all the blackness and defilement of that sink of hell, the human heart, and then the man stands aghast. " I never thought I was like this. Oh ! those sins I thought were little, have swelled out to an immense stature. What I thought was a mole-hill, has grown into a mountain ; it was but the hyssop on the wall before, but now it has become a cedar of Lebanon. Oh," saith the man within himself, " I will try and reform ; I will do good deeds enough to wash these black deeds out." Then comes the **Holy Spirit** and shows him that he can not do this, takes away all his fancied power and strength, so that the man falls down on his knees in agony and cries, "Oh! once I thought I could save myself by my good works, but now I find that

> ' Could my tears forever flow,
> Could my zeal no respite know,
> All for sin could not atone,
> Thou must save and thou alone.' "

Then the heart sinks, and the man is ready to despair. And saith he, " I never can be saved. Nothing can save me." Then comes the Holy Spirit, and shows the sinner the cross of Christ, gives him eyes anointed with heavenly eye-salve, and says, " Look to yonder cross, that man died to save sinners ; you feel that you are a sinner ; he died to save you." And he enables the heart to believe, and to come to Christ. And when it comes to Christ, by this sweet drawing of the Spirit, it finds " a peace with God which passeth all under standing, which keeps his heart and mind through Jesus Christ our Lord." Now, you will plainly perceive that all this may be done without any compulsion. Man is as much drawn willingly, as if he were not drawn at all ; and he comes to Christ with full consent, with as full a consent as if no secret influence had ever been exercised in his heart. But that influence must be exercised, or else there never has been and there never will be, any man who either can or will come to the Lord Jesus Christ.

III. And, now, we gather up our ends, and conclude by trying to make a practical application of the doctrine ; and we trust a comfortable one. " Well," says one, " if what this man preaches be true, what is to become of my religion? for do you know I have been a long while trying, and I do not like to hear you say a man can not save himself. I believe he can, and I mean to persevere ; but if I am to believe what you say, I must give it all up and begin again." My dear friends, it will be a very happy thing if you do. Do not think that I shall be at all alarmed if you do so. Remember, what you are doing is building your house upon the sand, and it is but an act of charity if I can shake it a little for you. Let me assure you, in God's name, if your religion has no better foundation than your own strength, it will not stand you at the bar of God. Nothing will last to eternity, but that which came from eternity. Unless the everlasting God has done a good work in your heart, all you may have done must be unraveled at the last day of account. It is all in vain for you to be a church-goer or chapel-goer, a good keeper of the Sabbath, an observer of your prayers; it is all in vain for you to be honest to your neighbors and reputable in your conversation, if you hope to be saved by these things, it is all in vain for you to trust in them. Go on; be as honest as you like, keep the Sabbath perpetually, be as holy as you can. I would not dissuade you from these things. God forbid; grow in them, but oh, do not trust in them, for if you rely upon these things you will find they will fail you when most you need them. And if there be anything else that you have found yourself able to do unassisted by divine grace, the sooner you can get rid of the hope that has been engendered by it the better for you, for it is a foul delusion to rely upon anything that flesh can do. A spiritual heaven must be inhabited by spiritual men, and preparation for it must be wrought by the Spirit of God. "Well," cries another, "I have been sitting under a ministry where I have been told that I could, at my own option, repent and believe, and the consequence is, that I have been putting it off from day to day. I thought I could come one day as well as another; that I had only to say, 'Lord, have mercy upon me,' and believe, and then I should be saved. Now you have taken all this hope away for me, sir; I feel amazement and horror taking hold upon me." Again, I say, "My dear friend, I am very glad of it. This was the effect which I hoped to produce. I pray that you may feel this a great deal more. When you have no hope of saving yourself, I shall have hope that God has begun to save you. As soon as you say, 'Oh, I can not come to Christ. Lord, draw me, help me,' I shall rejoice over you. He who has got a will, though he has not power, has grace begun in his heart, and

God will not leave him until the work is finished." But, careless sinner, learn that thy salvation now hangs in God's hand.
Oh, remember thou art entirely in the hand of God. Thou
hast sinned against him, and if he wills to damn thee, damned
thou art. Thou canst not resist his will nor thwart his purpose. Thou hast deserved his wrath, and if he chooses to
pour the full shower of that wrath upon thy head, thou cans
do nothing to avert it. If, on the other hand, he chooses to
save thee, he is able to save thee to the very uttermost. But
thou liest as much in his hand as the summer's moth beneath
thine own finger. He is the God whom thou art grieving
every day. Doth it not make thee tremble to think that thy
eternal destiny now hangs upon the will of him whom thou
hast angered and incensed ? Does not this make thy knees
knock together, and thy blood curdle ? If it does so I rejoice,
inasmuch as this may be the first effect of the Spirit's drawing
in thy soul. Oh, tremble to think that the God whom thou
hast angered, is the God upon whom thy salvation or thy condemnation entirely depends. Tremble and " kiss the Son lest
he be angry, and ye perish from the way while his wrath is
kindled but a little."

Now, the comfortable reflection is this :—Some of you this
morning are conscious that you are coming to Christ. Have
you not begun to weep the penitential tear ? Did not your
closet witness your prayerful preparation for the hearing of
the Word of God ? And during the service of this morning
has not your heart said within you, " Lord, save me, or I perish, for save myself I can not ?" And could you not now
stand up in your seat, and sing,

> " Oh, sovereign grace, my heart subdue ;
> I would be led in triumph, too,
> A willing captive of my Lord,
> To sing the triumph of his Word."

And have I not myself heard you say in your heart—" Jesus
Jesus, my whole trust is in thee ; I know that no righteousness of my own can save me, but only thou, O Christ—sink
or swim, I cast myself on thee ?" O, my brother, thou art

drawn by the Father, for thou couldst not have come unless he had drawn thee. Sweet thought! And if he has drawn thee, dost thou know what is the delightful inference? Let me repeat one text, and may that comfort thee: "The Lord hath appeared of old unto me, saying, I have loved thee with an everlasting love: therefore with loving kindness have I drawn thee." Yes, my poor weeping brother, inasmuch as thou art now coming to Christ, God has drawn thee; and inasmuch as he has drawn thee, it is a proof that he has loved thee from before the foundation of the world. Let thy heart leap within thee, thou art one of his. Thy name was written on the Saviour's hands when they were nailed to the accursed tree. Thy name glitters on the breast-plate of the great High Priest to-day; ay, and it was there before the day-star knew its place, or planets ran their round. Rejoice in the Lord ye that have come to Christ, and shout for joy all ye that have been drawn of the Father. For this is your proof, your solemn testimony, that you from among men have been chosen in eternal election, and that you shall be kept by the power of God, through faith, unto the salvation which is ready to be revealed.

SERMON XXVII

LOVE THY NEIGHBOR

"Thou shalt love thy neighbor as thyself."—MATTHEW, xix. 19

OUR Saviour very often preached upon the moral precepts of the law. Many of the sermons of Christ—and what sermons shall compare with them—have not what is now currently called "the gospel" in them at all. Our Saviour did not every time he stood up to preach, declare the doctrine of election, or of atonement, or of effectual calling, or of final perseverance. No, he just as frequently spoke upon the duties of human life, and upon those precious fruits of the Spirit, which are begotten in us by the grace of God. Mark this word that I have just uttered. You may have started at it at first, but upon diligent reading of the four evangelists, you will find I am correct in stating that very much of our Saviour's time was occupied in telling the people what they ought to do towards one another; and many of his sermons are not what our precise critics would in these times call sermons full of unction and savor ; for certainly they would be far from savory to the sickly sentimental Christians who do not care about the practical part of religion. Beloved, it is as much the business of God's minister to preach man's duty, as it is to preach Christ's atonement; and unless he doth preach man's duty, he will never be blessed of God to bring man into the proper state to see the beauty of the atonement. Unless he sometimes thunders out the law, and claims for his Master the right of obedience to it, he will never be very likely to produce conviction—certainly, not that conviction which afterwards leads to conversion. This morning, I am aware, my sermon will not be very unctuous and savory to you that are always wanting the same round of doctrines, but of this I have

but little care. This rough world sometimes needs to be rebuked, and if we can get at the ears of the people, it is our
business to reprove them; and I think if ever there was a
time when this text need to be enlarged upon, it is just now.
It is so often forgotten, so seldom remembered, "Thou shalt
love thy neighbor as thyself."

I shall notice, first of all, *the command ;* secondly, I shall
try and bring *some reasons for your obedience to it ;* and
afterwards, I shall draw *some suggestions from the law
itself.*

I. First, then, THE COMMAND. It is the second great commandment. The first is, "Thou shalt love the Lord, thy
God," and there, the proper standard is, thou shalt love thy
God more than thyself. The second commandment is, "Thou
shalt love thy neighbor," and the standard there is a little
lower, but still pre-eminently high, "Thou shalt love thy
neighbor as thyself." There is the command. We can split
it into three parts. *Whom am I to love ?* My neighbor.
What am I to do ? I am to *love* him. *How am I to do it ?*
I am to love him *as myself.*

First, whom am I to love? I am to love my neighbor.
By the word neighbor, we are to understand any person who
is near us. It comes from two old words, nae or near, (near)
and buer, (to dwell) persons residing, or being near us, and if
any one in the world is near us, he is our neighbor. The
Samaritan, when he saw the wounded man on the road to
Jericho, felt that he was in his neighborhood, and that therefore he was his neighbor, and he was bound to love him.
"Love thy neighbor." Perhaps he is in riches, and thou art
poor, and thou livest in thy little cot side-by-side with his
lordly mansion. Thou seest his estates, thou markest his fine
linen, and his sumptuous raiment. God has given him these
gifts, and if he has not given them to thee, covet not his
wealth, and think no hard thoughts concerning him. There
will ever be differences in the circumstances of man, so let it
be. Be content with thy own lot, if thou canst not better it,
but do not look upon thy neighbor, and wish that he were
poor as thyself, and do not aid or abet any who would rid him

of his wealth, to make thee hastily rich.   Love him, and then thou canst not envy him.   Mayhap, on the other hand, thou art rich, and near thee reside the poor.   Do not scorn to call them neighbors.   Do not scorn to own that thou art bound to love even them.   The world calls them thy inferiors.   In what are they inferior?   They are thine equals really, though not so in station.   "God hath made of one blood all people that dwell on the face of the earth."   Thou art by no means better than they.   They are men, and what art thou more than that?   They may be men in rags, but men in rags are men; and if thou be a man arrayed in scarlet, thou art no more than a man.   Take heed that thou love thy neighbor, even though he be in rags, and scorn him not, though sunken in the depths of poverty.

Love thy neighbor, too, *albeit that he be of a different religion*.   Thou thinkest thyself to be of that sect which is the nearest to the truth, and thou hast hope that thou and thy compeers who think so well, shall certainly be saved.   Thy neighbor thinketh differently.   His religion thou sayest is unsound and untrue; love him, for all that.   Let not thy differences separate him from thee.   Perhaps he may be right, or he may be wrong; *he* shall be the rightest in practice, who loves the most.   Possibly he has no religion at all.   He disregards thy God; he breaks the Sabbath; he is confessedly an atheist; love him still.   Hard words will not convert him, hard deeds will not make him a Christian.   Love him straight on; his sin is not against thee, but against thy God.   Thy God takes vengeance for sins committed against himself, and leave thou him in God's hands.   But if thou canst do him a kind turn, if thou canst find aught whereby thou canst serve him, do it, be it day or night.   And if thou makest any distinction, make it thus: Because thou art not of my religion, I will serve thee the more, that thou mayest be converted to the right; whereas thou art a heretic Samaritan, and I an orthodox Jew, thou art still my neighbor, and I will love thee with the hope that thou mayest give up thy temple in Gerizim, and come to bow in the temple of God in Jerusalem.   Love thy neighbor, despite differences in religion

Love thy neighbor, *although he oppose thee in trade.* It will be a motto hard to introduce upon the exchange, or in trade; but, nevertheless, it is one I am bound to preach to you that are merchants and tradesmen. A young man has lately started a shop which you are afraid will damage you. You must not hurt him; you must neither think nor say anything to injure him. Your business is to love him, for though he oppose you in your business, he is your neighbor still. There is another one residing near you, who is indebted to you, and if you should take from him all that he owes you, you will ruin him; but if you let him keep your money for a little, he may weather the storm, and succeed in his endeavors. It is your business to love him as yourself. Let him have your money, let him try again, and perhaps you shall have your own, and he shall be helped too. With whomsoever thou hast dealings in thy business, he is thy neighbor. With whomsoever thou tradest, be he greater or less than thou, he is thy neighbor, and the Christian law commands that thou shalt love thy neighbor. It doth not merely say that thou art not to hate him, but it tells thee to love him; and though he should thwart thy projects, though he should prevent thy obtaining wealth, though he should rob thee of thy custom— ay, though he should obscure thy fame, yet thou art bound to love him as thyself. This law makes no exception. Is he near thee, and hast thou any dealings with him? Thus says the law, "Thou shalt love him."

Again, thou art bound to love thy neighbor, *though he offend thee with his sin.* Sometimes our spirits are overwhelmed, and our hearts are grieved, when we see the wickedness of our streets. The common habit with the harlot or the profligate, is to drive them out of society as a curse. It is not right, it is not Christian-like. We are bound to love even sinners, and not to drive them from the land of hope, but seek to reclaim even these. Is a man a rogue, a thief, or a liar? I cannot love his roguery, or I should be a rogue myself. I cannot love his lying, or I should be untrue; but I am bound to love *him* still, and even though I am wronged by him, yet I must not harbor one vindictive feeling, but as I would desire God to forgive me, so I must forgive him. And if he so sins against the law of the land, that he is to be punished (and rightly so,) I am to love him in the punishment; for I am not to condemn him to imprisonment vindictively, but I am to do it for his good, that he may be led to repent through the punishment; I am to give him such a measure of punishment as shall be adequate, not as an atonement for his crime, but to teach him the evil of it, and induce him to forsake it. But let me condemn him with a tear in my eye, because I love him still. And let me, when he is thrust into prison, take care that all his keepers attend to him with kindness, and although there be a necessity for sternness and severity in prison discipline, let it not go too far, lest it merge into cruelty, and become wanton, instead of useful. I am bound to love him, though he be sunken in vice, and degraded. The law knows of no exception. It claims my love for him. I must love him. I am not bound to take him to my house; I am not bound to treat him as one of my family. There may be some acts of kindness which would be imprudent, seeing that by doing them I might ruin others, and reward vice. I am bound to set my *face* against him, as I am just, but I feel I ought not to set my *heart* against him, for he is my brother-man, and though the devil has besmeared his face, and spits his venom in his mouth, so that when he speaks he speaks in oaths, and when he walks, his feet are swift to shed blood, yet he is a man, and as a man he is my brother, and as a brother I am bound to love him, and if by stooping I can lift him up to something like moral dignity, I am wrong if I do not do it, for I am bound to love him as I love myself. O, I would to God that this great law were fully carried out. Ah, my hearers, you do not love your neighbors, you know you do not. You do not hardly love all the people who go to the same chapel. Certainly, you would not think of loving those who differ from you in opinion—would you? That would be too strange a charity. Why, you hardly love your own brothers and sisters. Some of you to-day are at daggers drawing with them that hung on the same breast. O, how can I expect you to love your enemies if you do not love your friends? Some of you have come here angered at your parents, and here is a brother who is angry with his sister for a word she said before he left home. O, if you can not love your brothers and sisters you are worse than heathen men and publicans. How can I expect you to obey this high and mighty command, "Love your neighbors?" But whether you obey it or not, it is mine to preach it, and not shift it to a gainsaying generation's taste. First, we are bound to love and honor all men, simply because they are men ; and we are to love, next, all those who dwell near us, not for their goodness or serviceableness toward us, but simply because the law demands it, and they are our neighbors. "Love thy neighbor as thyself."

2. But, now, what am I to do to my neighbor ? *Love* him —it is a hard word—*love* him. "Well I believe," says one, "I never speak an unkind word of any of my neighbors. I do not know that I ever hurt a person's reputation in my life. I am very careful to do my neighbor no damage. When I start in business I do not let my spirit of competition over throw my spirit of charity. I try not to hurt anybody." My dear friend, that is right as far as it goes, but it does not go the whole way. It is not enough for you to say, you do not hate your neighbor, you are to love him. When you see him in the street it is not sufficient that you keep out of his way, and do not knock him down. It is not sufficient that you do not molest him by night, nor disturb his quiet. It is not a negative, it is a positive command. It is not *the not doing*, it is the doing. Thou must not injure him it is true, but thou hast not done all when thou hast not done that. Thou oughtest to love him. "Well," says one, "when my neighbors are sick round about; if they be poor, I take a piece from the joint for dinner, and send it to them, that they may have a little food and be refreshed, and if they be exceedingly poor, I lay out my money, and see that they are taken care of." Yes, but thou mayest do this, and not love them. I have seen charity thrown to a poor man as a bone is thrown to a dog, and there was no love in it. I have seen money given to those who needed it with not one half the politeness with

which hay is given to a horse. "There it is, you want it. I suppose I must give it to you, or people will not think me liberal. Take it, I am sorry you came here. Why don't you go to somebody else's house? I am always having paupers hanging on me." O, this is not loving our neighbor, and this is not making him love us. If we had spoken a kind word to him, and refused him, he would have loved us better than when we gave to him in an unkind manner. No, though thou feedest the poor, and visitest the sick, thou hast not obeyed the command, unless thy heart goes with thy hand, and the kindness of thy life bespeaks the kindness of thy soul. "Thou shalt love thy neighbor."

And now some one here may say, "Sir, I can not love my neighbor, you may love your's perhaps, because they may be better than mine, but mine are such an odd set of neighbors, and I try to love them, and for all I do they do but return insult." So much the more room for heroism. Wouldst thou be some feather-bed warrior, instead of bearing the rough fight of love? Sir, he who dares the most—shall win the most; and if rough be thy path of love, tread it boldly, and still on, loving thy neighbors through thick and thin. Heap coals of fire on their heads, and if they be hard to please, seek not to please *them*, but to please *thy Master*, and remember if they spurn thy love, thy Master hath not spurned it, and thy deed is as acceptable to him as if it had been acceptable to them. "Thou shalt love thy neighbor."

Now, if this love for our neighbor were carried out—love, real love—it would prohibit all *rash anger*. Who is ever angry with himself? I suppose all wise men are now and then, and I suspect we should not be righteous if we were not sometimes angry. A man who is never angry is not worth a button. He can not be a good man, for he will often see things so bad that he must be angry at them. But, remember, thou hast no right to be more angry with thy neighbor than thou art with thyself. Thou art sometimes vexed with thyself, and thou mayest sometimes be vexed with him if he has done wrong. But thine anger toward thyself is very short-lived: thou soon forgivest thine own dear self; well, thou art bound just as soon to forgive him, and though thou speakest a rough word, if it be too rough, withdraw it, and if it be but rough enough, do not add more to it to make it too much so. State the truth if thou art obliged to do it, as kindly as thou canst. Be no more stern than there is need to be. Deal with others as thou wouldst deal with thyself. Above all, harbor no revenge. Never let the sun set on thine anger—it is impossible to love thy neighbor if thou dost that. Revenge renders obedience to this command entirely out of the question.

Thou art bound to love thy neighbor, then *do not neglect him.* He may be sick, he may live very near thy house, and he does not send for thee to call on him, for he says, " No, I do not like to trouble him." Remember, it is thy business to find him out. The most worthy of all poverty is that which never asks for pity. See where thy neighbors are in need ; do not wait to be told of it, but find it out thyself, and give them some help. Do not neglect them ; and when thou goest, go not with the haughty pride which charity often assumes, not as some superior being about to bestow a benefaction ; but go to thy brother as if thou were about to pay him a debt which nature makes his due, and sit by his side, and talk to him ; and if he be one that hath a high spirit, give him not thy charity as a charity, give it to him in some other way, lest thou break his head with the very box of ointment with which thou hadst intended to have anointed him. Be thou very chary how thou speakest to him : break not his spirit. Leave thy charity behind thee, and he shall forget that, but he shall remember well thy kindness toward him in thy speech.

Love to our neighbors puts aside every sin that is akin to covetousness, and envy, and it makes us at all times ready to serve them, ready to be their footstool, if so it must be, that we may be so proved to be the children of Christ.

" Well," says one, " I can not see that I am always to forgive ; you know a worm will turn if it is trodden upon." And is a worm to be your exemplar ? A worm will turn ; but a Christian will not. I think it foul scorn to take a worm for my exemplar, when I have got Christ for my copy. Christ did not turn—when he was reviled, he reviled not again ; when they crucified him, and nailed him to the tree, he cried, "Father, forgive them." Let love, unconquerable love, dwell in thy bosom, love which many waters can not quench, love which the floods can not drown. Love thy neighbors.

3. And now we have done with this command, when we have noticed *how we are to love our neighbor.* It would be a good thing if some ladies loved their neighbors as much as they loved their lap-dogs. It would be a fine thing for many a country squire if he loved his neighbors as much as he loved his pack of hounds. I think it might be a high pitch of virtue, if some of you were to love your neighbors as much as you love some favorite animal in your house. What an inferior grade of virtue, however, that appears to be! And yet it were something far superior to what some of you have attained to. You do not love your neighbor as you love your house, your estate, or your purse. How high then is, "Love thy neighbor as thyself" the gospel standard? How much does a man love himself? None of us too little, some of us too much. Thou mayest love thyself as much as thou pleasest, but take care that thou lovest thy neighbor as much. 1 am certain thou needest no exhortation to love thyself, thine own case will be seen to, thine own comfort will be a very primary theme of thine anxiety. Thou wilt line thine own nest well with downy feathers, if thou canst. There is no need to exhort thee to love thyself. Thou wilt do that well enough. Well, then, as much as thou lovest thyself love thy neighbor. And mark, by this is meant—thine enemy, the man who opposes thee in trade, and the man of another class. Thou oughtest to love him as thou lovest thyself.

Oh, it would turn the world upside down indeed, if this were practiced. A fine lever this would be for upsetting many things that have now become the custom of the land. In England we have a caste almost as strong as in Hindostan. My lord will not speak to any one who is a little beneath himself in dignity, and he who hath the next degree of dignity thinks the tradesman infinitely below him, and he who is a tradesman thinks a mechanic scarcely worth his notice, and mechanics according to their grades have their castes and classes too. Oh, for the day when these shall be broken down, when the impulse of the one blood shall be felt, and when as one family each shall love the other, and feel that one class depends upon the other! It were well if each would strive to help and love the other as he ought. My fine lady, in your silks and satins, you have gone to church many a day, and sat side by side with a poor old woman in her red cloak, who is as good a saint as you could be. But do you eve. speak to her? Never in your life. You would not speak to her, poor soul, because you happen to be worth more hundreds of pounds a-year than she is shillings. There are you, Sir John, you come to your place, and you expect every one to be eminently respectful to you, as indeed they ought to be, for we are all honorable men, and the same text that says, "Honor the king," says also, "Honor all men." And so we are bound to honor every one of them. But you think that you, above all men, are to be worshipped. You do not condescend to men of mean estate. My dear sir, you would be a greater man by one-half if you were not to appear so great. Oh, I say again, blessed be Christ, blessed be his Father for this commandment, and blessed be the world when the commandment shall be obeyed, and we shall love our neighbors as ourselves!

II. And now shall I have to give REASONS WHY WE SHOULD OBEY THIS COMMAND.

The best reason in all the world is that with which we will begin. We are bound to love our neighbors because *God commands it*. To the Christian there is no argument so potent as God's will. God's will is the believer's law. He doth not ask what shall it profit him, what shall be the good effect of it upon others, but he simply says, doth my Father say it? Oh, Holy Spirit, help me to obey, not because I may see how it shall be always good for me, but simply because thou commandest. It is the Christian's privilege to do God's commandments, "hearkening to the voice of his Word." But some other reasons may prevail more with others of you who are not Christians.

Let me remark, then, that *selfishness itself would bid you love your neighbor.* Oh, strange that selfishness should preach a suicidal sermon; but yet if self could speak, it might, if it were wise, deliver an oration like this, " Self, love thy neighbor, for then thy neighbor will love thee. Self, help thy neighbor, for then thy neighbor will help thee. Make to thyself, O self, friends of the mammon of unrighteousness, that when thou failest they may receive thee into abiding habitations. Self, thou wantest ease; make thyself easy by treating everbody well. Self, thou wantest pleasure, thou canst get no pleasure if those around thee hate thee. Make them love thee, dear self, and so shalt thou bless thyself." Ay, even if ye are selfish, I would ye were so pre-eminently selfish, and so wisely selfish that ye would love others to make yourselves happy.

The short cut to be happy yourself is to try to make others happy. The world is bad enough, but it is not so bad as not to feel the power of kindness. Treat servants well. There are some of them that you can't mend at all, but treat them well, and as a rule they will treat you well. Treat your masters well. Some of them are gruff and bad enough, but as a class they know good servants, and they will treat you well. There, now, if I would wish to be happy, I would not ask to have the wealth of this world, nor the things that men call comforts ; the best comforts that I should desire would be loving ones round about me, and a sense that where I went I scattered happiness, and made men glad. That is the way to be happy, and selfishness itself might say, "Love thy neighbor," for in so doing thou dost love thyself; for there is such a connection between him and thee, that in loving him the stream of thy love returns into thine own heart again.

But I shall not assail you with such a paltry motive as that ; it is too poor for a Christian ; it should be too base even for a man. Love your neighbor, in the next place, *because that will be the way to do good in the world.* You are philanthropists, some of you subscribe to missionary societies, you subscribe to the society for orphans, and other charitable objects I am persuaded that these institutions, though they be excel

lent. and good things, are in some respects a loss, for now a
man gives to a society one-tenth of what he would have given
himself, and where an orphan would have been kept by a
single family, ten families join together to keep that orphan,
and so there is about one-tenth of the charity. I think the
man who has the time is bound to give nothing at all to societies, but to give all away himself. Be your own society. If
there be a society for the sick, then if you have enough
money, be your own sick society. If you have the time go
and visit the sick yourself, you will know money is well spent
then, and you will spare the expense of a secretary. There
is a society for finding soup for the poor. Make your own
own soup. Give it yourself; and if every one who gives his
half-a-crown to the society would just spend half-a-sovereign
to give the soup away himself, there would be more done
Societies are good; God forbid that I should speak against
them; do all you can for them: but still I am afraid that
they sometimes thwart individual effort, and I know they
rob us of a part of the pleasure which we should have in our
own benefactions—the pleasure of seeing the gleaming eye,
and of hearing the grateful word when we have been our own
almoners.

Dear friends, remember that man's good requires that you
should be kind to your fellow creatures. The best way for
you to make the world better is to be kind yourself. Are
you a preacher? Preach in a surly way and in a surly tone
to your church; a pretty church you will make of it before
long! Are you a Sunday-school teacher? Teach your children with a frown on your face; a fine lot they will learn!
Are you a master? Do you hold family prayer? Get in a
passion with your servants, and say "Let us pray." A vast
amount of devotion you will develop in such a manner as that.
Are you a warder of a jail, and have prisoners under you?
Abuse them and ill-treat them, and then send the chaplain to
them. A fine preparation for the reception of the Word of
God! You have poor around you; you wish to see them
elevated, you say. You are always grumbling about the poverty of their dwellings, and the meanness of their tastes. Gc

and make a great row at them all—a fine way that would be to improve them! Now, just wash your face of that black frown, and buy a little essence of summer somewhere, and put it on your face, and have a smile on your lip, and say, "I love you. I am no cant, but I love you, and as far as I can I will prove my love to you. What can I do for you? Can I help you over a stile? Can I give you any assistance, or speak a kind word to you? Methinks I could see after your little daughter. Can I fetch the doctor to your wife now she is ill?" All these kind things would be making the world a little better. Your jails and gibbets, and all that, never made the world better yet. You may hang men as long as you like; you will never stop murder. Hang us all, we should not be much the better for it. There is no necessity for hanging any; it will never improve the world. Deal gently, deal kindly, deal lovingly, and there is not a wolf in human shape but will be melted by kindness; and there is not a tiger in woman's form but will break down and sue for pardon, if God should bless the love that is brought to bear upon her by her friend. I say again, for the world's good, love your neighbors.

And now, once more, love your neighbor, for *there is a deal of misery in the world that you do not know of.* We have often spoken hard words to poor miserable souls; we did not know their misery, but we should have known it, we should have found it out. Shall I tell you, my friend landlord, you went yesterday to get a warrant against a poor woman that has got three children. Her husband died a long while ago. She was three weeks back in her rent; the last time, to pay you, she sold off her late husband's watch and her own wedding ring; it was all that she had that was dear to her, and she paid you; and you went to her the next week, and she begged a little patience, and you think yourself highly exemplary because you had that little patience. "The woman," you have said, "I dare say is good for nothing, and if not, it is no particular business of mine whether she has got three children, or none; rent is rent, and business is business." Out she goes directly. Oh, if you could have seen that woman's heart when she stood penniless and houseless, and knew not where to send the children for the night, you would have said, " Never mind, my good woman, stop there; I can not turn a widow out of house and home." You did not do it yourself, did you? No, but you sent your agent to do it and the sin lay on you just as much for all that. You had no right to do it; you had a right in the eye of man's law but God's law says, "Thou shalt love thy neigbor as thy self."

A young man called upon you a little time ago. He said, " Sir, you know my little business. I have been struggling very hard, and you have kindly let me have some things on credit. But through the pressure of the times, I don't know how it is, I seem to get very hard up. I think, sir, if I could weather the next month, I might be able to get on well. I have every prospect of having a trade yet, if I could but have a little more credit, if you could possibly allow it." " Young man," you have said, " I have had a great many bad debts lately. Besides you do not bring me any good security; I can not trust you." The young man bowed, and left you. You did not know how he bowed in spirit as well as in body. That young man had a poor old mother and two sisters in the house, and he had tried to establish a little business that he might earn bread and cheese for them as well as for himself. For the last month they have eaten scarcely anything but bread and butter, and the weakest tea has been their drink, and he has been striving hard ; but some one, poorer than he seemed to be, did not pay him the little debt that was due to him, and he could not pay you. And if you had helped him, it might have been all well with him ; and now what to do he can not tell. His heart is broken, his soul is swollen within him. That aged mother of his, and those girls, what shall become of them ? You did not know his agony, or else you would have helped him. But you ought to have known You never should have dismissed his case until you had known a little more about him. It would not be business-like, would it ? No, sir, to be business-like is sometimes to be devil-like. But I would not have you business-like when it is so. Out on your business ; be Christian-like. If you be pro fessors, seek to serve God in obeying his commands—"Thou shalt love thy neighbor as thyself."

"Nay," says another, "but I am always very kind to the poor." There is a lady here who has got a tolerable share of money to spare, and to her, money is about as common as pins. And she goes to see the poor; and when she gets in, they set her a chair, and she sits down, and begins to talk to them about economy, and gives them a tolerably good lecture on that. The poor souls wonder how they are to economise any more than they do; for they eat nothing but bread, and they can not see that they can get anything much cheaper. Then she begins to exhort them about cleanliness, and makes about fifty impertinent remarks about the children's clothes. "Now," says she, "my good woman, before I leave you I will give you this tract, it is about drunkenness: perhaps you will give it to your husband." If she does he will beat her, you may depend upon it. "Come now," she says, "there is a shilling for you." And now, my lady thinks, "I love my neighbor." Did you shake hands with her? "No, sir." Did you speak lovingly to her? "Of course not. She is an inferior." Then you did not obey this command, "Love thy neighbor as thyself." Shall I tell you what happened after you left? That woman as soon as ever you were gone, began to cry. She started off to the minister for consolation. She said to him, "Do you know, sir, I am very thankful to God that I have had a little relief given me this morning, but my spirit was almost broken. Do you know, sir, we used to be in better circumstances. This morning Mrs. So-and-so came and talked to me in such a way, as if I had been a dog, or as if I had been a child, and though she gave me a shilling I did not know what to do. I wanted the shilling bad enough, or else I really think I should have thrown it after her. She did talk in such a way, I could not bear it. Now, if you come to see me, sir, I know you will speak kindly to me, and if you give me nothing you will not abuse me and find fault with me." "Oh," she said, "my heart is broken within me. I can not bear this, for we have seen better days, and we have been used to different treatment to this." Now, you did not love her. Your shilling, what was the good of that, if you did not put a little love on it. You might have made it as good as a golden sovereign if you had spread a little love upon it. She would have thought far more of it. "Love thy neigh-bors." Oh! would to God that I could always practice it my-self, and would that I could impress it into every one of your hearts. Love thy neighbor as thou lovest thyself.

And now the last argument I shall use is one especially ap-propriate to the Christian. Christian, your religion *claims your love*—Christ loved you before you loved him. He loved you when there was nothing good in you. He loved you though you insulted him, though you despised him and re-belled against him. He has loved you right on, and never ceased to love you. He has loved you in your backslidings and loved you out of them. He has loved you in your sins, in your wickedness and folly. His loving heart was still eter-nally the same, and he shed his heart's blood to prove his love for you. He has given you what you want on earth, and pro-vided for you an habitation in heaven. Now Christian, your religion claims from you, that you should love as your Master loved. How can you imitate him, unless you love too? We will leave to the Mahometans, to the Jew, and to the infidel, coldheartedness and unkindness; 'twere more in keeping with their views, but with you unkindness is a strange anomaly. It is a gross contradiction to the spirit of your religion, and if you love not your neighbor, I see not how you can be a true follower of the Lord Jesus.

And now I conclude with just a weighty suggestion or two, and I will not weary you. My text suggests first, *the guilt of us all.* My friends, if this be God's law, who here can plead that he is not guilty? If God's law demands I should love my neighbor, I must stand in my pulpit, and confess my guilt. In thinking of this text yesterday, my eyes ran with tears at the recollection of many a hard thing I had spoken in unwary moments. I thought of many an opportunity of loving my neighbor that I had slighted, and I labored to confess the sin. I am certain there is not one of all this immense audience who would not do the same, if he felt this law applied by the Spirit in power to his soul.

Oh! are we not guilty? Kindest of spirits, most benevolent of souls, are you not guilty? Will you not confess it? And then that suggests this remark. If no man can be saved by his works, unless he keeps this law perfectly, who can be saved by his works? Have any of you loved your neighbor all your life with all your heart? Then shall you be saved by your own deeds, if you have not broken any other command. But if you have not done it, and can not do it, then hear the sentence of the law. You have sinned, and you shall perish for your sin. Hope not to be saved by the mandate of the law. And oh! how this endears the gospel to me! If I have broken this law, and I have—and if I can not enter heaven with this law broken, precious is the Saviour who can wash me from all my sins in his blood! Precious is he that can forgive my want of charity, and pardon my want of kindness— can forgive my roughness and my rudeness, can put away all my harsh speaking, my bigotry and unkindness, and can through his all-atoning sacrifice give me a seat in heaven, notwithstanding all my sins. You are sinners this morning— you must feel it : my sermon, if blessed of God, must convince you all of guilt. Well, then, as sinners, let me preach to you the gospel. "Whosoever believeth in the Lord Jesus shall be saved." Though he hath hitherto broken this law God shall forgive him, and put a new heart and a right spirit into his bosom, whereby he shall be enabled to keep the law in future, at least to an eminent degree, and shall, by-and-by, attain to a crown of life in glory everlasting.

Now, I do not know whether I have been personal to any body this morning. I sincerely hope I have. I meant to be. I know there are a great many characters in the world that must have a cap made exactly to fit them, or else they will never wear it, and I have tried as near as I could to do it. If you would not say, "How well that applied to my neighbor," but just for once say, "How well it applied to me," I shall hope that there will be some good follow from this exhorta tion; and though the Antinomian may turn away, and say, "Ah! it was only a legal sermon," my love to that precious Antinomian. I do not care about his opinion. My Saviour preached like that, and I shall do the same. I believe it is right that Christians should be told what they should do, and that worldlings should know what Christianity will lead us to do; that the highest standard of love, of kindness, and of law, should be uplifted in the world, and kept constantly before the people's eyes.

May God bless you, and be with you, for Jesus' sake!